PEOPLE AND ORGANISATIONS

Core
Personnel
and
Development

MICK MARCHINGTON
AND ADRIAN WILKINSON

INSTITUTE OF PERSONNEL AND DEVELOPMENT

Design by Curve

Typeset by Fakenham Photosetting Ltd, Fakenham, Norfolk

Printed in Great Britain by
The Cromwell Press, Wiltshire

British Library Cataloguing in Publication Data

A catalogue record for this book is available from the British Library

ISBN 0–85292–622–7

The views expressed in this book are the authors' own and may not
necessarily reflect those of the IPD.

INSTITUTE OF PERSONNEL
AND DEVELOPMENT

IPD House, Camp Road, London SW19 4UX
Tel: 0181 971 9000   Fax: 0181 263 3333
Registered office as above. Registered Charity No. 1038333
A company limited by guarantee. Registered in England No. 2931892

CORE
PERSONNEL
AND
DEVELOPMENT

Mick Marchington is professor of human resource management at the Manchester School of Management, University of Manchester Institute of Science and Technology (UMIST), England. He has written extensively on employee involvement and on HRM and industrial relations. His most recent research activity has been in the areas of HRM in retailing and total quality management. He is chief examiner, core personnel and development, for the IPD.

Adrian Wilkinson is lecturer in human resource management at UMIST. He has many publications to his credit in the field of industrial relations and HRM, including books, monographs, and over 60 articles. His current research interests are business strategy and its links with the management of human resources, total quality management, and HRM in financial services.

IPD

Other titles in the series:

The Institute of Personnel and Development is the leading publisher of books and reports for personnel and training professionals and students and for all those concerned with the effective management and development of people at work. For full details of all our titles please telephone the Publishing Department on 0181 263 3387.

294439

Contents

Editors' foreword

People hold the key to more productive and efficient organisations. The way in which people are managed and developed at work has major effects upon quality, customer service, organisational flexibility and costs. Personnel and development practitioners can play a major role in creating the framework for this to happen, but ultimately they are dependent upon line managers and other employees for its delivery. It is important that personnel and development specialists gain the commitment of others and pursue professional and ethical practices that will bring about competitive success. There is also a need to evaluate the contribution that personnel and development approaches and processes make for organisational success, and to consider ways of making these more effective. Such an approach is relevant for all types of practitioner – personnel and development generalists and specialists, line managers, consultants and academics.

This is one of a series of books under the title *People and Organisations*. The series provides essential guidance and points of reference for all those involved with people in organisations. It aims to provide the main body of knowledge and pointers to the required level of skills for personnel and development practitioners operating at a professional level in all types and sizes of organisation.

The series has been specially written to satisfy new professional standards defined by the Institute of Personnel and Development (IPD) in the United Kingdom and the Republic of Ireland. The series also responds to a special need in the United Kingdom for texts structured to cover the knowledge aspects of new and revised National and Scottish Vocational Qualifications (N/SVQs) in personnel and training development.

Three 'fields' of standards have to be satisfied in order to gain graduate membership of the IPD: (i) core management (ii) core personnel and development and (iii) any four from a range of more than 20 generalist and specialist electives. The three fields can be tackled in any order, or indeed all at the same time. A range of learning routes is available: full or part-time educational course, flexible learning methods or direct experience. The standards may be assessed by educational and competence-based methods. The books in the series are suitable for supporting all methods of learning.

The series starts by addressing *core personnel and development* and four generalist electives: employee reward, employee resourcing, employee relations and employee development. Together, these cover the personnel and development knowledge requirements for graduateship of the IPD. These also cover the knowledge aspects of training and development and personnel N/SVQs at Level 4.

Core Personnel and Development by Mick Marchington and Adrian Wilkinson addresses the essential knowledge and understanding required of all personnel and development professionals, whether generalists or specialists. Practitioners need to be aware of the wide range of circumstances in which personnel and development processes take place and consequently the degree to which particular approaches and practices may be appropriate in specific circumstances. In addressing these matters the book covers the core personnel and development standards of the IPD, as well as providing an essential grounding for human resource management options within business and management studies degrees. The authors are both well-known researchers in the field, working at one of the UK's leading management schools. Professor Marchington is also a chief examiner with the IPD.

Employee Reward by chief examiner Michael Armstrong has been written specially to provide extensive subject coverage for practitioners required by both the IPD's new generalist standards for employee reward and the personnel N/SVQ Level 4 unit covering employee reward. It is the first book on employee reward to be produced specifically for the purposes of aiding practitioners to gain accredited UK qualifications. *Employee Relations*, by chief examiner Professor John Gennard and associate examiner Graham Judge, explores the link between the corporate environment and the interests of buyers and sellers of labour. It also demonstrates how employers (whether or not they recognise unions) can handle the core issues of bargaining, group problem-solving, redundancy, participation, discipline and grievances, and examines how to evaluate the latest management trends.

Employee Development, by chief examiner Rosemary Harrison, is a major new text which extends the scope of her immensely popular earlier book of the same name to establish the role of human resource development (HRD) and its direction into the next century. After reviewing the historical roots of HRD, she considers its links with business imperatives, its national and international context, the management of the HRD function, and ways of aligning HRD with the organisation's performance management system. Finally, she provides a framework that sets HRD in the context of organisational learning, the key capabilities of an enterprise and the generation of the new knowledge it needs.

These books, like Stephen Taylor's *Employee Resourcing*, are carefully tailored to the new IPD and N/SVQ standards, whereas Malcolm Martin and Tricia Jackson's *Personnel Practice* is focused on the needs of those studying for the Certificate in Personnel Practice. This also gives a thorough grounding in the basics of personnel activities. The authors are experienced practitioners and lead tutors for one of the UK's main providers of IPD flexible learning programmes.

In drawing upon a team of distinguished and experienced writers and practitioners, the *People and Organisations* series aims to provide a range of up-to-date, practical texts indispensable to those pursuing IPD and N/SVQ qualifications in personnel and development. The books will also prove valuable to those who are taking other human resource management and employment relations courses, or who are simply seeking greater understanding in their work.

Mick Marchington   *Mike Oram*

Acknowledgements

As with any book, the list of acknowledgements that could be made is extensive, but these are the most important. Much of our work over the last 10 years has been assisted by financial support from various funding bodies, and the ideas that emerge from these projects have inevitably been fed into the book. We wish to mention grants received from the Economic and Social Research Council, the Engineering and Physical Sciences Research Council, the Employment Department, the Institute of Personnel Management (as it was at the time of their grant) and the Institute of Management. Useful comments on drafts of some of the chapters have been received from Stephen Taylor, Jill Earnshaw, Phil Booth, Mike Oram and Matthew Reisz. Several people assisted with the word-processing of the manuscript, including Carol Ebbrell and Ann Coldicott, but the final document was put together by Lisa Bourne, who also sorted out the list of references for us; without her, we would probably have failed miserably in our attempt to meet the deadline. As usual, though, families and friends make the major contribution. Adrian would like to thank Jackie and his parents for their support, while Mick is indebted to Lorrie, Jack, and Lucy for trying to make him realise there is more to life than work – the problem is finding the time to do it!

Mick Marchington
Adrian Wilkinson
Manchester, March 1996

Part 1

INTRODUCTION

1 The professional standards and guide to the book

INTRODUCTION

The way in which people are managed at work is now seen by many observers as *the* key to improved organisational performance. At one level this is illustrated by the somewhat trite phraseology that 'people are our most important resource' or 'people make the difference'. Since this terminology has become so widely used its meaning has been devalued and questions are inevitably raised about the integrity and accuracy of such assertions. At a quite different level, recently a number of researchers have used case studies and quantitative data to argue that so-called 'best practice' human resource management/personnel and development (P&D) is associated with superior organisational performance. This has added a new dimension to the debate, hopefully facilitating a more systematic evaluation of the claim that people are a source of competitive advantage.

Serious doubts remain, however, as to whether or not managements do invest in 'their' human resources in practice, and equally whether or not this leads to competitive advantage in practice. There is no shortage of success stories, where links are made between P&D and business strategy, where a new customer-focused strategy has apparently led to superior levels of performance, or where the existing culture has been transformed by the creation of a learning organisation. The principles which underpin some recent developments, such as Investors in People, make the implicit assumption that organisations are likely to be successful if they commit themselves to more professional approaches to training, communications and total quality management for example. But other studies – especially those undertaken by independent observers – show that it is a lack of effective training, a failure to communicate with the workforce, or an unsystematic approach to recruitment and selection which still predominate. Even when 'best practice' P&D appears to be adopted, it is often implemented without clear and careful planning, and taken up as the latest fad or fashion without considering how it might actually contribute to competitive advantage. As with many other aspects of organisational life in Britain, short-termism and the requirement to achieve immediate returns assumes priority over the sustained development of policies that will be beneficial in the longer run.

The purpose of this book, therefore, is to delve beneath the surface by adopting an analytical and evaluative stance to P&D. It provides readers with knowledge and understanding in the core areas of human resource management/P&D, as well as facilitating the acquisition of skills which are central to the field. In this sense, the book has been written to provide an essential reference for students who are aiming to meet the IPD Standards in the area of Core Personnel and Development. It has relevance not only for those individuals who are studying full time or part time on college or university-based programmes, but also for those who are undertaking flexible learning or are aiming to meet the standards through experience and competence-based methods.

The book is ideal also for students who are taking modules in human resource management and employment relations on business and management studies degree courses. It differs from many of the existing prescriptive and descriptive texts by encouraging readers to raise questions, engage in a critical assessment of theory and practice, and basically evaluate the extent to which broad policies and procedures can be converted into reality. It repeatedly asks the question 'why', and demands of readers that they consider the relevance of specific human resource practices for different organisations.

CORE PERSONNEL AND DEVELOPMENT: THE KEY ASSUMPTIONS

The rationale behind the Core P&D syllabus specifies clearly the importance of acquiring a sound professional base for activities in the area, irrespective of the precise role which is occupied or the type of organisation for which he or she works. The skills, knowledge and understanding which are developed are even appropriate for individuals who do not undertake specialist P&D activities for an employer, but are employed as consultants, academics or line managers.

It is now increasingly common for practitioners to move between functions and organisations throughout their working lives, as well as between different forms of employment status. As a consequence it is important that all P&D practitioners are aware not only of their own area of specialist expertise but also of the wider contribution which P&D can make to organisational success. They need to be able to justify their contribution to organisational success and to understand the integration of P&D with other organisational activities. In addition, P&D practitioners need to understand how their own activities fit in with other areas of personnel and development, and the extent to which they may support or conflict with overall strategies. A major theme underlying this syllabus, and indeed the whole Professional

Qualification Scheme, is the need for P&D specialists to gain the commitment of line managers to their advice. Being able to persuade colleagues of the merits of particular ideas, and their contribution to organisational and departmental goals, is a skill of the utmost importance.

There are four key assumptions behind the Core P&D standards and syllabus, which are reinforced regularly throughout this book. First, the *subject area of P&D* is defined as those aspects of people management which need to be understood by all graduates of the IPD irrespective of their precise role or position in organisations. The standards represent those aspects of the job which cannot be ignored, even by those people who choose at an early stage in their careers to specialise in a particular area of P&D. Using Torrington's medical terminology (see Chapter 4), these are the standards which the 'general practitioner' needs to understand, and which remain important for the specialist consultant even though he or she is not explicitly aware that they are being used. These principles and practices are categorised in the Core P&D Standards, as well as in this book, into the four generalist areas of resourcing, development, relations, and reward. Included within this is information technology, a technique and way of thinking which is relevant for many aspects of P&D, and which cannot be compartmentalised into a discrete topic area.

Second, the notion of integration is central to the standards. This takes two forms: *vertical integration*, which refers to the links between P&D and wider business strategies and organisational contexts; and *horizontal integration*, which refers to the 'fit' between different P&D policies and practices, and the degree to which they support or contradict one another. Readers will find similar topics being addressed at a number of places in the standards. This should be recognised as a positive sign of complementarity, integration and reinforcement rather than unnecessary repetition. A key assumption behind the standards is that both vertical and horizontal integration need to be strengthened in order to maximise the P&D contribution, as well as minimise the likelihood of conflicting messages.

Third, a thread running through all the standards, not just the Core module, is that P&D specialists need to be able to *gain line management commitment* for their proposals and recommendations. It matters little that a course of action impresses other P&D specialists if it fails to convince line managers – the people who have to put most P&D policies into effect. This is not to say that P&D specialists should become the servants of line managers, merely recommending what the line managers want to hear in order to gain 'customer' approval. But it does mean that P&D specialists need to be acutely aware of their audience, of the purpose of human resource policies, and their contribution to organisational success. On some occasions the existing views of line managers will need to be challenged and the basis for their perspectives questioned, whilst on others their needs will have to be met with a professional judgement and sound practical advice.

The final thread running through the standards is that of *ethics and professionalism*. As we shall see in Chapter 4, P&D specialists might be able to make a distinctive contribution by adopting a clear ethical and professional stance on issues which some other managers might wish to ignore. This means that P&D can never be a simple technical exercise, whereby answers are read off according to well-known scientific formulae, and implemented without problem. P&D professionals have to become accustomed to the fact – especially as they reach the higher echelons of the occupation – that their work is going to be fraught with tensions and contradictions, and with situations that are characterised by uncertainty, indeterminacy, and competing perspectives.

THE OUTLINE OF THE BOOK

Following on from this introductory chapter are a further nineteen chapters organised into seven parts. Part 2 comprises three chapters on the Context for P&D, dealing with the nature of work, the legal and institutional framework, and the professional and ethical basis of P&D. We note in Chapter 2 that the employment relationship is characterised by conflict and co-operation, and that whilst one may assume prominence in particular workplaces or at particular times, the other is never totally absent. We also suggest (in Chapter 3) that even though the national and institutional context has a major influence on the practice of P&D, it does not determine it precisely; indeed, P&D is subject to some highly uneven developments. We also provide some material on equal opportunities, arguing that this is a prime example of how the ethical and professional bases of P&D come together well (see Chapter 4). Readers are advised, however, that equal opportunities and managing diversity need to be considered a key aspect of day-to-day P&D practice rather than being siphoned off and regarded solely as a topic which should be treated under a separate heading.

In Part 3 we move on to examine the Employee Resourcing aspects of Core P&D. In Chapter 5, we deal with human resource planning, a topic which is frequently stressed as a key element in a professional and strategic approach to P&D. The practice of human resource planning is altogether more mundane, however, and organisations are more likely to be typified by 'ad hocery' and reactive management than they are by systematic planning. In Chapter 6, we examine recruitment and selection, emphasising that decisions at this stage have a major consequence for subsequent employment relations. The increasing sophistication of selection testing means that P&D practitioners should be aware of the limits of their expertise in this area, and be ready to seek advice if necessary. Finally in Part 3 we focus on the management of performance and attendance, starting with induction training and going through to measures designed to ensure that employees perform at a satisfactory level; this chapter includes material on absence control and counselling through employee assistance programmes, all under the umbrella of performance management.

The subject of Part 4 is Employee Development. The first chapter (8) in this part looks at the theory and practice of learning, examining different approaches to how people acquire knowledge and skills, and focusing on continuing professional development, the learning organisation, and <u>Investors in People</u> as three examples of learning and training in practice. Chapter 9 reviews the complete training and development process, making use of the TDLB's Systematic Training Cycle to organise the material. The importance of identifying training needs correctly, of designing and delivering training programmes effectively, and of evaluating whether they have attained objectives, are all critical to the success of training interventions. The transfer of learning back to the workplace is the subject of Chapter 10, where we analyse six different types of training programme to see how well these work in practice; the six that are dealt with are outdoor-based development programmes, return-to-learning schemes, negotiating skills courses, customer care training, women-only management development exercises, and computer-assisted learning.

Part 5 focuses on Employee Relations, and here we attempt to convey some of the flavour of how employers manage employee relations, both in its collective form and in relation to individual employees. In Chapter 11, we analyse management styles in employee relations, and consider union and non-union organisations, comparing and contrasting these as appropriate. Here, we argue that the differences between union and non-union firms are probably exaggerated, given the sizeable differences within each of these broad categories, say between a large, 'household name' non-union firm and a sweatshop where unions are excluded. The processes of employee relations are the subject of Chapter 12; this includes a lengthy analysis of collective bargaining which, despite its decline in recent years, still remains a major influence on employee relations decisions and outcomes. We also consider other processes in the employee relations field, such as employee involvement and communications, custom and practice, legal enactment, and management prerogatives. Finally in this part we discuss the role of procedures in employee relations, with particular reference to discipline and grievance procedures, and to health and safety. We conclude that procedures still have an important role to play in the management of employee relations, and urge caution on those employers who might see them as little more than a legacy of previous bureaucratic rules which should be discarded in the pursuit of flexibility.

The fourth core area of P&D, Employee Reward, is dealt with in Part 6. Chapter 14 examines the motivational base for reward strategy and practice by analysing briefly the work of the classical management theorists (such as Taylor, Maslow and Herzberg) and its implications for reward management and choices of payment system. Also included in this chapter is a review of job evaluation and a consideration of equal value issues for the design of reward schemes. In Chapter 15, we address the subject of payment schemes, explaining their nature and reviewing their extensiveness, as well as considering the way in which these work in practice. A large part of Chapter 15 looks at performance-related pay. The final chapter in the Employee Reward Part is concerned with benefits (such as pensions and sick-pay schemes), harmonisation and non-financial recognition and reward. This last area is seen increasingly as one which can and should be developed, not only due to cost constraints on employers but also because the provision of more interesting work and prizes can have an important motivational and recognition effect.

In Part 7 we deal with the topic of integration, devoting three chapters to this because it is seen as so central to the IPD Standards, especially in the Core P&D module. Chapter 17 analyses vertical integration, and in particular the extent to which broader business strategies determine P&D, as well as the contribution which P&D can make to organisational success. We also address the way in which this contribution can be measured. In Chapter 18 the emphasis shifts to horizontal integration, and to an analysis of 'best practice' P&D which draws upon studies conducted in Britain and the USA to construct a list of ten practices which might be utilised by employers claiming to be at the 'leading edge'. We also consider in some detail the way in which the responsibility for P&D is divided between specialists and line managers, illustrating that, despite the trend to devolve more P&D issues to line managers and bring in consultants, specialists still have an important role to play. Finally in the Integration Part we present seven case studies of P&D in practice which aim to show its variety and diversity. The cases are drawn from the public and private sectors, from manufacturing and service-sector organisations, from large and small companies, and from employers who recognise trade unions through to those who aim to keep them out by a combination of fear and bribery.

Chapter 20 is the final chapter of the book, providing a useful review and assessment of the material that has been covered, and the opportunity to tackle the type of questions which appear in the examination. There are three sections to the Core P&D paper, comprising a compulsory case study in Section One, a series of compulsory questions which require paragraph-length answers in Section Two, and a Management Report or other practical exercise in Section Three. Some general advice is provided to students about how these questions should be approached, and in particular what to avoid in order to increase their chances of passing the examination.

Part 2

THE CONTEXT FOR PERSONNEL AND DEVELOPMENT

2 The work and employment context

INTRODUCTION

The employment relationship is central to personnel and development, whether in terms of the direct employment of staff by an organisation, or in the subcontracting of work to external bodies. It is a relationship which is characterised by conflict and co-operation, by confusion and contradiction, and by varying imbalances in the distribution of power between the parties. The employment relationship is never simple, but is influenced by many factors: broad political, legal, economic, social and technological trends; interactions between representatives of employers and employees at a national and international level; senior managers and employees (and in many instances their representatives) at an organisational or establishment level; and the actions of first line managers and individual employees on the shop floor or in the office. None of these influences is paramount in defining the way in which employment relationships are forged at the workplace, although some may have a stronger influence at some times than others. All may point in the same or different directions.

It is tempting to assume that the broader contextual influences leave little room for manoeuvre or choice at the workplace. Since the late 1970s there have been major amendments to employment legislation, the size of the manufacturing and public sectors has been greatly reduced, trade unions have lost members and have been excluded from the corridors of power, and unemployment has remained stubbornly high. Put together, these changes obviously exert a substantial influence on the employment relationship and on P&D practice, leading to assumptions that the work context has undergone significant and irreversible change.

However, it is important to stress that although these wider trends appear to have a significant impact on employment relations at workplace level, their precise influence remains heavily dependent upon the ways in which managers and employees interact whilst at work as well as the specific circumstances which characterise each area or establishment. An example may help to illustrate this point: during the 1980s and first half of the 1990s, employment in Britain has gone through many contextual changes which have strengthened the hand of the employer, and provided an opportunity for managers to exert firmer control over their staff. Many workplaces have seen unprecedented changes over this period, not only in terms of the employment relationship but also in patterns of customer care, quality management and organisational cultures. Despite this general trend, however, there remain organisations where line managers still have difficulty in persuading their staff to work harder and smarter, or in dealing with 'problem' employees. In other workplaces, managers may lack the skills or the power to encourage staff to operate more flexible patterns of working, to work without close supervision, or to take greater responsibility for their own quality control. In the contrasting situation – at times when environmental influences have placed more severe constraints on managements' freedom of action – there were still workplaces where employees were harshly treated and received little protection from arbitrary actions by managers. What matters therefore is the *combination* of these influences, and P&D practitioners need to be able to analyse situations in order to recommend actions which are appropriate for their own organisations.

In this section of this book we focus principally on general influences rather than those which are specific to particular workplaces; these are taken up more fully throughout the remainder of the book. In this chapter we examine the work context, using a broad PEST (political/legal; economic; social; technological) framework of analysis to help organise the material; at the same time it has to be acknowledged that there are overlaps between these categories, so we draw upon this framework to inform each of our sections – on 'The Nature of Work', 'The Legal and Political Framework for Employment', 'Labour Market and Employment Flexibility', and 'The Flexible Firm'. For readers who need reminding of the PEST terminology, the following are examples of what might be included under each heading:

- *political/legal*: government stability; attitudes towards the European Union; employment law

- *economic*: stages in the business cycle; unemployment; inflation; interest rates

- *social*: demographic and population change; income distribution; education and training; attitudes to work and leisure

- *technological*: new discoveries and developments; government spending on, and promotion of, research; speed of technology transfer.

According to Johnson and Scholes (1993: 82), PEST analyses can be used in at least four sets of ways: (1) as a checklist, a way of organising our understanding of the environment; (2) as a method of identifying a small number of key influences which are relevant for a particular situation; (3) as a technique for identifying long-term drivers of change in an industry or organisation; and (4) as a framework for examining the differential impact of external influences on organisations, either historically or in the future. Analysing external influences on an organisation can help in the construction of scenarios for the future, and for estimating which lines of action may be appropriate in the event of political, legal, economic, social and technological changes. Some of these can be predicted with greater certainty than others (eg the birth rate gives us some idea of the potential size of the labour force 15 years ahead whereas legal and political influences may be apparent only for very short timespans towards the end of a government's term of office). An ability to analyse the impact of external events on organisational policies and practices may help the P&D specialist to gain credibility and make a telling contribution to the establishment of strategic objectives.

Undertake a PEST analysis of your own organisation or establishment, determining what you believe are likely to be the key influences on its shape in the near future. What are the most important implications for P&D from this analysis?

By the end of this chapter, readers should be able to:

• apply a PEST framework to analyse the work context at their own organisation or establishment

• provide advice on the effect that major pieces of legislation have on the employment contract

• contribute to decisions about the use of flexible forms of working in their own organisation.

In addition, readers should be able to understand and explain:

• contrasting perspectives on the nature of the employment relationship

• the political/legal, economic, social and technological context in which P&D takes place

• the nature, meaning and extensiveness of the flexible firm.

THE NATURE OF WORK

Most texts on employee and industrial relations, as well as industrial and organisational sociology, include some material on the nature of work (see, for example, Blyton and Turnbull, 1994; Edwards, 1995). Typically, this characterises the employment relationship in terms of *conflict and co-operation*, both of which are present to differing degrees at all times. By way of contrast, it is unusual for texts on other aspects of P&D (eg recruitment and selection, performance management, training or development, reward management) to visualise the employment relationship in such terms. Instead there is likely to be some discussion of motivation or commitment, which deals with conflict solely in terms of management's failure to engender employee attachment to the organisation. In other words, the notion of conflict between the buyers and sellers of labour is compartmentalised as an employee relations issue.

Issues of conflict and co-operation are explicitly embedded in employee relations, most obviously in the analysis of collective bargaining between employers and trade unions, as well as in investigations of strike action. But conflict and co-operation also pervade other aspects of P&D as well. In employee resourcing, for example, it is apparent in questions concerning the selection of new staff and the desire to choose employees who are prepared to work effectively with a minimum of supervision. It is also central to management's approach to absence control. In employee development also, conflict and co-operation is ever-present, particularly in terms of individuals' attitudes to training, and their willingness to take on extra skills and responsibilities and to work towards the achievement of organisational goals as opposed to against them. The subject of employee reward also includes subjects which go right to the heart of the employment relationship, concerning equity and fairness, harmonisation, and internal and external differentials. Too often, however, these issues are treated in straightforward technical terms: for example, the shortcomings of interviews, or whether or not to use psychometric tests; the design and evaluation of training programmes; and the choice of payment systems for particular types of work. It is crucial that students are fully aware that each of these subjects raises issues which are central to the operation of the employment relationship, and they are not unique to employee relations.

There are many different perspectives on the employment relationship. Some of the early labour process writers (for example, Braverman, 1974; and R Edwards, 1979) saw it as typified solely by conflict and a struggle for control between managers and those whom they seek to manage. According to this viewpoint the interests of workers automatically collide with those of employers, since what is good for employers (capital) is inevitably bad for workers (labour) because surplus value – which is required in order to finance and reward capital – can only be achieved through the exploitation of workers. According to this viewpoint, workers who co-operate with employers, and who take part in participation and involvement schemes by offering their advice and ideas to management, are effectively doing themselves out of jobs by helping organisations to become more efficient. In addition, by sharing their expertise with management, workers also make it more likely that in the future their jobs will become deskilled (or disappear altogether) as employers replace labour with new technology. Some analyses (eg Smith and Morton, 1993) have assumed that employers have been engaged in a conspiracy to weaken and exclude trade unions since the early 1980s, and that all their initiatives have been designed with this as its principal objective.

Other writers are more interested in the balance between conflict and co-operation in the employment relationship. In relation to new technology, for example, Paul Edwards (1995: 13) notes that employees have shared interests with employers (eg in the development of new skills and the greater employment security which may come from a more successful business), as well as potential conflicts (eg in new demands upon them and disputes about levels of reward for taking on new responsibilities). Edwards (1995: 15) regards the employer–employee relationship as characterised by 'structured antagonism' which is created by the *indeterminacy* of the employment relationship. This relationship can never be constructed precisely enough to specify every aspect of an individual's work, and it relies upon both employer and employee to show some degree of trust and discretion for it to be discharged effectively. Because of this, Edwards (1995: 15) sees the employment relationship as both contradictory and antagonistic; it is contradictory because managers not only have to exercise control but also learn how to tap into and release creativity, whilst it is antagonistic because workers offer the only opportunity for employers to realise surplus value. Whilst employees may have much to gain from co-operating with employers, this should not disguise the fact that employers need to make a maximum of employees' efforts in order to make their employment of people worthwhile.

In short, just as an absence of overt conflict does not guarantee co-operation, neither does a bout of industrial action necessarily indicate a fundamental breakdown in the employment relationship. It is also likely that at the same time measures are being taken which seek to increase control over employees (say, in relation to timekeeping), other actions can be initiated which seek to develop their creative abilities (eg through an Employee Development and Assistance Programme). As many employers can testify, it is much easier to gain employee co-operation and changes at a behavioural level than it is to achieve deep-seated employee commitment to organisational goals.

Irrespective of their job, all employees possess 'tacit skills'; this refers to the knowledge and understanding that workers accumulate throughout their lives, which in many cases cannot be written down and copied. Tacit skills can be seen in many areas of paid and unpaid employment: in the ability to spot the sound of a machine or car engine, for example, which indicates that a problem may be on the horizon, in the 'simple' act of washing up dishes, or in gardening. Certain elements of these skills can be copied by watching other people or reading manuals, but others are 'learned' through practice or by doing similar jobs, sometimes outside of work.

Tacit skills can be used in a variety of ways (Marchington, 1992: 155). First, they can be employed as a potential weapon against employers, either as part of a collective dispute or as an individual response to managerial domination. Tacit skills can be used overtly by refusals to 'work beyond contract' or covertly in order to undermine a management instruction; in the latter case, the actions may need to be secret if they are unlawful or they may need to be hidden from management if employees are fearful that they will be dismissed if they are seen to be speaking out openly against their supervisors. 'Whistleblowing' is a good example of the latter. What unites each of these cases is the concept of using tacit skills to 'get back' at an employer, employees channelling their creative energies into opposing, rather than co-operating with, employer objectives.

The second use of tacit skills is in making life at work tolerable, in offering employers no more than the basic minimum which is required to fulfil the terms of the employment contract. Often this approach results in game-playing, what Burawoy (1979: 81–82) refers to as 'making out' and Marchington (1992: 156) terms 'getting by'. Under this scenario, employees dream up games to keep their minds occupied whilst at work. Anybody who has been employed on routine, mundane jobs will recognise how games can be used to pass the time: thinking up names for customers, producing a certain number of components in a 30-minute period, or reliving sporting highlights during the working week. In many cases, this may actually improve performance, as workers set themselves targets for achievement or prevent their getting bored by talking with other members of staff. As workers *apparently* consent to management rules, their low level of attachment comes to light only when they are asked to take part in the latest employee involvement initiative or sign up for a development programme. Since their major life interests are obtained outside of work, they resent what is seen as an intrusion into their private lives.

The third use of tacit skills is what employers would like to achieve – this is where employees actively contribute to the achievement of employer goals by 'getting on' at work. This takes several forms, such as working hard to gain promotion, taking on extra responsibilities to ensure that the organisation manages to satisfy customer orders, or in working hard because this is seen as the 'right' thing to do. The idea of doing a 'good job' – turning out high-quality work, resolving work-related problems, providing effective customer service, or co-operating with other team members – is central to much of our socialisation, and also to many of the activities which we undertake outside of paid employment. To a large extent our identities and feelings of self-worth are reinforced by 'getting on' at work, by resolving a series of problems, finishing a project, or just clearing the in-tray. As we shall see throughout this book, managements have recently been exhorted by various 'gurus' to tap into this knowledge, expertise and commitment, and get away from the syndrome whereby workers 'leave their brains on the coathanger' on the way into work.

> Think about three or four different types of job that you have either done or of which you have some knowledge. What was the mix of 'getting back', 'getting by' and 'getting on' in these jobs, and what might have been done to increase the likelihood of workers' wanting to 'get on'?

A number of the classic studies have analysed what employees want from their working lives. Writers like Maslow (1943) and Herzberg (1966) point to factors intrinsic to work, motivators such as interesting and varied work, the opportunity to develop, to be recognised for doing a good job, and so on. Others (eg Goldthorpe, Lockwood, Bechofer and Platt, 1968) suggest that factors such as job security and decent wages, which were seen as hygiene factors by Herzberg, are important, especially for people who do not regard work as of central life interest. Given that subjects such as these are covered in detail on the IPD Professional Management Foundation Programme, there is no point in repeating their findings here. However, since these studies were carried out some time ago, to what extent do their findings still have resonance today?

The Employment in Britain survey (Guest, 1995) provides some information about what people want from work. There are four broad sets of factors which seem to matter to people, in the sense that over 70 per cent of those questioned felt these were essential or very important:

- the type of work which they are doing, the opportunity to use their initiative and abilities whilst at work, in effect to be stretched in terms of problem-solving and creativity

- job security

- working with friendly and supportive people, having a good relationship with their supervisor

- good pay and satisfactory physical working conditions.

The fact that work is expected to fulfil an important social and creative role probably explains why such a large proportion of people indicate that they would continue working even if they no longer had any economic need to do so. The so-called 'lottery question' has been asked on many occasions, both in Britain and elsewhere. O'Brien (1992: 47) summarises the results and, although there are variations, a substantial majority of people state that they would continue to work if they won sufficient money to keep them comfortably off for the rest of their working lives. British workers had the lowest level of commitment to remaining in work, but even here it was over two-thirds of all those questioned; in Japan, the corresponding figure was over 90 per cent, whereas in the USA, Israel, the Netherlands and Belgium it was well over 80 per cent. Only in Germany was the figure anywhere near that in Britain. The reasons that are given for wanting to carry on working are instructive as well, with people regularly indicating the social and identity-related aspects of work, as well as its importance in structuring time (O'Brien, 1992: 45).

Other studies show how work is increasingly becoming harder, more intensive and less secure than it was in the past, and that more people feel it is unreasonable. In a survey for the IPD, Undy and Kessler (1995) found that about two-thirds of their sample felt they were working harder than when they first joined their current organisation compared with just 6 per cent who felt they were working less hard; the remainder felt it was no different. Even allowing for the fact that this response would be expected – it is unlikely that people would admit to working less hard – the proportions are still very high. This confirms other impressions of increased work intensification in recent years, exemplified by longer working hours, higher reported levels of stress at work, and greater levels of insecurity. Despite this, a substantial proportion of respondents to the IPD survey (Undy and Kessler, 1995) felt 'a lot of' or 'some' loyalty to people with whom they work, as Table 1 illustrates. Their levels of loyalty to the organisation for which they worked was somewhat lower, although 40 per cent felt a lot of loyalty, and a further 37 per cent some degree of loyalty, to their employer. Their level of trust in the organisation was lower still, with about a third of the respondents reporting that they had only a little or no trust at all. Given the number of redundancies since the beginning of the 1980s it is remarkable that the proportion of respondents indicating such low levels of trust is only one-third.

Table 1 Loyalty and trust (%)

	Loyalty to fellow employees	Loyalty to supervisor	Loyalty to organisation	Trust in organisation
A lot	64	52	40	26
Some	29	31	37	40
A little	4	9	15	20
None	2	6	8	13
Don't know	1	2	0	1

Recently there has been a renewed interest in the 'psychological contract' between employer and employee, first described by Schein (1988). This implicit 'contract' is based upon a series of assumptions about relations between employer and employee. These are outlined by Mayo (1995: 48):

• that employees will be treated fairly and honestly, and that information will be provided about changes at work, so as to meet the need for equity and justice

• that employees can expect to have some degree of security and certainty about the jobs in return for their loyalty to the employer, thus fulfilling the need for security and relative certainty

• that employees can expect employers to recognise and value their past and future contribution, so as to satisfy the need for fulfilment, satisfaction and progression.

This set of reciprocal arrangements may have been present in organisations during the 1970s according to Herriot (1995: 196), but it has now disappeared. The 1990s are characterised by instrumentality and uncertainty, an imbalance in what is offered by the individual compared with that which is offered by the employer. In 1990s Britain, he argues, the individual offers flexibility, accountability and long hours, and gets in return a job with a high salary, although for many peripheral workers none of this can be taken for granted (see below). The insecurities that now characterise the psychological contract are felt particularly by middle managers, as some of Herriot's (1995b) respondents show graphically in these quotations:

• 'Management are being put in a no-win situation, measured on performance when they have no control over targets and resources. Due to the recession, companies know that management are unlikely to complain, so they just pile on the pressure.'

- 'Only when the economic climate becomes less oppressive will the pendulum swing from an attitude of "do it or else", to one of worrying about staff turnover and loyalty instead of abusing it.'

- 'The company have not made any encouraging sounds regarding future structure and stability, and have therefore promoted this apparent lack of ambition, mobility and general lack of trust which is now commonplace among loyal and long-serving staff.'

> Do any of these quotations seem familiar to you from experiences at your own organisation? If so, how can we square the apparent contradictions between claims that 'employees are our most important asset' and these feelings of insecurity, powerlessness, and low levels of trust?

THE LEGAL AND POLITICAL FRAMEWORK FOR EMPLOYMENT

Legal and political issues set the scene for all aspects of P&D, and at each stage of the employment relationship. For example, there are clear legal standards influencing decisions about recruitment and selection, and at the induction stage of employment. Legislation affects issues relating to equal opportunities in all aspects of P&D, such as in access to recruitment (employee resourcing) and training (employee development), as well as in areas covered by employee relations (discipline) and employee reward (equal value considerations). Perhaps the most obvious political and legal influences are felt in the area of employee relations, and the period since 1979 has been characterised in the UK by a piecemeal, step-by-step process to reform and restrict the activities of trade unions. At the same time, most – though not all – of the legal infrastructure which was constructed in the 1960s and 1970s to provide a 'floor of employment rights' for workers has remained intact since then; see below for some of the changes. In a number of places it has been strengthened as a result of European Union legislation and following judgements of the European Court of Justice. Readers need to be aware that, at least until the late 1960s, Britain was regarded as unusual because the law played such a *minor* role in the employment arena, and it was seen as a country in which voluntarism reigned supreme (Clegg, 1970: 344).

The material in this section aims to set the scene for the more detailed analysis of P&D which comprises the rest of the book. Firstly, it outlines the nature of the employment contract, as this underpins most other aspects of work. It then goes on to focus on three areas, following a categorisation by Dickens and Hall (1995): employer–worker relations; employer–union relations; and union–member relations. It is important to state at the outset what this section does *not* do; it does not aim to provide a comprehensive and detailed coverage of all aspects of employment law, nor is it intended as a replacement for more specialised employment law publications. P&D practitioners need to be especially aware of the *limits* of their expertise in this area, and seek specialist advice if in doubt. We also mention legal and political influences elsewhere in the book, for example in relation to equal opportunities in Chapter 4, recruitment in Chapter 6, discipline in Chapter 13, and equal value in Chapter 16.

Employer–worker relations

Employer–worker relations are organised principally around the concept of the employment contract. The main terms of this contract are outlined in various texts (for example, Farnham, 1990: 252–255; Lewis, 1990: 16–26; and Pitt, 1995: 53–92), sources which should be consulted for further advice. At the outset, however, it is important to clarify the difference between the employment contract and the statement of terms and conditions. The contract may or may not be written, and in practice the parties enter into a contract after the stages of advertisement, interview, offer and acceptance. In most cases employers provide a statement of the main terms and conditions of employment or a written contract, but a contract is still formed even if no written material changes hands. It is also important to realise that a breach of contract, which can lead to an action for wrongful dismissal, is different from a claim for unfair dismissal. Not only is each case typically dealt with through different channels (wrongful dismissal through the court system, and unfair dismissal through the industrial tribunals), they each cover different issues (Pitt, 1995: 159). There are several sources of contractual terms.

Express agreement between employer and employee

These are the terms of the contract which are spelled out, either in writing or orally. These may include the terms of an advertisement, oral terms outlined at interview, or a written contract provided after the interview, either at the time the individual starts work or some time thereafter. The express terms may differ from what is contained in a job advertisement, but are clearly laid down as part of the individual contract or are expressly incorporated from a collective agreement (Lewis, 1990: 16).

Terms implied by common law

These are the terms which can be inferred from the courts as inherent in *all* contracts of employment. They can arise in two sorts of way. First, based upon the presumed intention of the parties, either through 'the officious bystander' test which means that a term is so obvious that it need not be stated, or through 'the business efficacy' test, in which it can be presumed that this was the intention at all events by both parties who are businessmen (*sic*). The second influence of common law is that certain terms are implied in every contract. Under this, the employer has a duty:

- *to pay wages* if an employee is available for work and there is no express term which limits this (eg in the event of being laid off)

- *to provide work* in certain circumstances, such as when an employee's earnings are dependent upon work being provided (eg if employees are paid by commission), or when the lack of work could lead to a loss of publicity or affect the reputation of the employee, or when the employee needs practice in order to maintain his or her skills

* *to co-operate with the employee,* in that the employee is treated by the employer in a manner which will not destroy any mutual trust and confidence upon which co-operation is built (eg making false accusations on the basis of flimsy evidence, requiring contractual obligations which are impossible to comply with, or persistently varying an employee's conditions of service)

* *to take reasonable care for the health and safety of the employee* by providing a standard of care which any prudent employer would take in the circumstances (eg providing safe premises and working environment, and avoiding risks which are reasonably foreseeable).

In return, the employee also has obligations under common law. These are:

* *to co-operate with the employer,* by obeying lawful and reasonable instructions so as not to impede the employer's business. The situation when employees are asked to take on duties which fall outside the scope of their contract is complicated; depending upon the nature of the request, this may be construed as a fundamental breach of contract, but the employer may be able to justify the decision on the grounds of a necessary business reorganisation and so avoid an accusation of unfair dismissal (Pitt, 1995: 195–196)

* *to be faithful to the employer,* and not engage in actions which cause a conflict of interest with the employer (eg in competing directly with the employer, in disclosing confidential information which may be of benefit to a competitor or some other third party, or in relation to patents and copyright)

* *to take reasonable care* in the performance of their duties such that they do not put themselves or other employees at risk.

Collective agreements

Terms may be derived from collective agreements as well as being individually negotiated, either by express provision or by implication. Pay and conditions of service are routinely incorporated into an individual's contract of employment if it contains an express provision that the contract is subject to the terms of a particular collective agreement. In addition, the terms of a collective agreement may be legally enforceable if trade union officers act as agents of their members for the purpose of making a contract on their behalf; this is really likely only where the number of workers is small.

Works rules

These can be incorporated into the contract in two ways: first, if employees are required to sign an acknowledgement at the time of entering employment that works rules will form part of the contract; and second, if 'reasonable notice' is given by the employer that works rules are to form part of the contract. Questions then need to be asked about the terms of variation of the contract, how adequately and prominently the rules have been displayed, and whether or not the employee would regard this notice as likely to include contractual conditions. Works rules are dealt with again in the Employee Relations section of the book (Chapters 12 and 13).

Custom and practice

In the absence of express terms, custom and practice may help to define what constitutes the employment contract. To be implied into a contract, custom and practice has to be 'reasonable, certain and notorious'. It is *reasonable* if it fits with norms in the industry in question, and would be interpreted in this way by a court. Custom and practice is *certain* if it is capable of precise definition, and not interpreted in substantially different ways by different people. Finally, it is *notorious* if the custom is well-known by all those to whom it relates. Given the requirement to provide written statements to employees, the scope for there to be customary terms in the contract is likely to be limited (Pitt, 1995: 81).

> What customs and practices operate in your organisation which are counter to formal rules and procedures? Who gains most from them – employers or employees?

Statute

These are terms which Parliament has decreed will be put into all contracts of employment, such as the provision for pay equality through the Equal Pay Act 1970, as amended by the Equal Value Amendment Regulations 1983.

The amount of employment legislation regarding employer–worker relations has expanded considerably in the UK since the early 1970s, under a whole series of legal enactments (eg Industrial Relations Act 1971; Trade Union and Labour Relations Act 1974; Employment Protection Consolidation Act 1978; Sex Discrimination Act 1975; Race Relations Act 1976; Equal Pay Act 1970 as amended by the Equal Pay Amendment Regulations 1983; Transfer of Undertakings (Protection of Employment) Regulations 1981; Data Protection Act 1984; Wages Act 1986; Trade Union Reform and Employment Rights Act 1993; Disability Discrimination Act 1995; Employment Rights Act 1995). The legislation in relation to equal opportunities and discrimination on the basis of sex, race and disability is taken up again in Chapter 4 when we examine the ethical and professional context of P&D.

The main statutory employment rights of individuals include the following (Farnham 1990: 255–260):

• a written statement of the main terms of employment

• an itemised pay statement

• maternity pay, time off and return to work

• not to be dismissed for trade union membership

• minimum periods of notice

- time off without pay for certain public duties
- redundancy pay for those with at least two years' service
- not to be unfairly dismissed for those with at least two years' service (dismissals on the grounds of pregnancy or trade union membership, for example, are automatically unfair)
- written statement of reasons for dismissal after two years' service
- time off with pay for trade union duties and training
- time off without pay for trade union activities
- time off with pay for safety representatives and for safety training.

A written statement of particulars should be provided for all employees working more than eight hours per week, within two months of their commencing employment. This should include the following:

- the names of the employer and employee
- the date on which the period of continuous employment commenced
- the scale or rate of remuneration, and the interval at which it is to be paid
- terms and conditions relating to hours of work, holidays and holiday pay, and sick pay
- terms relating to pensions arrangements
- length of notice that employees are required to receive and obliged to provide
- the title of the job
- the name of persons to whom the individual employee can apply in the event of a grievance or dissatisfaction with a disciplinary decision
- the place(s) of work at which the employee is required or allowed to work
- details regarding collective agreements which directly affect the employee's terms and conditions of employment.

These are impressive arrays of measures which seek to provide protection for employees at work, and compared with the situation prior to the 1970s employees have much greater opportunity to seek redress against employers who behave in an unreasonable manner. As we shall see in Chapter 13, this has led to considerable procedural reform in the area of P&D, in particular relating to unfair dismissal, and many employers now pride themselves on complying with the spirit, as well as the letter, of the law. On the other hand, it is less easy to be sanguine about the impact of these statutory changes on employment protection – as opposed to procedures. Since 1979 the period of service which employees are required to have completed before being eligible to take claims to industrial tribunals has been increased from six months to two years. Those winning their claims at an industrial tribunal remain very unlikely to regain their jobs, and find that their compensation for unfair dismissal is typically low; in 1993–94, for example, the median award made by tribunals was £2773 (Pitt, 1995: 202). Pre-hearing reviews have reduced the likelihood of full industrial tribunal hearings, and there is now a greater likelihood that both parties will be represented by specialists at a tribunal rather than stating their own case. In addition, those employed in industries which used to be covered by the Wages Councils have less protection now than for a long time (Dickens, 1988). When this is combined with labour market deregulation, the growing proportion of temporary contracts, and increased subcontracting of services by large employers to smaller firms, it could be argued that many individuals have less protection now than they did 15 years ago.

> Do you think that employees are now less secure than they were 20 years ago? To what extent do you think that changes in legislation have made it harder for employees?

Employees also receive some protection under the Data Protection Act 1984, which is highly relevant to P&D issues. Its main purpose is to 'regulate the use of automatically processed information relating to individuals and the provision of services in respect of such information'. The Act requires good computer practice with regard to the information which is held about them on personal files, and all those who hold such data are required to register with the Data Protection Registrar. Employees are entitled to receive a copy of any personal information that is held on computer, and if it is found to be inaccurate they can apply to have it amended or deleted. Eight principles underpin the holding of data (Lewis, 1990: 233–34): it must be obtained and processed lawfully and fairly; it must be held for lawful and specified purposes; it should not be used or disclosed in a manner incompatible with its purpose; the data must be adequate, relevant and not excessive; it should be accurate and up to date; it should not be kept for longer than necessary; individuals should be entitled to access to data at 'reasonable intervals', and to have it corrected or erased if it is inaccurate; security measures need to be taken to prevent unauthorised access to the data. The Data Protection Act covers many aspects of P&D; for example recruitment, provision of references, internal assessments, career planning, wage administration and payments.

Employer–union relations
This has been the principal area of government intervention since 1979, having been widely predicted prior to the Conservatives' taking up office in that year. Unlike the Industrial Relations Act 1971, which attempted to achieve wholesale changes in one piece of legislation to restrict the activities of trade unions, the period since 1980 has been characterised by a piecemeal and gradual reform of employer–union relations. At the same time it has been driven by a continuing and persistent objective: to weaken the power of trade unions, both by limiting their ability to engage in industrial action, and in making it harder for trade union leaders to gain mandates from the membership.

Not many employers have actually taken out injunctions to delay industrial action, and even fewer have gone beyond the injunction stage to seek damages against trade unions (Evans, 1987). On the other hand, the potential threat of the law has probably acted as a severe constraint on union leaders and members, and may well have prevented many deep-seated conflicts from being translated into strike action. Most commentators agree that the law has played a significant part in changing the balance of power since 1979, but it would be unwise to overestimate its influence, given other factors, most notably continuing high levels of unemployment and increasingly competitive product market pressures (Kessler and Bayliss, 1995).

The legislation that has been directed at employer–union relations includes the following: Employment Act 1980; Employment Act 1982; Trade Union Act 1984; Employment Act 1988; Employment Act 1989; Employment Act 1990; Trade Union Reform and Employment Rights Act 1993. Rather than take each Act in turn, which gives little feel for the overall impact of the legislation, two major areas of legal intervention are examined below. These are union organisation and recognition (and in particular the closed shop), and industrial action (strikes and picketing).

Throughout the twentieth century up until 1979, public policy in Britain had encouraged the support and development of collective bargaining. Most of this period was characterised by voluntarism which left employers and trade unions to sort out their own arrangements without any explicit state intervention. The law played an *auxiliary* role, persuading the parties that employee relations could be improved by the development and extension of collective bargaining; the terms of reference of ACAS are a prime example of this, in that up until 1993, it had a general duty to 'encourage the extension of collective bargaining', although there were no formal powers to impose changes on employers or employees. The period since 1979 has seen a gradual erosion of collectivist legal principles in employee relations, being presented as 'enhancing individual freedom, freeing employers from the abuses of union power, and improving efficiency and competitiveness' (Dickens and Hall, 1995: 275).

The dismantling of the legislation which allowed union membership to be a condition of employment (the closed shop), albeit with exceptions and escape clauses for employees with fundamental objections to the principle, was achieved through four pieces of legislation between 1980 and 1990. The Employment Act 1980 broadened the grounds on which employees could be exempt from union membership from 'religious reasons' to 'conscience and deeply held personal conviction to membership of any union or a particular union'. All new closed shops had to have the support in a secret ballot of at least 80 per cent of those covered by the arrangement, not just those who actually voted. In practice, given that it was unlikely that all employees would vote, this hurdle was set at a very high level indeed. In the Employment Act 1982, the balloting provisions were extended to all closed shops, and dismissal for failing to join a union was deemed automatically unfair if the closed shop had not been supported in a secret ballot in the five years preceding the dismissal by 80 per cent of those eligible to vote or 85 per cent of those actually voting. In addition, the compensation which was payable to individuals found to be unfairly dismissed in these circumstances was increased substantially, to a figure well above that for other unfair dismissals. Interestingly, a number of employers took steps to maintain closed shops by holding re-run ballots until the requisite percentage had voted in favour of its continuation (Roberts, 1984). The Employment Acts of 1988 and 1990 effectively outlawed the closed shop altogether by removing legal immunity protection from industrial action or other pressures to maintain compulsory union membership. The 1988 Act removed immunity for post-entry closed shops (those where employees were required to join a union within a certain period of starting employment), whilst the 1990 Act did the same for pre-entry closed shops (those where union membership was required in order to apply for a job). The Trade Union Reform and Employment Rights Act 1993 made it harder for unions to organise at the workplace by restrictions on check-off or DOCAS arrangements (deduction of contribution at source). Individuals now have to provide written consent every three years that they are prepared to have union subscriptions deducted from payroll. Again, there have been employer objections to this provision on the grounds that it can destabilise employee relations and lead to greater confusion and complexity at the workplace (see also Chapter 11).

The legislation on strikes and picketing has followed a similar gradualist route, to the point where it is now extremely difficult for trade unions to organise industrial action. Prior to the Employment Act 1980, picketing was allowed at any place other than an individual's home. In 1980 picketing was effectively restricted solely to a person's place of work, although there were exceptions for individuals with no fixed workplace. A Code of Practice issued by the Employment Department also recommended a limit of six on the number of pickets, although this has not been rigorously applied by the police, who have preferred to control picket lines via the use of public order offences. There have been a number of attempts to restrict strike activity, but broadly these fall into three categories:

- Definitions of a lawful trade dispute have been narrowed progressively since the Employment Act 1982. Inter-union disputes have been excluded from immunity, as are those deemed to be of a 'political character', that is, seen to be wider than those concerned wholly or mainly with conditions of employment. Secondary industrial action (ie that which relates to disputes beyond the initial employer–employee dispute) was also restricted in 1982, and is now effectively outlawed.

- The dismissal of strikers has been made easier following the Employment Act 1982. This prevented individuals who were dismissed during a lawful dispute from claiming unfair dismissal if *all* strikers at a workplace had been dismissed and none had been re-engaged within three months. The Employment Act 1990 allowed for the selective dismissal of strikers engaged in unofficial action.

- The requirement to hold ballots of members before taking industrial action has been extended, first on a voluntary 'auxiliary' basis by providing public funds to pay for postal ballots in the 1980 Act, and more recently through the removal of immunity if ballots are not held. At first unions were allowed to hold workplace ballots (Trade Union Act 1984) but in 1993 this was restricted to postal ballots alone. The wording on the ballot paper has been specified more precisely; there are now time limits regulating the use of industrial action after a ballot, and notice has to be given to an employer that a ballot is to be held. There is little doubt that these requirements now make it much harder for trade unions to organise, and much easier for employers to plan their defence against, industrial action, given that prior notice has to be given. Interestingly, the ballots provisions have tended to increase the support for industrial action rather than decrease it in a majority of cases (Martin, Fosh, Morris, Smith and Undy, 1991). As Kessler and Bayliss (1995: 242) note, unions have learned to use the results of strike ballots as a bargaining ploy in order to put pressure on employers at an early stage of the negotiation process.

> What is your view on the position of the law in relation to trade unions? Does the 'balance' between employers and unions seem about right or should it be adjusted? Do the current restrictions make it harder or easier for P&D practitioners? Why do you say this?

Union–member relations

Part of this has already been dealt with in the previous subsection, but there have been a number of provisions designed to give members a greater say or influence over union affairs, in addition to those relating to votes over industrial action. This is an example of the government's avowed intention to 'give unions back to their members', although some analysts believe that this comprises part of a broader programme to make life more difficult for trade unions. It needs to be recalled that up until 1980, union–member relations were broadly regulated by internal rules which were subject to scrutiny by the Certification Officer. There are three major aspects to the legislative changes since 1980 regarding union–member relations.

First, there are now legal requirements to allow all members to vote in union elections. As with strike ballots, the initial move in the 1980 Act was 'persuasive', providing funds for unions to hold postal ballots for elections to executive committees and for full-time officers, rule amendments and amalgamations. The Trade Union Act 1984 required that all *voting* members of a union executive committee should be elected every five years by secret ballot. By the 1988 Act it was specified that these had to be postal ballots, while subsequent Acts have made further minor amendments. Some of these changes merely served to reinforce 'good practice' among unions, while others have introduced new and more rigorous requirements. Second, there have been changes to the way in which trade union political funds are administered. The Trade Union Act 1984 required unions to hold a ballot at least every ten years to maintain the legality of their political funds. As with elections, the 1988 Act made it compulsory for these ballots to be postal. Third, a Commissioner for the Rights of Trade Union Members (CROTUM) was established via the 1988 Act, whose duties included assisting members who wished to take legal action against their union, for example if they felt they were being 'unjustifiably disciplined' by the union for refusing to take part if they felt they were industrial action. The services of CROTUM have not been widely used, and there have been allegations that the cost per claim is exceptionally high. In general, however, it is suggested that the unions have coped well with these legislative changes, although some may well have lessened direct democracy rather than extending it; for example, Smith, Fosh, Martin, Morris and Undy (1993) found that the requirement to conduct postal ballots has lowered the proportion of members who vote in elections rather than increasing turnouts.

LABOUR MARKET AND EMPLOYMENT FLEXIBILITY

The last two decades have seen major adjustments to the labour market and the structure of employment in Britain, in particular in sectoral shifts in employment and in the growing proportion of workers employed on what are termed 'atypical' contracts. Unemployment has remained well above levels regarded as politically unacceptable in the early 1970s, and patterns of strike action have also undergone sizeable change over this period. All of these have significant implications for P&D. Many of these issues are bound up with, and exemplified by, the growth of the flexible firm, and increasing distinctions between a core and peripheral workforce. Before analysing the nature and extent of the flexible firm in Britain we need first to describe briefly some of these major economic and labour market factors.

The last two decades have seen a fundamental sectoral shift in employment away from manufacturing and the public sector – sectors which are renowned for highly formalised P&D systems, high levels of trade union membership, and largish employment units – towards the more informal, relatively union-free, and smaller employment units of the service sector. For example, in 1970 nearly eight million people worked in manufacturing, a figure which fell to about seven million by 1980 and has now dropped to nearer four million; in other words, the number of people working in manufacturing in Britain has halved in about 25 years. Public-sector employment has also declined significantly in recent years, falling from around 30 per cent of all those employed in 1979 to nearer 20 per cent by the mid-1990s. Much of this decline has been due to long-running problems in the productive public sector (eg coal) and to privatisations of what were previously public service sector employers (eg gas, water, electricity, telecommunications). In addition, healthcare, local and central government organisations have seen declining numbers due to contracting-out of services, though some of these continue to employ large numbers of people. For example, local authorities employed over 2.5 million staff in 1993, 45 per cent of whom were in education, with another 370,000 working in further and higher education and grant-maintained schools (Winchester and Bach, 1995: 306). By contrast, the principal growth area has been the service sector. As a whole, including both public and private services, this grew from about 11 million employees in 1970 to over 15 million 25 years later; in short, whereas manufacturing lost four million jobs, services gained an equivalent number. The largest growth areas in terms of employment over this period were banking, insurance and finance (although these have seen substantial cuts in the 1990s), hotels and catering, retailing, and medical and health services.

There have also been significant changes in the nature of employment, with a sharp decline in the number of people in full-time (standard) jobs, and a corresponding increase of those in non-standard employment (part-time, temporary, self-employed). According to Nolan and Walsh (1995: 56–57), the number of employees in full-time jobs fell from 18 million in the late 1970s to 15 million by the mid-1990s, a trend which appears to be accelerating, given that about two million 'standard' jobs have disappeared since 1989. The proportion of the workforce in part-time employment increased from one in six in 1971 to almost one-third by the mid-1990s; there has been an absolute increase of about 1.5 million part-time jobs since 1979. However, many of these jobs are what Casey (1991) terms 'small' jobs, in that 70 per cent of all part-time workers are employed for less than 16 hours per week, with many of these working less than eight hours. The number of temporary jobs has remained more or less constant since the early 1980s, at around 5–6 per cent of all employees. Finally, there has been a substantial growth in the number of people who are classified as self-employed in the last 20 years; in 1979 just over 1.8 million people were self-employed, a figure which increased dramatically to over 3.2 million by 1989, only to fall back in the early 1990s to a little under three million (Kessler and Bayliss, 1995: 44). Many of the self-employed are people who were made redundant during the 1980s, and decided to set up their own businesses due to the relative scarcity of 'standard' employment opportunities; unfortunately, many of these businesses have since gone into liquidation or their owners have made only limited financial returns for their investments.

A third major change in the structure of employment since the late 1970s has been in the growing number of female employees and a corresponding decline in the number of men in employment. In 1959, for example, women comprised about one-third of the labour force (about 7.2 million), a figure which rose to over 40 per cent (9.4 million) by 1979, and over 48 per cent (10.2 million) in 1992. Over the same period, the number of men in employment fell from 13.8 million in 1959 to about eleven million in 1992 (Blyton and Turnbull, 1994: 49). On current projections, the proportion of men and women in the labour force could well equalise early in the next century. The labour market is heavily segmented, however, with many more women than men working part-time, and with women concentrated in the service sector (both public and private) and in lower-status jobs. The equal opportunities implications of this division of labour is considered in Chapter 4.

While the employed segment of the labour force may have been altered significantly since the late 1970s, unemployment levels have remained stubbornly high over this period. Back in the 1960s, unemployment typically stood at about 3 per cent, that is around 600,000 people. The effects of a variety of world-wide shocks on the system during the 1970s pushed the figure steadily up beyond one million and to over 5 per cent by 1979. Since then a number of changes in the way in which unemployment is defined have made it difficult to make precise comparisons, but it has oscillated between 1.5 and 3.5 million over this period. In percentage terms, the figure has varied from about 7 to 12 per cent; even at the lower levels this is way above that which came to be expected 30 years ago. At the end of 1995 unemployment stood at 2.27 million, over 8 per cent of the potential workforce, but a significant finding is that each trough in the figures over the last 25 years has been at a level which is higher than the previous one (eg 425,000 in 1973; 1.04 million in 1979; 1.59 million in 1990). Certain pockets of unemployment persist, chiefly among young people in inner-city areas, and in those in their fifties who have been made redundant and are unable to find comparable work.

The next 30 years are likely to see further pressures on the labour market due to an ageing population, and perhaps calls to lift the retirement age beyond 65. In Britain, for example, the ratio of pensioners to the working population is currently about 1:3, a ratio which could rise – on current projections – to over 2:5 by 2030. This is not just a British problem either, with estimates for Germany of over 3:5 by 2030, and for Italy of 7:10 (*The Guardian*, 27 January 1996). These demographic changes will have a major impact upon pensions provisions and on the ability of society to cope with the recent spate of early retirements – see Chapter 16.

The extent of strike action in Britain also illustrates the degree to which labour markets have changed since the 1970s. Table 2 shows the strike record for each decade since the 1950s.

Table 2 Britain's strike record since the 1950s (annual averages)

Decade	Number of strikes	Workers involved (000s)	Working days lost (000s)
1950-59	2119	663	3252
1960-69	2446	1357	3554
1970-79	2601	1615	12870
1980-89	1129	1040	7213
1990-95	318	208	748

The principal points to note about this table are that the number of strikes has declined dramatically since the 1970s, a trend which became very apparent during the 1980s and has continued throughout the first half of the 1990s. On the other hand, the number of workers involved in strikes, and the aggregate number of working days lost, has declined markedly only in the 1990s, and is very much influenced by the presence (or absence) of one or more large strikes. Kessler and

Bayliss (1995: 230) calculate that, as an example, excluding the year-long miners' strike of 1984–85 from the statistics for the 1980s would reduce the annual average to 4.6 million working days lost, a figure which is not that much higher than for decades other than the 1970s. They also show (1995: 231) that the proportion of strikes which last not more than one day has increased significantly since the early 1970s to nearly half of all recorded stoppages (compared with about 20 per cent during that decade).

> Have there been any strikes at your place of work in recent years, and if so what were they about? If there have not been any strikes, how have employees shown their discontent? Has this been easy to handle?

THE FLEXIBLE FIRM

Popular and managerial interest in the concept of the flexible firm emerged following the publication of Atkinson's work at the Institute of Manpower Studies in the mid-1980s (Atkinson, 1984; Atkinson and Meager, 1986; Atkinson, 1987). Since then other writers have taken up the idea, notably Handy (1991) with the terminology of a 'shamrock organisation'. Both make distinctions between a core and a peripheral workforce, albeit in slightly different ways and with different foci, but because Atkinson's was the first to be publicised it is used as the framework for this section. In addition, reference is made to Loveridge and Mok's (1979) less well-known, but arguably more penetrating, framework which divides labour markets into four categories on the basis of primary/secondary and internal/external distinctions. This is developed from yet earlier analyses by labour market economists, such as Doeringer and Piore (1971), and it shows how the notion of the 'flexible firm' has a pedigree which is much longer than that which emerged with the surge of interest in the 1980s.

In simple terms, organisations can be divided into a core and a periphery in employment terms, as illustrated by Figure 1. The core comprises workers who are drawn from the primary labour market, who have the security of 'permanent' (ie not fixed-term) contracts, and who have skills which are extremely important to the employer. In return, these core employees are expected to be functionally flexible, to apply their skills across a wide range of tasks. Flexibility can be both vertical and horizontal. *Vertical* refers to employees who take on tasks which are at a higher or lower skill level than that for which they have been recruited, for example, craft workers undertaking labouring duties – such as sweeping-up – in order to complete a piece of work, or semi-skilled employees assuming responsibility for certain skilled tasks, such as making minor repairs to keep production lines running. *Horizontal* refers to employees who undertake a wider range of tasks at the same broad skill level, as for example with engineering craft workers who agree to ignore previous demarcation boundaries by doing both mechanical and electrical work. Employees can also be both vertically and horizontally flexible when they work in teams that are responsible for a complete task, for example as with chemical workers who not only operate the production process but also undertake

routine maintenance tasks and take it in turns to act as the team leader
(Buchanan 1986; Marchington 1992: 115–123). Each of these forms
of functional flexibility is driven by employer needs for increased
productivity and quality in order to meet the demands of highly
competitive (often international) product market pressures.

Figure 1 **The flexible firm**

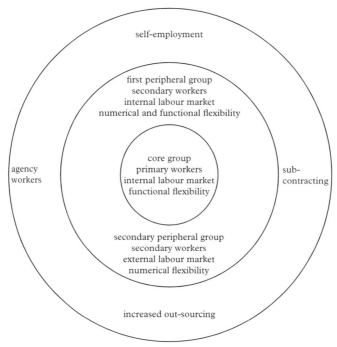

(Adapted from J Atkinson 1984: 29)

The periphery can be subdivided into several segments. The first
peripheral group comprises workers who come from the secondary
labour market, but are still internal to the organisation; they are
employed on contracts which have some degree of permanence and are
typically full-time (though some part-timers could also be included in
this category), but due to their lower level of skills these workers
cannot expect similar degrees of security as their colleagues from the
'core'. They may display some functional flexibility, but typically their
work will be characterised by little responsibility, low levels of
discretion and lower material rewards. These employees are
numerically flexible and can be laid off relatively easily with few
anxieties, since applicants with similar skills can be rehired quickly if
necessary.

The second peripheral group comprises individuals who find greater
difficulty breaking into internal labour markets and whose employment
experiences tend to be precarious. This group includes individuals with
little prospect of employment security: many part-timers, temporaries,
and public subsidy trainees would fit into this category, and for some
a move into the internal labour market is a possibility, provided work

continues and they are seen to do a good job and 'fit' with the organisational culture. As we saw in the previous section, the number of part-timers has increased substantially over the past 20 years and there has been a slight increase in the number of employees on fixed-term contracts who can have little prospect that their employment will be continued at the end of the contract.

Beyond the second peripheral group are those individuals who are clearly external to the organisation, that is, employed by another employer or in self-employment. As we noted above, the size of this group has expanded significantly since the 1970s, and it comprises not only those who own their businesses but also those individuals working for organisations to whom work is subcontracted. Agency workers would also fit into this category, with the types of people included ranging from secretaries to accountants, nurses and lecturers in further education. Whereas the Atkinson model views this group as very much within the secondary labour market, and at a major disadvantage to those in the primary internal labour market, Loveridge and Mok (1979: 123–126) see elements of this group as being in a relatively powerful position. The more highly skilled workers may be in great demand, and may choose to remain outside of mainstream organisational life in order to maintain greater control over their own lives, as well as earn larger amounts of money for their efforts. Obviously, some of the more successful consultants would fall into this category, as would other individuals whose skills are in demand (eg information technology specialists). This can be shown by the way in which the Loveridge and Mok model portrays the four groups; see Figure 2.

Figure 2 **A multi-segmented labour market**

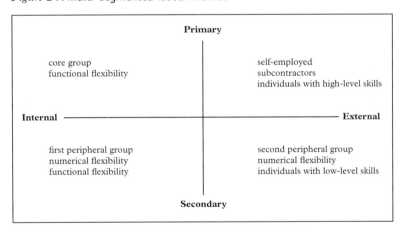

(Adapted from Loveridge and Mok, 1979: 123)

How well do these models compare with patterns of flexibility in your own organisation, and how easy is it to distinguish between these categories in practice?

There is a good deal of evidence to support the idea that organisations are becoming more flexible in their employment policies and practices, in particular in the increasing use of part-timers and in the growth of subcontracting and self-employment. The public sector has felt this change more than most over the last decade, with government requirements to extend compulsory competitive tendering (CCT), and through the increased use of fixed-term contracts (Pollert, 1988). But, despite some well-publicised success stories, there remain doubts about the extensiveness of the 'flexible firm' in reality, and considerable scepticism as to whether or not it represents a fundamental and strategic shift in the management of labour. There are four sets of concerns.

First, there are doubts about the conceptual standing of the terminology, with suggestions that the flexible firm model has a tendency to fuse together description, prediction and prescription into a self-fulfilling prophecy (Pollert, 1988: 50). Writings on the subject seem to veer between descriptions of flexibility at work, to predictions that the flexible firm is the design of the future, through to prescriptions that this represents what organisations ought to look like in order to be successful. At times it is difficult to tell which is being used, and it has led to allegations that government ministers and managerial spokespeople have tried to 'talk up' the whole topic of flexibility in order to support their ideological stance on market deregulation and 'lean' organisations (Legge, 1995: 172). It is also argued that, despite its obvious intuitive appeal, the model itself lacks clarity in terms of the core-periphery distinction. Taking part-timers as an example, it is clear that some part-time workers may be key to organisational success, given their contact with customers or their contribution to business goals (Hunter and MacInnes, 1991: 49). A question arises therefore as to whether these workers should be classified as core because of their roles, or peripheral because they are part-timers.

Second, there are doubts about the extensiveness of flexibility in practice, in particular whether functional flexibility is as widespread as some analysts seem to suggest. Many of the case studies which describe major changes to working practices have been selected precisely because they illustrate the concept of the flexible firm. We gain no feel from these about the *number* of employers who have introduced functional flexibility, nor do we find examples where flexible working practices have been resisted. An ACAS survey (1988a: 15) found that, while many more firms had increased flexibility than decreased it over the previous three-year period, an even larger proportion of managers reported no change. More recently, Beatson (1995: 52–53) makes a similar point in relation to comparisons between Britain and other countries; many more German and Japanese organisations had implemented new working practices than had their British counterparts, leading him to conclude that 'full-blown flexibility is a rarity.' Neither did Hunter and MacInnes (1991: 52) find much evidence of a comprehensive and systematic drive towards the flexible firm in the companies they analysed, cases which were selected on the basis of likely fit with the model.

One of the problems in trying to assess the extensiveness of flexibility is that many of the deals are 'enabling' agreements, designed to pave the way for local bargaining about how to implement new working practices. While the enabling agreement may look impressive in its scope, functional flexibility has little meaning unless there are clear improvements at workplace level. There are often major gaps between rhetoric and reality, as we shall see in Chapter 17. Nevertheless, there is little doubt that there have been sizeable adjustments to working practices in many organisations, although this is likely to be less widespread and less significant than some of the proponents of flexibility have claimed.

The third concern about the flexible firm model relates to the reasons for its growth, and especially the fact that it is not merely a 1980s and 1990s phenomenon. The proportion of people working part-time has been growing for decades, but this has also occurred in countries where labour market deregulation has not been pursued with quite the same vigour as in Britain. The proportion of the workforce employed on part-time or temporary contracts may have more to do with sectoral shifts (from manufacturing to services, for example) than it has to do with changes *within* organisations. The rationale used by employers for implementing flexibility deals is interesting. Rubery, Tarling and Wilkinson (1987: 147) noted that moves to functional or numerical flexibility were usually related to changes proposed elsewhere in their productive systems: 'Firms were therefore motivated by their own specific production and market objectives, and not by the opportunities to assert managerial control offered by excess labour supply and more quiescent trade unions.' On the basis of a more recent survey, Hunter and MacInnes (1991: 50) noted that employers appeared to be using part-time contracts when 'bundles' of tasks became available that did not equate with a full-time post, and that temporary contracts were used for tasks whose future was uncertain, or of a clearly-defined time period.

Finally, questions can be raised about the costs and benefits of flexibility. It is assumed that the flexible firm is naturally and automatically more efficient than its 'inflexible' counterpart, and that part-time workers, temporaries and subcontractors offer advantages over secure and permanent staff. This question is reviewed more fully in Chapter 18 when we analyse the arguments for 'best practice' human resource management and for horizontal integration between different aspects of P&D. There are doubts about whether part-time workers are more productive or whether they cost more because of high levels of absenteeism, a lack of commitment and loyalty, and lower levels of quality (Hunter, McGregor, MacInnes and Sproull 1993: 398). There have been major concerns about levels of quality in some of the catering and cleaning jobs which have been subcontracted by the NHS and local authorities (Kelliher and McKenna, 1988). Equally, it is doubtful that core workers maintain previous levels of commitment to their employers when many of their colleagues lose jobs through redundancy and rationalisation; if anything they are more likely to be fearful for their own future security and engage with the employer at a more compliant and superficial level.

> Who do you think gains most from flexible working, and why? Put together lists for employees and employers in relation to functional and numerical flexibility before making a judgement.

CONCLUSION

In this chapter we have reviewed some of the key contextual factors which influence P&D activities in organisations. We have sought to stress that analysts who assume that changes in the political/legal, economic, social and technological context have transformed work fail to take account of evidence which suggests that rival forces may have limited the extent of change at workplace level. First, contrary to the dominant assumption that employees are now highly motivated, committed and co-operative, some studies suggest that they may be little more than compliant, highly stressed and embittered, unable to contest what they see as unfair employer practices. Second, although there have been legal changes which have reduced significantly the ability of trade unions and their members to engage in collective action, EU legislation and judgments from the ECJ have forced the British Government to introduce some new protections for certain categories of staff (eg part-timers). Third, despite the enthusiasm with which the flexible firm is promoted in many quarters, there are doubts about its extensiveness, both in terms of numerical and functional flexibility. In other words, the factors we have reviewed in this chapter are often uneven in their effects and more complex in character than is often assumed.

USEFUL READING

ATKINSON, J. (1984) 'Manpower strategies for the flexible organisation', *Personnel Management*, August: 28–31.

DICKENS, L. and HALL, M. (1995) 'The State: Labour law and industrial relations', in P. EDWARDS (Ed.), *Industrial Relations; Theory and Practice in Britain*. Oxford, Blackwell: 255–303.

HERRIOT, P. (1995) 'The management of careers', in S. TYSON (Ed.), *Strategic Prospects for HRM*. London, IPD: 184–205.

HUNTER, L. and MACINNES, J. (1991) *Employers' Labour Use Strategies: Case Studies*. London, Employment Department Research Paper No. 87.

KESSLER, S. and BAYLISS, F. (1995) *Contemporary British Industrial Relations*, Second Edition. London, Macmillan.

LEWIS, D. (1990) *The Essentials of Employment Law*, Third edition. London, IPD.

LEWIS, P. (1992) *Practical Employment Law*. Oxford, Blackwell.

MANT, A. (1995) 'Changing work roles', in S. TYSON (Ed.), *Strategic Prospects for HRM*. London, IPD: 30–55.

NOLAN, P. and WALSH, L. (1995) 'The structure of the economy and labour market', in P. EDWARDS (Ed). *Industrial Relations; Theory and Practice in Britain*. Oxford, Blackwell: 50–86.

PITT, G. (1995) *Employment Law*, Second Edition. London, Sweet and Maxwell.

3 The institutional and national context

INTRODUCTION

In the previous chapter we analysed the way in which the work and employment context provided a backcloth for the practice of personnel and development (P&D) at workplace level. One of the key points to recall from that chapter is that work is characterised by both conflict and co-operation, and that the precise nature of employment depends upon the interplay between local, national and international forces. In this chapter we move on to analyse the role of some of the principal institutional and national bodies which influence P&D.

First we examine a range of bodies which, in one way or another, are connected with the legal framework. As we saw in Chapter 2, there has been a major growth in legislation over the past 25 years, and lawyers have played an increasingly important role in setting the parameters within which P&D is enacted. For the vast majority of employers, the most immediate and obvious influence on their activities, especially in the area of employment rights, comes from the industrial tribunal system. But the industrial tribunals are themselves overseen and explicitly influenced by the Employment Appeals Tribunal and higher-level courts. Increasingly, this includes European legal institutions – such as the European Court of Justice – whose influence over the adjudication of employment rights has grown enormously since the 1980s, and has led to major changes in employment law. Readers who are keen to find out more information about the legal institutions and framework might like to consult law books, such as those by David Lewis (1990), Paul Lewis (1992), or Pitt (1995), or specialist employee relations texts such as Towers (1992) or Farnham (1993). Other statutory bodies have also played a sizeable part in the P&D area. In relation to equal opportunities, this has been through the Equal Opportunities Commission and the Commission for Racial Equality, whereas the resolution of grievances, disputes and dismissal cases has comprised a key part of the Advisory Conciliation and Arbitration Service's duties.

Next we examine the part that has been played by organisations of employers and employees. In a sense these organisations are both external *and* internal to any single employer. They are *external* because their officials are not employees of that employer, and they have interests which extend way beyond the specific workplace in which P&D issues are played out. For example, employers' organisations have many different employers in their membership and speak on trade issues which are distant from the P&D arena, while most trade unions have members in many different workplaces and speak on political issues which are not always immediately relevant to all workplaces. On the other hand, they are *internal* in the sense that collective agreements which are negotiated between employers' organisations and trade unions can form part of the employment contract, and in the case of trade unions their members are also employees. One is reminded of the conversation between a chief executive and a union general secretary: the chief executive said that he 'employed 50,000 people of whom half happen to be union members', to which the general secretary retorted 'I have 500,000 members of whom 25,000 happen to work for your company!' We will describe briefly the role of the 'peak' bodies, the Trades Union Congress (TUC) and the Confederation of British Industry (CBI), as well as provide some material on membership levels in individual trade unions.

The final part of this chapter examines the changing nature of the training system, analysing this from its earlier roots in industrial training boards through to the role of Training and Enterprise Councils (TECs) in England and Wales, and Local Enterprise Companies (LECs) in Scotland. In this section we also venture into a short analysis of training standards through the lead bodies (occupational standards councils) and National/Scottish vocational qualifications. As with Chapter 2, readers should not expect to find a highly sophisticated and comprehensive analysis of these institutions here, but are advised to search for more detailed treatments elsewhere. Also, because NVQs are being reviewed during 1996, readers should ensure that their knowledge is up to date by accessing other sources of information – such as *People Management* – rather than relying on this chapter alone.

> To what extent do you think employers ought to be free of external influences such as these to determine their own P&D policies? What do employers gain from these external influences?

By the end of this chapter, readers should be able to:

- advise their management team on the services available from ACAS and the operation of the industrial tribunal system

- provide advice on the benefits which may be gained from membership of an employers' organisation

- explain the principles behind, and structure of, the NVQ/SVQ system to a group of trainees.

In addition, readers should be able to understand and explain:

- the role played by legal and national institutions in setting the standards for P&D

- the influence of employers' organisations and trade unions on the practice of P&D

• the emergence and development of training policy, and the current operation of national and local training organisations.

THE TRIBUNALS AND OTHER LEGAL INSTITUTIONS

Before describing the tribunal system, it is important that readers are aware of the differences between criminal and civil law. Although the vast majority of P&D issues are dealt with through the civil law, there are times when the criminal law comes into play, and individuals may be able to seek redress through either branch of the law. Criminal law is concerned with preventing breaches of society's rules, and with punishing offenders; cases are normally dealt with through the magistrates' courts or Crown courts. In contrast, civil law is concerned with settling disputes between private parties, such as between two individuals or between a worker and an employer. Employment issues are typically dealt with through the tribunal system, whilst other matters go through the County court or High Court system. Two examples of employment issues which could go through either or both routes are those concerned with safety and accidents, and with dismissal due to a breach of contract. The diagram below (Figure 3), reproduced from Earnshaw and Cooper (1996) illustrates this well.

The vast majority of P&D practitioners who become embroiled in legal issues are likely to be involved in industrial tribunal (IT) hearings. The ITs were originally set up under the Industrial Training Act 1964 to hear employers' appeals against levies, and their work was extended in 1965 to include redundancy payments issues. It was only really after the Industrial Relations Act 1971 that ITs started to play a major role in the P&D area, largely in dealing with claims for unfair dismissal, but more recently an increasing proportion of their case load has involved equal opportunities and redundancy payments issues. Over the years, the IT system has had a significant influence on the way in which managements handle employment issues, and it has led to an increasing formalisation of procedures in employing organisations; this topic is dealt with more fully in Chapter 13, when we examine grievance and disciplinary procedures. It should be noted that even at smaller establishments in the private sector (those employing 25–99 staff), procedures are firmly established in the vast majority of workplaces – for example, 85 per cent of establishments in this size band had disciplinary procedures and 79 per cent had grievance procedures according to Millward, Stevens, Smart and Hawes (1992: 189). It is highly unlikely that large private sector establishments and public sector workplaces will not have procedures for these issues.

Industrial Tribunals are able to hear the following sorts of issues:

• unfair dismissal

• health and safety at work

• race discrimination

• equal pay, sex discrimination and maternity

• redundancy, reorganisation and transfers of undertakings

Figure 3 The court structure in Britain

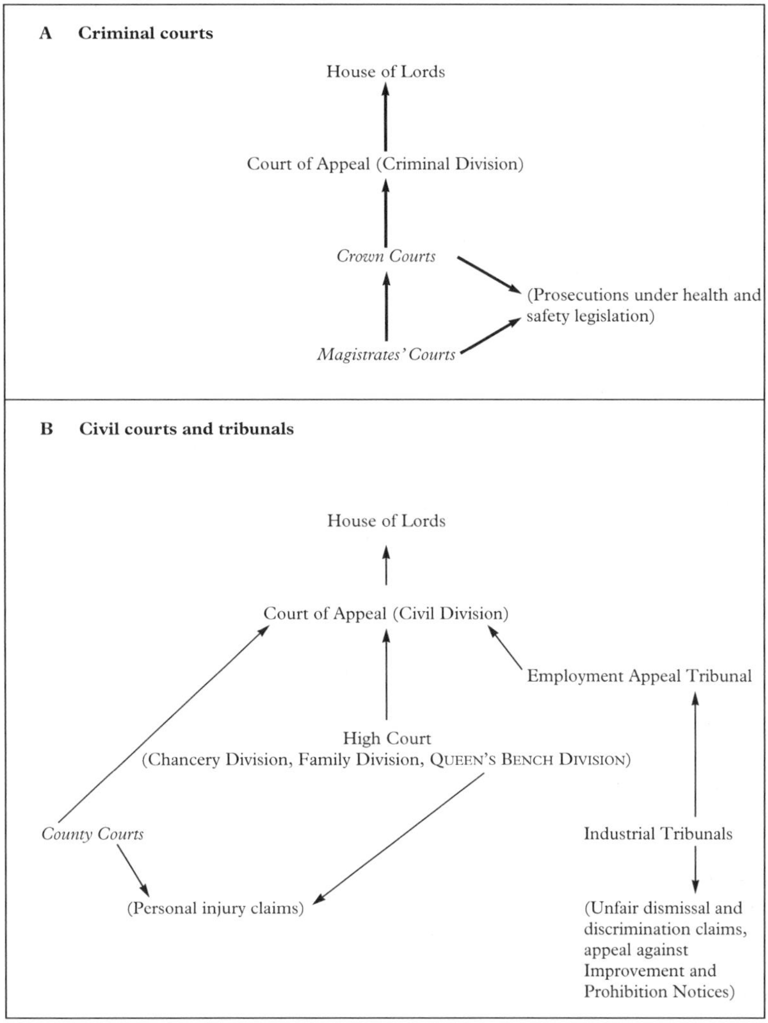

A   Criminal courts

House of Lords

Court of Appeal (Criminal Division)

Crown Courts

(Prosecutions under health and safety legislation)

Magistrates' Courts

B   Civil courts and tribunals

House of Lords

Court of Appeal (Civil Division)

Employment Appeal Tribunal

High Court
(Chancery Division, Family Division, QUEEN'S BENCH DIVISION)

County Courts

Industrial Tribunals

(Personal injury claims)

(Unfair dismissal and discrimination claims, appeal against Improvement and Prohibition Notices)

Reproduced from Earnshaw, J. and Cooper, C. (1996) *Stress and Employer Liability*, London, IPD.

- pay and other terms of employment
- trade union membership and non-membership
- time off for public duties.

Individuals who have a complaint against an employer start the process by completing an originating application (IT1), typically, though not necessarily, after consulting with their trade union, the Citizens Advice Bureau, a friend or a solicitor. After receipt of the application by the Central Office of Industrial Tribunals (COIT) and its reference to a particular regional office (ROIT), the Advisory Conciliation and

Arbitration Service (ACAS) can be used to achieve a conciliated settlement. ACAS conciliation officers have the task of making speedy and informal contact with the parties, and a duty under the law to seek a conciliated settlement if either party requests it or if ACAS believes there is a reasonable prospect that its intervention may be successful. Following conciliation, a substantial proportion of cases are settled, and in many cases this results in an out-of-court settlement to the applicant. It is rare for the individual to be reinstated or re-engaged, however.

On the other hand, the number of originating applications has risen sharply over the past decade to over 70,000 per annum, compared with about 35,000 in the mid-1980s. The range of cases has broadened as well, and matters have been complicated yet further by the influence of European judgements on British employment relations. This has prompted the government, through an Employment Department Green Paper in 1994 (*Resolving Employment Rights Disputes: Options for Reform*) to suggest ways in which to reduce the load on tribunals, to minimise delays, and to contain demands on public expenditure. A key aspect of any reform process is likely to focus on the role of procedures within the workplace – not only that they should exist but also that they should be used effectively by trained and skilled line managers. Given the increasing tendency for P&D practice (in particular grievance and discipline handling) to be devolved to line managers, the issue of effective usage is critical. We take this up again in Chapter 18, where we provide a more detailed analysis of the interplay between line and specialist managers.

Within the tribunal system itself there has been a continuing tension between its initial aim of providing a cheap, speedy and informal route to resolve employment rights problems, and the increasing tendency to legalism and reference to legal precedents (Dickens *et al*, 1985). The latter is inevitable as the body of case law builds up and both parties (respondent and applicant) seek specialist representation at tribunal. In addition to the increasing likelihood that both parties will be represented by solicitors, employers' organisations and trade unions also provide specialist expertise, and some employers have their own legal experts to deal with these cases. Given that the costs of losing a case can be quite high for an employer, not only in terms of direct employment costs, but also in compensation, payment for representation, and negative public relations, the incentive to win becomes even greater. Attempts are made to retain the informality by many IT chairmen, who have been encouraged to adopt a more inquisitorial approach, and assist unrepresented applicants or respondents with a line of questioning. The lay members of the IT provide knowledge and expertise from industry. Readers who wish to find out more about how to prepare for, and present a case to, ITs are advised to look at a more specialised publication, such as that by Paul Lewis (1992: 296–318).

Appeals against IT decisions are made to the Employment Appeals Tribunal (EAT), a body with the same status as a High Court, which was established under the Employment Protection Act 1975. It hears appeals on any question of *law* stemming from an IT decision, whereby it is claimed that the IT had misunderstood or misdirected itself as to the law that was applicable in the circumstances, where there is no evidence to support a particular finding, or where the IT has reached a perverse conclusion. Appeals can be remitted to the same or to a fresh IT for a rehearing if they are neither upheld nor dismissed. Appeals on a point of law are tightly circumscribed, and there have been repeated warnings that points of fact are not to be dressed up in the garb of points of law in order to bring an appeal. The EAT can also hear cases, both on points of law and fact, on issues concerning decisions of the Certification Officer, but these are unlikely to fall within the remit of most P&D practitioners. Appeals against EAT decisions can be made in certain circumstances to the Court of Appeal, thence to the House of Lords and to the European Court of Justice. In addition, individual ITs can refer matters direct to the ECJ for interpretations of community law. The ECJ is becoming increasingly influential in several areas of employment law – for example, in relation to equal pay, maternity rights, sex discrimination, and health and safety.

Go to the library and find a recent copy of one of the specialist employment law publications – such as the *Industrial Relations Law Reports* or the *Industrial Relations Law Bulletin*. Choose a recent case, examine the details, and write a short report for your manager outlining any lessons which can be learnt for your organisation.

The influence of European law is more complicated than that resulting from domestic legislation, partly due to Britain's opt-out from the Social Chapter at Maastricht in 1991 (Gold, 1993: 7). This ensures that on some issues (eg European Works Councils) employers in the UK are not bound by the same provisions as their European colleagues in, for example, France, Germany and Italy – see Chapter 12 for further discussion of this topic. It is also complicated, in the minds of many P&D practitioners at least, in that four separate sets of proposals can be put forward by the European Commission: these are *recommendations* which do not bind member states but it is hoped will be followed; *regulations*, which take immediate effect once adopted by the Commission; *directions*, which affect only the parties involved in a specific case; and *directives*, which are binding on member states but require appropriate legislation from each member state within a set period of time to comply with the objectives of the directive. In addition, the Commission has also issued *codes of practice*. Cases are heard at the European Court of Justice, which is responsible for interpreting European legislation and for providing preliminary rulings on disputed or unclear points of law. These then have to be incorporated into domestic law, such as with the changes to the equal value provisions in the early 1980s, or in relation to part-time workers more recently.

THE ADVISORY CONCILIATION AND ARBITRATION SERVICE (ACAS)

Although ACAS is a relatively new creation, being established by the Employment Protection Act 1975, there is a long history of conciliation and arbitration in Britain, stemming in particular from two pieces of legislation in the late nineteenth and early twentieth centuries. The Conciliation Act of 1896 gave general powers to the government to investigate the cause and circumstances of any dispute, and appoint a conciliator or arbitrator, as appropriate. The Industrial Courts Act 1919 set up a permanent tripartite arbitration body which could examine a dispute which had exhausted internal organisational or industry-wide mechanisms for its resolution. This body – the Industrial Court – was renamed the Central Arbitration Committee in 1975, and for a number of years had a sizeable influence over issues relating to union recognition. Nowadays its role is much reduced, being confined to arbitration in equal value and information disclosure cases (Salamon, 1992: 438).

The formation of ACAS brought a number of activities previously handled by the Department of Employment and other bodies into one organisation and under one structure. ACAS is run by a full-time chair and a council comprising a number of part-time members drawn from different areas, for example from academia, employers' organisations and employees' organisations (not just trade unions). ACAS is independent of government, even though it is staffed by civil servants from the Department of Trade and Industry, because of its statutory obligations under the 1975 Act. This is seen as vital in maintaining its reputation as a genuine third party in the employee relations area, and in its ability to help resolve problems at work, both of a collective and an individual nature. Its general duty, under the 1975 Act, was 'to improve industrial relations and to encourage the extension of collective bargaining', with the assumption that 'good' industrial relations were synonymous with the reform of collective bargaining and its development, where appropriate. The clause relating to collective bargaining was deleted in the Trade Union Reform and Employment Rights Act 1993. ACAS undertakes work in five main areas:

- Individual conciliation – which has already been referred to in the section on industrial tribunals – is a major aspect of the work of ACAS. This is also the way in which many P&D practitioners will come into direct contact with its services.

- Collective conciliation is where ACAS provides assistance through its officers at the request of either party to a dispute, or on its own initiative – although this needs to be done with great care and sensitivity. ACAS officers encourage the parties to use their own internally-agreed procedures to resolve disputes, but on some occasions the intervention of ACAS makes headline news, with reporters camped outside their offices in London. For the most part, however, the collective conciliation work is done quietly and unobtrusively (Farnham and Pimlott, 1995: 226). Mediation is sometimes used as an alternative to conciliation, whereby the ACAS officer makes recommendations to the parties who then resume their attempts to resolve the problem.

- Arbitration is not actually conducted by ACAS officials themselves, but by appointed independent experts – such as academics – who investigate the issue and produce a report under the auspices of ACAS. Some disputes procedures provide for ACAS arbitration following the exhaustion of internal procedures and a breakdown in negotiations; on some occasions both parties agree that the decision of the arbitrator will be binding on the parties, but frequently this is left open and it is assumed that both parties will voluntarily agree to abide by the decision. Arbitration can take several forms in practice, varying from the conventional practice of reaching a compromise, through to pendulum arbitration, in which a decision is made entirely in favour of one party or the other.

- Advisory work is undertaken by ACAS in order to help the parties prevent problems arising in the first place, and it is an area of activity which ACAS officers regard as very important. It is perhaps best viewed as 'fire prevention', rather than the fire fighting which takes place following a breakdown in negotiations, or the dismissal of an employee which is regarded as unfair by the rest of the workforce. The sorts of issues which are investigated include those relating to payment systems, the design of grievance and disciplinary procedures, and job evaluation. To some extent connected with this is the duty to issue codes of practice, which contain practical guidance on how to improve employment relations. ACAS has issued three codes of practice – on disciplinary practice and procedures in employment, on disclosure of information, and time off work for trade union duties and activities. As we shall see in Chapter 13, the first of these codes of practice has been widely used in the development of disciplinary procedures.

- Inquiries form the final broad aspect of the ACAS work load, into topics such as alcohol abuse, the use of quality circles, or labour flexibility. As with the codes of practice, ACAS seeks through this activity to improve industrial relations by fire prevention rather than fire fighting.

Has your organisation had any contact with ACAS? If so, in what capacity? How would you rate its contribution? Are there other areas in which ACAS could offer services to your organisation?

THE COMMISSIONS: EQUAL OPPORTUNITIES, RACIAL EQUALITY, HEALTH AND SAFETY, TRADE UNION ISSUES

The Equal Opportunities Commission (EOC) was established under the Sex Discrimination Act 1975 with the general duties of working towards the elimination of discrimination, promoting equality of opportunity between men and women generally, and reviewing the operation of the relevant legislation – such as on sex discrimination and on equal pay. The EOC is able to bring proceedings under the various pieces of legislation, carry out formal investigations on its own initiative, and publish reports and recommendations. Enforcement relating to employment matters falls within the domain of the ITs, and the last decade has seen a large increase in the number of cases which are on equal opportunities issues. Although the majority of cases which are brought before ITs relate to women's attempts to receive equal treatment with men, the EOC also investigates cases where men feel they are being discriminated against in favour of women – for example, in the case of a male secretary. The EOC has issued a code of practice on how to eliminate discrimination in employment, as too has the IPD of course, and it can issue 'non-discrimination' notices.

In many respects, the Commission for Racial Equality (CRE) performs a role similar to that of the EOC. It was established under the Race Relations Act 1976, with similar general duties to the EOC, but with an added requirement to promote good relations between persons of different racial groups. The CRE has three principal functions: to conduct formal investigations into any discriminatory matter, and (like the EOC) issue non-discrimination notices; to institute legal proceedings in the case of persistent discrimination and in relation to advertisements; and to assist individual complainants in taking their case to an IT. Like the EOC, it has produced a code of practice on how to eliminate discrimination in employment. Both these equal opportunities issues are taken up again in Chapter 4, when we review the ethical and professional context of P&D.

The Health and Safety Commission (HSC) has some similarities with ACAS in that it operates with a full-time chair and a council composed of part-time members drawn from a variety of backgrounds, but broadly representative of both sides of industry and commerce. The Health and Safety at Work Act (HASAWA) 1974 brought together the myriad different bodies which had previously held responsibility for safety and health issues, thus providing the HSC with a unified and integrated set of powers. The general duties of the HSC are: to assist and encourage people to secure the health, safety and welfare of persons at work, and protect those not at work; to undertake and encourage research, to publish findings, and to train and educate people in relation to the purposes of the legislation; to provide an advisory and information service; and to make proposals for regulations. The HSC therefore has a wide remit, including more obvious safety issues – such as the wearing of protective clothing and investigation of accidents – through to less obvious, but equally important, areas concerned with health at work; recently this has involved issues connected with stress-related illnesses and the provision of management support for employees who are under intolerable pressures at work. The HSC has an operational arm, the Health and Safety Executive, which is responsible for the work of the various inspectorates. The main instruments of enforcement open to inspectors are 'improvement notices' which require a fault to be remedied within a set period of time; 'prohibition notices' – which can lead to closures of workplaces and buildings as unsafe if insufficient attention has been paid to an improvement notice, or the risk of serious injury is considered to be high; and prosecutions. We return to the health and safety theme in Chapter 13, where the impact of the legislation at workplace level is considered, and in Chapter 7 when we analyse the role of employee assistance programmes in health promotion.

Which of these three Commissions do you consider has made the most impact on the workplace? Do you think that the impact has been broadly positive or negative? Why?

The Certification Officer was yet another result of the Employment Protection Act 1975, replacing the Registrar of Friendly Societies. This post has the following areas of responsibility:

• trade union political activities, such as approving the rules for a political fund, and dealing with complaints from union members about breaches of the rules in this respect

• trade union mergers and transfers of engagements, ensuring that these take place in accordance with union rules, and that individual members who complain have their cases dealt with

• maintaining a list of trade unions, and determining whether or not they can be classified as independent. This is a major role which requires the Certification Officer to establish whether or not a trade union is 'independent' of an employer, and able to continue in existence without support from the employer. A certificate of independence entitles trade unions to secure tax relief on parts of their income and expenditure, as well as to have access to information from employers about various proposals. To retain a certificate of independence, the trade union has to submit membership returns and agree to scrutiny of its rules

• ensuring that trade unions keep up-to-date membership returns for election purposes, and investigating complaints from members about the administration of elections.

As we saw in Chapter 2, the Employment Act 1988 established the position of Commissioner for the Rights of Trade Union Members (CROTUM). Broadly, this office is responsible for assisting union members who wish to complain about their trade unions, providing them with financial support to help progress their claims. Some argue that the role has been modelled on that of the CRE and EOC, but others suggest that this is a misleading comparison, and is evidence of attempts to undermine the union movement yet further (Farnham and Pimlott, 1995: 230). In support of this claim of alleged unfairness against trade unions, another recently-established role (under the Trade Union Reform and Employment Rights Act (TURERA) 1993 is that of the Commissioner for Protection against Unlawful Industrial Action. This is designed to provide assistance to any member of the general public who wishes to seek damages from a trade union which has engaged in unlawful industrial action and which has involved them in a loss. It should be recalled from Chapter 2 that CROTUM has not been widely used and the costs of administration are excessive given the work load; it is too early to establish whether similar complaints will be made about the new Commissioner.

TRADE UNIONS AND THE TRADES UNION CONGRESS (TUC)

The British trade union movement has a long and proud history, stretching back at least to the early part of the nineteenth century. As Britain became the cradle of modern industrialisation, unions were formed to provide workers with protection against unscrupulous Victorian employers. The union movement can be categorised in two ways: craft, general and industrial; or open and closed (Turner, 1962). Readers who wish to find out more about the union movement are advised to consult one of the specialist employee relations texts (such as Salamon, 1992; Towers, 1992; Blyton and Turnbull, 1994; Farnham and Pimlott, 1995; Edwards, 1995).

Taking the former categorisation, the earliest unions were for craftsmen (for it was *men*) who experienced a high level of autonomy in their work, and sought to maintain and extend job control by preventing a dilution of their skills. These *craft* unions were based on single trades – such as printing, carpentry and milling – and they were organised typically at a local and regional level, with no real attempt to form national federations before the 1850s. Each trade union jealously guarded its own specialist field, both against other craft unions and against encroachment by unskilled workers, and union strength came from the ability to regulate entry to a particular set of jobs by maintaining strict controls over numbers. These themes – strong local organisation, restrictions on membership, and strict demarcation lines between trades – have had a major impact upon the growth and development of the British union movement and upon its ability to respond effectively to the Conservative government's reforms of the last two decades. The fact that early developments were restricted to craft workers meant that unskilled and semi-skilled workers had to look elsewhere in order to build organisations for themselves. The traditions of this group – the *general* unions – are very different from their craft-based colleagues' in a number of ways. They were established in the 1880s and 1890s at national level (after a number of false starts) by people who adopted a more overtly political stance. They were willing to accept almost anybody into membership, and subscriptions were kept at a low level so as not to deter new members. These unions were also more willing to adopt aggressive strike tactics against recalcitrant employers. Typical among their number were gasworkers, dockers and matchgirls. The third category is *industrial* unions, formed to represent a wide range of workers in a particular industry or sector. These unions vary somewhat in structure and orientation, but prominent among the industrial unions were those for workers in coal mining and the railways, although in neither case did the principal union (the National Union of Mineworkers or the National Union of Railwaymen – now RMT) manage to achieve complete coverage and other unions maintained a presence in the industry. Other unions restricted their recruitment to workers in a particular sector, such as the 'old' National and Local Government Officers' Association (NALGO). In recent years, however, partly due to privatisation and major rationalisation in these industries, these unions have gone through major upheavals: the NUM has lost numbers, mostly due to pit closures although the formation of a rival union also had some impact; the NUR lost numbers and ultimately engaged in a defensive merger with the National Union of Seamen; NALGO, faced with privatisations such as those in gas and water, and the contracting-out of local government and health service jobs, joined with the Confederation of Health Service Employees and the National Union of Public Employees to form UNISON, now the largest union in Britain. Merger activity since the early 1980s has rendered the old craft/general/industrial classification increasingly obsolete, and the emergence of more 'super unions' over the next few years will make it even less appropriate as an instrument of categorisation.

The alternative classification – open and closed – has the benefit of focusing on the recruitment methods of the union, and the extent to which it seeks to expand or restrict membership. Good examples of *closed* unions were those originally formed for craft workers or in some industrial sectors – such as coal mining; few of these now remain in existence. In the print industry, for example, technological change has accelerated mergers of what were once closed unions. The *open* unions, by contrast, seek to expand membership in order to increase their strength and influence. Trade unions can thus be categorised in terms of the degree to which they are open or closed in nature.

The overall number of unions has declined consistently since the early part of the twentieth century, from nearly 1400 in 1920 to about 250 in the mid-1990s. Membership has become more concentrated as well, with the 25 unions whose membership is in excess of 50,000 accounting for about 85 per cent of all trade union members. It has been the aim of the Trades Union Congress for a number of years to create a small number of super unions which will work together rather than, as in the past on some occasions, channelling their disagreement into battles between each other. The fifteen largest unions in Britain are shown in Table 3.

The changing sectoral nature of employment, outlined in the previous chapter, has had significant implications for the trade unions. It is estimated now that about one-third of those in employment are union members, a dramatic decline since the zenith of 1979 when it stood at approximately 55 per cent of all employees. Yet, if the current figures are seen against a longer backdrop, the decline looks slightly less stark; between 1945 and 1970, membership density was relatively stable at 40 to 45 per cent, and it was only the major surge during the 1970s which took it well above half the workforce by the end of the decade. Nevertheless, there is no doubt that union membership and density of unionisation has declined considerably since the late 1970s. While the reason for some of this decline can be located in more aggressive government and employer policies towards the unions (as we shall see in Chapter 11 when we consider derecognition), there are many other structural and employment factors which help to

Table 3 The 15 largest British unions (1993)

Unions	Membership (000s) 1993	Summary Description
UNISON – The Public Service Union	1464	Public services; white-collar and manual.
Transport and General Workers Union	949	General/open; has white-collar section.
Amalgamated Engineering and Electrical Union	835	Ex-craft; now fairly open.
GMB (General, Municipal & Boilermakers' Union)	808	General/open; has white-collar section.
Manufacturing, Science and Finance Union	516	White-collar technicians and supervisors.
Royal College of Nursing	303	'Professional union', largest union not in TUC.
Union of Shop, Distributive and Allied Workers	299	Based in retailing, but wider.
Graphical, Paper and Media Union	250	Ex-craft, printing/paper industries.
National Union of Teachers	232	School teachers.
National Association of School Masters & Union of Women Teachers	207	School teachers.
Union of Communication Workers	180	Mainly Post Office workers.
Association of Teachers and Lecturers	162	School and some college teachers, second largest non-TUC union.
Banking, Insurance and Finance Union	141	Financial services union, competes with non-TUC staff associations.
Union of Construction, Allied Trades and Technicians	136	Building industry union; some craftworkers elsewhere.
National Communications Union	122	Mainly British Telecom workers.

Source: Calculated from Annual Reports of the Certification Office (Adapted from Goodman, Marchington, Berridge, Snape and Bamber 1996)

explain the decline (Farnham and Pimlott, 1995: 114). Among them are the following:

- high density in the 'old' areas of Britain, and low density in the 'new' areas

- decline in large units of employment and an increase in the number of smaller establishments

- high union density in the contracting sectors of employment and low density in the expanding sectors

- contraction in manual occupations and an increase in non-manual occupations.

> What are the levels of union membership at your workplace, and how have these altered over the last few years? If the density of unionisation has not altered markedly over the last few years, explain why there is a discrepancy between the situation at your workplace and the aggregate figures. (If you work in a non-union firm, compare your own experiences with that of a colleague working in a unionised environment.)

The peak body for the union movement is the Trades Union Congress (TUC). Founded in 1868, the role of the TUC has evolved since then from an organisation that attempted to unite the different trades, to one that, in addition to dealing with inter-union relations, also seeks to play a major role at national and international level. During the 1970s, the TUC – along with the Confederation of British Industry (CBI) – was closely involved on a tripartite basis with the Labour government of the time. The 1980s saw a substantial reduction in the influence of the TUC as various Conservative governments sought to exclude it from a number of principal advisory bodies, as well as lessen its role within others, such as ACAS and the IT system.

The TUC has the following as its major objectives (Farnham, 1993: 49–50):

- to promote the interests of all or any of its affiliated organisations

- to assist in the complete organisation of all workers eligible for union membership

- to improve the economic and social conditions of workers in all parts of the world

- to affiliate to, or assist, any organisation having similar objectives to the TUC

- to assist in settling disputes between members of affiliated organisations and their employers, between affiliated organisations and their members, and between affiliated organisations themselves.

The first two of these objectives are concerned with increasing levels of union membership and promoting the union movement as a whole. To achieve this, the TUC needs to be seen in a positive light by the general public and as a body which can gain their respect for its actions and contribution to society, not only in terms of the needs of existing and potential union members but also those sections of society which may lack knowledge of what unions actually do in practice. The third and fourth objectives relate to broader international aims, and in recent years the TUC has moved much closer to some of its European neighbours as well as to the broad direction of EU policy. Having been sceptical about the benefits of European Community membership until the early 1980s, the TUC now actively supports attempts to develop a more effective social dialogue. The TUC is part of the European Trades Union Confederation (ETUC) and the International Confederation of Free Trade Unions (ICFTU), and through these bodies it aims to promote the interests of trade union members both in Britain and elsewhere.

The final objective of the TUC – internal governance – is probably the area in which some of the most complex problems emerge. As Kessler and Bayliss note (1995: 173), we need to remember that the TUC is basically the servant of the British union movement, given that it was created by the unions in the first place. This led some commentators in the 1960s to view the TUC as akin to an old carthorse, slow and plodding in its actions but nevertheless steadfast and reliable. There have been many changes since then, in terms of its governing structure and the replacement of its policy and industrial committees with a single executive committee which is answerable to the General Council, and the introduction of task groups to examine important issues. For example, the TUC presented a paper to the 1994 Annual Congress on how the unions might respond to human resource management, given that it has been perceived as an assault on the practice of trade unionism (TUC, 1994). The report notes that this is not an inevitable outcome, however, and there are plenty of situations where employers pursue what are seen as HRM practices (such as appraisal, employee involvement, and performance-related pay) alongside – rather than in opposition to – partnerships with trade unions. The report states that the union movement is committed to 'a new approach to relationships at work' based on high-quality secure employment, a renewed emphasis on competitiveness, high-quality public services, a social partnership between employers and trade unions, and a profound commitment to equal opportunities. This can only be achieved, it is argued, with investment in the long term: in training and development of employees, in capital funding of employing organisations, and in the development of the economy as a whole.

> Is there still a future for the unions? Read the article by Sid Kessler and consider the views of leading practitioners reported in the July 1993 edition of *Personnel Management* before coming to your conclusion.

EMPLOYERS' ORGANISATIONS

Organisations of employers have a history as long as the trade union movement, but in recent times their prominence and influence over employment issues has also declined. This is illustrated well by the space devoted to the subject in academic industrial relations texts; whereas Clegg devoted a whole chapter to employers' organisations in 1970, they do not even get a mention in the index of Paul Edwards' edited collection 25 years later. Before examining the reasons for, and the extent of, this decline we will review briefly the way in which employers' organisations have developed since their emergence in the eighteenth and nineteenth centuries. They can be defined as 'any organisation of employers, individual proprietors, or constituent organisations of employers whose principal purpose includes the regulation of relations between employers and workers or between employers and trade unions' (Farnham, 1993: 40). Their numbers have declined in much the same way as have trade unions, from well over one thousand in the mid-1960s to about 250 in the mid-1990s (Farnham and Pimlott, 1995: 93). *The 1990 Workplace Industrial Relations Survey* (Millward *et al*, 1992: 45–46) illustrates the decline over the course of the 1980s; in 1980, for example, approximately one-quarter of all establishments were members of employers' organisations, a figure which had halved ten years later, and has probably fallen even further since then. It is likely that more manufacturing establishments will be in membership than those in the private service sector, and three sectors (engineering, textiles and construction) have much higher levels of membership. In the case of the latter, about three-quarters of establishments were members of the employers' organisation at the start of the decade.

Employers' organisations differ widely in their structure and organisation, and can be categorised into three broad groupings. First, there are national associations with local affiliates, such as the Engineering Employers' Federation (EEF) which has fifteen regional affiliate organisations, the largest of which is the West Midland Engineering Employers with about one thousand members (Farnham and Pimlott, 1995: 94). Also included in this category would be the Building Employers' Confederation with about 8,000 member firms. The second category comprises those with a national body and local branches, such as the Electrical Contractors' Association with about 2,000 members representing some 80 per cent of the firms and employees in the industry (Farnham and Pimlott, 1995: 96). The final category is the single association with national coverage; this includes bodies such as the Multiple Shoe Retailers Association, the Vehicle Builders and Repairers Association, and the Test and County Cricket Board.

Employers' organisations had a major surge in membership and influence around the turn of the century when they brought together, and acted as representatives for, groups of employers in the same industry in reaching agreements with trade unions over recognition, disputes procedures and the substantive terms and conditions of employment. Rather than allowing each firm in the industry to set its own wage levels and other terms and conditions of employment, they managed to negotiate deals across the whole industry, so 'taking wages out of competition' amongst employers competing in the same product market. As such, they provided a form of defence against trade unions keen to engage in wage bargaining at the level of the individual firm, and then make use of comparability claims to push up wages. The early employers' organisations also assisted individual members who were being targeted for union recognition, or who were suffering the effects of industrial action, by maintaining a unified defence and a common front against the trade unions. On occasions they went on the offensive, as in the 1896 engineering dispute when the EEF led a national 'lock-out' of workers in opposition to union pressure for an eight-hour day (Goodman *et al*, 1996). Other tactics explicitly promoted by employers' organisations included the use of 'blackleg' or replacement labour during a dispute, or the use of 'the document' in which new recruits agreed to give up their membership or not join a union once they were employed (Gospel and Palmer, 1993: 77).

Employers' organisations have traditionally offered four major sets of services to members:

Collective bargaining with trade unions

This role was central to the activities of employers' organisations for many years, and is still particularly important when collective bargaining is organised at industry level. In some industries, agreements are comprehensive in scope and coverage, specifying wage rates and other terms and conditions of employment which apply at each establishment in the industry. In the past such comprehensive agreements were prevalent in several industries, and they remain highly influential in local authorities and universities despite some moves towards single employer bargaining. Nowadays, with the decline in multi-employer industry-wide bargaining (see Chapter 12 for further analysis of this issue), most remaining national agreements are 'partial' in coverage, laying down minimum wage levels for particular grades, as well as rates for overtime working or holiday pay, and for the length of the working week. They are still influential in creating a climate of expectation about what is considered a reasonable increase, and in some organisations specifying levels of holiday pay in the absence of local negotiations. For some employers, such as conglomerates whose interests span many different industries or those organisations that prefer to negotiate locally or across the firm as a whole, the collective bargaining role does not offer any advantages. Conversely, for employers with a single industry focus and intense labour market competition in a specific region or area, the employers' organisation can fulfil a very useful role.

Assisting in the resolution of disputes

To some extent, this is linked in with the previous role, in that the employers' organisation and the recognised trade unions abide by joint grievance, disputes, and disciplinary procedures if there is a 'failure to agree' at establishment or firm level. The major purpose of these procedures is to allow for an independent view of problems in a particular workplace by individuals who have a good knowledge of the industry, and so assist the parties to reach an agreement. It also has the advantage of encouraging the parties to channel their discontent into agreed procedures rather than taking unilateral action – such as going on strike or dismissing a worker without appeal. While there are employers who still use these services, many others who have resigned membership of an employers' organisation have chosen to appoint their own appeals body rather than remain tied into these formal arrangements (see Chapter 13 for more on this issue).

Providing general advice to members

This can take a variety of forms, ranging from seminars for member companies on the impact of new legislation or important developments in P&D, through to informal assistance in the event of a query about how to resolve a human resource problem. Overall, Millward *et al* (1992: 47) report a reduced use of employers' organisations as a source of external advice between 1980 and 1990. Of employers seeking advice from an external body in 1980, the most likely source was an employers' organisation or a full-time trade union officer, with ACAS and outside lawyers being the next most popular, and management consultants rarely used. By 1990, lawyers were by far the most popular source of advice, followed by ACAS. The use of employers' organisations was much lower, and even less than management consultants and trade unions. Surprisingly, perhaps, more use is made of employers' organisations by P&D specialists and by larger establishments, rather confounding the view that it might be the less experienced employers who seek advice.

Representing members' views

This role takes two forms; first, employers' organisations, and in particular the Confederation of British Industry (CBI), acts as a pressure group for employers generally, both in relation to national government and with the European Commission. In some industries they play a major role in widening the awareness of the general public, say in relation to the employment consequences of tax increases on tobacco or alcohol, or on the value of attracting inward investment to a particular region. Employers' organisations also provide specialist representation for member firms which have to appear at industrial tribunals; as we saw above, however, some employers now prefer to use lawyers or consultants instead for this purpose.

Summarise the reasons why employers' organisations are now less widely used than they were 25 years ago. If your establishment is a member, what do you gain from this membership, and could you obtain these services as cheaply or effectively from other sources? If your establishment is not a member, what benefits might accrue from membership?

The peak body for employers is the Confederation of British Industry (CBI). It was formed in 1965 by a merger of three existing organisations so as to concentrate resources on the more effective co-ordination and representation of industrial opinion to government and other bodies. Many small employers were against the merger, feeling that their interests would not be well represented, and this feeling has remained to some extent. When formed, the CBI had a membership of 12,600 firms, the main nationalised industries, 104 employers' organisations and 150 trade associations. The principal objects of the CBI are, according to Farnham and Pimlott (1995: 200):

- to provide a voice for British industry and influence general industrial and economic policy, and to act as a national point of reference for those seeking industry's views

- to develop the contribution of British industry to the national economy

- to encourage the efficiency and competitive power of British industry, and provide information and advice to help do so.

In addition to the CBI, and of course the IPD, both of which aim to represent industrial and professional views to government, there are also other organisations which claim to speak for employer interests. In the last decade the Institute of Directors has achieved a higher profile, largely because its commitment to free market principles and its support for the Conservative government's policies have been more overtly forthright than that of the CBI. Indeed, there have been times when the CBI has quite openly criticised government action, especially in relation to the continuing demise of manufacturing industry, and in its expression of concerns about any drift towards to a low skill–low wage economy. At European level, employers are represented by the Union of Industrial and Employers' Confederations of Europe (UNICE).

TRAINING POLICIES AND GOVERNMENT INTERVENTION

The British 'training problem' has been with us a long time, having been recognised by governments of all political complexions. However, they have differed in their perception of the extent of the problem, and a variety of initiatives has emerged over the post-war period in an attempt to develop something of a national policy. The fact that most interventions have not been particularly successful has entailed regular reviews and revisions, and different periods have thrown up different prognoses and solutions, with shifts in the degree of state intervention and employer involvement. (Readers who require a more in-depth treatment of this material are referred to Harrison, 1992, especially Part One.)

The 1959 Crowther Report expressed concern over the poor provision of education and training for school-leavers in Britain. A consensus between the government, the CBI and the TUC led to the 1964 Industrial Training Act, which created the system of industrial training boards (ITBs). As Lane (1989: 72) puts it, 'this signified the recognition that voluntary policies could not overcome the problems of skills shortages which were connected with poor economic performance in the post-war period'. The ITBs were tripartite bodies with the power to impose a levy in order to fund training – this was based on the size of the workforce – and the money was then made available in the form of grants. It was hoped this would discourage poaching by employers who were unwilling to meet the costs of training their own labour. The record of the ITBs, as Keep (1989: 187) sees it, is not a bad one: 'They encouraged the setting up of training departments where none had previously existed; they were responsible for improvements in manpower policy; they sponsored the training of groups other than apprenticeships; they pioneered and promoted new training methods and they helped to raise standards in most areas.' At their height, the 27 ITBs covered 15 million employees. However, there were complaints that the ITBs were biased against small firms and that they failed to reform the apprenticeship system, with numbers falling from 389,000 in 1964, to 296,000 in 1974 (Aldcroft, 1992: 59). Indeed, the apprenticeship system – such as in engineering and printing – had its critics. School-leavers joined employers and qualified by serving time, and training was largely on-the-job (and variable in quality) with skills specific to the occupation. The numbers trained were relatively small, as entry was controlled by unions which were anxious to protect their craftsmen.

The Employment and Training Act 1973 was designed to make the system less bureaucratic by creating a system of exemptions for small firms and those which could demonstrate that they met the specified criteria. This seemed to indicate an end to the 'voluntarist' approach, as it created a national new body – the Manpower Services Commission (MSC) – to overhaul the ITBs, and in particular to fill in gaps caused by their concentration on the apprenticeship system to the neglect of youth employment and adult retraining. The worsening economic climate of the 1970s meant that measures designed to deal with unemployment became a major priority, and as a national body the MSC was better able to address these issues than the ITBs, which were based on occupational labour markets.

The election of a Conservative government in 1979 signalled a major shift in training policy. A number of beliefs shaped their approach, including the assumption that market forces, not statutory rights or duties, were the most appropriate way to determine training, both in its form and amount. It was felt that the key responsibility resided with employers, and to a lesser extent employees, with state assistance to help disadvantaged groups – such as the unemployed – and pump-priming in order to aid innovation. The tripartite apparatus was rejected, and it was stressed that training should be employer-led (Keep and Rainbird, 1995: 518–519). The Employment and Training Act 1981 abolished 17 of the 24 ITBs, although the MSC did expand its role by taking on responsibility for youth training (YTS) and later adult employment (ET). However, government policy remained 'voluntarist', with its role solely as providing support and infrastructure, but letting employers manage the training process. Ashton and Felstead (1994: 240–241) argue that this policy misunderstands the training problem: 'If employers are demanding only low skill levels, then placing them in control of the delivery of government training programmes and encouraging individuals to respond to employers' demands is merely to reproduce the low skills base of the UK economy.' In short, it does little more than increase the supply of skills for lower-paid jobs.

In 1983 the Youth Training Scheme was created, based broadly on the earlier Youth Opportunities Programme. In practice, off-the-job training had not been integrated with work placement and became simply a way of alleviating high unemployment, rather than creating high-quality training. The YTS was replaced by the Youth Training initiative in 1990. This was later reviewed so that it was 'customer driven' and the intention was to introduce training credits or vouchers which would allow the individual to achieve NVQs. ET, which was established in 1988, was designed to help the adult unemployed back into the labour market, but it was also criticised for providing opportunities for employers to utilise cheap labour.

By 1988 the corporatist tripartite approach to training finally ended as the MSC became the Training Commission, later the Training Agency, and then part of the Employment Department. With the exception of the Construction Industry Training Board, ITBs were abolished. Following the National Training Task Force recommendation, local training bodies (Training and Enterprise Councils – TECs – in England and Wales, and Local Enterprise Companies – LECs – in Scotland) were created by government in 1991; these are run by employers to assess training needs and co-ordinate programmes. At least two-thirds of each TEC board must be private-sector employers – who are chairmen or senior management of major local companies. The TECs are responsible for helping with the Technical and Vocational Education Initiative (TVEI), establishing business/education partnerships, being involved in youth training, and for accreditation of the Investors In People (IIP) initiative – see Chapter 8. Part of the rationale behind TECs and LECs was to influence *local* labour markets rather than sectors, and to provide assistance for the unemployed to become the main focus of concern, rather than training in general; because of this, their ability to achieve 'a step change in training activity in Britain' is doubted (Keep and Rainbird, 1995: 525). In addition to the TECs, there are voluntary industrial training organisations (ITOs) which are based at sectoral level, supported by organisations within the industry and overseen by a national body (NCITO). The largest of the old ITBs – the Engineering Industry Training Board – was reconstructed into a company – the Engineering Training Authority (Hendry, 1994: 410–415).

Another significant development has been the move towards a unified system of national vocational qualifications (NVQs) and Scottish Vocational Qualifications (SVQs). A number of assumptions provide the context within which NVQs/SVQs are established: the view that qualifications need to reflect real workplace needs if the learning is to be useful; that industries must own and develop their own qualifications; employers' views of what is required should dominate further education; the Single European Market requires a modern input to what will become a 'European' qualification (Reid, Barrington and Kenny 1992: 26). The National Council for Vocational Qualifications (NCVQ) was established in 1986 to rationalise and reform vocational qualifications in England and Wales, and SCOTVEC was formed in Scotland to fulfil a similar purpose. The basis of assessment is reaching a performance standard laid down by the lead body for an area of vocational work and, unlike traditional exams, assessment is undertaken on the job. While NVQs may require employees to be trained to reach a set of standards, it is not a training programme, nor is there a prescribed learning method. The main aim has been to create a national standard, with NVQs essentially based on occupational competence. There are four main principles of NVQs (IRS *Employee Development Bulletin* 40, 1993). Firstly, it is an industry-led scheme, in theory making the qualifications acceptable to employers rather than educationalists or trainers. Secondly, it is based on performance on the job rather than knowledge. Thirdly, it is aimed at making access to qualifications more flexible by removing barriers or restrictions on individuals. Finally, the qualifications are flexible and transferable because they comprise units of competencies which enable individuals to accumulate units over time. Furthermore, Accreditation of Prior Learning provides a way of giving evidence for past achievements. Given that NVQs specify outcomes and not learning methods, there is flexibility in teaching and learning.

There are five levels of the award, reflecting increasingly demanding competence requirements and more complex knowledge.

Level 1 Occupational competence in performing a range of tasks under supervision.

Level 2 Occupational competence in performing a wider range of tasks with limited supervision.

Level 3 Occupational competence required for satisfactory, responsible performance in a defined occupation or range of jobs.

Level 4 Competence to design and specify defined tasks, products or process and to accept responsibility for the work of others.

Level 5 Competence at a professional level with mastery of a range of relevant knowledge and the ability to apply it at a level higher than 4.

> Find out about NVQs/SVQs in an occupation of your choice, and assess how effective they are in providing a qualification structure for that occupation.

The National Advisory Council for Education and Training Targets (NACETTS) was established in 1993 to help assist the achievement of competitiveness. Targets include 50 per cent of medium or large organisations to be IIP by 1996, and by the turn of the century 50 per cent of workers to be qualified to NVQ Level 3 (or equivalent). However, a number of doubts have been expressed about the system. One problem is that TEC budgets are determined by outputs – for example, the number of people attaining NVQs and employers achieving IIP – and this merely rewards short-term goals. Secondly, a survey by the National Council for Voluntary Organisations argued that output targets force employers to select 'individuals who can be trained quickly rather than those most in need of training – such as the long-term unemployed or disabled people' (*Personnel Management Plus*, August 1993: 4). Thirdly, it is not clear how much employers really do value NVQs: they were cited as being acceptable only for one hundred civil service vacancies in three years (*People Management*, August 1995: 14). Fourthly, they have been criticised for being too narrow and task-specific, unable to cope with changing technology, work methods and skill requirements. Moreover, the skill level is seen as too low (Keep, 1994: 312). Wide-ranging criticism has led to a review prepared for the Department for Education and Employment by the Evaluation Advisory Group chaired by Gordon Beaumont. Broadly, this endorses the system in principle, while making about 80 recommendations designed to improve the qualification; these are concerned largely with making the system more accessible to employers, and for greater responsibility for assessment and quality to be given to employer-run lead bodies and occupational standards councils (Merrick, 1996: 14; Pringle, 1996: 150).

THE DEPTH OF TRAINING PROVISION

The 1980s saw major changes in work organisation, including increasing work loads, wider ranges of tasks, new technology, a greater emphasis on flexibility, and the elimination of entire levels in the hierarchy. Training has been seen as a key part in this change process. A new training culture is meant to have emerged in which employees identify and act on their own training needs, and thereby harmonise personal and corporate development (Roberts and Corcoran-Nantes, 1995). The early 1990s recession saw only a small reduction in training provision, but ironically the survival of the 'market model' appears to have been due largely to regulations which set a floor for training activity – such as on health and safety matters (as a result of economy-wide regulations on the control of substances hazardous to health and the Food Safety Act), or occupational or sector-specific regulation (for example the Financial Services Act). The training requirements of BS5750 have also been cited (Felstead and Green, 1994: 199).

Other research supports this estimate of maintained levels of training in recent years, with the great majority of those receiving training feeling it had clear benefits for them. As an issue it ranked close to job security, pay and supervision. Nevertheless, there remains evidence of a substantial training 'gap', with one in five of those who want training in the future feeling they are unlikely to get it (Gallie and White, 1993). Unlike initiatives such as BS5750 or TQM, which have been criticised for being too production/systems-oriented, IIP has been seen by some as providing the organisation with the necessary human resource element which other quality initiatives tend to neglect. Furthermore, training is often seen as a 'litmus test' for management commitment to staff (Keep, 1989). Management commitment to training has a symbolic value. It represents employers' commitment to staff, the recipients feel involved, and it can also signal a business strategy based on added value rather than on low cost (Storey and Sisson, 1993). Training also fits with recent ideas on the learning organisation (Senge, 1990), in which training and learning become central to the very essence of the organisation rather than just a set of processes – we consider the impact of these issues on organisations more fully in Chapter 8.

In the UK the *laissez-faire* and voluntarist approach to training has been predominant, and hence the onus for training has fallen directly on individual employers. Yet this does not seem to have been a success. Finegold and Soskice (1988: 23) note that 'Britain's relative failure to educate and train its workforce has contributed to its poor economic record in the post-war period.' Keep (1989: 331) also criticises the UK's 'persistent failure to evolve and maintain a coherent national system of vocational education and training', and points to low average per capita spending on training and development in British companies compared with their counterparts in many other countries. This derives partly from the traditional dominance of training by craft apprenticeships at the lower end of the hierarchy, with most other training expenditure concentrated on management or supervisory staff. Central to the UK problems has been its lack of a national infrastructure. Steedman and Wagner (1987) indicate that the superior training of German youth machinists results in less 'down-time', because the high level of training provided to the workforce means that they are able not only to run the manufacturing process but also to carry out maintenance. Others have also found British managers poorly educated and lacking in competence compared with managers in other countries (Constable and McCormick, 1987).

A central problem has been the division between education and training, and the lower significance accredited to vocational education. 'Vocational education is perceived as low-status because it provides little opportunity for career advancement and because managers who themselves enter employment without practical experience or technical training focus on academic examinations as the best means of assessing the potential of trainees' (Finegold and Soskice, 1988: 28). Moreover, structural problems inhibit the development of training: UK employers are inclined to shift productive capacity and investment abroad so that they can 'buy' pre-trained workforces; the short-termism of British industry, with mergers and take-overs undermining long-term commitment; the dominance of the finance function, which has a cost ideology; and the low adoption of coherent P&D practices (Keep, 1989). That these are long-term problems is illustrated by Hobsbawm (1968: 168), who described Britain 'entering the twentieth century and the age of modern science and technology as a spectacularly ill-educated people'.

Finegold and Soskice (1988) outline a number of reasons why Britain has failed to develop in the training area. First, the political parties – with the Conservatives opposed to intervening in the market and Labour seeing technical and vocational skills as incompatible with the provision of comprehensive education. Secondly, the lack of a structure to administer a national policy. Thirdly, the education and training system which has been biased against the acquisition of practical skills. Fourthly, the industrial structure of Britain, which is based on low-skill areas, and consequently provides little incentive for employers to train, and results in training being seen as a low-status function. Fifthly, the financial market – which emphasises short-term performance and so inhibits the development of training. Finally, conflictual industrial relations traditionally made it more difficult to introduce training for semi-skilled workers because of existing demarcations. As we have noted, apart from health and safety there is no general legislative requirement for training.

CONCLUSION

In this chapter we have reviewed the institutional and national context for P&D, focusing on three particular aspects of this infrastructure – the legal institutions and bodies which are most central to P&D, trade unions and employers' organisations, and the training system in Britain. There is little doubt that legal institutions, such as the industrial tribunal system and the various Commissions (Equal Opportunities, Racial Equality, Health and Safety) have had a major impact on P&D policies and practices. It is not just their direct impact on individual employers and employees which matters, but the indirect influence of their activities on all employers. For example, not only do the industrial tribunals hear a large number of cases each year, but their decisions also send messages to other employers about how to deal with dismissal and other employment issues; as we see in Chapter 13, procedures have been extensively formalised since the 1970s, to a large extent because of this influence. In addition, managements are now more likely to take care when advertising, recruiting and selecting, when dealing with equal opportunities cases, and in promoting health and safety awareness at work, than they were 25 years ago. In contrast, the aggregate impact of trade unions and employers' organisations on P&D has declined over the last 15 years, to a large extent due to their exclusion by successive Conservative governments, as well as to structural and sectoral changes in employment. But, there are many workplaces where trade unions continue to have a significant presence, and where employers' organisations are still used for specific advice and/or collective bargaining and dispute resolution. While a Labour government would place greater priority on social partnership than the Conservatives, and so re-establish some elements of tripartism, it is hard to imagine that trade unions and employers' organisations will regain the positions of prominence and influence which they enjoyed in the 1960s and 1970s. The position in relation to training policy looks even bleaker in some respects, as Britain has lacked any systematic and nationally-based infrastructure to develop training in all workplaces compared with some of our major competitors. The advent of NVQs and SVQs offers considerable potential, as these are employer-led and specifically related to workplace needs. On the other hand, this can also be a source of weakness, as the initiative rests ultimately with employers and employees rather than being driven by government; this means that developments are likely to be highly uneven, with most employees still failing to gain any training beyond that needed to satisfy the basic and immediate needs of their jobs. The future might bring a return to training levies or tax incentives, but at the time of writing the precise way forward is uncertain. In the meantime, P&D practitioners are best advised to develop training and learning opportunities which are appropriate for their own organisations (see Chapters 8–10).

USEFUL READING

BLYTON, P. AND TURNBULL, P. (1994) *The Dynamics of Employee Relations*. London, Macmillan.

FARNHAM, D. AND PIMLOTT, J. (1995) *Understanding Industrial Relations*, Fifth Edition. London, Cassell.

FELSTEAD, A. AND GRUN, F. (1994) 'Training During the Recession', *Work, Employment and Society*, Vol 8, 2; 199–219.

GOLD, M. (Ed.) (1993) *The Social Dimension: Employment Policy in the European Community*. London, Macmillan.

HARRISON, R. (1992) *Employee Development*. London, IPD.

KEEP, E. AND RAINBIRD, H. (1995) 'Training' in P. Edwards (Ed.) *Industrial Relations; Theory and Practice in Britain*. Oxford, Blackwell: 515–542.

KESSLER, S. (1993) 'Is there still a future for the unions?' *Personnel Management*, July: 24–30.

KESSLER, S. AND BAYLISS, F. (1995) *Contemporary British Industrial Relations*, Second Edition. London, Macmillan.

LEWIS, D. (1994) *Essentials of Employment Law*, Fourth Edition. London, IPD.

PITT, G. (1995) *Employment Law*, Second Edition. London, Sweet and Maxwell.

SAGGERS, R. (1994) 'Training climbs the corporate agenda', *Personnel Management*, July: 42–45.

4 The professional and ethical context

INTRODUCTION

In the previous two chapters we examined some of the major contextual influences on personnel and development, namely the nature of work and employment, and the role of national and legal institutions in shaping employment relations at workplace level. It was argued that, while both of these contextual factors played a major part in creating the environment within which P&D is practised, neither of these *determines* its precise operation. The direct influence of these contextual factors is limited by the way in which they are interpreted by managers and non-managerial staff in employing organisations, as well as by their uneven effects on P&D in different workplaces. In this chapter we move on to examine the third set of contextual factors, the professional and ethical bases of P&D. As we shall see later, ethics and professionalism are key elements in the functional map of one of the lead bodies in the area (the Personnel Standards Lead Body), which joined with the Training and Development Lead Body and the Trade Union Sector Development Body to form the Employment Occupational Standards Council (EOSC) in 1994.

The notion of standards is central to this discussion, both in its historical context and its contemporary expression through the work of the lead bodies. Personnel management had its origins in activities which were designed, in part at least, to ameliorate the worst effects of industrial capitalism, and its pioneers were individuals with a strong social conscience – such as Seebohm Rowntree and Jesse Boot. On occasions, the P&D function has been characterised as the employers' conscience, there to ensure that in the pursuit of more productive and efficient work the human dimension is not overlooked. The ethical and professional perspective is demonstrated by what some would see as an obsession with rules, a compliance with legal standards, and ensuring the expression of alternative views. But professionalism also has another side to it, which can lead to better employment relations (and, by inference, to more productive and efficient employing organisations) through the adoption of up-to-date and proven P&D policies and practices. In this regard, efforts to persuade line managers to implement 'best practice' P&D practices is a clear sign of professionalism, in much the same way that accountants and engineers would disseminate new ideas in the areas of finance and new technology.

One area in which the professional and ethical influences coalesce is that of equal opportunities, and for this reason the final part of the chapter focuses on employer policies in this field. Here we review the development of equal opportunities policies in employing organisations, and examine the way in which these have been influenced by legal measures and broader ethical and professional considerations. As with many aspects of P&D, there are essentially two distinct sets of arguments which are used to extend equal opportunities – the moral and the economic. The *moral* case rests upon injustice and inequality, on the limited access that women, the disabled, and minority ethnic groups have to employment in certain occupations, and especially into more senior management. The *economic* case is built around ideas of wastage and inefficiency and the claim that it makes good business sense to increase access – in terms of productivity and quality, customer care, and managerial skills – in order to ensure the most effective use of all talents in the workforce. Although this theme is taken up again in most chapters in this book, we advance a number of arguments here to support the 'business case' for equal opportunities.

By the end of this chapter, readers should be able to:

- review their own P&D activity, and define more precisely how they might enhance their professional and ethical reputation

- convince line managers that it is worthwhile adopting a professional and ethical stance with regard to P&D issues

- make out a 'business case' for the implementation, extension or maintenance of equal opportunities.

In addition, readers should be able to understand and explain:

- the principal features of P&D work, its major tensions and contradictions

- the meaning of business ethics and the role which P&D specialists can play in its implementation

- the key differences between equal opportunities and managing diversity.

THE NATURE OF PERSONNEL AND DEVELOPMENT

A number of books provide potted histories of personnel and training management, with some describing the major developments from its early roots in Victorian Britain (see, for example, Crichton, 1968; Farnham, 1990), while others develop a more sociological critique of the occupation (Watson, 1977; Legge, 1995). Rather than dwell on these details here, we focus on two key features of P&D – the range of activities it covers, and the tensions and contradictions in its meaning – illustrating these with examples drawn from historical sources, as appropriate. Readers who are keen on a fuller treatment are advised to consult one or more of the sources mentioned above.

First, it is clear that P&D covers a *wide range of activities*. The early roots were in *welfare*, championed by social reformers who displayed a genuine paternalistic concern for their workers. Often driven by strong religious motivations, such as Quakerism and non-conformism, they were keen to improve working conditions and provide their employees with assistance should they fall on hard times. At the same time the reform programmes were implemented within a clear business framework, in which tight controls were maintained in relation to discipline, time-keeping, and output (Crichton, 1968: 15). Many of the earliest welfare workers were women, especially in munitions factories during the First World War, and they were brought in specifically to make work more tolerable for the female workers who were drafted in at this time. Some of the first companies to invest in personnel and welfare are still household names today: Boots, Cadbury's, Lever Brothers, and Rowntree (now owned by Nestlé). Welfare issues resurface at various stages in this book, most notably in the Resourcing part, when we examine Employee Assistance Programmes (EAPs) and counselling.

While most analysts are agreed that the roots of P&D can be found in the welfare tradition, there are alternative viewpoints about how it has developed since then. The history of P&D can be viewed sequentially, with different aspects of the subject coming to the fore in different time periods to reflect changing pressures, or it can be seen in a summative fashion, with each new set of activities representing an addition to the P&D portfolio (Torrington, 1988). In a sense, both perspectives have validity, given the range of different types of employing organisations and the different pressures with which each is confronted. The other activities are:

Administration
This comprises many of what are seen as the mainstream aspects of P&D, and those which often form the largest element of a new personnel assistant's or training officer's job. Included within the administrative duties would be recruitment advertising, writing letters to candidates, organising induction programmes, setting up training sessions, keeping employee records (on matters such as absence levels and discipline), and payroll. In other words, it is not possible to pigeon-hole this set of activities into any one of the 'generalist' categories (resourcing, development, relations, reward) as they cover all aspects of the employment contract. Administrative activities have formed a central part of the P&D role since the 1940s. Although it is typically seen as reactive, the administrative role is increasingly important as a support and trigger mechanism within a fully integrated computerised personnel information system.

Negotiation
This activity reached prominence in the 1960s and 1970s, as employers responded to a growing trade union involvement in P&D affairs. The context for the negotiation role is one where trade unions have high levels of membership and are prepared to use (or threaten to use) their bargaining power to force a change in employer-employee relations. It is most apparent in the set-piece negotiations which take place between employers and trade unions at the time of wage settlements, although it is also seen when managements enter into discussions about changes to working practices, redundancies or

subcontracting of services. The skills which are needed for this set of activities are somewhat different from those required in welfare or administration duties. Good negotiators not only need to demonstrate competence in interpersonal skills such as persuasion, but should also work well in teams, be able to operate under extreme stress, and keep calm while under pressure. We take up some of these issues in the employee relations section of the book, but leave the full treatment of negotiating skills to the generalist book in the series.

Legal expertise

As we have already seen, employment relations in Britain remained relatively free from the law until the 1960s. Since that time there has been a mass of legislation which P&D professionals need to understand, both in the field of employment protection and individual rights, and in the area of collective regulation. In the employment protection area, in particular, this has led to a considerable amount of procedural reform, with the consequence that most P&D managers today need to have a decent working knowledge of the law; in the 1970s this was principally in the area of unfair dismissal, but more recently industrial tribunals have dealt with a growing number of increasingly complex equal opportunities cases. Many chapters in the remainder of the book include a consideration of legal issues, but these are integrated as appropriate: for example, recruitment advertising in the Employee Resourcing section, health and safety in Employee Relations, and employee share ownership in Reward.

Organisation development (OD)

Although there was some interest among a number of large multinational companies in OD models during the late 1960s and early 1970s, this has become a new element in the P&D area during the last decade. It is often connected with ideas on change management, with a strong emphasis on organisation culture and restructuring, evidenced by terms such as delayering, empowerment and the learning organisation. It coincided with a period of intense competitive pressures, being influenced by writers such as Tom Peters and Rosabeth Moss Kanter, and the examples of large US organisations which 'turned themselves around' during the 1980s. We deal with this aspect of P&D again in the Employee Development section of the book, but it also forms the backcloth to a number of issues which we consider in the Resourcing, Relations and Reward sections as well – for example, performance management, non-union firms, and harmonisation.

Many of these aspects of P&D are now pulled together or used selectively under the *human resource management* banner. Of course, much depends upon the version of HRM which is employed, and whether the emphasis is on 'human *resource* management' or the 'management of resourceful humans'. We do not address the differences between the various forms of HRM here, nor do we consider whether or not HRM is different from personnel management or industrial relations, although throughout the remainder of the book we do use examples of P&D practices which can form part of these different versions of HRM. Some consider the debate about the meanings of personnel management and HRM to be rather sterile

(Gennard and Kelly, 1994: 27), whilst others (eg Legge, 1995; Storey, 1995) provide detailed analysis of the theory and practice of HRM. Torrington (1988: 7–8) advocates use of the medical metaphor of the general practitioner to understand the contemporary role of the P&D professional. He argues:

> The general practitioner enjoys professional standing and respect because of a wide-ranging expertise, while acknowledging the specialist expertise of consultants. The personnel manager is a general practitioner deploying similar wide-ranging expertise. Sometimes there is a need for special skills, so the consultants are called in or the 'patient' is referred to a training school, assessment centre or other source of special treatment.

How appropriate is this 'general practitioner' metaphor in your experience and, if it was more widely used, could it help P&D specialists to enhance their contribution?

The second key feature of P&D is its ambiguity, and the tensions and contradictions which characterise it both conceptually and practically. Legge (1995: 10) summarises this as a 'tension between two potentially incompatible orientations'; the 'caring' and the 'control' elements of the role. Both of these were apparent in its initial formulation as a welfare agent, whereby employees were given assistance at work, largely – though not exclusively – to ensure their contribution could be enhanced. It can also be seen in the dual usage of the term 'counselling', on the one hand denoting an activity which is undertaken in a non-directive way to help staff come to terms with anxieties, whilst on the other being used as a shorthand for the preliminary stages of a disciplinary process. The fact that the expertise of P&D practitioners is bound up in their dealings – either directly or indirectly – with the 'human' resource, as opposed to other inanimate resources, means that they are inextricably linked with questions of caring and control. For other managers, human resource considerations tend to be hidden and implicit in their thinking rather than overt and explicit; the staffing implications of their inventions would not figure prominently in the work of research scientists, for example.

Many people still view P&D practitioners as intermediaries between management and employees, ready to listen to both but on the side of neither. Applicants for P&D posts are often prone to say at interview that the reason they want to go into the occupation is because they 'like working with people', or because they visualise their role as akin to a United Nations envoy who brings together the warring factions. The reality of P&D, especially in its variant as strategic HRM, is that specialists are clearly and directly involved in making a contribution to management objectives. The main issues which confront P&D professionals toward the end of the twentieth century are all about their contribution to the business, in terms of improving recruitment and selection decisions, training employees to achieve targets, working with the unions through partnerships to reduce conflict at work, and designing reward strategies that help employers to gain maximum productivity from all employees. In each of these respects P&D is just as much a part of management as production, finance or marketing, and it is on these criteria that its contribution is increasingly being assessed (see Chapter 17 for a discussion of service-level agreements). If P&D fails to make a positive contribution which can be measured and evaluated it is seen to be at risk of being subcontracted, or having its activities devolved in their entirety to line managers. At the same time, as we shall see in Chapters 17 and 18, the move to measurement and quantification also has risks attached to it, as P&D seemingly embraces an accountancy perspective on the world (P. Armstrong, 1989).

Connected with this is the continuing debate about who is responsible for P&D, and whether it is a specialist occupation or an activity which forms part of every manager's job. To some extent, of course, both perspectives are correct; obviously, any employee who manages other people at work has responsibilities in the P&D area, since he or she deals with issues of motivation, discipline, reward, learning and training on a regular basis, irrespective of whether or not a specialist function is in existence. In organisations which do have specialists, the balance of responsibilities between P&D professionals and line managers is important. Research by Hutchinson and Wood (1995) for the IPD shows that, despite greater devolution of P&D issues to line managers, there tends to be a distinction between policy and practice; line managers are increasingly taking over the *practice* of P&D while functional specialists retain responsibility for drawing up *policy* and reviewing procedures. We explore this question of responsibility for human resource issues more fully in Chapter 18.

Tensions can also occur between different elements of P&D, especially if the function is highly specialised and differentiated, or if certain issues fall within the province both of P&D and other management functions. The latter is best illustrated in the area of corporate communications, which may be the responsibility of specialist functions such as sales and marketing, public relations, or planning, instead of P&D. Equally, it is likely that the line managers would expect to control the dissemination of information without interference from specialist support functions. It is also possible, given different traditions and backgrounds, that different parts of P&D will have contrasting 'solutions' for employment problems; the employee relations manager, for example, may regard many of the 'new' HRM initiatives as little more than 'soft and naïve' management, whereas the OD manager might see his or her employee relations colleague as a throwback to the collectivist world of the 1970s. One of these might be keen to pursue policies that are designed to strengthen individualism, while the other might be keen to strengthen a collectivist stance, maintaining co-operative relations with local trade union officers. These themes are examined more fully in Chapter 18 when we analyse the meaning of horizontal integration and 'best practice' P&D.

> What do you see as the philosophies which underpin different aspects of P&D, exemplified by the generalist subjects of employee resourcing, employee development, employee relations, and employee reward? Are there tensions and contradictions between them, or are such distinctions a thing of the past?

PROFESSIONALISM AND STANDARDS IN PERSONNEL AND DEVELOPMENT

Although there is evidence of P&D practice during the nineteenth century, the first attempt to create a professional body did not take place until 1913 when Seebohm Rowntree invited firms to send representatives to a conference of welfare workers in York. The 48 people present decided to form an Association of Employers 'interested in industrial betterment and of welfare workers engaged by them' (Niven, 1967: 36). The Welfare Workers' Association, as it became known, joined with the North Western Area Industrial Association six years later to form the Welfare Workers' Institute, with a membership of 700 (Farnham, 1990: 22). After the First World War membership fell as the welfare tradition lost ground, and the association was renamed the Institute of Labour Management in 1931, a name it kept until after the Second World War. During this time the type of duties undertaken by practitioners in the P&D field broadened to include wages, employment, joint consultation, health and safety, employee services and welfare, and education and training (Farnham, 1990: 22–23). In 1946 the Institute of Personnel Management was formed, thus reflecting this broader orientation, remaining in existence until 1994 when the IPM joined with the Institute of Training and Development to form the Institute of Personnel and Development (IPD).

Since 1913 membership has grown dramatically, although there were periods in the early part of the century when numbers fell. Table 4 illustrates the growth of this main professional body, and shows how membership has almost quadrupled since the beginning of the 1980s.

Table 4 Membership of the main professional body for P&D

Year	Number of members
1913	48
1919	700
1939	760
1956	3980
1971	14,260
1981	22,620
1990	41,000
1994	75,500
1996	76,760

By the spring of 1996 members of the IPD were distributed amongst grades in the following way:

Companions	236
Fellows	5,951
Corporate Members	23,205
Graduates	17,080
Licentiates and Associates	14,851
Affiliates (studying and non-studying)	15,437

The IPD is Europe's largest professional body for individuals specialising in the management and development of people. Its mission is to:

• lead in the development and promotion of good practice in the field of the management and development of people, for application both by professional members and by their organisational colleagues

• to serve the professional interests of members

• to uphold the highest ideals in the management and development of people.

The Institute is a charity and it has specific charitable objectives:

• to promote and develop the science and practice of the management and development of people (including the promotion of research and the publication of the useful results of such research for the public benefit)

• to establish, promote and monitor standards of competence, good practice, conduct and ethics for those engaged (or about to engage) in the practice of management and development of people, for the public benefit.

The IPD aims to fulfil its objectives in a number of ways:

• by establishing, monitoring and promoting standards and ethics for the profession

• by seeking opportunities and pursuing activities, using the specialised experience of professional members supported by staff and other resources, to advance the practice of the management and development of people

• by influencing developments and issues relating to the management and development of people through effective representation of the views of the profession

• by disseminating and exchanging information, experience and the results of research and development for the public benefit and the continuing professional development of members

• by establishing programmes of education and training and

continuing professional development with recognised standards of achievement, to support the systematic development and accreditation of members

- by providing a wide range of member services at local, national and international levels to support the professional needs of members

- by developing and maintaining appropriate links with other bodies and organisations at local, national and international levels in order to positively influence decisions and thinking affecting the management and development of people

- by providing relevant commercial activities which support the professionalism of the Institute and its members and which earns commercial returns for reinvestment into its main purposes.

To what extent does the IPD fulfil criteria typically associated with a professional body, and do its members deserve the title 'professional'? Freidson (1973: 22) defines professionalisation as:

> a process by which an organised occupation, usually but not always by virtue of making a claim to special esoteric competence and to concern for the quality of its work and its benefits to society, obtains the exclusive right to perform a particular kind of work, control training for and access to it, and control the right of determining and evaluating the way their work is performed.

In terms of exclusivity to perform specialist work, the IPD cannot claim to have in membership all individuals responsible for P&D activities at work. We have seen already that many aspects of P&D practice are actually undertaken by line managers, but it is common for a P&D specialist to have designed the policies and procedures which govern and structure this work. Moreover, even if an employer does not employ a dedicated P&D specialist, 'good practice' in the field may well have been developed initially by experts in the P&D area – either through research or the experiences of other employing organisations which do employ P&D specialists. On the other hand, it is estimated that only about half of those individuals who claim to be in the P&D occupation are members of the IPD.

In relation to the other elements in Freidson's definition, the IPD meets some criteria better than others. The Professional Qualification Scheme lays down a set of standards which have to be met by all aspiring members, and which have to be maintained through Continuing Professional Development for the remainder of their working lives. CPD is particularly important when it comes to upgrading decisions, and all members have to demonstrate not only what they have done in the area but also indicate the impact this has had on their employing organisations and the broader specialist community – CPD is considered further in Chapter 8. Standards for the majority of new entrants are maintained by a formal coursework and examination assessment scheme which is overseen by the IPD vice president and director for membership and education, as well as by chief examiners appointed for their expertise in the area. For those members who gain graduate membership through other routes (say, through exempted courses or by the professional assessment, Accreditation of Prior Certificated Learning or NVQ/SVQ routes), the IPD sets standards to be achieved which are monitored continuously by external examiners and professional advisers and are subject to regular re-accreditation – typically on a five-year basis. Of course, there is nothing to prevent an individual practising P&D without an IPD-approved qualification, thus making any claim to exclusive control over entry standards much weaker than for some other occupations, eg doctors and dentists. Compared with other managerial functions, apart from accountancy, the IPD is in a much stronger position due to its well-developed qualification system and its growing voice in the area of people management. The IPD is obviously able to expel members for failing to pay their subscriptions and they are not eligible for upgrading if CPD requirements cannot be met, but this does not prevent these individuals from continuing to practise P&D if their employer does not insist on membership. Since it is unlikely, and is seen by some as undesirable, that IPD membership will become a condition for employment as a P&D specialist, this lack of exclusivity means that questions will always remain about full professionalisation, especially in comparison with medical and legal occupations. But in terms of qualifications, standards and influence, the IPD comes close to fulfilling many of Freidson's criteria.

> Why did you join the IPD, and what benefits have you gained from membership so far? Arrange to talk with a Corporate Member and ask him or her about the benefits he or she has gained so far, as well as what more the IPD might do to improve its services to members.

During 1996 it is expected that sets of standards will be approved by the National Council for Vocational Qualifications and the Scottish Vocational Education Council for NVQ/SVQ Levels 3 and 4 for personnel, and Level 5 for personnel strategy, as well as Level 5 for training and development strategy. National Standards for Training and Development at Levels 3 and 4 were approved in 1994. In this section we focus on the personnel standards since these provide specifically for elements and performance criteria for ethics and professionalism at Levels 3, 4 and 5. The training and development standards are reviewed in Chapters 8 to 10 when we examine Employee Development.

In the first chapter we explained how the standards had influenced the design of the IPD Professional Qualification Scheme. For example, the PSLB standards were derived from a combination of functional analysis and stakeholder interests (Gibb, 1994). The former was provided by research into the activities of practising P&D managers, whereas the latter occurred at a later date as various interested parties – including the IPD – commented on the findings, and suggested alternative ideas and categorisations. Whatever their precise genealogy, there is little doubt that the standards will have a major influence on P&D by providing a benchmark against which organisational practice can be judged, as well as a set of performance criteria which may amend educational provision in the area (McKiddie, 1994; Whittaker, 1994; Gibb, 1994).

One area (out of seven on personnel and general work) relates to ethics and professionalism, being included at Levels 3, 4 and 5. At each level one of the Units (F2) describes those activities which individuals need to display in order to maintain high standards of professional and ethical behaviour in carrying out personnel duties, irrespective of their position in the organisation, since they are integral to all aspects of P&D work. There are four elements to this Unit:

- *Satisfy client requirements for personnel services*, which includes compliance with Codes of Practice, the needs of clients for personnel services, their objections to any recommended techniques, as well as the costs and benefits of personnel work.

- *Obtain support and advice from other professionals when client requirements exceed one's own level of expertise.* As we argue in Chapter 6, this is particularly important when P&D practitioners are dealing with psychometric tests.

- *Keep up to date with relevant information, theory, techniques and processes in one's own area of personnel practice*, an area which is well covered by the IPD Professional Qualification Scheme and CPD requirements.

- *Enable others to learn from, and benefit from, one's own experience*, which is concerned with how individuals convey ideas to other people, both within and external to their own employing organisation.

Other Units are included at Levels 4 and 5. At Level 4, the standards specify contributions to the delivery of personnel services by non-personnel practitioners, covering any process whereby P&D specialists act in a facilitating or consultancy role. The elements incorporated in this Unit are process design, assistance in implementing best practice, and evaluations of performance. At Level 5 the focus is on the internal consultant role, in particular assisting line managers to take responsibility for P&D practice, providing support for them as appropriate, and gaining their commitment to implement a wide range of personnel policies. At this level, the emphasis is on providing a cost-effective service which can be benchmarked against 'best practice' elsewhere. The issue of line manager involvement, and vertical and horizontal integration, is dealt with in much greater detail in Chapters 17 to 19.

BUSINESS ETHICS AND SOCIAL RESPONSIBILITY

In recent times, there has been a considerable degree of scepticism about the concept and practice of business ethics, and suggestions are made that business ethics is 'a contradiction in terms' (Chryssides and Kaler, 1993: 5). It is not hard to see why people may be sceptical, given the range of examples which can be used to illustrate a lack of ethics: allegations of sleaze in public life; whistleblowing; environmental catastrophes; and arms sales to military dictatorships. In addition to these general examples, others can be quoted which are firmly within the realm of P&D activity – eg levels of boardroom remuneration at a time of pay restraint and redundancies on the part of staff, misappropriation of pension funds, and racism, sexism and ageism in organisational practice. On some occasions P&D specialists may even be accused of duplicity, such as in relation to low wage levels, selective redundancies, and the use of selection tests which have not been properly validated. Perhaps this scepticism (and indeed, on some occasions, cynicism) is understandable, given the public commitment of many employers to high standards of ethical and professional behaviour through their mission statements.

On most occasions the criticisms are directed at management as a whole, but in a scathing attack on human resource management in particular, Hart (1993) has placed the blame for falling ethical and professional standards at the door of the P&D practitioner. He argues (1993: 29) that HRM is 'amoral and anti-social, unprofessional, reactive, uneconomic and ecologically destructive', and as such it needs to be exorcised from organisations to be replaced by the 'old' welfarist version of personnel management. P&D practitioners are used to being criticised for their contribution, but now they find themselves blamed for the destruction of the planet as well! Hart's basic argument is that P&D has lost any pretence of professionalism because it has sided with employers, casting itself firmly as a part of the management process, and seeking to develop arguments which are principally economic and business-oriented in character. For example, in pursuing the extension of equal opportunities, fairness and justice within organisations, P&D specialists are concerned solely with whether and how they 'add value', not with their inherent moral and ethical qualities. A professional, by way of contrast, would expect to signal the potential divergence between professional and managerial values, and if there was conflict between them automatically pursue the professional line. Hart (1993: 36) reckons that the way forward for P&D specialists is to 'embrace' the ambivalence in their role, to stress the importance of pluralism, and to adopt a line which is critical of and distanced from other management functions. It is only by pursuing 'deviant innovation' (Legge, 1978) that P&D can really make a significant contribution. Many of the arguments in Hart's polemical article have been rebutted by Torrington (1993a), but nonetheless his critique is interesting in that it challenges P&D specialists to analyse their position within management and consider how their contribution can be most effective.

Unethical behaviour is not confined just to managerial staff acting explicitly or implicitly to further employer policies, but is also evident in the actions of non-managerial staff. Johns (1995: 33) lists some of these:

• giving gifts or gratuities to buyers in the hope of influencing them

• dishonesty towards customers and clients

• theft of the employer's property and materials

• 'slagging-off' the employer, internally or externally, without good reason

- reading other people's mail for personal advantage

- insider trading.

Examples such as these have stimulated a growth of interest in business ethics and social responsibility, in seeking to extend managerial concern to include objectives other than short-term profit maximisation and the satisfaction of shareholders. As we shall see below, this leads us into an analysis of stakeholder interests, but some commentators believe that the only social responsibility that a business has is to maximise profits. The leading proponent of this view is Milton Friedman (1970), who argues that there is 'one and only one social responsibility of business – to use its resources and engage in activities designed to increase its profits so long as it stays within the rules of the game ... [that is] engages in open and free competition without deception or fraud.' It is claimed that businessmen (*sic*) who talk of social responsibility in terms of environmental protection, the prevention of discrimination or the provision of employment, are guilty of 'pure and unadulterated socialism', and are 'unwilling puppets of the intellectual forces that have been undermining the basis of a free society' (taken from readings in Chryssides and Kaler, 1993: 249). He argues that by using their employer's resources to fund policies such as these, managers are spending other people's money (shareholders, customers, employees) for societal interests without having any mandate to do so. He sees social responsibility solely in terms of costs to the employing organisation, while promoting 'good' values should be the responsibility of government, and should only be undertaken if it has electoral support for such a programme.

In a sustained critique of his position, Chryssides and Kaler (1993: 230–237) stress that Friedman misunderstands the nature of ethics and responsibility on a number of counts. First, not only can social responsibility be seen in terms of costs, it can also secure benefits as well, both in the short term (by lowering pollution levels, for example) and in the longer term (by contributing to the prevention of global warming). Second, not only should social responsibility be seen as a force to stimulate good, it should also be recognised for its contribution to the elimination of evil; if employers are seen to be serious about rooting out racial discrimination, for example, this sends a clear message to the public at large. Third, they argue that Friedman fails to appreciate the fact that profit can be enhanced by processes (means) rather than just being seen in terms of ends and outputs; this leads us into 'the business case' for ethical behaviour which is mentioned below. Finally, they suggest that Friedman's emphasis on shareholders neglects the concerns of other stakeholders in the organisation – employees, customers, suppliers, and the local community – and that managers have to learn how to strike a balance between these groups. In short, Chryssides and Kaler (1993: 233) reject the assumption that the common good is best achieved by each individual's pursuing his or her own interests: the so-called 'invisible hand' approach advocated by free-market economists.

Where do you stand on this argument? Do you believe it is right for employers to try to promote business ethics and social responsibility, or should these be left to government and society at large?

The IPD Code of Professional Conduct defines the kind of behaviour which is expected of a P&D practitioner. IPD members are required to observe the code and are subject to disciplinary action by the Institute for non-observance. This includes several issues which have an ethical slant to them:

- *accuracy*: members must maintain high standards of accuracy in the information and advice they provide to employers and employees

- *confidentiality*: members must respect their employer's legitimate needs for confidentiality and ensure that all personnel information (including information about current, past and prospective employees) remains private

- *equal opportunities*: members must promote best employment practices that do not result in unfair discrimination

- *fair dealing*: members must maintain fair and reasonable standards in their treatment of individuals.

While some of these principles are relatively easy to interpret, others rely on the terminology of 'fair and reasonable' which may change over time, and from one issue to another. Equally, there may be times when adherence to one principle (say, accuracy) can conflict with another (say, confidentiality). If this is the case, questions arise about which principle takes precedence and about the meaning of fairness to different stakeholder interests. A survey by Carroll (1990) in the USA asked groups of managers and business studies students which of a series of principles they considered to be paramount. The two which were rated first and second by each group were the Golden Rule (do unto others as you would have them do unto you) and the Disclosure Rule (if you are comfortable with an action or decision after asking yourself whether you would mind if all your associations, friends and family were aware of it, then you should act or decide). Carroll argues (1990: 22–23) that the Golden Rule 'personalises business relations and brings the ideas of fairness into business deliberations', while the Disclosure Rule places decisions firmly within the context of public exposure. There ought to be little here to which P&D professionals would object on principle, but it might be harder to justify some practical decisions on these issues – say, about the extent of a redundancy programme, the decision not to appoint a particular individual, or the use of certain negotiating tactics. However, the idea of public exposure might have more resonance within professional circles than those within which a petty criminal moves, for example. The third most important principle for the managers was the Intuition Rule (do what your 'gut feeling' tells you) whereas for the students it was the Utilitarian Rule (follow the principle of the greatest good for the greatest number).

The idea that ethical principles make good business sense developed rather earlier in the USA and in some other parts of Europe than it did in Britain, according to Donaldson and Davis (1990: 29). In the last few years, some organisations have publicised their ethical stance more widely, using it to demonstrate to shareholders and customers that it is worth doing business with them; two prime examples here are the Co-operative Bank and the Body Shop, although this has not prevented critics from attempting to question the depth of their commitment to an ethical stance. In the environmental sphere, for example, some organisations have taken steps not only to improve their record and image, but also to implement 'green' policies and set up mechanisms to ensure that these issues are taken into account more fully in the future – for example, appointing environmental or ethical advisers to senior positions, and training staff in the importance of environmental protection (Elkington and Burke, 1989: 228–237). During the late 1980s, for example, one of the components in ICI's appraisals system for managerial staff, used to establish performance-related payments, was their ecological and environmental record (Snape, Redman and Bamber, 1994: 134).

Chryssides and Kaler (1993: 27) suggest that there is 'a substantial congruence between morally correct behaviour and commercial success', whilst Donaldson and Davis (1990: 30) claim that, by following ethical principles five goals can be achieved by managers which are central to business success. These are:

• an enhancement of managerial legitimacy

• a strengthening of coherent and balanced organisational cultures

• greater trust in relationships between individuals and groups

• greater consistency in the standards and quality of products, services, working procedures, and levels of output and achievements throughout the enterprise

• greater sensitivity to the impact of the enterprise's message to its customers and its image in the marketplace.

In order to be successful in this area, it is clearly important for employers to demonstrate their commitment to ethical and responsible stances, and for individuals to believe in the principles of ethical behaviour. However, on its own, this is insufficient, and some commentators feel that employer commitment to business ethics is superficial, at the level of rhetoric rather than reality. Ethics 'in use' may be somewhat different from the broad and benign visions which are publicised in the mission statements. For example, there may be an expectation that staff work long hours despite a public commitment to healthy working practices. Equally, some staff may be paid low wages despite a commitment to the concept of employees as a key resource, or training may be non-existent or poorly managed despite an objective stipulating that employees are encouraged to engage in long-term development. There is a danger that ethical and socially responsible practices will become even more elusive as organisations devolve P&D activities to line managers who are required to meet corporate targets which stress production and service goals as their first priority; we return to the issue of responsibility for P&D in Chapter 18. It is acknowledged that ethical issues are not capable of being considered in the same way as straightforward technical decisions, but that they are 'ambiguous, multi-faceted and confusing' (Johns, 1995: 34), open to competing solutions and perspectives. The way in which ethical decisions are made may also vary, according to Pearson (1995), depending upon the organisation's stage in the life cycle. At the survival stages (start-up or faltering), ethical considerations may be low on the agenda, treated with only scant regard: 'directors of businesses which are threatened with extinction often take heroic personal risks, behaving illegally, fraudulently, and without regard for the whole truth, with the aim of steering the business through its crisis' (Pearson, 1995: 81). During more secure times it may be easier for senior managers to articulate ethical principles, although middle and junior managers who are put under pressure to meet targets may find it harder to maintain a consistent ethical stance at all times.

> Does your organisation have an ethical policy, and are there gaps between the rhetoric and the reality? If there are, what have you done, or what could or should you do, about it?

In what ways might P&D specialists contribute to the development of an ethical stance? Connock and Johns (1995: 159) suggest that the P&D function is particularly well placed to be the guardian of ethical policies and practices, reflecting the 'conscience', of the organisation rather better than, say, marketing or production. At the same time they remind us that it is important for P&D not to commandeer the promotion of organisational ethics for fear that other functions will not take it seriously. According to Pickard (1995: 23), P&D can help the organisation to raise its awareness in three ways:

- by deploying professional expertise to develop and communicate an ethics policy, hold training sessions to generate awareness, and monitor the policy so as to bring about further improvements

- the inclusion of ethical values and vision in the formation of corporate strategy

- role-modelling across the organisation by virtue of its own ethical policies and practices.

Yet it is rare to find much mention of ethical issues in books on human resource management or personnel and development. Miller (1996: 5–8) outlines the principles on which the ethical management of human resources might focus; these are systems justice (fairness and correctness), procedural justice (the provision of checks and balances in organisations), and outcome justice (comparison with other organisations and workers). In the 1990s we have seen a weakening of some of these principles as trade unions have lost power and influence, and not many employers have put in place alternative structures and systems to ensure that fairness, correctness and equality can be established and monitored. As we saw in Chapter 2, the changing nature of the psychological contract has left many employees relatively powerless in relation to their employers, and unsure about how their legitimate concerns might be articulated and dealt with – unless by the 'conscience' of the organisation. Miller (1996: 16) worries that ethical considerations are often overlooked so that, in the short term, 'employees may be as expendable as the ozone layer'.

Connock and Johns (1995: 209–221) produce a list of fourteen critical success factors for organisations which aim to practise ethical leadership. These include:

- a clear and cogent link between ethical values/leadership and vision/strategic direction

- systematic policies and procedures (such as for reward, punishment, appraisal, communication, involvement, employee development) which reinforce and promote the principles of ethical leadership

- visible support and role-modelling from top management

- approaches to the implementation and monitoring of ethical leadership which are seen as open and fair

- the involvement of all parts of the organisation in the implementation of ethical leadership

- a refusal to shelve hard and unpleasant decisions, and encouragement to employees to report improper, unethical or illegal activities

- regular review and updating of codes of ethics and values.

EQUAL OPPORTUNITIES AND DIVERSITY

In this section we review material relating to equal opportunities and the management of diversity in employing organisations. Rather than attempt to deal with all aspects of disadvantage and discrimination, we restrict our analysis to three areas which are particularly central to the work of P&D practitioners – gender, race and disability. The *principles* which are outlined in relation to these issues can also be applied to questions of ageism and homosexuality, for example, albeit without the well-established legal frameworks which govern sex, race and disability discrimination. Before moving on to outline briefly the legal situation and the actions which employers have taken (or could take) to remove the barriers to equal opportunities, it is worth noting some indicators of disadvantage (see Dickens, 1994: 254–259; Kandola and Fullerton, 1995: 21–28).

We noted in Chapter 2 that women now comprise almost half the workforce, but that the labour market remains heavily segmented. Over 40 per cent of all women employees work part-time compared with a very small, but admittedly growing, proportion of men. The great majority of women are employed in the service sector, more than five times as many as work in manufacturing. The occupational division of labour is equally unbalanced, with twice as many male managers and administrators as women, nearly six times as many computer analysts and programmers, and about five times as many sales representatives. Conversely, women outnumber men in sales assistants' jobs by two to one, in clerical and secretarial work by three to one, and sewing machinists by almost twelve to one. Women with higher-level academic and professional qualifications (degrees and diplomas) are more likely to go into teaching or healthcare work, while their male equivalents are more likely to end up in science and engineering. Despite over 25 years of equal pay legislation, women on average are paid less than 80 per cent of the male average, primarily due to segmented labour markets.

The position in relation to ethnic minority groups is more complicated, and is heavily influenced by the specific group (black, South Asian and Chinese) as well as between women and men (Kandola and Fullerton, 1995: 21–24). Levels of unemployment tend to be much higher for Asians and blacks, especially for young males, but even when groups with similar educational achievements are compared, whites fare considerably better than ethnic minorities. One notable exception here is the proportion of Indian men employed in professional occupations, which is higher than for whites. Overall, though, people from ethnic minorities are disadvantaged compared with whites, not just in terms of the type of work which is undertaken, and their average pay levels (at least 10 per cent less than whites), but crucially in their access to employment.

Disabled people suffer problems with access to work as well. According to Doyle (1991: 94), less than one-third of disabled adults who are of working age are in employment compared with over two-thirds of the population as a whole. In addition, for those seeking work the rate and length of unemployment for disabled people is twice that for the whole population. Over half the disabled adults under 30 are not working (Kandola and Fullerton, 1995: 24). For those in employment, disabled workers are paid approximately 20 per cent less than their able-bodied counterparts.

> These figures demonstrate quite clearly that certain groups of people are disadvantaged in relation to the population as a whole. How can you explain this? To what extent do you think this is due to discrimination (overt or covert) on the part of employers as a whole or by individual managers?

The legislation on disability has a long pedigree, but it has only recently been strengthened through the Disability Discrimination Act 1995. Prior to this, the Disabled Persons (Employment) Acts 1944–58 set up a scheme whereby employers having twenty or more employees had to give employment to a quota (3 per cent) of disabled people. If the proportion of disabled people fell below this figure, the employer was not allowed to employ an able-bodied person without getting a permit. As Pitt (1995: 50) notes wryly, the Act was 'effectively a dead letter' given that there were no civil remedies for its breach and permits were provided readily to employers on request.

The 1995 Act seeks to remedy these shortcomings, being viewed by *Equal Opportunities Review* (*EOR* No 60, March/April 1995) as the 'most important discrimination legislation in a generation'. It has been framed in a manner different from the laws on sex and race discrimination in not making consideration of disability impermissible. Instead, it prohibits discrimination only where the employer's decision which is being challenged is held to have been unreasonable, taking into account in that assessment any duty on the employer to make a reasonable 'adjustment' to the working conditions or working environment of the disabled person. *EOR* (1995: 25) finds this to be 'gravely flawed', allowing employers, if they so desire, to justify discriminating against disabled people on grounds of customer preference or the prejudice of their employees. Although the quota scheme is to be replaced, at least complaints will be heard in future by industrial tribunals (rather than through the criminal law as before) which will be allowed to award unlimited compensation. In addition, a National Disability Council is established with advisory, not statutory, powers.

The basic framework of legislation relating to sex and race discrimination came into force in the mid-1970s, with the Sex Discrimination Act 1975 and the Race Relations Act a year later. These cover not only employees (that is, people working under a contract of service), but also those who apply for a contract as well. The legislation is important for many stages in the employment relationship, as we shall see throughout the remainder of the book: in Chapter 6, we analyse recruitment and selection, in Chapter 10 we examine women-only training courses, and in Chapter 14 the equal value considerations in job evaluation. Readers are encouraged, however, to consider questions of equal opportunities throughout the whole text, not just in this chapter or in others where it is dealt with explicitly. The two major institutions in the area – the Equal Opportunities Commission and the Commission for Racial Equality – were described briefly in Chapter 3. Both these bodies publish booklets providing guidance on a variety of P&D issues – such as advertisements, job evaluation, and grievance procedures.

Three forms of race and sex discrimination are defined in the Acts: (1) *direct* means less favourable treatment of a woman (or a man) because of their sex, or of an individual on racial grounds. It is usually fairly easy to recognise, but less easy to prove (Pitt, 1995: 28). Among larger organisations this form of discrimination is now likely to be relatively rare, and even less likely to be admitted; (2) *indirect* discrimination relates to the situation where it was not the intention of the employer to discriminate against an employee, but nevertheless the outcome results in one group being disadvantaged in comparison to another. Indirect discrimination is established if four conditions are satisfied: first, a requirement or condition must be applied to all applicants or employees; second, the condition or requirement is such that the proportion of (say) women, married people, or members of a racial group which can comply with this is considerably smaller than that of the comparator group; third, the condition is not justifiable; and fourth, it is to the detriment of the complainant that he or she cannot comply with it (Pitt, 1995: 35); (3) *victimisation*, which is defined as the less favourable treatment of an individual who has complained under the Acts or who is assisting someone in this regard. This aims to prevent people being discouraged from complaining under the Acts.

There is one major exception to this general rule, termed a Genuine Occupational Qualification (GOQ), which allows job offers to be restricted to applicants from a particular group in certain circumstances. The list of GOQs includes situations where, for example, physical authenticity requires a part in a play to be performed by a man/woman/black person; where the job is at an all-male institution such as a prison; where the law outlaws the employment of women; or where – in the case of overseas appointments – local customs or laws preclude the job being undertaken by a woman. In the race area one of the most contentious examples has been where personal services (such as welfare or education) are provided to a specific racial group, and it is felt that this can be done most effectively by a member of that group (Pitt, 1995: 40).

> Think of examples where indirect discrimination *may* exist in your organisation. What evidence would you need to collect to show that it is *actually* indirect discrimination, and how would you attempt to deal with this?

In the sex discrimination area, legislation also covers the rights of pregnant women in four ways (Pitt, 1995: 114–123). First, women cannot be dismissed on the grounds of pregnancy from the date at which their employment commences – up until the implementation of a 1992 European directive in TURERA 1993, women had to have been employed for two years to gain this right. Second, pregnant women have the right to time off for ante-natal care, although the employer is entitled to written proof of the appointment (and of the pregnancy). Third, women are entitled to maternity pay, the amount depending not only upon the employee's wage or salary, but also upon the length of time for which the employee has been employed. For example, women with over 26 weeks' continuous employment by the fifteenth week prior to the expected week of childbirth, and whose earnings are at or above the lower earnings limit for the payment of National Insurance contributions, are entitled to Statutory Maternity Pay for a period of 18 weeks. Finally, women have a right to maternity leave, the amount depending upon length of service; all pregnant women are entitled to a minimum of 14 weeks leave irrespective of length of service and hours of work, whereas women employed for at least two years by the eleventh week prior to the expected week of confinement have a right to return to work at any time up to 29 weeks after the actual week of confinement. Some of the details relating to maternity leave are cumbersome and rather complex (Pitt, 1995: 121), requiring women to give notice at set dates in order to qualify for these rights. It should be noted in passing that in 1996 no right to paternity leave existed in Britain despite the fact that the European Commission has been pushing for a directive since 1983.

This sets the backcloth for the development by employers of equal opportunities policies and practices in the P&D area. Although some employers may be driven by moral and philosophical beliefs, there are basically two distinct sets of reasons why employers might want to take action to remove obstacles to equal opportunity (Dickens, 1994: 260–269): penalty avoidance, and organisational self-interest, the latter often termed 'the business case for equal opportunities'. The *penalty avoidance* case rests principally upon the need to comply with the legislation which has been outlined above, and there is little doubt that it has led to changes in organisational practice, most visibly in relation to equal value cases (such as at J Sainsbury in the late 1980s) and in recruitment and selection procedures. The threat of numerous industrial tribunal claims has undoubtedly persuaded some employers to review grading structures (see Chapter 14 for more discussion of equal value cases and job evaluation). On the other hand, the 'penalty avoidance' route to equal opportunities is unlikely to produce a fundamental change in attitudes and behaviour in organisations, but instead a line of 'avoidance rather than compliance, with organisations seeking to minimise the likely impact of the law' (Dickens, 1994: 274). There are several elements to the *organisational self-interest* case:

Labour market competition

Due to skills shortages, employers have been more inclined to consider recruiting staff from 'non-traditional' sources, that is those other than white, able-bodied males. This argument works on the assumption that women, ethnic minorities and disabled people represent an untapped source of expertise, and that measures can be taken to increase the likelihood both that they will apply for jobs and that they will wish to continue working for the employer. Evidence suggests (Dickens, 1994: 262) that part-time workers and employees from ethnic minority groups are often *overskilled* for the types of jobs they undertake.

'Best practice' P&D

The argument here is that employers who implement equal opportunities policies and practices are conforming with good practice, and that this can help contribute to better organisational performance, quality and customer service. In addition, because it resonates with ethical and professional values, it can help to reinforce the position of the P&D specialist in an employing organisation.

Better employee relations

Not only can equal opportunities policies and practices help to increase the motivation and commitment of employees (particularly those from disadvantaged groups), it may lessen the likelihood of industrial unrest. This is well illustrated by the experience at Ford in the spring of 1996, when it was found that a number of black faces had been painted white for an advertising poster to be used in Poland. After a short stoppage of work and complaints from the trade unions, Ford management soon issued an apology in order to prevent a further deterioration in employee relations.

Organisational image

Not only do employers want to avoid a bad press – both locally and nationally – they also want to convey a more positive image as a 'good employer' which attracts high-quality applicants. In addition to having a direct impact upon applicants (potential employees), organisational image also has an impact upon customers and citizens in the local community. This has led many service organisations (both public and private) to publicise their equal opportunities policies and reflect the wide mix of employees in their advertising and P&D policies.

Gaining from diversity

This argument rests upon the assertion that organisations actually gain from employing a wide mix of staff from different backgrounds and groupings. This comes not only from the benefits which may be gained from multi-culturalism – such as better-focused customer service, a wider range of ideas, more balanced teams – but also from the fact that employing people from disadvantaged groups may lead other staff to question their stereotypical views and prejudices.

While this list indicates *potential* benefits for employers in adopting the business case for equal opportunities, this does not mean they are automatic and universal. Kandola and Fullerton (1995: 35) make a distinction between 'proven' benefits, 'debatable' benefits, and 'indirect' benefits, and caution readers to question whether the potential benefits will actually apply in their own organisation. Table 5 provides examples of the benefits under the three categories.

Table 5 **The perceived benefits from equal opportunities**

Proven benefits:
•   easier to recruit scarce labour
•   reduced costs due to lower levels of labour turnover and absenteeism
•   enhanced organisational flexibility.
Debatable benefits:
•   team creativity and problem-solving
•   better decisions
•   improved customer service
•   increased sales to disadvantaged groups
•   improved quality.
Indirect benefits:
•   improved morale and job satisfaction
•   better public image
•   better competitive edge.

Adapted from Kandola and Fullerton, 1995: 35.

Doubts remain about the durability and likely conversion of these potential benefits into equal opportunity practice within organisations. The 'business case' can be quite fragile since it depends upon the specific circumstances which confront each organisation, as well as changes in the wider legal/political, economic and social context; these may lead management to downgrade equal opportunities arguments if they are not seen to be of pressing concern. For example, the 'defusing' of the demographic timebomb in the early 1990s, caused by economic recession, led some employers to 'backslide on the detail and extent of their equality provisions' (Dickens, 1994: 270). Similarly, some employers may be unconvinced by the cost-effectiveness arguments because they may gain substantially (in the short term, at least) from pockets of low-paid labour which enable them to keep down the organisation's cost base. Moreover, despite the existence of national policies that support the extension of equal opportunities, union officials may find themselves under pressure from existing male, white, and able-bodied members to protect their interests rather than those of disadvantaged groups. Furthermore, while having the potential to overcome negative stereotyping, employing people from disadvantaged groups may merely reinforce the prejudices of some workers and lead to *worse* – rather than better – employee relations. At the heart of effective equality provision is, of course, a new set of attitudes, beliefs and values; it is very difficult to change ideas which may be deep-rooted, implicit, and resistant to alternative arguments. Dickens (1994: 273) is worried that the entire business case might be based on dubious grounds, as 'such arguments may encourage action, but only in areas where it is clear that equal opportunities and business needs immediately coincide'.

Make out a case for equal opportunities at your workplace, either to extend current provision or to ensure that it is not reduced due to other pressures. To what extent would you draw upon the 'business case' to convince line managers of the value of equality provisions?

The form that equal opportunities policies and practices can take in organisations varies enormously along two dimensions, according to Goss (1994: 157). The first, the depth of management's commitment to equality, can range from shallow and instrumental through to deep and principled, whereas the second, the breadth of its focus, ranges from a narrow list of practices driven largely by economic and legal expediency through to a broad set which includes not only race, sex and disability provisions which are governed by law, but also age and sexual preference. This allows for four alternative agendas in practice: the *short* agenda is shallow and narrow, little more than a lip-service commitment to legal imperatives; the *broad* agenda combines a broad focus with a shallow commitment to equality, and is similar to the short except that a wider focus is adopted; the *focused* agenda is built upon a narrow base, but at least has the advantage of a deep management commitment to achieve real change; finally, the *long* agenda is broad and deep, essentially concerned with changing how the whole organisation is managed, and aiming to develop the talents of all employees. This final agenda is rare according to Goss (1994: 159), except in some local authorities and large private-sector employers where an essential component of the equality policies is likely to be positive action. Under this agenda, employers aim to ensure that members of under-represented groups have the skills and credentials necessary to reach the selection pool, prepare for the selection interview, gain training in areas where their skills may be lacking, and so on.

An alternative categorisation has been developed by Jewson, Mason, Drewett and Rossiter (1995), which appears to resemble five steps along the route to full-blown equal opportunities:

- serendipity: equality by virtue of happy accidents and *ad hoc* solutions

- dissociation: the presence of written procedures but little in the way of concrete actions

- accommodation: despite the presence of equal opportunities policies and procedures, there is an absence of strategic thinking about equality, and it is not integrated into business plans

- integration: equal opportunity practices which are comprehensive, proactive and focused around an elaborate, ongoing and formal set of policies, and operationalised through dedicated units, committees and support structures

- assimilation: characterised by the absorption of all aspects of equal opportunities practice into business strategies and everyday routines, perhaps best summed up by the use of the term 'diversity' and its associated concepts. Under this scenario, there is a danger that, in the absence of specialist structures and units, equality issues will disappear into other broader developments, so becoming obscured.

Based on their survey of 285 organisations, Kandola and Fullerton (1995: 56) identify the ten most frequently implemented equal opportunity initiatives; these were derived from a list of 40 such initiatives which were put before respondents. These are as follows, the figures in brackets indicating the percentage of organisations participating in each particular initiative:

- a policy on equal opportunities (94 per cent)

- equal opportunities monitoring in place (76 per cent)

- a strategy on equal opportunities (74 per cent)

- fair selection training to recruiters (74 per cent)

- physical changes to the working environment to improve access (69 per cent)

- eliminating age criteria from selection decisions (68 per cent)

- an explicit policy on harassment (67 per cent)

- flexible hours arrangements (66 per cent)

- time off to care for dependants (64 per cent)

- ongoing contact with specialist bodies such as the CRE and disability groups (64 per cent).

By contrast, some of the less extensively implemented initiatives included the facilitation of support groups and networks (say, for employees on career breaks), assessing managers on equal opportunities as part of their appraisal, target setting, and the provision of training for disadvantaged groups. Monitoring initiatives is a critical aspect of equal opportunities, and it is surprising to note that one-third of the 52 organisations which had harassment policies (in itself, only about 20 per cent of the total sample) had not conducted any assessment of its effectiveness. At the same time, respondents claimed that the principal reasons for taking action on equal opportunities were 'good business sense', legislation, and senior management commitment (Kandola and Fullerton, 1995: 64–71). Perhaps these employers have not yet worked out that monitoring is an essential requirement of equal opportunities just as much as it is for other aspects of business plans.

Are equal opportunity policies at your workplace monitored? If so, what does this show, and where does it place your organisation on the categories outlined by Goss or Jewson *et al*? If equal opportunities policies are not monitored, why is this the case, and what do you intend to do about it?

During the 1990s the language of 'equal opportunities' has been replaced in some quarters by that of 'managing diversity' (Greenslade, 1991). The differences between these two terms, according to Kandola and Fullerton (1994: 49) are clear, as Table 6 illustrates.

Table 6 The key differences between equal opportunities and managing diversity

Equal opportunities	Managing diversity
• concentrates on removing discrimination	• focus on maximising employee potential
• seen as an issue for disadvantaged groups	• seen as relevant to all employees
• seen as an issue to do with P&D practitioners	• an issue which involves all managers
• relies on positive action.	• does not rely on positive action.

Adapted from Kandola and Fullerton, 1994: 49.

A good example of the differences between equal opportunities and managing diversity can be seen in their approaches to the concept of 'family-friendly' policies (IRS *Employment Trends* 593, 1995). The former would focus primarily on the way in which employers could introduce policies and practices which make it easier for women to balance the competing demands of childcare (or eldercare) and continued employment. The emphasis would therefore be on flexible working patterns – such as part-time employment, term-time only contracts, flexitime, and extended career breaks – as well as consideration of nursery and crèche provision. The key point, however, is that equal opportunities would focus on the *obstacles* to women's continued employment, and how these might be overcome to allow women to reduce the tension between work commitments and domestic responsibilities. As Dickens (1994: 288) notes, the main problem is that the equal opportunities prescription rests upon an inadequate conceptualisation of the 'problem', and it pays insufficient attention to the resistance that may be created by such interventions. Moreover, the prescription generally focuses on 'helping individuals from disadvantaged groups get in and get on within existing organisations, with no real challenge being mounted to the nature, structure and values of the organisations themselves'. Since the prevailing norms and cultures have for the most part been created by members of 'advantaged' groups, it is not surprising that even the best achievements have fallen well short of equality in employment.

By contrast, managing diversity starts from the assumption that the focus should be on the workforce as a whole and what it can contribute, rather than on the removal of obstacles for *specific sections* of the workforce. It is appreciated that differences can actually be strengths for the organisation as a whole, and that different people can introduce alternative perspectives and ideas which lead to a wider range of options for consideration. It is only when what are seen as 'women's issues' are recast as 'people's issues' that any real moves towards equality are likely, and diversity is recognised and commended – both in its own right and for its contribution to improved organisational performance.

CONCLUSION

In this, the final chapter in the Context part of the book, we have examined the professional and ethical aspects of P&D. It will be recalled that this is a mandatory element in the Personnel Standards at NVQ/SVQ Levels 3, 4 and 5 developed by the Employment Occupational Standards Council. Notions of professionalism and ethics also provide P&D practitioners with the potential for a distinctive contribution to organisational success, one which recognises the need for consistency, fairness and equity in the handling of people management issues. Other managers will not always appreciate the value of this contribution, and P&D practitioners who do their jobs effectively may well make life uncomfortable for their colleagues at times. There are likely to be disagreements about the validity and suitability of their recommendations, especially in the short term, but it is up to P&D specialists to demonstrate that they are beneficial for the organisation as a whole. This may be achieved through 'best practice' human resource policies which enable both employee and employer goals to be satisfied at the same time. On the other hand, however, P&D practitioners may need to put forward recommendations which require downsizing, dismissals, and pay cuts. On these occasions, simplistic unitarist versions of ethical management are clearly insufficient. P&D practitioners will therefore need to ensure that their recommendations are based upon thorough and systematic analysis, an accurate portrayal of the facts, and a sensitive, fair and professional handling of the situation. P&D practitioners may not find that they are 'loved' for their contribution, but hopefully they will be respected.

USEFUL READING

CHRYSSIDES, G. AND KALER, J. (1993) *An Introduction to Business Ethics.* London, Chapman and Hall.

CONNOCK, S. AND JOHNS, T. (1995) *Ethical Leadership.* London, IPD.

DICKENS, L. (1994) 'Wasted resources? Equal opportunities in employment', in K. SISSON (Ed.), *Personnel Management in Britain.* Oxford, Blackwell: 253–296.

DONALDSON, J. AND DAVIS, P. (1990) 'Business ethics? Yes, but what can it do for the bottom line?' *Management Decision*, Vol 28, 6: 29–33.

GREENSLADE, M. (1991) 'Managing diversity: lessons from the United States'. *Personnel Management*, December: 28–33.

HART, T. (1993) 'Human resource management – time to exorcise the Militant Tendency'. *Employee Relations*, Vol 15, 3: 29–36.

KANDOLA, R. AND FULLERTON, J. (1994) *Managing the Mosaic: Diversity in Action.* London, IPD.

LEGGE, K. (1995) *Human Resource Management: Rhetorics and Realities.* London, Macmillan.

MILLER, P. (1996) 'Strategy and the Ethical Management of Human Resources', *Human Resource Management Journal*, Vol 6, 1: 5–18.

PITT, G. (1995) *Employment Law*, Second Edition. London, Sweet and Maxwell.

Part 3

EMPLOYEE RESOURCING

5 Human resource planning

INTRODUCTION

Most commentators agree that human resource planning is a key aspect of personnel and development, especially if it links together business strategy and people management. In many respects, human resource planning forms the starting point for the establishment of an organisation's human resource strategy as it seeks to integrate the operational requirements of the business with a labour force equipped to provide the services and products that customers demand. Matching these two factors is particularly important in enabling employers to sustain competitive advantage in the increasingly complex and tough international trading environment of the late twentieth century.

Doubts exist, however, about whether this integration is being achieved in reality, or indeed whether or not human resource planning is a worthwhile activity, given the turbulence and unpredictability which characterises contemporary organisational life. If plans turn out to be inaccurate, for example, one may ask why organisations bother to spend time creating a plan in the first place. Equally, if major decisions are made elsewhere in the world (say, as in a large multinational employer) which have significant implications for employees working in the British arm of the company, how useful is it for British managers to develop sophisticated models for linking together business and human resource strategies? On the other hand, the pressure to control labour costs, and at the same time deliver high levels of customer service, increases the need for effective human resource planning. Perhaps now the contribution of well-organised and appropriate human resource planning models and approaches is greater than ever.

The use of computers to assist with human resource planning is also relevant, and a recent survey shows this as likely to be one of the major growth areas in IT usage over the next few years. Blum (1996: 4) found that only about one-third of the organisations he surveyed currently made use of computers for human resource planning, compared with much higher figures for training, payroll, absence control, and the management of temporary staff. However, human resource planning is identified as one of the three most important features to be needed by organisations by the end of the century. This reflects a feeling that P&D professionals will become more strategically-focused. Interestingly, it is also estimated that more issues can be devolved via local area networks connected into a mainframe. There is a clear implication – not just in relation to human resource planning, but across the whole subject area – that the P&D function needs to become more familiar with, and confident at using, IT systems so as to enhance its contribution to business success.

Questions such as these set the theme for this chapter, which analyses the role of human resource planning within the personnel and development process. It provides definitions of human resource planning, explains why it is an important aspect of personnel and development, outlines the process and models by which human resource planning is conducted, and discusses some of the shortcomings of engaging in planning of this kind.

By the end of the chapter, readers should be able to:

- provide advice on how to predict future staffing requirements and utilisation

- undertake a wastage analysis on an employing organisation

- access sources which provide up-to-date and relevant published information about labour market trends.

In addition, readers should be able to understand and explain:

- the differences between 'soft' and 'hard' human resource planning

- the main processes of human resource planning

- the major shortcomings of human resource planning.

THE NATURE OF HUMAN RESOURCE PLANNING

The subject of human resource planning first entered the body of personnel management thought in the 1960s, under the term 'manpower planning'. Building upon work conducted in a number of large organisations (such as the Civil Service, the Armed Forces, the National Health Service, ICI, BP, Shell, and ICL), the topic achieved prominence through the formation of the Manpower Society and several publications during that era; see, for example, the Department of Employment (1968), Smith (1971), and Bartholomew (1976). 'Manpower planning' was seen to be at the junction of a number of disciplines – economics, statistics, operational research, organisation studies, and politics – and to be highly relevant for employers who were confronted with skill shortages as well as problems of how to plan careers for their managerial staff. The influence of statistics and operational research was considerable, and some of the early publications (eg Bartholomew, 1976) went into great detail about the basis for, and operation of, the statistical and mathematical models that were employed. Other writers (eg Bowey, 1975) used rather less complex formulae for estimating wastage and retention rates, but nevertheless these still required some powers of numerical reasoning. A typical definition of manpower planning under this formulation is that of Bowey (1975: 1): 'the activity of management which is aimed at co-ordinating the requirements for and availability of different types of employee'.

The prospect of having to apply techniques such as these no doubt frightened off many personnel managers and prevented a more widespread adoption of 'manpower planning'. The use of such obviously gender-blind terminology presumably also served to limit the development of the subject. Recently a new set of publications have emerged which make use of the 'human resource planning' phraseology (Torrington and Hall, 1995; Beardwell and Holden, 1994; Bramham, 1994; Sisson, 1994; Storey, 1995), and a distinction has been made between 'hard' and 'soft' human resource planning. The former is characterised by manpower planning models which aim to ensure that the right amount of the right type of labour is available in the right place at the right time. This is based upon quantitative analysis. 'Soft' HR planning is more explicitly focused on creating and shaping the culture of the organisation so that there is a clear integration between corporate goals and employee values, beliefs and behaviours. While 'hard' human resource planning can be criticised for its lack of width and its focus on numbers of staff, its 'soft' counterpart is effectively synonymous with the whole subject of human resource management, given that virtually all aspects of the employment contract are included within its definition. The former might over-emphasise techniques and be far too elaborate in its attempts to apply mathematical models, but the latter is vaguer in its approach, lacking explicit practical application or specification. Torrington and Hall (1995: 78) suggest that the purpose of human resource planning is to maintain and improve the ability of the organisation to achieve its objectives through strategies designed to enhance the contribution of employees in the foreseeable future. Bramham (1994: 155) goes even further and suggests that there is a 'big difference' between manpower planning and human resource planning. He argues that the former is concerned with 'the numerical elements of forecasting, supply/demand matching and control – in which people are a part', while the latter is about motivating people. In our view, his conception of human resource planning is synonymous with HRM in its entirety, and as such loses any distinctive sense. Indeed, while Bramham's earlier books on manpower planning (1975–1988) described in detail the planning process as it is applied to the number and type of staff required, his more recent book devotes just one chapter to these issues, preferring to focus on other aspects of personnel and development (eg reward management, employee relations, equal opportunities, and quality and customer care).

Do you find the term 'manpower planning' offensive, and do you think it has implications for the employment of women?

It is important to acknowledge both the hard and soft variants, but to come up with something which is broader than the pure quantitative models, yet narrower than the concept articulated by Bramham or Torrington and Hall. For our purposes, human resource planning is defined as:

> The process of matching future organisational requirements with the supply of properly qualified, committed and experienced staff in the right place at the right time. These staff can be drawn both from the internal and the external labour market.

This requires a focus on the following:

- an assessment of future product market trends and requirements

- a specification of the type and numbers of staff required to satisfy these product market trends and requirements

- an estimate of the type and number of staff likely to be employed by the organisation in five years

- a specification of the numbers/type of staff to be recruited or made redundant

- a development plan for retraining and re-focusing existing staff and, if appropriate, for recruiting additional staff from the external labour market

- a re-examination of broader business strategies in the light of this analysis.

It is crucial to recognise that human resource planning can take quite different forms depending upon organisational goals and projected product market demand, the quantity and quality of existing staff, and future external labour market trends. Organisations which operate in a relatively stable market environment and employ a large proportion of well-qualified staff are much more able to engage in career management and succession planning than are those whose environment is characterised by turbulence and unpredictability. In the latter, human resource planning is more likely to be dominated by considerations of rationalisation and redundancy, major job redefinitions, and for most staff a lack of career advancement. Human resource planning is no less important in this type of organisation than it is in the former case, but it will take different forms and focus on different aspects of personnel and development.

In a similar vein, human resource planning will have quite a different emphasis in organisations which are opening greenfield sites from those which operate from old-established premises with a shortage of suitably qualified staff on the external labour market. In the former, it might well be that the lack of qualified staff in a particular region or country would lead the employer to re-assess organisational goals and consider whether objectives could be equally well met by the choice of a different location or product market niche. In the case of the latter, the question may be how to retain existing skilled staff or how to attract new recruits to replace staff as they retire. While human resource planning is typically downstream from business strategy, as indeed are most human resource decisions (Purcell, 1989), there are occasions when they can and should form part of the broader corporate plan.

> What form might human resource planning take in the following types of organisation: a large secondary school; a medium-sized factory in a highly competitive, international market; an expanding supermarket chain; a charity?

THE IMPORTANCE OF HUMAN RESOURCE PLANNING

In all walks of life we are encouraged to think ahead and give proper consideration to planning for the future, and this is just as important in P&D as elsewhere. At a time when world markets were characterised by greater stability and predictability than now, this was a much more straightforward task which could be undertaken via sophisticated modelling techniques with a fair degree of certainty about the outcome. Thus, commentators refer to the 'golden age of manpower planning' and to the fact that it 'caught a cold in the chill economic winds of the 1980s' (Cowling and Walters, 1990: 3). It is sometimes implied that planning is at best irrelevant, and at worst misguided and dangerous, in the turbulent and increasingly insecure competitive environment of the late twentieth century.

Such a view, however, misunderstands the nature and uses of the planning process, and can be used to justify 'ad-hocery' and reactive management. Planning is just as important, if not more so, during turbulent times to ensure that employers have staff of the right quality and numbers available at the right time. Compared with some of our international competitors, Britain has been typified by continuing and recurrent skills shortages both at a national and organisational level. More effective long-term human resource planning can help to minimise the problems associated with this. Indeed, it could be argued that current pressures to control labour costs and protect tighter profit margins demands an increasing, rather than decreasing, emphasis on human resource planning. This applies not only to the numbers of staff to be employed but also to their quality and commitment, which is crucial at a time when high levels of customer service are seen as necessary in order to achieve competitive advantage. In other words, rather than being seen as an anachronism, human resource planning may now be more important than ever.

Similarly, employers who are faced with declining markets are able to start planning at an earlier date for reductions in numbers employed, and so avoid some of the more difficult aspects of compulsory redundancy. Managements can consider alternative forms of contract, or choose to subcontract work that is unpredictable in nature. Accordingly, long-term human resource planning has obvious implications for many features of the psychological, as well as the legal, contract.

Human resource planning is therefore important for at least four sets of reasons:

It encourages employers to develop clear and explicit links between their business and human resource plans, and so integrate the two more effectively. There are two ways in which this linkage can be viewed (Sparrow, 1992); first, solely in terms of its 'fit' and alignment with broader strategic plans, and the ability of human resource plans to deliver precisely what is required by the business as a whole. Second, the relationship between corporate and human resource plans can be seen interactively, with the latter contributing to the development of the former, and at least demonstrating that longer-term business goals may not be appropriate, given the expected supply of suitably qualified staff. Either way, human resource planning is viewed as a major facilitator of competitive advantage. Of course, this assumes that employers do actually have broader business strategies, and there is some doubt about whether or not this happens in practice (Marchington and Parker, 1990: 60).

It allows for much better control over staffing costs and numbers employed. It is important for employers to make projections about expected numbers of staff to be employed in future years, irrespective of whether a growth or decline in numbers is predicted. By so doing, employers are better able to match supply and demand, and make decisions about recruiting from the external labour market, relocating staff, or preparing for reductions in numbers employed. In each case, better control over staffing costs is the likely result. For example, if product market demand over the next five years is expected to be highly variable, then decisions can be made about the balance between employed and subcontracted labour, between temporary and open-ended contracts, or between full-time and part-time staffing arrangements. The employer who is faced with this set of environmental pressures would be well advised to place great emphasis on the employment of non-core peripheral staff, or to consider subcontracting activities out to other organisations.

It enables employers to make more informed judgements about the skills and attitude mix in the organisation, and prepare integrated personnel and development strategies. While it is important to ensure a match in *numbers* employed, it is just as necessary to achieve the right *skills* mix and desired levels of commitment among the workforce. Decisions about employee attitudes and skills can be linked in with expectations about the future shape and nature of the business, and shifts can be planned well in advance. For example, management in an organisation which is becoming more customer-oriented in its approach needs to consider whether new types of employees should be recruited (at all levels), how they might best be selected, inducted and appraised, the nature of their training and development, the reward systems which are most appropriate to deliver high levels of customer service, and the employee relations arrangements which might be most beneficial to the employer. Often this is seen merely in terms of succession planning for senior managers, but achieving the best skills and attitude mix for *all* staff is of crucial importance, especially those who are most regularly in contact with customers. Each of these issues is taken up again at various stages throughout the remainder of the book.

4 *It provides a profile of current staff (in terms of gender, race and disability, for example) which is necessary for moves towards an equal opportunities organisation.* Without accurate and up-to-date figures of existing staff, subdivided by grade and position, it is impossible for employers to make decisions about how equality management can be achieved (Schuler and Huber, 1993: 129). In each of the areas discussed above, but especially here, the use of information technology makes this a much more manageable task.

> Do you believe that human resource planning is worthwhile in your organisation (or in one with which you are familiar)? Why do you think this, and is it justifiable?

THE FRAMEWORK FOR HUMAN RESOURCE PLANNING

Before moving on to examine the main techniques which are, and have been, used for human resource planning, we need to establish a framework for this activity. Within the UK human resource literature two different frameworks have been suggested – by Bowey (1975) and Bramham (1975) – both of which derive from more general planning models. It is important to remember that planning processes should not be viewed in a simple unilinear, top-down way, suggesting a beginning and an end (Bramham, 1975: 20), but involve continuous feedback and further refinements to emergent plans. Indeed, Walker (1992: 161) specifically highlights the essential role of 'bottom-up' forecasts in establishing accurate and meaningful estimates of future demand. We take up this view of policy and planning again in Chapter 17 – on vertical integration – when we question the validity of 'classical' models of business strategy.

Bowey's framework (1975: 4) involves the subdivision of human resource planning into three broad categories of activity. First is an assessment of future labour requirements, which presumably ought to be derived from projected business expectations. Second, she refers to an assessment of the organisation's ability to retain its current labour force, and any replacements which may be necessary. This takes us into questions of projected labour turnover, and considerations of whether to plan for growth or reductions in the size of the labour force. Indeed, a large section of her analysis focuses on different measures of labour turnover, wastage and stability. Finally, some predictions have to be made about the ability of the organisation to acquire or attract different kinds of staff from the external labour market. As with more recent versions of 'soft' human resource planning, this framework obviously extends beyond straightforward number counts and into choices about reward management, employee development, employee relations and employee resourcing policies and plans.

Bramham's framework was central to his original book on manpower planning (1975: 21), but it has now been relegated to a minor position in his more recent work on human resource planning (1994: 163). It comprises four main phases – investigating, forecasting, planning, and utilising – of which the first two are the most relevant for this chapter. The *investigation* stage provides an analysis of the external environment (and in particular to business plans, organisational strengths and weaknesses, market share, and so on), a review of the external labour market (such as the quality and quantity of graduates or school leavers, and broader government policies towards employment and educational issues), and an audit of the internal labour market. The second phase is *forecasting* future and projected requirements (the demand for labour) and the potential supply of that labour from within and outside the organisation. Bramham (1975: 28) emphasises the fact that forecasting should not be viewed as creating tablets of stone, but as a continuously changing frame of reference against which human resource decisions are made. This is where most of the statistical modelling techniques were used with such vigour by certain large employers in the 1960s and 1970s, in order to make estimates about wastage, flows of labour through various grades, and succession planning. The next phase is *planning and control*, which involves turning forecasts into personnel and development policies for recruitment, training and development, absence control, motivation and reward; each of these aspects is dealt with more fully elsewhere in this book. The final phase, according to Bramham, is *utilisation*, which requires the human resource plans to be compared against defined and important measures of organisational success, in terms of factors such as labour productivity, product quality, customer satisfaction, and organisational performance. Perhaps evaluation is a better term than utilisation for this phase.

Which of these frameworks do you think is more useful in trying to understand how organisations develop their human resource plans? What are the major drawbacks of these frameworks?

TECHNIQUES FOR HUMAN RESOURCE PLANNING

Over the years a number of techniques or methods have been used for determining 'hard' human resource plans, especially in terms of the numbers of staff required by, or available in, the organisation. Broadly these have been applied to three sets of issues: forecasts of the demand for labour; forecasts of internal supply; and forecasts of external supply. Each of these is considered in turn, with the greatest emphasis on the internal supply forecasts, since this has traditionally been the area where human resource contributions have been most sought after.

Methods for forecasting future demand

There are basically two sorts of method for assessing future demands for labour, the objective and the subjective. The former relies upon the projection of past trends and, to be of any value, needs to take into account shifts brought about by changes in technology and organisational goals. Simple projections from the past to indicate the amount or type of labour required in the future can be related to results from work study exercises or ratios of customers to staff. For example, in the case of education, certain norms become established for the number of full-time equivalent (FTE) students per member of staff, or class sizes which are deemed to be appropriate for effective learning to take place. Arguments for increases, decreases or replacements are typically made with these figures in mind, and comparisons are made with similar schools/departments in similar situations. However, technological changes may lead to major reductions in the demand for certain types of labour and increases in demand for others, or perhaps a lower demand for labour overall; examples can be found from changes in the nature of labour demand in the printing industry or from the continuing shift from manual to white-collar staff over the last 50 years. But, in the short term at least, comparisons with other departments or over time are widely used to justify numbers employed.

A good example here is that of the leading food retailers, which cope with massive variations in customer demand during the course of the week by linking aggregate staff hours for any store to previous patterns of trading – in formulae which are established centrally via computer models. If there are quirks or changes to the system, store managers can make a case for exceptions to be applied, but broad parameters are set at headquarters. Given the tight margins with which food retailers typically operate, there is a premium on keeping staff numbers low, but this can create tensions with other commitments made by the companies, such as those to minimise queue lengths and open more checkouts to serve customers more quickly.

Fears that centralised systems such as this may be unresponsive to local needs has fuelled arguments that subjective methods are more appropriate for assessing future staff demand. At its most basic this takes the form of managerial judgement about future needs, and in some cases it can be an excuse for speculation and even 'guestimates' based on limited amounts of data. The subjective approaches can be either 'top-down' or 'bottom-up' or, indeed, be a mixture of both. A top-down approach relies heavily on estimates from senior managers, a group of people who *ought* to have a clear idea about the direction in which the organisation is moving. The bottom-up method, conversely, focuses on departmental and workplace managers making estimates about future staffing requirements based upon their experience and judgement (Walker, 1992: 162). Although this is likely to be formulated with a good knowledge of current demand locally, it does not necessarily reflect future prospects, nor are these managers aware of wider corporate goals. In addition, first-line managers often learn to ask for more than is required – on the grounds that this will be negotiated down by their senior colleagues. In reality, of course, both methods are used in conjunction in order to form a more meaningful estimate of likely future demand.

One method which relies on managerial judgement is the Delphi technique. According to Schuler and Huber (1993: 135), experts take turns in presenting their forecasts and assumptions to others, who then make adjustments to their own forecasts. The process continues until a viable composite forecast emerges. Torrington and Hall (1995: 84) also refer to the Delphi technique, but their description indicates that the process is undertaken *anonymously* until the plans converge. Either way, the technique is designed to bring together different estimates on the grounds that the combined judgement will be superior to any individual estimate.

Forecasting the demand for staff is, of course, heavily dependent upon assumptions about the nature of product demand in the future, and the implications which this has for the numbers and type of employees who are required. This is not a task which is central to human resource specialists, but is more likely to involve business planners, finance and marketing managers. It is much easier to forecast future demand in certain sectors than in others. For example, based upon past projections, reasonable assumptions can be made about *overall* levels of demand for health care, primary school education or food products in the next five years, and this allows for meaningful estimates of future labour demand to be made. However, it is much more difficult to estimate the numbers of patients, schoolchildren or shoppers likely to attend a *particular* hospital, school or supermarket, given mobility patterns and, in principle, a wider degree of choice for consumers. Since classes at school are run in broad unit sizes (say, 30), difficult decisions have to be made if an extra ten children are enrolled across two age groups. Also, the decision to take on extra schoolchildren to satisfy demand raises critical questions about the need for more facilities, buildings and other aspects of the infrastructure. Staffing plans are even harder to determine for companies which operate in highly competitive international markets, especially those which are prone to political volatility, because of extreme difficulties in predicting future patterns of demand.

Forecasting internal supply

Once an employer has forecast the likely demand for labour, attention can then turn to how that demand can be satisfied, and in particular to establish the balance between recruiting from the external labour market, developing staff internally, or if necessary, seeking workforce reductions. This section examines factors internal to the organisation, while the next considers external supply.

The techniques which are used here principally cover two sorts of estimate: wastage/labour turnover, and internal job and grade movements. Data about these issues can be used for a variety of purposes, and can point to problems which are likely to emerge for the organisation in years to come. The presence of high levels of labour turnover, for example, can indicate problems with a whole range of P&D policies and practices, ranging from inappropriate recruitment methods and selection criteria, through to badly designed payment systems and uncompetitive levels of pay, inappropriate grievance and disciplinary procedures and practices, inadequate levels of training and development, and major blockages in communication systems. There are external factors which could account for these problems as well, including the presence of new competitors for labour in the area or a reduced provision of public transport to the establishment. While human resource planning will not *per se* remove these problems, a clear knowledge of the source of the labour turnover problem can at least ensure that managers know where to look for appropriate solutions. Similarly, it is essential to have accurate data on grade movements, or the age and gender distribution of the workforce, if other personnel and development issues are to be tackled properly.

> How is labour turnover measured in your organisation? Are line managers provided with information on labour turnover on a departmental basis? If not, why not?

Two sorts of measure are typically used to calculate wastage. First, there is a labour turnover index, which divides the number of staff who leave in a given period by the number of staff employed overall; the formula is presented in Figure 4. Both the numerator and the divisor can include different features and be applied to different departments in the organisation; for example, leavers may refer solely to those people who leave the organisation voluntarily, or it can include those made redundant, those at the end of fixed-term contracts, or those dismissed, each of which inflates the figure to some extent. The divisor can be calculated on the basis of the number employed at the beginning of the year, at the end, or the average of the two figures. Comparisons of raw data are inevitably clouded by such considerations, and care needs to be taken in interpreting material without a clear understanding of the basis on which the statistics are derived. Exit interviews may shed some light on the problem but people are often unwilling to provide an honest answer to explain their resignation. The most fundamental problem with raw wastage indices, however, are that they do not differentiate between leavers in terms of their length of service, grade or gender. It is clear that the solution to a problem of high labour turnover is likely to be quite different if this is caused by the departure of women in managerial grades with short periods of service, than if it is long-serving male manual workers. In the former case, there is probably a need to investigate training and development practices, support systems and mentoring, whereas in the latter problems may be indicated in the working environment and the demands of physical labour.

Figure 4 Indices of labour turnover

$$Wastage\ rate = \frac{\text{leavers in year}}{\text{average numbers of staff in post during year}} \times 100$$

$$Stability\ rate = \frac{\text{number of staff with one year's service at date}}{\text{number of staff employed exactly one year before}} \times 100$$

Problems such as this have led to the development of the second type of measure – 'stability' indices. In these, the number of staff with a certain minimum period of service (say, one year) at a certain date is divided by overall numbers employed at that date; see the diagram in the box below for the formula for determining this. Bowey (1975: 44) devises a slightly different measure which takes into account two years' service, but the principle is the same. Stability indices provide a good indicator of the proportion of staff who have been with the organisation for a longer period, and conversely the extent to which labour turnover is a problem specific to staff with shorter periods of service. Indeed, in many large organisations, quite a high proportion of staff – at all levels and grades – have in the past typically had very long periods of service; the recent fragmentation of the labour market and reductions in the number of 'tenured' employees (staff who are not on fixed-term contracts of one sort or another) has probably reduced this significantly.

The census method provides an effective way in which to portray measures of labour turnover since it produces a picture, via a histogram, of the percentage of leavers with specific periods of service. This allows analysts to observe when staff are most likely to leave the organisation, and then start to determine the reasons why this is happening. Torrington and Hall (1995: 95–100) provide an example of how this applied to a hotel complex, which illustrates the problem that many of the leavers have only short periods of service, often under six months.

The histogram below provides a census analysis of leavers for one store in a leading supermarket chain. The store employs a total of 224 staff, and during the last year there was a wastage rate of 41 per cent and a stability index of 85 per cent. The wastage rate was highest among young part-time staff; stability was highest among the middle-aged full-timers.

Write a short report explaining the results to the store manager and suggesting lines of action to remedy the problem.

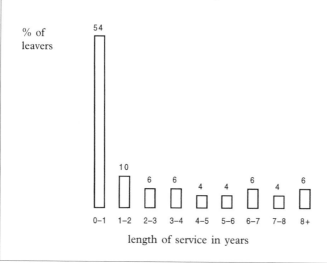

According to Walker (1992: 170) there are two fundamental types of model used in internal supply forecasting: supply 'push' and demand 'pull' models, although there are variants on this theme, as we shall see below. Each type relies, to a greater or lesser extent, on mathematical modelling techniques and the probability that historical movements of staff will be reproduced in the future. Driven by operational researchers, these models became increasingly complex during the 1960s and 1970s, and a variety of different approaches were put forward, in many cases used by large employers through their computerised personnel information databases; Bartholomew (1976) has collated a series of readings on these techniques for those who wish to understand the mathematical reasoning behind them, and who have knowledge of linear and non-linear programming, and parametric and non-parametric statistics.

The supply-push approaches are typically derived from Markov models, which are drawn from two demographic models of staffing. The first is a model of staff wastage based upon the log normal law of distribution, which asserts that 'staff leave an organisation according to a clearly definable pattern of length of service' (Sisson and Timperley, 1994: 156), and that once this pattern is modelled then staffing and promotion information is available for decision-making. The second model is based upon staff profile analysis which assumes that recruitment, promotion and wastage patterns are stable over time, so the probability that a member of staff in a particular grade will be in some other grade later in their working life can be determined from recent career histories. If gaps become apparent, then remedial action can be taken to seek further recruitment at certain levels or develop internal staff for subsequent promotion. More recently, the use of Markov chains has been superseded in some US organisations by tables of transition rates or probabilities (Walker, 1992: 171; Schuler and Huber, 1993: 138).

To have any chance of success, however, these models rely upon large numbers of employees in an organisation, a relatively stable and predictable career structure, and broadly consistent aggregate wastage rates. It is likely to be of little use to a small firm operating in a volatile product market, or to an organisation which has decided to delayer its management structure and, as an example, halve the number of grades in the hierarchy. Equally, given that rates of labour turnover are heavily influenced by factors external to the firm, such as the level of local and/or occupational unemployment and the availability of jobs elsewhere in the labour market, decisions are often beyond the control of human resource planners in organisations. Also, technological or other changes may render existing job definitions irrelevant, so great care needs to be exercised in applying these techniques too rigidly. As a guide, however, this type of analysis can throw up at an early stage potential problems which can then be tackled before the event.

The pull/renewal models are based upon movements out of grades and release from the organisation as a whole, such that flows of staff are triggered by vacancies or promotions. At the top of the organisation the only movement can be through retirement or resignation, so a change here then sets in motion a search for a replacement external to the organisation or a series of internal movements to fill the vacancies which are created. The situation then becomes more complicated as the analysis shifts to lower levels in the hierarchy, as it also does when decisions may be made not to seek a replacement, or to undergo a more radical reorganisation of the management structure. According to Walker (1992: 174), the demand-pull models are not as widely used in the USA, but are particularly helpful in considering promotion and succession decisions.

A useful way in which to portray these demand-pull approaches is through the use of 'camel' models or career progression diagrams (Bramham, 1994: 167). Broadly, these seek to plot a matrix, with age distribution as one axis and grade as the other, and then to assess the proportion of staff in any one grade at a particular age. It is then possible to establish the age distribution of the organisation as a whole, or of a particular subset, and predict likely shortfalls and blockages within the system. This can then activate the search for solutions to overcome the problem. For example, if it appears that there will be major gaps at certain levels in the organisation in several years' time – say, due to a lack of suitably qualified and/or experienced internal staff – then action can be taken to recruit, retrain or relocate specific employees. Alternatively, the information may instead activate a search for different solutions, such as restructuring the department or redefining the nature of work to be undertaken. In the converse situation, where a major promotion blockage appears likely in the near future, senior management can take steps to limit recruitment, encourage people to leave the organisation, or re-orient the culture of the firm such that 'lateral' moves are recognised as a route to further career development

What can you establish (without doing detailed calculations) from the diagram below about recruitment and promotion opportunities over the next five years in this insurance company? Assume that the company has just four grades of staff (with 1 as the highest), and that numbers employed are likely to remain broadly the same as now. Wastage rates (excluding retirements) are 10 per cent p.a. in grades 1 and 2, 15 per cent in grade 3, and 25 per cent in grade 4. The figures refer to numbers of staff in each grade/age range.

Grade	20–29	30–39	40–49	50–59	60+
1	0	1	1	4	4
2	1	2	7	5	5
3	12	23	11	3	1
4	56	19	21	4	0

Age

Forecasting External Supply

Most of the texts on human resource planning devote rather less attention to forecasts of external supply than they do to internal supply, and this is probably a major reason why so many employers were shocked to find out about the so-called 'demographic timebomb' which was publicised in the late 1980s. It will be recalled that this suggested that, due to a decline in the birth rate in the late 1970s, the number of school and college leavers entering the labour market in the early-to-mid 1990s would be significantly less than in previous years. This stimulated a spate of recruitment and advertising schemes designed to attract school leavers, but also the introduction of new policies to retain existing female and elderly staff – for example, through career break schemes for women in the banks, and the employment of individuals past the normal age of retirement in retailing. The aversion to national, centralised and regulated planning which has been so common in Britain since the early 1980s can also explain some of this lack of attention. As Bramham (1994: 160) notes, although this is an area where human resource managers should have an important interest, it is not one where they are able to exert much influence. This is at odds with other aspects of corporate planning, however; awareness of market prospects is an important aspect of product market decisions, so it seems strange that it is so lacking in the labour market area, especially given the renewed emphasis on 'people making the difference'. In addition, such a stance ignores the influence that employers are able to exert locally – either directly or indirectly – on educational and employment issues through their membership of TECs, on boards of school governors, or through local councils. Equally, through their participation in the activities of employers' and trade associations, influence can be exerted on government, higher education establishments or through the media. It is just not accurate, nor is it particularly business-like, to conceive of managers as powerless in the face of external pressures.

But too often this is precisely what appears to happen, as Atkinson's analysis of employers' responses to shortages of labour in the late 1980s indicated. He suggested (1989) that four main types of response were possible, basically divided into tactical and strategic. Among the former were to 'take it on the chin' by doing nothing or allowing hiring standards to decline, and 'competing' with other employers for a declining pool of labour, with the attendant worries that this may stimulate a spiralling of wage and other recruitment costs. Most employers fell into these categories. A few took a more strategic stance by finding 'substitutes' through the recruitment and retention of older workers or reducing wastage, and being 'creative', principally through training and development programmes.

There are a number of factors which determine the supply of staff from the external labour market, both at a local and a national level, which are influenced by economic, social and legal issues. Obviously, local labour market and social information is more important for certain grades and types of staff, such as manual workers, whereas national trends and educational developments matter more for professionally qualified personnel. We will return to this point in the next chapter, on recruitment and selection, when sources of labour supply and job advertising are examined in more detail. Broadly speaking, among the major factors which influence external labour supply locally are:

- the level of unemployment in the travel-to-work area

- opening and closure of other workplaces in the area which compete for the same types of labour

- number/qualifications of school and college leavers from the local educational system

- housing and transport developments

- the reputation of the employer compared with that of others in the area, measured by such things as wages and working conditions, employment record, and general public relations image.

The major factors which influence labour supply at a national level, and by implication locally, include the following:

- the level of unemployment in general, and in particular occupations

- the number of graduates in general, and in specific fields

- the UK and EU legal frameworks governing working hours, equal opportunities, employment protection, and employee relations

- government and industry-wide training schemes.

> There are many sources of information on labour market issues. Find a recent copy of the *Employment Gazette* to establish the level of unemployment nationally and in your region. Consult *IRS Employment Review* to find out the going rate for pay increases in the economy as a whole and in the industry within which you work. What are the major implications of these statistics for your own organisation's human resource plan?

HUMAN RESOURCE PLANNING IN PRACTICE

So much for the theory of human resource planning; what about the practice? The evidence, both from Britain and the USA, indicates that rather more employers involve themselves in 'ad-hocery' and muddling through than in strategic planning and the use of well-developed computerised personnel information systems for this purpose. Respondents to a number of surveys have implied that systematic human resource planning is undertaken, but when questioned further or asked for details of the usage, it is found that little is done (Storey, 1992a: 84; Rothwell, 1995: 177), and the subject is often regarded as 'academic and tedious' (Sisson and Timperley, 1994: 167).

A number of US and UK surveys report results on the extensiveness of human resource planning, and with it the use of computers and information technology to assist the process. Cowling and Walters

(1990: 5) present the results of an IPD survey undertaken in the late 1980s which showed that the major uses of human resource planning were for identifying training and development needs, analysing labour costs and productivity, and assessing the need for structural change. In quite a number of cases, however, this was still done on an *ad hoc* and reactive manner, rather than being part of a wider business plan. The public sector lagged behind the private in this area. Computers were used in certain areas, including career development and succession planning, manpower supply and demand, and monitoring productivity. A more recent survey, again for the IPD, by Kinnie and Arthurs (1993), found that although computer-based personnel systems were present in about three-quarters of the organisations surveyed, less than one-third of those with systems used them for more strategic purposes such as human resource planning. The authors note that the use of computers is limited mainly to routine operational tasks and, for that reason, employers miss a tremendous opportunity to model strategic and more long-term issues. An exception might be the case of Abbey National (Storey and Sisson, 1993: 115), which developed a database for matching the competences of staff with the required competences for specific jobs.

The situation in the USA hardly appears much better. Greer, Jackson and Fiorito's (1989: 110) survey of human resource managers in 137 organisations in the mid-1980s found that qualitative techniques – such as replacement charts, personnel inventories and supervisor estimates – were far more common than quantitative methods for estimating internal supply; for example, Markov models were used by just 6 per cent, and computer simulation by 12 per cent, compared with nearly 50 per cent who used supervisor estimates. The major uses of human resource planning techniques (if the qualitative approaches alone are worthy of this title) were for career planning and human resource development, avoiding shortages of key personnel, and affirmative action. Mathys and Burack (1993) illustrate the application of human resource planning to decisions on 'strategic downsizing', which is more in keeping with the dominant issues affecting organisations in the late twentieth century. Huselid's survey of nearly 1,000 firms (1993: 38) shows that the use of human resource planning varies greatly across the sample, with many organisations still at what is termed the 'traditional' phase, with little in the way of long-term planning. The employers most likely to make use of human resource planning techniques were large, research-and-development-intensive organisations, with sophisticated business planning systems and an active involvement of human resource managers in overall business planning.

Even though most managers probably agree with assertions about the *need* for human resource planning, and appreciate the contribution which such plans can make to organisational success, there still appears to be an aversion to its practice. Similarly, the increased profile of computerised personnel information systems does not seem to have stimulated the use of quantitative models either. There are a number of explanations for why such a massive gap should exist between the theory of human resource planning and its reported use in employing organisations.

First, there are arguments that the models and techniques which have been established are not really rooted in the real world, and merely seek to impose a level of mathematical sophistication on to a messy, and ultimately indeterminate, process. The heyday of modelling appeared in the late 1960s and early 1970s, led by operational researchers and the Institute of Manpower Studies (Bell, 1989). Bartholomew's edited book contains a number of articles, written by practitioners as well as academics, which explain the proofs for formulae and their subsequent use in employing organisations. However, the models should not be used slavishly, acting as a replacement for managerial judgement and interpretation, but as a valuable source of information which can guide choices in other areas of personnel and development – such as whether or not to recruit, and if so, at what level; who should be trained, and in preparation for what; whether induction programmes need to be revised to reduce high levels of labour turnover; how effective payment systems might be for retaining key sets of individuals; whether or not employees are losing motivation and commitment due to blockages in the promotion system; and so on. Also, there is an underlying suspicion that managers may have eschewed the application of human resource planning models because of their anxieties about mathematics and statistics; in other words, highlighting the shortcomings of the more sophisticated techniques as a way of justifying their avoidance of them, and reliance upon 'muddling through'.

Second, it is apparent that many organisations do not actually hold data in a sufficiently user-friendly form to establish even simple human resource planning models (Storey, 1992: 84). It is rare for organisations to maintain detailed records of their staff which can be accessed for multiple purposes, and often there are separate data banks for different issues; for example, separate parts of the P&D function produce reports on equal opportunities, absence and labour turnover figures, training and development programmes attended, and appraisal results, without proper integration of these data. The importance of integrating human resource systems is not often questioned, but it rarely gets done apart from in some of the large, centralised employers, such as the leading food retailers and in multinational chemical companies. The theme of horizontal and vertical integration, dealt with in detail in Chapters 17–19, is right at the heart of a comprehensive human resource planning system.

Third, as we have already seen, in order to be effective, there need to be links between business and human resource plans. This is obviously important when trying to assess the demand for labour, but it is also crucial to determine whether the skills and experience of the current workforce is adequate to meet future business goals. There is a series of problems here. Despite considerable exhortation, many commentators believe that much business planning and strategy is uncoordinated, reactive and inchoate (Storey, 1986: 49). Clearly, it is impossible to develop a comprehensive human resource plan if no business plan has been prepared. There is evidence that human resource plans rarely find their way into a business strategy even if one does exist, and it has been a continuing concern that P&D

specialists are not adequately represented at board level. Some are, and are known to have a major influence over discussions about the business as a whole (Wilkinson and Marchington, 1994), but in most cases the consideration of human resource issues is typically downstream from other corporate decisions (Marchington and Parker, 1990: 51–54).

A final point, to some extent connected with the previous one, is that senior line managers show little interest in, or commitment to, human resource planning, and it is a matter of low priority. This has been found not only in Britain (Cowling and Walters, 1990: 6), but also in the USA (Greer *et al*, 1989: 112). There clearly appears to be a contradiction between vague assertions that 'people are our most important resource' and the lack of attention typically devoted to effective human resource planning. This means that much of the effort which goes into techniques such as psychometric testing, the implementation of competence-based training plans, performance-related pay, new-style union agreements, and other management fashions of the 1990s takes place within a vacuum, and without proper integration.

> Given that senior managers show so little interest in human resource planning, how might personnel and development specialists seek to demonstrate its value and contribution to the business?

CONCLUSION

Human resource planning represents the first stage in an organisation's P&D practices, and in many respects it sets the tone for the remainder of an employer's human resource policies. If planning is not carried out in this aspect of P&D, it is hard to imagine it being done effectively elsewhere. At the same time, relatively little is known about human resource planning in practice, and it is often dismissed as a worthless paper exercise until problems arise; as, for example, when an organisation is forced to restructure, and management realises that it has recruited too many staff or those with the wrong skills, and panic measures are taken. Given the turbulence and highly competitive product markets within which organisations operate at the current time, the case for human resource planning is now probably greater than ever. However, human resource plans should not be seen as a substitute for managerial judgement, but as an aid to management decision-making. The major advantage of planning in advance is that it allows managers to consider a range of solutions rather than feeling pressurised into adopting the only realistic option which remains open to them as a last-ditch attempt to avoid a crisis.

USEFUL READING

ATKINSON, J. (1989) 'Four stages of adjustment to the demographic downturn', *Personnel Management*, August: 20–24.

BRAMHAM, J. (1988) *Practical Manpower Planning,* Fourth Edition. London, IPM.

BRAMHAM, J. (1994) *Human Resource Planning,* Second Edition. London, IPD.

COWLING, A. AND WALTERS, M. (1990) 'Manpower planning – where are we today?', *Personnel Review,* Vol 19, 3: 3–8.

KINNIE, N. AND ARTHURS, A. (1993) 'Will personnel people ever learn to love the computer?', *Personnel Management,* June: 46–51.

MATHYS, N. AND BURACK, E. (1993) 'Strategic downsizing: human resource planning approaches', *Human Resource Planning,* Vol 16, 1: 71–85.

SCHULER, R. AND HUBER, V. (1993) *Personnel and Human Resource Management.* New York, West Publishing Company: Chapter 4.

SISSON, K. (Ed.) (1994) *Personnel Management in Britain.* Oxford, Blackwell: Chapter 5.

TORRINGTON, D. AND HALL, L. (1995) *Personnel Management: Human resource management in action.* London, Prentice Hall: Chapter 5.

WALKER, J. (1992) *Human Resource Strategy.* New York, McGraw Hill.

6 Recruitment and selection

INTRODUCTION

Recruiting and selecting people to fill new or existing positions is a crucial element of personnel and development activity in all organisations, irrespective of their size, structure or orientation. Over the last two decades this area of management practice has become much more sophisticated, with some large organisations using organisational psychologists or consultants to improve the reliability and validity of the selection decision. After all, provided there is an adequate supply of labour, newly-appointed staff provide management with an opportunity to acquire new skills as well as adjust attitudes and cultures within organisations. Too often, however, decisions are made in an informal, *ad hoc* and reactive manner, without a proper analysis of whether or not specific jobs are needed (beyond filling a vacancy), of the characteristics required by post-holders (beyond a continuation of previous practice), or of the most appropriate techniques to be used for recruiting and selecting staff (beyond an unplanned interview).

It is the purpose of this chapter to review the entire recruitment and selection cycle, from job analysis through to appointment. The process incorporates a number of stages, each of which needs to be done well to increase the likelihood of making a satisfactory appointment. Jobs have to be analysed in order to isolate the key characteristics and competences which are required, and this then leads to the derivation of accurate and relevant job descriptions and personnel specifications. The recruitment process needs to be managed in terms of choosing the most appropriate media to be used (informal contacts as well as advertising), and ensuring that the right messages are conveyed about the job as well as the organisation's image. Once a suitable pool of candidates has been attracted, selection methods have to be chosen which are relevant for the task; these can range from the most frequently used (interviews) to the least (graphology), from a focus on values and beliefs (eg personality tests) to direct assessments of performance (eg work samples). It is advised that multiple methods should be employed to increase the validity of selection decisions.

The implications of poor selection decisions for all aspects of P&D, and on the business as a whole, are enormous and can be catastrophic. They may be very expensive in terms of the management time required to deal with disciplinary cases, in retraining poor performers, and in having to recruit replacements for those individuals who have been wrongly selected and who choose to leave soon after starting work. The effects on customer service and product quality are more readily apparent, whether staff are employed on a supermarket check-out, an engineering factory or a hotel. It is not solely a problem of recruiting someone who is under-qualified, lacks the relevant skills or is uncooperative, even though this is what inevitably comes to mind. Equally serious problems may arise with an employee who is over-qualified, who soon becomes bored with routines, or challenges managers who are accustomed to issuing instructions. It is selecting the *right* person for the task which matters. The chances of this can be enhanced by a thorough understanding of the recruitment and selection techniques which are most useful for specific circumstances.

By the end of this chapter, readers should be able to:

- undertake a job analysis and compile a job description and person specification
- identify the most appropriate media through which to advertise specific vacancies
- contribute to the design, implementation and evaluation of a selection decision.

In addition, readers should be able to understand and explain:

- the most important and widely-used methods of job analysis
- the nature of the recruitment process and its principal components
- the major differences between a range of selection methods, their value and shortcomings in the selection process.

JOB ANALYSIS

Job analysis represents the first stage of the recruitment and selection process, and it is crucial in identifying the range of tasks that the new recruit will be expected to undertake. In firms with relatively buoyant product markets and high levels of labour turnover, in which recruitment takes place on a frequent and continuing basis, job analysis is obviously not required prior to the filling of all vacancies. However, it is useful as a tool for examining whether or not existing job descriptions are appropriate for future needs. Indeed, it may even demonstrate that there is no need for further recruitment or that the type of job and person required is somewhat different from that which is anticipated. Given increasing financial pressures on employers to redesign and restructure work by allocating it among existing staff, decisions about whether or not to fill vacancies are likely to have become more frequent. For many organisations, particularly in the manufacturing sector, recruitment and selection of *new* staff may be a rarity, and rather more attention has been focused on redeploying employees who would otherwise be made redundant. Job analysis is clearly equally relevant in this context.

Job analysis refers to the process of collecting and analysing information about the tasks, responsibilities and the content of jobs.

This emphasis on process reinforces the distinction between job *analysis* and the job *description*, with the latter being seen quite clearly as an output of the former. One of the leading American texts (Schuler and Huber, 1993: 153) focuses on the process aspect of job analysis: it is defined as 'describing and recording the purpose of a job, its major duties and activities, the conditions under which it is performed, and the necessary skills, knowledge and abilities.' However, an IPM publication (Pearn and Kandola, 1993: 1) suggests that the term *job* analysis is too narrow, and should be extended to 'job, task and role analysis' in order to emphasise the importance of the activity. This is defined as 'any systematic procedure for obtaining detailed and objective information about a job, task or role that will be performed or is currently being performed.'

Job analysis is also useful in a variety of other P&D situations, apart from as an aid to recruitment and selection decisions. In employee reward it can help with the classification and ranking of different jobs, and in determining internal and external pay relativities. In employee relations it can be used to identify necessary changes in work design and in discussions with trade union representatives about working arrangements. Job analysis is also useful in the employee development field in relation to training requirements and plans for individual employees, and in other areas of employee resourcing such as induction and appraisal. Each of these is taken up in subsequent sections of the book.

> Can you think of any other ways in which job analysis might be useful in the P&D field? Can you envisage any conflict over the process of conducting job analysis or its outcomes?

A number of methods can be used for job analysis, and readers who are in need of more detailed information should refer to Pearn and Kandola's book (1993) which provides an evaluation of a range of methods, or to the relevant sections in Smith and Robertson (1993). Broadly, methods vary in terms of their sophistication, cost, convenience and acceptability, and these factors need to be borne in mind when deciding which method to employ. The issue of cost is particularly pertinent, as the benefits to be gained from any technique always need to be compared with the time, effort and money involved in its application. Similarly, the methods which are used need to be acceptable to the staff involved and be capable of gaining their agreement and commitment. If not, there is a danger that spurious results will be obtained from the analysis, as employees seek to give the impression that their jobs are more demanding than they really are.

No one method is inherently more suitable than any other; so much depends upon the need for the information, the jobs which are to be analysed and the context in which job analysis takes place. For example, the use of sophisticated techniques is unlikely to be cost-effective if the number of jobs to be analysed is small and relatively low-skilled. Moreover, the employment of untrained or unqualified staff to undertake job analysis may actually be counterproductive, and more may be gained from using relatively straightforward methods. According to Smith and Robertson (1993: 19), the use of more complex methods is justified in the following sets of circumstances: when large numbers of recruits are involved; when the costs and consequences of employing the wrong people are high (eg when dealing with dangerous products); when the results of job analysis can also be used for other purposes.

There are four broad types of method which can be used: observation, diaries, interviews, and questionnaires. The first three of these are relatively simple to employ and are probably most widely used in organisations. Indeed, Smith and Robertson (1993: 15) note that in most selection contexts a simple approach incorporating documentary analysis, interviews and observation is sufficient to yield an increase in efficiency. They also suggest that, if at all possible, analysts should attempt to do the job themselves, provided it would not break health and safety rules.

Observation is potentially the most straightforward and readily available method, and in any event it would form part of job analysis even if other techniques were employed. It is also likely to be one of the least costly methods. Not only would observers be able to see jobs being undertaken for themselves, they would also seek clarification from job holders about what work is entailed. There are also a number of problems with this method, particularly if it is used in isolation. It may be difficult to interpret precisely what work is being undertaken, especially if there is a high intellectual or cognitive content to the job. The mere fact that someone is being observed can also have an impact upon job behaviour, of either an intended or unintended nature. Moreover, there are doubts about the reliability of observation, in that different observers may come up with quite different analyses, depending upon their approach. Furthermore, the tasks may vary from one day, week or month to the next.

Work diaries are also commonly employed as a method of job analysis. This operates on the principle that job holders keep a record of their activities over a period of time – say each hour over the course of a week, or every time they change the task on which they are engaged. To be done effectively this requires a high degree of commitment and co-operation from the job holder, and a willingness to spend time with the job analyst explaining items in the diary. It is heavily reliant on job holders keeping a comprehensive record of their activities, and not excluding items because they are deemed unimportant, or omitting items which are done frequently or seem like common sense and are not worth recording. A job analysis of local authority manual workers conducted by the authors illustrated that women in support jobs (such as social services or canteens) often failed to include in their diaries major items of their work because these were deemed to be 'common sense' or 'what we do at home as well as at work'. By way of contrast, men who were driving cranes or operating machinery emphasised the technical nature of their work, even though many of them utilised similar skills outside of work. Job analysis is clearly not immune from equal opportunity considerations.

Interviews are the third broad type of method employed, and these range from the relatively unstructured (in which job holders are asked to describe their job while the interviewer probes to get more detail) through to the more standardised format where similar questions are asked of each job holder. Two variants of the interview are co-counselling, in which two job holders interview each other about the job, and the critical incident technique which, as its name suggests, focuses on specific and important events in the job (Pearn and Kandola, 1993: 23–30). Job analysis interviews have much the same sorts of benefits and drawbacks as do interviews in any other area of P&D. The major advantages are to do with cost and convenience, and the opportunity for interaction between interviewer and interviewee. The major disadvantages are concerned with bias and reliability, and interviewer skills, for it is too often assumed that this is a task which can be done by any manager. A further and rather more sophisticated technique which has been used for job analysis is the repertory grid, although this requires skilled specialist interviewers (Pearn and Kandola, 1993: 31–35; Smith and Robertson, 1993: 32).

Questionnaires are typically the most sophisticated and complex of the methods employed for job analysis, and indeed some of these use computer packages. There is a range of techniques on offer: the Position Analysis Questionnaire (PAQ) which contains 194 job elements, and is relatively well-known in the USA through a massive job bank (Schuler and Huber, 1993: 163–164); the Work Profiling System (WPS), a technique developed in the UK by Saville and Holdsworth, which provides organisations with a large amount of information for use in many areas of P&D (Pearn and Kandola, 1993: 51–57). Watson (1994: 190) reports that this instrument was designed with the help of occupational psychologists, the EOC and CRE in order to prevent building discriminatory assumptions into the questions. The Work Performance Survey System (WPSS), also American in origin and used by AT&T: this questionnaire is designed for computer analysis, although it is time-consuming to administer (Pearn and Kandola, 1993: 69–70). More detailed analysis of these methods is beyond the scope of this book, because they require specialist training and expertise.

> Has your organisation ever used the more sophisticated methods of job analysis? If so, evaluate their use and consider whether or not this could be extended to other types of job. If these methods have not been used, explain why.

JOB DESCRIPTIONS AND PERSON SPECIFICATIONS

Various pieces of information need to be included in the job description, some of which were mentioned in Chapter 2 when we dealt with the contract of employment and requirements for a statement of terms and conditions. The precise categorisation is obviously a matter for specific employers and jobs, but the following list indicates what might be included.

1) *Job title*: a clear statement is all that is required, such as personnel director, employee relations manager, training officer, wages clerk.

2) *Location*: department, establishment, organisation.

3) *Responsible to*: job title of supervisor to whom the member of staff reports.

4) *Responsible for*: job titles of members of staff who report directly into the job holder, if any.

5) *Main purpose of the job*: a short and unambiguous statement indicating precisely the overall objective and purpose of the job, such as 'assist and advise customers in a specific area', 'to drill metals in accordance with manufacturing policy'.

6) *Responsibilities/duties*: a list of the main and subsidiary elements in the job, specifying in more or less detail precisely what is required. For a customer-service position, for example, this might include demonstrations of equipment, and organising deliveries or providing after-sales service.

7) *Working conditions*: a list of the major contractual agreements relating to the job, such as pay scales and fringe benefits, hours of work, overtime, holiday entitlement, access to pension scheme, etc. There could also be a note relating to union membership.

8) *Other matters*: this could include information about career prospects, mobility, and performance standards.

9) *Any other duties which are reasonable.*

In recent years, job descriptions have come in for criticism as being outmoded and increasingly irrelevant to modern conditions, symptomatic of an earlier collectivist, inflexible and more rules-oriented culture. No longer, it is argued, should employers be concerned with the precise detail of what employees are expected to do as a minimum and/or norm, but rather the emphasis should be on improving levels of customer service through the use of employee initiative and empowerment. Instead of 'working to contract' and abiding by explicit and published rules, staff should be encouraged and assisted to work 'beyond contract' in order to ensure that customers receive excellent service. The terminology used by these organisations includes 'high-performance work systems', 'blame-free cultures', 'high-trust philosophies' and so on. Some of these were apparent in the companies analysed by Storey (1992: 82–83), especially in terms of the expectation that staff would be willing and able to go beyond contract in the performance of their duties, and that each job title would cover a much broader area than in the past. He quotes Ford as having reduced the number of job titles from 500 to 50 (Storey, 1992: 95). Wickens (1987) also reports on the use of flexible job descriptions at Nissan. Wood and Albanese (1995: 8) regard the introduction of more flexible job descriptions not linked to one specific task as one aspect of 'high commitment management'.

'High-commitment management' has now become more widespread in

British industry, though it should be reiterated that there are still many bureaucratic organisations which have remained relatively untouched by these philosophies, retaining long and detailed job descriptions which were last reviewed a long time ago. We should also be aware of the fact that job descriptions are still important in that they provide potential recruits and existing employees with information about what is expected from work. There is a danger that commentators are seduced by the notions of liberation and empowerment which go along with some of these ideas, without being aware that some employers exploit and manipulate their new-found freedom to redesign people's jobs without consultation or negotiation. These issues are analysed again in the Employee Relations and Employee Reward sections of the book.

> Have detailed job descriptions gone from your organisation, and if so, what has replaced them? Do you think their removal has led to greater autonomy or greater stress? If detailed job descriptions still exist at your workplace, do employees stick rigidly to them when performing work?

Whereas job descriptions are concerned with the jobs for which people are to be recruited, *person specifications* relate to the human characteristics and attributes which are seen as necessary to do the job. The best known and most widely used methods are the seven-point plan (Rodger, 1952) and its later adaptation by Fraser (1966) in the form of the five-point plan. These describe and categorise the principal features required for any job, and all that P&D specialists need to do is apply these to the vacancy in question. The person specification should then distinguish between those aspects which are *essential* to perform the job and those that, in an ideal world, are *desirable*. The two plans are outlined in Tables 7 and 8, with examples to illustrate the terminology.

Both these sets of personnel specifications are somewhat dated, relating not only to a working environment which was much more stable but also to a social and legal framework where it was considered acceptable to ask questions about an individual's domestic circumstances or private life. Although the broad framework may still be valid, it is now unethical, inappropriate and potentially discriminatory to probe too deeply into some of these areas of the person specification. Moreover, it may not make much business sense either to restrict applications to people with specific educational qualifications or a certain length of experience in an industry or occupation. Plumbley (1991: 16) notes that there are many employees with minimal academic or professional qualifications holding down senior posts, and older staff who possess more drive than their younger counterparts.

> Looking over Tables 7 and 8, identify examples under each of the points where there may be tensions between the plans and your own professional standards. Pay close attention to the whole range of equal opportunity and ethical issues.

Table 7 **Rodger's seven-point plan**

- *Physical make-up*: this is concerned with the physical attributes which are considered essential or desirable for achievement of the task, such as ability to lift heavy loads, discriminate between colours, or be able to communicate with customers.

- *Attainments*: this includes educational/professional qualifications, licences, and work experience. Some of these may be obligatory for the performance of certain jobs (eg a doctor), while others may be desirable or generally accepted as important for the achievement of tasks.

- *General intelligence*: this involves the ability to define and solve problems, for example to learn new skills within specified periods of time, or to use initiative in dealing with stressful situations. The recent growth in the use of tests as part of the selection process illustrates the way in which this is now assessed in some organisations.

- *Special aptitudes*: this highlights specific skills, abilities or competences deemed necessary or desirable for performing a job. Again, this is an area where tests have become more common in recent years (eg in the areas of numerical and verbal reasoning, manual dexterity) although some at least can be assessed by examining work samples or probing past experience.

- *Interests*: these refer both to work-related and leisure pursuits which may be relevant to the performance of the job, such as chairing committees, team sports, outdoor interests. These are more likely to figure in person specifications for graduate trainee positions or jobs for school leavers.

- *Disposition*: this deals with attitudes to work and to other people, measured sometimes by personality tests. It refers to attributes such as friendliness, ability to cope with stress, stability and assertiveness.

- *Circumstances*: this involves domestic commitments, mobility, family support, ability to work on certain days of the week or for long hours. In some jobs, these may be essential (eg it is not acceptable for professional footballers to say they are unavailable for work on a Saturday or Sunday), but in many jobs it may be unethical to delve into this aspect of a person's life.

Table 8 **Munro Fraser's five-point plan**

- *Impact on others*: this covers much the same sort of area as 'Physical make-up' in Table 7, but it is also slightly different in conception, relating specifically to impact upon other employees and customers.

- *Acquired knowledge and qualifications*: this covers much the same areas as Rodger's second category.

- *Innate abilities*: this covers much the same areas as Rodger's category 'General intelligence'.

- *Motivation*: this refers to a person's desire to succeed in particular areas and his or her commitment to doing so. It could, for example, relate to the ability to cope with mundane tasks or to longer-term career objectives, and it can be illustrated by previous experience, by test results or through interviews and discussions.

- *Adjustment*: this involves characteristics which are related specifically to the job, such as ability to withstand pressure, cope with difficult customers, or work well in a team.

RECRUITMENT METHODS

Recruitment is often regarded as the poor relation of selection, with rather less space devoted to it in most publications. While the latter has caught the attention of organisational psychologists keen to increase the reliability and validity of selection methods, the former has received scant attention. However, as Watson (1994: 203) argues, 'Recruitment provides the candidates for the selector to judge. Selection techniques cannot overcome failures in recruitment; they merely make them evident.' Important decisions have to be made about whether or not to recruit, from which sources, using which media, and at what cost. Moreover, the documentation which is used in the recruitment exercise has an impact much wider than employee resourcing alone, in that it conveys images of the organisation, its products and its overall philosophy. Mercury Communications recognised that recruitment advertisements provide a general impression of the company and 'send out messages to potential employees, clients, customers, partners and shareholders' (IRS *Employee Development Bulletin* 49, 1994: 5). Furthermore, if the recruitment process generates insufficient applications, or too many unsuitable ones, it will prove expensive to make appointment decisions.

Rather than produce a long list of recruitment methods, with associated advantages and disadvantages, it makes more sense to classify them into four broad categories. The first of these is internal recruitment, where management seek candidates by searching internal records, and redeploy employees from one task or area to another. At its best this might be seen as a form of career management in which staff are moved around the organisation so as to make effective use of their skills and abilities as part of a wider human resource plan. At its worst, however, in situations where external recruitment is frozen, it may simply entail shifting existing staff from one department to another, resulting in untrained and/or demotivated employees.

A second method is to rely on existing staff to identify potential recruits, or to rehire former employees, casual callers, or people whose records are on file from previous recruitment exercises. For many years methods such as these dominated hiring decisions in many organisations, particularly those with close-knit communities and where whole families were employed by a particular firm – such as printing and dockworkers. As with internal recruitment, this is a cheap and relatively easy option, in that recruits are readily available, are known to existing members of the workforce, and their selection requires little in the way of sophisticated techniques. Although methods such as these are often criticised as inefficient because they fail to tap into wider labour markets, and for perpetuating existing cultures, they can also act as a source of discipline over new recruits as well; rather than having to build teams, they come ready-made! On the other hand, 'ring-fencing' may serve only to reinforce existing imbalances (gender, race and disability), thwarting attempts to encourage greater workforce diversity.

Thirdly, employers can utilise their own specialist P&D staff to manage and operate the recruitment and selection process. In large organisations there may even be a separate recruitment and selection section within the human resource department, whereas in others this may be facilitated by a generalist, and administered predominantly by line managers or even teams of workers themselves. The precise methods to be used are likely to vary depending upon the vacancies to be filled and the resources which the employer is prepared to commit to the exercise. The state of the external labour market is also a relevant consideration, and the most appropriate methods will vary depending upon local and/or national levels of unemployment, on specific skills shortages, and on competition from other employers for the same types of labour.

Three examples may help to illustrate this point. A company which is seeking to recruit a semi-skilled manual worker for a job that requires little training may target the local job centre and put advertisements in local newspapers at no, or minimal, cost. This may generate sufficient adequately-skilled applicants, at a cost-effective price, especially if there is a satisfactory supply of labour available in the area.

A second example might be where technical staff are required for the organisation's engineering department. In this case it is more likely that specialist trade magazines will be targeted, as might schools and further education colleges, and regional newspapers. Given the fact that professional qualifications would probably be required (or the individual might be expected to acquire these during his or her employment), the local paper would typically not generate a sufficient quantity or quality of acceptable applications to be cost-effective. If there had been a major redundancy from a similar employer in the area in recent months, or the employer was so attractive that employees would be prepared to leave existing jobs, then local sources may be cost-effective after all.

In the final example, large employers might visit higher educational institutions on the 'milk round' and advertise in the national press in order to recruit management trainees. In this situation, the cost of recruitment is likely to be high, but it may well be justified in terms of the expected contribution from graduates in general, and some potential high-fliers in particular. There is even an element of competing with other leading employers for the best labour, rather like Premier League football teams. In some cases there is targeting of specific universities for new recruits, driven either by positive experiences in the past or even blind prejudice on the part of managers who believe that recruits from their old university are inherently superior to other applicants.

The final category of recruitment methods is where employers subcontract this activity to an outside body. Depending upon the level and nature of the recruit who is sought, this could include headhunters (executive search consultants), management selection consultants and commercial employment agencies. Each of these charges a fee for their services, although some require this to be paid only in the event of filling the vacancy – rather like an estate agent. The cost of using consultants is higher than for any other method, although if the salaries and expenses of specialist staff are taken into account, it can prove more cost-effective than some of the other methods. In addition, if the appointment is to be at a very high level, and senior managers in other organisations are to be targeted, commercial and personal confidentiality may make this a more attractive method. So too might the purchase of specialist expertise and a wider range of contacts from the consultancy.

> Which of these methods have been used in your organisation, which have been most widely used, and have they been cost-effective?

RECRUITMENT ADVERTISEMENTS AND APPLICATION FORMS

Recruitment advertisements and application forms are two of the most important written documents which provide potential recruits with information about an image of the organisation. The advertisement is what typically attracts individuals to apply for jobs in the first place. If it is well designed, and conveys a realistic and accurate image of the employer and the job(s) which are to be filled, it will succeed in encouraging people to apply. If it is poorly designed, contains typographical mistakes, and conjures up pictures of a boring, drab and lifeless organisation, it may succeed in putting off suitable candidates – unless of course the organisation really is boring, drab and lifeless, in which case it might be of some value! But too often, according to Lewis (1985: 122), recruitment advertisements are amateurish, drafted at short notice, with the vague objective of 'producing suitable applicants'. Compared with product advertisements, recruitment advertising is often undertaken with low budgets, a lack of clear planning, and without proper evaluation of whether or not it has worked. Snape et al (1994: 23) report that a majority of advertisements for management jobs were less than useful, over half failing to provide clear and unambiguous instructions about how to apply for the job. Information technology can now be used to analyse responses to advertisements, and identify which media have been the most useful in generating high-quality and relevant applications (IRS Employee Development Bulletin 49, 1994).

Lewis (1985: 22–23) indicates that four 'rules' have been suggested for cost-effective recruitment advertising. These are: the right audience should be targeted by choosing the most appropriate media; an adequate number of replies should be generated; the advertisement should minimise the number of wasted replies, so reducing the amount of work to be done by recruitment staff, but also limiting the number of disappointed applicants; and the organisation should be promoted as a good employer, as this may attract future applicants without even needing to advertise jobs. In short, not only must the advertisement be prepared properly perhaps by commissioning a specialist agency, but it must also appear in the right places. It is not sensible to attract large numbers of applicants just for the sake of it, as may be the result of a loosely-worded and vague advertisement, for valuable time will be taken up looking through letters from candidates who do not measure up to the person specification. Recruitment agencies provide not only specialist expertise in the design of advertisements, but also – because of their commercial muscle – may be able to place the advertisement at a lower price than the employer would have had to pay.

Recruitment advertising has very clear equal opportunities connotations, both in terms of ensuring that employers comply with various Codes of Practice (including that of the IPD) and that they are able to attract a wider pool of applicants. Paddison (1990: 55) demonstrates clearly that recruitment advertisements can portray images which are indirectly discriminatory because of the copy which is used (for example, omitting pictures of women, black people, or those with disabilities while at the same time claiming to be equal opportunities employers). She also reports that Rank Xerox increased not only the proportion of men applying for a particular occupation (where they were under-represented) but also, by skilful copywriting, increased the number of female applicants as well. A similar result was achieved by Channel Four when it targeted people with disabilities (Paddison, 1990: 56–57).

> Design a short advert for your own job which will attract a sufficient pool of suitable applicants, choose where to place it, and estimate the costs involved.

Similar comments can be made about application forms, although of course these are only seen by those people who actually respond to the job advertisement. Poorly designed application forms may put off good applicants or fail to provide assessors with information necessary for the selection process. According to IRS (*Employment Development Bulletin* 51, 1994a: 2), it is strange that so little thought is given to application forms, and they are seldom acknowledged as 'an effective and integral part of a selection strategy.' Jenkins (1983: 259) demonstrates that a large proportion of applicants decide not to pursue the vacancy after receiving the application form. Although there are a variety of reasons for this, some of which are obviously beneficial to the employer if unsuitable applicants drop out at this stage rather than later, it is also likely that some high-quality applicants are also lost at this point as well. The recruitment field is no different from many other areas of P&D in that employers consistently fail to integrate their people management practices with their broader business objectives.

The most effective application forms ensure that the information provided ties in with the person specification and core competencies required for the job in question. This is now done for executive officers in the Employment Service, in terms of seven competencies: getting on with people; communication skills; planning and prioritising work; adapting to and managing change; making decisions; managing a team; developing others (IRS *Employee Development Bulletin* 51, 1994a: 4–5). For each competency, applicants are asked to provide examples of how they have dealt with specific situations. For example, under 'getting on with people', the form states 'Executive officers have to be able to deal with people, relate to colleagues and the public, even in difficult circumstances. Please give an example of when you have had to deal with difficult or uncooperative people.' Most of the leading food retailers also use a competence-based approach for recruitment and selection of graduate trainees, and this forms a central feature of their application forms. Payne (1995) reports that there is some degree of overlap in the competencies sought by these companies, with most seeking the following: self-motivation; business awareness; planning and prioritising; conceptual thinking; self-confidence; influencing skills; and analytical skills. At the same time, Feltham (1992: 96), despite advocating their use, urges caution in taking a too mechanistic view on linking competences to sections on the application form.

THE CHOICE OF SELECTION METHODS

Having dealt with recruitment, the remainder of the chapter now moves on to examine a number of selection methods, principally those which are used most extensively within organisations, or represent what are sometimes called 'modern' techniques. We cover interviews and tests in some detail, but there is also a brief review of assessment centres, graphology, and random selection. At the outset it is necessary to stress several important features in the selection process. It should be borne in mind that selection is a two-way process (Torrington and Hall, 1995), and that many potential applicants withdraw from consideration at various points; after receiving details about the post and the organisation, perhaps because they are not impressed by the material which is sent to them; after submitting an application form, perhaps because an alternative job looks more interesting; after interview, perhaps because they did not like the image which the organisation portrayed. Of course, many of these withdrawals may be beneficial to both parties as applicants become aware that they might not 'fit' in the organisation, but some good candidates may also be lost along the way. Although it is the employer who makes the offer to a candidate, the selection process is only completed when that person *accepts* the offer and reports for work.

None of the techniques, irrespective of how well they are designed and administered, is capable of producing perfect selection decisions that predict with certainty who is or is not bound to be a good performer in a particular role. In recent years the growing interest in psychometrics and the use of tests as part of the selection process may have given the misguided impression that they offer a perfect solution to the problem of selection. The use of statistical analysis reinforces the 'semblance of being objective and scientific ... [as well as] ... efficient' (Townley, 1989: 92), whereas all that has happened is that selection decisions are now somewhat *less imperfect*. We return to this issue later in the chapter when tests are reviewed; not only do P&D professionals need to be aware of the limits of testing and the circumstances in which its use might be most suitable, they also need to know when to seek specialist advice about the choice of which tests to employ – if any – in specific situations.

In the vast majority of selection decisions employers use more than one method. Interviews are used on a very large proportion of occasions and in most organisations, along with application forms and the taking up of references. Practice varies as to whether references are sought prior to or after interviews, whether they are consulted before or after interview, or merely sought as a final vetting device prior to making an appointment. Although references may be taken up, the weight which is given to them also varies, and indeed most P&D practitioners will know of cases when 'excellent' references have been provided for staff that the existing employer would be happy to release. Langtry (1994: 251) reproduces data showing that most techniques are hardly better than chance in making selection decisions; this is not just confined to those techniques which are most typically condemned as unscientific – such as references and interviews – but also to personality tests and biodata. Assessment centres are reckoned to produce the best results, but even here it is less than 20 per cent better than chance.

A variety of surveys (Robertson and Makin, 1986; Shackleton and Newell, 1991) provide evidence on the extent and popularity of different techniques across British industry. For the selection of managers, both in the private sector and in local government, interviews, references and application forms are used extensively. Interviews are very popular irrespective of organisation size, although application forms are not so widespread in smaller companies. By way of contrast, tests are used in the majority of selection decisions in fewer than a quarter of organisations (Shackleton and Newell, 1991: 27). Assessment centres are even less widely used, except for the recruitment of graduates where they were used by almost half of those employers who responded to Keenan's (1995: 315) questionnaire. A cross-European comparison of selection techniques, put together from a variety of sources, suggested that psychometric tests had increased in popularity during the early part of the 1990s (Sparrow and Hiltrop, 1994: 341), but the table is rather vague and its results should be treated with caution.

What really matters, though, is choosing the most appropriate selection techniques for each exercise, as it is clear that no one method is a panacea. A range of criteria need to be used to assess the value of each method (see Smith and Robertson, 1993: 93–145 and Watson, 1994: 205–207 for further details); these are practicability, sensitivity, reliability, and validity.

Practicability is, according to Smith and Robertson (1993: 94), the most important criterion of all. The method chosen has to be acceptable to all parties (senior managers and candidates, as well as statutory bodies such as the EOC and CRE, and professional institutes, such as the IPD and The British Psychological Society). It also has to be economical in terms of costs and benefits, the time which is required to administer the exercise, and within the capabilities of those people who are to run the selection process. The issue of cost is particularly critical. There is little point in administering a sophisticated and complex personality test if the field of candidates from which to draw comprises just one candidate who fulfils all aspects of the person specification. Equally, there is little or no point in using tests to differentiate between applicants for an unskilled post to be filled on a short-term contract basis.

Sensitivity is a key feature in the choice of selection methods, as this represents the ability of any particular technique to discriminate between candidates. Such discrimination is desirable provided it relates to the applicants' ability to do the job, and is not used as a smokescreen for making employment decisions which disadvantage particular groups of applicants on grounds of race, gender, age or disability.

Reliability is a concept which is referred to regularly in the selection literature. Although there are several different aspects of reliability, it broadly means that the method 'should not be influenced too much by chance factors ... [it] should be consistent in the results it gives if used to assess a person on more than one occasion' (Watson, 1994: 205). Smith and Robertson (1993: 106) provide details of the various forms of reliability: between different raters; when the same technique is used on different occasions; between different methods. If inter-rater reliability is low, for example, great care must be exercised when using a number of interviewers, as one is likely to reject candidates that others would have selected. Tests may prove to be unreliable if it is shown that applicants are able to improve their performance from one occasion to the next. This inevitably disadvantages those who are taking a test for the first time, and may be beneficial to individuals who have been coached in how to approach tests or have learned how to adapt their answers for a particular audience.

The final criterion is *validity*, which means the correctness of the inferences which can be drawn from the selection method, in terms of 'measuring the characteristic which it purports to measure' and 'predicting future behaviour or performance that it is required or assumed to predict' (Watson, 1994: 205). Much of the competency debate has revolved around this sort of issue, as selectors attempt to define the key attributes and skills which are demonstrated by existing high performers (and therefore seen as being required in new recruits) and then assess these during the recruitment and selection exercise. It is a very difficult task to undertake, for a variety of reasons. Not only is it hard to find proxies for these characteristics (eg the best questions to ask about an individual's effectiveness at running a team or managing change) but caution also needs to be displayed in drawing inferences about future job performance from statements made at interview or characteristics displayed during an assessment centre. A whole host of other variables influence subsequent job performance, many of which occur outside of the workplace, and their effects may be unknown at the time of appointment. As with the concept of reliability, validity has a number of different elements. Although it may not carry the same scientific weight as other elements, face validity is important as it maximises the degree to which a technique is acceptable to senior managers, since it is based upon their *perception* of what is appropriate. As with all aspects of P&D, the ability to convince line managers of the value of a particular technique is just as important as its academic or professional credibility.

INTERVIEWS

We have already noted that interviews are the most widely used selection technique, not just in Britain but also in many other European countries as well. They are also amongst the most widely condemned of all selection techniques, criticised in particular for their unacceptable reliability, poor predictive validity and low sensitivity, although they do have the advantage of being relatively cheap – at least in terms of direct costs. Frequently, however, the interview (as a technique) is blamed when the real problem resides with the way in which it is planned and conducted by untrained and underprepared interviewers.

There are two rather contrasting perspectives on the interview which illustrate a potential tension between P&D practitioners and occupational psychologists; as an example of the former, Torrington and Hall (1995: 272) describe it as 'a controlled conversation with a purpose', the purpose being to 'collect information in order to predict how successfully the individual would perform in the job for which they have applied, measuring them against predetermined criteria.' The idea of a conversation, albeit controlled, conjures up images of a pleasant chat to share experiences, and plays down the fact that the selector is in a rather more enviable and powerful position, especially at times of high unemployment. On the other hand, the approach adopted by occupational psychologists (see Smith and Robertson, 1993, for example), perhaps in search of the 'perfect' selection device, is to focus on ways of making the interview more scientific, with higher levels of reliability and validity, and of minimising the degree to which the interviewer is allowed to contaminate the selection decision. It is anticipated that problems may be reduced by placing interviews and interviewers into a pre-programmed and structured format, one which can at least increase their reliability.

> Which of these perspectives do you favour? Why?

Interviews for selection purposes can take a number of forms. They can be between *individuals*, on a one-off and one-to-one basis, and these have the advantage of greater informality, the encouragement of rapport, and the generation of more open and frank discussions. They also suffer from problems of interviewer bias (both the halo effect and negative prejudices), from low levels of reliability, and lack of coverage of the subject matter. This type of interview is particularly prone to the accusation that the interviewer makes up his or her mind about an applicant in the first few minutes, before spending the remainder of the interview finding reasons to justify this viewpoint. The sequential interview is a slight adaptation of this format, in that candidates are seen by a series of managers in one-to-one situations, with each probing for evidence about different aspects of the job. It also has the potential advantage that each manager is able to make an independent judgement (at least initially) about the candidates before the final decision is made. In this case, what might be thought of as low inter-rater reliability (when an individual is rated first by one interviewer and last by another) may in fact be assessments about the individual's ability to perform different aspects of the job.

The second broad variant is the small group or *tandem* interview, whereby two people interview a candidate together, making their judgement on the same event; the two may be exploring different aspects of the job, however, or may even take on specific roles during the interview. In the case of a supervisory appointment, for example, it may be appropriate to combine a line manager and a personnel and development specialist to explore both the technical elements of the job and the individual's likely style of management. This has the advantage of enabling the key selectors to observe the candidate first-hand and come to a joint decision about the appointment; as well as strengthening the validity of the interview, it may also act as an aid to team-building and the encouragement of shared visions within the organisation. Of course, it might also expose contrasting judgements.

The final type of interview is the *panel*, typically comprising between three and five interviewers drawn from different parts of the organisation, and fulfilling (if their roles have been allocated beforehand) different duties. Panel interviews for senior academics and public servants can often be conducted by twelve or more people, in which case the interview really does become something of a ritual or trial, depending upon which side of the table one is sitting. The arguments in favour of using a panel are much the same as for the tandem interview: it allows a number of different people to see a candidate at the same time; it minimises the potential for *overt* bias; and it ensures (in theory at least) that the decision is made by a number of managers within the organisation who are likely to work with the appointed person. The disadvantages are also well known: it is more difficult for the interviewers to build up rapport with the candidates; some interviewees may be extremely nervous about the prospect of facing a large number of people in a formal setting; and the panel members need to be clear about their purpose at the interview, as well as being adequately trained. The notion of bias is particularly interesting here, as there is evidence that some panel members exert rather greater influence over the decision than others. Sometimes, this is acknowledged before the event, as certain panel members admit that they are only really there to 'see that fair play takes place' or 'to make up the numbers'. On other occasions, panel members may accept too readily the views of senior managers present or use the interview as a stage upon which to play out other political games, in which the candidate is a pawn. Panel interviews can be difficult to control, especially if some members move away from their agreed area of questioning or break in before it is supposed to be their 'turn'. On the other hand, the exercise can appear excessively formal if all interviewers stick rigidly and mechanically to their allocated area.

Many commentators stress that the selection interview is riddled with problems, most of which are due to shortcomings in the interviewers rather than the interview itself. These have already been mentioned, but the major problem is well summed up by Plumbley (1991: 103); he notes that interviewing is 'an everyday occurrence and is the most widely used assessment technique; it is part of the popular vocabulary;

it looks easy, and everyone is inclined to believe they are good at it. Therein lies the danger and the confusion.' Much of this can be explained by attribution theory, the view that applicants are defined as 'good' if they obey the rules of the interview as seen by the interviewer, and 'bad' if they do not comply (Smith and Robertson, 1993: 201). Similarly, people are often selected who mirror those attributes which the interviewer regards as important, and rejected if they display contrary behaviours. The possibility that such frames of reference tend to consolidate existing cultures within organisations, and make it more difficult for candidates from different backgrounds to gain employment, has serious equal opportunities implications.

Which of these types of interview would you advise should be used for selecting a) a bank clerk, b) a production supervisor, c) a sales manager? Justify your answer.

The interview remains extremely popular despite increasing awareness of such problems, and Lewis (1985: 153–156) provides a set of rules for the selection interview. The ritual of interviewing may be more important than is often admitted, as both parties (interviewers and interviewees) perceive it as a key aspect of the recruitment and selection decision. It would be very strange indeed for hiring decisions to be made without any face-to-face contact, as employers would feel uncomfortable recruiting an individual they had not seen and applicants would hardly want to work at a place they had not visited. The likelihood of unsatisfactory decisions being made by either party is high. Fletcher (1991) reports that the vast majority of employers and candidates on the university milk round felt that the interview was a fair method of selecting people, most clearly in one-to-one situations; the face validity of interviews is certainly high.

So-called *structured interviews* are seen as a way of improving the validity and reliability of the exercise. According to Smith and Robertson (1993: 198–200), three features are particularly important: questions should be developed based upon a job analysis; each candidate should be asked standard, though not necessarily identical, questions; and a systematic scoring procedure should be used, preferably based upon a behaviourally anchored rating scale. In addition, there need to be regular reviews of selection decisions which have been taken, and training of interviewers in best practice; Smith and Robertson (1993: 202) suggest that CCTV exercises in which interviewers practise their skills are less effective than observing 'model' interviews.

These sorts of ideas seem to have influenced the way in which panel interviews are now conducted in many local authorities, as part of a drive to ensure that selection decisions are free from gender and race bias. In some of these, applicants are asked precisely the same set of questions which are agreed in advance, and rated in a systematic manner. Interviews are then conducted by councillors, with line managers and trade union officials in attendance. The likelihood of improved reliability is very high, but there remain major problems with validity. For example, some individuals may be extremely good at articulating their achievements and plans, but poor at putting these into effect, whereas others may do the job well but not act in a very convincing manner at the interview. Moreover, the lack of line manager influence over the decision may create team-building problems in the future. These sorts of interview aim to replicate the standardised and pseudo-scientific nature of tests, even down to the extent of training interviewers to follow the one best way of interviewing. Not only may such attempts be foredoomed, they may also be misguided.

Discuss with your colleagues whether structured interviews are likely to have greater validity than other types of interview.

SELECTION TESTING

Selection testing has become a more popular and extensively used technique over the last few years, as dissatisfaction with interviews has grown and employers have sought to achieve higher levels of validity from their selection decisions. According to various surveys (Bartram, 1991; Newell and Shackleton, 1993; Baker and Cooper, 1995), tests are now used in some form or another by a large number of organisations. Baker and Cooper (1995: 3) provide the most conservative of these estimates, and even they reckon that over half of all employers who employ more than 200 staff have used tests. They are most likely to be used for selection to junior and middle management, supervisory and professional positions, and especially when assessing graduates (Newell and Shackleton, 1993: 18); in the latter case tests are used regularly as part of a battery of selection techniques. Of course, tests are also used for other P&D decisions, but their use in the selection context far outstrips that in training and development or career planning (Baker and Cooper, 1995: 4).

To some extent this increase in usage has led to a number of problems, particularly in the choice of tests and in their deployment. Major concerns have been raised by professional bodies such as the IPD and the BPS about the emergence within the field of disreputable providers and untrained assessors who do not know how to interpret the results of tests (Fletcher, 1993). In addition, a number of cases have led to concerns from various statutory bodies (such as the CRE) with the result that codes of practice on psychological testing have now been produced; these are outlined later in this section.

The purpose of this section should be clarified at the outset; it is *not* designed to provide students with knowledge, skills and competencies to design, administer, and interpret tests, but rather to make them aware of the major types of tests which are available, their principal merits and shortcomings, and their part in selection decisions. It is crucial that P&D practitioners understand the *limits* to their own role in this area, knowing when to seek advice on test usage, and from which suppliers. The implications of acting beyond their own professional knowledge and skills can have severe consequences, not only in the area of recruitment and selection, but also for the public relations image of the organisation as well as on applicants.

Psychological tests have been defined as 'carefully chosen, systematic and standardised procedures for evoking a sample of responses from a candidate, which can be used to assess one or more of their psychological characteristics by comparing the results with those of a representative sample of an appropriate population' (Smith and Robertson, 1993: 161). This definition highlights several important features: the fact that tests should be chosen carefully and appropriately; that they should be applied systematically in a standard manner; and that the results should be capable of comparison with norms for the particular group in question. They can be divided into two broad categories according to Toplis, Dulewicz and Fletcher (1991: 15) – psychometric tests and psychometric questionnaires/ personality tests. As we see below, it is the latter which has encountered the most stringent criticisms in recent years. Readers who require more detailed analysis of these techniques are advised to consult Lewis (1985), Herriot (1989), Toplis *et al* (1991), Smith and Robertson (1993), or the series on selection testing which appeared in *Personnel Management* during 1994. This series provides the names and addresses of a number of respected suppliers and consultants, and further expert advice can be obtained from the IPD and the BPS.

Psychometric tests are designed to measure mental ability, and they take several different forms in practice. First, there are tests of attainment or ability, which purport to measure the degree of knowledge and/or skill a person has acquired *at the time the test is administered*. This would include school examinations, for example. Second, there are tests of general intelligence which are designed to assess 'the capacity for abstract thinking and reasoning within a range of different contexts and media' (Toplis *et al*, 1991: 17). Among the better known of these are Wechsler's Adult Intelligence Scale (WAIS), AH4, and Raven's Progressive Matrices (RPM). The third set of psychometric tests are for special aptitudes or abilities, such as for assessment of verbal, numerical or spatial ability, and manual dexterity. A number of these are outlined in Toplis *et al* – (1991: 19–26), including tests for clerical speed and accuracy, computer aptitudes, or sales skills. Sometimes, these are compiled into batteries of tests for use in organisations.

The second broad grouping is *psychometric questionnaires or personality tests*. These are based around 'trait' or 'type' theories, which involve 'the identification of a number of fairly independent and enduring characteristics of behaviour which all people display but to differing degrees' (Toplis *et al*, 1991: 28). No one trait is inherently superior to any other, but each may be considered more suitable for certain contexts, occupations and sectors. The choice of what is considered appropriate is clearly a matter of judgement, based upon existing evidence and perceived organisational needs. There are now many of these types of test on the market, some of which were designed and tested on the American market and therefore need to be treated with caution if they have not been validated in Britain. The most common types of personality questionnaire are Cattell's 16PF, the Saville and

Holdsworth Occupational Personality Questionnaire (OPQ), the Myers-Briggs Type Indicator and the Californian Psychological Inventory (CPI). There are sometimes several versions of each type as well. In addition to personality questionnaires, there are also interest questionnaires (such as the Rothwell-Miller Interest Blank and a range of Saville and Holdsworth questionnaires for different levels), values questionnaires, and work behaviour questionnaires. So many of these are available that just to list them would cover several pages, so readers are advised to seek further information from the sources already provided.

The controversy which surrounds the use of personality tests is much greater than that for ability or aptitude tests. In the early 1990s, *Personnel Management* invited a number of psychologists to respond to a sustained critique by Blinkhorn about the role of personality tests (Fletcher, 1991). The basis of his critique is that there is a dearth of research literature supporting the case for personality testing, and that the way in which data are presented exaggerates the value of these tests; in short, he argues that there are 'no grounds for supposing that personality tests predict performance at work to any useful extent, except in a minority of rather extreme kinds of work' (Fletcher, 1991: 38). Most of the occupational psychologists who were asked to comment on the Blinkhorn critique acknowledged that the level of research support for them was less than for aptitude tests, but none the less felt they had a useful role to play in selection decisions *provided* they were used properly, preferably in tandem with other tests or selection methods. Indeed, Newell and Shackleton (1993: 22) are adamant that tests should never be used in isolation, but always as part of a broader selection process.

There are other concerns with testing as well, many of which relate to their administration and ethical standing. Smith and Robertson (1993: 189) provide a list of ten ethical considerations, which includes the following: tests should only be sold to qualified users, carried out under standard conditions, and only released after adequate research; people should not be coached for tests; the results should be confidential and held with the full knowledge of those tested; and tests should not be used which are known to discriminate against particular groups of individuals, such as ethnic minorities, women or the disabled. Wood and Baron, (1992: 34–35) report on cases in the early 1990s involving British Rail, among other employers, regarding the use of tests for the selection of guards. These were found to discriminate unfairly against ethnic minorities, and the company took action to produce an open-learning pack which the guards could work on before retaking the test. The result was that the majority of the guards were selected second time around. It was claimed that the tests did not take account of different cultural norms in the use of time, answering questions purposively, and keeping calm.

The IPD Code of Practice on Psychological Testing provides guidance on the appropriateness, choice and administration of tests, as well as interpreting their results. If there are omissions, or the supplier is unable to answer the questions posed, the test should not be used. In relation to the choice of tests, which is here what matters most, the following guidance is given to users:

- tests should actually measure attributes that are directly relevant to the employment context

- the test should have been rigorously developed

- data should be provided on the reliability, validity and effectiveness of tests

- evidence should be supplied that the test does not disadvantage certain groups

- the norms provided by the test supplier and the manual accompanying the tests should be comprehensive, answering all the employer's queries.

> If selection testing has been used in your organisation, find out how closely the principles in the IPD Code of Practice were followed. If tests have not been used, find out why.

Perhaps the major concern about testing is that it often looks more accurate than it actually is, and confidence inspired by its apparent objectivity can be seriously abused by inappropriate tests and unsatisfactory use. The idea that any selection technique can be 'objective' is plainly wrong, as decisions have to be made along the way which render the exercise open to management choice: for example, in terms of the choice of test, the items contained within it, the perceived validity for the job in question, as well as the cultural norms which surround their use. On the other hand, to extend the point made by Lewis (1985: 157), testing may be useful as one element in the selection decision, which helps to minimise its implicit subjectivity. There are still Orwellian undertones to the use of personality tests, however, and concerns that employers are seeking to clone what are seen as model employees. This may limit the degree to which organisations are able to achieve 'diverse' workforces.

ASSESSMENT CENTRES AND OTHER TECHNIQUES

The *assessment centre* (AC) comprises an amalgam of selection methods rather than any one technique and, as such, overcomes many of the criticisms that have been made of any one of the methods which have been discussed so far in this chapter. Feltham (1989: 401) defines it as a 'process by which an individual, or group of individuals, is assessed by a team of judges using a comprehensive and integrated set of techniques.' It is built upon a set of dimensions which are felt to be indicative of future performance (Smith and Robertson, 1993: 226), such that assessment centres are most frequently used for managerial or graduate appointments. The numbers to be assessed at any one time can range from 6 to 12, with a ratio of one assessor for every two candidates. There has been a sizeable growth in the use of ACs in the last few years, the concept having been developed by the War Office Selection Board back in the early 1940s.

The types of exercise which are used in ACs vary depending upon the position to be filled and the organisation involved. Most typically, there are four broad types of exercise. First, there are written tests – such as writing a memorandum, completing an in-tray exercise, or analytical tests – which also test the ability of the individual to prioritise work, choose the most appropriate form of response, or solve a problem. Second are one-to-one exercises, such as role-playing a standard encounter between a member of the sales staff and a customer or between a manager and a problem employee. Thirdly, ACs usually involve group exercises such as a negotiation, a problem-solving session, or a planning exercise. Sometimes these will be run with designated roles, while on other occasions leaderless groups are employed despite some criticism of this approach (Woodruffe, 1993: 98). Finally, some assessment centres require each candidate to make a presentation to a group of existing staff/managers, typically on a topic that has been circulated in advance of the AC and which is relevant to the organisation. Not only does this test an individual's ability to access sources of information, it also requires them to tailor their knowledge to a specific situation, display speaking skills, and work within time constraints. Computers can also be used for interactive exercises in an AC, as well as for analysing and presenting results; as more people use personal computers at work, or to work from home, this is likely to becomes a more central feature in the design of ACs. Readers who need further information on the types of exercises which can be used in an AC are referred to Woodruffe (1993).

Assessment centres are not cheap to set up and run. As Feltham (1989: 409–410) illustrates, good ACs involve job analysis, the purchase or development of tests, training of assessors, and other incidental expenses such as accommodation and travel. It is widely acknowledged that, if done properly, ACs have a higher validity than other techniques, but there are concerns that some organisations have introduced ACs as a fad or fashion without comprehensive analysis and training (Smith and Robertson, 1993: 230). When properly designed and administered, ACs probably represent a cost-effective way in which to recruit key personnel who manage major budgets or whose mistakes can have serious consequences for organisational performance or safety.

Biodata refers to a set of biographical information (such as age, marital status, number of dependents, previous employment, average tenure in jobs, educational achievements, place of residence, and health impairment) which is available from application forms or curricula vitae. It works on the principle that a 'factually-based view of a person's life thus far' may be a good predictor of his or her future performance and potential, and studies have shown that there is an association between biodata and subsequent job behaviour (Smith and Robertson, 1993: 234). However, there are also statistical and ethical concerns about its use as a selection device, and even greater anxieties about the blanket rejection of candidates on the basis of their gender, age or race. There are fears that this discriminates between individuals on the basis of factors which are not related to specific job competences.

Graphology – the analysis of handwriting – has been used extensively in other fields, not least in forensic cases for identifying suspects, given that there is a reliable pattern to people's writing across different situations and over time. Within the selection area, graphology has only really achieved much coverage in France; estimates vary, but it is claimed that more than 50 per cent of French organisations use this method, though not for all vacancies (Smith and Robertson, 1993: 246; Sparrow and Hiltrop, 1994: 341). This makes graphology the fourth most popular selection device in France, compared with hardly any use in the rest of Europe. There are major doubts about its validity as a predictor of future performance, and indeed it has been shown to be little better than chance in identifying an individual's occupation from an analysis of their handwriting; graphologists actually did worse than psychologists in this test and no better than other untrained assessors (Ben-Shakhar, 1989: 475).

What are your views on the use of graphology? If you know anyone who works for a French-owned firm, ask him or her whether graphology is used in the organisation, and if so, in what ways.

Random selection is hardly a technique at all, but it has been used to prune down a large field of applicants, all of whom meet the essential requirements of the person specification. Broadly, employers either deal with applicants on a first-come first-served basis, or select at random applicants who meet the selection criteria. While not really advocating its use, Lewis (1985: 145) suggests that it may be an efficient and cheap way of dealing with large pools of unqualified staff or for filling temporary posts for highly qualified professional staff. Random selection is usually carried out with the aid of a computer to generate random numbers, which supposedly gives the technique a scientific gloss. Claims that random selection is legally acceptable have been tempered by arguments that it may be discriminatory if the organisation is failing to attract many applications from certain groups in the community (IRS *Employee Development Bulletin* 51, 1994b: 15). However, other solutions are available to overcome the problem of large pools of applicants, most obviously by searching for ways to reduce them at the outset, perhaps by more focused advertisements based upon comprehensive job analysis. In other words, rather than viewing a large pool of applicants as a problem to be resolved by random selection, it is better seen as a problem caused by ineffective recruitment practices.

CONCLUSIONS

This chapter has reviewed briefly the major elements in an organisation's recruitment and selection policies and practices, and it has argued that recruitment should not be treated as the poor relation of selection. Because of increasing sophistication in selection decisions, it is often forgotten that without effective recruitment practices the field of applicants from which to choose is likely to be small and unsuitable. It is easy to identify the problems that are caused by poor recruitment and selection, and which can lead to unsatisfactory performance at later stages in the employment relationship. It should be clear, however, that effective policies and practices at this stage provide the right kind of staff who are capable of meeting, and indeed exceeding, targets. This is one area of P&D where assistance might usefully be sought from consultants and specialists, especially in relation to recruitment advertising and psychometric testing. Being aware of the limits to one's expertise may be just as important as knowing what techniques can be employed. The devolution of selection decisions to line managers makes this even more important, ensuring that these activities are well organised, delivered and evaluated, and advice is sought where appropriate.

USEFUL READING

BAKER, B. AND COOPER, J. (1995) 'Fair play or foul? A survey of occupational test practices in the UK', *Personnel Review*, Vol 24, 3: 3–18.

FLETCHER, C. (Ed.) (1991) 'Personality tests: the great debate', *Personnel Management*, September: 38–42.

HERRIOT, P. (Ed.) (1989) *Assessment and Selection in Organisations.* Chichester, Wiley.

INDUSTRIAL RELATIONS SERVICES, (1994) 'The changing face of recruitment advertising', *Employee Development Bulletin* 49: 2–5.

INDUSTRIAL RELATIONS SERVICES (1994) 'Ensuring effective recruitment: developments in the use of application forms', *Employee Development Bulletin* 51: 2–8.

LEWIS, C. (1985) *Employee Selection.* Hutchinson, London.

NEWELL, S. AND SHACKLETON, V. (1993) 'The use and abuse of psychometric tests in British industry and commerce', *Human Resource Management Journal*, Vol 4, 1: 14–23.

PADDISON, L. (1990) 'The targeted approach to recruitment', *Personnel Management*, November: 54–58.

PEARN, M. AND KANDOLA, R. (1993) *Job Analysis*, Second Edition. London, IPD.

SMITH, M. AND ROBERTSON, I. (1993) *The Theory and Practice of Systematic Personnel Selection.* Basingstoke, Macmillan.

TOPLIS, J., DULEWICZ, V. AND FLETCHER, C. (1991) *Psychological Testing: A manager's guide*, Second Edition. London, IPM.

WOODRUFFE, C. (1993) *Assessment Centres: Identifying and developing competence*, Second Edition. London, IPM.

7 Managing performance and attendance

INTRODUCTION

By now it should be clear to readers that horizontal and vertical integration are key themes in the IPD Core Personnel and Development module, and it is these which distinguish it from the generalist and specialist modules. It might be worth reiterating the meaning of these terms before introducing this chapter, given their relevance to its subject matter. It will be recalled that horizontal integration is concerned with the degree of 'internal fit' between different aspects of P&D, between each of the core areas of resourcing, reward, relations and development. Vertical integration, conversely, relates to the degree of 'external fit' between P&D activities and strategies, the management of the organisation as a whole, and the competitive environment within which it operates (Baird and Meshoulam, 1988). While horizontal integration aims to achieve a greater degree of complementarity, rather than conflict, between different aspects of people management, vertical integration is concerned with the congruence between P&D policies and broader business strategies. The greater the degree of integration, the less the opportunity for critics to claim that human resource managers are out of step with the rest of the organisation, or, worse still, that they are developing packages which are in direct contradiction to existing policies and procedures in the area.

Review your understanding of vertical and horizontal integration by applying it to your own organisation, and assess the degree to which this exists at your workplace.

Nowhere is the concept of integration more important than in the management of performance and attendance at work. As we shall see below, performance management (which is discussed in the first part of this chapter) aims directly to link together individual goals, departmental purposes and organisational objectives. It incorporates issues which are central to other parts of the IPD scheme, such as appraisal and employee development, performance-related pay and reward management, and individualism and employee relations. Indeed, it has been argued that performance management is synonymous with the totality of day-to-day management activity since it is concerned with how work can be organised in order to achieve the best possible results (Fowler, 1990a: 47).

In this chapter we stretch beyond conventional definitions of performance management – the setting of objectives and standards, and their review – to include other aspects of the employment relationship. Here we deal with the induction of new staff – following on from the previous chapter where we considered recruitment and selection – as this is a key component of employee resourcing activities. While it is obviously crucial to select the right people, it is also imperative to ensure that, from the outset of their employment, employees understand not only the nature of their tasks but also how these fit into broader organisational cultures – which may emphasise customer service, quality management or entrepreneurship. Some employers make major efforts to socialise new staff, 'educating' them about the mission, values and beliefs upon which the organisation is predicated. If staff are selected with care and inducted effectively it is less likely that problems will emerge during their subsequent employment, but of course there is no guarantee. At different stages in an individual's employment history, there may be lapses in commitment and motivation, brought about either by events outside of work (relating to family issues, for example) or within work (relating to missed career opportunities or a change in management style, for example). These can manifest themselves in poor attendance, in a lack of interest in work, or in psychological problems – with which management may be able to assist through counselling or welfare policies. In other words, our focus here is on the management of effective *and* ineffective performance. It is impossible to deal with the whole of this issue within a single chapter, however, so chapters elsewhere in the book examine aspects such as the learning organisation (Chapter 8), the handling of disciplinary matters (Chapter 13) and performance-related pay (Chapter 15).

By the end of this chapter, readers should be able to:

• advise line managers about the key issues involved in handling performance appraisals

• prepare for, and conduct, a return-to-work interview

• identify sources of information and expertise regarding employee assistance programmes.

In addition, readers should be able to understand and explain:

• the nature of performance management systems, their benefits and limitations

• the contribution that effective induction programmes can make to the achievement of organisational goals

• the role that the attendance management can play in a comprehensive personnel and development strategy.

PERFORMANCE MANAGEMENT SYSTEMS (PMS)

Since gaining access to the lexicon of personnel and development terminology towards the end of the 1980s, performance management has grown considerably in coverage and has become well known among specialists in the area. From being 'at the crossroads' in the early 1990s (Bevan and Thomson, 1991), it is now firmly on the agenda. There are many reasons for this growth in popularity and extensiveness, but drawing from Connock (1991: 130) and Storey and Sisson (1993: 134–35), these can be summarised as: increased competitive pressures which put an emphasis on performance improvement; attempts to achieve a clearer correlation between organisational goals and individual targets; restructuring and devolution which have put a primacy on delegating tasks and responsibilities down organisational hierarchies; the shift from collectivism to individualism during the last decade, which has allowed for a more rigorous specification of individual performance standards and measures.

Like many supposedly well-known terms in management, however, performance management has a variety of meanings and has been used to describe just about any P&D initiative. For most writers it is seen as a system which 'translates the goals of strategic management into individual performance' (Anderson and Evenden, 1993: 248) and enables the achievement of optimum results through the effective organisation of work (Fowler, 1990a: 47; Walters, 1995: x). Mabey and Salaman (1995: 189) see the essence of performance management as establishing 'a framework in which performance by individuals can be directed, monitored, motivated and refined'.

Both in theory and in practice, performance management systems are seen to have a number of central characteristics (Bevan and Thomson, 1991: 38; Walters, 1995). These include:

- mission statements which are communicated to all staff, not only during induction but also at later dates, in order to reinforce corporate messages or to cascade down information about changes in formal organisational cultures

- regular communications about business plans and progress in achieving objectives

- integration with total quality management or other organisation-wide initiatives

- a clear focus on the performance of senior managers, and links between this and remuneration packages

- performance expectations expressed in terms of SMART (specific, measurable, appropriate, relevant and timed) targets which are reviewed regularly and, wherever possible, agreed with staff

- systematic performance appraisal processes which form a key part of the review process

- the adoption of performance-related pay systems

- the use of formal and ongoing reviews of progress to identify training and development needs which enable the achievement of individual performance requirements and organisational goals.

Performance management is typically characterised as a system (Storey and Sisson, 1993: 131), a systematic model (Mabey and Salaman, 1995: 188), or a cycle (Torrington and Hall, 1995: 317). The elements in each of these frameworks is broadly similar, in that they each link together planning, doing and supporting, and reviewing progress, some being explicit about integration with broader business and departmental goals. The principal components of the process are illustrated by Figure 5.

Figure 5

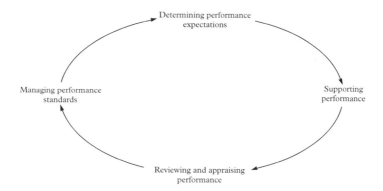

Determining performance expectations is the stage at which employees are made aware of the performance standards that are expected of them. Typically, this would be expressed through mission statements and organisational goals, mediated through departmental purpose analyses, and agreed with the individual. Much of the literature on performance management assumes that this phase of the cycle/process is concerned with corporate communications, job descriptions and key accountabilities, each of which are considered elsewhere in this book. Induction training and initial socialisation into employment in an organisation are rarely mentioned, but this is a critical time for establishing understanding about, and commitment to, wider corporate or departmental goals; this is dealt with in the next section.

Supporting performance is the second part of the Torrington and Hall cycle, and is neglected in most of the other texts on the subject. This refers to the day-to-day informal interaction between managers and their staff, to the provision of resources and systems which facilitate achievement of individual targets, and to accessibility (Torrington and Hall, 1995: 317). Support can come either from line managers and peers, or from P&D specialists, taking the form of mentoring, coaching, welfare provision, and of course assistance with the removal of barriers that may prevent excellent performance. While it is clearly necessary to establish formal mechanisms, such as those which are sometimes developed for women managers (see Chapter 10), performance management requires ongoing and unsolicited support in order to be effective; that is, the telephone call or the 'chance' conversation just to check that all is going well, which many busy managers tend to overlook in their efforts to satisfy formal organisational demands.

The third stage in the process is *review and appraisal*, which is often seen as synonymous with performance management. Later in this chapter we shall deal with the appraisal process, but it is important to stress that annual (or twice-yearly) reviews should be seen only as the formal part of the cycle, the opportunity to review performance against objectives over the last period, and determine goals and training needs for the immediate future. As with any formalised management system, there are dangers that the appraisal interview comes to be viewed as *the* sole event at which performance is reviewed, when staff are praised (or criticised) for meeting (or not meeting) targets, and when training and development needs are identified.

The final stage in the process is the *management of performance standards*, when actions are taken to deal with issues which are highlighted during reviews of progress. In many cases, and in particular when appraisals are assessment-based, the key purpose of this phase is to determine the level of performance-related pay or bonus which is due to the individual employee; this is dealt with in Chapter 15. But with developmental appraisals the emphasis is on how improved performance can be facilitated and sustained, on training and development, and on assisting staff to achieve targets that have been set for the next few years. In some parts of higher education, for example, the appraisal process is used to identify ways in which academic staff may seek to manage their careers and gain promotion by writing papers, supervising research students, or developing new courses in collaboration with users. However, it is important to note that this phase might just as easily focus on failures to achieve standards, on poor performance, and on problems which may be affecting work. The management of attendance – as well as welfare and counselling – is dealt with later in this chapter.

> Is there a performance management system (PMS) in your organisation? If so, how successful is it? How could it be made more successful? If your organisation does not have a PMS, what value might it add? How could you sell the idea of a PMS to a senior manager?

The development of performance management in ICI Pharmaceuticals (now Zeneca) has been quoted extensively in books and articles on the subject (Sheard, 1992). The pressures which led the company into performance management were similar to those facing most organisations, most notably international competition. The company had a task-oriented culture in which staff felt disassociated from the business as a whole, and it was decided to shift towards a learning organisation, one in which there was a holistic understanding of issues. The focus at ICI was development-based rather than assessment-based, and the system was introduced and integrated by 'performance management' coaches – who were line managers. Two key features of the system which are particularly worthy of note are the close involvement of individuals in setting their own targets, and the fact that the administration of the performance-related pay system is devolved to departmental and functional level.

Local authorities have also ventured down the path of performance management in recent years, as cited by over 40 per cent of employers who responded to an IRS survey (*Employment Trends* 594, 1995) and either had a system already or were in the process of introducing one. This had been stimulated in some cases by governmental pressures to introduce compulsory competitive tendering, and by moves to increase employee involvement, to seek better ways of identifying training needs, and to monitor employee performance more effectively – all of which were aimed at improving service delivery. A large number of councils saw performance management as a very significant development in their activities, tied in with appraisals and attendance management. As with private-sector employers, local authorities are keen to ensure that individual members of staff work towards clearly defined and agreed targets, although in this case the targets are established through decision-making channels which involve elected representatives and council committees.

Performance management systems (PMS) are not without problems of course, and there have been warnings that they represent nothing more than yet another managerial fad (Fowler, 1990a: 51). The danger that performance management (and in particular, appraisal) is little more than an annual burden is well documented by Egan (1995: 34), who reports of managers several years behind in their formal reviews of progress but whose organisations continue to flourish. As mentioned above, some performance management systems are little more than appraisal or performance-related pay schemes, in which other parts of the cycle are ignored or treated in a superficial or ritualistic manner to satisfy the requirements of the system (Wilson, 1992). In addition, many line managers in the Wilson study did not feel any ownership of the PMS, viewing it as a brainchild of the personnel function. Egan (1995: 35) notes that if appraisal becomes the centrepiece of performance management, then the system is purely retrospective; it should be prospective and ongoing, concerned with performance *improvement*. There are also some doubts about the correlation between the existence of a PMS and organisational success (Bevan and Thomson, 1991: 38), but this is difficult to prove for a number of reasons.

INDUCTION AND EMPLOYEE SOCIALISATION

Induction can be defined as 'any and all arrangements made to familiarise the new employee with the organisation, safety rules, general conditions of employment, and the work of the section or department in which they are employed' (Skeats, 1991: 16). Many definitions also mention the importance of helping employees 'settle into their new jobs' (ACAS, 1983: 2), welcoming them into the organisation (Reid and Barrington, 1994: 332), and arranging for them to get to know other workers. Writers stress that a formal induction programme need not be expensive, and certainly the benefits to be gained from a systematic process far outweigh the costs of recruiting new staff if large numbers of people leave at the time of the so-called 'induction crisis' (ACAS, 1983: 11).

Irrespective of whether or not a formal or structured programme is in place, all employees go through an induction phase on joining a new organisation or department. In many organisations, especially those which do not have a specialist P&D function or manager, this can be little more than a rudimentary greeting before being shown to their place of work. New recruits may be told to ask questions if they need assistance or just to get on with the job, as they obviously have the required technical or administrative skills to cope. In many workplaces the introductory phase may consist of practical jokes and tricks (for example, 'go and find a left-handed screwdriver') as the new recruit is socialised into the norms of the workplace and the workgroup. There may be little attempt to explain anything about the company mission, its policies on customer service or quality assurance, or its underlying philosophy. Even information about health and safety, disciplinary rules and company procedures may be dealt with in an informal way, despite their importance in setting the tone of the workplace and what are seen as acceptable behaviours.

The problems associated with this lack of systematisation are obvious: employees often feel isolated and confused, unaware of company rules and procedures; they may struggle to learn how to do the job because they have received only limited assistance at the outset; they may break safety or disciplinary rules, receive a warning and become embittered about the employer; they may decide that the initial enthusiasm which was associated with the new job was misplaced, and leave to take up a position elsewhere. Each of these problems represents a cost to the employer, either in direct financial terms (poor-quality work, time spent on disciplinary issues, re-advertising jobs) or in public relations terms, as potential recruits and customers choose to go elsewhere. Fowler (1990b: 7) contrasts the care which employers take in dealing with the installation of new plant and equipment with the cavalier attitude which is sometimes taken towards induction of new staff. In circumstances such as these it is hardly surprising that employees question the depth of employers' commitments to people as their most important resource.

For organisations which do invest time and effort in induction, there are three broad perspectives on the nature and purpose of the process: the first views it as an *administrative* exercise, in which the sole purpose is to impart information about the job, the procedures and the organisation. From this perspective the principal points at issue appear to be what topics to include and when to deal with them so as to prevent information overload. Drawing on the lists produced by Fowler (1990b: 50–52), Skeats (1991: 66–71) and Reid and Barrington (1994: 335–336), the following are seen as necessary elements in the induction package:

- terms of employment, such as information about hours of work, shift arrangements, timekeeping and clocking-on and -off systems

- housekeeping and security issues, such as catering facilities, energy conservation and speed limits on site

- health and safety regulations, such as safety procedures, protective clothing and hazards of office equipment

- wages and benefits, such as starting salary, holiday and sick pay, profit sharing, expenses claims, welfare

- company rules and policies, such as disciplinary and grievance procedures, trade union membership, works rules, time off for statutory or trade union duties, equal opportunities

- employee development opportunities, sports and social amenities

- information about the company and the industry, such as a mission statement, history, product markets, organisation structure, communications

- job performance issues, such as job description, standards, appraisal, and role within the department.

Having determined the content, all that is required from the administrative perspective is to work out how it should be delivered. Advice is provided about the ordering of items (safety should be dealt with early), the importance of letting new employees actually undertake some work as soon as possible, and the use of visual aids to ensure better information retention. The role of the P&D specialist is seen as particularly relevant in maintaining quality assurance standards during the induction process, as well as in delivering some parts of the programme – such as information about welfare, wage and salary administration, grievance and disciplinary procedures. Fowler (1990b: 85–92) suggests that specialists can assist line managers to enhance their contribution to induction programmes by designing policies and training in conjunction with them, and by monitoring the effectiveness of existing systems. Data could be presented on labour turnover crisis points, on the results of exit interviews, on the degree to which all aspects of the induction checklist are being covered, and by inspecting progress reports on recent recruits.

The second and third perspectives differ not so much in the type of information which is to be imparted during induction, but on the underlying philosophy of the process and its interpretation. The *welfare* perspective is best illustrated by Plumbley (1991), whose tone is more social worker or nurse than manager. He argues that during the 'period of after-care' when people start employment with an organisation, the personnel manager must try to 'settle the new person in quickly'. Readers are told that employees cannot work effectively if they are 'worrying about settling in the family' and everyone they meet is a 'stranger'. Benevolent paternalism is clearly an important part of the initial phase of employment, but this is reminiscent of personnel management in the early part of this century. On the other hand, there may be groups of workers for whom some cosseting is particularly appropriate: school leavers who are entering employment for the first time, young catering staff who have just left home to work in a hotel, or women returners who are coming back into the labour force after a long gap. Other workers may face special problems at work, and also need a fair amount of initial assistance; for example, employees with disabilities will need to know immediately where and how special arrangements can be made for them, and members of ethnic minorities may need to be put in touch with support groups soon after taking up employment.

The final perspective views induction as an altogether more hard-nosed business issue, in which employers make use of various techniques to 'educate' employees about the company ethos, aiming to integrate them with existing organisational cultures. This, the *human resource management* perspective, is rarely to be found in mainstream P&D publications, which view induction as a relatively value-free device for helping employees to settle down in a new job. Accordingly, the advice is mainly prescriptive about the design of induction programmes or the balancing of different activities to ensure that effective learning takes place. It is hardly acknowledged that induction can be a powerful device for integrating new employees into organisations, gaining their commitment, and inculcating them with a sense of belonging and identity which forms a basis for effective performance 'beyond contract'.

Skeats (1991: 18) goes some way towards this by acknowledging that induction can engender 'a feeling of belonging to the company [which] develops a commitment to organisational goals. The employer then maximises the contribution of the workforce and gets a faster return on investment'. She argues (1991: 27), however, that this should not lead to organisational cloning, but should '*produce* individuals' who function effectively without accepting all aspects of the company culture. Harrison (1992: 283) suggests that dialogic learning is a major element of induction in that new recruits are 'oriented to the mission and culture of the organisation, to its beliefs and ways of doing things'. By placing some interpretation on the policies and practices which are administered by the employer, new recruits are able to appreciate the meaning and purpose of them in practice. With reference to equal opportunities or quality service, for example, employees are provided with a clear understanding of what this means in practice, and the fact that this is an important aspect of organisational life.

There is some evidence that dialogic learning and the human resource management perspective comprises a major component in the employment strategies and practices of many Japanese and US companies, exemplified by artefacts such as similar uniforms, badges, baseball caps and company credit cards. Harrison (1992: 284) mentions the fact that new recruits at Fujitsu are invited to join the 'family of employees' and some American computer companies are noted for their commitment to philosophies which emphasise open communications (Peters and Waterman, 1982). Reitsperger (1986: 576) describes how high levels of employee satisfaction in a Japanese company were achieved by reinforcement of the 'corporate community' message at all stages of the employment relationship. Similarly, Delbridge and Turnbull (1992: 61) report on a process known as 'intensive induction' during which new recruits are developed into loyal and trusting members of staff. There are numerous other examples of the HRM approach to induction which is utilised by Japanese companies, involving team activities and physical exercises, as well as learning about the philosophy and motives of the company (Oliver and Wilkinson, 1992: 47). This approach has now been copied by some leading British employers such as Rover (Oliver and Wilkinson, 1992: 102–103). Analysis at this deeper and more critical level might lead some to argue that induction is more appropriately termed 'indoctrination'.

Is there any substance in the view that induction can be interpreted as indoctrination? Might it be beneficial for employers if induction was based more on dialogic learning?

PERFORMANCE APPRAISAL

The review stage of the performance cycle usually incorporates appraisal on an annual or more frequent basis. The formal appraisal of staff is not a new phenomenon, and Randell (1994: 223–26) provides details of its development in Britain from the time of Robert Owen and the New Lanark textile mills through to the current day. There have long been conflicting viewpoints about the principal objectives of appraisal, with some seeing it as a technique for assessing and rewarding performance whilst others consider its major purpose to be the identification of future development needs. According to Randell (1994: 228), the British approach has been predominantly person-centred and skills-based whereas US companies have emphasised a work-centred and mechanistic philosophy.

In broad terms, performance appraisal is defined by Randell (1994: 221) as 'the process whereby current performance in a job is observed and discussed for the purpose of adding value to that level of performance'. In itself this seemingly simple definition contains a number of contentious issues, not least who has responsibility for, and what is included in, appraisals. In the case of the latter, three types of performance criteria can be appraised: *traits* – that is, personal characteristics such as loyalty, dependability or leadership skills; *behaviours* – that is, how work is performed, including persuasion or listening skills or sensitivity; and *outcomes,* such as the number of products sold or defects reported. Some criteria may be more relevant for certain circumstances than others, although each has drawbacks as well as advantages (Schuler and Huber, 1993: 285–286). It is not appropriate here to enter into a detailed discussion of the format for performance appraisals – such as the use of ranking or comparisons, or behavioural observation scales (BOS) or behaviourally-anchored rating scales (BARS) – because these are dealt with in the generalist and specialist modules of the Professional Qualification Scheme.

Choices about the person(s) who should act as appraiser also have to be made, and again much depends upon prevailing organisational cultures and the group to be appraised. Redman and Snape (1992: 33) suggest that there can be as many as seven options, and some systems involve several of these for the same appraisal; adopting in part a familial terminology, these are:

- the individual's immediate supervisor (this is also known as 'parent' appraisal)

- his or her supervisor's supervisor ('grandparent')

- colleagues at the same grade/level ('peer')

- internal customers for the individual's services ('aunt/uncle')

- external ('client') customers for the individual's services

- the appraisee's subordinates ('upward')

- the individual him- or herself.

In recent years there has been a shift away from relying solely or predominantly on 'parent' appraisals in order to incorporate a greater number of independent reviews of performance and so build up a more rounded picture of the individual. As Grint (1993: 74) argues in an insightful analysis of appraisal schemes, we need to escape from the labyrinth which suggests that schemes can be objective, and instead accept our subjective fate by collating a number of different perspectives on performance, including those of subordinates; we return to the issue of 360-degree appraisals later in this section.

One of the major problems with performance appraisal is that it has been used for many different and conflicting purposes, the pursuit of one often creating obstacles which prevent achievement of the others. Fletcher (1993a: 34) identifies three principal objectives of appraisals: first, they are used as a vehicle for motivating staff and improving performance through the setting of objectives and realistic targets for achievement over the course of the next period. In this case, the appraisal is essentially forward-looking, aiming to integrate individual performance levels and direction with that of the organisation as a whole. Second, appraisals are used for assessing employee performance and distributing payments within organisations, rewarding staff for their effort and contribution to the achievements of the previous period. In this case appraisals are reviews of past performance and recognition of how well or poorly staff have managed to achieve targets. Finally, appraisals are useful for development purposes, for identifying training needs in the forthcoming period, and assisting employees to manage their careers. Used in this way, appraisals are designed to encourage employees to reflect on shortcomings in their current performance, to establish ways in which it might be improved in the future, and identify training needs which may facilitate it. These conflicting purposes can clearly cause potential problems both for appraiser and for appraisee; it is difficult for the appraiser to be both 'judge and helper' (Torrington and Hall, 1995: 319), whereas the appraisee is unlikely to admit to the possibility that performance could be improved for fear that it might lead to a lower rating – and hence lower rewards through performance-related pay. Development needs are often overlooked in this situation (Fletcher, 1993: 34).

Because of this, Anderson (1992: 189–191) argues that appraisal ought to be divided into two distinct and separate phases: one for development purposes and another for assessment and reward. The principal advantage of separating development from assessment is that the former will be seen as important, with employees prepared to be open and look for ways to improve performance in the future, rather than seeking to influence appraisers to give them a good rating. The major disadvantage is that development appraisals are not taken as seriously, because they are not explicitly linked to rewards, and it may be difficult for organisations to develop a performance-oriented culture if the two are separated. Whilst acknowledging that the two probably ought to be split in theory, Carlton and Sloman (1992, pp 86–87) argue that this is difficult to achieve in practice. Drawing upon their experiences at County NatWest, they show how P&D specialists can assist line managers to appreciate the way in which assessment and development are linked over time; the training need identified during an appraisal at period one can lead to improved performance and higher rewards in period two.

This conflict of purpose is not the only criticism which is made of performance appraisal in practice. A second problem is that many line managers regard appraisals as a bureaucratic and irksome exercise which is done solely to satisfy the personnel and development function (Carlton and Sloman, 1992: 85–86; Grint, 1993: 62; Torrington and Hall, 1995: 327). Appraisal is not seen as a practice which 'adds value' to the organisation, and appraisers are neither rewarded nor recognised for conducting appraisals on time; too many managers leave their appraisals until forced to do them, and then go through the motions with little interest or commitment. Only if appraisals are seen to be worthwhile, leading to change and demonstrable outputs, can P&D practitioners ever hope to gain line management commitment to, and ownership of, the process, so that it is seen as a key contributor to a high-commitment performance-oriented culture.

There are also problems inherent in the formal appraisal process as well, not least in the ratings which are given by appraisers. Grint (1993: 63) describes the 'distortions' which are likely to occur in assessment of performance; the 'halo' effect leads to overestimations, whereas the 'horn' effect results in a lower assessment than might otherwise be expected; the 'crony' effect is caused by closeness of the personal relationship between appraiser and appraisee; the 'Veblen' effect results in central tendencies, so-named after the tutor's habit of giving all his students C grades irrespective of their quality; finally, the 'doppelganger' effect occurs when appraisers reward similarities between themselves and appraisees, whereas differences lead to adverse ratings. This obviously has significant equal opportunities implications given that, with traditional top-down appraisals, women and ethnic minorities have been prone to lose out due to imbalances in the hierarchical structure of organisations. Appraisers also face problems when confronted with appraisees who have not performed well during the year, especially if appraisal is linked with financial rewards, given the general reluctance to be a purveyor of bad news (Grint, 1993: 63). The fact that managers often feel uncomfortable in dealing with the poor performers probably explains why ratings drift occurs and, even in an organisation which is not performing particularly well, a large proportion of its staff still end up with above-average ratings.

> Are many of these shortcomings apparent in your organisation, and how are the problems manifested? What has been done to overcome them?

Over the last few years there has been increasing interest in more open approaches to appraisal, involving both subordinates and other 'customers' of a manager's services. There are a number of reasons why upward and 360-degree appraisals have become popular (Redman and Snape, 1992: 33–37):

- They fit well with notions of employee involvement and empowerment, ideas which have become more significant in management thinking recently. The point that subordinates are often in closer contact with their managers than any more senior staff helps to increase the relevance of this approach, as too does the fact that they are on the receiving end of his or her actions. Also, it is expected that by involving staff in appraisals of their supervisors and other colleagues, their commitment to the organisation will be enhanced.

- With flatter organisations and greater spans of control it is more difficult for any one manager to appraise a large number of staff with any degree of accuracy or knowledge. Appraisal by other customers is a useful way of extending the information base on which to make judgements.

- Now that employees have greater access to their personal files, including job references in some organisations, there is a need to ensure that the results of appraisal are known to the appraisee. Having a more open approach which draws upon a wider range of viewpoints facilitates this and lessens the likelihood of legal action against the appraiser.

- Traditional top-down approaches provide only a single viewpoint, and that may be influenced by factors which are subject to personal bias or prejudice, either positive or negative. Having upward or 360-degree appraisals provides an instrument with potentially much greater validity, and one which stands a greater chance of acceptance by the appraisee.

- Managers may find comments about their performance actually useful and constructive, and it may cause them to amend their behaviour (Grint, 1993: 73). If an organisation genuinely believes in a spirit of continuous improvement, the provision of views from a variety of perspectives – particularly customers of an individual's services – is to be welcomed as a means to enhanced performance.

Peter Ward, the senior manager responsible for introducing 360-degree appraisals into Tesco, is convinced that this form of appraisal is far superior to any other approach, in that it provides the manager with feedback from all angles. It is also very 'real' in that it relates clearly and explicitly to the performance of the managers involved, and is not reliant on their skills of impression management during a formal annual review. He stresses (Ward, 1995: 20–22) that 360-degree appraisal is not a replacement for other forms of review, but is part of a process of which the aim is to seek as many views as practicable about performance in order to achieve improvements. 360-degree appraisal is not without its problems, however, and care has to be taken to ensure anonymity in the presentation of views and the avoidance of judgemental statements; Ward (1995: 21) compares feedback where the appraisee is told that 'your listening skills are bad' with the more constructive alternative suggestion, 'I notice that you don't look at people when they are talking to you'.

Although upward appraisals can be seen as part of a move towards more open styles of management, their success depends upon managers being prepared to accept criticism and feedback from those they manage. A domineering supervisor may receive very few, if any, criticisms from his or her subordinates if they are scared about the consequences of their comments about performance and behaviour. The supervisor, on receiving no adverse comments, may then feel that his or her approach is acceptable. Unfortunately, all that the upward appraisal has done is to provide a veneer of legitimacy for existing behaviour, and it is essential that alternative mechanisms are available for expressing views. In addition, upward appraisals also rely on subordinates being prepared to act in an open and honest manner, and not using them as an excuse for registering unjustified complaints against their supervisors.

> Identify the ways in which P&D professionals can contribute to the effective implementation and operation of any form of appraisal, but especially upward appraisals.

THE MANAGEMENT OF ATTENDANCE

Much of the literature on new human resource management styles (eg Storey, 1992) describes situations in which employees have been prepared to 'work beyond contract' or 'go the extra mile' for the employer in order to achieve competitive advantage: such as the hotel porter who used his initiative to return a briefcase to a guest, the secretary who redrafted a letter to incorporate new information while her boss was away, or the production worker who ignored instructions and changed a machine setting to override a fault. Although such examples are quoted regularly, they are probably less extensive than the number of cases where employees fall short of targets or, worse still, fail to turn up for work at all. Data from a CBI survey in April 1995 (IRS *Employment Trends* 591: 2) suggests that 3.4 per cent of available working time is lost in any one year, equivalent to one-and-a-half weeks of absence per person – in addition to statutory and paid holidays. According to the survey the estimated direct cost of absence in 1994 was £10 billion, with a further £6 billion lost in indirect costs. Although it is clear that not all absences are avoidable, many are undoubtedly the result of minor ailments or are for reasons which do not necessitate a day off work.

The management of attendance is a topic which is integral to all aspects of P&D. There are links with other parts of employee resourcing in terms of induction, welfare and counselling, and with employee development regarding training sessions for line managers who are required to handle attendance issues. Questions about sick pay, pensions schemes and attendance payments link it with employee reward, and there are a multitude of connections with employee relations – as well as being part of disciplinary procedures, the causes of absence have much to do with morale, commitment and conflict at work. The indirect costs of poor levels of attendance are seen in inadequate levels of customer service, cancelled commuter trains, unanswered telephone calls, and overworked staff who cover for their absent colleagues, only to run into problems when attempting to complete their own work on time.

Much of the blame for high levels of absenteeism rests with managements who fail to take the absence problem seriously – by not keeping adequate records or making it clear to employees (both at induction and following bouts of time off) that absence is not to be seen as a 'normal' part of the contract. It is not suggested that all absences would be prevented by the systematic management of attendance, but it is argued that the culture which prevails in the organisation has a major impact on how people relate to work, and whether or not they decide it is worth getting out of bed at 7 am on a Monday morning (Sargent, 1989: 11). As with performance appraisals, it is often difficult for managers to deal with staff whose performance or attendance is not good, especially if they feel that their actions will not be supported by more senior managers or may be overturned on appeal.

It is important to define clearly what is meant by absenteeism, to identify measures of absence, and to understand its main causes in order to set up effective control systems. Huczynski and Fitzpatrick's (1989: 156) ALIEDIM model is one which has been widely quoted and is relatively straightforward. This comprises:

A *assess* the absence problem, consider how significant it really is, and establish the costs (direct and indirect) which are incurred because of it

L *locate* the absence problem by identifying where in the organisation it is most problematic, and which groups, departments or establishments need to be targeted

I *identify* and prioritise the absence causes, using a model such as that of Steers and Rhodes (outlined below), to see whether the causes of absence is related to the job, the groups of staff employed, their supervision, or whatever

E *evaluate* current absence control approaches, assess whether these are the most appropriate for the causes which have been identified, and whether the systems which have been established actually work properly (eg are staff phoning line managers to report absence?)

D *design* the absence control programme by considering a range of options before choosing which is most appropriate for your own organisation. Important factors to consider here are the culture of the organisation, its geographical spread, and the cost of implementation

I *implement* the absence control programme by preparing the ground for any changes, and anticipating and overcoming any resistance to proposed changes

M *monitor* the effectiveness of the absence control programme against established benchmarks and performance criteria, including an assessment of the benefits achieved from the new system.

Absence measures do not normally include anticipated and legitimate spells away from work, such as holidays, jury service, or attendance at a training course. Other forms of absence are typically divided between authorised and unauthorised; broadly, the former deals with situations in which employees are genuinely unwell and have a valid medical certificate, whereas the latter typically refers to cases in which it is not clear that the employee is actually unwell or has an acceptable reason for being away from work. With the growth and extension of self-certification, the distinction between these two categories has become blurred. It is obvious, however, that cases in the two categories may need to be treated in different ways. For example, if an employee has been absent for a series of single days over a specified period, a quiet word may lead to improved attendance patterns, whereas if the employee has been off sick for several months a warning is hardly likely to speed up his or her return.

Collecting data on absence levels, and then disaggregating this, is a crucial first step in trying to resolve attendance problems. There are several measures which can be used to quantify the level of absence on an individual, departmental and organisational basis (Torrington and Hall, 1995: 637). First, it is important to determine the overall *number of days lost*; 0–2 per annum is considered low, 8 is regarded as the median, while anything above this is worthy of further investigation. Second, it is necessary to know the *number of absences in any one year*; 0–2 spells is reckoned to be low, four is the median, and anything above this needs to be analysed further. Third, employers need to collect data on the *reasons for absence* given that a multitude of factors may be behind any one period off work, and it is virtually impossible to recall it several months later. Recorded reasons for the absence may pinpoint bad weather, influenza, dizzy spells, a sick child or relative, or some other factor. Some elaborate models have been devised to analyse absenteeism, breaking it down into a mass of different causes, but probably the best known and most straightforward is Steers and Rhodes' process model (1978), which differentiates between the *motivation* to attend and the *ability* to attend. This sort of data is easily held on a computer, and dispersed systems allow supervisors much easier access to records, so taking these out of the preserve of the P&D function. Individual or departmental records can be triggered once levels reach a certain point.

Does your organisation keep absence records on computer? If so, what information is held, what is it used for, and who has access to these records? How could the system be improved so that line managers could play a greater role in the management of attendance? If your organisation does not use a computerised system, how are records kept, how easy is it to identify problem cases, and what problems have emerged due to the lack of IT in this area? Work out whether it would be cost-effective to use a computer for this purpose.

Recently there have been a number of publications addressing the issue of attendance management, in particular in devices to tighten up control systems and encourage employees to attend work rather than take time off. Two of these are of particular interest: the use of triggers to identify cases for further investigation, and the implementation of automatic return-to-work interviews after a period of absence. About three-quarters of the private and public sector respondents to an IRS survey (*Employment Trends* 568, September 1994) used both triggers and return-to-work interviews.

Triggers for further investigation are relatively easy to introduce for organisations which have a computerised personnel information system, with print-outs available on a monthly, quarterly and annual basis, for example. The provision of this information directs the line manager to consider whether or not to take the matter further, and if so, how. As Evans (1991: 45) cautions, computers only provide information which can then stimulate management action, they do not solve the absence problem if the information is not used effectively. In addition, care is needed in interpreting the data, especially if the employee concerned is known to have suffered a major problem in recent months, or the behaviour is not consistent with the individual's long-term employment history. In situations such as these, a crude triggering of a disciplinary interview may serve only to make matters worse, and counselling or independent help may be more appropriate.

The information provided to line managers includes data on the length and frequency of absences, whether or not it was certificated, and the recorded reason for the absence – in categories such as back or heart problems, headaches, or feeling sick. The criteria for triggering may be in terms of the number of days off in a given period, the number of absences, or both. Employers may therefore choose to trigger records on any individuals who have had more than three separate absences in the previous quarter, or have had more than six days off during this time. The trigger varies widely, with some employers being rather more stringent (seven days or three absences in a rolling twelve-month period) whilst others have more relaxed rules (five separate absences per annum or ten days in any one month). Some employers agree 'accepted' levels of absence with recognised trade unions – say, 8 per cent (IRS *Industrial Law Bulletin* 530, 1995: 8) – although there are dangers that this may come to be seen as the norm, with employees manipulating the system in such a way to accumulate what they believe are approved levels of absence. On the other hand, having agreed levels of absence may enhance an employer's case at an industrial tribunal, especially if levels are well above what is considered reasonable, and appropriate disciplinary procedures have been followed; this matter is dealt with again in Chapter 13.

Return-to-work interviews have also become more popular in recent years, especially in local government, as a way of tackling unacceptable levels of absenteeism. According to an IRS survey (*Employment Trends* 594, 1995: 11), over 90 per cent of local authorities have made changes to their absence control procedures since 1990, and the most frequently-mentioned initiative was the introduction of return-to-work interviews. Typically, this was in conjunction with a range of other measures – such as better monitoring of attendance levels, the use of computers to trigger potential problems, the publication of sickness absence figures on a departmental basis, information on absence levels sent to chief officers, sickness counselling, and the appointment of an occupational health specialist. Half of the local authorities surveyed reported reductions in absence levels over five years, and in only 10 per cent did levels increase; surprisingly, 25 per cent were unable to say whether absence levels had changed.

The return-to-work interview provides a useful opportunity to enquire about the reasons for absence, to follow up any serious problems and suggest further assistance if required, or to make it clear that attendance is expected unless there are good reasons for being absent. It focuses attention specifically on the absence, helping to generate an attendance culture, one in which genuine illness is acknowledged but malingering is dealt with severely. As with all people management issues, this message is important not only for the individual concerned but also for other workers, many of whom suffer the immediate consequences of colleagues' absence by having to undertake extra work as well as do their own. Interestingly, where shop floor employees have been given responsibility for overall team performance (including absence control), they have often taken a firmer line than their supervisors (Marchington, 1992a: 117).

Sargent (1989: 75–77) provides a checklist of how line managers can prepare for and conduct return-to-work interviews, and by implication this highlights the support which can be provided by P&D professionals. This includes the following:

- *Preparation.* Before the meeting, the line manager needs to have information about the employee's previous record, the reason cited for the absence, and any relevant out-of-work issues. Advice may be sought from other people, such as a shop steward or a former supervisor. A P&D specialist may be able to help the line manager clarify his or her feelings about the employee, especially if these are negative and may influence the conduct of the interview.

- *The interview.* At the meeting, Sargent advises that the manager gets straight to the point of the interview by explaining its purpose, and then asking open-ended questions to elicit information. The meeting must be treated both with gravity and sensitivity, and it should not deteriorate into a mutual blame session: tempers should not be allowed to rise. Attempts need to be made to seek joint solutions, and the meeting should conclude with a clear action plan and a date for further review if appropriate. P&D practitioners can here support line managers through the provision of training courses in absence control – not just in how to handle meetings, but also in how to ensure records are kept up to date and the right climate is created.

- *Follow-up*. Notes should be written up promptly, copies need to be sent to relevant managerial colleagues and to the employee concerned, and support should be provided to the employee if a serious matter has been uncovered.

> It is essential that absence control is dealt with by line managers in order to ensure that it is taken seriously. Compare the experiences at your own organisation with the material provided in this section of the book, and suggest ways to improve your systems.

COUNSELLING AND EMPLOYEE ASSISTANCE PROGRAMMES

The previous section hinted that there are problems that emerge in the working environment which have their roots outside of work, and equally that problems at work can affect other spheres of an individual's life. For example, issues outside of work to do with childcare or family responsibilities, alcohol and drug abuse, depression brought about by changes in life stage, or marital problems, all have an impact on the way in which an individual performs at work. Similarly, problems at work – due to racial or sexual harassment, bullying, post-traumatic stress, or blocked career opportunities – all have an impact on relations outside work (Summerfield and van Oudtshoorn, 1995: 89–127). This interrelationship between domestic and paid employment has not really been examined fully in the past, but with increasing numbers of women at work the issue now appears to be taken more seriously. Although the changing balance of the workforce may have spawned interest in the work-home interface, it should not be taken to imply that it is solely a 'women's' issue. As we argue elsewhere in the book, equal opportunities is a subject which applies to *all* employees irrespective of gender, race or disability.

It would be wrong to argue, however, that employers have only just started paying attention to the resolution of work-home issues, since the early roots of the personnel profession were based around the welfare image. As Berridge and Cooper (1994: 7) note, welfare schemes date from Victorian times and, as such, are often still imbued with a philosophy of charity and paternalism, and the tacit superiority of middle-class moral values. Some employers provide subsidised loans to employees who run into financial difficulty, some offer support systems for the partners of newly-appointed managerial and professional staff, and some sponsor local charities and sports teams. Similarly, a concern for welfare and counselling has been demonstrated by occupational health departments and the friendly nurse with whom one can talk about personal problems – although in many cases, the agenda is principally concerned with physical health and well-being.

The emergence of Employee Assistance Programmes (EAPs) is relatively new to Britain. They appeared in the late 1980s, and were seen by some as an American import given that the pedigree of EAPs is much longer in the USA (Highley and Cooper, 1994: 46). EAPs differ from the welfare and occupational health provisions which went before them in two major respects: comprehensiveness and integration. The EAP seeks to bring together under one umbrella each of the activities which was previously dispersed, and often uncoordinated, throughout organisations. Also, unlike the welfare image, which conjures up connotations of do-gooding and tangential activities, EAPs are clearly integrated into attempts to enhance organisational well-being, not only in terms of improved attendance patterns but also in profitability and productivity. The EAP is defined by Berridge and Cooper (1994: 5) as:

> a programmatic intervention at the workplace, usually at the level of the individual employee, using behavioural science knowledge and methods for the recognition and control of work- and non work-related problems which adversely affect job performance, with the objective of enabling the individual to return to making her or his full work contribution and attaining full functioning in personal life.

Readers who wish to find out more about EAPs should consult the special edition of *Personnel* Review edited by John Berridge and Cary Cooper, Vol 23(7), 1994. Many types of issue can be dealt with by an EAP, and these vary somewhat, dependent upon the organisation involved. The following is typical, however (Berridge and Cooper, 1994: 10):

- AIDS
- disability
- gambling
- marital problems
- retirement
- alcohol abuse
- divorce
- legal matters
- racial harassment
- verbal abuse
- bereavement
- financial advice
- literacy
- redundancy
- weight control

Evaluation of EAPs suggests that they provide many benefits to the individuals concerned as well as to their employers. Individual employees may find they are able to function more effectively both within and outside of work, to operate with reduced stress levels, to work better within teams, and to produce better-quality work if they are not worried about personal or work-related problems. Employers may benefit through lower levels of labour turnover, reduced absenteeism, higher productivity, and better customer service, all of which can make an important contribution to higher profitability and competitive advantage. Indeed, Highley and Cooper (1994: 47–48) itemise a series of American studies which used cost-benefit analyses to demonstrate that EAPs had been financially worthwhile; for example, McDonnell–Douglas estimated savings of $5.1 million, General Motors $500,000, and the US Department of Health and Human Services reckoned savings of almost $300 per client served. As with all studies which attempt to quantify savings in the human resource area, such figures need to be treated with caution for a number of reasons, not least because of the influence of other external variables, but at least they do suggest that EAPs can be of value. The British studies have been less clear-cut about the benefits, but the number of organisations which now have EAPs presumably shows that there must be some value in them.

One of the most important questions involved in the setting up of an EAP is whether or not it should be run internally or externally. Internally-administered EAPs predominate in the USA, but in the UK there has been a surge in independent companies and consultants who offer the service at prices varying from £8.50 to £25 per employee per year (at 1995 prices). Typically the external agency provides a telephone help-line which staff can use for anonymous advice and support, and the option of meeting with a trained counsellor if needed (IRS *Employment Trends*: 591, 1995b: 12). Confidentiality is a key feature of the schemes, and some feel that this can be guaranteed more effectively via an external service. If the EAP is provided in-house, the counselling service is usually part of the human resource function, and in this case it is crucial that the individuals who deal with employees maintain their independence from senior management and protect the anonymity of their clients (Summerfield and van Oudtshoorn, 1995: 24–27). The advantage of dealing with issues in-house is that the counsellors are aware of existing organisational cultures, and may be in a better position to influence changes in company policy if needed.

Details of a number of recent EAPs can be found in the IRS study referred to above (IRS *Employment Trends* 591, 1995b: 12–16). Each of the four organisations surveyed had contracted an independent company to run the EAP: Whitbread, widely quoted as the first UK company to set up an EAP, started its scheme in 1988, covering 40,000 employees, and run by FOCUS (The Forum for Counselling and Unemployment Services); UNISON launched its scheme in 1992 covering 1,200 employees, and managed by Independent Counselling and Advisory Services (ICAS); South London Housing Association employs EAR (Employee Advisory Resource) to run its EAP, set up in 1993, which covers 500 staff; finally, Nottingham City Council contracted Mentors Counselling Consultants to deal with its 4,000 employees in 1995. Each of these organisations is registered with the British Chapter of the Employee Assistance Professionals Association (EAPA) which lays down certain rules and standards for members. These require the maintenance of agreed client–counsellor ratios, the insistence that all counsellors have professional qualifications, abide by the Data Protection Act, offer full training to specific groups of managers in the companies served, and have adequate indemnity and insurance. The address of the Employee Assistance Professionals Association (EAPA) is 2 Dovedale Studios, 465 Battersea Park Road, London SW11 4LN, Tel: 0171–228 6768.

Consider whether it is ethically acceptable for counselling to be done in-house rather than by an independent consultant, or is it actually advantageous to the employees concerned to have their problems dealt with by a manager who is a member of a professional body, such as the IPD, with its own ethical principles.

CONCLUSIONS

Performance Management Systems (PMS) are now much more widespread than they were in the early 1990s, and in some cases they are seen as synonymous with 'new' ways of managing human resources: focusing on the four stages of: determining performance expectations; supporting performance; reviewing and appraising performance; and managing performance standards. Many of these issues are taken up again in later chapters in the book, for example during our analysis of learning organisations and performance-related pay. Each stage of a PMS is important, but often too little attention is paid to the critical role which induction can play in creating the right cultural expectations amongst new recruits. Employers who are serious about a PMS need to realise that this stage of the cycle makes a significant contribution to the socialisation of new staff, and it is so much more than a routine administrative exercise. In a similar vein, a PMS needs to be designed so that performance which is below standard can be dealt with in an appropriate way – that is, through counselling and assistance if an employee has a genuine problem or through disciplinary procedures if the employee is thought to be guilty of misconduct. In short, rather than viewing a PMS solely as a route to gaining yet further performance improvements, it should also be seen as part of the process for removing poor performers.

USEFUL READING

BEVAN, S. AND THOMSON, M. (1991) 'Performance management at the crossroads'. *Personnel Management*, November: 36–39.

CARLTON, I. AND SLOMAN, M. (1992) 'Performance appraisal in practice'. *Human Resource Management Journal*, Vol 2, 3: 80–94.

GRINT, K. (1993) 'What's wrong with performance appraisals? A critique and a suggestion'. *Human Resource Management Journal*, Vol 3, 3: 61–77.

HUCZYNSKI, A. AND FITZPATRICK, M. (1989) *Managing Employee Absence for a Competitive Edge*. London, Pitman.

INDUSTRIAL RELATIONS SERVICES, (1994) 'Sickness absence monitoring and control: A survey of practice'. IRS *Employment Trends 568*, September: 4–16.

REDMAN, T. AND SNAPE, E. (1992) 'Upward and onward: can staff appraise their managers?'. *Personnel Review*, Vol 21, 7: 32–46.

SARGENT, A. (1989) *The Missing Workforce: Managing absenteeism*. London, IPM.

SKEATS, J. (1991) *Successful Induction: How to get the most from your new employees*. London, Kogan Page.

SUMMERFIELD, J. AND VAN OUDTSHOORN, L. (1995) *Counselling in the Workplace*. London, IPD.

WARD, P. (1995) 'A 360-degree turn for the better'. *People Management*, 9 February: 20–25.

Part 4

EMPLOYEE DEVELOPMENT

8 Individual and organisational learning

INTRODUCTION

Traditionally, organisations used to employ specialists whose job was merely to *instruct* and *teach* people how to do tasks more efficiently. Nowadays, as the title of this chapter suggests, the emphasis is on *learning* – both from the standpoint of the individual and from that of the organisation. The 'good' organisations are those which engage in facilitating learner development, in encouraging people to enhance their skills and knowledge, and to foster their creativity and initiative as part of a drive for continuous improvement. There are many reported cases of organisations that supposedly recognise the importance of employee development and have incorporated this into their human resource management vision for the future (in the car industry, for example, initiatives have recently taken place at Ford, Peugeot Talbot, and Vauxhall – see IRS *Employee Development Bulletin* 53, 1994: 2–5 and *EDB* 60, 1994: 5–10). The shift from training (in the form of teacher-driven courses) to learning and development is also emphasised by the IPD through its Continuing Professional Development policy.

Most publications on human resource management stress the importance of training and development for individual and organisational growth and success. For example, Keep (1989: 125) argues that human resource development is 'the vital component' in HRM (p 111), an 'integral part of wider (employment) strategies' (p 116), and a 'useful litmus test' of the reality of human resource management. Storey and Sisson (1993: 155), drawing upon Lane's comparison of European policy and practice, refer to the 'virtuous circle' of training and development, whereby a high investment in this aspect of P&D can lead to the more effective utilisation of high technology, higher skill levels, higher wages and lower unit labour costs, leading ultimately to competitive advantage. In Wickens's (1995:

219) description of the ascendant organisation, one in which there is high control over work processes and high levels of employee commitment, 'every worker is a knowledge worker' who is able to contribute to the achievement of strategic goals.

Unfortunately, as we have already indicated in Chapter 3, not many organisations live up to this image of 'the learning organisation', one in which all employees are actively encouraged to take responsibility for their own development with clear and effective support mechanisms provided by management. Compared with other European countries such as France and Germany the amount of investment in training and development in Britain is low, and the proportion of people (managers *and* non-managerial staff) with formal academic qualifications is well below that of our major competitors. In addition, the infrastructure which is meant to support the drive for improvement lacks direction and co-ordination. Far too many employees receive no training at all, even in the most basic forms of instruction about how to do their jobs, let alone in how to develop their skills or improve their contribution to organisational success. As with recruitment and selection, despite the rhetoric, much of the practice in British industry and commerce is based upon *ad hoc*, unplanned and poorly-conceived ideas about how to improve employee performance. The lack of training and development in most organisations is due to the short-termism so characteristic of British employers (Storey and Sisson, 1993: 76). But some is also due to an imperfect understanding of how adults learn, and many learners are themselves wary or dubious about further training and development opportunities, given their unsatisfactory experience in formal educational settings (Rogers, 1989: 9–25). Equally, many line managers probably regard the provision of 'learning opportunities' for manual workers or clerical staff as pampering the workforce, and as an unwarranted distraction from their departmental targets and duties.

Consider how you might persuade a sceptical line manager to release staff for learning and development activities.

The purpose of this chapter is to introduce the Employee Development part of the book, by providing an outline of how people – but especially adults – learn, and how this has been incorporated into training and development practice. We then focus on a number of aspects of learning and training, paying particular attention to Continuing Professional Development, the Learning Organisation, and Investors in People. After providing this base, the emphasis in the next two chapters shifts to deal with the ways in which the training cycle is managed, and an analysis of specific training and development interventions in practice.

By the end of this chapter, readers should be able to:

- advise colleagues on how to complete a record of their continuing professional development

- provide advice on how to become and remain a 'learning organisation'

- explain what organisations need to do in order to become Investors in People.

In addition, readers should be able to understand and explain:

- the meaning of terms which are widely used in employee development, such as learning, training, development, education, continuing professional development, learning organisation

- the major principles of learning, and their implications for the design of training and development programmes.

- the contribution which learning and development can make to other aspects of P&D, as well as to organisational effectiveness.

THE TERMINOLOGY OF EMPLOYEE DEVELOPMENT

Although terms such as training, development, learning and education are often used interchangeably, there is a need to be aware of the major distinctions between them, at least in their pure form. In reality, of course, some of the distinctions are less clear cut, there is sometimes overlap between the concepts, and one may feed into the other; for example, the educational process ought to involve learning, hopefully leads to development, and may even contain some training in specific techniques. In addition, as the use of NVQs spreads, the distinction between education and training is likely to become even more blurred.

Education has been defined as 'activities which aim at developing the knowledge, skills, moral values and understanding required in all aspects of life. Its purpose is to provide the conditions essential to young people and adults to develop an understanding of the traditions and ideas influencing the society in which they live' (Reid and Barrington, 1994: 7). This is a very wide definition indeed, and arguably excludes many university degree courses other than those in the social sciences. A focus on the learning of principles and concepts, on the importance of analysis and critical appraisal, and on the development of theoretical constructs, might be nearer to the mark.

Training on the other hand is a much narrower concept than education, referring to a 'planned process to modify attitudes, knowledge or skill behaviour through learning experience to achieve effective performance in an activity or range of activities' (Reid and Barrington, 1994: 7). The notion of predetermined standards is important here, as too is the rather more limited purpose and coverage of training (Harrison, 1992: 4) and a more explicit reference to instruction (Sparrow and Hiltrop, 1994: 363). Although recognising that the distinctions are not altogether clear cut, Reid and Barrington (1994: 45) summarise the principal differences between education and training as:

- the former is more abstract, the latter more specific

- education typically takes longer than training

- the latter is more mechanistic than the former, more explicitly linking stimuli and responses

- training is workplace-based whereas education is generally off-the-job.

But these represent two polar extremes, and just because a two-day course (in negotiating skills, for example) takes place away from the employer's premises, this does not qualify it as education unless it comprises part of a wider product, such as a professional qualification or an MBA. Similarly, full-time students on a Masters' programme in P&D who take part in an outdoor-based development programme undertake this as an element in their education even though the course may be run by trainers.

If education and training typically refer (albeit implicitly) to the process by which an individual's attitudes, behaviour or performance is changed, learning focuses explicitly on the changes which take place within the individual and to the process by which the learner acquires knowledge, develops a skill, or undergoes a transition in attitudes. While training may be seen typically from the perspective of the *deliverer* (the trainer), learning starts out from a different standpoint, that of the *learner*. Indeed, rather than define ourselves as lecturers, teachers, or tutors, the authors might prefer to be described as 'facilitators of structured and developmental learning'!

Learning is 'the process by which a new capability is attained' according to Reid and Barrington (1994: 6), or 'a process within the organism which results in the capacity for changed performance which can be related to experience rather than maturation' according to Ribeaux and Poppleton (1978: 38). In both definitions, the emphasis is on attainment of something by the individual learner, although the latter differentiates between the root of the changed performance; for Ribeaux and Poppleton, changes which occur solely through the process of ageing or moving into another stage of maturity are insufficient to qualify as learning. This implies that learners have an explicit awareness that learning is taking place, and some attempt is made to relate this to concepts or principles by a process of reflection or reinforcement. In other words, the learner has to understand *why* a particular action or approach is required, and have some awareness of when it may or may not be appropriate in the future. It is also important to recognise the distinction between learning and performance. Stammers and Patrick (1975: 23) note that 'changes in the level of learning may not be reflected by changes in behaviour'; that is, employees may learn something without it leading to changes in performance. Equally, unless individuals are allowed to demonstrate and reinforce their learning, it is likely to be forgotten.

There is less agreement among writers about the definition of *development*. Collin (1994: 274–275) views development as a broader term than learning, in terms of its complexity and elaboration, as well as its continuity, but nevertheless sees it as rooted in the individual. Others see employee development in the same way as the IPD – as the blanket term to describe the employer's strategy for managing the learning and training process. For example, Reid and Barrington

(1994: 7) define it as 'the planning and management of people's learning', while Harrison (1992: 4) refers to employee development as 'the skilful provision of learning experiences in the workplace in order that performance can be improved.' For the purpose of this book we will take the latter definitions.

Do you think it is possible for people to learn without being aware that they are learning? Do they need to consolidate the learning or relate it to abstract principles for learning to be effective?

LEARNING OUTCOMES

Formalised learning has to have some purpose, typically measured by a series of outcomes, as is evident from the core, generalist and specialist syllabuses for the IPD Professional Qualification Scheme. By the end of a module, the learner should be able to perform a set of skills, display understanding of particular issues, and demonstrate competencies in specified areas. In addition, however, it is important to remember that most learners come to a new learning situation with existing skills, understanding and competencies. Often, learners may be unaware that they possess these, or be unable to articulate them to a third party; these are referred to as 'tacit' skills and knowledge. Skills, understanding and competencies developed in one situation are also frequently transferable to another, and on many occasions all that the learner requires is tutor support and an awareness of their relevance to the new context.

Skill and understanding are those aspects of behaviour which are practised in the work situation, and which individuals need to be able to perform at an acceptable level in order to do the job satisfactorily. They comprise motor skills, manual dexterity, social and interpersonal skills, technical skills, analytical skills, and so on. Skills are frequently seen in terms of a hierarchy, in which the lower levels are perceived as prerequisites for the higher levels; for example, Bloom's taxonomy (reproduced in Collin, 1994: 288–289) views learning as a series of building-blocks:

a) knowledge

b) comprehension (understanding the meaning of this knowledge)

c) application (ability to apply this knowledge and comprehension in new situations)

d) analysis (breaking down material into constituent parts and seeing relationships between them)

e) synthesis (reassembling the parts into a new and meaningful relationship)

f) evaluation (the ability to judge the value of the material).

Understanding and knowledge, and the ability to explain things to other people, are therefore incorporated within this conception of the term 'skill'. For most observers, however, skill has a commonsense, everyday meaning, typically connected with these lower levels, and seen in the application of motor skills rather than the powers of analysis, synthesis and evaluation. It is also important to recognise that 'skill' is a socially-constructed phenomenon rather than some objective characteristic of an individual or task (Sturdy *et al*, 1992: 4); the skills which are valued are likely to be very different if your car has broken down in the desert from those which are seen as useful when negotiating in a foreign language or managing a superstore.

Do you think that basic motor skills, such as typing, are entirely devoid of higher-level skills? Why/why not?

Competency is a newer term than 'skill', growing in importance since the publication of *The Competent Manager* by Boyatsis in 1982. The competence/competency terminology has been widely used in Britain in recent years, and it underpins the work of the National Council for Vocational Qualifications, as well as that of lead bodies such as the Employment Occupational Standards Council (see Chapter 3). But there is also much confusion about the terminology. According to Woodruffe (1992: 17), 'competency' is 'the set of behaviour patterns that the incumbent needs to bring to a position in order to perform its tasks and functions with competence'. In other words, competency is concerned with the *individual* and his or her behaviour, whereas competence is related to dimensions of the *job or task* in question.

At issue is whether or not it is possible to derive a list of generic competencies which are appropriate to all situations, or whether they are organisation- or function-specific. A number of lists of generic management competencies have been published, containing similar sorts of headings, albeit with different titles (Woodruffe, 1992: 18–24). Most include the following competencies:

• breadth of awareness and strategic perspective

• oral and written communication

• leadership, decisiveness and assertiveness

• team working and ability to work with others

• analysis and judgement

• drive and persistence

• organisation and planning

• sensitivity to others' viewpoints

• self-confidence and persuasiveness

• flexibility and adaptability.

> How adequately do you think this list of competencies relates to the personal characteristics which are required to perform satisfactorily in your particular job?

Tacit skills and knowledge are harder to define, and are frequently overlooked when considering the outcomes of learning. These refer to 'know-how' (Collin, 1994: 286), the ability to perform a task without being able to explain how it is being done. Sometimes it this knowledge or skill may be held at a subconscious level without individuals being aware that they have ever learned how to do certain things, and on other occasions individuals may lack the linguistic resources to transmit this knowledge to others. For example, female catering workers and home-care staff often belittle the acquired skills and knowledge that is used in the performance of their tasks, somehow regarding their attributes as being ingrained and natural. Since this know-how is typically acquired through experience, rather than formal instruction, it is hard to specify and quantify. There is little doubt, however, that tacit skills represent 'a reservoir of knowledge and ability which remains untapped because of traditional job demarcations' (Myers and Davids, 1992: 45); these demarcations exist between all types of employee, managers and non-managerial staff, and often represent a potential threat to middle managers who have not been accustomed to 'open' management styles.

As we saw in Chapter 2, employees may use tacit skills in a variety of ways, both to assist managements in the performance of duties and to resist managerial instructions. Much of the interest among employee relations experts has been directed at the latter, given that individuals may use their tacit skills to sabotage new initiatives or react against overbearing managers who are insensitive to employees' needs and interests. As well as using their know-how to 'get back' at managers, however, employees may also use these skills to make work more efficient, to 'get on' with work by smoothing over problems. This can take place in relation to technical and interpersonal relations; in the case of the former, employees may choose to override what they know to be faulty computer signals on chemical plants, whereas in the latter, secretarial staff often cover up for their managers' failings. These are skills which are essential to organisational effectiveness, but are rarely the subject of training courses or (apart from Collin's work) considered in texts on employee development.

THE PROCESS OF LEARNING

The way in which people learn is of obvious importance to all P&D professionals, given its centrality to most aspects of organisational life. Learning is important at the time of induction, not only in terms of basic instructions about the tasks to be performed and safety regulations which govern the workplace, but also in appreciating organisational norms and cultures. It is equally relevant throughout the rest of an individual's employment, both in terms of learning to comply with disciplinary rules, and in learning how to manage other people, improve product quality and write effective reports. The processes by which *adults* learn is particularly apposite given that they comprise the vast majority of the working population.

There are a range of different theories analysing the learning process, but there is neither the space nor the need to discuss these in detail here; readers wanting a fuller explanation of these theories are advised to consult one of the core psychology texts such as Atkinson, Atkinson, Smith and Bem (1993). Gagne's (1977) classification is one of the better known, seeing learning in terms of a hierarchy, moving from lower- to higher-order skills. Although it is suggested that this sequence forms the optimal conditions for learning, this does not mean that learning can take place *only* in this order (Stammers and Patrick, 1975: 81). Gagne's eight classes of learning are:

- signal learning (see below)

- stimulus-response learning (see below)

- chaining (two or more stimulus-response connections)

- verbal association (learning chains that are verbal)

- discrimination learning (making different responses to different stimuli)

- concepts learning (making a common response to a class of stimuli that may differ in physical appearance)

- rule learning (a chain of two or more concepts)

- problem-solving (the combination of two or more rules via a process of thinking).

In this section we draw upon the classifications proposed by Stammers and Patrick (1975), Ribeaux and Poppleton (1978) and Hilgard, Atkinson and Atkinson (1979), as well as Gagne, re-categorising these as appropriate to make them more relevant for P&D specialists.

The first category is learning by *association*, incorporating signal and other type of stimulus-response learning. Signal learning is most obviously apparent in the behaviour of household pets, which run to the kitchen when they hear food being placed in a dish on the floor (Gagne, 1977: 77). It is the classical conditioned response which has been popularised by the Pavlovian dogs experiment, although sceptics might suggest that it can also be found in the fixed smile which appears on a salesperson's face the moment a customer walks through the door. Conditioning can be either classical (whereby the stimulus automatically leads to a response) or operant, in which case a desired response is rewarded and reinforced *after* it has been delivered. In the latter case, the behaviour may be natural and unconditioned, in the sense that it has not been trained into the individual, in which case appropriate behaviour is often learned by a process of trial and error. This is regularly used with young children who are rewarded with a chocolate or a cuddle for using their potty instead of soiling a nappy. In organisations, operant conditioning can be seen in the recognition which is shown by a line manager to high-quality performance by a newish recruit, and this can then act as a powerful reinforcement for learning how to do the job well. It is also apparent in bonus schemes where employees are rewarded at the end of the week for achieving high production figures or low reject rates, in the hope that they will learn about the importance of good levels of performance. Even in adults, reinforcement must occur soon after the event for it to be meaningful, and without appropriate reinforcement learning soon becomes extinct.

This sort of learning (termed associative) may be appropriate for some situations, such as the acquisition of automatic physical activities or habit formation. Even in these cases, however, a variety of conditions are necessary for learning to be successful (Ribeaux and Poppleton, 1978: 45):

- the learner should be active rather than passive

- frequent repetition is needed

- reinforcement of the learned activity is important, especially if it is positive

- practice is necessary for generalisation, and determining the conditions under which specific actions are appropriate.

Stimulus-response reinforcement paradigms have been extremely influential in psychology, but there are serious concerns that they fail to account for all types of learning. In particular, given that the experiments were originally conducted on animals, the paradigm does not give sufficient weight to the dynamic and interactive complexity of human beings (Stammers and Patrick, 1975: 23). Also, given the range of stimuli in a work (as opposed to a laboratory) situation, it may prove difficult to determine the precise influence of one stimulus over a defined response.

> How adequately do you think theories of learning based on laboratory experiments – on animals or human beings – can account for learning at work?

The second category of learning is *cognitive*, which is not based upon stimulus-response theories but upon stimulus-stimulus connections. The classic example here is of a chimpanzee locked in a cage with a piece of fruit some distance away. After first trying to escape, and later using a short stick which is placed near the cage, neither of which enable it to reach the fruit, the chimpanzee eventually realises that the short stick could enable it to reach a longer stick which is capable of pulling the fruit towards the cage (Hilgard *et al*, 1979: 208-209). The idea of insight, what is referred to as the 'aha' experience, is central to cognitive learning, and in many situations we take the insights for granted. But the pleasure of gaining an insight acts as a powerful reinforcer of learning, and a significant stimulus to memory. A case study which helps learners to link theories and practical applications is a good example of this, as is group problem-solving, which can have a highly positive effect on team-building if properly structured. According to Hilgard *et al* (1979: 210), three features of insight (cognitive) learning are worth stressing:

• insight will only occur if the essentials for the solution are arranged so that their relationships can be perceived

• once a solution occurs with insight, it can be repeated promptly

• solutions achieved by insight can be applied in new situations because a relationship has been established between a means and an end.

Whereas stimulus-response applications might be suitable for training in basic practical skills, cognitive learning is more appropriate for mental skills. These types of theory rely on the learner's connecting together different concepts or actions to form a chain of stimuli which enable him or her to arrive at the ultimate goal.

Cybernetics represents the third strand of theories which attempt to explain the process of learning. This approach regards learning as an information-processing system in which a signal containing information is passed along a communication channel subject to interference from a variety of sources (Collin, 1994: 290). Stammers and Patrick (1975: 27–35), drawing upon earlier work by Crossman, outline the essential elements of this communication process. Signals have to be encoded to enable them to be transmitted along the communication channel, and decoded before they can be received. All messages are subject to 'noise' which acts as an obstacle to learning – this does not mean just audible noises but also other factors which interfere with the transmission process. Learning may be hindered, therefore, by the presence of other stimuli which interfere with the receipt of messages and cause them to be confused or imperfectly picked up (eg when domestic problems are bothering learners). There are also limits to the amount of information which can be transmitted along a channel. Feedback is an important aspect of these models; it may be intrinsic to the learning itself, in which case the individual is aware of this during the acquisition or application of the skill, or it may be extrinsic, in which case it becomes available at a later date and can influence future performance. This form of feedback may be derived from the individual learner or it may be provided by a trainer, or a set of figures which demonstrate the impact of learning upon performance. In any form of learning – whether it be intellectual development or practical skills – feedback is crucial to enable learners to evaluate how well they are performing and to help them correct any defects. Without such feedback a lot of time and effort can be wasted, with detrimental consequences for both the individual and the organisation.

The final category in this section is *social learning theory*, which works on the principle of learning by imitation (Bandura, 1977). Through this, individuals learn to do specific tasks by watching other people perform them, then trying for themselves, generalising from this as appropriate. Long ridiculed as 'sitting by Nellie', these forms of learning may actually enable the transfer of 'tacit' skills from one employee to another, and they can result in more effective work performance (Myers and David, 1992: 47). Many basic skills can be learned in this way, although reinforcement through doing (often repeatedly) is crucial to their success. Social and interpersonal skills are also be learned through this process, and many of the so-called 'tacit skills' discussed in the previous section are certainly acquired in this way, typically without the individual being aware that learning has actually taken place. Women, in particular, are prone to downgrade them and refer to these skills as 'common sense'. Because of this, they may be ignored in job analysis and evaluation exercises because these skills have not been taught during a structured training session nor been subject to a formal test. One of the major problems with unstructured training (social learning), which does not incorporate feedback or evaluation, is that people may learn inefficient ways of working or they fail to decipher some of the tacit skills which are used by experienced workers. There are also dangers that individuals learn behaviour by imitation which are not welcomed by management or society – for example, bullying or aggressive behaviour, fiddles and

Keep a diary for a week, and note all the times when you learned something new, either at work or elsewhere. Categorise these learning experiences according to the different theories outlined above. Make sure you include all learning events, not just those which took place at work.

scams, racism and sexism. In addition, Ribeaux and Poppleton (1979: 50) report on studies which show how an individual's learning is influenced by the social power of the controller or role model; accordingly, the individual is more likely to imitate people wielding the greatest power or controlling the more valued resources. Unfortunately, this can pose problems in organisations where P&D specialists have low status.

EXPERIENTIAL LEARNING, CYCLES AND STYLES

Much of the mainstream psychology literature has focused on what is seen as 'traditional' learning – the importance of building-blocks, hierarchies of skills, and reinforcing theory with examples. Clearly, this may be particularly appropriate to educational situations and in child development, but it may be less appropriate for adults as it is apparent that not all individuals learn in the same manner. Carl Rogers (1969: 5) is the major proponent of experiential learning, which he sees as having the following components: personal involvement; self-initiation; pervasiveness; evaluation by the learner. The essence of experiential learning resides in its meaning to the learner. This makes it quite different from traditional learning, and potentially quite exciting for employees who left school early and feel threatened by the classroom situation. It provides the individual employee with a responsibility to learn, although of course it also requires skilful management of the learning situation by professional staff; as Mumford (1988: 171–172) warns, experiential learning can be 'a very inefficient, hit-or-miss operation ... guidance helps the process to be both quicker and easier'.

The experiential approach is best known in the P&D field through the work of Kolb, and Honey and Mumford, on the learning cycle, and indeed it forms a centrepiece of the IPD's guidance for Continuing Professional Development. Kolb, Osland and Rubin (1995: 49) view the learning process as both active and passive, concrete and abstract, and conceive of it as a four-stage cycle. The model is:

Figure 6

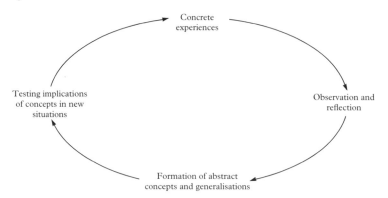

(From Kolb D. *et al*, 1995, *Organisational Behaviour; An experiential approach.* Prentice Hall, New Jersey: 49).

Several important features of this model need to be stressed (Kolb *et al*, 1995: 50). First, the learning cycle is continuously recurring, as concepts are tested in practice, and modified as appropriate. Second, as the direction that learning takes is governed by one's own felt needs and goals, these have to be clarified in order to prevent the process of learning from being erratic and inefficient. Third, learning is highly individual both in direction and process, so our learning styles have weak and strong points, determined by preferred modes of operating.

From this Kolb developed a Learning Styles Inventory based upon the four stages of the learning process. He argues that effective learners rely on four different learning modes, and each individual has an orientation toward one or more of these.

• An orientation towards *concrete experience* means that individuals adopt an intuitive stance, relying upon their personal judgement rather than systematic analysis. These individuals enjoy relating to people, being involved in real situations, and adopt an open-minded approach to life.

• An orientation towards *reflective observation* leads individuals to view situations carefully, considering their meaning, and drawing out the implications of ideas. These people prefer to reflect on issues rather than acting, looking at questions from different points of view, and they value patient and thoughtful judgement.

• An orientation towards *abstract conceptualisation* implies that learners emphasise the use of logic, ideas and concepts, opposing intuitive judgements. These individuals are good at systematic planning and quantitative analysis, and they value precise formulations and neat, conceptual systems.

- An orientation towards *active experimentation* means that the individual enjoys practical applications, active involvement in change, and a pragmatic concern with what works in practice. Achieving results is important for this group of learners, and they value having an impact on their working environment.

Sangita is a senior research scientist who runs a small team of professionals and technicians working for a large chemical company. She has a PhD in biochemistry, and spent many years working at the bench before being promoted to more senior jobs. She reports direct to the research and development director who has been very successful in promoting the development of profitable new products in the past, but requires a lot of convincing before agreeing to proceed. Sangita also works closely with line managers and shop floor employees in trying to exploit the practical application of new ideas.

Which learning styles do you think are most likely for each of the groups/individuals (her team, her boss, line managers, shop floor employees) with whom Sangita deals, and what advice would you give her on how to approach these different sets of people?

Honey and Mumford (Mumford, 1988: 175–177) have developed a similar instrument to that of Kolb, also comprising four learning styles, with norms based on the scores of management educators and trainers. Their Learning Styles Questionnaire categorises people into the following types, and readers who want more information on how to use this instrument are referred to Honey and Mumford (1986):

- *Activists* who learn best by active involvement in concrete tasks, and from relatively short tasks such as business games and competitive teamwork exercises.

- *Reflectors* who learn best by reviewing and reflecting upon what has happened in certain situations, where they are able to stand back, listen and observe.

- *Theorists* who learn best when new information can be located within the context of concepts and theories, and who are able to absorb new ideas when they are distanced from real-life situations.

- *Pragmatists* who learn best when they see a link between new information and real-life problems and issues, and from being exposed to techniques which can be applied immediately.

This focus on learning cycles and learning styles has major implications for the training and development process, and for the choice of particular techniques and learning technology. If a group comprises theorists alone, it is unlikely that these individuals will feel comfortable with case studies or role-play situations, whereas a group of pragmatists would find this a particularly fruitful way in which to learn. Similarly, while reflectors only really make sense of a situation after they have had time to evaluate its impact, activists are keen to put ideas into practice at the earliest possible opportunity, getting frustrated if too much time is spent reviewing previous learning situations. Of course, it is more likely that groups contain a mix of different types of learners, in which case the tutor needs to be able to design learning situations to maximise strengths and improve on areas of weakness.

> Explain to a friend or colleague Kolb's and Honey and Mumford's work on learning styles. Then attempt to sort yourselves into one or more categories. How adequate are these models, and what is their major value?

Despite their value, there are doubts about the use of learning styles questionnaires as well. Given that the four categories represent 'ideal types', it is unlikely that people conform totally or even principally to a single learning style, and indeed, they may be strong on two apparently dissimilar axes. The precise questions which are asked of individuals are also capable of differing interpretations, depending upon the context in which they are set; for example, an individual may be a reflector in response to certain questions or situations, and a pragmatist in others. Moreover, the combination of people in a working group may lead individuals to adopt other styles than they might do in a formal learning situation in order, say, to cajole a group of theorists into action, or to encourage a set of activists to reflect on their proposed course of action. This implies that people's preferred learning styles may alter over time rather than remaining static.

An alternative conception of the learning cycle is developed by Engeström (1994: 32–35). This is termed 'integral learning', and it comprises six steps, each of which demands specific learning actions. The six steps are:

- *motivation*; the awakening of interest in the subject

- *orientation*; the formation of preliminary hypotheses on the subject which explain the principles and structure of the knowledge necessary for problem-solving; by fashioning a 'lens' through which to assimilate information, the learner creates an active model which enables essential points and linkages to be made

- *internalisation*; new knowledge is added to enrich and extend the model, as well as render it meaningful to the learner

- *externalisation*; applying the model to solve concrete problems, in so doing testing and evaluating its utility in a practical situation; application enriches and corrects theory, raising new questions and stimulating creativity

- *critique*; a critical evaluation of the validity and applicability of the model, identifying situations in which it might be useful or inappropriate

- *control*; by examining the way in which learning has taken place, the learner evaluates its effectiveness and tries to improve his or her learning methods.

CONTINUING PROFESSIONAL DEVELOPMENT

Ideas about learning styles and learning cycles have influenced the growth of interest in continuous development, both in a broad sense and in relation to the IPD. There are a number of essential features of continuous development, according to Wood (1988: 9–13). It enables the integration of learning with work in a way which is meaningful and relevant to the individual. The learning which takes place is self-directed, as job-holders are uniquely placed to understand their own development needs; at the same time, many individuals will need assistance in being able to identify their own learning needs. It is important to recognise that continuous development is a process, not a technique, which has relevance for all employees. In recent years there has been an increasing awareness among some British employers that learning is not something which is reserved for managers alone, but is an important component for manual and clerical jobs as well. Within continuous development, learning is seen as an attitude of mind, one in which learning becomes a habit, 'thinking positively about problems and viewing them as opportunities for learning' (Wood 1988: 12). Finally, continuous development should lead simultaneously both to individual growth and improvements in organisational efficiency, especially if it is rooted in teams.

The whole concept of continuing development is underpinned by the phrase 'learning to learn', and material on the 'learning organisation' (reviewed in the next section) paints a very positive picture of current practice. It is seen as automatic and inevitable that employees will be motivated to learn and search for continuous improvements at work, but this cannot be taken for granted. Many employees see little point in investing time and energy in work beyond the minimum which is required, and the growing insecurity of employment only serves to reinforce feelings such as these. Equally, not all individuals look forward to being given the opportunity of being 'stimulated' to learn at work, preferring to focus their creative energies on leisure activities. Not all employers are enamoured by concepts of continuing development and learning organisations either, if analyses of the extent of training provision in Britain are to be believed. Many employers still adopt the view that 'manual workers are not paid to think', and that any investment in training and development is wasted due to lost production time or labour turnover among trained staff.

But there are benefits to be gained, both by individuals and organisations, from continuous development, as the IPD Policy on Continuing Professional Development (CPD) makes clear. There are at least four reasons for P&D professionals to engage in CPD: it ensures that they remain up to date; it encourages them to aspire to improved performance; it ensures that they are committed to learning as an integral part of their work; and it ensures that the reputation of the profession as a whole is enhanced and remains high. Other professional bodies – such as lawyers, accountants and surveyors – are required to record their CPD to remain in membership, and this is inspected at times of upgrading.

CPD can take many forms for IPD members: involvement in courses, seminars and conferences; professional work-based activities, such as secondments, project management, and contributions to strategic planning; self-directed and informal learning, such as reading professional journals and books, and updating of knowledge. The basic point behind CPD is that IPD members are expected to remain up to date with P&D activities, and actively *learn* from them. As Judy Whittaker (1992: 29) pointed out at the time the original IPM CPD was launched, 'Attendance at courses is not enough. If the policy is to have any meaning, it should ensure that development has actually taken place.' The wider significance of CPD was also stressed in this article, when she wrote 'It will have been successful if personnel professionals become known as people committed to their own professional development, professionals who are always up-to-date and committed to the development of their own organisation' (Whittaker, 1992: 30). In other words, as the occupation most directly interested in improving the contribution of employees to organisational success, we need to demonstrate our own personal commitment to continuing patterns of learning and development.

Leaving aside your attendance on an IPD or other formal course, note the amount and types of CPD in which you have engaged during the past two years. How much time have you really spent on this activity, and what exactly has been learned from this?

THE LEARNING ORGANISATION

The learning organisation has been the subject of much interest in Britain and elsewhere for a number of years, initially articulated by Argyris and Schon (1978), and subsequently developed by people such as Morgan (1986), Senge (1990), and Pedler, Burgoyne and Boydell (1991). In fact, Pedler and his colleagues prefer the term 'learning company' to learning organisation, as they feel it conveys less of a mechanical feeling, and a more comradely, collectivist perspective. Whilst we would not disagree with Pedler *et al*'s reasoning, we will use learning 'organisation' as it more obviously includes all forms of employment situation. The Pedler *et al* definition (1991: 1) is nicely succinct, capturing the essential principle that it is 'an organisation that facilitates the learning of all its members *and* continuously transforms itself.' Drawing from a variety of sources, but mostly Pedler *et al* (1991: 18–23) and the Pearn Kandola toolkit (reported in IRS *Employee Development Bulletin* 45, 1993), the principal characteristics of a learning organisation are:

• the creation of opportunities for learning, not just in a formal sense but also from everyday actions which are debated, reviewed and questioned

- the design of structures and cultures which ensure that all employees feel that they are encouraged to learn, to question existing rules and practices, to experiment with new ideas, and are empowered to contribute to decisions at all levels

- the development of managers who are totally committed to facilitating learning by the adoption of 'open' and participative approaches to decision-making

- the acceptance that mistakes will be made, but that they are an essential part of the learning process; as Pedler *et al* (1992: 23) note, 'We will never learn if we do not try out new ideas [and] new ways of doing things'

- the provision of learning opportunities for *all* employees, not just managers, and the assumption that, with appropriate guidance, each employee should assume responsibility for his or her own learning and development

- the implementation of systems (accounting and other data) designed to be accessed by users rather than experts

- the breaking down of barriers between different individuals and departments to encourage open communication and ways of working, and the creation of internal supplier-customer relationships

- the learning approach to strategy, meaning, according to Pedler *et al.* (1992: 18) that 'Managerial acts are thus seen as conscious experiments rather than set solutions.'

> How does your own workplace compare with these characteristics of a learning organisation, and what might it do to improve things?

Some of these ideas sound rather futuristic and idealistic, especially the notion that managers engage in experiments and that employees are empowered to contribute to decisions at *all* levels. Many managers in traditional organisations might respond that not only are these ideas unworkable but they are downright revolutionary. If mistakes result in financial losses or dissatisfied customers, the consequences could be severe both for the organisation and, one imagines, for the employees concerned. Employees may also be wary about taking responsibility for actions which go wrong, after a lifetime of advice which stresses caution, and so shun the opportunity to become involved.

On the other hand, the concept of the learning organisation, especially that articulated by Pedler and his colleagues, has obvious similarities to some of the underpinning principles of total quality management and business process re-engineering; ideas of continuous improvement, breaking down barriers, customer-supplier chains and empowerment all echo the proposals of those extolling the virtues of the TQM and BPR (Wilkinson, Marchington, Ackers and Goodman, 1992). The concept also has the major advantage of viewing the organisation in its *totality*, of consciously looking for links between different management functions, departments and specialisms, and of regarding continuous improvement as a never-ending process. Examples of learning organisations are provided in the book edited by Wood (1988), and reports in *People Management* (or its predecessor, *Personnel Management*) show evidence of how other companies are faring in their search for new organisational forms.

A key feature of learning organisations is that they are designed to overcome many of the obstacles which traditionally prevent learning and development from taking place. These can either be individually- or organisationally-rooted. In the case of the former, employees may have emotional or motivational barriers to learning, carried over from earlier educational experiences, or they may lack the intellectual skills or learning styles to enable effective learning to be achieved. In the case of the latter, the organisation may display few signs of obvious commitment to learning, or line managers may make it known that they are not supportive of their staff engaging in further development (due to time constraints or anxieties that their authority will be usurped). These types of organisation are a long way from even understanding the meaning of a learning environment.

Other employers may be part-way on the route to the creation of a learning organisation, but stuck with what is known as 'single-loop learning' (Morgan, 1986: 88); this rests in an 'ability to detect and correct error in relation to a given set of operating norms', and it is located firmly within existing decision-making frameworks. While there is some element of inquiry through single-loop learning, bureaucracy creates boundaries and fragmented structures which do not encourage employees to think beyond their own role or department. Moreover, people are typically rewarded for their ability to operate within existing rules, norms and customs. Furthermore, as managers are accountable for their performance, there is an incentive to cover up mistakes and to take ready-made solutions to senior managers rather than present problems which are then investigated thoroughly in teams.

In contrast to this is 'double-loop learning', which depends upon 'being able to take a "double look" at the situation by questioning the relevance of operating norms'. In this context, employees are actively encouraged to query whether existing ways of working are the most effective, and whether alternative approaches might yield better results. In other words, under double-loop learning, as with the learning organisation, there is a shift away from bureaucratic structures which are seen as unnecessarily stifling. How then can an organisation which engages in single-loop learning be transformed into one where double-loop learning is the norm?

According to Morgan (1986: 89–95), there are four major guidelines. First, senior managers need to encourage openness and reflectivity, accepting error and uncertainty as inevitable features of organisational life. As with TQM, the philosophy of a blame-free culture, in which employees admit mistakes and seek ways to improve processes, is a crucial element in the move to double-loop learning. Second, within problem-solving, there should be a primacy on the expression of different and competing viewpoints, in the expectation that constructive debate can lead ultimately to more effective and better accepted solutions. Third, every attempt should be made to avoid imposing stifling structures on problem-solving techniques, and encouraging an inquiry-driven, open approach to organisational problems. Morgan (1986: 93) acknowledges that this can be an extremely time-consuming process, but 'When a decision is made, one can be fairly certain that most errors will have been detected and corrected, and that the decision will carry the commitment of those involved.' Finally, double-loop learning can be facilitated by the creation of structures and processes which help implement the above three principles.

When written about in the abstract, there is often a real feeling of excitement about the potential for double-loop learning, the development and use of creativity, the breaking down of barriers, the achievement of commitment, and so on. Try to think of teams in which you have taken part when this state may have been reached. Was it all good and liberating, or were there also problems with it? While constructive conflict can be beneficial, where is the boundary between that and destructive, negative and cynical contributions?

When thinking of teams, do not just confine this to the employment situation, but draw upon examples from your part in sports or social groups, political activities, and even your own family or friendship circles.

INVESTORS IN PEOPLE

The notion of the national standard – originally conceived by the National Training Task Force – was established in November 1990 by the Department of Employment and follows the training policies adopted by leading UK companies. It aims to encourage businesses to invest in their future by developing staff in line with business objectives, and hence give training a higher profile. It is designed to be applicable to all types of organisation whether large or small, private or public sector, manufacturing or service industry. As the literature states 'At the heart of Investors in People is the national standard for effective investment in people. This represents a standard towards which an organisation can work, and a benchmark against which progress can be measured. Being recognised as an Investor in People will increasingly be of value, in the eyes of potential recruits as well as current employees and customers and shareholders in public companies' (Toolkit 1991: 1).

For an organisation to be an Investor in People, it has to comply with the four principles of the standard:

First, an Investor in People makes a public commitment from the top to develop all employees to achieve its business objectives.

- Every employer should have a written but flexible plan which sets out business goals and targets, considers how employees will contribute to achieving the plan, and specifies how development needs in particular will be assessed and met.

- Management should develop and communicate to all employees a vision of where the organisation is going and the contribution the employees will make to its success, involving employee representatives as appropriate.

Second, an Investor in People regularly reviews the training and development needs of all employees.

- The resources for training and developing employees should be clearly identified in the business plan.

- Managers should be responsible for regularly agreeing training and development needs with each employee in the context of business objectives, setting targets and standards, linked, where appropriate, to the achievement of NVQs/SVQs.

Third, an Investor in People takes action to train and develop individuals on recruitment and throughout their employment.

- Action should focus on the training needs of all new recruits, and on continually developing and improving the skills of existing employees.

- All employees should be encouraged to contribute to identifying and meeting their own job-related development needs.

Finally, an Investor in People evaluates the investment in training and development to assess achievement and improve future effectiveness.

- The investment, competence and commitment of employees, and the use made of skills learned should be reviewed at all levels against business goals and targets.

- The effectiveness of training and development should be reviewed at the top level and lead to renewed commitment and target setting.

A total of 24 assessment indicators exist for the four principles, and details of these can be obtained from the Training and Enterprise Councils (TECs), which are responsible for delivering the initiative. The Department of Employment has developed a 'tool kit' to help potential Investors, which provides planning and diagnostic materials to enable organisations to measure themselves against the performance indicators they need to meet in order to achieve the standard.

Once an organisation makes a commitment to achieving the standard there is a four-stage process it has to go through before it can call itself an Investor in People and be qualified to use the logo. This commences with management contacting the awarding body (the local TEC) who send an assessor or adviser to explain more about IIP. Having agreed that this is what they wish to pursue, a formal commitment is made and signed by a senior manager. Before devising a training and development plan, an employee survey and interviews are often conducted to provide a benchmark and identify any problems

– usually involving someone outside the organisation, such as a consultant. Clearly some organisations do not need to go through all these steps if they have a well-developed training and development programme which meets the criteria of IIP, as indeed occurred with a number of recognised employers in the IMS study (1994). An action plan and portfolio of evidence are then produced which take account of the 24 assessment indicators. Once the organisation believes it meets the criteria, an assessment is undertaken – with the time involved depending on factors such as the size of the organisation and the number of staff. If the organisation meets the criteria it can then call itself an 'Investor in People'. If it does not, the assessor will explain 'the deficiencies' and specify the improvements required.

Assessment against the performance indicators is carried out by qualified independent assessors, and organisations are reassessed every three years to ensure continued adherence to the standard. Assessment of potential Investors examines the culture of the organisation and the process by which management aims to develop staff. Training targets can be linked to the achievement of external standards such as NVQs/SVQs. Provided there is measurable evidence of a system which works, it does not have to be rigidly bureaucratic and procedure-bound. Experience so far shows that the last aspect of the standard – evaluation – is the area in which many organisations fail.

According to the Department of Employment, (*A Brief for Top Managers*, 1991: 5–6), the main advantages of IIP are:

• improved earnings – as people are better skilled and motivated

• reduced costs – reduction in waste as people are more skilled

• quality – as people produce better goods or services

• motivation – as personal development is given priority

• customer satisfaction – as there are closer links between business needs and training

• organisational reputation – as IIP is a prestigious award.

An Incomes Data Services Study (No 530, May 1993) found that there were several reasons why employers committed to the scheme. This includes identification of training gaps in existing programmes, a highlighting of business objectives, demonstrating a commitment to staff, placing greater emphasis on personnel and human resource policies, enhancing reputations through publicity, and promoting quality in all aspects of business performance.

A Manpower/Institute of Management Survey (1993) reported that while IIP was generally welcomed, it has not yet made the breakthrough to become a widely recognised standard. Whilst 60 per cent of respondents were aware of IIP, only 30 per cent were familiar with any detail concerning the initiative. Moreover, only 1 per cent of organisations surveyed were recognised. Although a further 13 per cent were committed and 15 per cent were planning to commit, no fewer than 50 per cent had no plans in this area. A report by the National

Advisory Council for Education and Training Targets found that, while the aim is for half of all medium- and large-sized employers to become recognised as Investors in People by 1996, so far only 25 per cent have achieved it.

A number of concerns have emerged from recent research (IDS, 1993; Rix, Parkinson and Gaunt 1993; IMS, 1994). Firstly, there is the issue of its (so far) uneven distribution. Finn (1994: 33), argues that the initiative is in danger of becoming industry-specific, which of course defeats the original all-embracing objective. He also points out that perceived problems of bureaucracy and assessment costs need to be addressed. These criticisms were also apparent in the CRG report (Rix *et al*, 1993) in which some respondents (uncommitted to IIP) saw the scheme as primarily designed for larger businesses and some also reported that they were too involved with other initiatives to take part in IIP. As there are no sanctions against organisations which do not adopt IIP, doubts must remain as to how far it can provide a solution to the British training problem.

Secondly, a major problem with IIP is that it is not *developmental*, in that it requires the repeated achievement of a minimum standard. Rix *et al* (1993) noted tensions between viewing the initiative as an award or as a process, with those employers who saw it as an 'award' less likely to agree that they had received large-scale benefits from the scheme. In contrast, organisations which took a 'process' approach perceived the initiative as a significant part of their changing training and development function, and indeed many saw the actual process of IIP to be as useful as the recognition itself. According to Pickard (1991: 18) 'It is evident from talking to companies which have taken part in the development of IIP that it is not uniformity of approach which matters, but evidence of having arrived at the same destination – having become a "learning organisation" in which training is embedded, applies to all employees, is linked to business needs, and is regularly evaluated.'

Thirdly, there is the issue of IIP and performance. The Institute of Manpower Studies (1994) examined the relative performance of those organisations which have achieved the award, those which are committed to it, and those which are not involved at all. They reported that over two-thirds of employers who have achieved the standard or are committed to achieving it, have introduced changes in practice as a direct or indirect result, thus indicating a raised priority for training. Of the remainder, half believed that being involved in IIP would lead to such a change. Organisations involved with IIP were more likely to have mission statements, business plans and human resource strategies, and while an assessment of training needs appeared to be carried out by all employers, those involved with the initiative used more formal methods. However, the report acknowledges that the direction of causality is not clear. Employers who had achieved IIP claimed they had achieved the benefits which were expected at the outset of the process, and a third believed they would not have done so if they had not been involved with IIP. However, implementing IIP did involve costs for employers, with around half identifying costs associated with taking staff away from work, increased spending on training, and consultancy fees. Prior to becoming involved with IIP, employers expected benefits such as improving their training system and improving staff morale. Two-thirds of those who had achieved the standard, and a third of those in the process of achieving it, believed that their involvement with IIP had improved the quality of their workforce. Three-quarters of those awarded the standard felt it had contributed to a positive change in business. Those employers who have achieved the standard appear to be positive about the process, with most stating their intention of maintaining the award after the review period.

However, a number of those who achieved the standard claimed they had not altered their training plans or reviewed the criteria on which training decisions were made. These employers had merely used the process to 'badge' their current system, already having good P&D systems and procedures. The IMS refers to others as 'changers', those who have changed working practices, but who would have made the same changes in the absence of IIP, and 'partial changers' who would have made changes, but not on the same scale. They estimated the latter represented 50–60 per cent of employers in the sample (IMS 1994).

A positive picture also emerges from research by Cranfield School of Management and The Host Consultancy (IPA, 1995). This reports that recognised employers had stronger overall performance in terms of profitability than committed or non-involved organisations. These employers were more likely to see a clear link between human resource management and business performance. Moreover, 54 per cent of the recognised and committed organisations felt that they had achieved 'a major gain in performance and competitiveness, through Investors in People'.

However, doubts about the efficacy of IIP still remain as the methodology employed in these reports is not particularly rigorous. For example, the self-reporting of organisational success is open to question, as are other features about whether IIP justifies its expenditure; whether it provides a focus for existing initiatives; and what precisely are the direct benefits accruing to employers achieving recognition. Evaluating training investment is one of the four principles of IIP, so it is therefore critical to quantify the business benefits that are gained as a result of its achievement.

Fourthly, we have very little knowledge concerning employee attitudes to IIP. The CRG report has a very brief section which describes low awareness and limited understanding, with IIP seen as 'a management secret to be launched on staff at an appropriate time' (Rix et al, 1993: 8), and a reluctance of employers to publicise IIP for fear of raising expectations. A small-scale survey of employees in the IMS study (1994) indicated that 40 per cent welcomed IIP as having a positive effect on the workplace, but most reports pay little attention to employee attitudes. Certainly much more needs to be known about employee attitudes, and this should be a central rather than side issue in assessing IIP; after all, employees are the main target of IIP and they play a critical and active role in the training and development process.

Finally, we have little knowledge of the role played by P&D professionals, and the function in general, in the IIP process. Given the emphasis on 'people as a resource', IIP certainly represents an opportunity for P&D to raise its profile and ensure an input to training and development programmes which are recognised as contributing to corporate objectives. In the IMS study (1994), in 56 per cent of cases the decision to involve the organisation in Investors in People came from the board of directors, as against just 6 per cent where it came from the human resource or personnel director and 11 per cent from the personnel or training manager. Once the decision had been made, responsibility for implementing IIP was more likely to be shouldered by other managers (38 per cent) than it was by personnel or training managers (15 per cent) or HR/personnel directors (1 per cent).

CONCLUSION

This first chapter in the Employee Development section of the book has been designed to provide a clear and concise analysis of some of the major differences between learning, development, education and training. This is particularly important as many organisations are at least attempting to move away from 'traditional' approaches to training – based on instruction – and towards the idea that individuals need to take responsibility for their own lifetime learning and development. Being able to appreciate the range of ways in which people learn and, as appropriate, facilitate their development, is likely to become a more significant aspect of the P&D practitioner's core skills in the future. Three examples of individual and organisational learning were discussed in the chapter, each of which focuses on different aspects of P&D. Yet there are also links between them, in that learning organisations are only likely to flourish if their employees are prepared and able to manage their own continuing development. Similarly, the achievement of IIP may be one step on the way to the creation of a fully-fledged learning organisation, and some of the IIP principles are based upon the need for continuous improvement, at both an individual and an organisational level.

USEFUL READING

FINN, R. (1994) 'Investors in People: counting the dividends'. *Personnel Management*, May: 30–33.

GAGNE, R. (1977) *The Conditions of Learning*. Holt Saunders, New York. 1977.

HARRISON, R. (1992) *Employee Development*. London, IPD.

INDUSTRIAL RELATIONS SERVICES (1993) *The Learning Organisation. Employee Development Bulletin* 45: 5–8.

KOLB, D., OSLAND, J. AND RUBIN, I. (1995) *Organisational Behaviour: An experiential approach*, Sixth Edition. New Jersey, Prentice Hall.

PEDLER, M., BURGOYNE, J. AND BOYDELL, T. (1991) *The Learning Company: A strategy for sustainable development*. London, McGraw Hill.

REID, M. AND BARRINGTON, H. (1994) *Training Interventions: Managing employee development*, Fourth Edition. London, IPD.

RIX, A., PARKINSON, R. AND GAUNT, R. (1993) 'Investors in People: a qualitative study of employers'. Employment Department, Research Series, No. 21.

STAMMERS, R. AND PATRICK, J. (1975) *The Psychology of Training.* London, Methuen.

WOOD, S. (Ed.) (1988) *Continuous Development.* London, IPD.

9 Managing the training and development process

INTRODUCTION

In earlier chapters we have emphasised repeatedly the role that training and development is expected to play in organisations which regard their employees as an important resource. While recruiting and selecting staff is an effective way in which to transform the nature of the workforce, the opportunities for it are limited except in organisations which are expanding rapidly and/or opening new sites. For the majority of larger organisations – especially those in the public sector and in manufacturing – the training and development of *existing* employees offers a much greater opportunity for generating improvements in productivity and quality. It has been estimated that of those who will be employed by the year 2000, over 80 per cent were already in work by 1993 (Rainbird and Maguire, 1993: 34); accordingly, training and developing the existing workforce is essential if employers in Britain are to upgrade and reskill along the lines of our major competitors.

In the previous chapter we focused on organisations as learning environments, and on the processes by which individuals learn new skills, attitudes and knowledge. Having understood how learning takes place we can now move on to analyse the way in which employers tackle training and development, and to some of the models which are available to manage the training process. For many years, from the days of the industrial training boards through to that of the lead bodies (for example, the Training and Development Lead Body, the Personnel Standards Lead Body, and their successor, the Employment Occupational Standards Council), there has been encouragement for a systematic and comprehensive approach to training. Although the models and the terminology may differ, as we see in the next section, training and development is portrayed as a series of logical steps or stages which progress from an identification of the need through to an evaluation of its effectiveness. While there may be criticisms that these models are too rational, prescriptive and static, as well as out of touch with the realities of organisational life, they do nevertheless provide a framework by which to analyse and manage the training process.

After reviewing models that describe the training process we then go on to analyse the different elements that comprise the model: the identification of training needs, and training needs analysis; the determination of learning objectives; the delivery of training, and different training methods; and the evaluation of training and development. We conclude with a consideration of whether or not training is cost-effective, and the measures which can be used to assess that.

By the end of this chapter, readers should be able to:

- conduct a training needs analysis

- contribute to the design of a training and development programme

- evaluate the effectiveness of training and development practice in their own organisation.

In addition, readers should be able to understand and explain:

- the nature and meaning of the training and development process, its benefits and shortcomings, and its relevance to employing organisations

- the range of learning methods available for use by P&D professionals, and the circumstances in which they may be used

- the importance of assessing the costs and benefits of training and development to employers and employees.

THE TRAINING AND DEVELOPMENT PROCESS IN THEORY

There are a number of alternative models which describe and prescribe how training and development is supposedly managed by employers. Each of these is presented briefly.

Reid and Barrington (1994: 126) use the term the 'training process' to describe the logical sequence covering pre-planning, planning, implementation, and evaluation, in six stages:

- identification of training needs

- setting learning objectives

- determining a learning strategy

- designing and planning training

- training

- assessing results.

In this approach there is a major focus on the early stages of the training process, those which are undertaken *before* the training and development of employees actually takes place, and relatively little on the choice of techniques and learning strategies which might be employed by P&D professionals.

The Bees (1994: xvi) use the concept of a 'training wheel' as the organising framework for their IPD book. In many respects it is similar to the Reid and Barrington approach, including around the 'rim' of their wheel the identification and specification of training needs, their translation into action, and evaluation. It differs in two ways; first, the Bees make much more explicit reference to the business context in which training is enacted and to the importance of environmental scanning. Second, their representation of training as a 'wheel' has people at the hub of the process, thus reinforcing the image that training and learning are inextricably linked. Like Reid and Barrington, however, there is hardly any consideration of how training itself might be conducted or of the conditions under which different techniques might be most appropriate.

Harrison (1992: 244) outlines three alternative analytical approaches for establishing organisational employee development needs and plans, although each share many of the same stages in the process. The *comprehensive* and *problem-centred* approaches each have eight steps: identify major needs; agree possible solutions; select training options; create a training plan; prioritise learning events; apply budgetary constraints; communicate results; and monitor and evaluate implementation. There is a greater recognition here of the realities of organisational life, since she stresses the importance of gaining agreement for solutions and being aware of whether or not these initiatives are likely to be financed. The former approach, she argues, is more suitable for organisations in relatively stable environments where long-term training plans are feasible and likely to be accepted, whereas the latter might appeal more to employers who feel the need for focused training in response to organisational crises and environmental uncertainties. The third approach – the *business strategy approach* – has five steps (Harrison, 1992: 254) as outlined below:

- defining strategic company objectives

- identifying key skill needs in every function/sector of the organisation in order to meet these objectives

- setting standards for individual tasks related to these objectives

- setting specific training objectives for every training event

- reviewing training outcomes in relation to strategic objectives.

Organisational and occupational psychologists have also articulated models to describe how training and development takes place. For example, Arnold, Robertson and Cooper (1991: 247) divide the 'training process' into six stages, which cover ground similar to those described above, even though the terminology differs: assess training needs; analyse jobs/skills/tasks; specify aims and objectives; determine content and nature of training; conduct training; collect evaluation data. In their model, feedback is expected to take place at each step in the process, and there is a rather greater emphasis on the systematic design of evaluation systems to monitor the effectiveness of training interventions. In particular, Arnold *et al* (1991: 258) stress the need for control groups, and preferably more complex design models, to be confident that it was the training (and not some other factor) which has led to changes in employee attitudes and behaviour. Patrick (1992: 122) reviews instructional systems development (ISD) models before proposing his own learning systems development (LSD) model which has three phases: analyse; design/develop; and implement/control. Although covering similar ground as the other models, once again the emphasis differs, and additional factors are highlighted. For example, part of Patrick's analysis phase is a review of existing courses, while his design and development phase incorporates more specific references to the need to consider assessment methods.

The final group of models refer to the 'training cycle', although the precise details vary; both Bramley (1991: 6) and Storey and Sisson (1993: 157) have five steps in the cycle (identification of training needs, training objectives, selection and design of programmes, delivery of training, and evaluation). The model which is likely to have the greatest influence over the rest of the decade, however, is that which has guided the National Standards for Training and Development – the systematic training cycle; this has four stages (A, B, C, E) which are known as areas of competence. This is derived from existing approaches, and it is illustrated in Figure 7.

Figure 7

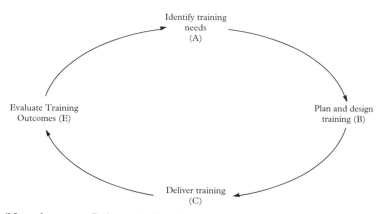

(Note that stage D is not included here; this relates to the assessment and progress of individuals only.)

The key purpose of training and development, according to the TDLB, is to 'develop human potential to assist organisations and individuals to achieve their objectives'. The functional map breaks down the standards further into areas (which comprise the key parts of the training cycle), sub-areas, units, and elements. For example, for the N/SVQ Level 4 in human resource development, the seven core units are:

A13 Identify organisational training and development needs.

B12 Devise a plan for implementing an organisation's training and development objectives.

C11 Co-ordinate the provision of learning opportunities with other contributors to the learning programme.

E21 Evaluate training and development programmes.

E22 Improve training and development programmes.

E31 Evaluate and develop own practice.

E32 Manage relationships with colleagues and customers.

There are clear advantages in using structured and sequential models for describing the training process, especially if they establish a framework within which managers can operate. As Patrick notes (1992: 123), these models are applicable irrespective of organisational context, but for large employers in particular they provide a way in which to subdivide training and development tasks between individuals so that their input can be monitored. In addition, they enable a valuable quality assurance check on the progress of training, and a systematic framework into which new trainers can easily slot.

On the other hand, there is a feeling that these models represent an 'ideal' state of affairs rather than conveying an accurate and realistic picture of organisational practice. The idea that training and development regularly follows this logical and sequential cycle is open to question, and – as with other aspects of P&D – there is likely to be rather more *ad hoc* and reactive management of training than planned and proactive strategies (Reid and Barrington, 1994: 125–126). Patrick (1992: 124) also comments that these models typically describe *what* training is required rather than *how* it might be undertaken; they are 'skeletons without flesh'. A more serious concern is that training and development often lapses into a 'closed' cycle, in which there are few, if any, links with other aspects of P&D, let alone broader business plans and objectives. As Bramley (1991: 6) argues, 'The result of this is often efficient rather than effective training because training objectives, once defined, become synonymous with training need and the system becomes a closed cycle.' In other words, the effectiveness of training is assessed against the training needs identified by the trainers themselves, and not measured in relation to their contribution to business goals.

> To what extent does your organisation follow this sort of logical and sequential approach to training? If it does not, what benefits might be gained from so doing? If this sort of approach is already used, what further improvements might be made to the management of training?

THE IDENTIFICATION OF TRAINING NEEDS

The first stage in the training cycle is an identification of training needs (ITN), which is often reviewed in conjunction with a training needs analysis (TNA). Although used interchangeably on many occasions, ITN is concerned with the process required to *detect and specify* training needs at an individual and organisational level, whilst TNA refers to the process of examining training needs to determine how they might actually be met. A training need exists when:

• there is a gap between the future requirements of the job and the current capabilities of the incumbent, whether this is measured in terms of skills, attitudes or knowledge, and

- it is anticipated that systematic training will overcome the deficiency (Boydell, 1971: 4) or barrier (Arnold *et al*, 1991: 248).

We have to be certain, however, that training represents the best or the only solution to these problems, and that it is not being suggested as a panacea for all organisational ills. In some circumstances training may not be the most effective option, and the choice of a specific programme might be totally inappropriate. The problem may reside elsewhere, and there are dangers that employers prescribe training as a universal solution ('training is the answer irrespective of the question') without considering any alternative lines of action. Actions such as job redesign, better systems of communication and involvement, adjustments to organisational cultures and structures, or disciplinary action to tackle a gap between actual and required performance, may be more appropriate. It may even make sense to do nothing (Bee and Bee, 1994: 59), as there are often as many dangers in providing too much training as there are in providing too little; for example, excessive levels of training cost money and use up valuable resources, and may even result in job dissatisfaction if employees are unable to practise their new-found skills back at the workplace (Arnold *et al*, 1991: 247). Indeed, training can often become an end in itself, a closed loop, which is not measured against its contribution to broader organisational goals.

> Are you aware of any circumstances when training has been put forward as a solution and it has been inappropriate? What happened in these cases, and why? What might have been done instead?

Training can be used in a range of different circumstances and contexts, and this clearly has an effect on the design of programmes. Drawing on Harrison (1992: 283), there are broadly three principal categories. First, training is used as a *socialisation initiative*, a mechanism for inducting new employees, and ensuring that they learn about the job/tasks they are to undertake, as well as the organisation and department of which they are a part. In these circumstances making employees aware of the broader cultural norms of the organisation may be just as important as any specific skill or knowledge transfer. As we have already seen in Chapter 7, effective and comprehensive induction programmes are an important element in the shift by some employers to an HRM philosophy. Second, training can be used as a *development initiative*, for example by preparing employees for promotion, helping them cope with new technology, or as part of an organisational change programme. In this situation training may be part of a formalised and well-established system within an organisation, and there is likely to be little consideration of the needs of individual members of staff compared with pressures to meet organisational requirements; these programmes are sometimes unkindly referred to as 'the sheep dip' approach to training. Finally, training is used as a way in which to correct unsatisfactory performance, perhaps as part of a *disciplinary initiative* in cases where individuals are found to be working below acceptable quality, output or customer service standards. The training need in these circumstances may be concerned with technical skills, such as how to operate a piece of machinery, or with highlighting problems in an individual's attitudes or behaviour. For example, a manager who has been harassing or bullying his staff might need very careful and sensitive training in how to relate to women employees.

> These examples show some of the links between training and other parts of core P&D, and emphasise the importance of 'horizontal integration'. Try to identify three links which are relevant to your own organisation.

Training needs can be identified at three different levels – organisational, job/occupational, and personal – and it is assumed that all three can be integrated. Most publications stress the importance of commencing the ITN process with a review of organisational training needs in order to establish how specific training programmes may contribute to broader strategic goals (see, for example, Bramley, 1991: 10; Harrison, 1992: 254). Walters (1983: 181) outlines nine sources of information which help to identify training priorities. These are:

- *organisational goals and corporate plans*, which guide the trainer as to the direction in which the organisation is moving, and the implications for future training and development

- *human resource and succession planning*, which provides information about future training needs for key managers, and indicates areas of priority

- *personnel statistics*, which provide information regarding labour turnover and absence, for example, which directs the trainer to possible sources of problems; this includes training, but may also suggest other reasons

- *exit interviews*, which may highlight information about potential management and supervisory training needs

- *consultation with senior managers*, which provides an understanding of the views of key opinion formers and of organisational culture

- *data on productivity, quality and performance*, which provides clues about the relationship between actual and required performance

- *departmental layout changes*, which provides information about future developments and can highlight training needs (skills or knowledge) at an early stage

- *management requests*, which indicate perceived needs and ideas for further development

- *knowledge of financial plans*, which is essential to determine whether or not training requirements are likely to be adopted by senior management, and may encourage fresh approaches if resources are limited.

The principal advantage of lists such as this is that they highlight the importance of locating training and development firmly in its corporate context, and ensure that this aspect of P&D can be undertaken with broader strategic goals in mind. It also provides a useful template against which to assess the contribution of training and development to organisational objectives. In short, it offers a logical and sequential process for establishing training needs within realistic organisational parameters. But there are also shortcomings with this top-down approach, especially if it is conducted as part of a wide-ranging formal review of training activity. It can be time-consuming and expensive, and it may be difficult to collect all the data in the time available (Reid and Barrington, 1994: 178). If the review takes a long time, there are bound to be questions about the prioritisation of training over the period during which the organisational analysis takes place.

The second level is job or occupation analysis, the purpose of this stage being to identify more specific training needs. There are many similarities here with job analysis which we dealt with in Chapter 6 on recruitment and selection. Harrison (1992: 263) terms this 'job-training analysis' so as to differentiate it clearly from its recruitment and selection counterpart; for her it is the 'process of identifying the purpose of a job and its component parts, and specifying what must be learned in order for there to be effective work performance.' A range of methods can be used to collect information at the job training analysis level, including an examination of job descriptions and job specifications, the use of questionnaires, group discussions, observation of the task in hand, work diaries, and even getting analysts to do the job themselves. Interviews are particularly useful, not just with the job-holder, but also with his or her supervisor and customers or clients; 'customers' in this sense of the word can apply equally well to internal as well as external contacts. Walters (1983: 195) puts forward a contingency model for choosing which assessment methods to use, taking into account the extent of employee and managerial involvement in the process, as well as the cost and skills required to undertake the exercise. Interviews, for example, are time-consuming and relatively costly, but high on employee involvement. He argues that they are low on management involvement, but this would not be the case if the manager was one of the principal sources of data collection – as one might expect if training needs are established from discussions with managers as well as the job-holder. Reid and Barrington (1994: 253) also note the value of self-observation as a technique for identifying training needs at the job level, and in some respects this is one of the best ways to determine precisely what the job entails. But, they note, there are also problems with this methodology, as individuals may be too close to their jobs to identify training needs effectively, they may not keep an accurate record of events during the course of the day, and indeed they may over-emphasise certain aspects of the job which they enjoy or dislike in order to gain training. There is also the problem that confusions arise between training needs which are identified for the *job*, irrespective of who undertakes it, and those which relate to the *person* who is currently in the post.

> Identify the training needs for a colleague's job and prepare a training needs analysis, including organisational considerations as well.

The final stage is a person-level analysis, which has some similarities with the methods discussed above. Bramley (1991: 13–14), for example, advocates the use of interviews and questionnaires, observation and work sampling, and testing the knowledge of job-holders on specific issues. In addition, he suggests the use of performance appraisal and assessment centres for identifying development needs rather than for selection purposes. Harrison (1992: 303) regards appraisal as 'at the heart of training and development', which is true, but it is also at the heart of other aspects of P&D, where it has quite different connotations. Holden and Livian (1992: 17), in their review of training and development in ten European countries, note that in Britain appraisal is the most important method for analysing training needs, rating much higher than analyses of business plans, line management requests and training audits. Both appraisal and assessment centres have already been considered in earlier chapters (see Chapter 6 for an analysis of assessment centres as part of the selection process, and Chapter 7 for an analysis of appraisal as a key element in performance management), so here we focus on the issues which are particularly applicable to the identification of training needs.

The key point is one of purpose; appraisal and assessment centres are used in training to identify *development* needs whereas in performance management or selection, they tend to be used as part of an *assessment* process. When appraisal is part of performance management, it is often linked with reward packages and levels, with future promotion opportunities, or with disciplinary matters. Understandably in situations such as this, job-holders may treat the appraisal interview as an opportunity to impress their supervisor if it is linked with payment or upgrading, or to withhold information if it is part of the disciplinary process. In these situations employees are likely to be fully aware of the power imbalance in the employment relationship, and 'use' information to further their own cause. Appraisals which are conducted under these circumstances are unlikely to unearth training needs which can lead to improvements in customer service or product quality.

Conversely, when appraisal is part of a development initiative and is conducted with this as its clear purpose – as in an organisation which purports to operate with a 'blame-free' environment, for example – then the whole process is likely to be more open. If employees are encouraged to acknowledge that there are areas of their work which are not being performed at full capacity, or with inadequate knowledge or skills, then appraisal interviews may help to identify important training and development needs. Harrison (1992: 303–304) stresses that if appraisal is to succeed as part of training and development, four conditions must apply in the appraiser–appraisee relationship:

- a shared perception of the purpose and value of the discussion, and a shared commitment to its objectives

- mutual learning and understanding, and a willingness to learn from each other

- avoidance of any tendency to blame or judge the appraisee, and a preparedness to be supportive

- an accurate diagnosis of learning needs, and an agreed plan of action, monitoring and review.

Training is most likely to be effective, according to Fairbairns (1991: 45), when three conditions apply, and a training needs analysis is conducted using the 'three circle' model. The three conditions are: training is seen as important for the future; there is a need for training to meet individual job and development goals; and there is a likelihood of recognition or reward by the organisation. In many cases, she argues, the last condition is left unmet, and employers express surprise that training has made such a limited impact on the organisation. For training to be truly effective, it needs to receive a positive reception at the workplace and trainees need to feel that the training has been worthwhile and can be incorporated into future plans and actions. Too often, of course, individuals return from a training programme full of ideas, only to encounter blockages and barriers within the organisation, and suspicion or derision from workmates.

DEVISING A LEARNING PLAN

The traditional approach to devising training plans focuses on the need to determine clear aims and objectives which are relevant to the learners concerned and enable the performance gap to be bridged. Both Harrison (1992: 331) and Arnold et al (1991: 251) make similar distinctions between aims and objectives in the devising of learning programmes: aims are expressions of general intent, such as 'to grasp the basic principles of x' or 'to be aware of the influence of y on z', and they make no attempt to specify measurable outcomes. Objectives, on the other hand, are more precise, giving a clear focus for the learning in terms of competencies, abilities, or understanding at the end of the training event. Harrison (1992: 331) suggests that 'The most helpful behavioural objectives are those which describe not only the kinds of behaviour to be achieved at the end of the learning event, but also the conditions under which that behaviour is expected to occur and the standards to be reached in that behaviour.' The expression of standards in the IPD Professional Qualifications, for example, is phrased in terms of learning outcomes (objectives) with a broad statement about each of the modules (aims).

A major feature to consider when devising learning plans is the characteristics of the trainees themselves, and the 'baggage' which they bring with them to the learning event; their prior knowledge, skills, attitudes, motivations and expectations. Trainees may well differ in terms of their level of educational achievement, their attitudes towards learning, their ability to absorb new ideas or maintain concentration, their team working skills, and so on (Jenkins D, 1983: 221–222). They are likely to have very diverse sets of reasons for being involved in the learning event, just as students do on degree programmes. Some may be there because they enjoy learning, while others have a clear instrumental purpose, such as to enhance their chances of promotion. Yet others may attend a formal training programme because it is deemed to be their turn, or because a colleague dropped out at the last minute. Some may be there under duress, determined to put little effort into the sessions, and keen to demonstrate their lack of interest at every possible opportunity. There may also be variations in the extent to which trainees have been briefed beforehand about the learning event or in the amount of preparation which has been undertaken before the workshop gets under way, for example. In order to be effective, and for learning to transfer back to the workplace, training and development has to be embedded in the norms and cultures of the organisation involved. This is particularly important with off-the-job training and with longer courses.

Obviously it is important to establish the aims and objectives for a learning event, and to take into account factors which influence the choice of training methods to be employed – such as the characteristics of the learners, and their motives for attending training sessions. But for effective learning to occur it is also crucial that P&D professionals gain agreement for their recommendations from key decision-takers, and that this learning is located in its organisational context. Unfortunately, this *political* dimension to training is often overlooked in publications which concentrate on the theoretical bases of learning and development, on ensuring that course content matches with outcomes, and that training is designed logically and sequentially.

As we saw above, the second part of the N/SVQ Level 4 in human resource development is the planning and design of training, with the core module being to 'devise a plan for implementing an organisation's training and development objectives'. This focuses, *inter alia*, on issues concerned with gaining agreement and support from key managers, on dealing with negative reactions to training, and on the costs and benefits of training interventions. In other words, it recognises that there is more to training than choices about the most appropriate methods for establishing training needs or learning techniques.

Regardless of the technical quality of training plans, without senior management support to resource and champion the initiative it will prove worthless. As Moorby (1992: 20) stresses, 'To succeed with approaches to employee development, it is essential to form a realistic view of what those who hold the power in an organisation will support, and then to match the strategy adopted to reflect this.' Once it is acknowledged that employee development managers have only limited power, the key objective is to gain the support of those senior managers who control expenditure, and to be aware of their motives and priorities even if these appear less suitable and more expensive than one's own solutions. Moorby (1992: 25) argues that there are six steps in this process:

- identify the key players in the employee development area, and those who influence the success or failure of initiatives

- assess the importance of employee development in helping these key players to achieve their objectives

- assess the degree of support from these players

- estimate the strength of skill and knowledge of employee development for each player

- identify the political implications for each player

- estimate future posture and actions for each player.

> Apply this six-step process to an employee development initiative relevant to your own organisation, and assess whether or not it helps you to sharpen up your approach.

An awareness of costs and benefits is a key feature in gaining agreement for training interventions, and it is one in which P&D practitioners are not always well versed. This is especially the case when costings are concerned. It is relatively easy to reel off a list of general benefits from training, especially those which relate to other aspects of P&D. Such a list might include (Reid and Barrington, 1994: 132–133):

- training helps new staff to learn jobs more quickly

- trained staff are less likely to make costly errors or to have accidents at work

- an organisation with a reputation for training may find it easier to recruit high-quality staff

- trained workers are likely to be more flexible and able to undertake a range of jobs

- trained employees may be more committed to the organisation and less likely to leave for other jobs

- training can help to focus employee attention on how to achieve high levels of quality and customer service.

It is somewhat harder to demonstrate unequivocally that training has a *direct and measurable* impact on organisational performance levels, although this does not stop people making the claim; for example, Moorby (1992: 72) suggests that measures might include an increase in market share from x to y, an improvement in sales per square metre from £a to £b, or that 95 per cent of trains will arrive within five minutes of published time. Ever the pragmatist, he notes that 'careful examination of the business plan and listening to senior managers who are oriented towards performance measurement will provide clues as to what they are prepared to buy'! But it might prove difficult to sell these solutions on more than one occasion, or to convince senior managers who want to have 'hard' estimates of costs and benefits.

Costs are easier to determine, although much depends on the items to be included in the equation (Bee and Bee, 1994: 162–163). First, there are overhead or fixed costs such as permanent accommodation or training equipment, as well as standard charges for heating and lighting, and managerial and administrative salaries. Obviously these account for a much higher proportion of costs in an organisation with its own training centre than for one which subcontracts all or most of its training activities. The second item is fixed costs which are allocated over the lifetime of a training programme, such as the salaries and on-costs of trainers and/or consultants employed in organising and managing the training and development activity. Included in this would also be the cost of developing training materials, as well as evaluation tools. Finally, there are direct or variable costs, which vary according to the amount of training which is undertaken, and include the costs of trainers and one-off speakers, travel and residential costs, costs of duplicated training materials, and so on. It is more difficult to decide whether or not to include the costs of delegates in the figures, either as a pro rata element of their wage and salary bill or the costs of replacements.

Costing is not altogether straightforward, however, as Reid and Barrington (1994: 135) show with their distinction between *learning* costs and *training* costs. The former is the cost to the organisation of learning how to do the job through an unplanned and unstructured approach to development. Learning costs include things such as payments to employees when learning on-the-job, the costs of wasted materials or rejected products due to less-than-competent employees, or the time which supervisors and other employees spend in correcting mistakes or dealing with problems caused by untrained staff. Training costs, on the other hand, are specifically identifiable, as the above list shows. In other words, to consider the costs of training fully we also need to be aware of the costs of *not training*, of relying on informal and *ad hoc* methods for improving performance.

It is also important to make comparisons with the amount spent by other organisations on training and development. We have already seen in Chapter 3 how employers in Britain spend relatively little on training compared with many of their foreign competitors, but comparisons should also be made with similar types of organisations in the same sector or area of the country. If figures are low, this information may prove helpful to the employee development manager who is seeking to justify training expenditure, or if comparisons are favourable it may prove helpful in public relations terms. Benchmarking is just as useful in the training field as it is in all the other areas of P&D activity.

How much does training cost your organisation, and how does it compare with other organisations' costs, either in the same sector or in the same area of the country? How can this information be used to make your training and development activity more effective?

A REVIEW OF TRAINING METHODS

There is a multitude of methods which can be used to train and develop staff, both on- and off-the-job, ranging from the relatively unstructured and informal – such as 'sitting by Nellie' – through to the carefully programmed and structured – such as computer-assisted learning and project management. Most texts on the subject provide lists of different methods, their nature and meaning, their advantages and shortcomings (see, for example, Reid and Barrington, 1994: 399-409). While useful at one level, these lists are lacking in two respects. First, they are not organised into any coherent conceptual framework which differentiates between techniques according to learning principles or the characteristics of the learning situation. This makes it difficult for readers to 'locate' different methods within a structure, and to recall them, other than as a list which is to be regurgitated parrot-fashion in an examination. The second problem is that while the lists describe concisely the key features of different methods, as well as outlining their major advantages and disadvantages, there is little attempt to identify the conditions under which particular techniques may be appropriate for facilitating effective learning.

Therefore it is important to recognise that no one method is inherently superior to any other, but that different methods are suitable for different sets of circumstances. Choosing when to employ the right methods, and why, is a much more critical consideration than being able to note the advantages and disadvantages of each method in the abstract. While the lecture may be inappropriate for most training situations, it may be the ideal technique for a newly-appointed marketing director to open the annual sales conference and so set the tone for the detailed sessions which follow. Conversely, computer-based training can be very effective for reinforcing basic language skills but it offers rather less towards the development of team working and group problem-solving.

Rather than produce yet another list, we analyse training methods in four distinct categories, differentiated according to the main approach which is adopted, and whether the training is individual or group-based. Snape *et al* (1994: 73) make the distinction between *andragogical* and *pedagogical* approaches to training and development. The former, more accurately titled 'auto-didactic', is essentially self-directed and participative, with the trainer providing a facilitative or supportive role. The latter, by contrast, is largely trainer-driven and allows little room for student input into the learning situation. The second distinction is between individual and group-based training. This categorisation is illustrated in Figure 8, with an example of each type of training for illustrative purposes; this forms the basis for the remainder of the section.

Figure 8 Categories of training methods

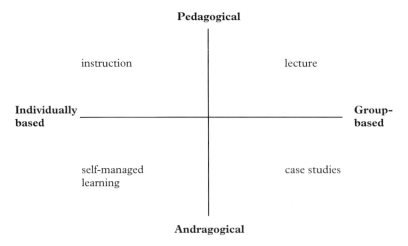

The top left-hand quadrant includes methods which are principally pedagogically-oriented and individually-based, such as one-to-one instructional techniques and simulations. These are particularly useful for the acquisition of standard programmable skills, for the transfer of routine information and ways of working, but those which also require practice and application in real-life situations. This can cover the extremes of the scale in terms of traditional job levels. At one extreme might be simulators for pilots in the early stages of training when they need to learn basic operating rules and principles in order to ensure the safe carriage of passengers or freight. At the other extreme would be the basic stages of an assembly operation or the standard training in customer care which is given to checkout operators in supermarkets. The major point behind these techniques is that there is seen to be no room for discretion or creativity, or for employee input into the choice of how to serve customers, fix together parts of a piece of equipment, or land planes safely. Of course, once employees actually start to do the work themselves and become more experienced there may be much more room for manoeuvre, or for the use of initiative in an emergency.

The basic principles of these kinds of training intervention are of the 'tell-show-do-review' variety, in which skills, knowledge and operating routines are transferred progressively to trainees until they have mastered the task. The trainer decides how quickly to move to a position of trust when he or she feels that the trainee has acquired sufficient skills and knowledge, and has demonstrated competence in them, to feel confident that the trainee can progress to the next stage of the instruction process. There is no room for vagueness or confusion in the instruction, especially if it relates to a task which can have serious health or safety consequences if it is done wrong. On the other hand, instructing staff to follow established routines can lead to motivational problems if the employees concerned feel that they already have the required skills or they do not share senior management's commitment to them. As we shall see in the next chapter, this has sometimes been a source of annoyance for staff in customer service organisations who feel sceptical about the messages which they are being told to convey.

The top right-hand quadrant includes methods which are pedagogically and group-based, such as lectures, presentations and videos, and these are particularly appropriate in situations when a large number of people need to be given information at the same time, or it is cost-effective to deliver training in this way. Most learners have been subjected to lectures at some times during the lives, and are often fully aware that there are limits to the amount that can be retained during a session; estimates vary, but it is reckoned that less than a quarter of what is said is recalled, and the maximum concentration span is typically less than 20 minutes. Given that many lecturers have not received professional training in how to deliver lectures, and many more seem incapable of conveying information or ideas, let alone enthusing their learners, it is to be wondered why this technique is still practised so widely. But it is a cost-effective way of providing information, at least to the extent of class contact hours, although whether or not it represents a cost-effective way of learning is another matter. On the other hand, most of us will have listened to an individual speak for an hour or more at a conference or in higher education, and have been enthralled by what he or she said. Management gurus such as Rosabeth Moss Kanter are renowned for keeping audiences transfixed for a couple of hours without interruption and with very little in the way of visual aids. But for most lecturers it is essential to use overhead projections or slides, distribute short summaries of the lecture, and litter the talk with examples and anecdotes to ensure that some retention takes place. Enthusiasm and knowledge of the subject matter are also seen as essential, as is an awareness of learner needs, an ability to present information in a clear and concise manner, and a recognition that tone and cadence need to vary to maintain attention.

One of the major problems with lectures and presentations is that they are often used inappropriately, for example to transmit information which can more easily be distributed as written documents or videos. The latter are now rather more common as teaching aids, and can provide a useful interlude in the training programme, and a change of technology to facilitate learning. But there are also dangers with videos as well; they have to be chosen carefully to ensure that they are specifically directed at the issue in hand; they need to be realistic and relevant, and they need to be contextualised in the programme with specific learning outcomes attached to them. Given that watching videos is a passive exercise, and it allows for connotations with leisure and relaxation at home, it is possible that the benefits gained in enjoyment and acceptability may be lost in a lack of effective learning.

Choose what you think has been a successful lecture, or feel to be a good lecturer, and identify the attributes of both which have led to that evaluation. Can they be taught to other people? Why/why not?

The bottom right-hand quadrant is the andragogical/group-based category, which includes case studies, projects, group role-playing exercises (such as in a negotiating exercise), and business games, some of which are managed through the use of computerised models. The basic point about this set of techniques is that they are essentially team-oriented and allow the group to propose their own solutions and ideas to problems with a minimum of trainer intervention during the process. The job of the trainer is to support the team, help it to arrive at conclusions, and generally facilitate the process of learning through a sharing of ideas. In effect, learning should take place through a process of *induction,* in which examples and incidents are generalised to arrive at a better understanding of the principles and processes which underpin management issues. This set of methods allows for the development of a number of the core competencies we have considered in previous chapters as being central to any manager's job: decision-making, planning and time management, drive and persistence, ability to work under pressure, oral and written communication, flexibility and adaptability, self-confidence and persuasiveness. In the case of projects that are initiated during a formal training course, but which are then continued back at work, other skills are developed as well, especially the ability to persuade senior managers that the project is worthy of time and effort.

Case studies provide a good avenue for 'real-life' problem-solving, for working out solutions in teams, and for presenting recommendations to other people. Like any other training technique, they need to be well-managed, have clear learning outcomes associated with them, and be relevant to the needs and abilities of the trainees. They need to be of an appropriate length and degree of difficulty for the student group, as well as containing sufficient information and enough flexibility to allow for competing solutions between different teams (Jenkins D, 1983: 231). The case study can also prove problematic as well. There are dangers that individuals who are working together in a team may come into conflict, or that one or more individuals will dominate discussion in a way that excludes others and may lead to unsatisfactory solutions. Some trainees undoubtedly feel dissatisfied with the amount of information provided by the trainer, either becoming stressed because they feel that there is too much to analyse in the time provided, or insecure because they reckon there is too little to make a recommendation.

The final set of methods is the individually-based self-directed category, and this is where the use of computer-based training (CBT) has come to the fore in recent years. This group includes language laboratories, computer-assisted learning, and role-plays of individual employee relations issues – such as grievance and disciplinary interviews. Perhaps the principal point about these forms of training is that they are typically self-managed and can be undertaken at a pace, time and possibly location which is suitable for the individual concerned. With increased access to electronic media, both at work and at home, and new generations of computers which use artificial intelligence to interact with learners, the opportunities for this type of training are considerable. This set of techniques has the major advantage of being responsive to individual needs in a way which allows for a better fit between learning and domestic or work commitments. The self-management of learning is especially appropriate for the acquisition of impersonal techniques (such as accounting or computing), the development and reinforcement of basic language skills, and for gathering information for reports. Although these techniques have been used for interpersonal skills training (Snape *et al*, 1994: 74), it is unlikely that their use will become extensive given the importance of face-to-face contact for improving these skills. In this sort of situation, individual role-playing (either with a colleague or friend/partner) offers a much better route to improved competency and confidence in coping with an aggressive senior manager or in counselling a poor performer.

> Next time you are confronted with an aggressive boss or a member of staff whose performance is not satisfactory, try role-playing the encounter in advance with a friend or partner. Obviously, you will need to brief them well first and be totally open about the issue, but assess how it has improved your performance. What did you learn from it?

EVALUATING THE EFFECTIVENESS OF THE TRAINING PROCESS

It is widely acknowledged that the evaluation of training is one of the most critical steps in the process, and it is one which is frequently not done in any comprehensive or systematic fashion. Although Holden and Livian (1992: 17) found that 84 per cent of the UK employers in their survey claimed to monitor the effectiveness of training (incidentally, a figure higher than for any of the other nine European countries investigated), the method of evaluation most commonly used was informal feedback from line managers and trainees; this was used twice as often as tests, and much more regularly than formal evaluations conducted some time after the training had been completed. In other words, as with many other aspects of P&D, the extent of formal and systematic evaluation is limited.

Perhaps this is why the Training and Development Lead Body has placed such a strong emphasis on evaluation in its N/SVQ Level 4 standards for human resource development. As we saw earlier in the chapter, of the seven core areas of competence which are specified, four of these relate to evaluation. The elements and performance criteria include: selecting methods for evaluating training and development programmes; being clear about the purpose and scope of evaluation, and the criteria against which judgements are to be made; identifying potential improvements to programmes; evaluating their own performance and development needs, including the preparation of personal action plans; and managing relationships with colleagues and customers. P&D practitioners clearly need to be aware of the ways in which evaluation is to be carried out, as well as being able to demonstrate the value of training to broader business objectives and corporate performance.

Evaluation can take many forms, so it is important to clarify these at the outset, as well as identify the principal purposes to which it is put. Evaluation has been defined by Davies (1983: 241) as 'any attempt to obtain information (feedback) on the effects of a training programme, and to assess the value of the training in the light of that information'. The effects can be assessed at a number of levels (this is considered below) and in terms of their impact on a number of different stakeholders – not just on the trainees themselves, but also on their line managers, the organisation or department as a whole, and the trainers and designers of programmes. The effects can be assessed using a variety of instruments, such as observation of work behaviour, interviews and questionnaires, and collection of performance data. Each of these can form a valuable component in the overall evaluation of training effectiveness.

There have been several attempts to identify the major *purposes* of evaluation. Bramley and Newby (1984: 11–13) put forward five major reasons for conducting an evaluation of training effectiveness. First, it provides feedback for the trainers and the trainees, in terms of the design and relevance of the course or in the achievement of individual learning objectives. Second, it enables organisations to establish whether or not training offers a more cost-effective and relevant solution to problems than other P&D actions such as recruitment or dismissal. Third, it serves a valuable research purpose, for example in identifying the factors which help people to transfer learning back into the workplace. Fourth, it can be used as a form of organisational intervention which triggers reappraisal of existing approaches, criteria and policies relating to training. Finally, evaluation in 'real' organisations becomes part of a political process, a 'power game' in which different factions within management use the results of training exercises to gain approval for their ideas; in this process, outside consultants and academics may prove to be unwitting pawns in an internal struggle between departments or managers.

Easterby-Smith and Mackness (1992: 43) identify four purposes for evaluation, to some extent based on their work with a government department which was introducing a new computerised system. These are *proving* that a course has particular outcomes and consequences, *improving* the quality of courses by using data from the evaluation exercise, *learning* to help trainees sharpen up on what has been gained from the course, and *control* of how the training or educational initiative is implemented. Each of these purposes has relevance for different stakeholders in the training process.

Finally, the Bees (1994: 174) and Reid and Barrington (1994: 291–92) suggest a number of reasons why the evaluation of training is necessary in organisations. Some of these are similar to those already mentioned above, such as improving the quality and effectiveness of training courses, giving feedback to trainers to help them improve their performance, justifying the courses and the expenditure on them, and finally acting as a contribution to the learning process. Reid and Barrington also point out that evaluation should be part of the learning cycle, not only in causing trainees to reflect on what has been learned, but also in assisting them and their managers to identify future training and development needs.

> Given your own experience of training and development, what do you feel is its major purpose? What do you think of the view that evaluation may be part of a wider power game within organisations?

Once we have established why evaluation is being undertaken, it should then be possible to determine what should be evaluated, and when and how it might be done. Most ideas in this area stem from the work of Kirkpatrick (1967), who differentiated between four levels of evaluation: reaction, immediate, intermediate, and ultimate. Although each of these is considered in turn, it is important to recognise that evaluation at *all* levels needs to be undertaken in order to form a full picture of training effectiveness – the 'circle of evaluation' as Davies (1983: 243) terms it. Of course, the most important level of evaluation may differ according to the circumstances and the needs of the stakeholders. For example, while trainers may be more interested in how well they are performing in front of the group, the finance director may be more concerned about the cost-effectiveness of training programmes, and the departmental manager may be keen to assess the precise impact of training on job performance.

The *reaction* level is the one most commonly used during or at the end of courses, and it is often termed the 'smile sheet' since it assesses the performance of trainers in both absolute and relative terms. This form of evaluation aims to establish the views of one stakeholder, the trainees themselves, about the training event, and these judgements are particularly relevant for assessing the adequacy of facilities and organisation. Views are typically elicited through short questionnaires, filled in at the end of training or soon after it has been completed. The views of trainees can be highly useful to trainers, provided the latter see them as valuable and are prepared and able to act upon them.

Evaluations at the reaction level have recently become more widespread throughout the British higher education system, as departments are assessed on the quality of their teaching, and lecturers find they need to produce evidence of how well or badly they are performing in the classroom in order to be considered for promotion. It is a system which is well-established in North America, and has long been used on management courses, but it is a much newer development for undergraduate programmes. The concerns which are expressed generally about 'smile sheets' find resonance here, as a whole series of anxieties emerge about their use. There are worries that trainees (in this case, students) merely react to the quality of the performance, the lecturer's ability to maintain surface-level interest or tell jokes to the class, so setting up expectations amongst both parties which may be of dubious educational merit. There are also doubts about the students' ability to evaluate the lecture in its wider context, as part of a broader educational programme or for its relevance to future performance in work (Reid and Barrington, 1994: 295). Indeed, it might be argued that there is no reason why positive reaction-level assessments should provide any indicator of subsequent job performance and the transfer of learning into the workplace.

Secondly, there is the *immediate* level of evaluation, which attempts to measure directly the extent to which training objectives have been achieved, in terms of knowledge, skills and attitudes. The Bees (1994) produce a series of alternative questionnaires which can be used to assess whether or not these standards have been achieved following the completion of a disciplinary skills training course. The alternatives are:

- a list of true/false statements (such as 'the sole purpose of discipline is punishment')

- a forced-choice questionnaire where trainees must select one answer from three or four options (such as 'The main purpose of discipline is: a) punishment, b) teaching a lesson, c) improved performance, and d) don't know')

- a series of questions which require short five-minute length answers, such as 'What information should be included in the record of the disciplinary hearing?'

Of course, the last of these options now forms one part of the final examination assessment portfolio in the IPD's Professional Qualification Scheme. Although forced-choice or true/false questions attract a lot of interest from certain quarters, and are seen by some to be eminently superior to essays or more open questions (Bramley, 1992: 42), there are also problems with these as well. They guide the student towards an answer by providing signposts and parameters which are typically lacking in a management environment; in industry and commerce, for example, employees (and especially professionals) are asked for answers to *general* questions and problems (for example, what should we do about x?), which are then translated into terms of reference which guide subsequent activity. Managers are not usually provided with a series of forced-choice options, and asked to indicate which represents the best solution, but instead to come to that judgement after researching the issue. Indeed, this is probably the best way to encourage creativity in organisations which preach continuous improvement and empowerment.

> List the ethical and professional issues associated with evaluation at these first two levels, as they affect both trainers and trainees.

The third level of evaluation is the *intermediate*. This refers to the impact of training on job performance and how effectively learning has been transferred back into the workplace. As the Bees (1994: 233) note, there is little point engaging in training if transfer does not take place, unless of course the objective of the programme is merely to keep employees away from work! But evaluation at this level is much less common than at the first two levels, in many cases because it is harder to undertake but also due to the problem of isolating the impact of training from the effect of other variables. Intermediate-level evaluation takes many forms, including interviews, self-report questionnaires, diaries, and observation. The latter technique may be effective for evaluating the transfer of technical skills (such as changing the wheel on a car), but may be more difficult to assess the extent of changes in time-management skills when a diary or a series of verifiable outputs might provide better data. For interpersonal skills a mixture of observation and self-reporting may be the most useful approach, given that part of the training objective is to encourage greater self-awareness of how relationships are handled. Evaluating the impact of training on a manager who has been accused of bullying may be even more difficult to determine, especially if victims lack the confidence to report incidents, or the manager concerned refuses to recognise that he or she has a problem. The chances of successful evaluation can be enhanced by a clear statement of objectives for the training, consultation with all those involved, and a careful design and testing of assessment instruments (Bee and Bee, 1994: 244).

Finally, there is *ultimate*-level evaluation, which attempts to assess the impact of training on departmental or organisational performance, and on the individual's total job; the distinction here between intermediate- and ultimate-level evaluation is somewhat blurred, but the former usually refers to performance in a particular *task or set of tasks* for which training has been provided, whereas the latter evaluates the impact of training on overall *results*. The best indicators for ultimate-level evaluation obviously vary enormously depending upon what are deemed to be key performance criteria, but typical examples would be:

- number of customer complaints

- levels of sales

- productivity levels

- number of rejects

- number of accidents

- number of lost industrial tribunal cases

- level of unauthorised absenteeism

- proportion of letters answered within two days

- number of students submitting work on time

- amount of labour turnover during probation period.

As the name implies, ultimate-level evaluation is the most difficult of all to measure and therefore to determine the precise impact of training on performance. In some situations there may be no clear and simple measures to employ, or data may not be collected in a form which allows for evaluation to take place. There are many factors other than training which could affect the measure, especially at higher levels in the organisation when external influences can have a significant impact (for example, the influence of unemployment on labour turnover). In addition, only a small proportion of staff within a department or establishment might have been trained, and although *their* performance may have improved this would have relatively little effect on results. For many analysts, training interventions which can be shown to have an impact at the ultimate level are what really matters, but Rainbird and Maguire (1993: 37) rightly point out that there are dangers in becoming obsessed with organisational needs to the neglect of those relating to personal development. As we saw in the previous chapter, learning organisations attempt to satisfy both these demands at the same time. We return to the issue of how P&D managers add value to the organisation in the final section of the book, when we consider horizontal and vertical integration in more detail.

CONCLUSION

In this chapter we have stressed the importance of having a systematic and well-organised structure for managing training and development in organisations. Although there are a number of models and frameworks which can be used for this, each covers broadly the same cycle: identifying training needs, devising plans, delivery, and evaluation. It is worth reiterating that there is no single best approach to training interventions since the most suitable method depends on the purpose of the training, its subject matter, the size of the audience, and the finance which is available for the programme. Instead, P&D practitioners need to be able to choose the approach that is most appropriate for the specific circumstances in which the training is to be undertaken. At the same time, however, a thorough evaluation of training is critical, especially in assessing transfer back to the workplace for courses which take place off-the-job. This forms the centrepiece of the final chapter in the Employee Development section of the book.

USEFUL READING

BEE, R. AND BEE, F. (1994) *Training Needs Analysis and Evaluation*. London, IPD.

BRAMLEY, P. (1991) *Evaluating Training Effectiveness: Translating theory into practice*. Maidenhead, McGraw Hill.

EASTERBY-SMITH, M. AND MACKNESS, J. (1992) 'Completing the cycle of evaluation', *Personnel Management*, May: 1 42–45.

FAIRBAIRNS, J. (1991) 'Plugging the gap in training needs analysis', *Personnel Management*, February: 43–45.

HARRISON, R. (1992) *Employee Development*. London, IPD.

MOORBY, E. (1992) *How to Succeed in Employee Development: Moving from vision to results*. Maidenhead, McGraw Hill.

REID, M. AND BARRINGTON, H. (1994) *Training Interventions: Managing employee development*, Fourth Edition. London, IPD.

10 Transferring learning to the workplace

INTRODUCTION

In the previous two chapters we considered the ways in which learning takes place, both at an individual and an organisational level, and how the training and development process is managed. In these chapters we emphasised the importance of understanding the processes by which people learn, and the ways in which this may be achieved by the provision of realistic training and development policies covering the whole cycle. Transfer of learning to improve everyday workplace performance is especially critical in this respect. Not only does this require managers to have a clear set of objectives for training and development programmes, it also demands integration with wider corporate goals as well as with other aspects of P&D strategies. Too often, training courses receive highly positive ratings at the reaction and immediate levels, only to achieve little at the intermediate and ultimate levels; in other words, individuals find the courses and the learning enjoyable but are unable to make full use of what they have learned, either because it is inappropriate, or due to obstacles imposed by prevailing organisational cultures.

In this chapter we move on to examine a number of specific training, learning and development practices which are used by employers in Britain. Any of a number of practices could have been analysed, but we have chosen to focus on six which provide a range of experiences, contexts and learning methods. The six are:

- outdoor-based development programmes

- return-to-learning schemes

- negotiating skills courses for employee relations

- customer-care training

- women-only management development exercises

- computer-assisted learning.

In each case we outline the specific practices and programmes before providing some evaluation of their effectiveness in terms of transferability and impact. We do not consider how to set up these schemes, nor the specific mechanics of how they are run, as this is far too specialised and detailed for consideration in the Core Personnel and Development syllabus; issues such as these are taken up in the generalist and specialist modules in Employee Development. Instead, the aim is to provide readers with a number of examples of training, learning and development in practice which can be used as a vehicle for analysing the employee development agenda.

By the end of this chapter, readers should be able to:

- identify sources of information and expertise for specific forms of training, learning and development

- convince other managers, especially line managers, of the value of training and development programmes and learning exercises in their own organisation

- specify how skills, attitudes and knowledge acquired through development exercises may lead to improved performance at work.

In addition, readers should be able to understand and explain:

- the range of training, learning and development practices which can be used by employing organisations in Britain

- the advantages and disadvantages of specific training, learning and development activities

- the contribution of employee development to broader organisational goals.

OUTDOOR-BASED DEVELOPMENT PROGRAMMES

Outdoor-based development programmes are a relatively recent addition to the training scene, with little mention of them prior to the 1980s, except in very specific circumstances such as the Armed Forces. Since then they have grown enormously both in popularity and extent, and have been used by organisations in many different industries for developing leadership and team-working skills, especially among managerial staff. For example, a survey by Industrial Relations Services (*Employee Development Bulletin* 34, 1992) listed over 50 organisations which made use of this form of training, including the following: Glaxo, John Laing, Thomas Cook, Norweb, Vickers, Royal Bank of Scotland, Continental Can, and Gardner Merchant. At the same time outdoor-based development programmes have been castigated as little more than a fad or fashion with limited application to commercial situations or, more seriously, unsafe and potentially dangerous. In a small number of cases this may be accurate but, if used properly and managed by experienced and qualified trainers, outdoor-based development can offer a highly effective tool for improving managerial performance.

It is important to recognise that outdoor-based development is more than 'training outdoors', in which participants are confronted with a range of exercises and problems which need to be resolved within a set period of time. A key feature of outdoor-based development is that it is rooted in experiential learning theories, such as that of Kolb *et al* (1995) which was discussed in Chapter 8. In addition, active participation in outdoor exercises may form less than half of all the time that is devoted to the development programme, and members are required to reflect upon their experiences in order to draw out learning points which are likely to be relevant to workplace problems and issues. Moreover, those who design and administer programmes need to be acutely aware of the composition of their groups, the prevailing organisational cultures, and the limits to which individuals can be stretched. As Tuson (1994: 2–3) notes, it is important to understand the differences between the 'comfort zone', the 'challenge zone' and the 'panic zone', and that very little effective learning will take place in the last of these zones. As stress levels rise and we move from the comfort zone into the challenge zone, the potential for learning and creativity increases, only to deteriorate rapidly when panic sets in. The safety of participants is paramount in the design of these types of programme, and one which all reputable providers should be able to guarantee, especially when the exercises involve physical activities such as abseiling, rock climbing, orienteering and canoeing. The key point about outdoor-based development, however, is that although the tasks are not 'normal' in the sense of being part of the everyday life of the managers concerned, they are nevertheless 'real' in that the results of their actions are immediately apparent, providing clear evidence of their performance (Lowe, 1992: 46).

The types of skills which outdoor-based programmes are intended to develop look rather like any other set of generic management competencies. Combining the lists provided by IRS (1992: 4), Hogg (1988), and Tuson (1994: 13–17), five of these seem to be central. *Leadership skills* are a major focus of these programmes, in that individuals are encouraged to take the initiative for coping with unusual situations, especially if there is no designated leader for the group. Clearly connected with this are concepts such as motivation, delegation and effective communication. *Team working skills* are developed through taking part in exercises which are not based around typical work exercises, thus giving individuals the opportunity to occupy different roles from those which dominate their work situation. Accordingly, leaders may be able to play a supporting role and learn better how this might be achieved, while juniors may have leadership thrust upon them, or feel confident away from the workplace to lead their more senior colleagues. Co-operation with other team members is also necessary to enable the achievement of most tasks, and this may help to build trust among work groups which can be transferred back to the workplace; as one of the supervisors in Lowe's study commented about a colleague, 'because I learnt how he ticked, I learnt how to get the best out of him' (1992: 54). *Problem-solving and creativity* are enhanced as individuals and teams learn how to cope with difficult situations, and look for alternative types of solution. In a sense, unimpeded by organisational norms, rules and traditions of what is the best way to resolve problems, participants are forced back on to first principles and encouraged to find new ways of looking at problems. Various *personal competencies* – such as time management, coping with stress, planning and decision-making – are also facilitated by outdoor-based courses, especially if teams are put into previously unknown situations or are required to meet deadlines for the completion of a task. Employees who are not renowned for displaying certain skills at work may suddenly be seen in a new light on these courses, and find that they go back to the workplace much more confident of their abilities and potential contribution. Finally, outdoor-based courses can help individuals to be more *self-aware and self-confident*, more at ease with themselves and aware of their impact on other people. For managers who are keen to engage in CPD and are actively searching for ways to improve their performance at work (and outside of work), these courses may provide an ideal vehicle for critical self-appraisal and realising limitations in their performance, as well as ways to tackle obstacles and problems.

This is a list of the benefits which outdoor-based development might offer to organisations, but what does it actually achieve in practice? Respondents to the IRS (1992: 4) survey felt that leadership and team-building were the skills which were most commonly developed on these courses, followed by interpersonal skills, problem-solving, planning, decision-making, self-confidence and self-awareness. Much less important in the survey were time management, assertiveness, networking and risk-taking. Nevertheless, about two-thirds of the sample organisations felt that these courses had been very effective, with less than 5 per cent assessing outdoor-based development as ineffective (1992: 6). Lowe (1992: 51) reports that all but one of the 41 participants in his study felt that the programme had a significant positive impact at the reaction level, with many viewing it as one of the most important development activities ever undertaken by the company. The impact on their job behaviour and the organisation as a whole was much less impressive, however. Just under half the participants reckoned the course had a significant impact on their behaviour, with about 20 per cent estimating it had made no impact; remember that this survey tested *perceptions* rather than changes in actual and observable behaviour. Well over half the sample felt it had made no impact at all on the organisation.

This highlights one of the major problems with any employee development activity, but especially those which are conducted away from the workplace and involve only a limited proportion of employees. In the case of the company analysed by Lowe the courses were voluntary, which inevitably meant that some of the more sceptical supervisors did not attend, and they felt even more defensive after the others had returned from the course in such a positive frame of mind about their time away. Moreover, attendance on the course was drawn principally from supervisors and production managers, and no one from senior management took part in the exercise. Both these factors limited the possibility of transference back to the workplace, and supervisors complained that the organisation was as 'unchanged and immobile as ever' (1992: 56).

While this may be a common reaction to off-the-job training courses, there are other concerns which are particularly apposite to outdoor-based development programmes. There are dangers that the participants become so involved in the physical exercises that they forget what the course is supposed to achieve. Given that exercises are so obviously removed from the workplace context, leaders need to be particularly skilled in helping participants to see the relevance of what they are doing and seek to transfer learning back to the workplace – as opposed to seeing the course solely as 'good fun', important though that may be for team development. In addition, some individuals find great difficulty coping with the physical activities due to their state of health, or are scared by some of the situations into which they are placed; although likely to be less at risk when abseiling down a rock face or jumping into the sea from five metres under experienced supervision than they are when driving to and from work, for some individuals this can feel like the panic zone rather than a challenge. There are also arguments that outdoor-based development programmes may be discriminatory against women on the grounds of physical stamina or that the exercises tend to reinforce male-bonding. Interestingly, several of the respondents to the IRS survey who had abandoned this form of development pointed to its negative impact on women or staff with health problems (1992: 8). But most respondents to the survey stated that they were not convinced of the effectiveness of outdoor-based programmes, given the high cost per delegate.

It is important to stress, however, that outdoor-based development programmes vary enormously, and while some are very poor indeed others offer genuine and transferable learning, as well as being good fun. Drawing on the experience of a number of organisations as well as an IRS survey (*Employee Development Bulletin* 14, 1991: 9) it should be noted that several ground rules are important to increase the chances of successful programmes. Broadly, these relate to:

- integration with other training activity and with organisational goals

- clear and achievable objectives which are monitored and relate back to the workplace; these need to be established in conjunction with the outdoor trainers

- rigorous checks on safety offered by providers

- tutors and trainers who are skilled at undertaking on-going reviews of the courses, both of a structured and unstructured nature

- programmes tailored to individual and company needs

- a sense of ownership on the part of the delegates.

> Prepare the outline of a case to line managers in your organisation which aims to persuade them that it would be cost-effective to send their staff on outdoor-based development programmes.

RETURN-TO-LEARNING SCHEMES

It has been acknowledged for years that the level of educational qualifications held by British employees is lower than that of many of their European counterparts. As we described in Chapter 3, there has been a series of initiatives nationally in recent years to tackle this problem, not least by redesigning academic/vocational qualifications for school pupils, and by encouraging an increase in the number of students attending higher and further education post-18. In addition to governmental responses, some employers have also taken action to increase the likelihood of their staff returning to learn.

Probably the best known of these initiatives is the Ford Employee Development and Assistance Programme (EDAP), a concept which was first mooted in Britain during the 1987 national pay negotiations following a long discussion about vocational training. John Hougham (then personnel director at the company) proposed that the company would fund non-job-related training without having any clear ideas about what this would entail or how it would be managed (Hougham, Thomas and Sisson, 1991: 81–82). A scheme with a similar name had been running at Ford in the USA for some years, but the rationale for the British initiative was continuing development for staff who were to remain employed by the company, rather than to help redundant workers increase their employability. As Ken Mortimer (1990: 309), then manager of education and training at the company, notes, the key objective was to 'provide opportunities for personal development and training outside working hours for all employees'. Given that a large proportion of employees had left school by the age of 16 (Hougham *et al*, 1991: 79), the EDAP provided an opportunity for many to re-enter education with a different, and possibly more mature, frame of reference. Mortimer (1990: 313) stresses that a key feature of the EDAP is to create an awareness and 'desire' for continuing education and growth among employees who may have negative experiences from their time at school and are suspicious of any activity which reminds them of formal education (see Chapter 8).

There were also other reasons for embarking on the scheme, most notably with regard to employee relations, which demonstrates clearly the importance of integrating different aspects of P&D. There was an implicit understanding that the EDAP would help to produce improvements in the industrial relations climate at the company, at both national and local levels, as the unions and management became used to working more closely with each other in a non-adversarial framework. There were several features to the EDAP scheme which illustrate this move to 'jointism', and which have been reflected in other aspects of management-union relations. These are:

- that the EDAP should be administered jointly by a steering committee comprising union representatives, line and personnel managers

- that the EDAP should have national and local joint committees which are responsible for allocating funds to applicants

- that local education advisers (LEAs) should be appointed who were independent of the company and unions, who were able to provide 'neutral' advice to staff; by 1991, there were 18 of these professionals working across the company

- that all development activities should be undertaken outside of working hours, that involvement in the scheme should be voluntary, and that all training should be *unrelated* to current work activities (where existing training provisions would apply).

The EDAP is funded by the company, and obviously the money allocated (approximately £12 million between 1988 and 1994, according to IRS *Employee Development Bulletin* 68, 1995) comprises part of the overall labour costs for any one year. Each member of staff is eligible for up to £200 per annum for approved courses of study, although individuals who choose to spend their entitlement on leisure or sport activities (eg golf lessons) do not receive tax exemption. Estimates vary as to the number of employees who have taken advantage of the EDAP, but it is likely to be a majority of the workforce now. The most popular subjects for study have been health and fitness (eg aerobics), sport and leisure, languages and craft skills, and first aid training. More general academic and educational courses, such as business studies or information technology, have also proved fairly popular, as have arts, crafts and music. Many more of the courses are now run in-house at Ford sites, and some have been accredited to allow staff to gain exemption from parts of degrees or other formal qualifications offered by academic institutions or internally (eg the Halewood Bachelor of Philosophy degree).

Ford is not alone in offering these forms of employee development programme, having been followed by a number of other car manufacturers. For example, Peugeot Talbot introduced an assisted development programme (ADP) in 1991, also as a joint initiative between management and unions, which had the principal aim of directing educational opportunities towards a wider pool of employees than usually gain from such activities. Like Ford, there are joint steering committees locally and nationally, and much of the groundwork was undertaken by a local authority careers service professional. Employees receive tokens to the value of £250 for most courses, although only half of this is available if staff want to pursue leisure studies. The ADP also provides assistance for staff who have been out of education for a long time through 'return-to-learn' courses and English workshops (IRS *Employee Development Bulletin* 53, 1994). Similar initiatives have occurred at Vauxhall, Rover and Rolls-Royce Motor Cars through schemes such as 'Pathways for Personal Development'. An interesting feature of these schemes has been the major involvement of employees in their implementation and management; at Rolls-Royce, for example, the leader was an ex-trade union convenor, while at Vauxhall two employees undertook an opinion poll to identify the level of interest in an open learning initiative. The Employers' Forum for Education and Development Programmes was established in 1991 with the aim of improving the take-up of education and training opportunities, and increasing their effectiveness. This is an informal network with a core of about ten employers, and some commitment from a further twenty at the end of 1994 (IRS *Employee Development Bulletin* 60, 1994). The Forum is organised by NIACE (the National Organisation for Adult Learning).

Although car companies may have been prominent in the development of these schemes, their application has not been restricted to the motor industry alone. Since 1993 a number of companies (including Sainsbury's and Royal Mail) have introduced systems for careers guidance under the Gateways to Learning initiative. This aims to develop comprehensive local information, assessment and guidance services for adults under the auspices of the TECs. Credits are offered which can be used by individuals to buy guidance and assessment services. Sainsbury's, for example, has been at the forefront of these initiatives, viewing them as a useful device to help individuals think carefully about their future working lives, as well as about the transfer of competencies between leisure pursuits and their paid employment duties (IRS *Employee Development Bulletin* 37, 1993).

While employee development and assistance schemes are novel, it is important to ask whether they make much impact in the workplace or whether they lead to improvements in individual, team and organisational performance. Here, the evidence is rather limited. Ford management and unions are clear that the EDAP has played a major part in sustained improvement in industrial relations at the company since the early 1980s, and it has served as an emblem of the new 'partnership' approach which is built upon the enhancement of a non-adversarial approach; see Chapter 11 for more detail on these types of arrangement. The fact that managers and unions administer the scheme jointly, and that it has not become a bargaining issue, stands testimony to its success. The company reckons that the EDAP has contributed to the achievement of a more committed and flexible workforce, enhanced relationships at work, and greater self-confidence, given the shift to a new learning culture (Moore, 1994: 10). It is much harder to evaluate its contribution in quantitative terms, in relation to increases in productivity or decreases in defects, given that outputs such as these are susceptible to a range of other influences. Research by NIACE does suggest, however, that there are reductions in absenteeism and labour turnover, better relationships and a greater willingness to accept responsibility. When he was personnel director, John Hougham was quite bullish about the question of impact, arguing that unions and management should be given 'a vote of thanks' for setting up a scheme which is of benefit to the whole workforce.

> What benefits do you think can be gained from setting up an employee development programme, in which employees can opt to take courses in a wide range of activities which are not explicitly related to their jobs (eg in first aid training, learning languages, or craft skills)?

Although it may seem logical that participation in employee development schemes would lead to improvements in individual performance, at least in the long run, this has not been firmly established. Similarly, despite the obvious attractions of such schemes to employers who claim to be interested in developing a learning community, it is rather more difficult to demonstrate tangible evidence of improvements because of the EDAP. Nevertheless, a number of leading employers seem happy to continue with schemes, so there must be some advantages. On the other hand, this does not prevent line managers from enquiring about whether the benefits outweigh the costs.

NEGOTIATING SKILLS COURSES FOR EMPLOYEE RELATIONS

In one sense everybody engages in bargaining and negotiations all their lives, whether at work, in social situations, or in domestic and family relationships. We negotiate about our work loads, our contribution to the Parent–Teachers Association, and our turn to do the washing up or the ironing. In many cases individuals are unaware that they are actually involved in negotiations, but the use of precedents, comparability and sanctions confirms that that is what is taking place. Because bargaining is so commonplace, it can be viewed as an underlying trait, a set of skills which cannot be taught (or learned), and leads to assertions that negotiators are born and not made.

On the other hand, employee relations negotiating is often surrounded by a mystique which renders it inaccessible to most managers and employees. Because it is often conducted behind closed doors between highly specialised groups of people it is very difficult to observe that form of negotiation in practice. In employee relations negotiators rarely operate on their own but are usually members of teams, perhaps working in pairs when dealing with a grievance, or in large groups when faced with an annual pay claim which covers thousands of staff. Negotiations can also have a high public profile, the outcome of which may affect many constituencies way beyond the parties to a particular discussion, as for example in wage bargaining in the public sector or for a large private sector employer (such as Ford) which has a settlement date early in the annual pay round. It is critical that such negotiators do not make mistakes for the consequences can be catastrophic. But even when dealing with departmental issues, it is important that line managers are able to strike the best possible deal which is acceptable both to the employer and to the employees concerned. It is of little value to force through a deal which fails to gain employee co-operation or is found to be unworkable.

Negotiating can be defined as 'the process of resolving conflict through compromise' (Hawkins, 1979: 189), and the implication behind employee relations negotiating is that one or both parties (management and trade union) will move from their initial position in order to gain an agreement. The skilful negotiator is therefore someone who can encourage the achievement of a jointly acceptable position on a divisive issue (Kniveton, 1974: 30). For managers, this should also be achieved within the parameters which are laid down by the employing organisation, in terms of wage costs, comparability with other establishments, or the avoidance of industrial action at a time which is detrimental to the employer. It should also be recognised that negotiation is not concerned solely with pay issues which are dealt with by specialists on an annual basis, but is inherent in the work of all line managers. As more employee relations activities are devolved to the line, P&D practitioners need to be aware of the basics of the negotiating process in order to support their line management colleagues.

> Identify a number of occasions during the last year when you have been involved in a negotiation; choose events which are both work-related and concerned with non-work activities. In each case, consider whether or not you were prepared for the negotiation, how the negotiation proceeded, and how it was resolved. What did you learn from these events?

Employee relations negotiating skills sessions for managers may be organised as specialist courses, say on a residential basis, or as part of general management training along with other core activities. Typically they have the following learning outcomes, achieved by a mixture of instruction, practice and reflection rather than by experiential learning alone. By the end of a course participants are usually expected to understand and be able to explain:

- the differences between distributive and integrative bargaining (Walton and McKersie, 1965), and have an awareness that issues which appear on the surface to be distributive (haggling over how to share out a fixed size of cake) can sometimes be repackaged as integrative (searching for win-win results)

- the principal bargaining conventions which underpin employee relations negotiations, and the shared understandings about what is regarded as legitimate or unacceptable; for example, the fact that offers (once made) are not withdrawn or that key decisions are recorded in writing (Brewster, 1989: 122)

- the major sources of bargaining power, that provide the context within which negotiations take place, including labour and product market conditions, the willingness of workers to take industrial action, and the pressure on employers to achieve agreements. As we noted in the introductory section of the book, the period since 1980 has seen a major realignment in bargaining power which has been buttressed by substantial changes to trade union law.

In addition, by the end of a course it is expected that participants should be able to:

- contribute to preparations for negotiating, by clarifying their own and their opponent's objectives in terms of goals which *must* be achieved, those which they *intend* to achieve, and those which both parties would *like* to achieve (often referred to as the LIM – Like, Intend, Must – approach). These are recorded on paper, and reviewed at the end of the negotiation. A major element in the preparatory stages is the ability to gather information, either from written sources or informal conversations, which helps to strengthen one's own case and find flaws in that of the opponent.

- contribute to the management of negotiations in terms of understanding the stages in the process, identifying and overcoming deadlocks, and reaching agreements. Being aware of this whole process is one of the keys to becoming competent as a negotiator (Fells, 1986).

- occupy a number of roles in a team negotiation – such as chair, secretary, expert, spokesperson, observer – and in some cases play the part of aggressor, peacemaker or scapegoat (Brewster, 1989: 133).

One of the most important parts of any negotiation is the preparation which goes on before the sides meet at the bargaining table. The negotiator who goes into a meeting with employee representatives claiming 'We'll see what they have to say' is either remarkably skilled or incredibly ill-prepared. Consider your own work situation, or one with which you are familiar, and assess the principal strengths and weaknesses in the employer and employee cases, assuming negotiations were about to commence now.

Most negotiating skills courses make extensive use of closed-circuit television (CCTV) to record the negotiations and feed the results back to participants. This can prove an enlightening experience as negotiators observe their own performance, the way in which points have been made, and how they have been received by opponents. It also provides individuals with a chance to see themselves in action and highlight any facial or other mannerisms of which they may be unaware, or which they may wish to hide during a proper negotiation. Individuals can also discover that as the tension rises during a mock negotiation their behaviour changes, and they start to exhibit characteristics which may act as an obstacle to achieving an effective outcome; for example, a negotiator who becomes irritated by an opponent may hinder progress by aggressive or threatening postures and gestures. Observing these for oneself, or having them pointed out by a colleague or the tutor, may lead to improved performance at the negotiating table. Of course, the individual has to be prepared to change and accept that his or her actions may be counter-productive, but if the right climate has been created during the course this ought to be facilitated (Kniveton and Towers, 1978: 131–135).

A major advantage of role-playing and CCTV is that individuals gain the opportunity to occupy roles which may be unavailable at work – either in a different capacity on the team, or indeed as a trade union negotiator rather than a member of management. This latter experience, role reversal, is very useful for helping negotiators to view employee relations issues from a different angle, and moreover to act out the role of opponent. Gaining insights into how an employee representative might perceive a particular incident can throw new light on how it could best be tackled by management in order to reach an acceptable agreement. The incidents have to be realistic and relevant, and participants need to take the role-play seriously for it to be effective (Reid and Barrington, 1994: 403). It is not unknown for managers who are role-playing trade union officials to don a flat cap and speak in a mock northern accent!

Although the use of CCTV for negotiating skills courses is widespread, other approaches have been used as well. One of these, controlled-pace negotiation, operates rather like a role-play in slow motion, in that one party prepares a statement which is delivered to their opponents for them to analyse. After evaluating the statement, the opponents respond and rate the initial statement according to an agreed classification system. The process of exchanging statements and rating them continues, and both sides learn immediately, and in some detail, how their views are received by the opponents. It is a very slow and time-consuming process, and it can be criticised for focusing on *what* is said, rather than *how* it is said; it is widely acknowledged that the latter is a crucial component of the negotiating process (Kniveton and Towers, 1978: 122).

The most important advantage of negotiating courses, however, is that individuals have the opportunity to practise skills away from real-life collective bargaining or grievance-handling situations. Mistakes which are made on the course are not costly to the employer, although they may result in some loss of face by the individual manager. There is always the danger that the exercises may be defined by the participants as nothing more than games, and therefore unreal, but practice can help to generate improvements in performance. Employee relations negotiating is rather like sport, in that training and regular practice can help to make good players even better, while also fine-tuning the skills of the most gifted.

CUSTOMER-CARE TRAINING

There has been a sizeable growth in customer-care training in British organisations over the last decade, as employers have sought to differentiate themselves from the rest of the market through an emphasis on first-class customer service. British Airways has been regularly quoted as one of the first major organisations to invest in training in this area, as all staff have attended two-day workshops to raise their awareness of customer needs and learn ways in which to provide excellent levels of service (Storey and Sisson, 1993: 162). The 'Putting People First' Programme was designed to help all employees, initially those with a direct interface with the customer, recognise how they responded to treatments from other people. This was then followed up by a series of further courses, each of which have aimed to improve customer service, either directly or indirectly through a better understanding of how the company fits together (IDS/IPM, 1989: 110–113).

This lead has now been followed by leading retailers, hotel chains, fast-food outlets, financial services firms, computer companies, and even local authorities and railways; indeed, the language of the customer has now become so widespread that it is beginning to lose any distinctive meaning. As we shall see later, employees (and customers) are growing increasingly sceptical about the real depth of commitment and understanding associated with high-profile customer service programmes (Heery, 1993: 286); do employers really 'listen' to their customers if what they hear requires expenditure for no immediate financial return?

Compared with each of the other training practices which have been reviewed in this chapter, customer-care training is directed at all employees, or at least those who come into direct contact with external agents. It is often based around the provision of standard packages applicable to all groups of employee, relying on Taylorist principles about the one best method to undertake a job. The training itself can be quite limited in scope, concerned with guidance on how to answer the telephone, reply to letters, or establish eye contact with customers. Standard phrases are taught as employers seek to specify what Hochschild (1983) has termed the 'emotional' side of labour. To be effective, it is argued, all employees need to ensure that they use the same forms of words to 'greet customers' or 'delight guests', so that the service which is provided will be comparable across all establishments. This obviously has major implications for the ways in which training is delivered with a tendency, given the numbers of staff involved as well as the desire to convey standard messages, to use instructional techniques through videos and company literature. The IDS/IPM survey (1989: 41) did find, however, that many companies used workshops for customer-care training in which employees were encouraged to express their views about services provided, as well as being given some awareness exercises.

> Discuss with your colleagues what 'good customer service' means to you, and identify the most appropriate way in which training could be conducted in order to achieve this.

Customer-care programmes have been widely used by the leading food retailers, initially during induction but also when the messages or the vision changes (Marchington, 1992: 98–103). During induction, employees are shown videos by a staff trainer, with employees drawn from different parts of the store in order to minimise disruption to activities there. There is no attempt to use these sessions as a vehicle for team-building, and it is rare for line managers to attend meetings. The messages conveyed in these sessions tend to be simple and straightforward, although they vary in the degree to which they take a prescriptive line about the 'one best way' to serve customers. The image of the customer as all-powerful is central to these programmes, and the phraseology reflects unitarist assumptions. For example:

> 'Customer care is the Number One skill all Superco employees must have. Our future success will depend upon how well you apply this skill.'

> 'Remember it is not what you are doing that is the most important thing, it is what the customer *perceives* you are doing.'

> 'Make sure that you always say good morning, please, thank you; use the customer's name, if known; always apologise if something is wrong or there is a delay; take customers to a display; always show concern.'

Some of the more experienced staff in the stores found these customer care videos extremely simplistic, and actually became annoyed by them. They resented the way in which the message was put across, the patronising and condescending tone of the whole presentation, and the image which was conveyed by the stores in which the films were made. In these, the actors who were playing staff worked at a very leisurely pace, and had time to laugh and joke with the actors who were playing customers. On the other hand, senior management saw these devices as necessary in order to maintain the emphasis on quality service, while customers also appear to approve of these attempts to improve their experience as shoppers. More critical assessments of the British Airways programme (Hopfl, 1993: 120–123) have also questioned the depth of changes which may be achieved in employee behaviour, and pointed out that some employees remain sceptical about the showmanship and stage management which accompanies these customer service training 'events'.

Local authorities have also ventured down the customer-care training route; IRS provide details of two schemes at Elmbridge Borough Council (*Employee Development Bulletin* 44, 1993) and Leicester City Council (*Employee Development Bulletin* 46, 1993). At Elmbridge training took place in the housing department, which comprised about 100 staff. Unlike some of the top-down approaches, this series of two-day seminars placed great emphasis on participation and practice, as well as encouraging staff to conceive of the general public as customers – something which has not been particularly common in local government in the past. There were opportunities for role-playing situations with an awkward customer, and for exercises which were designed to assist staff avoid communications breakdowns with customers. These sessions were conducted as part of a wider programme, which involved visits to other departments, and so helped to embed customer care within a broader cultural change initiative. At the same time, the Council has found it difficult to evaluate the costs and benefits of the programme; the costs of employing consultants to undertake the initial training were high, but then much of the necessary groundwork and continued support for the initiative falls upon departmental managers and directors. The benefits can be seen through better relations with service users, according to questionnaire surveys, and through a series of further developments to improve service provision and change the predominant culture at the authority. At Leicester customer-care training has taken a number of forms, but in particular one set of courses has sought to define and categorise complaints so as to develop better staff skills in handling the. Again a major emphasis has been the identification of customers.

One of the major concerns with customer-care training is whether or not improved levels of service will be maintained far into the future. The 'sheep dip' approach to training, in which employees are all processed through a series of one-off courses, is hardly likely to bring about changes in attitudes, even if there may be improvements in behaviour. Equally, if employers are serious in their assertion that employees represent the organisation's most important resource, it seems strange to impose conformity rather than empowering staff to use their initiative in deciding how to deal with customers. Furthermore, because the training focuses on specific aspects of behaviour, rather than on the complete job, it is hardly surprising that some employees feel that customer-care sessions lack depth and any real attempt to understand the customer-employee-manager relationship.

WOMEN-ONLY MANAGEMENT DEVELOPMENT EXERCISES

The provision of single-gender training courses is probably one of the most contentious issues in the employee development area, not least because it highlights issues of sexuality and male-female relations which often tend not to be confronted head-on while at work. These issues are not absent from organisational life, but are often hidden under the surface and are consequently less amenable to rational discussion and critique. But an increasing number of organisations, such as British Telecom and Barclays Bank, have developed women-only courses as an adjunct to their other training activities, and as an integral part of their broader development strategies.

Three major arguments are typically put forward against the provision of women-only training courses (Colwill and Vinnicombe, 1991, pp 42–43). First, that this mode of training serves only to highlight further the differences between women and men, thus making integration in the workplace even more problematic. To focus on distinctions between the sexes merely reinforces the differences rather than building upon the similarities. Second, training which takes place in single-sex groupings is artificial and out-of-touch with organisational realities whereby women have to interact with men, either in teams or on an individual basis. Learning to work with men might be facilitated more effectively in mixed groups, it is argued, where gender issues are confronted explicitly. The third reason against women-only training is to do with men's perceptions of the courses, and the view that the training is seen as frivolous and of low status precisely because it involves women and not men (Vinnicombe and Colwill, 1995: 81). There is probably also an element of resentment here on the part of men, who feel that women are being given privileges which are not open to them. Attitudes such as this are not restricted solely to men, however, and many women are not convinced of the value of single-sex training either; Vinnicombe and Colwill (1995: 75) report that half the women who opted for the 'Women in Management' elective on Cranfield's MBA programme felt that working with an exclusive set of women managers was 'dangerous because it was contrived, and because it had the potential to become a session in which participants simply cosseted their own values and behaviour through blaming men'. It is also argued that treating women as a homogeneous group tends to obscure the diversity among women, failing to allow for the fact that there are likely to be quite substantial differences in working motives and preferred career patterns (Sinclair and Ewing, 1993: 25).

There are also three broad arguments in favour of women-only training courses. First, it is argued that women have a quite different set of backgrounds, experiences and life issues from men, and that it is only through separate sessions that these can be discussed. Their preferred styles of managing are likely to be different, with a much greater emphasis on co-operation and teamwork than men, with the latter tending to be more competitive and individualistic (Limerick and Heywood, 1993: 26).

Second, it is argued that women-only training courses can be run in a way which is more suitable for women than is the case with mixed sessions. Research indicates that mixed courses tend to be dominated by men, with sessions focusing on issues which are derived from existing organisational cultures – principally male issues, therefore. Courses are more likely to be tutored by men than women, and women's problems (that is, problems which are not considered by employers to be relevant to men while at work, but which obviously relate to men's positions in society and family) are often ridiculed or marginalised. Many tutors and managers will know only too well that senior management courses which are open both to men and women rarely include more than one or two females, and many are all-male. A women-only course can allow for consideration of issues which have traditionally been more important to women – such as balancing work and childcare commitments, or dealing with aggressive or sexist male behaviour – and these can be facilitated by a female tutor.

Third, attendance at a women-only course can act as a stimulant for further activities back at the workplace, through networking, women's support groups, mentoring arrangements, and the opportunity to identify role models (Limerick and Heywood, 1993: 27–28). Each of these helps to establish a stronger awareness among women, especially in managerial positions, of how to succeed at work, how to manage difficult relationships, and how to increase the likelihood of gaining promotion. On their own, and in isolation from the development of other mechanisms, women-only courses are unlikely to achieve much, and they may even leave women feeling yet more vulnerable. Colwill and Vinnicombe (1989: 48) stress that women-only training needs to be seen as an 'adjunct to, rather than a substitute for, more traditional organisational and occupational training. Such training must be treated merely as one specific part of a comprehensive career development programme for female employees.'

British Telecom has been a major force in this area, with a programme for females which has a women-only management development course at its core (Vinnicombe and Sturges, 1995: 116–118). The course was devised in conjunction with Cranfield based upon an analysis of what women managers felt were the most important training and development needs; these included personal development, career planning, assertiveness, political skills, leadership, and balancing career and home life. The philosophy behind the programme aims to release untapped potential amongst the participants by overcoming blockages and barriers (see also Burnett and James, 1993). British Telecom runs courses to develop women managers at first line, middle and senior levels, and the results have been highly positive, not only in terms of increasing self-confidence and personal effectiveness, but also in their contribution to the business as a whole. An important spin-off from these courses has been the creation of a BT Women's Network. In other words, it would appear that the development of women-only training courses here has worked precisely because it has been integrated into the

wider male and female organisational culture, and has not been
allowed to fester at the margins.

> Has women-only training and development got a part to play in your
> organisation? Why/why not? Do not consider this question until you have
> collected data on the proportion of women in managerial positions (first-
> line/middle/senior) and an analysis of current policies.

COMPUTER-ASSISTED LEARNING

Most individuals who have been employed for more than a decade
will have had little opportunity to learn other than in traditional ways:
through reading textbooks, watching television programmes, taking
part in group exercises, or conducting experiments in the laboratory.
The last decade has seen a major expansion in forms of computer-
based training, and most children at school are gaining competence in
how to use information technology. Accordingly, P&D professionals
need to be aware of the type of training options based upon computers
which are available, as well as understand what these are able to
deliver. The basic point about computer-assisted learning, however, is
that the process is managed by the learner, and it can take place at a
time, place and speed which is appropriate for him or her (Reid and
Barrington, 1994: 407).

Computer-assisted learning comprises at least three different broad
forms. First, users in libraries or at the office can access CD-ROM
packages to gather information on particular topics by typing in one
or more key words. This allows users to identify publications that
contain information which is needed for an assignment or a
management report (say, on works councils, 360-degree appraisal,
performance-related pay, or even computer-assisted learning). Users
are presented with a set of article and journal titles, and they can
choose whether or not to seek further information through an abstract
of the publication. In some cases users are able to access the full
publication, but at the time of writing not many journals are available
in electronic form. CD-ROM provides a read-only facility, however, so
this is little more than a speedy, flexible and convenient way of
gathering information. There are some obvious drawbacks with CD-
ROM facilities: not all publications have details on compact disc and
a search may be limited because of this; this form of data-gathering
does not allow for lateral development and thinking, which can
sometimes emerge from a general search in the library; some keywords
may throw up a mass of publications in the search, most of which
may be unhelpful; the whole system is dependent upon the choice of
keywords from the author or programmer.

> Make use of the CD-ROM and a periodical which is available in hard
> copy with an index (such as *Industrial Relations Services*) when doing your
> next assignment for Core Personnel and Development. Compare and
> contrast the two sources of data, and evaluate their respective
> contributions.

The second form of computer-assisted learning is much more interactive, in that an opportunity is provided for some learner participation in the process. In these situations, sometimes referred to as computer-based training (CBT), learners work their way through a package, and are then tested at the end of a section. Depending upon the accuracy of the answers, the learner may or may not be allowed to proceed, or there may be need to contact the tutor for further discussion. This form of learning has become popular in the financial services sector, especially for professional examinations where large numbers of people are involved and it is sometimes difficult to allow learners time off work to attend a college course.

The Chartered Institute of Bankers, for example, has used CBT for a number of years to provide a set of stand-alone learning programmes which are linked with workbooks produced in hard copy. The programmes can be undertaken on an individual basis or in groups. According to the users (Young, 1991: 20), CBT has many advantages over more conventional forms of tuition: it offers a flexible and adaptable form of learning, as users are able to control the pace of their work and are able to revise at times which suit them; it provides instant feedback on exercises so that mistakes are immediately identified, rather than having to wait until a tutor marks the assignment some weeks later; and it is cost-effective, especially in cutting down the time of travel to and from college. Young (1991: 18) also comments that the system enables tutors to spend more time assisting learners who have problems, now that they are released from the task of presenting standard information to a whole class. The experiences of CBT at Yorkshire Bank broadly support these claims, although Pearson (1994: 49) is keen to point out the complexity of costing computer-assisted learning, given the high initial outlay on equipment and software. He suggests that, to be cost-effective, CBT needs to be used extensively over a five-year period. Commenting upon its use at Sun Alliance in training staff about new products, Cole (1994: 64) argues that CBT is 70 per cent more effective at transferring knowledge than traditional forms of training, with higher levels of retention as well. The company estimates that this is much cheaper than traditional forms of training, although it is stressed that CBT acts as a complement to these rather than a replacement for them. Like the bankers and insurance services, the accountancy profession has also entered into the field of CBT.

Evans (1991: 65–67) illustrates the use and advantages of CBT for organisations with multiple outlets, such as Whitbread Inns and Post Office Counters Ltd, for training staff at the workplace. At Whitbread, for example, use was made of the existing computerised sales information system for providing training to staff at their place of work; after completing exercises, learners are able to test their knowledge via a battery of multiple-choice questions, with answers available immediately after completing the test. Learners are performing much better now on the tests but, more crucially, the use of CBT has helped to foster a learning environment where individuals are keen to gain NVQs in food hygiene.

Perhaps the most novel form of computer-assisted learning is interactive video (IV), whereby learners are able to interact with the computer, make choices and decisions, answer questions and generally establish a dialogue with the computer. As with CBT, learners are able to find out immediately how they have performed – in much the same way that a trainee pilot practises landing an airplane in a simulator. This may be a particularly effective method to employ when learning skills that require an interface with sophisticated equipment, and results for the US military indicated vastly superior performance through IV than with traditional methods (Griffith, 1987: 48). The advantages which are claimed for other forms of computer-assisted learning also apply here as well, particularly cost-effectiveness, flexibility, and the opportunity for experimentation in a safe environment.

The use of IV has not been restricted solely to training in how to handle technical operations. The British civil service introduced IV during the late 1980s for training managers in how to handle appraisals, with a programme entitled 'Appraising Anita' (Cann, 1986). Trainees watch various extracts from Anita's work over the past year (eg letters from customers, reports, dealing with colleagues) before writing an appraisal report; this is then compared with a 'model' version stored on the computer. After this the next and largest step is to conduct the appraisal; during this stage there are opportunities to interrupt the programme, make choices and be guided by an instructor. The programme speeds up as the trainee gets further into the programme, so that instant decisions are required as well. Assessments by users have been positive about IV, and most schoolchildren testify to the fact that this is an enjoyable form of learning.

This is not to say that computer-assisted learning is a panacea, or that it is suitable for all types of learning situation or for all types of learners. Learning may be effective at one level, and for the acquisition of a simple skill that may be acceptable; but for situations requiring groupwork and social interaction there are limits to the effectiveness of computer-assisted learning. Some learners feel the need for group solidarity and support while studying, the opportunity to check an idea with a tutor, or the desire to go further than is allowed by the computer software. At a somewhat deeper level there are concerns that too great a reliance on computer-assisted learning will encourage learners to believe that there is always one correct answer, or that conflict and alternative perceptions are illegitimate. As with the use of personality tests, there are worries that computer-assisted learning, and especially IV which is used for interpersonal skills training, somehow seeks to create organisational clones and downplay diversity.

CONCLUSION

Each of the forms of learning, training and development which have been reviewed in this chapter have been assessed against the yardstick of transferability back to the workplace. In each case we have seen that the potential for transfer is present, but that much depends upon the way in which the course is designed, organised and integrated. In the case of outdoor-based development, for example, the most effective courses meet, and sometimes exceed, the expectations of the trainees and their organisations, whereas the worst fail to achieve much in the way of useful learning, and in some cases are actually dangerous for the participants. There are a number of key features which enhance the value of all these forms of training and improve the likelihood of transfer taking place. These are clear objectives, jointly-devised and developed courses, skilled tutors who work closely with the client organisation, well-organised and relevant tasks, and – most important of all – integration with existing cultures and practices at the workplace. As with any aspect of P&D, the need for integration with wider business objectives is paramount.

USEFUL READING

DEAN, C. AND WHITLOCK, Q. (1992) *A Handbook of Computer-based Training*. London, Kogan Page.

FELLS, R. (1986) 'Managing deadlocks in negotiation'. *Employee Relations*, Vol 8(2): 2–7.

HOUGHAM, J., THOMAS, J. AND SISSON, K. (1991) 'Ford's EDAP scheme: a roundtable discussion'. *Human Resource Management Journal*, Vol 1, 3: 77–91.

INCOMES DATA SERVICES/INSTITUTE OF PERSONNEL MANAGEMENT (1989) *Customer Care: the Personnel Implication'*, London, IDS/IPM.

INDUSTRIAL RELATIONS SERVICES (1992) 'The role of outdoor-based development: a survey of 120 employers'. *IRS Employee Development Bulletin* 34, October: 2–17.

INDUSTRIAL RELATIONS SERVICES (1994) 'New approaches to employee development'. *IRS Employee Development Bulletin* 60, December: 5–10.

KNIVETON, B. AND TOWERS, B. (1978) *Training for Negotiating*. London, Business Books.

REID, M. AND BARRINGTON, H. (1994) *Training Interventions: Managing employee development*, Fourth Edition. London, IPD.

TUSON, M. (1994) *Outdoor Training: For employee effectiveness*. London, IPD.

VINNICOMBE, S. AND COLWILL, N. (Eds.) (1995) *Women in Management*. London, Prentice-Hall.

Part 5

EMPLOYEE RELATIONS

11 Managing with or without unions

INTRODUCTION

Employee relations issues are central to work. Indeed, the way in which employers choose to manage their employees has for a long time been a source of interest to academics and practitioners alike. Different approaches have gained prominence in line with a variety of internal and external pressures on the employing organisation; these include the growth of trade unionism, changing product and employment market conditions, labour law and new technology.

During the 1970s employers were encouraged to recognise and work with trade unions, required to improve the floor of employment rights for workers, and prompted to conciliate with rather than confront staff. However, during the 1980s the climate became more hostile for unions and changes in the political and legal context removed much of their statutory support. Moreover, the government encouraged employers to reassert their control, and high levels of unemployment in the United Kingdom also shifted the balance of power. Hence, some commentators have talked of a 'new industrial relations' or 'employee relations', which reflects a fundamental shift in the nature of the employment relationship. The use of the terminology of employee relations is itself indicative of a shift in perspective on the subject. This terminology has emerged for three reasons: first, through slippage, whereby the term becomes fashionable and enters ordinary vocabulary for no reason other than that it is used widely; second, because it is increasingly used by practitioners to label that part of personnel and development concerned with the regulation of relations (collective and individual) between employer and employee; third, there may be actual differences from industrial relations, most notably in the focus on management alone rather than on all parties to the employment relationship, and on contemporary practices rather than on history and development. We have used 'employee relations' principally for the second reason and, therefore, references to industrial relations can be seen as interchangeable, simply reflecting alternative labels (Marchington and Parker, 1990: 7–8)

Those who have argued that change has characterised the last 15 years point to the decline in union membership, from a peak of 13 million and a 55 per cent density of unionisation in 1979 to 8 million and 33 per cent in 1995. The extent of industrial action has also fallen dramatically, with days lost through strikes at a very low level, and a whole generation of personnel managers is now unaccustomed to dealing with collective disputes at work. Collective bargaining now has lower levels of coverage and scope than at any time since the 1930s, and trade unions have lost their national prominence and voice to an extent which would not have been thought possible in the 1970s. Such indicators suggest that the last two decades can be characterised as a period of fundamental and deep-rooted change.

However, it is important to see these changes in perspective. While trade union membership has declined substantially, it has not disappeared altogether. Trade unions are recognised by employers in about half of all workplaces employing 25 or more people, and over ten million employees work in unionised establishments. Although collective bargaining is less central to employee relations in the mid-1990s, it is still the mechanism by which pay is determined for about half the workforce. Findings such as these support the notion that employee relations have been subject to continuity rather than change.

While both interpretations are valid at one level, they overlook the point that different patterns of employee relations are found in different workplaces, sometimes in the same industry or sector. Two commentators sum this up in the following way:

> 'Diversity is more noticeable than similarity, uneven developments are more typical than common trends, and changes take place in different directions in different workplaces' (Marchington 1995: 82).

> There is no doubt that there has been a _transition_ away from the traditional system, although towards what is unclear' (Metcalf 1993: 1).

Compare and contrast these two viewpoints on changes in employee relations. Do they contradict each other, or are both perspectives valid?

In this chapter we discuss the concept of an employee relations system in order to locate developments in a broader context and understand the nature of different pressures on the various actors at workplace level. Secondly, we examine management objectives for industrial relations. Thirdly we look at the concept of management style and explain the reasons for variations in styles. Fourthly we discuss shop stewards and workplace union organisation. Finally we take up the subject of union recognition and the nature of union and non-union workplaces.

By the end of the chapter, readers should be able to:

- provide advice to management on the employee relations objectives which are appropriate for their own organisation

- specify an employee relations management style which could be used by their own organisation

- contribute to the design of an employee relations policy which explains how trade unions will be dealt with, or how a non-union strategy will be effected.

In addition, they should be able to understand and explain:

- the nature of employee relations and the concept of an industrial relations system

- the meaning of management style in employee relations, and the reasons why it varies from one organisation to another

- the processes of union recognition and derecognition.

THE EMPLOYEE RELATIONS SYSTEM

While industrial relations are often associated solely with conflict and strikes, a view reinforced by media representations, in reality it is much broader that this, incorporating issues such as employee participation, management style and collective bargaining. The centrepiece of employee relations is the relationship between employers and employees, and it is endemic to this relationship that there are common and divergent interests (see Chapter 2). It is clear that both sides of industry (ie buyers and sellers of labour) have some common interests. For the employer and employee, co-operation can serve both sides well, since employees get a wage which they require to sustain their living standards and employers receive in return the product of their investment, whether in the form of a manufactured product or a service. It is in neither party's interest for the organisation to perform poorly with consequent negative effects on profits (for the employer) or wages (for the employee). Hence, these common interests suggest that employers and employees can work together. However, while there are clearly common goals there are also divergent interests. In simple terms, the employer is likely to wish to buy labour at the lowest possible price or cost so as to maximise profits, whereas employees wish to sell their labour at the highest possible price. This produces a conflict of interest which does not necessarily result in open conflict, but means that the arrangements which are reached may be unstable depending on relative bargaining power. Because employees are relatively weaker than employers, employees may gain advantage from organising themselves into trade unions in order to boost their bargaining power.

Thus employee relations are characterised by both *conflict* and *co-operation*. For some people industrial relations is inextricably linked with conflict, since this is the only time it obtains much media coverage. It is now accepted that the so-called 'British disease' of industrial conflict in the 1970s was largely a myth, as Britain has a record no worse than many other countries in the developed world. Co-operation is necessary to produce goods and services, and both parties have an interest in co-operating to some degree: employers need co-operation so as to produce their products and employees need co-operation so as to provide them with a wage. However, conflict is also inherent in the employee relations process since it is unlikely for there to be a consensus over the sum which is paid out in wages as opposed to profits. Conflict may manifest itself through a strike or it may be contained or institutionalised through procedures (see Chapter 13).

However, this notion of two sides is also too simplistic. Firstly, neither side is consistently unified and much bargaining and disagreement takes place *within* each party as well as between them. Within management there are likely to be conflicting objectives between different functions and between different levels; for example, the objectives of the sales team may conflict with those of the production function. Similarly, the demands placed upon line managers in terms of adherence to procedure agreements may cause conflict between them and the P&D function. To some extent, though, the overriding objective of companies to secure profitability can help integrate the various sub-objectives. On the union side matters are more complex, with conflict between members in different departments and in different trade unions, as well as between different levels in the shop steward hierarchy. There may also be differences between different trade or interest groups or between the leadership and the ordinary rank and file members.

It is also too simplistic to think of only two parties in industrial relations, because of third-party governmental intervention. This can take several different forms. For example, legislation on employee relations has developed considerably since the 1960s and it played a key role during the 1980s – legislation on the closed shop, industrial action, and ballots, for example, as we saw in Chapter 2. The government has also played a role in pay regulation since the Second World War, either through a formal mechanism – such as incomes policy during the 1960s and 1970s – or the imposition of cash limits for the public sector in more recent times. This highlights a second role; the government is a key employer, and hence has a managerial side to its role as an actor in the system. In addition, via the agencies of independent tripartite bodies such as ACAS, it has played a role in the resolution of disputes in both the public and private sectors.

Write down two lists, one specifying the common interests of employers and employees, and the other divergent interests. Apply this to your own organisation and see if it helps you to evaluate the quality of employee relations.

A useful way of conceptualising the subject is to use the systems model developed by Dunlop, who argued that the industrial relations system was a sub-system of society, overlapping the economic and political systems. His model conceived of the system as 'comprised of certain actors, certain contexts, an ideology which binds the industrial relations system together and a body of rules created to govern the actors at the workplace' (Dunlop, 1958: 7).

Actors include management, employees (and their representatives) and the government. The *contexts* which influence actors' actions include technology, labour and product markets, and the laws and distribution of power within the wider society. For example, technology influences workplace characteristics such as the size of the workforce, the nature of the workgroup and managerial control. Legislation reflects power within society and hence may restrict the actions of the various parties. According to Dunlop an *ideology* (or set of core beliefs) acts as an integrating force binding the actors together in providing a set of common assumptions about the nature of industrial relations and the roles the actors play. For example, for much of the post-war period a philosophy of 'voluntarism' was paramount, characterised by a shared ideology between employers and employees whereby the processes of employee relations should be changed only by 'voluntary' action and not third-party intervention. The output of actors, contexts and ideology is a body of *rules* concerned with regulating industrial relations, which includes things such as procedural matters (eg management/union agreements or disciplinary and grievance procedures) as well as substantive issues such as levels of payment.

There have been a number of criticisms of this model of industrial relations (Wood, Wagner, Armstrong, Goodman and Davis, 1975). In particular, a central criticism has centred on the extent to which the systems approach takes a functional view of industrial relations and assumes that the system is naturally stable with the emphasis on creating rules and order. Nevertheless, Dunlop's ideas have continued to be utilised by students of the subject, and the model is a useful way of encapsulating the subject matter of employee relations in context.

It is also important to recognise that the system operates at a number of levels. For example, there is a *national* level where we can observe the legal framework, the nature of unionism (eg craft and general unions) which reflect historical developments in Britain, and so on. At *industry* level we can see the agreements made between employers and unions on matters such as holidays or safety regulations for certain industries. At *workplace* level there may be less formal agreements and more evidence of custom and practice. These may diverge within the same industry, and even within the same company or workplace with informal agreements reflecting local differences. In this chapter, our principal focus is on workplace employee relations.

MANAGEMENT OBJECTIVES FOR EMPLOYEE RELATIONS

Before looking at the employee relations objectives of management, we need to remind ourselves of the nature of management itself, and especially the sharply differing contexts within which employee relations are enacted. Three aspects are worthy of mention. First, there is the distinction between different types of employing organisation on grounds of orientation (manufacturing or service) and capital ownership (private or public). This leads to four types of employing organisation: private businesses, public corporations, public services, voluntary bodies (Farnham, 1990: 24). Second, there are major differences between employment in large, multi-establishment enterprises and small single-unit firms. Third, we need to be aware of the position of strategic employee relations decisions in comparison with other corporate-level issues (see Chapter 16).

A number of writers in the USA have developed a 'strategic choice' model whereby employers are seen as the key movers of change, and industrial relations policies are seen as strategic in that they form part of a long-term plan (Kochan, McKersie and Cappelli, 1985). This is important in recognising both the element of choice which faces managements, and also the extent to which management is able to set the agenda to which other actors (eg trade unions) then react.

It might be expected that employee relations objectives would be in line with corporate strategy, although this does assume that employers are proactive enough to have devised such strategies, and are not just muddling through. Even if we do assume that employers have some idea about what they are doing, and why they are doing it, their objectives may be implicit rather than explicit, and in many cases these would not be committed to paper. In any event, employee relations objectives typically include the following:

- minimising disruption at work and reducing the likelihood of overt conflict

- reducing unit labour costs, though not necessarily wages

- achieving greater stability in employee relations by channelling discontent through agreed procedures

- increasing productivity and the utilisation of labour

- increasing co-operation and commitment so as to increase the likely acceptance of change

- increasing control over the labour process.

There are problems with a number of these objectives on their own; for example, while management clearly want to minimise disruption this should not be at the expense of high productivity, and the latter may also be achieved in the long term by engineering a strike. Some of these objectives may be more appropriate for certain stages in an organisation's development, or for some types of employer. Equally, although no employer would ever admit it, some analysts would argue that control over the labour process is management's prime concern, and all the other objectives are subordinate to this, merely a means to achieving this end.

> Think of examples of conflicts that occur in your organisation between different objectives. To what extent do objectives change over time?

Over the last 20 years a variety of bodies have argued that managements must adopt a more strategic approach to industrial relations, largely because fire fighting was seen as leading to problems as short-term, *ad hoc* solutions merely stored up trouble for the future. In contrast, it was suggested that devising a strategy could provide a greater likelihood of success as this would increase consistency and harness commitment. Starting with Donovan in 1968, and continuing through the Commission on Industrial Relations in 1973 and ACAS in 1981 (and thereafter), the emphasis has been on the idea that strategy/planning is equated with good industrial relations. Industrial relations strategy has been defined by Thurley and Wood (1983: 198) as 'long-term policies which were developed by the management of an organisation in order to preserve or change the procedures, practices or results of industrial relations activities over time'.

However, the research evidence has tended to suggest that managers have adopted opportunistic and pragmatic tactics to managing employees rather than the much-heralded strategic approaches extolled by the human resource management texts (Armstrong, 1992). Companies tend to consider personnel issues at the implementation stage of decisions to do with the production process or acquisitions, rather than forming part of the initial decision.

If an employer does have a clearly thought-out strategy for the management of people at work, it then needs to be broken down into constituent policies for particular parts of the employment relationship. Management also needs to be aware of potential contradictions between policy in one area and that in another. Again there are doubts about the degree to which employers do plan ahead in industrial relations – and, even if they do, room for manoeuvre must be left so as to cope with change. Nevertheless, employers would probably consider issues such as whether or not there should be a role for trade unions, methods for determining pay, employee involvement, flexibility of working arrangements, controls over work, and procedures.

MANAGEMENT STYLE

The subject of management style in employee relations has evolved since Alan Fox's categorisation in 1974 of management/employee relations on the basis of his distinction between unitary and pluralist approaches. Purcell and Sisson (1983) identified five ideal typical styles which are outlined below.

Traditional (authoritarian)
This is the style typical of the small owner-managed organisation in which employee relations are seen as relatively unimportant until something goes wrong, whereupon a fire-fighting approach is utilised. The culture of the organisation tends to be tough and the employers pay as little as they can get away with. There is an authoritarian style of management in which there is seen to be no need for trade unions, the attitude towards them being unreservedly hostile.

Sophisticated human relations (paternalistic)
While this kind of organisation shares with the previous category a view that there is no need for trade unions, this belief is founded upon the

premise that trade unions are unnecessary because of the forward-looking and essentially co-operative stance of the employer. Paying above the market rate, the employer takes great care to select the right kind of people and then puts considerable effort into engendering employee loyalty to corporate goals. The culture of the organisation is primarily entrepreneurial.

Consultative (problem-solving)

This kind of organisation operates through a mixture of formal and informal mechanisms in its employee relations, but both are based upon forward planning and proactivity in managing people. Trade unions are welcomed as partners in the enterprise and as essential to represent employee opinion, as well as being central to the communication process. Considerable emphasis is placed upon consultation with unions and employees, and a problem-solving approach is encouraged in an attempt to reach agreement. Pay may or may not be negotiated centrally, but local managers and union representatives will remain free to work together to improve work organisation, productivity and welfare at establishment level. All of this takes place, however, within a shared management perspective about employee relations.

Constitutional

While this kind of organisation shares a number of characteristics with those outlined in the previous category, there are a number of different assumptions and attitudes which underpin this style. In common with the consultative style, there is considerable attention to forward-planning, managers work with trade unions at workplace level, and participation is typically achieved through trade union channels. This style differs from the consultative category in that the approach to employee relations is more combative and adversarial, there being more focus upon formal and regulated agreements, with peace being negotiated between two strong partners in the workplace. Consultation is very much subsidiary to negotiation for both parties.

Opportunist

While all of the previous categories identify a dominant style or broadly shared management perspective, the central element of this style is that it rests upon devolution to establishments and a pragmatic approach to employee relations depending upon local circumstances. It is typical of conglomerates operating in a wide range of industries, in which a contingency approach to management might be utilised and establishments are purely responsible to the parent for profitability, although some central services are provided. Thus trade unions may or may not be recognised, employee participation may or may not be extensive, and pay is more likely to be determined at local level within broad limits set by senior management.

Purcell (1987: 535) has now refined his approach. First, he has provided a more precise definition of style which implies 'the existence of a distinctive set of guiding principles, written or otherwise, which set parameters to and signposts for management action in the way employees are treated and particular events are handled'. Style is less about outcomes than about originating principles and policies which influence action, and about links with business strategy. His second refinement is to differentiate between management attitudes and policies towards employees on an individual and collective basis. The former relate to the extent to which employees are treated as a resource while the latter reflects management recognition of the collective interests of the group.

> What is the management style in your organisation? Does it differ between different workplaces? Has it changed over time? Why is this?

While it is important to describe differences between the styles used by employers in managing their employee relations, it is crucial to be able to isolate the factors which help to account for these differences in style. Obviously the style of employee relations management used in Shell is different from that used by the small family butcher, but there are also differences in style between a health authority and Ford, between GEC and Marks & Spencer, and between a public corporation and a local authority. It is important to be able to establish why styles may or may not change over time, or why indeed they may vary between different parts of the same organisation. As we discuss in more detail in Chapter 16, the external environment does not *determine* or dictate a style that in some way can be 'read-off' from the contingent circumstances. The history of any industry shows that such determinism is inaccurate, and that the preferences of senior managers play an important part in deciding which policies are adopted, as well as in influencing some of the so-called external factors such as the product market or the technology employed. So, too, do the attitudes of other staff – be they managers, supervisors, trade union representatives, or other employees – and the relationships between them. What does seem apparent, though, is that the external environment sets some limits as to what is feasible for any organisation.

A number of factors can influence the style of employee relations management adopted by senior managers in an organisation. Each of the five factors may be mediated (sometimes affected) by the different actors in the workplace, especially the most senior managers in the organisation. These factors are:

• the *product market* factor, which has three subdivisions. First, there is orientation which refers to the nature of customers served, and to whether this is dominated by industrial as opposed to domestic consumers, whether the principal products are fashion-oriented and therefore subject to regular change, as opposed to those products which are sold more on the basis of high quality or durability. Secondly, there is the intensity of competition in the market place, the size of market held by each organisation, and the number of major players on the scene. Thirdly, there is the rate of change in the size of the market, whether it is growing or declining, whether it is stable or subject to regular swings of either a predictable or unpredictable nature. All of these can influence the management style which is (or should be) adopted by the employer. An organisation selling high-quality products on a business-to-business basis in a stable or growing market which is dominated by a very small number of competitors is likely to be able to pursue a different management style from one which is fighting for survival in a highly competitive, fashion-oriented or declining market.

- the *technology* factor, also comprising three subdivisions. First, there is the degree of capital intensity, which relates to the cost of labour as opposed to capital equipment, to the proportion that the wages/benefits bill takes of value added by the company. The rate of technical change is the second factor, in particular the degree to which the introduction of new technology leads to changes in job definitions and prospects, and the extent to which this stimulates employee resistance to change. Finally, there is the degree of interdependence in operations, the extent to which different jobs, departments and establishments are linked together in the manufacture of goods or provision of services. An organisation for which labour costs are a small proportion of overall costs, which has a phased introduction of new technology, and in which different functions operate independently of each other, has a greater opportunity to pursue a consultative style, for example.

- the *labour market* factor, also comprising three subdivisions. First, patterns of labour supply, which refers to the number and quality of potential recruits for the employer, and is of course heavily influenced by the level of unemployment, the number of school leavers, skills shortages and so on. Second is the history/traditions of trade unionism in the organisation or industry as a whole, and whether it is feasible to consider alternative approaches to the notion of collective representation – for example, non-union or single-union deals. Finally, there is the occupational mix of the workforce and the degree to which labour is recruited on the basis of mental as opposed to physical abilities. All these factors are particularly relevant for the setting up of new sites.

- *organisational characteristics* is the fourth factor. This includes the size of the company – large, medium or small – which has been identified regularly as a critical factor in influencing the management style which is adopted. Secondly, the structure of the organisation is important for the evolution of P&D practices, and this may vary between single-establishment firms, through highly centralised multi-site organisations or decentralised multi-plant companies, to conglomerates which show little interest in the specialist policies adopted as long as the profit centre or unit makes money. The key elements in this category are the degree of central control over the management of human resources and the promulgation of a corporate HR philosophy. Thirdly, ownership is also a key element; for example, according to recent studies, US or Japanese-owned organisations are more likely to pursue a consultative style, whereas public-sector bodies are less likely to do so. Finally, the funding element may have a key influence on the approach of the organisation.

- the *social, legal and political environment*. The first four factors help to create the environment within which companies operate, and thus provide tools or straitjackets for the styles of employee relations management in practice. The effect of economic factors such as employment levels has both actual and perceived influences over employee relations, as too does the political climate in terms of inspiring confidence in certain approaches. The legal environment similarly places obstacles or ladders in the path of employers. All of this is interwoven in the social climate within which business operates and the degree to which it influences employer, employee and public opinion about issues relating to social responsibility.

The other issue confronting senior managers is how to reconcile an organisation's or unit's management style if a number of these factors tend to suggest different approaches; for example, if there is conflict between the preferred options *vis-à-vis* the product market situation and that in the labour market, say a strong demand for high-quality employees for a company with a mature and declining product, or a highly centralised organisation where labour costs are a substantial proportion of value added. One way around this is to differentiate between core and peripheral employees, while another is to adjust organisation design or culture, and a third is to divest certain businesses.

To what extent is management style dictated by these external contingencies, or does management have room for manoeuvre in selecting appropriate policies? How does this analysis apply to your own organisation?

While some writers have argued that control over labour is the primary and overriding objective for employers, others have criticised this view (see Chapter 2). Firstly, they point out that companies are in business for profit and are not primarily about employee relations. While the decisions which managers take, such as over new technology, may well have implications for employees this does not necessarily mean that such policies were formulated with this in mind. Secondly, others argue that labour is of *secondary* importance in management decision-making. This suggests that management make decisions on the basis of business considerations and consider P&D issues later. A third view is that P&D considerations are one factor among many and management's role is to balance various interests by serving customers, rewarding shareholders and generating profits, as well as attempting to satisfy employees.

WORKPLACE UNION ORGANISATION

Shop stewards exist in most workplaces where trade unions have a presence. These individuals are not full-time paid union officials but paid for by the employer, irrespective of how much time is devoted to union duties. In short, they act as unpaid representatives of the union and are usually responsible for grievance handling and even negotiation for their members. Often their importance is not formally recognised in union rule books, and the range of their functions and responsibilities is not fully acknowledged, especially as much of their role depends on informal custom and practice rather than explicit written agreements. They represent small groups of workers and are generally elected from among them.

During the 1970s workplace union organisation was formally strengthened. This was indicated by a rise in the number of shop stewards, with two-thirds of large establishments (those with over 1,000 employees) having at least one steward who spent all his or her time on union business. Other indicators – such as time off for training, check-off arrangements and joint shop steward meetings – also reflected this formalisation. In 1978 the closed shop covered some 3.5 million employees, over 40 per cent of union members according to Dunn and Gennard (1984: 17). The formalisation of industrial relations and the increase in legal intervention meant that stewards had less to do with negotiating payments and much more to do with workplace rights in relation to issues such as dismissal, health and safety, and redundancy. During this time management increasingly came not only to accept stewards in the workplace but also to sponsor their development and organisation through the judicious granting of facilities, and also indirectly through the implementation of procedures. Hence, management felt it more appropriate to work *with* the stewards than work against them, although clearly union pressure was a key factor in persuading managers that simple opposition was not a realistic option.

Most people join trade unions primarily for instrumental reasons – for example, for protection against arbitrary management decisions or for insurance against accidents. They may not necessarily believe in the notion of collective action but join for individual defensive purposes, as for example did some employees in the financial services sector in 'fear for their jobs' and the possibility of arbitrary treatment after the 1987 crash in the city. The insurance function in the event of discipline, dismissal, injury or dispute may be central. On the other hand, some people may join unions because of peer-group pressure or because they feel it is morally right to be in a union.

This predominantly instrumental attitude partially explains why participation in union affairs is generally so low, although it does increase considerably if there is a concrete problem or specific issue in employee relations. It also explains why unions tend to be seen in local and economic terms since this is where the union performs its service and is most visible to the ordinary member, especially through the activities of its lay representatives. This 'local' perspective helps us understand why questions of whether unions in general are too strong can be answered in the positive, but if the same question is asked about unions at the individual workplace the answer is negative.

Sweeping changes in the political, economic and legal environment during the early 1980s appeared not to have had a dramatic effect on workplace union organisation for, while union membership fell substantially, much of this could be explained by changes in sectoral employment and by unemployment. Indeed the role of shop stewards actually increased between 1980 and 1984. However, the 1990 WIRS data (Millward *et al*, 1992: 110) revealed that between 1984 and 1990 there was a reduction from 54 per cent to 38 per cent of workplaces which had a shop steward. This was seen as reflecting a broader decline in union influence, including fewer employees covered by collective bargaining, fewer closed shops and fewer strikes. It was suggested that the distinctive British system of adversarial collective bargaining is no longer characteristic of the economy as a whole, although where it remains there has been little in the way of institutional change. At a chemical company codenamed Scotchem, for example, the *institutions* of collective bargaining and joint consultation changed little during the 1980s, but it was clear that their importance declined significantly as management sought to communicate directly with employees and less attention was paid to the established committee structure (Wilkinson, Marchington, Goodman and Ackers, 1993: 32–34).

> How does this view of weakened shop stewards compare with experiences at your own organisation? If you work in a non-union organisation, ask this question of friends and colleagues.

THE EXTENT AND NATURE OF UNION RECOGNITION

The issue of union recognition lies at the very heart of employee relations, and policies and practices in this area have changed more than most in the last two decades. In the mid-1970s it was assumed that most employers would automatically recognise and deal with trade unions, support their activities in the workplace, and attempt to build close working relationships with senior shop stewards so as to lubricate relations at work and minimise the likelihood of disruption to business. But in the 1990s many commentators suggest that this has changed as employers have introduced new working patterns without even consulting, let alone negotiating with, union representatives. While derecognition is limited, the lack of new recognition is more significant. For example, in the private sector, management in workplaces which were less than ten years old recognised unions in only 23 per cent of cases compared with 52 per cent of them that were more than 20 years old (Metcalf, 1993: 2).

Despite this decline in recognition and union membership, many industries and certain sectors still boast a considerable union presence in the 1990s. For example, according to WIRS union density was in excess of 50 per cent in nearly half of all industries, and over half of all workplaces in metals and mineral products, textiles, post and telecommunications, energy and water, central and local government, education, and banking, finance and insurance had unions recognised for collective bargaining purposes. Of course, following privatisations of public sector organisations, unions have been derecognised at some of these workplaces in the first half of the 1990s. Within manufacturing, unions were recognised at approximately 80 per cent of all larger manufacturing workplaces (those employing more than 200), with only a slight decline over the latter half of the 1980s

(Millward *et al*, 1992: 72). While there has been a decline in the overall number of shop stewards during the last 15 years, this has not been at the same rate as the decline in union membership, thus leading to a reduction in the ratio of members:stewards in recent times.

There is no legal or compulsory route for unions and employers to follow in order to grant recognition, something which makes the British system different from those operating in many other industrialised countries in Europe and North America. If they so desire, British employers may choose to grant recognition to a union which has no members in the workplace; indeed, this is precisely what happened at some of the greenfield sites when deals with a single union were signed before any employees were recruited, as at Nissan (Wickens, 1987: 129–137). Conversely, employers may also choose not to recognise a union at a workplace where *all* employees are union members, although this is extremely unlikely and in practice would be difficult to sustain. In short, the ultimate decision to grant recognition remains the prerogative of management.

For most of the 1970s statutory recognition procedures did exist in Britain through the Commission on Industrial Relations (CIR) and with the recognition route provided under the Employment Protection Act 1975. This allowed for an independent trade union to refer a recognition issue to ACAS, which was then required to consult with employers, unions and employees (typically via a secret ballot) before making a recommendation about recognition. However, even where recognition was recommended there was no guarantee that it actually happened; employers could simply refuse to comply with the recommendations. Some employers, such as Grunwick Processing Laboratories, refused to allow ACAS access to employee records in order to conduct the ballot, this bringing the provisions down at the first hurdle. Problems such as these meant that there was little resistance to the Conservative government's repeal of these sections of the Act in 1980. The TUC has discussed the re-introduction of a legally-enforceable system for recognition (Beaumont and Towers 1992: 129–130), and more recently it has been suggested that at workplaces with more than 50 per cent membership, unions should be granted recognition. However, so much still depends upon employers and their preparedness to recognise and deal with unions at the workplace. Should such legislation be adopted, the unions will continue to face opposition from employers who are set against working with them. It would therefore appear that we are witnessing an increasing divide between those workplaces where unions have maintained a presence, and one often supported by managements; those where they are being edged out and are in danger of becoming extinct; and non-union workplaces. We will now analyse these three options.

Imagine that you have just started work at an establishment where 50 per cent of the workforce are union members. As the P&D specialist, specify the questions which you would need to ask in order to make a recommendation to the management team about the matter of recognition.

WORKING WITH THE UNIONS

There are a number of reasons why employers should choose to work with, rather than against, unions at the workplace. Firstly, management may regard trade union representatives as an essential part of the communication process in larger workplaces. Rather than being forced to establish a system for dealing with all employees, or setting up a non-union representative forum, trade unions are seen as a channel which allows for the effective resolution of issues concerned with pay bargaining or grievance handling (Marchington and Parker, 1990: 25). It is also the case that reaching agreement with union representatives, in contrast to imposing decisions, can provide decisions with a legitimacy which otherwise would be lacking. It can also lead to 'better' decisions as well. Even if this method of decision-making appears more time-consuming than the simple imposition of change, less time is spent in trying to correct mistakes or persuade employees after the event of the efficacy of management ideas.

Secondly, employers may desist from the use of aggressive strategies when the balance of power is firmly with them for fear that, should conditions change, shop stewards may seek to settle old scores. Compromise may be attractive because – as we have already noted – one of management's major employee relations objectives is to achieve order and stability in the workplace, especially in persuading employees of the sanctity of procedures for resolving industrial disputes. As a quid pro quo, employers have to be prepared to use procedures themselves for resolving differences at work, especially in the area of disciplinary matters. Indeed, it has been argued that 'responsible' workplace union organisation and 'responsive' management is mutually reinforcing (Marchington, 1982: 50).

Thirdly, some employers have taken the view that, given the nature of their workforce, the industry, and the region in which establishments are located, unionisation is inevitable. In this case, rather than engage in a fight with a number of prospective unions for recognition – and suffer both employee relations and employee morale consequences in the process – it is far better to reach an agreement with a preferred union from the outset. Thus, Peter Wickens at Continental Can and later at Nissan points out that 'the view was that if we sought to be non-union we could end up in a multi-union situation. Recognition claims would come from a variety of trade unions – skilled and unskilled, engineering, supervisory and administrative. There would then have rapidly developed a situation which would be difficult to control' (Wickens, 1987: 129).

It is also important to keep the trade union issue in perspective. Employers have many other concerns than those relating to trade unions and, provided the latter do not present a major obstacle to the realisation of more important goals, a union presence can be tolerated or even promoted. This is even more relevant if trade unions are not engaged in a continual struggle with employers, but see co-operation as a more appropriate stance in 'difficult' competitive circumstances.

Finally, even if employers wish to reduce the role of unions at the workplace, they may lack the power to carry through their intentions because of local constraints – for example, skill shortages of particular grades of labour may make wholesale dismissals unrealistic, as may fears that the tacit skills of workers will be lost, with the consequence of less effective and efficient organisations.

After a period during the 1980s in which it appeared that the notion of working with the unions disappeared from the employee relations agenda, there has been a recent revival of interest in notions of 'partnership' (IPA, 1993). This refers to the situation in which management is prepared to support the activities of the trade union(s), and for their part employees are more likely to regard union membership as an important aspect of their employment conditions. A good example of this is the IPA report (Towards Industrial Partnership), which is publicly endorsed by leading trade union and management representatives as well as a number of well-known academics. While not seeking to deny differences of opinions and goals, the report recognises the high degree of common interests shared by employers and unions, and stresses the need to accept the legitimacy of representative institutions. For example, at Staveley Chemicals (part of Rhone-Poulenc), there has been a major shift from classic adversarialism to co-operation between the company and five separate unions. The process of building trust is shown to be a long and time-consuming process, with initial and understandable reluctance on the part of unions to accept the 'new' management style. But, over a six-year period, it was felt that each party came to accept the legitimacy of the other, and started working together through single-table bargaining to enhance the prosperity of the company as a whole (IPA 1995). Godfrey and Marchington (1996) show that shop stewards' reactions to partnership programmes depend fundamentally on their trust in management. At some sites stewards were highly supportive, referring to a 'new dawn', more open styles of management and an increased influence over decisions. In other organisations, conversely, union representatives were highly sceptical about the extent of managements' attempts to create partnerships, viewing them as nothing more than the latest fad or fashion, a device to weaken unions via incorporation.

Perhaps the most persuasive case for 'working with the unions' has been articulated by Purcell (1979b), in his strategy for management control in industrial relations, part commentary on, and part prescription for, the post-Donovan period. The basis of his argument is that management will have greater success in achieving its objectives by working with trade unions, in particular by encouraging union membership and participation in union affairs, as well as assisting unions to work together through support for joint shop steward committees. A key notion in his discussion is 'cumulation' (Purcell, 1979b: 31), the idea that early experiences of industrial relations in an organisation influences subsequent behaviour. There are many detailed aspects to his argument, most of which still have relevance for some employers in the 1990s even allowing for the vast changes in the economic, political, legal and social context in which employee relations are conducted. Some of the policies bear a remarkable similarity to those utilised by employers, such as Nissan or Komatsu, which set up on greenfield sites during the 1980s, or to more established manufacturing or service companies which maintained their support for workplace trade unionism throughout the years of Conservative governments. The following are examples of the policies, adapted to fit with circumstances in the 1990s:

- prompt union recognition, even courting of 'appropriate' unions for specific groups of employees, in order to reduce the likelihood of being caught up in a recruitment battle

- assistance with 'check-off' or DOCAS (deduction of contribution at source) to ensure that employees remain union members, although this is likely to demand greater efforts on the part of management following the requirement in the Trade Union Reform and Employment Rights Act 1993 that this arrangement is confirmed by ballot every few years

- time off and facilities for all union members to attend union meetings at the workplace (maybe at lunch time or after work) and for provision for voting in union elections

- agreement on time off for union representatives to undertake prescribed union duties, attend consultative meetings, and take part in training courses

- encouragement of inter-union committees at work, especially those designed to operate via single-table bargaining – see Chapter 12 for further discussion of this arrangement which has become more fashionable in the 1990s.

Union Recognition at Bosch

Most of these ideas featured heavily in the decision by Bosch to recognise the EETPU (now AEEU) as the sole trade union at its Cardiff plant where it started production in 1991 (IRS *Employment Trends* 501, 1991: 5–6). Its Director of Human Resources (Martin Wibberley) was the first employee to be appointed by Bosch at the site, and he decided that it would be sensible to establish a 'working relationship' with a union at the outset. Given the traditions of unionism in South Wales, and the fact that many prospective employees would already have experience of union membership, it was felt that recognition would be inevitable in the long run. Attempting to remain non-union would lead to disorderly employee relations structures and persistent pressures for recognition. A number of unions were approached and asked how they would respond to the company's proposed employment practices. Of these, the EETPU was considered to be the 'most experienced in negotiating single union, no-strike agreements and ... the most progressive in terms of training and development, flexible working and new technology'. Recognition was bolstered by the implementation of a check-off agreement, a slot for a full-time official during induction, and a clear statement by the company during recruitment that it supports union membership. Membership participation is also assisted through facilities for the union to hold meetings with its members, and training courses are provided for representatives. Martin Wibberley was concerned that Bosch should not have 'a vacuum that would exist if we had an EETPU single union recognition deal here but they had a very low penetration. So, as a sort of risk limitation strategy, we wanted to encourage membership'.

If you were about to set up a new manufacturing plant in the late 1990s, would your approach be the same as at Bosch or would it differ? Why?

EDGING OUT THE UNIONS

While some employers have sought to develop their relationship with unions, others have opted for marginalisation or derecognition. In these situations employers have decided that their objectives are more likely to be achieved by reducing or removing the union presence. In some workplaces there may have been disputes which have slowed down or prevented changes in working practices, or managers may be concerned about whether or not they can work with trade unions. Others may simply have taken advantage of a superior power base to remove or restrict the activities of unions, to reduce wage costs, and enforce a stricter managerial regime, perhaps in line with some deep-seated antagonism among senior managers towards unions. Some of the reduction in union influence has occurred as part of a broader management strategy rather than an attack on unions as such, and the removal of the union is undertaken in conjunction with a shift to more direct methods of employee involvement. For example, some managements have placed considerable emphasis on cultures which stress personalised customer service and performance-related pay schemes rather than collectively-negotiated rates. In short, management is seeking to deny, rather than legitimise, the role of one or more unions.

Even when trade unions are marginalised they retain a presence in the workplace, and in many cases maintain the right to collective bargaining. In these situations, even though the institutions of collective employee relations remain in place, they represent a much less important aspect of human resource policies and practices. A number of changes are typically associated with marginalisation: substantial reductions in the number of shop stewards at establishment level; a severe tightening-up on access to time off for trade union activities and facilities for undertaking union-related work; withdrawal of full-time shop steward positions, often subsequent to the dismissal (usually through redundancy or early retirement) of the existing role-holders; lack of support for check-off arrangements; a lower priority accorded to collective bargaining with unions and (in some cases) the upgrading of information-passing meetings of management and stewards; a greater emphasis on individualism and direct communications from line managers to all employees.

Certainly in recent years, as unions have become less able and willing to take industrial action, employers have pruned the collective bargaining agenda and relied more heavily on written and oral communications to all staff as opposed to going through union channels alone. Perhaps this stance is best summed up in the words of a manager from a food factory, who said 'it's pushing negotiations down to consultation, and consultation down to communication' (Marchington and Parker, 1990: 144). In short, employers 'freeze out' shop stewards by allowing them less access to management, whilst at the same time making it more difficult for them to interact with their members.

Beyond marginalisation is derecognition, an idea that entered the vocabulary of British employee relations only in the 1980s (Gall and

McKay, 1994). It is important to appreciate at the outset that derecognition is not a homogeneous concept. In its most straightforward form derecognition refers to the complete withdrawal of collective bargaining rights and trade union organisation for some or all employees at a workplace, or throughout a complete employing organisation; in other words, no trade union is recognised for the employees involved, even though by law they retain the right to join unions of their choice. Alternatively, derecognition can mean the removal of bargaining rights for one or more unions in a multi-union environment, while allowing for, and even encouraging, the transfer of membership to other unions in the workplace. In this situation management might seek to simplify existing arrangements and reduce the number of unions with which it deals, and the end result could well be levels of union membership little different from before the derecognition. While it is clear that one union loses, another has the potential to gain in terms of membership.

We can get some idea of the *extensiveness* of derecognitions from the 1990 Workplace Industrial Relations Survey (Millward *et al*, 1992). They estimate that just 3 per cent of workplaces which recognised unions in 1984 no longer did so in 1990, although it should be noted that a similar percentage of workplaces which were non-union in 1984 did have recognition by 1990 (1992: 74–75). They suggest (1992: 75) that 'it seems plausible that in many of these workplaces union negotiating rights simply withered away through the lack of support from employees.' That is, it was unlikely there had been any major struggle over derecognition. Derecognition seems to be a small but increasingly significant practice across Britain. The types of employees most likely to lose their bargaining rights have been managers and other professional staff, with specific and well-publicised cases involving manual workers such as at Unipart, Tioxide and Esso.

Employers have derecognised for three main reasons. First, it occurs where union organisation and membership is in the process of withering away, and the actual act of derecognition by management is opportunistic. It is neither dramatic nor fiercely contested by the staff involved. Secondly, partial derecognitions have been implemented so as to 'tidy up' union arrangements at a workplace, and in many cases these are likely to be in situations where particular unions have low levels of membership; sometimes this will be part of a move to single-union agreements or as an aspect of company reorganisation or privatisation, as in the water industry with shifts to single-table bargaining following the dissolution of national negotiating arrangements (IRS *Employment Trends* 516, 1992). At the same time it should be noted that employers may take advantage of the simplification of bargaining units as an opportunity to derecognise unions and marginalise the shop stewards with whom they have had most difficulty. Thirdly, some managements have taken the view that 'collectivisation' is no longer appropriate for the organisation's future regime of employment relations. In some cases, as at Tioxide, this has been associated with a package to harmonise conditions between manual and white-collar staff. Esso's 270 drivers moved from collective bargaining to a system of individual contracts in late 1991, with merit pay being determined solely on the basis of performance appraisal; they are now known as 'distribution technicians' and have much broader responsibilities for the whole task. At the other extreme, according to the Incomes Data Services report (IDS, 1992: 13), there have been cases in the printing and publishing industry of unions not even being informed in advance by management that recognition was to be withdrawn.

Some people would argue that derecognition is morally offensive, a denial of workers' rights. What do you think?

However, while there is little doubt that derecognitions have become more popular in the last few years, it should be noted that in comparison to other sources of membership decline (such as shifts in employment from areas of high to low union density), the absolute impact of derecognitions is not that large. Moreover it is often forgotten that trade unions perform a number of functions in the workplace, many of which are likely to assist the management of employee relations. In a non-union organisation following complete derecognition the onus falls upon management to perform an even greater range of tasks, and there are suggestions that it has proved difficult to sustain alternative representation arrangements, as well as satisfy employee expectations about a 'new environment'.

MANAGING WITHOUT UNIONS

Just as derecognition did not figure at all in publications on employee relations until the 1980s, neither did the notion of non-union firms receive much attention prior to this time. It was well known that there were large numbers of small, usually independent, companies which did not recognise or deal with trade unions, but they were generally labelled as 'traditionalist', unitarist or 'sweatshop' employers, and castigated (usually quite rightly) for their poor treatment of staff. It was only with the growing awareness of what Beaumont (1987: 117) refers to as the 'household name' group – companies such as IBM, Marks & Spencer, Hewlett Packard – that academic and practitioner interest started to blossom. These companies were praised for their employee relations policies, which were designed to offer employees more than could be achieved by trade unions through negotiations. At last it appeared that non-union firms could actually feel proud of their approach to employee relations.

Non-unionism is more extensive in certain parts of the country (such as the south-east of England) and in certain sectors of the economy (such as retailing, professional services, and hotels and catering) than in others. Younger and smaller establishments are also more likely to be non-union, and there has been some debate as to whether the high technology sector is adding to the stock of non-unionism. But non-unionism can take many different forms, varying from the sophisticated, and arguably more pleasant, employment practices which characterise the 'household name' groups through to the sweatshops and 'bleak houses' (Sisson, 1993) of the 'Dickensian' employers. One of the problems with studies of non-union firms has been the lack of differentiation between these highly contrasting forms of employee relations, which have little in common beyond the refusal by employers to recognise trade unions for collective bargaining. Guest and Hoque (1994a) argue that the term 'non-unionism' is actually limiting, in that firms are only analysed 'in relation to' unionised organisations. They suggest a fourfold categorisation of non-union firms – the good, the bad, the ugly and the lucky.

First, and most celebrated by commentators, are employers who are probably leaders in their product market, who would be classified by Guest and Hoque as 'good'. These are often large employers, who have a clear strategy for managing people and operate with a wide range of human resource policies. These employers have tended to operate a 'union substitution' policy (Beaumont, 1987: 136) that offers a complete employment package which is intended to be seen by employees as an attractive alternative to trade union membership. Such an approach might include a highly competitive pay and benefits package which is typically in excess of those offered by other firms recruiting from the same labour market; a comprehensive battery of recruitment techniques (including psychometric tests) designed to select individuals who 'match' organisational norms and discard those who do not fit with the company profile (eg those with a history of union activism); a high priority accorded to induction programmes which are geared up to socialising employees into the company ethos; a stress on training and development opportunities, related both to the employees' work and more broadly to their role in the company and society (eg employee development and assistance programmes and career counselling); a focus on employee communications and information-sharing within the enterprise, such as through team briefing; a system (such as speak-up) enabling employee concerns and anxieties to be dealt with by management (rather than a union), as well as for contributing ideas which may help to improve organisational efficiency; a commitment to providing secure and satisfying work while employed by the organisation, often involving regular moves to different types of job; single status and harmonised employment policies between blue- and white-collar employees; an individualised pay and appraisal system differentiating between staff in terms of previous performance and future potential, designed to reward those who contribute most to organisational success, (eg performance-related or merit pay). This theme is taken up again in Chapter 18 when we consider 'best practice' P&D.

For example, a company such as IBM, with a highly-qualified workforce, has for years utilised most of these employment practices (Bassett, 1987), and indeed in some areas has been credited as the architect of these sorts of policies – for example, speak-up and open-door programmes. The company also made use of regular employee attitude surveys and had a high commitment to training and development of staff well before many other leading employers realised the advantages which could be gained from such initiatives. IBM's practice of job security was also well publicised for many years, helping the company through its relocation from London to the south coast in the 1970s. In recent years, following increasingly severe competition and over-capacity in the international computer market, this practice has lapsed as management have sought to 'right-size' (an attempt to find a neutral term for redundancies and lay-offs). In the early 1990s, IBM cut over 100,000 jobs worldwide, including almost one-third of the British workforce.

The leading food retailers, such as J Sainsbury and Safeway, are also worthy of being considered under the same banner, offering way in excess of their competitors at the low-cost and no-frills end of the market, although rather less than IBM in terms of employment practices. In addition, as the market segments further, these firms are aiming to differentiate themselves from the remainder of the competition, and as such are extending horizontal integration of P&D (see Chapter 18). Recent years have seen improvements to their recruitment and induction programmes, a greater stress on communications and involvement, and management development courses which emphasise open styles of supervision. As with IBM, these two companies have preferred to regulate employee relations without recognising trade unions for collective bargaining, and as such have seen the need to implement a range of policies which ensure that managers pay close attention to employee relations issues. Even in IBM and Marks & Spencer, however, employees are free to join trade unions if they desire and are legally protected against dismissal or other forms of disciplinary action on the grounds of their union membership. Many other 'household names' do not recognise trade unions for bargaining purposes, even though they have pockets of union membership and allow officials or workplace representatives to accompany employees who are subject to disciplinary action or have a grievance against the company.

However, these organisations have not escaped criticism. It could be argued that 'sophisticated' employment practices are merely an illusion designed to obscure the true nature of human resource management regimes in these types of company, or that workers are merely 'conned' by their overt appeal into working harder, not for their own benefit but for that of the company. Similarly, it has been suggested that employers will continue to provide superior employment practices only under favourable economic and competitive conditions, and that product market problems will lead to their permanent or temporary withdrawal; in other words, the supposed employer commitment to employees as their 'most valuable resource' is both superficial and trite. The argument that these sophisticated non-union organisations offer good benefits only because of the previous and continuing efforts of trade unions across the economy as a whole also has a fair degree of credence.

The second type of non-union firm is the traditional, sweatshop employer, often a small independent single-site company operating as

> The P&D practices used by these 'good' firms certainly look attractive to employees. Assess whether or not they represent a cost-effective alternative to trade unions.

a supplier to one of the sophisticated non-union organisations analysed above. Managements which deliberately deprive workers of their rights are categorised as 'ugly' whereas those which offer poor terms and conditions without such a manipulative intent are referred to as 'bad'. The subordinate role many of these small suppliers have with a larger company – dependent, dominated and isolated – leaves them with little control over their own destiny and places a primacy on labour flexibility. These firms are under considerable pressure to control costs and enhance flexibility, goals which many of these employers believe to be achievable only without what they see as interference by trade unions. In these circumstances pay rates are likely to be low, while formal fringe benefits and welfare arrangements would be virtually non-existent. The regime in these small firms is highly personalised (Scott, Roberts, Holroyd and Sawbridge, 1989: 42). Recruitment practices are also likely to reflect the owner/managers' deep distrust of unions. The lack of formal disciplinary procedures means that employee protection is haphazard and arbitrary at best, totally absent at worst.

Millward *et al* (1992: 363–365) confirm this picture of few procedures, highly personal relations and harsh discipline. WIRS showed that one-fifth of companies which did not recognise trade unions had no disciplinary procedure, one-quarter had no mechanism for handling grievances, and a similar number had no health and safety machinery. Although managers in some non-union firms claimed that there was a substantial flow of information, formal meetings were rare and at about half the establishments there was no regular dissemination of financial information to employees. Moreover, dismissals in non-union firms as a whole occurred at twice the rate of their unionised counterparts. The picture which emerges is one of harsh informality, somewhat at odds with the claim that 'small is beautiful'. As Scott *et al* (1989: 45–46) note, 'What often passes for good communication is usually the more negative situation in which no one has said anything' – they must be happy because no one has complained!

The final type of non-union firm is the 'lucky', the organisations in which there is neither much in the way of sophistication nor a concerted attempt to manage by fear and union suppression. These are organisations with little formalisation of procedures for recruitment and selection, induction, payments, grievance and discipline, health and safety, or communications, and none of these will be characterised by innovation or best practice. Equally, pay rates are likely to be towards the lower quartile, while formal fringe benefits and welfare packages reflect what the company can afford at the time. Owners/managers in these firms, however, are unlikely to hold deep reservations about trade unions, and indeed have probably hardly ever thought about them at all. Their non-union status owes more to 'straightforward avoidance or opportunism rather than to any HRM-derived sophisticated "substitution" strategy designed to obviate the need for union representation' (McLoughlin and Gourlay, 1992: 685). Accordingly, employment policies are likely to be fragmented, often poorly developed, and even non-existent until a need arises to resolve a particular issue at work. There is unlikely to be a personnel specialist on site, and if a personnel manager has been appointed this person will in all probability have been transferred from another function (for example, engineering) once his or her useful contribution there has been exhausted. At the same time, given the familial nature of these kinds of organisation, communications channels are likely to be open and workers are unlikely to feel any great threat from the owner/manager. In a sense, unitarism and team spirit are combined in an attempt to 'see off' the competition, in so doing displaying elements of patriotism and patriarchal relations.

CONCLUSION

It is important to reiterate that employee relations, like all aspects of P&D, are characterised by conflict *and* co-operation. At certain times, and in certain workplaces, one of these assumes predominance, sometimes leading to the misguided impression that employee relations at one site or at one point in time are solely about conflict, whereas at other establishments or times are seen only in terms of co-operation. Just because conflict is not expressed overtly, this does not mean that it is absent, and neither can it be assumed that the workplace is a haven of consent. In a similar vein, debates about whether the British employee relations system has been subject to change or continuity are also rather sterile, since it is the mixture of developments and their unevenness which is more noticeable.

It would appear that employee relations are becoming increasingly bifurcated, not so much *between* union and non-union organisations, but *within* each of these broad categories. Given the degree to which labour markets have been deregulated since the early 1980s, employers now have greater flexibility in choosing appropriate styles and structures for managing employee relations, as well as a greater opportunity to integrate people management strategies with those affecting the business as a whole. To do this effectively, however, requires employers to embrace a more strategic and externally focused approach to the management of employee relations, to be aware of the techniques which are adopted by other employers, and to disregard the latest fads and fashions if these are inappropriate for their own workplace. How many do this, of course, is another question.

USEFUL READING

BLYTON, P. AND TURNBULL, P. (1994) *The Dynamics of Employee Relations*. London, Macmillan.

FARNHAM, D. (1993) *Employee Relations*. London, IPM.

GALL, G. AND MCKAY, S. (1994) 'Trade union derecognition in Britain, 1988–1994' *British Journal of Industrial Relations*, Vol 32, 3: 433–448.

GUEST, D. AND HOQUE, K. (1994) 'The good, the bad and the ugly: employment relations in new non-union workplace', *Human Resource Management Journal*, Vol 5, 1: 1–14.

INVOLVEMENT AND PARTICIPATION ASSOCIATION (1995) *Towards*

Industrial Partnership: Putting it into practice – Rhone Poulenc Stavely chemicals: a case study in movement to single status. London, IPA.

McLOUGHLIN, I. AND GOURLAY, S. (1992) 'Enterprise without unions: the management of employee relations in non-union firms', *Journal of Management Studies*, Vol 29, 5: 669–691.

MARCHINGTON, M. (1995a) 'Employee relations', in S. Tyson (Ed.), *Strategic Prospects for HRM.* London, IPD: 81–111.

MARCHINGTON, M. AND PARKER, P. (1990) *Changing Patterns of Employee Relations.* Hemel Hempstead, Harvester Wheatsheaf.

WICKENS, P. (1987) *The Road to Nissan: Flexibility, quality, teamwork.* London, Macmillan.

WILKINSON, A., MARCHINGTON, M. AND ACKERS, P. (1993) 'Strategies for human resource management: issues in larger and international firms', in R. Harrison (Ed.) *Human Resource Management.* Wokingham, Addison-Wesley: 85–109.

12 The processes of employee relations

INTRODUCTION

In this chapter we discuss how the 'rules' of employee relations are made. By rules we do not simply mean those which are laid down formally in the company handbook, but the wide range of imposed or agreed rules which operate at the workplace. Rules establish ways of working in organisations and hence are a key feature of workplace employee relations.

Rules may be established by management 'diktat', actually making rules without negotiation and consultation, such as deciding to introduce a new initiative without reference to other parties. On the other hand, rules may be established by custom and practice, so that a way of working (eg leaving five minutes early to wash up) may become the norm without formal agreement. Rules may be established through a process of negotiation and bargaining – as in the introduction of a new payment scheme – with part of the deal being that workers who do badly from the scheme are red-circled and protected. Equally, it might be that workers are only consulted or informed about the change but it is not actually negotiated. Finally, rules may be established by the law, for example over what are acceptable reasons to dismiss employees.

In short, we find that rules are made by a series of processes. These fall into five categories: management prerogatives; custom and practice; third-party involvement and legal enactment; negotiation and bargaining; and involvement and consultation. In the workplace, employee relations are 'messy' and it may well be that practices evolve from a combination of the rule-making processes. For example, in making employees redundant the employer has to abide by certain legal regulations which require consultation with the workforce, yet management prerogatives may be enforced regarding the choice of employees to be made redundant. To complicate matters yet further, custom and practice – such as a last in, first out policy – may also influence the outcome.

By the end of this chapter readers should be able to:

- contribute to the design, implementation and evaluation of employee relations processes

- review the effectiveness of collective bargaining at their workplace, and make recommendations about changes to its structure

- provide advice as to the appropriateness of adopting different forms of employee involvement within their organisation.

In addition, they should be able to understand and explain:

- the way in which rules are made at the workplace

- the nature and meaning of collective bargaining, and its place within the employee relations framework

- the principal differences between industrial democracy and employee involvement.

MANAGEMENT PREROGATIVES

To try to understand management's approach to employee relations, it is useful to draw upon the concepts of 'frames of reference' developed by Alan Fox (1966) in his research paper for the Donovan Commission. These embody the main selective influences employed by managers and which cause them to supplement, omit and structure what they see. Thus, two people may see the same event in a completely different manner and may judge its meaning, significance and outcomes in contrasting ways. The unitary perspective sees the organisation as a team (like a football team), with all employees striving towards a common goal. All members of the team are assumed to work to the best of their ability, accept their place in the hierarchy, and follow their appointed leader. There is no room or reason for factions. Given that unions are unnecessary (since everyone is on the same side), conflict is seen as pathological or abnormal, the result of misunderstanding and troublemakers. In contrast, pluralism conceives of the organisation as comprising varied interest groups with common and divergent interests, and management's job is to balance these competing demands. Trade unions may be seen as a natural reflection of varied interests, rather than a cause of conflict. Conflict is not regarded as illegitimate, but needs to be channelled or managed through rules and procedures.

In simple terms, the principal difference between the two frames of reference rests upon a willingness to accept the curbing of management prerogatives at the workplace. Managers with a unitary perspective would expect employees to trust them to make the 'correct' decision, and since everyone supposedly has the same interests there should be no conflict between what is the best for the company and what is the best decision for employees. In contrast, the pluralist, who accepts the role of a union in the workplace, believes in a policy of gaining the support of unions and employees to achieve an 'acceptable' solution. Pluralists believe that shop stewards should be consulted about changes which may have a fundamental effect on employees. On many occasions the *substantive* outcome of joint decision-making may be little different from that which would have been achieved by direct management action. However, the *procedural* element is different and is critical.

Managers may vary in their willingness to accept a curbing of managerial rights, both between individuals and with the subject matter under consideration. For example, managers may well be willing to negotiate on matters relating to payment methods, job design and work practices, but be unwilling even to consult about matters such as investment and pricing policy, and product development. At any event, while management may be willing to consult, involve and even bargain, they will also insist that they have a 'prerogative' to make the final decision. Hence, in certain areas of employee relations – such as promotion and training – management prerogative is the norm. In organisations where unions are absent, management is able to vary terms and conditions of employment at will.

Since the 1980s managements have rediscovered their prerogative (Purcell, 1990). While cases of macho management showed how employers could transform their employee relations practices by sacking senior shop stewards, withdrawing recognition and tightening disciplinary standards, this is now recognised as having been relatively rare. However, it is clear that practices have changed in the workplace, with managements being more prepared to make use of their superior bargaining power. Purcell (1990: 33–34) argues that radical changes in the institutional map of industrial relations have been reflected in the replacement of multi-employer bargaining with single employer bargaining, and within that concentration of decentralised unit-specific arrangements which is associated with organisation-based employment systems. This is in contrast to the reliance on industry wage-fixing institutions to set terms and conditions of employment. Within these new systems the role of the union may be marginalised as the employer focuses on direct communication with individual employees and the implementation of P&D practices, such as performance-related pay, which are managerially determined. In short, the scope of managerial prerogative has been extended.

> Write down a list of decisions which you feel are the prerogative of management in your organisation. Does this equate with what you think *should* be determined solely by management?

CUSTOM AND PRACTICE

Although management may be able to devise coherent strategies it cannot be assumed that, once formulated, these are actually implemented in practice. As Brown (1973: 85) notes in his study of piecework bargaining, the rules that prevailed had little or no resemblance to those that had originally been laid down by management or through formal agreement. One reason for this is the existence of custom and practice on the shopfloor. This can be defined as rules which are produced and/or reproduced in the workplace through day-to-day interactions between the parties at work. It is important to appreciate that custom and practice is not simply a device operated and applied solely by employees alone, in attempts to mitigate the worst effects of management pressure which they can do little to prevent. Indeed, it is often supervisors and line managers who not only allow custom and practice to flourish, but also help to create it by their own interpretation of organisation rules.

This can occur in a number of ways; firstly, even if the formal rules are presented in a clear and unambiguous manner, line managers still have some discretion in whether and how to apply these rules – in the same way that a police officer 'decides whether to ignore, warn or report the speeding motorist' (Purcell, 1979a: 1040). One example of this is described by Armstrong, Goodman and Hyman (1981: 87) in the case of the 'whistling forelady':

> About an hour after the official morning break ... the forelady cruises around whistling an odd little tune through her teeth ... without a single word the girls flock to the lavatories ... on mornings when *he* (the works director) is around, the girls do not get their extra break.

Secondly, line managers may fail to implement rules precisely so as to allow themselves discretion and leeway in their handling of workers. One well-known example is a rule requiring workers to report lateness of over three minutes to the supervisor who has authority to accept or reject the excuse, with rejections resulting in the loss of fifteen minutes' pay. In practice, supervisors tolerated lengthier period of lateness as well as a long list of acceptable excuses. This process took place because 'It seemed to be the case that these concessions of lateness were made by the foremen to try to get co-operation from the workforce over issues which were unpopular with the shopfloor' (Terry, 1977: 80).

In these circumstances custom and practice is created by conscious acts of managers. In other circumstances supervisors find that they are unable to accept a senior management rule as either sensible or legitimate, and so apply the rule 'without enthusiasm'. In addition, custom and practice can be created not just by acts of commission or omission, but also by an error or a failure to see that shopfloor practices may be flouting formal rules; hence the informal practice continues and becomes established. A famous example is train drivers' invoking a 'work to rule' whereby they followed every rule and regulation in existence. This meant the service could never run on time as every door had to be shut before the train left the platform. In short, following every rule and regulation can mean that the organisation grinds to a halt. Sometimes, custom and practice can be created unwittingly by more senior managers during walkabouts on the office or shopfloor. Finally, it should be noted that it is actually possible for rules to be applied more strictly than in the procedure as line managers try to push through an issue or interpret a formal rule from above so as to quash worker demands.

With regard to your own organisation, produce a list of 'rules' made by custom and practice which are at odds with official rules and regulations.

LEGAL ENACTMENT AND THIRD-PARTY INTERVENTION

In Britain the law has traditionally played a minor role compared with many other countries. As we saw from Chapter 2, there has been a minimum of legal intervention here, and the character of the British system has been moulded more by the employers and trade unions rather than legal enactment by the state. 'Voluntarism' has been the prevailing philosophy with 'collective *laissez-faire*' (Kahn-Freund, 1959: 224) seen as the appropriate process to resolve employee relations issues; the law was seen only as a mechanism of last resort to be used when other voluntary means had failed. However, legal intervention has to be assessed not only against its desirability but also against its likelihood of attaining the modifications which are expected from its operation.

According to Kahn-Freund (1965: 302), the law performs a number of different roles in the rule-making process. Firstly, there is the *auxiliary* role through which the state provides a statutory framework of what is called 'organised persuasion'. This provides benefits - financial or otherwise – for those who observe agreements, and a number of pressures are applied against those who do not. A good illustration of this type of role can be seen in the action of ACAS which provides services such as conciliation, mediation and arbitration. Until the Trade Union Reform and Employment Rights Act 1993, ACAS also had the duty of 'encouraging the extension of collective bargaining, and where necessary, reform of collective bargaining machinery' but its public policy commitment to collective bargaining has now been removed. Secondly, the law has a *restrictive* role in that it provides a set of rules which stipulate what is allowed and what is forbidden in the conduct of industrial relations. Thus, rules which define legitimate strike action and picketing have existed for a long period, but have been the subject of major reforms during the last 15 years. Thirdly, the law has a *regulatory* role in that it sets a 'floor of employment rights' for employees. Again, this is a long-standing role which dates back to the nineteenth and early twentieth centuries when it was introduced to provide protection in industries such as mining, and over issues such as pay in sweatshops. In the 1970s the employment protection legislation took on a wider remit, incorporating all employees rather than just those in particular industries or working under particularly harsh conditions. Apart from actively setting certain rules and regulations, the law also has a wider impact. For example, the legislation on unfair dismissal has led to changes in the way people are recruited and selected, the formalisation of disciplinary procedures and the keeping of records (see Chapter 13).

Voluntarism came under attack due to the poor performance of the British economy, leading the state to intervene more in employee relations, through both economic policies and the legislative arena – for example the Industrial Relations Act 1971 which attempted the replacement of voluntarism with a more American-style legal regulation. Despite its failure, it did signify increasing concern over what were seen as the costs of voluntarism. The Conservative government which was elected in 1979 saw industrial relations at the centre of the 'British disease' and intervened with a step-by-step dismantling of union protections, ostensibly designed to free up the labour market. More recently a number of EU decisions have strengthened the position of workers – for example, in relation to redundancy, maternity, equal value and hours of work.

> To what extent do you think the state *should* intervene in employee relations? Discuss this question with colleagues on your course, and consider who has gained most from state intervention over the years.

COLLECTIVE BARGAINING

Collective bargaining has long been a significant component of British employee relations, certainly from the end of the First World War through to the 1980s, when it was the principal method by which wages and conditions were determined for a majority of the workforce. In addition, collective bargaining outcomes (in terms of wage levels, hours worked and holiday entitlements, for example) also influenced the terms and conditions of employees whose pay was determined by management alone. Indeed, as we saw in Chapter 11, one reason the sophisticated paternalist employers offer terms and conditions of employment superior to those which are negotiated by trade unions is to ensure that they remain union-free. In recent years, however, as we shall see below, the prominence of collective bargaining has declined.

A standard definition of collective bargaining is 'negotiations about working conditions and terms and conditions of employment between an employer, a group of employers or one or more employers' organisations, on the one hand, and one or more representative workers' organisations on the other, with a view to reaching an agreement' (Farnham and Pimlott, 1995: 143). This definition tends to emphasise the formal and institutional aspects of employee relations, and the image which is conjured up is of annual pay negotiations conducted at national level between large groups of employers' representatives and union officials, typically interrupted by threats about industrial action or final offers. While this is one perspective of collective bargaining, and one which is highly visible to the entire population through media coverage, it is a somewhat limited example. Collective bargaining is by no means restricted to these kinds of set-piece confrontation, and indeed the mass of negotiations take place continually between shop stewards, supervisors/line managers and personnel managers at workplace level, incorporating a wide range of matters concerned with working conditions, health and safety, discipline and grievance cases, and welfare/social concerns. The definition offered by Gospel and Palmer (1993: 180) captures this wider perspective rather better: 'an all-pervasive social process which involves the interaction between two or more individuals or groups which are attempting to define or redefine the terms of their relationships ... [it] may be covert or overt, it may result in informal or formal outcomes'. Thus, collective bargaining is a process which occurs principally (in terms of the time involved and the number of issues dealt with) at workplace level through unwritten deals and custom and practice, while some of the more important and long-term decisions about pay and working conditions are the subject of infrequent company-wide or multi-employer negotiations.

Collective bargaining is concerned with both substantive and procedural issues, the former referring to *what* is determined while the latter relates to *how* the matters of substance are to be decided between the parties now and in the future. Many of the blockages in bargaining occur not because of disputes about substantive matters (such as marginal increases in pay), but are due to disagreements about how employee relations are to be managed in the future – for example, union derecognition or the removal of the senior shop steward's facilities. Perhaps the multi-faceted character and purpose of collective bargaining is best understood with the help of Chamberlain and Kuhn's (1965: 113) distinction between the marketing, govern-mental/political and managerial concepts. Under the *marketing* concept, bargaining can be viewed as a means of contracting for the sale of labour and as a method for remedying economic inequalities. The *governmental* concept considers collective bargaining as a technique for setting a constitutional system of rule-making, for providing channels through which major disputes or workers' grievances may be handled. Finally, within the *managerial* concept, collective bargaining offers a mechanism for non-managerial employees to contribute their ideas and alternative perspectives, perhaps through joint consultation, to achieve improvements in organisational performance. In short, collective bargaining is both an adversarial *and* a co-operative process, one in which employees not only oppose managerial plans with which they disagree but may also wish to improve management decisions which they feel to be inadequate. In rare circumstances unions may unilaterally set the rules, the other side of the coin to management prerogative. This was seen historically with the craft societies which imposed their own employment rules on employers, often insisting on a specific period of apprenticeship and requiring all new workers to have a union card.

The extensiveness of formal collective bargaining can be estimated from the WIRS3 data. This shows (Millward *et al*, 1992: 91) that the proportion of employees (in establishments which employ 25 or more people) whose terms and conditions are formally negotiated by collective bargaining fell from 71 per cent in 1980 to 54 per cent a decade later. There are variations between sectors, with the public sector showing the highest extent of coverage and the private service sector the lowest. In total, according to WIRS3, over eight million workers had their terms and conditions determined by collective bargaining in 1990, of which over half were from the public sector.

CHOICES ABOUT BARGAINING LEVELS

The shape and character of collective bargaining varies considerably between workplaces, in particular in relation to the *level* at which bargaining takes place and the size/structure of the *unit* of employees who are covered by any agreement. The concept of bargaining level refers to the point(s) at which collective bargaining takes place, and it can range from workplace/section through to establishment, division, company and industry/multi-employer at its most complex. In many cases terms and conditions are the subject of negotiation at more than one level in the hierarchy, as for example with the setting of holiday entitlements at industry level, pension arrangements at the company level, and wages and flexibility issues locally. In other words, bargaining can take place both on a multi- and a single-employer basis, as well as at a range of levels within a multi-establishment organisation.

For a large part of this century, and certainly until the 1950s, multi-employer bargaining was considered to be the norm in the UK, and in some industries there was very little difference between the nationally-negotiated wage rate and an individual's actual pay. It was estimated that in 1948 the national rate in engineering comprised over 95 per cent of the standard pay package, although by 1968 the Donovan Commission reckoned that wage drift at local level had reduced this to nearer half. Although there was some closing of the gap during the 1970s, the national agreement collapsed when the Engineering Employers' Federation withdrew from national bargaining following the trade union campaign for a shorter working week in the late 1980s; this reduced by about 900,000 the number of employees who had at least part of their terms and conditions negotiated by multi-employer bargaining. In the 1980s, several other multi-employer agreements came to an end, including baking and milling, meat traders, multiple food retailers, national newspapers, banking, and the bus and coach industry (IRS *Employment Trends* 544, 1993).

In most cases employers have argued that national, multi-employer arrangements are increasingly inappropriate, and that they would prefer to negotiate terms and conditions which can be tailored to company- or site-specific goals and targets. Inevitably, this has been influenced by pressures from increasingly competitive international product markets and the fact that trade unions have been less able to resist moves to decentralise negotiations in recent years. For example, Leopold and Jackson's (1990: 186) analysis of the decision by Coats Viyella to withdraw from Knitting Industries Federation negotiations with the National Union of Hosiery and Knitwear Workers shows that decentralisation fitted well with the devolution of responsibility to profit centres, in addition to allowing for greater managerial control over wage costs and productivity. Government policies have also provided triggers for the abolition of multi-employer arrangements, either directly following the privatisation of major utilities such as water and electricity, or indirectly through the encouragement of local deals which more closely reflect company or plant-specific problems, such as in the ports following the abolition of the National Dock Labour Scheme in the late 1980s. Overall, therefore, the last decade has seen a significant reduction in the extent of multi-employer bargaining.

How are pay and working conditions determined at an organisation of your choice, and has this changed in the last few years? Why has it changed or why has it not changed? Review your answer after completing this section.

However, it is important to see this decline in multi-employer bargaining in perspective. While there was a sizeable reduction in the importance of multi-employer bargaining during the late 1980s, this still remained the basis for the most recent pay increase in a quarter of establishments in 1990 compared with nearly 40 per cent in 1984 (Millward *et al*, 1992: 218). In comparison, single-employer bargaining formed the basis for the most recent pay increase in less than 20 per cent of establishments. But this aggregate prominence of multi-employer arrangements owes a considerable amount to its centrality in the public sector where it was four or five times as important as single-employer bargaining. Even though the system is under strain and some local authorities have introduced local agreements, the vast majority of employees continue to rely heavily on national negotiations for large elements of their pay and benefits packages (Beaumont, 1992: 112–114). Within the private sector as a whole, the decline has been rather more pronounced, and Brown (1993: 195) estimates that single-employer bargaining is four times as likely as its multi-employer equivalent. The latter is least important among non-manual employees in the private service sector and most important (in comparative terms) across manufacturing where there remain national agreements in industries such as printing, electrical contracting and construction (Kessler & Bayliss, 1995).

In the case of single-employer bargaining further questions arise about the level at which decisions concerning pay and other terms and conditions of employment are to be taken, and whether or not to confine bargaining to just one level. The data from WIRS3 shows quite different patterns for the three main sectors of employment. In manufacturing, where rather fewer establishments were covered by collective agreements, plant-level deals were about twice as important as company-level agreements for both manual and non-manual employees. Employees in larger establishments were much more likely to have their wages determined by plant-level negotiations, and this was especially marked for manual workers (Millward *et al*, 1992: 22–27). As might be expected, single-employer bargaining in the private service sector was much more centralised, and it was uncommon for non-manual employees to have access to local negotiations. Bargaining at single-employer, multi-site level increased substantially in the private service sector during the 1980s, affecting nearly twice as many establishments as in 1980 (Millward *et al*, 1992: 229). We have already noted the importance of centralised multi-employer arrangements in the public sector, a picture which is mirrored among the small minority of establishments which are covered by single-employer bargaining.

The last decade has seen shifts away from centralised bargaining arrangements towards a greater emphasis on site and unit-level negotiations. In the early 1990s, for example, Philips brought to an end its system of centralised bargaining as part of a wider move to restructure the business and devolve management decision-making to local business unit level. Purcell and Ahlstrand's (1989: 409–411) case studies on multi-divisional companies also demonstrated the move away from centralised bargaining, although they found a wide variety of structures.

There are a number of factors which influence employer choices about the level at which negotiations are most appropriately conducted in multi-establishment organisations, some of which relate to industrial/economic characteristics of firms while others reflect more deep-seated political and ideological pressures. It should be stated at the outset that choice of most appropriate bargaining level is not a simple technical decision, and much depends upon judgements about the balance of power between employer and union, as well as the previous history of employee relations within the company itself. Centralised or decentralised bargaining may prove highly attractive to one employer for reasons which would make this totally illogical for another. Decisions about pay determination, or indeed any other employee relations practice, are not made in isolation from other business policies; priorities in other parts of the business may take precedence over what appear to be appropriate for employee relations. According to Ahlstrand and Purcell, 'Without exception, motivations for changing bargaining levels derived from changes in a wider business structure/style and not for industrial relations reasons ... The stated aim has been to tie industrial relations and bargaining outcomes to the business performance of the operating units' (1988).

Bearing these cautionary comments in mind, there are three principal advantages to employers of centralised single-employer bargaining. First, it encourages employees to identify with the company as a whole, and relate their pay and conditions of employment to the performance of the enterprise in its entirety. This approach is particularly prominent within parts of the financial services sector, such as building societies. Secondly, it enables head office to control labour costs directly and remove the possibility of leapfrogging claims within the organisation, or the use of coercive comparisons to supplement pay levels. Where unions have the potential for effective workplace organisation and are less likely to challenge management decisions at corporate level, centralisation may offer an attractive choice for employers. Thirdly, it allows for the use of specialist expertise in negotiating with unions at company level, and the concentration of managerial resources within one corporate personnel/human resource unit. Centralised single-employer bargaining is most likely in organisations with large numbers of standard employing units across the country (as, for example, in much of the private service sector such as in supermarkets or banks), where there is little point in providing for local bargaining given standard product ranges at each site. The major disadvantage of bargaining at company level in these circumstances is that it denies local managers the opportunity to control one of their most significant costs.

However, there are at least three major advantages to local bargaining, which have to be balanced against its limitations. It allows pay and other terms and conditions of employment to be linked more closely with local labour market pressures and establishment performance. This is especially important if there are significant variations in labour market circumstances which lead to shortages for particular types of labour in one area of the country, but not in others. Equally, it allows plant managers to reward workers for high performance – or penalise them for low performance – to introduce flexibility deals, and to ensure that labour costs are kept in line with other key performance ratios. Secondly, it encourages employees to identify more closely with the local establishment, something which is especially important in a conglomerate which trades under a range of names and is not seeking commitment to, and identification with, the holding company. The association between effort and reward is more easily made in these circumstances. Thirdly, it minimises the opportunity for trade union negotiators to build links with their counterparts at other establishments, and reduces the likelihood of comparability with other sites.

There are also suggestions that employers opt for specific collective bargaining arrangements in order to ensure that trade unions are kept away from the level at which key managerial decisions are made, or from the individuals who make them; this is known as 'institutional separation' (Purcell, 1983; Kinnie, 1985; Marchington and Parker, 1990). Typically, this describes the situation in which bargaining is conducted at establishment level, whereas decisions about capital investment, product and pricing policies, and unit labour costs are reserved for managers at corporate headquarters. The idea of institutional separation can be refined further by arguing that any autonomy apparently afforded to local unit managers is in fact illusory as their activities are closely monitored by head office personnel. As Marginson, Edwards, Martin, Purcell and Sisson (1988: 238) note, corporate officers reported that they were 'either directly involved in negotiations or pay determination, or indirectly involved through the issuing of guidelines or instructions or the convening of meetings to discuss offers'.

BARGAINING UNITS

This refers to the specific groups or categories of employees covered by a particular agreement, and it can range from narrow to wide, from a single category and sometimes small number of employees, through to a mass of different jobs or grades incorporated within the same negotiations. Interest in recent years has focused on the increasing width of bargaining units, especially at workplace or company level, and the supposed attractions of single-table bargaining (STB). However, this needs to be seen in the context of multi-unionism, which has been one of the distinctive features of British employee relations compared with other European countries (Millward *et al*, 1992: 77). The 1990 WIRS survey found (p 81) that an average of 2.5 unions operated at each establishment where there was recognition, and two or more unions were recognised at about two-thirds of all these workplaces. However, recognition of ten or more unions is now rare in manufacturing. By way of contrast, the simplest bargaining structures were found in foreign-owned and newer firms in the private sector.

It has been estimated by Gall (1993: 13) that the number of organisations which utilise STB doubled between 1990 and 1993. Furthermore, the number of employees whose terms and conditions of employment are negotiated via STB increased over the same period from 30,000 to nearly a quarter of a million, although it should be noted this is only a very small proportion of the workforce.

Recent examples include British Steel, Ilford, Southern Electric, Vauxhall, several of the water companies, and some of the NHS Trusts. In the case of Ilford, for example, the first single-table deal occurred in 1992, replacing previous arrangements whereby the five recognised unions had operated under four separate bargaining units. There had been discussions between management and the unions (through the Joint Shop Stewards Committee which covered both the blue- and white-collar unions) for several years about how to simplify pay bargaining and overcome demarcations between different groups of employees.

It is apparent that both management and unions can gain from STB. For the unions, the advent of STB can prevent 'divide and rule' tactics on the part of management and, provided the unions have clear objectives, help to develop closer working relationships and reduce the likelihood of inter-union disputes. The rationalisation of unions at establishment level, whereby some of the smaller unions (in terms of membership levels at the establishments involved) lose representative rights to larger unions, can also increase the effectiveness of union organisation and cohesiveness on the ground. There is also a feeling that STB deals have prevented employer-driven single union arrangements, and they have gained a measure of TUC support (Gall, 1993: 14).

STB has a number of advantages for employers. It helps to encourage a common view across the site or company from all the unions which are represented, and remove the possibility of leapfrogging claims. It reduces the amount of time which has to be devoted to negotiating, an important consideration in some organisations where specialist industrial relations managers traditionally have three or more separate sets of negotiations with different unions at different times of the year. STB also allows employers to involve union representatives in questions of how to allocate overall pay and benefits packages *between* different grades of employees. Since harmonisation and single-status considerations have been a major impetus behind the drive for STB, persuading both blue- and white-collar union representatives to negotiate together has eased the process of change – see Chapter 16 for a fuller discussion on harmonisation.

STB is not without its drawbacks, however. Issues of employee representation are of major importance to each of the unions, and agreements have to be achieved about how to allocate seats at the table, especially to unions with a minor presence. Although there may be sizeable advantages in meeting with all the unions at the same time, this also limits the potential to agree separate deals with different groups of employees; in effect, it reduces the likelihood that one union can be 'played off' against another. There are also doubts about the relevance of all single-table business to each participant, and the danger that some members will find meetings a waste of time and resources. Each of these concerns may lead employers to opt for a rationalisation of bargaining structures, but go for a compromise arrangement such as two-table bargaining – as at Seeboard in the early 1990s where management felt it was inappropriate for supervisors and professionals to have their terms and conditions indirectly determined by those they supervise.

> What are the implications of single-table bargaining for other aspects of P&D – employee resourcing, employee development and employee reward?

FROM INDUSTRIAL DEMOCRACY TO EMPLOYEE INVOLVEMENT

In recent years there has been considerable interest in the growth of employee participation and its relationship with collective bargaining, conditions of employment in particular being determined less by bargaining and more by consultation and involvement. Interest in the subject of employee participation has swung dramatically over the last thirty years, with different models of participation being proposed in the 1980s and 1990s from those advocated in the 1970s (Roberts and Wilkinson, 1991).

The 1970s model of participation reached its high point with the 1977 Bullock Report on 'Industrial Democracy', which addressed the question of *how* workers might be represented at board level. This emerged in period of strong union bargaining power and the Labour government's 'Social Contract', an atmosphere which provided the Bullock approach to industrial participation with several distinctive features. It was partly union-initiated, through the Labour Party, and based on collectivist principles which saw trade unions playing a central part in future arrangements. In addition, it was wedded to the general principle of employee rights established on a statutory basis (Ackers, Marchington, Wilkinson and Goodman, 1992: 272).

Experiments were initiated at the Post Office and the British Steel Corporation, but both had been discontinued by the early 1980s. In contrast, the 1980s produced a quite different agenda for participation, retitled 'employee involvement' (EI). The context was reduced union power and an anti-corporatist Thatcher government, which resisted statutory blueprints (excepting some tax breaks for profit sharing), and encouraged firms to evolve the arrangements which best suited them. This agenda differs from that of the 1970s in several ways. First, it is management-initiated, often from outside the industrial relations sphere, and with scant reference to trade unions. Second, the new EI is individualist, and stresses direct communications with the individual employee. Third, it is presented as driven by business criteria concerning economic performance and the 'bottom line', stressing the influence on employee motivation and commitment (Ackers *et al*, 1992: 272). Thus, employer interest in participation in the 1980s continued, although less concerned with the concept of joint negotiation and with much greater emphasis on quality circles, team briefing and profit sharing.

Unlike notions of industrial democracy, which is rooted in notions of employee rights, EI stems from an economic efficiency argument. It is seen to make business sense to involve employees, as a committed workforce is likely to understand better what the organisation is trying to do and be more prepared to contribute to its efficient operation. But it is management that decides whether or not employees are to be involved. Thus, EI tends to be individualist and direct (as opposed to collective and conducted via representatives); it is championed by management, often without any great pressure from employees or trade unions, and it is directed at securing greater employee commitment to, and identification with, the employing organisation. The terminology of EI is very apt as it relates to managers giving employees more information or, in a few cases, more influence at workplace level. EI could be characterised as a move away from 'you will do this' to 'this is why you will do this' (Wilkinson *et al*, 1993: 28).

According to Millward *et al* (1992: 175), there was a sizeable growth in direct EI and communications during the 1980s as management stepped up their communication with employees as a whole, a trend which is likely to have continued throughout the first half of the current decade. The implementation of 'new' EI initiatives speeded up during the latter part of the 1980s, and the 'systematic use of the management chain' was described by respondents as the most frequently employed method of communication (1992: 166). Regular meetings between managers and employees also grew, as did suggestions schemes and newsletters (1992: 167). Again, there were variations between sectors, with the highest level of activity being in the public sector and the lowest in manufacturing, with a spurt in growth in private services. Research by Marchington, Wilkinson, Ackers and Goodman (1992: 14) shows that many organisations practised multiple forms of EI, and if anything a wider range of techniques was employed in unionised firms than in their non-union counterparts. This study also demonstrates the variety and diversity of EI techniques which operate in practice, and the way in which the 'mix' of these depends crucially upon managerial choice and organisational context. The influence of key groups within an organisation has a substantial impact upon the range and type of schemes which are introduced, as well as upon their ultimate success. 'Champions' played a key role in shaping this process (Marchington *et al*, 1993a: 558).

What forms of employee involvement operate at your organisation? What purpose is served by each form of EI, and could its practice be improved?

EI takes a number of forms:

Downward communication from managers to employees, the principal purpose of which is to inform and 'educate' staff so that they accept management plans. This includes techniques such as team briefing, informal and non-routinised communications between managers and their staff, formal written media such as employee reports, house journals or company newspapers, and videos which are used to convey messages to employees about the organisation's financial performance or to publicise some new managerial initiative. These techniques provide employees with greater amounts of information from managers than most enjoyed previously, but whether or not this is of interest or relevance to them is open to question. In theory, employers gain because employees are 'educated' about the needs of the business and utilise their greater knowledge-base to improve customer service or product quality, so helping to sustain competitive advantage. These gains may not always be achieved in practice due to a lack of managerial commitment or skills, and a lack of employee interest.

Most organisations which practise team briefing hold meetings on a regular, scheduled monthly basis at most, and in many cases briefings are abandoned should more pressing business appear on the agenda, or management lose interest in the device. In contrast, daily team briefings are practised in many Japanese-owned companies operating in Britain (such as Nissan and Komatsu), and there are now signs that these ideas are spreading to other organisations (for example, Rover). Regular meetings at the start of each shift provide managers and employees not only with an opportunity to share information, but also to develop a team spirit as well. Team briefings may not be appropriate in all types of organisation, however, and other methods for communicating information need to be established. For example, J Sainsbury has a long-established and well-polished house journal, which communicates company-wide information to all staff, and is supplemented by notice boards and other forms of written information at each store.

Upward problem-solving, which is designed to tap into employee knowledge and opinion, either at an individual level or through small groups. The objective of these techniques is to increase the stock of ideas within an organisation, to encourage co-operative relations at work, and to legitimise change. These include quality circles, or action teams, suggestion schemes, attitude surveys and total quality management – at least in some of the forms that it takes in practice (Wilkinson *et al*, 1992). In theory these schemes offer employees the prospect of greater opportunities to contribute to discussions about work-related issues, and employers the possibility of higher levels of productivity and quality.

Task participation, in which employees are encouraged or expected to extend the range and type of tasks undertaken at work. As with the previous categories, these are also a form of direct EI of an individualist nature, some of which have their roots in earlier quality of working life experiments in the 1960s and 1970s (Buchanan, 1992). Examples of task participation are horizontal job redesign, job enrichment and teamworking, each of which has figured in a number of chemical and vehicle components companies which operate their production systems on a teamwork and relatively autonomous basis. Task-based participation is probably the most innovative method of EI, given that it is focused on the whole job rather than comprising a relatively small part of an employee's time at work. In addition, unlike team briefing or quality circles, which can be viewed as additional or incidental to working arrangements, task-based participation is integral to work itself. This has led to claims that 'workplaces have never been so democratic', even though such techniques do little to challenge existing patterns of power and authority (Marchington, 1995b: 55).

Financial involvement, which encompasses schemes designed to link part of an individual's reward to the success of the unit or enterprise as a whole, has been the object of much attention since the 1980s. This takes a variety of forms in practice, ranging from profit sharing and employee share ownership schemes through to ESOPs (employee share ownership plans) which are slowly beginning to emerge in Britain (Pendleton, 1992; Wilkinson, Marchington, Ackers and Goodman, 1994). Financial involvement shares similar objectives to the techniques already discussed but also operates under an assumption that employees with a financial stake in the overall success of the unit/enterprise are more likely to work harder for its ultimate success. Of course, much depends upon whether employees also perceive such a link, and how much control they have over the performance of the unit concerned. In the case of employee share ownership arrangements tied to profits, the most popular of these schemes, this is negligible. See Chapter 15 for a further discussion on financial involvement.

REPRESENTATIVE PARTICIPATION

Joint consultative committees (JCCs) are the best-known example of representative participation in Britain, having had a long and somewhat chequered history, comprising various periods of growth and decline. Indeed, JCCs were effectively 'written-off' in the 1960s, being viewed as unable to survive the development of strong shop steward workplace organisation, only to undergo a resurgence during the 1970s and decline slightly (especially in manufacturing) since then (Millward *et al*, 1992: 153). JCCs are likely to be present in about one-quarter of all workplaces now, compared with approximately one-third in the mid-1980s. This decline owes more to the changing structural and sectoral composition of workplaces, in particular the falling number of larger establishments, than to any concerted attempt by employers to terminate existing arrangements, or by unions to boycott committees (Millward *et al*, 1992: 154).

Unlike the methods of direct EI discussed in the previous section, JCCs are built upon the notion of indirect participation and worker representation in joint management–employee meetings. Joint consultation represents the most formal and potentially influential form of consultation, although of course it differs from collective bargaining in that its scope is typically wider – for instance, including financial matters – and in that the issues discussed are not formally negotiated. For some, they represent a diluted form of collective bargaining, and the shift in interest towards consultation reflects a decline in collective bargaining. It is probably the closest that we get in Britain to models of representative participation practised throughout the rest of Europe. But JCCs can take a number of forms, often contrasting sharply with each other in terms of their objectives, structures and processes (Marchington, 1994: 669–672). There is continuing debate concerning the nature of joint consultation. Some researchers suggest that joint consultation has been revitalised in order to cover issues traditionally dealt with through collective bargaining, and involve stewards more closely with management issues in order to convince them of the 'logic' of their decisions. Others have argued that the committees have largely been concerned with trivia and are thus marginal to the employee relations processes of the organisation. Consequently, in some organisations JCCs can act as a safety valve (ie an alternative to industrial action) through which to address more deep-seated employee grievances, while in others they can be used as a device to hinder the recognition of trade unions or undermine their activities in highly unionised workplaces. In yet others they may be irrelevant to management–employee relations, merely existing as a forum to debate various forms of trivia (Marchington, 1992a: 136–141). The relationship between collective bargaining and joint consultation in unionised workplaces can be a source of tension, particularly if management is trying to 'edge out' the unions.

> Do JCCs exist in your organisation? If so, what forms do they take and are they successful? How could they be improved? If there are no JCCs, what mechanisms are in place to consult with the workforce? Would a JCC be useful? Why/why not?

An important contemporary issue in this area is the European Works Council Directive. The centralist philosophy which underpins this initiative is in sharp contrast to the voluntarist approach promulgated by successive Conservative governments since the early 1980s, whereby employers have been encouraged to adopt measures which suit their own circumstances and predilections, with a minimum of statutory enforcement (Department of Employment, 1989). Since Britain entered the EU in the early 1970s there have been a number of attempts to create a more coherent and uniform 'social' framework, and to harmonise certain standards of employment and company law across the member states. Commencing with the Fifth Directive back in 1972 (which proposed a two-tier board structure for all companies employing 500 or more, with at least one-third of the supervisory board drawn from employees), the idea of high-level representative participation has re-emerged in various guises since that time. More recently, in the late 1980s through to the mid-1990s, further attempts have been made to harmonise policies in the areas of information, consultation and participation.

Member states covered by the EWC Directive – that is, all states except the UK which opted out of the Social Chapter at Maastricht in 1991 – are required to implement its provisions by September 1996. EWCs, or an equivalent information and consultation procedure have to be set up in all multinational enterprises with at least 1,000 employees within the 16 states covered by the directive, including at least 150 employees in at least two of these countries. There is scope for the negotiation of customised agreements, but in the event of failure to agree, a standard package will apply. In broad terms this provides a template for the composition of the EWC and its remit, as well as a stipulation that an annual meeting should take place. At this meeting the EWC convenes with central management to be informed and consulted about the enterprise's progress and prospects in a number of areas, including the broad economic, financial and employment situation, as well as trends in employment and substantial changes in working methods. Obviously a key point here is future employment projections – in particular closures, cutbacks and redundancies. The Commission is to review the operation of the Directive in 2001.

The Directive does not have statutory force in relation to employees of multinational companies employed in Britain. In a similar vein, although the provisions do apply to British companies which employ people elsewhere in the EU, managements are not required to include in an EWC workers employed in Britain. Both of these create the potential for internal divisions, even more so because Hall, Carley, Gold, Marginson and Sisson (1995: 12) estimate that just as many British companies will be affected by the provisions as are French or German organisations. As the authors note, this is something of a 'grey area' as data are not always available on employment patterns, but they reckon it will affect at least 140 British-owned companies; this can be compared with 150 German, 136 French, and 48 US organisations. The list includes employers such as Barclays, British Aerospace, Coats Viyella, Glaxo, Kingfisher, Lucas, Marks & Spencer, Rolls-Royce, United Biscuits and Zeneca. It will be interesting to note how many of these companies choose to exclude their UK employees from an EWC.

There is nothing to prevent British and overseas employers with employment units elsewhere in the EU opting of their own volition to set up EWCs, so as to keep up with 'good' practice and be seen as model employers (Ramsay, 1991; Hall, 1992). By the end of 1994, for example, approximately 40 EU-owned companies had already taken this opportunity (Hall *et al* 1995: 15), nearly two years before this becomes a requirement. Among the companies with voluntary existing arrangements are Bayer, Nestlé, Volkswagen and Thomson (whose first EWC was set up in 1985), and by 1994 the first British-owned companies – BP Oil and United Biscuits – were signed up. Quite a number of these were not known as EWCs, and the list of titles includes Employee Forum, European Group Committee, European Trades Union Committee, and European Information and Consultation Forum. Hall *et al* (1995) reprint the constitutions of a number of existing EWCs, and of those with employees in the UK some do appear (for example, Bull and Thomson) to invite representatives from these establishments to the committee.

It is interesting to examine the United Biscuits European Consultative Council (UBECC) because it was one of the first two to be agreed in Britain. The Council comprises 20 representatives from around the company's operations in Europe, of which 13 are drawn from UK sites. Members are nominated by the unions or works councils, and up to four full-time union officials are eligible to attend in addition to the worker representatives; Hall *et al* (1995: 17) note that the company has placed limitations on membership of UBECC, most importantly in being able to object to nominees if they are deemed 'inappropriate'. UBECC is chaired by the group human resources director, attended by the group chief executive and other divisional managers, and it is scheduled to take place annually. The Council focuses on the performance of the United Biscuits Group, on its overall strategic direction, on jobs and employment policy, and on the broad commercial factors which affect the operations of the company. It is expected that UBECC will consider how, if at all, the Council might need to be adjusted once the Directive comes into force in late 1996 (IRS *Employment Trends* 574, 1994).

UBECC is precluded from dealing with issues which are the preserve of national or local negotiating or consultative processes, operating rather like the 'adjunct' consultative committees described in Marchington (1994: 680–683). JCCs which have a long history of co-operation and have been used to dealing with strategic issues, albeit on an information-sharing basis, may be able to adapt their existing arrangements to fit with the Directive. It is clear therefore that, despite the generally negative response from employers and the Conservative government to these proposals, organisations which already have workable structures for multi-level consultative committees may have little to fear from EWCs.

> Do you think that your organisation – or one with which you are familiar – has much to fear from EWCs? How might an EWC be introduced into your organisation?

CONCLUSION

It should be clear from this chapter that the 'rules' of employee relations can be made and influenced in many ways. Although most analyses have focused on collective bargaining as the main rule-making institution, it must not be forgotten that some rules are made unilaterally by managements, and are not open for discussion or negotiation. Similarly, despite the growing coverage of formal and written procedures, many aspects of workplace employee relations are subject to informal customs and practices which have existed for years; on some occasions, managements turn a 'blind eye' to these, and in others they explicitly condone these adjustments to working practices in order to ensure that they gain co-operation at work. Yet other 'rules' are laid down by legal enactment or established by communication and consultation with the staff involved.

Collective bargaining remains a central aspect of employee relations in Britain, although in recent years its aggregate coverage has declined, and in some workplaces it is taking new forms – such as single-table bargaining. In this chapter we have sought to emphasise that patterns of collective bargaining vary greatly between workplaces and between organisations, and that P&D managers are able to exercise some degree of choice and influence over their eventual shape. In order to do this, however, P&D practitioners need to be aware of the different types of bargaining arrangement which exist, and their suitability for particular organisational contexts. It is important not to be seduced by the latest fads and fashions, but to make informed decisions about which bargaining levels and units are most appropriate for each employment situation. Similar options are also available for the mix of EI arrangements which might 'fit' with the needs of employers as well, and for the remainder of the century a significant issue in this area is likely to be European Works Councils or some equivalent representative body.

USEFUL READING

ADVISORY CONCILIATION AND ARBITRATION SERVICE (1991) *Health and Employment*, ACAS Advisory Booklet 15. London, HMSO.

BROWN, W. (1993) 'The contraction of collective bargaining in Britain', *British Journal of Industrial Relations*, Vol 31, 2: 189–200.

CARLEY, M., (1995) 'Talking shops or serious forums', *People Management*, 13 July.

FARNHAM, D. AND PIMLOTT, J. (1995) *Understanding Industrial Relations*, Fifth Edition. London, Cassell.

GOSPEL, H. AND PALMER, G. (1993) *British Industrial Relations*, Second Edition. London, Routledge & Kegan Paul.

INDUSTRIAL RELATIONS SERVICES (1995) 'European works councils and the UK'. *IRS Employment Trends* 581, April: 13–16.

INDUSTRIAL RELATIONS SERVICES (1995) 'Single table bargaining: an idea whose time is yet to come'. *IRS Employment Trends* 577, February: 10–16.

KESSLER, S. AND BAYLISS, F. (1992) 'The changing face of industrial relations', *Personnel Management*, May: 34–38.

KESSLER, S. AND BAYLISS, F. (1995) *Contemporary British Industrial Relations*, Second Edition. London, Macmillan.

MARCHINGTON, M. (1992) *Managing The Team: A guide to employee involvement in practice*. Blackwell, Oxford.

MARCHINGTON, M., WILKINSON, A. AND ACKERS, P. (1993) 'Waving or drowning in participation', *Personnel Management*, March: 30–33.

13 Employee relations procedures at work

INTRODUCTION

Procedures are very much a product of the employee relations environment of the 1960s and 1970s in which there was a more explicit struggle for control at the workplace. This had two principal effects. First, it produced the need for clear procedures so that all employees were aware of works rules and the action which could be taken against them if these rules were flouted. Second, it made for greater clarity and consistency in management action.

In contrast, the 1990s environment is one in which trade unions are weaker, and management prerogatives have replaced the archaic and bureaucratic rules which supposedly constrained managers' ability to manage in the earlier period. Moreover, as the principal activities of many P&D practitioners have shifted away from employee relations to employee development, employee resourcing and employee reward, the main guides to management action are now 'business need, flexibility and commitment' rather than 'procedures, consistency and control', (Storey 1992b: 28). Appeals to consistency, compromise, rules and regulations have been displaced by a new language of competitiveness, customers and commitment. Storey's research (1992a: 178) highlighted the following criticisms of procedures.

> From the hard side of [HRM] comes the criticism that the long drawn out appeals and referrals are simply inappropriate in a fiercely competitive and fast-changing climate. The efficient and effective utilisation of human resources, it is argued, requires tough decisions – for example, on downsizing, closures and divestment – decisions of a kind which almost by their very nature do not readily lend themselves to negotiated compromise. And from the soft side, with its emphasis on individual selection, direct communication by managers to 'their employees', investment in training and development, direct involvement of employees, tailoring individual pay to individual performance and similar nostrums, the regulator's arguments about dual process and about honouring agreements and observing custom and practice are anathema.

However, this interpretation has a number of problems. Firstly, it is by no means obvious that an emphasis on rules and procedures is outdated. Indeed, a belief in consistency and fairness is central to gaining the commitment of employees in any organisation (Clark,

1993); what may appear as flexibility to managers may seem arbitrary treatment to an employee. Secondly, even the new ideas of HRM do not necessarily mean the absence of procedures; recruitment, selection, training and appraisal are much more formalised now than in previous eras.

Some procedures are written to meet external legislative requirements rather than internal purposes. The non-formal system which operates in small firms takes the form of the owner speaking to an employee, who in turn speaks to the 'problem' employee. Rarely is the employee addressed directly by the owner on the issue, and this can lead to emotions running high when the problems come to a head and the employee is ordered to leave. The fact that the small firms are disproportionately represented at industrial tribunals for unfair dismissal claims does not reflect the fact that employers have to move quickly because of their small size, but instead describes a situation where a long history of problems is never formally addressed before it finally explodes. Consequently, procedures – if followed – could stabilise important areas of employee relations within the firm and could actually be beneficial to them (Scott *et al*, 1989: 97).

This chapter examines the role of procedures in the management of human resources, explains the functions which procedures serve, and provides guidance on how to assess them. It discusses how procedures are designed and how they operate in practice. It also looks at health and safety issues in the management of employee relations.

By the end of the chapter, readers should be able to:

- assess the role of procedures in achieving fairness and consistency at work
- advise line managers on how to handle disciplinary issues
- provide advice on how employers can meet their health and safety obligations.

In addition readers should know and understand:

- the principal components of, and differences between, disciplinary and grievance procedures
- the way in which P&D specialists may provide support for line managers in operating procedures in all areas
- the key requirements of health and safety legislation, and how it affects their own workplace.

THE NATURE AND EXTENT OF PROCEDURES

A government social survey in 1969 found only 8 per cent of the establishments which were surveyed actually operated with a formal disciplinary and dismissal procedure. The Donovan Commission (1968: 30), took up the cause of procedural reform, wanting 'procedures which are clear where the present procedures are vague, comprehensive where the present procedures are fragmented, speedy where the present procedures are protracted, and effective where the present procedures are fruitless'. It was felt that a lack of proper procedures was a major cause of industrial disputes.

There is evidence that procedural reform has taken place, at least formally. As Millward *et al* (1992: 212) observed, 'The 1970s saw a massive spread of formal disciplinary and dismissal procedures across British industry and commerce', so that by the 1980s they had become 'almost universal in all but the smallest workplaces'. In addition, grievance and health and safety procedures also become commonplace, as Table 9 illustrates.

Table 9 The extent of procedures in employee relations
(% of establishments with a formal procedure)

Type of procedure	1980	1984	1990
Discipline and dismissal	81	90	90
Individual grievances	77	88	87
Health and safety	–	89	87

Part of this growth has been caused by the growing involvement of the law, and in particular the Industrial Relations Act 1971 which introduced the notion of unfair dismissal; before 1971 it should be recalled that the employer did not need to give a reason for dismissal, and the only recourse open to employees was through ordinary courts of law. However, it also reflected a general principle that industrial relations needed to be reformed, and proceduralisation was part of the new recipe.

There has been a considerable degree of formalisation since then, with agreements usually being written, and greater precision and uniformity in procedures have been achieved across all industries. Within multi-plant organisations, standardisation has been accompanied by the growing involvement of corporate management in dismissal and disciplinary appeals. A major reason for this development can be seen in the growth in cases being taken to industrial tribunals. Of course, this does not necessarily mean that the procedures are followed; they may be no more than empty paper policies. Moreover, it is important to remember what procedures *cannot* do. Thomson and Murray (1976: 84) note that a procedure 'cannot solve the underlying causes of conflict ... it is very limited in the extent to which it can institutionalise conflict if there is not a basic consensus about the legitimacy of the roles of the parties. It cannot of itself make up for deficiencies in the structure of the relationship.'

A procedure agreement can be defined as 'a set of rules whose purpose is to influence the behaviour of management, employees and trade union representatives in a defined situation. The rules are, in effect, an agreed code of voluntary restraints on the use of power' (Hawkins, 1979: 132). Procedures can be adopted in a number of different areas:

- *Recognition*: specifying the rights of unions to recruit, organise and represent defined groups of staff in the workplace. Details may be included covering bargaining units (see Chapter 12), and the facilities for, and duties of, shop stewards (see Chapter 11).

- *Disputes*: indicating the route to be followed in the event of a collective or departmental type issue, including reference to a joint employers' organisation – trade union agreement.

- *Grievance*: indicating what is to be done in the event of an individual issue or complaint. Following the Employment Protection (Consolidation) Act of 1978, employees need to be made aware of the person to whom they can complain. This would normally be included in a statement of their terms and conditions of employment (see Chapter 3).

- *Disciplinary*: setting the standards of conduct expected from employees, specifying what is to be done following behaviour or conduct which is deemed unsatisfactory.

- *Redundancy*: this covers the organisation's approach to consultation about redundancy, methods of selection, compensation and assistance in finding other employment.

- *New technology*: covering agreements and policy for the introduction of new plant and machinery

- *Equal opportunities*: covering the organisation's policy on the provision of equal opportunities, outlining its commitment to the provision of equal opportunities regardless of gender, race or disability (see Chapter 4).

> Write down three procedures which operate at your workplace and explain their purpose. How successful are they in meeting their purpose?

Of course, this list is not exhaustive but merely indicative of the most common procedure agreements to be found in organisations. The main objective of any procedure is to have an agreed set of rules so as to channel any discussion or discontent through the appropriate mechanisms for its resolution. By themselves, procedures do not eliminate discontent, rather they provide a means of institutionalising it.

THE CASE FOR PROCEDURES IN EMPLOYEE RELATIONS

There are a number of reasons why employers implement procedures in the area of employee relations. These are:

- They help to clarify the relationship between the two parties and recognise explicitly the right of employees to raise grievances. This helps to focus conflict within the agreed mechanisms and facilitates its resolution within these. In short, it can create a framework for good employee relations.

- They provide a mechanism for resolution by identifying the individuals or post-holders to whom the issue should be taken initially, and by specifying the route to be followed should there be a failure to agree at that level.

- They act as a safety-valve and provide time within which to assess the issue that has been raised. It can consequently 'take the heat out of the situation' by providing time to reflect.

- They help to ensure that there is likely to be greater consistency within the organisation. They can reduce reliance on word of mouth or custom and practice, and minimise arbitrary treatment, as issues can be examined within the context of a procedure.

- They lead to the keeping of more adequate records, and consequently to improved management control and information systems.

- If they are written down and applied appropriately, and meet the criteria of natural justice, they are important in industrial tribunal cases.

- The process of drawing up procedures involves both parties working together to decide on the agreed mechanism for resolving matters that arise. Thus, joint ownership of the procedure may indicate a willingness to make the agreed procedure work.

> Do these reasons seem important to you, or is there no longer any need for managers to observe procedures?

As with all lists, this must be read with caution, for the potential advantages may not operate in all situations and at all times. It is also likely that different levels of management may have different perceptions of the need for operating such procedures. For example, line managers may regard procedures as little more than red tape and bureaucracy, seeing all procedures as taking them away from their main role of production or service. Equally, line managers may feel that the disciplinary process is long-winded, taking them too much time to get rid of an unsatisfactory employee. However, it is up to senior managers, and especially P&D professionals, to train line managers in how to use procedures and explain the value of using them by pointing out problems and difficulties. For example, it can be stressed that arbitrary or hasty action can lead to unfair dismissal claims. As Millward *et al* (1992: 185) observe, 'Procedures play a key role in bringing fairness and consistency to employment relationships. In defining rules of discussion they provide avenues through which potential or actual conflicts over pay, conditions and working arrangements can be addressed positively and constructively by management and workers. In providing opportunities for appeal against management decisions they require both employees and managers to consider what they are doing and why.'

For procedure agreements to be of value, the parties have to be willing to use them rather than settling their differences through other means, such as strike action by employees before procedures have been exhausted, or perhaps unilateral management changes to working practices. If managers, for example, continually flout the spirit of a procedure, then it would be little surprise if union representatives adopted a similar attitude. In short, if procedures are to be successful they require a degree of normative agreement as to their utility. Thomson and Murray (1976: 32–33) describe this as 'a "collaborative" orientation in which grievants are equally willing to satisfy the others' concerns as they are to ensure that their own are satisfied, which leads to a situation in which new approaches are sought which satisfy both parties'. In general terms, procedures have to be agreed which reflect current practice. If the *process* of grievance resolution is vastly different from the formal requirements, then it is likely that the latter will fall into disrepute. Because of this it is not surprising that the language of procedures tends to be broad and general, and the duties and obligations which agreements place on the parties remains imprecise. Flexibility continues to be valued more highly by many managers and trade union officials than clarity and definiteness (Millward *et al*, 1992: 212).

ASSESSING PROCEDURES

According to Marsh and McCarthy (1968: 3), there are two main criteria for assessing procedural adequacy: acceptability and appropriateness. Firstly, for a procedure to operate effectively it needs to be broadly *acceptable* to all parties. Clearly, it is unlikely to operate to the complete satisfaction of each party since there may well be differing expectations. For example, managers may be more interested in 'the consistency of decisions' and for the procedures to filter out 'local' matters so enabling the more important issues to move upwards. However, unions and employees may be interested more in speedy resolutions to problems as well as the opportunity to participate in the operation of procedures. Secondly, a procedure has to be *appropriate* to the structure of the industry and group within which it operates, and has to be related to the levels of decision-making within such a group. Thus, it may not be sensible for organisations always to impose a uniform procedure on departments or subsidiaries if these are in a wide range of industrial contexts. Indeed, it may well be that in such circumstances – where the procedure is seen as inappropriate within a particular context – the procedure itself becomes a *cause* of conflict rather than a way of dealing with it.

Ultimately, however, the procedure is not an end in itself, and there may be times when it might be sensible to override the procedure to sort out a pressing problem. Thus 'the process of grievance resolution may not always accord with the formal procedure' (Marchington, 1982: 118). For example, some stages may be missed out or employee representatives can be involved even before line managers are notified of grievances. Similarly, procedures might be avoided altogether, or 'external' people can be involved at an earlier stage. The key issue is to maintain the right balance between 'regarding procedures as vehicles of convenience and instruments of regulation' (Thomson and Murray, 1976). In short, organisations require procedures and flexibility *and* there is always likely to be a tension between these two different priorities.

While procedures reflect circumstances which are appropriate for different organisations and workplaces, there remains a remarkable similarity in terms of the main components. For example, while there may be variations in the number of stages in the procedure, the use of time limits or the provision for an external involvement, the underlying philosophy is to structure expectations so that procedures are viewed as the most appropriate mechanism for voicing discontent rather than using strike action. There are three parts to procedures which are worthy of further discussion.

The preamble and 'spirit' behind agreements

Most procedures contain an introduction or preamble which outlines the principles behind the scheme and the spirit in which it is to operate. For example, some refer to the agreement being in the mutual interests of both parties while others emphasise the need for a speedy resolution of differences. Some procedures make specific reference to industrial action, and the stage at which this can be considered legitimate, and it is common to state that neither party should invoke sanctions prior to the exhaustion of procedures. While such provisions are not legally binding, the clause is in effect seen as a gentleman's agreement. Management often accepts a mutual obligation on itself to process issues through the relevant procedure as speedily as possible, with time limits specified to ensure that issues do not get bogged down, and hence slow the resolution of the problem or grievance. The main aim behind the inclusion of a time limit is to demonstrate the employer's commitment to speedy resolution after allowing the heat to be taken out of the situation. Having said that, time limits can also be used as a stalling device by management.

Role of the personnel and development function

Personnel and development specialists are often seen as the guardians or custodians of procedures. The emphasis in procedures is that grievances and disputes are a line management responsibility, with personnel specialists available to provide advice and assistance when required. Given that the P&D function may have been instrumental in designing the procedures, they have an influence over arrangements whether or not they have been formally involved at each stage.

Indeed, it may be important that P&D specialists are involved at an early stage if line managers lack human resource and legal skills. However, if line managers see P&D only as providing information or interpreting procedures, this may not be achieved. Given this, personnel and development specialists need to have a good idea of what is happening at ground level, as well as understanding the legislation and the customs and practices of a particular workplace. If they lack, or are seen to lack such characteristics, they may be excluded from decision-making and relegated to a back-seat role, with their involvement in issues of grievance or conflict resolution arising *after* rather than before the conflict has arisen. Their contribution to organisational effectiveness is then perceived as limited and they get locked into a vicious circle whereby, because they lack power and authority, their role is continually down-graded (Legge, 1978). A common criticism of the personnel function is that it 'always passes the buck' and is 'out of touch' with reality in the workplace. Consequently it is important that P&D specialists have good relationships with line managers and that lines of responsibility are clear.

How can P&D practitioners convince line managers that it is worth using procedures and that they can make a contribution to organisational success?

Role of external third-party involvement

Some procedures provide an automatic role for third-party intervention with reference to ACAS, whereas others may be tied to an agreement between an employers' organisation and a trade union. Yet others make use of an independent arbitrator on an *ad hoc* basis. Intervention by a third party can be in one of three forms: conciliation, mediation and arbitration. With conciliation and mediation, assistance is provided when the parties have reached an impasse but the parties themselves must resolve the issue. With conciliation, the third party must confine itself to facilitating talk and discussion; while with mediation they can actually come up with specific recommendations. Arbitration involves the third party actually coming up with a decision to resolve the issue. It should be noted that ACAS should not be used as a substitute for the establishment of joint union–management procedures for dispute resolution. This can lead to a 'narcotic' effect where ACAS is used to help resolve issues, thus allowing the parties to avoid taking responsibility. Employee relations could be damaged if commitment to agreed procedures withers away. Millward *et al* (1992: 212) note that, whilst third-party intervention does continue to be envisaged as a possibility, in many procedures it is seen as an option the parties might consider rather than a binding obligation, and one whose form could be determined as and when the occasion demands rather than by detailed prior agreement. This is in contrast to the USA, where it is more common for a formal procedure to specify binding third-party arbitration as the final stage.

DISCIPLINARY PROCEDURES

We have already noted that the concept of unfair dismissal was first introduced by the Industrial Relations Act 1971, with changes subsequently in the Employment Protection (Consolidation) Act 1978 (EPCA) and later legislation. It is up to an industrial tribunal to determine whether or not the dismissal is fair or unfair. There are five potentially 'fair' reasons within the Act:

- a reason related to the capability (including health) or qualifications of the employee for performing work of the kind he or she was employed to do
- reasons related to the employee's conduct
- that the employee was redundant
- that the employee could not continue to work in the position that he or she held without contravention (either on his or her part or on that of the employer) of a duty or restriction imposed under or by a legal enactment
- some other substantial reason of a kind to justify the dismissal of an employee holding the position which that employee held (eg reorganisation of business).

Once the substantive case has been established, the question of whether the dismissal was fair or unfair can be determined, having regard to the reason shown by the employer. Fairness depends on whether in the circumstances (including the size and administrative resources of the employer's undertaking) the employer acted reasonably or unreasonably in treating it as a sufficient reason for dismissing the employee; and that question shall be determined in accordance with equity and the substantial merits of the case (EPCA 1978, as amended by Employment Act 1980). Such matters include the fairness of procedures.

The ACAS Code of Practice – 'Disciplinary Practice and Procedures in Employment' – first appeared in 1977. While the code is not binding in itself, in the absence of other procedures, or poorly designed ones, it can be admissible in evidence to an industrial tribunal that is attempting to gauge the fairness of dismissal – see the ACAS handbook: *Disputes at Work*. It recommends that discipline procedures should:

- be in writing

- specify to whom they apply

- provide for matters to be dealt with quickly

- indicate the disciplinary actions which may be taken

- specify the levels of management which have the authority to take the various forms of disciplinary action, ensuring that immediate superiors do not normally have the power to dismiss without reference to senior management

- provide for individuals to be informed of the complaints against them and to be given an opportunity to state their case before decisions are reached

- give individuals the right to be accompanied by a trade union representative or by a fellow employee

- ensure that, except for gross misconduct, no employees are dismissed for a first breach of discipline

- ensure that disciplinary action is not taken until the case has been carefully investigated

- ensure that individuals are given an explanation for any penalty imposed

- provide a right of appeal and specify the procedure.

In addition, disciplinary procedures should:

- apply to all employees, irrespective of their length of service

- be non-discriminatory and applied irrespective of sex, marital status or race

- ensure that any period of suspension for investigation is with pay, and specify how pay is to be calculated during such a period (if, exceptionally, suspension is to be without pay, this should be provided for in the contract of employment)

- ensure that, where the facts are in dispute, no disciplinary penalty is imposed until the case has been carefully investigated and it is concluded on the balance of probability that the employee committed the act in question.

> To what extent do the disciplinary procedures in your organisation reflect those recommended by ACAS? How and why do they differ?

According to an IRS survey (*Employment Trends* 591, 1995), the ten most common offences (in rank order) are the following:

1) absenteeism

2) poor performance

3) poor time-keeping

4) refusal to obey a reasonable instruction

5) theft/fraud

6) sexual/racial harassment

7) verbal abuse

8) health and safety infringements

9) fighting

10) alcohol/drug abuse.

Minor misconduct is usually dealt with by informal warnings – so being five minutes late, for example, is very unlikely to lead to dismissal. Clearly, actions must be appropriate to the circumstances. Managers should not look simply to punish employees but to counsel them, especially over inadequate performance. If performance is not up to standard, then management should attempt to find the reasons rather than just deal with the 'offence'. Employee performance may vary for reasons other than employee laziness or ineptitude. Lack of training, or problems in the employees' domestic circumstances need to be considered and employees should be 'assisted' rather than simply punished. Indeed, counselling should be seen as a positive rather than punitive action. It should also be recognised that indiscipline at work can have wider ramifications for the management of employee relations, as dismissal and other disciplinary measures were the fourth most common cause of strike action in 1994 (Industrial Relations Services, 1995c, 591). A typical disciplinary procedure is reproduced below.

Disciplinary Procedure

1. General

It is mutually agreed by the Company and Union that management have a positive role in encouraging and ensuring that all employees perform responsibly and effectively at work.

The process detailed below is designed to make the individual employee aware as early as possible of a need for improvement in performance so that serious disciplinary action is taken only after opportunities for improvement have not been satisfactorily responded to by the employee.

While the emphasis is on correction, in the interest of the company as a whole, disciplinary action will be taken where it is necessary to uphold the high standards of performance.

2. Principles

The following general principles will apply in all cases where disciplinary action is contemplated. The procedure will:

a) be generally known and available (this knowledge will be emphasised by issuing this revision through briefing groups)

b) be seen to be fair and effective by all employees

c) provide adequate opportunity for the employee to make the necessary improvement in performance required

d) provide for the employee to have the right to state his case before a decision is made

e) provide for the employee to have the right to be accompanied by his employee representative at any stage of the procedure and provide for written copies of any warnings to be issued to the employee representative

f) provide for previous recorded oral and written warnings to be disregarded if the specified time period has elapsed without further disciplinary action

g) except for gross misconduct, no-one will be dismissed for a first offence.

h) provide for a right of appeal to all formal disciplinary action.

3. Process

a) *Informal stages*

By normal day-to-day corrective action and by individual counselling and advice, management will make employees aware of the improvements in standard required.

Minor offences will be reprimanded by management informally but formal written records will not be kept at this stage.

cont'd

It is hoped that most matters can be speedily and effectively resolved at this level. However, in the event of failure to improve conditions to the required level, the following procedure will be invoked.

b) *Formal procedure*

While the procedure below will be followed in normal circumstances, the entry level for disciplinary action will be determined by management depending on the severity of the offence. The procedure may therefore be commenced directly at Stages II and III without previous warning.

At each stage, the offences will be comprehensively investigated by the appropriate members of management, and there will be full provision for the employee to hear the case against him and give his own explanation of the circumstances leading to the investigation. Following the enquiry, disciplinary action may be invoked at any of the following stages.

Stage I – Formal oral warning

Personnel present

The employee's immediate boss

The employee

If requested by the employee, his representative

Procedure

The immediate boss will make it clear to the employee that this is the first stage of the formal procedure and then will discuss the matter concerned with the employee explaining fully what is required and, where appropriate, what time period is given for corrective action. An opportunity will be given to the employee to put his point of view.

The formal oral warning will be recorded on the employee's personal file and issued in the presence of his representative if required.

If the employee fails to improve his performance to the required standard, Stage II of the formal procedure will follow.

A formal oral warning will remain in force for six months.

Stage II – Formal written warning (final warning)

Personnel present

The employee's immediate boss and his boss

The employee

A member of the personnel department

If requested by the employee, his representative

cont'd

Procedure

If improvements are not made or there are other incidents of a failure to sustain standards or of a serious first offence, a formal written warning will be issued by the immediate boss's boss. This will fully specify the problem, the corrective action necessary and the consequences if performance is not improved to the required standard. An opportunity will be given to the employee to put his viewpoint.

The warning will be issued in the presence of the employee, his representative if requested, and a member of the personnel department.

A copy of the warning will be placed on the employee's personal file.

If improvements are not made, the final stage of the procedure will follow.

A warning at this stage will remain in force for 12 months.

Stage III – Final stage – dismissal

Personnel Present

A senior member of the personnel department

The employing manager

The employee

If requested by the employee, his representative

Procedure

A full investigation into the circumstances of the case will precede the decision. This will consider all relevant factors including previous employment record and allow the employee concerned to state his case with the involvement of the trade union divisional organiser when appropriate.

4. Right of appeal

All employees have the right to appeal against any formal disciplinary action to the next level of management. The appeal must be in writing, giving the grounds of the appeal, which must involve information or evidence not previously considered.

All appeals must be lodged with the personnel department within two working days of the date of the hearing.

5. Representation

In all cases where formal disciplinary action is implemented, the individual's employee representative will be informed of the outcome in writing by the member of management responsible for issuing the warning.

cont'd

At the request of the employee his or her representative will be present at any meetings held with the employee to investigate the offence or issue a decision on the disciplinary action.

6. Gross misconduct

Serious offences which constitute gross misconduct will result in the final stage of the disciplinary procedure's being activated without previous warnings or notice of termination.

The employee will be regarded as suspended with pay while the hearing takes place.

Examples of offences which will be regarded as gross misconduct include:

- theft, or attempted theft, of company or employee property
- use of or threat of violence
- falsification of company documents
- serious disruptive or abusive behaviour
- being under the influence of drugs or alcohol on company premises
- wilful neglect or damage to company or employee property
- serious breaches of safety regulations
- disclosure of confidential information
- prolonged unauthorised absence
- serious negligence of duty
- gross insubordination or persistent refusal to carry out a reasonable working instruction
- refusal to be stopped and searched.

This list is by no means exhaustive but merely provides examples of behaviour which will be regarded as gross misconduct.

Source: Komatsu UK Handbook

GRIEVANCE PROCEDURES

Grievance procedures are used for handling individual issues, while collective issues are usually dealt with by disputes procedures. However, in practice some organisations have a combined procedure which reflects the fact that grievances are often likely to affect more than one employee, and others allow for grievances which can be referred to the collective disputes procedure. A grievance procedure is a parallel mechanism to the disciplinary procedure.

Problems can arise if agreements and rules are not written down, and the effect of custom and practice produces some ambiguity as to their status. Often it is possible to separate disputes of interest (what should be in the agreement) from disputes of right (what is in the agreement). During the 1960s, grievance procedures were parts of national agreements and this led to problems because of the time it took to get a grievance to the end of the procedure. Consequently industrial action sometimes took place before the procedure had been exhausted. Nowadays, however, it is much more common to have local grievance procedures, agreements which cover establishments or single employers.

The aim of a grievance procedure is to prevent issues and disagreements leading to major conflict or employees leaving – that is 'voting with their feet'. Even if an employee's cause for grievance may be the result of a fellow employee's action (eg as in harassment) the grievance is against management for failing to protect him or her from such harassment.

As with discipline, the spirit with which the grievance procedure is approached is significant. It is too easy for management simply to follow the letter of the procedure, making it a hollow sham, and once this is known employees will not bother to refer issues to the procedure, believing that nothing will be done as a result of their concerns. Consequently, it is important that P&D professionals encourage the proper use of procedures to uncover any problems which may exist, and which line managers may wish to hide since they fear it puts them in a bad light. At IBM an 'open-door' system operates which allows employees to take up grievances with managers directly rather than follow a lengthy procedure. However, this relies on management's taking the system seriously and being prepared to devote time and effort to keep it going.

Disputes procedures specify how collective grievances should be raised and the various points in the procedure should the problem not be resolved. For example, the chain of complaint may go from the supervisor, or immediate line manager, to the departmental manager or personnel manager to senior management. It may provide for matters to be referred to a third party such as ACAS if matters have not been resolved. It is also important that the procedure is efficient and relatively quick. Clearly there is a balance between the time needed to reflect on the issue at hand, while ensuring that it is not 'lost' in the process because of the length of time involved.

Get a copy of your own organisation's grievance procedure, and compare this with one from another organisation of your choice. What are the major differences between them? How might your procedure be adapted, if at all, to make it work better?

LINE MANAGERS AND PERSONNEL AND DEVELOPMENT

So far in this chapter we have discussed the importance of procedures, stressing the value of being proactive, taking the initiative and establishing/enforcing their use. Management has been treated as if it were a unified group, sharing common interests and perspectives. However, in reality, there may well be conflict between the perspectives held by personnel and development specialists and that of line managers.

To understand this one needs to appreciate the line manager's role in organisations. Research has documented the open-ended nature of the job, the heavy work load and the conflicting demands on time. As Mintzberg (1973: 171) puts it, the job is one 'characterised by brevity, variety and fragmentation. The vast majority (of contacts) are of brief duration, of the order of seconds for foremen and minutes for chief executives. A great variety of activities are performed, but with no obvious patterns. The trivial is interspersed with the consequential so that the manager must shift moods quickly and frequently. There is great fragmentation of work and interruptions are commonplace.' One result of this is continual adjustment to crises which require snap decisions, and a lack of similarity between formal rules and workplace practice.

To explain why this happens we need to examine the conflicting pressures placed on line managers. One set of pressures comes from the product market, which accords a priority to the consumer, production and profit, while on the other side there are the pressures of labour which places a priority on fairness, consistency and possibly some involvement in decision-making. Personnel and development procedures clearly fit into this latter group of priorities. The problem for line managers is that the more they satisfy one, the more they are likely to experience difficulties with the other.

In practice, it seems likely that production values expressed through the pressure of immediate and measurable targets will take priority over personnel considerations In short, directives and procedures from P&D specialists tend to have less force than those coming from a production director. Indeed, this could be interpreted as simple common sense as employers are not in the market to 'produce' good personnel practices or good employee relations, and hence it seems to make good sense to sacrifice one for the other. For example, rules may be applied leniently so as to ensure co-operation in a rush job.

This helps to explain why line managers are often hostile to rules which are seen to emanate from the P&D function, as these specialists are often castigated for not 'living in the real world'. Thus, a personnel policy which appears well formulated, embodies the basic rules of good management practice, and ensures uniformity and consistency may appear very differently when viewed from the position of the line manager from how it does at the level of senior management or from the personnel and development perspective.

Under such circumstances, P&D specialists need to be able to persuade line managers that the rules and procedures are valuable tools and guidelines rather than millstones. One argument might take the line that the procedures are no more than the codification of good practice; so, for example, the disciplinary procedure represents a helpful prompt to some managers, following actions which they should be doing in any case. Moreover, by not following procedure they are laying themselves and their employer open to the likelihood of appeals and time spent at an industrial tribunal, and even financial penalties. A short-cut by line managers may cost dearly later. A second argument might be that, by breaking rules or condoning new custom and practice, this merely lays down the seeds of greater trouble subsequently. For example, if line managers concede demands to employees in exchange for greater co-operation to meet a production target, this creates an expectation that all extra effort will be so rewarded. In short, a short-term decision can create long-term trouble. Thirdly, the observance of procedures sets the tone for dealing with other issues in the workplace; if managers are seen to be fair and prepared to follow procedures, it is much more reasonable for employees to do the same if they are unhappy with some aspect of management behaviour. Rather than taking industrial action to settle differences, employees can be encouraged to ensure that procedures are exhausted first. This allows employers to maintain production or services while resolving problems at work.

Procedures therefore have a role in giving line managers a clear perspective on the direction in which the organisation is moving, its objectives, and the general standards applied in relation to all aspects of the employment relationship. Whilst line managers may not have the time to become experts in all these matters, they must know the broad parameters of actions, as well as where and when to look for advice. Personnel specialists clearly play a key role both in providing information and acting as a sounding board for proposals (Hutchinson and Wood, 1995).

Indeed, the IRS survey quoted above suggests that P&D managers tended to deal with most of the work involved in taking disciplinary action, despite the written procedures providing a central role for line managers. In almost eight out of ten organisations, line managers spent 5 per cent or less of their time on disciplinary issues. However, discipline represented a more significant work load for the P&D professional. The research reported that in many organisations a personnel presence is required at all disciplinary hearings to ensure the procedure is applied consistently and fairly. As IRS (1995c: 16) notes, 'The involvement of personnel, particularly in the latter stages of the disciplinary procedure, may also be a reflection that employers believe line managers do not have the expertise to operate the disciplinary procedures unsupervised.'

Many employers reviewed their disciplinary procedures following the 1987 House of Lords decision in *Polkey* v *A E Dayton*, which made it clear that a dismissal is likely to be seen as unfair if a fair procedure is not followed prior to dismissal. Other issues which have lead to recent changes in disciplinary rules and procedures include sexual and racial harassment, smoking at work and the need to differentiate between appraisal and disciplinary procedures. It is also now required that sanctions which may be used against employees – in the event of a misdemeanour – are set out in the disciplinary procedure so as to form part of the employment contract.

While procedures may be formalised, management remains the

'leading party', especially since the 1980s when weakened union power has meant that 'the practice of discipline still leaves a great deal of discretion to management in deciding what is acceptable conduct and how it is to be enforced' (Edwards 1994: 572). For example, in case study research, there was found to be tightening up on the regulation of attendance, but this was not explained to workers, merely determined by management and then implemented. The IRS survey (*Employment Trends* 591, 1995) revealed that, when appropriate, most organisations took action short of dismissal – including transfer to other work in the same grade, downgrading, suspension without pay, or withdrawal of merit pay.

> What is the division of responsibility between line managers and P&D in relation to discipline in your organisation? Does this work well? How could it be improved, if at all?

HEALTH & SAFETY

Prior to the Health and Safety at Work Act (HASAWA) in 1974, later augmented by the Safety Representatives and Safety Committee Regulations (1977), the law on health and safety reflected a piecemeal development to deal with pressure from unions and the public over some 200 years. By 1970 there were almost 30 different statutes, with some 500 legal regulations and seven separate inspectorates. The Robens Committee Report in 1972 said that there was too much law, that much of it was unsatisfactory and unintelligible, and that there was overlapping jurisdiction between those responsible for enforcing the law. This resulted in a feeling of apathy in the day-to-day implementation of safety rules (Selwyn 1975). Furthermore, the TUC estimated that there were some eight million people not covered by the existing legislation.

HASAWA was therefore a milestone which was designed to deal with these problems. The overall aim was to promote safety awareness and effective safety organisation and performance by schemes designed to suit the particular industry or organisation. Within this there were three intentions:

• to prevent accidents happening in the first place

• to make safety a matter of concern for everyone in the workplace, as awareness was raised as recommended by the Robens Committee

• to require management to take specific responsibility for the provision and maintenance of adequate safety standards, and a requirement to draw up a safety policy which is enforced.

Under HASAWA, it is the duty of employers to ensure, so far as is reasonably practicable, the health, safety and welfare of their employees. This includes:

• providing safe plant and buildings and safe systems of work; this covers all existing plant and any new introductions, provision for emergency plans, the monitoring of the environment for toxicity levels, and protective clothing

- ensuring the safety of employees when using, handling, storing or transporting articles or substances; this includes audit, labelling and instructions in relation to obvious hazards

- providing information, training, instruction and supervision in relation to potential hazards connected with a substance, pieces of machinery or the environment

- maintaining a safe workplace with provision of means of entry and exit; this includes keeping buildings up to standard with fire exits etc

- providing a safe working environment and adequate facilities.

The employer also has a duty to non-employees, whether they are visiting the site or are likely to encounter risks due to management even if they are trespassing. Such duties might include putting up fencing or other barriers to prevent children from entering a site, or taking precautions such that dangerous fumes are not likely to affect the public in the locality.

The list of duties and obligations appears quite comprehensive, but all are subject to the phrase 'where this is reasonably practicable'. Thus it may be *practicable* to take action since this is achievable with the current state of knowledge, but it may not be *reasonable* to expect an employer to do so. In other words, the time, trouble and expense of implementing safety measures need to be weighed against the foreseeable risk involved. It would be reasonable for the employer to take the steps necessary to keep them in line with most other employers.

> Despite the legislation and the guidance, health and safety rules still tend to get broken. Why is this? What can employers do to ensure compliance?

One key factor stressed by the Health and Safety Commission (HSC) is the requirement to prepare (and revise) a written safety policy that is brought to the attention of all staff. This is seen as the centrepiece of health and safety strategy, and hence the policy and responsibilities therein should be clear to all in the organisation. While there is no prescribed model policy, because the HSC believe the organisation should be able to come up with its own specific requirements, a framework for such a policy is laid down.

- The general policy statement should be a 'declaration of intent'; if appropriate, more than one formulation may be requested so that sub-groups can interpret policy realistically.

- It should contain names and addresses of the executive responsible for fulfilling the policy and key individuals/appointments with specifically defined responsibilities.

- It should make it clear that the ultimate level of responsibility is that of each and every individual employee.

- It should specify the organisation of safety committees and include a list of people involved, including safety representatives.

- It should specify the need for training and supervision. It is vital, for example, to spell out the key role of the supervisor and to consider how best to equip the supervisor for his or her responsibilities.

- It should identify the main hazards and lay down procedures to deal with accidents or dangerous occurrences. These, should they occur, need to be recorded.

Employees have the legal right to be represented by safety representatives, appointed by recognised, independent trade unions. Employers have a duty to consult with these representatives and, if asked for by two or more of them in writing, to establish a safety committee. Some industries that have traditionally been high-risk, such as coal mining, had such representatives (and sometimes committees) well before 1974.

The regulations give some guidance on these matters in relation to three areas. First of all, the appointment of safety representatives is the duty of trade unions and not employers. They should normally have at least two years' service or experience in a similar industry or workplace, and the number to be appointed should relate to factors such as the size of the workplace, variety of locations, numbers employed and, crucially, the degree and character of any inherent dangers in the workplace.

Secondly, safety representatives have a number of functions to perform in their duties which may require assistance from employers. These include a right to information from employers and inspectors; to investigate hazards and complaints and inspect the workplace on a regular basis; and to facilities, such as a filing cabinet and telephone, and clerical assistance. In addition, they should be allowed to represent their constituents in consultations with employers and inspectors, attend safety committees and receive basic training. Safety representatives, however, are not liable except in the general duty of care as an employee. With the emphasis on health and safety awareness, employees have a duty to take reasonable care for their own safety and those of others affected by their actions, and co-operate with others (eg employer and inspector) regarding any duty imposed by the Act.

Thirdly, the employer is obliged to set up a safety committee, if requested (in writing) to do so by at least two safety representatives; this must be completed, after due consultation, not more than three months after the request is made. The guidance notes suggest that the committee should not be unduly large, should be chaired by a senior manager, should have a balance of managers from different functions and levels (including the safety officer), and should normally include fewer managers than representatives. It should have a separate entity and not be merged or interposed with other matters. The committee should be seen as a place where experience is 'pooled', and its effectiveness is best achieved by speedy management decisions, effective management action, effective publicity, regular meetings, and the involvement of personnel in action items. The proportion of establishments with safety committees remained stable over the 1980s at around one-third. However, there was also an increase in the number of establishments where management decided safety matters, with or without consultation (Millward *et al*, 1992: 162).

The Health and Safety Executive (HSE) which enforces the legislation can issue 'improvement' or 'prohibition' notices, although they are more likely to try to persuade employers to take the appropriate action. The Social Trends Survey published by the Central Statistical Office, reported that in 1991 2.7 per cent of the working week was lost to illness or injury, a very high rate compared to the rest of the European Union. Research by the Health and Safety Executive suggests that accidents cost employers directly and indirectly £900 million per year (at 1990 prices), with the overall cost of work-related accidents coming to 1–2 per cent of GDP. Although trade unions have managed to retain a central role in this issue, if not others, a general weakening in union influence has led employers to push labour harder, with a consequent increase in injuries (Nichols, 1990). Nevertheless, research suggests that establishments with joint consultative committees for health and safety (with representatives chosen by employees) have fewer injuries than where management deal with such matters alone.

Health and safety is also covered by European legislation and the 1992 'Framework directive of the European Commission' laid down minimum standards, some of which are already covered by HASAWA. This is one area of policy where there appears a broad consensus amongst EU member states. Indeed, it is suggested that legislation here is more likely to be 'maximalist' rather than lowest common denominator, as without such regulation the forces of the internal market would fragment health and safety legislation in member states (Teague and Grahl, 1992; Reilly, Paci and Hall, 1995). In addition, provision has been made for so-called 'daughter' directives which are designed to address particular issues. The 'framework' directive was incorporated into UK law by the Management of Health and Safety at Work Regulations in 1992, and other regulations incorporate the 'daughter' directives. The new set of regulations – known as the '*Six Pack*' – became law in January 1993. They incorporate the following:

Management of Health and Safety at Work Regulations
This requires employers to:

- assess risks to employees and other individuals affected by their work activity

- following risk assessment, to manage health and safety through planning, control, monitoring and review

- provide necessary health surveillance

- appoint competent people to devise and implement measures.

Manual Handling Operators Regulations

This relates to shifting loads and required assessment to be used to remove the risk of injury.

Health and Safety (Display Screen Equipment) Regulations

Minimum standards must be met for workstations – equipment and lighting for example – and employees must be provided with training and allowed breaks from the screen.

Personal Protective Equipment at Work Regulations

This includes all equipment worn to protect against risk, such as safety glasses, safety harnesses and life jackets. Employees must be provided with the appropriate equipment and trained in its use.

The Provision and Use of Work Equipment Regulations

Equipment is defined broadly to include hand-tools and machinery. Equipment needs to be suitable, to be maintained regularly, and employees need to be trained in its use.

Workplace (Health, Safety and Welfare) Regulations

This lays down minimum standards for working conditions, environment and hygiene, replacing aspects of the Factories Act 1961 and the Offices, Shops and Railway Premises Act 1963. The main parts include:

- maintaining a good working environment

- maintaining a safe place of work

- providing adequate facilities, including rest and eating facilities

- ensuring cleanliness of the workplace.

In recent years there has been a trend away from concerns with safety towards concerns about health. In 1994 fewer than 300 people were killed at work, but ten times that number died of the delayed effects of asbestos. Twenty thousand retire early due to ill health and some 60,000 are estimated to change jobs because of health problems (Rimington, 1995). This also reflects increasing recognition of the importance of health issues and the move to prevention as seen in the 'health of the nation' strategy. The idea of viewing employees as key assets has also led to a broader, more proactive approach from employers, and recent years have seen a redrawing of the health and safety regulations to include issues such as stress, AIDS, smoking and harassment (Bristol Business School, 1995)

Indeed, threats of job losses, changes in responsibilities, new skill requirements and intensification of work have all led to problems of absenteeism, turnover and poor morale. Research by McHugh (1993) suggests that stress-related illness is on the increase, but few employers appear to be addressing these issues, with many regarding them as 'external' to the organisation, unlike traditional work environment health and safety issues such as chemical hazards. As we saw in Chapter 7, EAPs may now be taking some of the strain off other mechanisms for dealing with health issues at work.

> Identify the ways in which health and safety issues are integrated with other aspects of P&D as well as with the business as a whole. Could health and safety be taken more seriously at your organisation?

Baxi, a manufacturer of domestic gas boilers and heaters, had for some years made risk assessment part of its workplace design, and health and safety meetings preceded the legislation which made them a requirement. According to Heathcote and King (1993), Baxi responded to the 'Six Pack' by:

- appointing a full-time health and safety manager

- linking health and safety policy to quality, and encouraging ownership by each business unit through a safety team led by a unit manager, with members elected from within the unit

- requiring team managers to sit on the safety management continuous improvement teams (CIT) which are responsible for assessing risks in their part of the company

- implementing a corporate safety committee, which is chaired by the managing director and includes safety representatives from each of the units, to deal with strategic issues

- training each safety team manager in risk management

- providing ergonomic training for product support engineers

- measuring safety awareness against a detailed checklist

- incorporating safety issues into the performance appraisal of directors and general managers.

CONCLUSION

In this chapter we have reviewed a number of the procedures which aim to provide a framework for employee relations, and which have grown extensively in coverage since the early 1970s. In the current climate – where concepts of flexibility, empowerment and delayering reign supreme – procedures are seen by some commentators as an anachronism, a legacy of the so-called 'old' collectivist and bureaucratic industrial relations of the 1970s. But we need to remember why procedures were introduced in the first place, and the purposes they have been expected to serve: one of the major rationales behind the emergence of unfair dismissal legislation in the early 1970s was to reduce the likelihood of employees' taking industrial action to protect fellow workers whom they felt had been badly treated by management. The procedures which were established as a result of this legal intervention helped to change attitudes and behaviour, and few P&D managers (or their line management colleagues) would welcome a return to the days of industrial disputes. As we noted in Chapter 2, many employees now feel that the psychological contract is too one-sided, and while they may lack the resources or the will to engage in industrial action, feelings of unfairness can easily translate into demotivation, a lack of interest in quality and customer-care, and more serious social problems in the community at large.

Procedures are an essential element of good employment relations and P&D practice (see Chapter 18), as they provide a clear framework within which issues can be resolved. In the absence of procedures, each new problem has to be tackled from first principles, and managers and employee representatives would spend considerable amounts of time trying to establish ground rules before being able to resolve the issues. Moreover, there would be no incentive for managers or employees to attempt to resolve disputes (to do with either discipline or grievances) in an orderly manner. The end result would be that both parties would seek to use their superior bargaining power to impose their own preferred solutions on the other. Whilst this may be acceptable to some managements nowadays, they would do well to recall that the balance of bargaining power can change; this provides a further reason why employers should maintain procedures (Edwards, 1991).

USEFUL READING

ACAS CODE OF PRACTICE (1985) *Disciplinary Practice and Procedures in Employment.* London, HMSO.

CLARK, J. (1993) 'Procedures and consistency versus flexibility and commitment in employee relations: a comment on Storey', *Human Resource Management Journal*, Vol 4, I: 79–81.

EDWARDS P, (1991) 'Industrial conflict: will the giant wake?' *Personnel Management*, September: 26–28.

FARNHAM, D. (1993) *Employee Relations.* London, IPM.

HUTCHINSON, S. AND WOOD, S. (1995) 'The UK Experience', in *Personnel and the Line: Developing the new relationship.* London, IPD: 3–42.

INDUSTRIAL RELATIONS SERVICES (1995) 'Employment Trends, No. 591'. *Discipline at Work – the Practice.*

INDUSTRIAL RELATIONS SERVICES (1995) 'Employment Trends, No. 592', *Discipline at Work 2 – the procedures.*

McHUGH, M. (1993) 'Stress at work. Do managers really count the costs?' *Employee Relations*, Vol 15, I: 18–32.

MILLWARD, N., STEVENS, M., SMART, D. AND HAWES, W. (1992) *Workplace Industrial Relations in Transition.* Aldershot, Dartmouth Publishing.

STOREY, J. (1992) *Developments in the Management of Human Resources.* Oxford, Blackwell.

Part 6

EMPLOYEE REWARD

14 Motivation and reward strategy

INTRODUCTION

The sight of employees sprinting away from the workplace as the factory hooter sounds suggests that well-motivated staff are not necessarily the norm in industry. There is also comparative research evidence which points to UK employees' being less committed to their employers than their counterparts in other countries. Studies also show that even where labour turnover is limited (one indicator of employee satisfaction), this may obscure deep-rooted discontent, as employees feel they have little choice but to remain with their current employer because of the economic situation or their lack of transferable skills.

Yet given the increased emphasis in recent years on people as a key source of competitive advantage, often being regarded as the key differentiator between organisations, it is not surprising to see corporate initiatives such as total quality management (TQM) or profit sharing in attempts to 'buy' employee commitment. But how successful are such campaigns, and on what assumptions are they based? It seems sensible to take a step back and try to understand the complexities of motivating people at work. This is important at three levels. First, for management, who clearly need to know and understand what motivates people, as it affects work performance, recruitment and retention. Second, employees need to think through what expectations they have of work and whether they are happy with their lot. Finally, for P&D professionals, issues such as these influence the design and implementation of reward structures and systems which they implement or monitor.

Certainly money is a factor which can motivate people at work, but even here things are not straightforward. Is it purely a financial issue, that is, how much cash we are paid which matters, or is payment more significant as recognition of our worth? It is worth recalling that in the famous lottery question (see Chapter 2), the majority of respondents indicated that they would continue to work even if they were financially secure for life. Clearly, there are other benefits from being at work as well as money. Warr (1982) identifies activity, variety, status and social contacts as being other possible benefits. This chapter examines the ideas of a number of well-known writers on motivation and analyses the significance they attach to monetary reward. Clearly, an understanding of motivation is of vital importance when designing a reward strategy.

In recent years there has been a growing emphasis in the literature that reward management should be utilised as a strategic tool, not just as a technique to recruit, retain and motivate staff, but also a device to manage corporate performance and to influence corporate values and beliefs (Armstrong and Murlis, 1995; Snape et al, 1994). Reward management has been defined as 'the design, implementation, maintenance, communication, and evolution of reward processes which help organisations to improve performance and achieve their objectives' (Armstrong and Murlis, 1995: 23). 'Reward management' is very much a phenomenon of the 1980s and 1990s with an associated upbeat rhetoric, and it is often set against an alleged backcloth of earlier approaches which were criticised for being inflexible and bureaucratic. The way in which employees are rewarded is seen as a critical issue in the strategic approach to HRM for a number of reasons: firstly, it is a mechanism by which employers aim to elicit effort and performance; second, the actual payment system may require adjustment to develop motivation; and third, it is often a significant part of the employer's financial strategy (Hendry, 1994: 343).

Such an approach, stressing that remuneration policy should reflect corporate strategy, reflects the idea that P&D policies should fit with corporate objectives. It ties in well with the HRM ideal, which sees policies designed around strategic choices – rather than simply reflecting environmental pressures. This means that there is unlikely to be a state-of-the-art, 'one size fits all' set of practices suitable for all organisations, and managers need to develop a 'fit' between remuneration policies and the strategic objectives of the organisation. However, the extent to which remuneration is used as a strategic tool in practice is more open to doubt. Managements tend to assess or reassess one part of the remuneration package but fail to analyse the whole system. Furthermore, managements have a whole host of objectives for their remuneration policy but these sometimes contradict one another, and their wider implications are not always clearly thought through.

In this chapter we examine the ideas of a number of writers on the links between motivation and reward before looking at the environmental context in terms of setting an agenda for management policy on remuneration. We go on to analyse the range of factors which affect salaries and wages, as well as the choices which management have to make when designing reward systems from a strategic perspective. We also discuss the wage–effort bargain and the importance of fairness in pay policy. Finally, we discuss job evaluation and equal value.

By the end of this chapter, readers should be able to:

- provide advice to the management team on how to design an integrated employee reward strategy which contributes to organisational performance

- advise management on whether or not to introduce or retain job evaluation, and if so, which schemes are most appropriate for their own organisation

- design a non-discriminatory job evaluation scheme.

In addition, readers should be able to understand and explain:

- the importance that key writers have attached to monetary rewards as a motivational tool, and its implications for the design of payment systems

- the role of reward strategy in an organisation and its potential for achieving change when integrated with P&D strategies

- the factors that affect reward philosophies and policies, and the basis upon which they are formulated and integrated with business strategies.

MOTIVATION AND REWARDS

Most texts on social psychology divide theories of motivation between *content* and *process* theories. The former focus on what are seen as fundamental human needs (for example, physiological, food and safety needs), while the latter try to understand the psychological processes involved in motivation (Robertson, Smith and Cooper, 1992; Fincham and Rhodes, 1988).

F W Taylor, the father of scientific management, viewed employees as rational and economic in their approach but basically lazy and having to be motivated by management through the pay system. Given that employees were motivated primarily by money, according to him, it was important to ensure that the jobs they were doing were capable of providing the opportunity to maximise earnings. Because of this, jobs needed to be examined scientifically through time and motion studies, broken down into their constituent parts, and then put back together in the most efficient manner. This 'best' method was devised by observing the 'best' workmen on each particular task. Once the 'best' method had been established, it could then be taught to other workers, who could be retrained if necessary. However, his approach has been widely criticised, in particular for his tendency to equate people with machines, his assumption that there was one universal best method, and that the individual incentive to earn money is the primary motivating factor at work (Rose, 1978: 62). Others have noted that his conception of rational–economic person led to a self-fulfilling prophecy in that 'If employees are expected to be indifferent, hostile and only motivated by economic incentives, the management strategies used to deal with them are likely to train them to behave in precisely this fashion' (Schein, 1965: 49). Taylor's ideas can be seen clearly in payment-by-results schemes, and in particular piecework, which make explicit the link between reward and effort.

The human relations movement emerged by the 1920s, presenting a picture of 'social man' against the 'economic man' of the scientific management school. This idea developed originally from research on fatigue and its link with productivity. The groups at the plants under investigation were studied over a period of time and changes were introduced relating to alterations in rest periods, refreshments, starting and finishing times, payment schemes and environmental conditions such as lighting. However, in contrast with the prevailing wisdom, variations in these conditions did not appear to correlate with productivity. Even when the experiment ended and conditions returned to their original state, production was some 30 per cent higher than at the start. These results were then interpreted as resulting from increased worker satisfaction through being given special attention, working as a close-knit group, and being involved in decision-making. Hence, as Schein (1965: 51) puts it, 'The initiative for work shifts from management to the worker. The manager, instead of being the creator of work, the motivator and the controller, becomes the facilitator and sympathetic supporter.' It was clear that workers did not always respond to incentive schemes as managers had expected, often having their own goals (as a group) which acted against management objectives. However, as with scientific management, the human relations approach has also been criticised for its unitarist philosophy, its 'one best way' approach and indeed for its methodology. The implications of this approach for reward strategy are not that payments are irrelevant, but that new payment schemes may have a once and for all Hawthorne effect which may increase productivity. However, this school of thought suggests that rewards need to be seen in a broader work context, one in which employee objectives, other than the simple maximisation of earnings, are important.

By the 1940s Maslow had developed the 'hierarchy of needs' approach to motivation. To some extent this incorporated the previous two theories of motivation, in that rather than identifying a single source of motivation it suggested an ascending hierarchy of needs. The theory suggests that people are motivated by a number of factors at work, aiming to satisfy one particular need before moving on to attempt to satisfy the next in the hierarchy. Thus, basic security needs such as food, jobs and housing have to be achieved before individuals begin to consider their social and affiliative needs. Once these needs are satisfied they can then look to satisfy their personal needs for ego satisfaction and self-actualisation. One implication of the 'hierarchy of needs' approach for reward management is that for those on low wages, and consequently operating at the lower end of the hierarchy, money may loom more important than for those earning considerably more; these people have satisfied their basic needs, and may move on to higher-level needs, although the controversy over executive rewards which led to the Greenbury Report appears to contradict this notion. However, there is little research evidence which supports the notion of a universal hierarchy. It is also apparent that, on the same day, employees may demand not only more money but also more satisfying work, and are thus operating at more than one level of hierarchy at one time. Maslow's work is also reflected to some extent in McGregor's

(1960) distinction between theory X and theory Y managers. Theory X managers believe workers are lazy and uninterested in their work, and therefore needed to be highly controlled and offered incentives to get them to work harder. In contrast, theory Y managers believe workers can be motivated by goals of self-esteem and the desire to do a good job; consequently, management's role is to facilitate this.

Herzberg's two-factor theory of motivation was very influential in the 1960s, especially with large companies such as ICI. His research found that satisfaction and dissatisfaction were not necessarily related, and that just because a person did not feel satisfied about a particular aspect of his work it did not mean that he was necessarily dissatisfied. Equally, if workers did not feel dissatisfied, this did not imply automatic satisfaction. The motivators that tended to be identified with the good feelings included factors such as achievement, responsibility, recognition, advancement and the work itself. The so-called 'hygiene' factors which were associated with bad feelings included company policy, working conditions, supervision and pay. Thus, if an employee spoke about feeling good, it was related to having achieved something or having been granted recognition, and so on. Conversely, when speaking about feeling bad, this referred to factors such as poor supervision or insufficient pay. However, the key point here is that unless the hygiene factors are satisfied, motivators are of little use, and Herzberg felt that many firms did not even satisfy the hygiene factors. If this theory holds true then it has similar implications to Maslow's work, in that pay is only significant as a 'hygiene' factor and that an appropriate level needs to be found which meets employee expectations. However, there will be no motivating effect by paying above this level. The theory also has implications in relation to the need to restructure or enrich jobs to provide satisfying work, as 'true' motivation is seen to derive from factors associated with the job itself and opportunity for achievement, involvement and recognition. We return to this concept in Chapter 16 when we deal with non-financial rewards and recognition.

More recent theory has posited the existence of people as complex animals. This does not lend us any automatically universal picture of the employee, but one in which he or she 'has many motives which are arranged in some sort of hierarchy of importance, but this hierarchy is subject to change from time to time and situation to situation' (Schein, 1965: 60). Goldthorpe and his colleagues (Goldthorpe et al, 1968) found in their research a group of manual workers, termed 'instrumental', who appeared to want little else from work other than enough money to enable them to enjoy life to the full outside the workplace. Few of the respondents seemed particularly satisfied with their work but neither were they dissatisfied; as a priority in their lives, work was unimportant. They came to work for purely instrumental reasons and their attachment to workmates, company and union was of a similar order. In contrast, other workers – while valuing their pay – also stressed the importance of the work group and the sense of achievement in their work.

> Do you think workers are prepared to put up with dull, boring jobs if
> they are paid high wages?

In contrast to the content approaches, the alternative *process* approach
is to explore the psychological processes that are involved. Expectancy
theory is based on the expectations that people bring with them to the
work situation, and the context and way in which these expectations
are satisfied (Vroom, 1964). This is not a static model, and indeed
there may well be different sets of expectations at different times.
Expectancy theory implies that management need to demonstrate to
employees that effort will be recognised and rewarded, in both financial
and non-financial terms. The importance of this theory is that the onus
is on management to establish schemes to reward the behaviour it
wants. Moreover, it helps to explain why employees do not always
respond in the desired way as they do not believe management's word
that, for example, co-operation with the introduction of new
technology will not lead to job losses.

Three concepts are central to this theory. First, *performance–outcome
expectancy*: this means that employees believe that if they act in a
particular way, there are foreseeable consequences. For example,
employees might believe that, if they exceed work quotas they will get
bonuses, or if the target is not met pay will be docked. Secondly,
valence, which refers to the value to the employee of an outcome
deriving from behaviour. For example, one employee might value being
promoted, while another would prefer to continue working doing the
same job within the same department, as he or she places a strong
value on friendship at work. Thirdly, *effort–performance expectancy*,
which is the employee's perception of the likelihood of achieving the
desired objective. For example, if an employee believes it is impossible
to meet a sales target because the product is not a good one or that it
is simply unrealistic, he or she may not even deem it worth the effort
to try. In simple terms, the employee focuses on three questions:

- Can I perform at this level, if I try?

- If I do manage to perform at the set level, what are the
  consequences?

- What do I feel about the consequences of that action?

The theory implies that low motivation will be the product of jobs
where there is little worker control. Nadler and Lawler (1979) draw out
the implications for managers and organisations. Managers need to:

- discover what outcomes/rewards are valued (have higher valence)
  for each employee, and whether it is monetary reward or recognition,
  for example

- be specific about the desired behaviours

- ensure that performance targets are attainable, otherwise employees
  may not bother to try very hard

- ensure there is a direct, clear and explicit link between desired performance and rewards; if staff value intrinsic rewards, such as interesting work, then management can concentrate on redesigning jobs rather than increasing pay

- check that there are no conflicting expectancies

- ensure changes in reward/outcome are significant, for as Nadler and Lawler (1979: 227) put it, 'Trivial rewards will result in trivial amounts of effort and thus trivial improvements in performance', or, in more popular language, 'If you pay peanuts you get monkeys'

- check that everyone is treated fairly by the system.

Organisations need to:

- design reward systems so that desirable performance is rewarded, and the relationship between performance and reward is clear

- design tasks and jobs so that employees can satisfy their needs through work

- individualise the organisation, reflecting different needs for different people (different valences); this includes not only the work but the benefits they receive, and might point to a system of cafeteria benefits.

A central concept of expectancy theory is the view that other approaches to motivation – such as Taylor, Mayo or Maslow – are based on the assumption that all employees are *alike*, motivated by money, recognition or whatever. In addition, all situations are alike and hence there is one best way to motivate employees (Nadler and Lawler, 1979). For further discussion of this see Robertson *et al* (1992: 29–30).

> How realistic is it to design reward strategies which take account of individual goals and objectives, allowing for these to change over time?

REWARD MANAGEMENT IN CONTEXT

When trying to understand the strategic choices made by management, the environmental context is clearly important. For example, the political and economic context in the UK have been important in the development of remuneration policies in organisations. In the 1960s and 1970s, for example, Bowey, Thorpe, Mitchell, Nicholls, Gosnold, Slavery and Hellier (1982: 37–53) found that the main reason employers introduced incentive schemes was to provide a way of giving workers pay increases at a time of government restraints. Because of this lack of strategic intent, few employers achieved reduced costs and less than half increased output. In recent times the Conservative government's free–market philosophy – and its attempt to cultivate an 'enterprise culture' – have had an influence on remuneration policies.

This has been ideological, in the sense of shifting ideas towards the concept of paying people for their performance (rather than their attendance), but also more directly in terms of lower rates of income tax, the trend towards heavier taxation of fringe benefits, and new fiscal incentives for share ownership which changed the relative tax efficiency of cash and non-cash forms of remuneration. In addition, privatisation and the attempt to create quasi-markets in the public sector also have had an influence. In terms of the economic context, lower levels of inflation in the last few years have reduced the significance of general cost-of-living pay rises, and hence provided greater scope for the individualisation of annual pay increases. Skills shortages lay behind many of the innovations in remuneration policies, particularly in the south-east of England during the late 1980s and early 1990s. Product market developments also provided an impetus for change, with the intensification of international competition, product development, new technology, privatisation, deregulation, and competitive restructuring, all leading to a search for new ways of competing and responding (Snape *et al*, 1994: 127). Table 10 provides an illustration of the changing influences on pay.

Table 10 **Changing influences on pay**

FROM	TOWARDS
Limited competition	More intense competition
Standardised work	Flexibility
Standard products	Innovation
Long runs	Short runs
Product-driven systems	Customer-driven systems
Quantity	Quality
Individual output	Teamworking
Fixed tasks	Continuous improvement
Re-work	Right first time
Making for stock	Just-in-time
Being told what to do	Involvement
Skills for life	New skills
Jobs for life	Less security
Measuring output	Appraising contribution
Rewarding seniority	Rewarding achievement
Job-based systems	People-based systems

Source: Cannell and Wood (1992: 6)

The political and economic contexts have major implications for remuneration policy. They can remove some of the obstacles to the strategic use of remuneration, for example through tax changes and lower levels of inflation, which allow managements to experiment with pay in a way which would not have been feasible previously. They may also place new demands on organisations, requiring greater effectiveness and responsiveness to customers. Remuneration policy has increasingly been seen as a key management tool in meeting such demands (Snape *et al*, 1994: 127–128).

There are several factors which influence salary and wage levels (Curnow, 1986). Firstly, job 'size' has traditionally been the main determinant of pay. This includes factors such as responsibility, level in the organisational hierarchy, required knowledge, skills or competencies, external contacts, complexity and decision-making. Hence, the individual's hierarchical position in large organisations has been central to the design of internal pay structures, with performance rewarded by promotion. However, since the 1980s, job size has been seen as less important than individual contribution. Secondly, individual characteristics – such as age, experience, qualifications and special skills, contribution and performance – are also significant factors. Thirdly, labour market factors – such as the supply and demand of particular skills both locally and the 'going rate' in the particular labour market – are important. Fourthly, product market conditions and the employers' cost structure – such as its position in the market, profitability and market ambitions and strategies – have a major influence on pay strategy. Finally, the remuneration philosophy of the organisation also has an influence on wage and salary levels. An organisation with the reputation for being a 'good employer', and wishing to attract the most able staff, is likely to offer higher wages than one where staff are valued less positively.

According to Lawler (1984: 128), reward systems can influence a number of areas which in turn have an impact on organisational performance. First, rewards influence who is attracted to apply to and work for the employer, and also who continues to work for him: 'Those organisations that give the most rewards tend to attract and retain the most people' (Lawler, 1984: 128). High wages attract more applicants, which allows greater choice over selection and hiring decisions, which in turn may reduce labour turnover. In addition, better performers need to be rewarded more highly than poor performers. The type of payment system (not just the level of rewards) also has an effect on recruitment and retention, so performance-based systems are more likely to attract high performers.

Secondly, employees see reward systems as signalling the importance the employer places on various activities or behaviours. Hence, reward systems have a motivational impact and need to be integrated with the corporate behaviour which is being sought. Devanna, Fombrun and Tichy (1984: 49) suggest that a key strategic issue is how to use the reward system to overcome the tendency towards short-sighted management. If rewards are tied too closely to annual performance, managers may not devote time and energy to long-term objectives and may 'mortgage the future for present performance'.

Thirdly, the way in which employees are rewarded has a major influence on corporate culture. For example, reward systems which provide benefits to long-serving staff are likely to shape the existing culture into one where loyalty is seen as central to the corporate ideology. In contrast, a system which rewards innovative behaviour is likely to help create an innovative culture. Banks and building societies, for example, have dismantled pay structures based on seniority and service, often introducing performance-related pay so as to emphasise the new enterprise culture (Snape, Redman and Wilkinson, 1993: 46). As the general manager of one society put it, 'We needed a set of human resource strategies which would change the culture of the society into a more dynamic, commercially orientated, market- and customer-led and profit-conscious organisation' (Murphy, 1989: 42).

Fourthly, the reward system can help define the status hierarchy and the decision-making structure. For example, if rewards are related directly to the position in the hierarchy, horizontal career management is unlikely to be valued by staff, as they see it as not being rewarded. Wage compression can produce high performance as there is less incentive to waste time on 'gaming the system' (Pfeffer, 1994: 51). De-emphasising pay can help enhance other bases of satisfaction with work. According to Crystal (1991), American chief executive officers earn 160 times more than the average worker, while in Germany the ratio is 21:1 and in Japan 16:1. However, the message that wage compression can help performance is not one of the Japanese lessons that Britain managers have been keen to promote!

Finally, cost is a key factor in reward systems, and for service-sector organisations labour costs are a significant proportion of their overall costs. The employer might wish to achieve flexibility so that labour costs can be brought down if the organisation is under financial pressure. Having a lower cost ratio than competitors might be another aim. However, lower wages do not always mean lower labour costs as this depends on productivity, and high wages may be correlated with higher levels of performance.

> Review the reward strategies at your workplace in the light of these five areas which are identified by Lawler as having an impact on organisational performance. How might you redesign reward strategy because of this?

INTEGRATION OR CONTRADICTION IN REWARD STRUCTURES

One potential problem is that these aims may conflict with or contradict each other, and this is a particular danger if those responsible for remuneration policy are unclear as to its specific objectives. Duncan (1992), for example, lists nine possible objectives which management might have: ensuring that firms can recruit the appropriate quantity and quality of staff; reducing labour disputes; motivating high performance; achieving equitable pay differentials; reducing labour turnover; controlling costs; increasing labour flexibility; increasing company loyalty; and compensating for adverse working conditions.

Another potential problem is that there may well be differences in the expectations of different groups of workers from the payment system, as we saw from the discussion on expectancy theory earlier in this chapter. While much of the literature discusses the functional and dysfunctional role of reward systems, it is not always matched by discussion of the *strategic* role of such systems. It is usual to regard the reward system as dependent on the business strategy and the management style of the organisation concerned. However, as we have seen from the previous section, existing human resources and reward systems may also exercise a constraint on corporate strategy, so the relationship is not simply one way.

When considering the strategic design of reward systems, Lawler (1984: 131) suggests that there are two dimensions to consider. These include a *structural* content dimension (formal procedures and practices) and a *process* dimension (communication and decision process parts). In relation to the *structural* decisions, there are a number of questions to consider:

- *Basis for rewards*: are people to be paid on the basis of what jobs they do (ie through job evaluation techniques) or for what skills or competencies they have? Skills-based pay is seen as more appropriate for those organisations that have a flexible, relatively permanent workforce that is oriented towards learning.

- *Pay for performance*: should staff be paid on the basis of seniority or performance? Because of the problems in implementing performance-based schemes, some believe individual pay should be based on seniority, as in Japan, with motivation to be achieved through other means (such as personal growth or recognition). If managements decide to pursue the performance route, then decisions need to be made on the behaviours to be rewarded and how they should be rewarded (for example, by individual or group plans).

- *Market position*: the market position and stance of an organisation will influence organisational climate. If management considers the organisation to be an élite and feels it is important to be a leading player, there is likely to be a different reward system from one in which staff are seen as less critical to business success.

- *Internal–external pay comparison*: managements need to decide the extent to which they value internal equity – someone doing similar work is paid the same even if they may be in different regions or in different businesses – or external equity, which focuses on the labour market as the key determinant of what employees should be paid. This issue depends on the extent to which the organisation wishes to have an overall corporate identity (eg everyone working for Ciba to have similar conditions of service) or product market differentiation (bulk chemicals and pharmaceuticals to be seen as distinct business or product lines).

- *Centralised–decentralised reward strategy*: organisations with a centralised strategy usually have a corporate P&D department which develops standardised pay and wage guidelines. This creates a feeling of internal equity and shared values. In decentralised organisations flexibility allows for local options.

- *Degree of hierarchy*: managements can choose whether they employ a hierarchical approach to reward, where people get paid depending on where they are in the hierarchy and are often also provided with symbols of their status, or a more egalitarian approach where the climate is more team-based and there are fewer status symbols.

- *Reward mix*: this refers to the type of rewards given to individuals (benefits, status symbols, etc) or indeed the choice employees are given through a cafeteria-style approach where individuals can make up their own package (see Chapter 15). Again, the form of rewards should reflect the culture or climate the employer wishes to create and reinforce.

Assess where your organisation fits with regard to the eight structural issues raised by Lawler, and whether they support or contradict each other. Explain why this is the situation, and what might be done to achieve greater horizontal and vertical integration.

In relation to the *process* dimensions of reward systems there are two key issues:

- *Communication policy*: how far the employer wants to have an open or closed policy on rewards depends on its philosophy.

- *Decision-making practices*: the issue here is whether or not to involve employees in system design and administration. Involvement can lead to important issues being raised and expertise being provided, which is not always the case if a top-down approach is taken. Moreover, involving employees and their representatives helps the acceptance of any changes since there is a greater sense of legitimacy bestowed on decisions.

There is no right or wrong approach, so what matters is choosing a position which is supportive of the culture and systems, and which produces the behaviour necessary to achieve organisational effectiveness. 'Reward system design features are not stand-alone items. There is considerable evidence that they affect each other and, as such, need to be supportive of the same type of behaviour, reflect the same overall managerial philosophy, and be generated by the same business strategy' (Lawler, 1984: 145).

He illustrates this by showing how two contrasting management philosophies call for two quite different approaches to reward practices – see Table 11.

Table 11 Appropriate reward system practices

	Traditional, or Theory X	Participative, or Theory Y
Reward system		
Fringe benefits	Vary according to organisation level	Cafeteria – same for all levels
Promotion	All decisions made by top management	Open posting for all jobs; peer group involvement in decision process
Status symbols	A great many, carefully allocated on the basis of job position	Few present, low emphasis on organisation level
Pay		
Type of system	Hourly and salary	All salary
Base rate	Based on job performed; high enough to attract job applicants	Based on skills; high enough to provide security and attract applicants
Incentive plan	Piece rate	Group and organisation-wide bonus, lump sum increase
Communication policy	Very restricted distribution of information	Individual rates, salary survey data, all other information made public
Decision-making locus	Top management	Close to location of person whose pay is being set

Source: Lawler, 1984: 146. (Reprinted by permission of John Wiley & Sons, Inc.)

Moreover, the issue of congruence or fit needs to be consistent with the P&D system as a whole. As Lawler (1984: 145–146) notes, this 'means that the reward system needs to fit such things as the way jobs are designed, the leadership style of the supervisors, and the types of career tracks available in the organisation ...' Unless this kind of fit exists, the organisation will be replete with conflicts and, to a degree the reward system practices will potentially be cancelled out by the practices in other areas. In short, a contingency approach which takes into account particular organisational and environmental factors is likely to be superior to an off-the-shelf solution which reflects current fads and fashions.

Much of the literature in the field tends to the prescriptive: we are told how management *should* tackle the subject of reward management but not what actually happens in practice. Those who have examined the *practice* of reward management paint quite a different picture. Kessler (1994: 270) argues that reward management policy has been 'driven by relating crude and unplanned attempts to relate pay to performance in a manner detached from contextual factors'. Changes in reward policy appear to have been driven by short-term cost considerations and the need to respond to immediate labour market pressures rather than any strategic intent. Kessler points out that there is little research on the evolution of reward systems or on the decision-making process itself. Indeed, a major concern is that few managements attempt to evaluate their pay schemes in any real depth. They appear not to have clear criteria against which the schemes can be evaluated, but rather tend to rely on a 'gut feel' assessment that, for example, because of its performance emphasis, a PRP system must be conducive to good performance. Conversely, any contra-indications or problems are dismissed as mere 'teething problems' which relate to issues of implementation.

Employees enter into a relationship with their employer which assumes that they will give their time to the organisation in return for a reward, which will certainly include money but may also include other factors such as status or job satisfaction. However, this is by no means a simple process as often the actual work is not specified and/or different employees may expect different rewards. Because many factors are not specified in the contract – work intensity and supervision for example – the effort bargain can only be established over time by custom and practice. However, because factors change, the relationships may be perceived by one party as unfair and hence the effort bargain is potentially unstable. For example, at a time of recession managers may attempt to change working practices to increase productivity, whereas workers may perceive this as a breach of custom and practice, so leading to potential conflict (Baladamas, 1961). The achievement of fairness is central to the issue of payment, and however well the bonus scheme or payment is devised it is unlikely to be effective if it is perceived to be unfair – see the discussion in Chapter 2 on the psychological contract. As Brown and Walsh (1994: 443) observe, 'the prudent personnel manager devotes far less time to devising new pay incentives than to tending old notions of fairness'. However, as they point out 'there is nothing absolute about fairness in pay', as it is 'a normative idea' based on comparison.

In general, it appears comparisons are taken more seriously if there is little social or geographical distance between the comparators. Secondly, convention and tradition are central to the concept of fairness, with any change from the *status quo* tending to cause concern. Given that changes as a result of new technology and other factors are inevitable, it is essential for management to justify decisions in terms of consistency and legitimacy. If unions have traditionally been involved and management then chooses to ignore them, such action may be seen as illegitimate. Hence, procedural matters are often as significant as the reward itself, in that fair rewards need to be paid in a fair manner. Job evaluation is one method of dealing with the problem of differentials. There is also the issue of external pay relativities – as expressed in the term 'rate for the job' – which reflects the view that employees should be paid an appropriate wage; the issue of affordability is a management problem, not one for employees. In recent years there has been a marked political and ideological swing away from the 'rate for the job' to a philosophy which tries to relate individual pay to individual and corporate performance. However, the issue of differentials and comparability is unlikely to disappear. Firstly, top managements justify their own pay increases by reference to external pay (for example, underpaid within the industry, or underpaid compared with managers abroad). Secondly, if organisations fail to pay the 'going rate', they risk losing staff to competitors.

Take a sample of five occupations for which you can gather information about pay levels – for example, Member of Parliament, train driver, checkout operator, nurse, P&D manager. Place these in rank order. Do you consider these pay levels to be fair in relation to each other? Why/why not? Discuss with your colleagues the notions of fairness and differentials.

JOB EVALUATION

Job evaluation can be defined as a process whereby jobs are placed in a rank order according to overall demands placed upon the job-holder. It therefore provides a basis for a fair and orderly grading structure (ACAS, 1991) but it is best regarded as a systematic rather than a scientific process. It is a method of establishing the relative position of jobs within a hierarchy, which is achieved by using criteria drawn from the content of the jobs. However, there is sometimes considerable confusion concerning the process. The process of writing job descriptions (which was dealt with in Chapter 6) is central to job evaluation, but it is *not* intended to evaluate the person or job-holder on his or her performance, to establish the pay for the job, or to reduce the need for collective bargaining. Job evaluation has existed since the 1920s but was given considerable impetus in the 1960s and 1970s because of government incomes policies. WIRS reported a broadening in coverage of job evaluation between 1980 and 1990, and the proportion of workplaces with 25 or more employees using job evaluation rose from 21 per cent to 26 per cent by 1990, with a notable increase in the public sector. It is found most commonly in manufacturing and nationalised industries, and its incidence increases with establishment size. Job evaluation has a number of benefits. It provides a formula for dealing with grievances about pay, and decisions are likely to be more acceptable if there is a formal system rather than *ad hoc* ways of dealing with pay issues. Millward *et al* (1992: 266–269) suggest that, given the legislation on equal opportunities, it is surprising that analytical schemes have not grown further and they suggest that the weakening of union power over the 1980s has reduced pressure on employers to use job evaluation to justify pay differentials.

Table 12 Nature of job evaluation scheme (% of establishments with any scheme)

Basis of largest scheme	1980	1984	1990
Points rating	46	46	45
Factor comparisons	9	7	15
Ranking	13	10	21
Grading	27	27	15
Other/not stated	5	10	4

Source: Millward *et al*, 1992: 267.

As we can see from Table 12, there are a number of job evaluation techniques, but in broad terms they fall into two types of scheme – non-analytical and analytical.

Non-analytical schemes use a simple ranking method, with jobs placed in rank order and no attempt to evaluate or compare parts of each job. They have declined in favour in recent years as they are unlikely to be a defence in an equal value claim. They are termed non-analytical because they do not break the job down into its constituent parts. There are various forms of non-analytical scheme.

Job ranking

Under this system, job descriptions or titles are placed in a rank order or hierarchy to provide a 'league table'. It is a very simple method as the job is considered as a whole rather than broken down into constituent parts. It is usually seen as suitable for small organisations where the evaluation team is likely to know all the jobs. It is simple and cheap to implement but tends to be very subjective. Furthermore, while job Y can be identified as more difficult than job X, it is not clear how much more difficult it is (Duncan, 1992: 277). For example, the following is a simple categorisation.

Grade 1 Supervised manual labour.

Grade 2 Unsupervised manual labour following prescribed procedures.

Grade 3 Tasks involving interpretation of procedures.

Grade 4 Tasks involving interpretation of procedures and responsibility for work groups.

Paired comparison

This approach is similar to the above but more systematic in that each job is compared with every other job, and points are allocated depending on whether it is less than, equal to, or more than the other jobs. The points are added up to provide a league table. It is more objective than job ranking but can be time-consuming unless there is computer support, given the comparisons which need to be made.

Job classification

This is the reverse of the above process in that, under this technique, the number of grades is first decided upon, and a detailed grades definition is then produced. Benchmark (representative) jobs are evaluated with non-benchmark jobs before being slotted in on the basis of the grade definitions. The main drawbacks are that complex jobs may be difficult to assess as they may stretch across grade boundaries.

The main drawback of these 'whole job' approaches is that they are highly subjective. Given that they are not analysed systematically, it is likely that implicit assumptions about the worth of jobs may be left unquestioned: physical strength, for example, may be given undue weight. This has significant implications for equal opportunities, as 'women's' jobs may be rated lower than 'men's' jobs for historical reasons.

Analytical schemes involve a systematic analysis of jobs by breaking them down into constituent factors. There are two principal categories of analytical scheme.

Points rating

This is the most popular technique, and it involves breaking down jobs into a number of factors which may include skill, judgement, knowledge, experience, effort, responsibility, pressure, and so on. Each factor receives a weighting, which is then converted to points, with the total points determining the relative worth of a job. It is more objective than non-analytical methods, and by breaking down the jobs helps overcome the danger that *people* are assessed rather than *jobs*. However, it is a time-consuming process which is prone to grievances as small changes in job content can lead to regrading issues.

Factor comparison

This attempts to rank jobs and attach monetary values simultaneously. Jobs are analysed in terms of factors (mental and physical requirements, responsibility, etc) and benchmark jobs are examined, one factor at a time, to produce a rank order of the job for each factor. The next step is to check how much of the wage is being paid for each factor. Where employees are shown to be overpaid for the job they do, the usual practice is red-circling which protects the individual's pay in the post (sometimes for a set period of time), but a successor would be paid the newly evaluated (lower) rate. This system is not popular in Britain, partly because the allocation of cash values to factors is seen as too arbitrary and it assumes that a pay structure already exists.

Despite the growth of more 'scientific' forms of job evaluation, ultimately the process is subjective, as assumptions are made about the design of the scheme, the factors and weights chosen, as well as the judgement of those doing the evaluating. Because of this, employee involvement in the scheme is important to lend credibility to something which would otherwise be seen as management-driven.

What are the main strengths and weaknesses of job evaluation in your organisation?

Armstrong and Murlis (1991: 136) suggest a number of reasons why job evaluation is in a transitional phase. First, equal pay legislation has meant that it has been necessary to re-examine schemes to ensure they are analytical and gender-neutral. Secondly, new technology is changing roles, eliminating job differences and introducing new skills – for example, by reducing the emphasis on physical skills and increasing the relevance of more conceptual skills. Thirdly, there is now greater flexibility in working arrangements, and a growth in teamworking, for example. Fourthly, information technology has reduced the number of layers in organisations which means decisions are being made by employees lower down the hierarchy. Hence, more is being demanded of employees, and their horizons may be narrowed rather than widened by job descriptions which define a single job. Fifthly, labour market pressures due to skill shortages can lead to comparisons based on external relativities rather than internal relativities. Finally, the notion of individual contribution is growing more important, a trend that is evidenced by the introduction of performance-related pay schemes.

> Is job evaluation in your organisation being affected by new technology.
> If so, how?

Recent criticism of job evaluation has pointed to its costly and bureaucratic nature – for example, in the NHS appeals on the clinical grading structure. Grayson (1987) points out that most job evaluation schemes pre-date changes in delayering, work methods and skills, and hence the original assumptions on which the schemes were based have become less valid. Job descriptions assume stability and hierarchy in the world of work, a situation which no longer appears to exist. The language of flexibility would also suggest that fixed job descriptions are a thing of the past; at Nissan, for example, there are no longer any job descriptions as such, and only 15 job titles (Wickens, 1987: 117). As Brown and Walsh (1994: 448) observe, the 'high tide of job evaluation is probably past. The more that pay is linked to the careers and knowledge of individuals, and the more that "adjustment to change" factors are seen to be part of the employees' duties, the less appropriate it is to link pay rigidly to the particular basket of tasks currently being performed by an individual employee.'

We have already noted that formal job evaluation processes began in the 1960s and 1970s, when, for many organisations, the main interest was in establishing internal equity, with a focus on jobs rather than on people. External labour markets were regarded as relatively homogeneous, and issues of individual performance and contribution were to a large degree optional extras, or accommodated by highly structured systems in which employees gained automatic progression (Murlis and Pritchard, 1991: 49). Nowadays employers are pursuing flexibility with flatter structures and fewer grades, but with wider pay bands attached to each grade. However, as Duncan (1992: 284) argues, these are by no means incompatible with job evaluation since 'the evaluation process may provide an agreed hierarchy of jobs from which a grading structure can be built, but need not determine the actual structure, and the setting of pay differentials and ranges is also normally quite separate from the evaluation process.' Indeed, job evaluation has been utilised in the reform of pay structures in both the private and public sectors to assist new grading arrangements which reflect a more flexible remuneration strategy (Duncan, 1992).

Recent work by Armstrong and Baron (1995) concluded that the death of job evaluation had been greatly exaggerated, although they do acknowledge that new perspectives are evolving – such as competence-based job evaluation associated with broad banding. With changes such as delayering and the growth of teamwork, employers appear to be attempting to value jobs in ways that fit with the need for operational and role flexibility. Hence there has been a growth of broad-banded or job-family pay structures which facilitate rewards for people who adapt to new challenges, and develop and expand their role. In the Armstrong and Baron survey (1995: 280–81), 55 per cent of the responding organisations operated a formal job evaluation scheme, and a further 22 per cent which were currently without formal job evaluation intended to introduce it. The greatest criticism of job evaluation was its inflexibility, and its inability to cope with knowledge workers, team working or flatter structures. Conventional job evaluation was seen as exaggerating small differences in skill and responsibility by the attachment of points in a way which impeded flexibility. Managements stressed the need to evaluate employees and not just jobs.

The research also found that competence-based factors had been added on to an existing points factor scheme and/or replaced existing factors. Job descriptions were being replaced by generic role definitions setting out core competences (encouraged by the take-up of NVQs). Competence-based job evaluation aims to value the work employees do in terms of the competences required to perform effectively in different roles and at different levels in the organisation. If a role requires a particular level of competence, this can then be translated into a standard of competence performance for the individual in that role (Armstrong and Baron, 1995: 97). 'A family' of closely related jobs – such as research scientists for example – can be constructed as a hierarchy of levels with employees paid according to the range and depth of their competencies (Armstrong and Murlis, 1995: 359–360). However, managements are interested in outputs (ie results/contribution) and not just inputs (competency levels). Alternatively, new factor plans were being developed which were wholly competency-based. However, Armstrong (1995: 35) warns that it is not enough for organisations to rid themselves of a structure and leave a vacuum: 'Structures have to be replaced with processes which provide guidance on how individuals will be paid and their progress within broad bands or job-family groups in which they are placed.' There is a growing awareness of need for gender-neutrality in schemes. Armstrong (1995: 35) argues that the methodology has to be flexible, with job evaluation seen as a dynamic evolutionary process being reviewed and modified in line with changes to processes, technology and values: it is not a separate stand-alone entity. Research by the IRS (*Employment Trends* 551) also found that job evaluation is being used as a tool to underpin pay structures but not to determine the pay rates of individual employees. Thus it will no longer represent the ultimate technique for pay decisions. Computer-assisted job evaluation eliminates the need for time-consuming panel meetings, and is therefore likely to become more widespread in large applications. As Armstrong (1995: 35) argues, the real issue is whether or not job evaluation adds value, and what effect it has on motivation, commitment and performance. He suggests that 'job evaluation will increasingly be seen as an integral part of the overall reward and people-management process. The onus will be to ensure that any methods used to assess the relative worth of jobs reflect the core values and culture of the organisation, and further the achievement of strategic objectives.'

EQUAL VALUE CONSIDERATIONS

The Equal Pay Act 1970 which came into operation in 1975 gave men and women the right to equal treatment in contracts of employment, and was concerned with wages as well as with other terms and conditions. In simple terms, this meant that an employer was required to employ women and men doing the same work on the same terms and conditions. The Equal Pay Act did not originally provide for equal pay for work of equal value. It envisaged dealing with situations where men and women were doing the same or broadly similar work (which meant that the scope of comparison was narrow), where a voluntary job evaluation scheme had evaluated the work as equal, or where terms and conditions were laid down in collective agreements, employers' wage structures or statutory wage orders. While the earnings gap between men and women has narrowed since 1970, there remains a 20 per cent difference in average gross hourly earnings (McColgan, 1994).

The Equal Pay (Amendment) Regulations 1983 broadened the scope of the original 1970 Act. A woman or man is entitled to 'equal pay for work of equal value' (in terms of the demands made on a worker under various headings, for instance effort, skill, decision). Hence, if a woman is doing work of the same *value* as a man, even if it is a different job, she can claim equal pay (EOC, 1995). The change means that women performing jobs in which traditionally few men have been employed are now within the scope of the Act (or the reverse – the Act gives the same rights to men), whereas prior to this, women could not claim equal pay because they were doing jobs not done by men employed by the same employer. Equal value claims can be made across sites, provided employees are deemed to be in the same employment (that is, working for the same or an associated employer). For example, in *Leverton v Clwyd County Council* (1989), the House of Lords ruled that establishments were covered by the same 'purple book' agreement, even if there were variations in individual terms and conditions.

This has far-reaching implications for organisations and their pay systems, and many employers have sought to introduce a new scheme or reassess their existing job evaluation system. Clearly job evaluation systems should reflect published objective criteria which can enable the employer to justify why particular rates are being paid to men and women. However, it is important to ensure that the scheme itself does not reflect discriminatory values, perhaps by overrating 'male' characteristics such as strength. In *Bromley and Ors v H and J Quick Ltd* (1988), the Court of Appeal held that paired comparisons in a whole job approach was inadequate, and a valid job evaluation scheme must be 'analytical'. It is believed that an integrated analysis job evaluation scheme (*all* employees) is the most defensible, and the case is helped if the system has been negotiated with a trade union and there is employee involvement in the operation of the scheme.

However, it has been argued that job evaluation acts not in an objective, independent way but merely serves to reinforce existing hierarchies. This is partly the result of the objectives of job evaluation, which tend to emphasise stability and acceptability, and hence do not disrupt established differentials (see Armstrong and Baron, 1995, for a summary of the research on this area). Non-analytical scenes are particularly prone to bias because they produce a 'felt-fair' rank order which can be based on stereotypes. However, even with analytical schemes, problems can occur in factor choice and weighting. For example, caring and human relations skills are often missed or misunderstood. Table 13 illustrates that the choice of different factors can produce quite a different rank order for the same jobs.

As Rubenstein (1992) puts it, 'since the work women do is undervalued because it is performed by women, the effect of traditional job evaluation which emphasises acceptability is merely to perpetuate the *status quo*. In such circumstances, job evaluation does not get rid of pay discrimination against women. All it does is to make pay discrimination more subtle, more covert and more difficult to prove' (quoted in Armstrong and Baron, 1995: 188).

An employer can justify differences in pay only where the variation between the terms and conditions is due to a 'material' (ie significant and relevant) factor, and not the difference in gender. That is, even when 'like work' is proved, a woman has no right to equal pay if an employer can show there is a material difference (not based on sex) between the two employees which justifies the differences in payment. Material factors held by case law to justify a difference in pay are market forces (for example, increasing the pay of a particular job to attract candidates), and 'red-circling' (ie where a job is downgraded but pay is not reduced) (Armstrong and Baron, 1995: 177–178). Equal value cases cannot be defended on the ground of implementation costs or of the impact on employee relations. Moreover, in *North Yorkshire County Council* v *Ratcliffe and Ors*, the House of Lords ruled that a local authority which paid women catering workers less than a group of male workers doing equivalent work – so that it could compete with a commercial firm for a tender – had not established that the difference in pay was due to a material factor other than gender. Other material differences could be experience or a qualification. However, this is to be evaluated on a one-by-one basis, as experience may be deemed relevant in one instance but irrelevant in another. For example, if a man is being paid more than the comparator because of certain skills he has which the applicant does not, it needs to be shown that these are necessary for the job and do not represent, for example, a past pay agreement.

The basis of comparison is each individual term of the contract. In *Hayward* v *Cammell Laird*, a cook claimed equal pay with a painter, joiner and insulation engineer. The report by the independent expert noted that her work was of equal value and should be paid at the same rate. The argument that some of Hayward's terms and conditions were more favourable than those of the comparators, and therefore could offset the difference in pay rates was ultimately rejected by the House of Lords (Armstrong and Baron, 1995: 179).

As well as job evaluation systems being biased, it is also possible for the process to reflect discriminatory principles. Ghobandian and White (1987) suggest that the following are more likely to lead to an unbiased process:

Table 13 Job evaluation using discriminatory and non–discriminatory factors

Discriminatory factors		
Factor	Maintenance fitter	Company nurse
Skill		
experience in job	10	1
training	5	7
Responsibility		
for money	0	0
for equipment and machinery	8	3
for safety	3	6
for work done by others	3	0
Effort		
lifting requirement	4	2
strength required	7	2
sustained physical effort	5	1
Conditions		
physical environment	6	0
working position	6	0
hazards	7	0
Total	64	22
Non-discriminatory factors		
Factor	Maintenance fitter	Company nurse
Basic knowledge	6	8
Complexity of task	6	7
Training	5	7
Responsibility for people	3	8
Responsibility for materials and equipment	8	6
Mental effort	5	6
Visual attention	6	6
Physical activity	8	5
Working conditions	6	1
Total	53	54

Source: EOC, 1985

- formal scheme

- analytical scheme

- a high number of factors

- a high proportion of women covered by the scheme

- job evaluation as the sole determinant of pay

- transparency in communications on the aim and methods of the scheme

- presence of female staff on working parties and panels

- union representatives as analysts and members of panels/committees

> Is your job evaluation scheme free of gender bias?

CONCLUSION

It is clear that there are certain fads and fashions in the reward area, as in many other aspects of P&D, which are influenced by prevailing theories of motivation, as well as external and internal contingencies. In this chapter we reviewed the way in which dominant reward philosophies tend to reflect the views of leading management thinkers (such as Taylor, Maslow and Herzberg), who make significantly different assumptions about what motivates workers. Accordingly, incentive schemes are typically founded upon the assumption that money is the sole motivating force, while time-based systems which also incorporate a range of other benefits are more likely to reflect the view that employees have hierarchies of needs. By way of contrast, some of the process theorists argue that motivation is a highly personal concept, and therefore reward policies need to be flexible, allowing for cafeteria benefits and individualised packages. External contextual factors – such as incomes policies, taxation systems, and the management of the economy – also have an important influence over the choice of appropriate reward systems, as does the employer's overall business strategy and his position in the product market.

Perhaps most important of all, at least for employees, is the idea that reward systems should be fair and equitable, that overall benefits and payments should be consistent with what is perceived as the quality of the individual's contribution, and his or her comparisons with other people, both internal and external to the organisation. The debate in the mid-1990s about the reward packages of top managers and executives sums this up well. Most manual and non-manual workers would deem it reasonable that these people should earn rather more than they do themselves, although there may be disagreements about the precise ratio. However, they would consider it totally unfair that such individuals are not subject to an open regulatory system, that they are able to benefit from well-designed share option schemes, and gain perks which appear excessive. The question of whether job evaluation is a legacy from an inflexible and bureaucratic past or a necessary element in efforts to achieve fairness, openness and consistency also illustrates this point. In addition, it illustrates the persistent dilemma which faces employers in the design of reward systems, between the pursuit of flexibility and the goal of equity.

USEFUL READING

ACAS (1991) 'Job evaluation – an introduction', *ACAS Advisory Booklet No 1*.

ARMSTRONG, M. (1995) 'Measuring work: the vital statistics', *People Management*, 21 September: 34–35.

ARMSTRONG, M. AND BARON, A. (1995) *The Job Evaluation Handbook*. London, IPD.

ARMSTRONG, M. AND MURLIS, H. (1995) *Reward Management*, Third edition. London, Kogan Page.

CANNELL, M. AND WOOD, S. (1992) *Incentive Pay*, London, NEDO/IPM.

CURNOW, B. (1986) 'The creative approach to pay', *Personnel Management*, October: 70–75.

DUNCAN, C. (1992) 'Pay, payment systems and job evaluation' in B. Towers (Ed.), *A Handbook of Industrial Relations Practice*, Third edition. London, Kogan Page: 258–291.

EQUAL OPPORTUNITIES COMMISSION (1995) *Equal Pay for Work of Equal Value, A guide to the Amended Equal Pay Act*. EOC, Manchester.

FINCHAM, R. AND RHODES, P. (1988) *The Individual, Work and Organisation*. London, Weidenfeld & Nicolson.

ROBERTSON, I., SMITH, M. AND COOPER, D. (1992) *Motivation*. London, IPD.

SNAPE, E., REDMAN, T. AND BAMBER, G. (1994) *Managing Managers: Strategies and techniques for human resource management*. Oxford, Blackwell.

15 Payment schemes

INTRODUCTION

According to Torrington (1993b: 149), since the 1940s arrangements for payment have had one or both of two underlying philosophies. First the *service* philosophy, which emphasises the acquisition of experience, implying that people become more effective as they remain in a job so that their service is rewarded through incremental pay scales. These scales are typically of five to eight points, encouraging people to continue in the post for several years as there is still some headroom for salary growth. Second is the *fairness* philosophy, which emphasises getting the right structure of differentials. The progressive spread of job evaluation from the 1960s onwards was an attempt to cope with the problems of *relative* pay levels that were generated by increasing organisation size and job complexity (see Chapter 14). Legislation on equal value in the 1970s gave further impetus to this approach.

Accompanying the growth of pay systems emphasising service and fairness, was a steady decline in incentive schemes. These had been developed almost entirely for manual workers from the early part of this century until the late 1960s, but had then begun to decline due to years of battling with union representatives, employees using their ingenuity in outwitting the work study officer, and changes in production technology. Since the 1980s there has been a return to the incentive idea and a new *performance* philosophy has arisen. Length of service is useful, fairness is necessary, but what really matters is the performance of the employee (Torrington 1993b: 149).

As we saw in the previous chapter, job evaluation often provides a structure for basic pay. However, basic pay comprises only part of the overall pay package, and different types of scheme may be used which reflect distinct philosophies of pay. While interest in pay systems has been influenced by faddism, Mahoney (1992: 337–338) argues that 'interest in a variety of pay plans is warranted as a means of enhancing the complementarity of compensation systems and forms of organisation and systems of management. Careful matching of compensation systems and organisational systems, rather than the implementation on the basis of fad, provides the opportunity to truly reinforce organisational strategy.'

In this chapter we examine the varieties of reward system and the different elements in the reward package. As we have seen in the previous chapter, it is important that the reward philosophy and policy reflects the overall objectives of the employer, and that the different elements of the package send a clear and consistent message to employees. One problem in this field is that the various terms and concepts are used inconsistently; not only is this confusing for the manager or reader, it also makes comparisons difficult, given that it is quite likely that terms are being used in different ways.

It is important that P&D professionals see the payment system not solely as something in its own right, but also see the links with organisation strategy and other human resource practices. Simply adopting a policy of selecting a scheme because it is seen as the latest thing to do is likely to be a recipe for failure. Nor should managements regard the adoption of a payment system as the complete and final solution to problems of pay policy. Indeed, there is a view that every scheme which is implemented, however satisfactory, contains the seeds of its own destruction (Watson, 1986: 182–183). As individuals or groups bring their own interests to bear on the system, this means that subsequently it becomes very difficult to manage as interests become embedded, and the system serves certain groups rather than the organisation as a whole Furthermore, as technology, business objectives, work organisation and labour supply alter, a system may need to be re-evaluated (Lupton and Gowler, 1969).

It is also crucial to understand that the choice of payment system depends on the particular circumstances of the organisation, the technology, the characteristics of the labour market and employee attitudes, and managers need to think carefully about the conditions under which a scheme will operate and the messages it will send to various audiences. A contingency approach, in which managers pick a scheme appropriate to their organisational needs, is more likely to be successful (Kessler, 1995: 257–258). For example, an employer who stresses the importance of quality (through a Total Quality Management initiative, for example) is likely to undermine this philosophy by the introduction or maintenance of a payment-by-results scheme (such as piece work) which sends a message that output is the key aim of the employer. Equally, an organisation which is not doing well financially may find it difficult to introduce a system of performance-related pay (PRP) as employees are likely to see few benefits for themselves. Indeed, research suggests that PRP schemes need to be 'greased in' to facilitate a trouble-free introduction. Moreover, the paucity of systematic evidence on the incentive effects of various payment systems should urge us to be wary of swallowing a consultant's line that their package will improve performance where other schemes or strategies have failed.

While pay may be only part of the broader package of benefits – which include recognition, achievement and the intrinsic qualities of the job (see Chapter 16) – a well-designed, strategically integrated remuneration policy can help signal changing priorities within the organisation. Moreover, as organisations become flatter and promotion opportunities lessen, this may place even greater emphasis on recognition and reward elements of the pay system.

By the end of this chapter, readers should be able to:

- advise management on the circumstances under which different payment systems may be appropriate for their organisation

- outline the case for and against the introduction of performance-related pay and specify the conditions under which it is appropriate

- explain the benefits of financial participation to the organisation and its employees.

In addition, readers should be able to understand and explain:

- the principal differences between different types of pay scheme

- the importance of linking the pay system to wider organisational goals and other P&D strategies

- the criteria for assessing whether a pay structure is effective.

In this chapter we examine the different type of pay schemes which can be implemented.

> What payment schemes exist in your organisation? Explain their rationale.

TIME RATES OF PAYMENT

These are usually expressed as an hourly rate, a weekly or monthly wage, or an annual salary. Some three-quarters of British employees are paid on pure time rates (Brown and Walsh, 1994), although in some cases a payment by results component may be added. There are two forms of time rate. The first is a flat rate per period of time, while the second incorporates fixed scales, with increases based on length of service (Duncan, 1992: 259). Such schemes are simple and cheap to administer, are easily understood by employees and are unlikely to cause disputes in themselves. Having said that, they are limited in providing work incentives (ACAS, 1991b). Time rates are often found in managerial work, although many managers put in more than their contractual hours, or in complex and process industries (such as in chemicals) where it is difficult to measure individual contributions to performance. With time-based systems, work effort and work quality is ensured by supervisors or custom and practice, although measured day work (see below) reflects a work-measurement approach to calculate work load.

There has been a shift from simple wage systems, with a single rate attached to all jobs of the same description, to salary systems where there is a range of pay for each job grade. Different rules apply for movement within grades, which typically use an incremental system, from those for promotion between grades where a more demanding system would typically be employed (Brown and Walsh, 1994: 451). While time rates should be simple, in practice additional payments such as overtime, especially among manual workers and junior management, add complexity. An additional problem with time-rate schemes, is grade drift whereby – over time – jobs bunch up in the higher ranks of the structure. Also there can be a proliferation of job grades, as new grades are used to 'buy' employee acceptance to a change in the job, which then requires restructuring every few years in order to simplify the structure. However, Brown and Walsh (1994: 454) argue that allowing grade drift in order to facilitate change – knowing there will be restructuring at a later period – is preferable to haggling over 'fair' cash shares from productivity improvements. In other words, one-off payments are granted in return for productivity improvements.

PAYMENT BY RESULTS (PBR)

Individual PBR

The philosophy here is straightforward; as conventional time-based schemes do not provide a clear and tangible link between reward and work effort, systems which do establish a link, so that a uniform price is paid per unit produced, are regarded as more motivating. Such schemes reflect the ideas of F W Taylor, the father of scientific management who, by standardising work processes through time and motion studies, laid the groundwork for such schemes to operate. As we saw from Chapter 14, views that workers are motivated solely by money led to payment schemes being designed to reflect this.

Individual PBR schemes vary in practice, and they can relate either to the whole of the employee's pay or be part of an overall pay package. They may also have a payment varying in relation to output, or payment of a fixed sum on the achievement of a particular level of output. Most schemes have a fallback rate and guarantee payments for downtime. The principal advantage of individual PBR schemes is that the incentive effect should be strong as workers can see a direct link between individual effort and earnings. By way of contrast, the major disadvantages of individual PBR are that they are expensive to install and maintain, often requiring a dedicated team to establish the system. Moreover, standards are often disputed and considerable effort is spent on both sides to apply the standards they believe are appropriate, or renegotiating in the light of any changes, such as new technology, problems with components supplied and so on. Finally, there is often friction between employees because of the emphasis on personal performance. Employees may also point to external factors which have an impact on performance but are not within their own control.

The most popular form of individual PBR is piece work. Such schemes have a long tradition in British industry, in particular in the textiles, footwear and engineering industries. They are based upon work study methods whereby the employee is simply paid a specific rate or price per unit (ie piece) of output. Although piece work survives in some industries, such as clothing, the evidence suggests that few new schemes are being introduced. While 47 per cent of all male manual workers received PBR payments in 1983, this had fallen to 37 per cent by 1990. The proportion of earnings which is covered by PBR is around 20 per cent for men and 26 per cent for women (Cannell and Wood, 1992: 10). The IPD/NEDO survey found only 3 per cent of responding organisations had introduced new piece work schemes in the previous five years, and 25 per cent of schemes introduced before the mid-1980s had been withdrawn in the previous five years (Cannell and Wood, 1992: 12). Outside of the production arena, PBR finds expression in commission paid to sales staff in sectors such as insurance and estate agencies.

Three major issues need to be considered in relation to PBR schemes: control, erosion and complexity. It has been argued that under PBR, less personal or direct supervision is necessary as it is in the worker's own interest to be productive. The age-old problem of buying workers' time, but not their effort, is supposedly eliminated. On the other hand, to some extent workers have greater discretion over their work, and responsibility for the quality of their outputs, so supervisors need to watch for short-cuts which may lead to lower quality or to health and safety risks or hazards. With frequent changes in technology, management now want to have closer control over production, and hence individual PBR has become less popular.

Schemes can degenerate through rate drift as a result of a learning curve, new technology (which had not led to remeasuring of jobs), and various worker fiddles which can hide slack rates. One other key problem relates to problems of leapfrogging and poor morale as a result of changes in rates which other workers then try to negotiate. PBR can rarely be applied uniformly to all employees in an organisation and hence may seem out of place in a harmonised environment.

Finally, for PBR to operate properly, standards of performance need to be set. In the past, rate fixers who had expertise in the industry would set standard prices or times, but more recently standards are set by using work study techniques. This requires both work study and the personnel to maintain it, not to mention a quality department. However, changes in product, material, specification or method are likely to require a new set of standards, which in turn may stimulate a bargaining process that can lead to employee relations problems, especially when workers who have become proficient in a specific task resist new methods.

Group PBR
This is often used where the production process makes it difficult to attribute performance to any one individual, so it is therefore based around the group. Similar considerations apply here as they do with individual PBR, but it is also important to recognise that a group scheme is likely to have a more positive effect if it is based on a natural work group, in which cohesiveness and solidarity can reinforce the scheme. However, the motivational effect of group PBR schemes is likely to decline as group sizes increase, the group loses its ethos, and there is a greater distance between effort and earnings.

Measured Day Work (MDW)
This was a popular response to the problems of PBR, representing something of a half-way house between an output-related scheme

such as PBR and a time-based payment system. Measured day work offered employees a fixed sum for maintaining performance at a predetermined level (Duncan, 1992: 265). An incentive is provided for good performance, but bargaining is not needed on each job or task. The system has a wider applicability than PBR. The first advantage is that disputes over time and prices which characterise PBR are avoided, while an incentive element which is not provided by time-rates is gained. Secondly, management has greater control over wage costs and hence can plan ahead more easily. In addition, employees should be more flexible in relation to changes in working methods because their earnings will not be threatened in the same way. Set against this is the extra cost of introducing and maintaining schemes which can be expensive, and the need to take action if employees fall below standard. This latter issue should not be a problem with PBR as an ineffective employee does not cost the employer in the same way. However, the onus is put on supervisors and line managers to spot problems and deal with them appropriately. Measured day work has also fallen from favour in recent years, and the 1988 ACAS survey reported that only 6 per cent of respondents used this scheme.

> Can you think of any jobs in your organisation for which any form of PBR might be suitable? Why would it be suitable, or inappropriate? Could PBR rise again?

PLANT/ENTERPRISE-BASED SCHEMES

While PBR or MDW can be effective for particular industries or groups, it may do little for overall performance, especially if there is friction between the different groups, which produces a negative effect on output. Enterprise- or plant-wide bonus schemes (sometimes called gainsharing) encourage staff to identify more widely with the organisation as a whole (see ACAS 1991a; Marchington, 1992a; IDS 547, 1994).

Scanlon plans (named after their inventor, an ex-union official who was responsible for a number of schemes in the US steel industry in the 1930s and 1940s) are based on the ratio of total payroll costs to sales value of production, which is estimated as a norm from inspection of figures over a representative period prior to the introduction of the technique. The smaller the ratio, the higher the bonus. The payment aspect of Scanlon plans is supplemented by a participation element often incorporating both a suggestion scheme and some form of consultative structure at departmental and/or unit level.

The Rucker plan (and its UK variant, the Bentley plan) is similar in many respects, but the wage calculation is based on the ratio of payroll costs to production value added (PVA), that is the difference between the sales value of output and the cost of materials, services and supplies. It represents the commercial value of the process of conversion from raw (or bought-in) materials to the finished product, so that value added is then available for the payment of all internally-controllable costs such as wages, profits and investment. The amount that constitutes wages is a proportion of the value added, fixed at a rate determined after inspection of records over the preceding years. For example, assume that for every £1,000 received for the sales value of output £500 is spent on the cost of materials, supplies and services. The £500 which remains is the production value added. An inspection of previous accounts suggests that labour's share of PVA is 40 per cent, that is wages have typically taken £200 of the £500 value added. Wages will then increase or decrease in future depending upon the absolute size of PVA, and this can be increased by greater sales value of output or lower costs of services, supplies and materials. Either of these will increase the amount available for distribution as wages, profits and investment. Increasing the sales value of output can be achieved by higher sales or prices, and costs of materials can be reduced – among other actions – by greater control over their usage, a higher proportion of output which is 'right first time', more efficient utilisation of energy, and so on. The incentive for employees to improve these aspects of their work is recognised in an explicit manner and can be rewarded by higher payments; gainsharing is therefore institutionalised and becomes a non-negotiable bonus for the employee. In addition, so as to protect workers against loss-sharing, minimum wage levels are set, and a reserve account is set up to cope with this eventuality.

However, the payment element is only one part of the scheme. Central to the whole scheme is a structure which enables employee representatives to contribute to decision-making via a works council or JCC arrangement. Employee representatives meet on a regular basis to hear the bonus announcement, to listen to explanations about the derivation of the figures, to question management about the factors which have influenced these, and to put forward suggestions about how things might be improved. Managers are charged with the responsibility of ensuring that employees understand the figures and with listening to worker suggestions about the operation of the system and the establishment. Thus a key feature of the scheme is formalising the relationship between employee participation in decision-making, organisational efficiency and individual reward.

In general such schemes have the advantage that employees see their contribution to the total effort of the enterprise and do not see themselves as individual units. In this way it can facilitate achievement of corporate identity. As this form of financial participation is often part of a wider consultation process, this can lead to a greater understanding of business issues as employees take more interest in the overall performance of the enterprise. There may be a greater willingness on the part of employees to accept and even push for change; managers may feel more able to discuss issues with workers; and greater productivity and efficiency can be achieved.

Set against the advantages are some potential disadvantages. Firstly, while gainsharing plans are implemented on the assumption that employees can see the connection between their own efforts and the rewards which are generated by the scheme, in many cases they have little control over the size of the bonus. External factors – such as increased costs of raw materials or services – may limit the bonus, as too may management decisions to delay an increase in prices due to competitive pressures. Secondly, rather than encouraging co-operation between different groups in the organisation, the schemes may increase inter-group hostility and recriminations if the bonus levels fail to meet employee expectations. Not only can this be problematic for employers and run counter to their objectives, it can also create conflicts within and between unions. Thirdly, some unions fear that gainsharing plans will lead to a progressive marginalisation of their role, either because collective bargaining will become less important in determining wage levels, or due to the fact that employees will develop greater commitment to the goals of the company and 'give away' hard fought-for gains.

Probably most important of all, some schemes may fail because managers are not prepared to accept a modified role, listen to employee suggestions for improvements, and act upon these ideas. A reassertion of managerial prerogatives is likely to undermine employee commitment to the scheme. Thus, a key issue is that employers who initiate gainsharing schemes need to be aware that more open management styles are central to potential success, and that schemes cannot simply be bolted on to existing structures and cultures. Such schemes embody the idea that the workforce represents a reservoir of creativity and experience which needs to be tapped, and that this can

> Read Marchington (1992: 166–173) for more information on plant-wide incentive schemes. Given the current vogue for empowerment and the gaining of employee commitment to organisational goals, why are these schemes not more popular?

be achieved more easily if employees are able to share in the gains of the whole unit (establishment, division or enterprise).

MERIT RATING

This system has been a long-standing feature in many organisations, working on the principle that individual employees receive their basic pay or a bonus according to an assessment of their performance. The latter might be assessed by factors such as output, quality of work, initiative and attendance, with these factors possibly weighted to reflect the demands of the specific job. Historically, merit rating has been utilised mainly for managers and indirect workers in the private sector, because incremental salary scales in the public sector reduce the scope for rewarding individual performance.

The attraction of merit rating is that it rewards qualities not always recognised by other schemes because it focuses on several factors rather than just one. It also provides a way of making bonus payments to staff whose work cannot be measured easily, so it is often suitable for managers and white-collar workers whose output is difficult to assess. However, a corresponding danger is that employees can regard it with suspicion because of the subjectivity of assessment of performance factors. Furthermore, many factors require a long period of time to be evaluated properly, leading to frustrations not only for the assessors but also for those being assessed.

PERFORMANCE-RELATED PAY (PRP)

The early 1990s have seen employers from both the private and the public sectors putting a much greater emphasis on 'paying for performance' and attempting to 'incentivise' remuneration in order to improve individual and organisational performance and create a new performance-based culture. These schemes base pay on an assessment of the individual's job performance. While such schemes are not identical they are 'usually based on a systematic salary structure, a formal appraisal system and a more or less systematic link between appraisal, performance and individual rewards' (Snape *et al*, 1994: 132). Accordingly, pay is linked to performance which is measured by a number of specific objectives (for example, sales targets or customer satisfaction) in contrast to merit rating which assesses behavioural traits. This reflects a move towards rewarding output (rather than input), using qualitative (rather than quantitative) judgements in assessing performance, a focus on working objectives (rather than personal qualities), and an end to general annual across-the-board pay increases (Fowler, 1988).

PRP became popular as a reflection of the 'enterprise culture'. A survey in 1991 found that two-thirds of organisations had PRP for managers and professional staff, and there is evidence that such schemes are spreading to the shop floor, including clerical and manual workers (Kinnie and Lowe, 1990; Cannell and Wood, 1992). It has also become more widely used in the public sector (for example, local government, the NHS and the Civil Service) where the Conservative government have strongly promoted the concept, which it sees as commercialising staff by instilling in them the disciplines of the private sector. Similarly in banking it was felt that the traditional system of reward valued seniority and long service, but not performance (Wilkinson, 1995). However the recession of the early 1990s, added to growing criticisms of PRP in practice, has slowed the momentum.

PRP is different from the types of incentive scheme that we have discussed so far in this chapter, which have run in manufacturing industry for many years, and which still continue – about one manual worker in three still has an incentive element in their pay packet. The difference is that many traditional incentive schemes are collectively-negotiated and based on standard formulae, whereas PRP is designed on an individual and personal basis. Accordingly, some workers do better than others – or some do worse than others – and it is this which makes PRP for manual workers a recent phenomenon. A common approach has been to have PRP on top of a general award, so that, say, 2 per cent is awarded to all employees to cover inflation, and additional payments are made to reward above-average performance. Alternatively, there may be no across-the-board increase but all pay increases are dependent on performance.

It is hard to find evidence to measure the achievements of PRP. While it has been widely promoted and practitioners in particular seem to retain great faith in its merits, in recent years there has been a more cautious, and indeed critical, evaluation of the ideas behind PRP. According to Cannell and Wood (1992: 51–65), there are several reasons why PRP has become more prevalent in recent years. First, there have been problems with traditional incremental systems – which in theory can provide both 'carrot and stick' by withholding or offering increments. In practice, the lack of a systematic appraisal system and high employee expectations meant automatic increments tended to be the norm. This means that staff bunch at the top of a grade, so making it expensive for employers to fund.

Secondly, the aim of rewarding better performance has been seen as paramount to the newly-introduced schemes. Thus, one interviewee from a financial service organisation said that 'With a small number of relatively senior people at our head office, we want people who have individual initiative. We don't have hordes of people doing the same thing but want people to be involved and exercise their initiative. Therefore we want to pay them on a system which demonstrates that we recognise initiative' (Cannell and Wood, 1992: 53). Rewarding good performance is seen as more important than motivation, although PRP can be linked with appraisal to provide motivation through recognition and feedback.

Thirdly, PRP has been seen very much as fitting alongside other changes in the environment. One of the interviewees in the IPD/NEDO project put it thus: 'Introducing PRP was a key event, really. It was a break with the past which said "You'll always get an increase every year, you'll always get a minimum increase and on top of that you'll get something else, and it doesn't matter how you perform". Now what we're saying is "Nobody owes anybody a thing. Nobody gets a pay rise unless they earn a pay rise" so it is a total break' (Cannell and Wood, 1992: 53–54). Such a break was also emphasised in the public sector organisations which were being told to act as if they were a private company. Focusing on the 'customer', driving down costs, paying for performance, and introducing initiatives such as TQM and customer care, reinforced the new culture. Moreover, PRP served as a control mechanism to get managers to focus on key targets.

Fourthly, PRP has been important in communicating the message that performance is critical, so good performance will get paid more than poor performance. It can also have a positive impact on general communications via the appraisal system, which can be reinforced by PRP as individuals place a great emphasis on being properly appraised. It also encourages line managers to see the process of objective-setting as part of their approach to managing their department or unit.

Fifthly, in addition to motivating people, PRP also has a retention role and has appeared to have had an effect on halting the loss of key employees. At the same time PRP reduces the 'golden handcuff' effect whereby poor performers decide to stay with an employer because they continue to be rewarded well.

Finally, greater individual responsibility was also a theme in some of the IPD/NEDO case studies, the idea being to break up the collective idea of payment for groups of staff into payment for individual staff members. This fitted in with a broader move to individualism in these organisations.

Marsden and Richardson (1994) analysed PRP in the Inland Revenue; it was introduced in 1988 with a central justification that it should act as a motivator. They questioned over 2000 staff about the impact of PRP on their own behaviour as well as on others. Judgements concerning performance were made through the staff appraisal system, which involved three key stages. Firstly, there was an annual discussion of individual work objectives for the coming year between each staff member and his or her supervisor. Secondly, there was a review of achievements in relation to job plans which could lead to a revised plan being produced. Finally, there was evaluation of staff performance at the end of year according to thirteen criteria; these included standard of work (quality and quantity), personal skills (planning, problem-solving, negotiation, decision-making), management (of staff and resources), communication (oral and written), working relationships (with colleagues and the public), and knowledge (both professional and technical). Staff are placed in one of five categories – outstanding performance; performance significantly above requirements; performance which meets the normal requirements; performance which is not fully up to requirements; and unacceptable performance. Payments are made in the form of additional increments, which are usually permanent (that is, the same as normal service increments) even if in principle they could be withdrawn after unsatisfactory performance. The research found that a majority of Inland Revenue staff (57 per cent) supported the principle of PRP, although a significant minority (40 per cent) felt hostile to it. Marsden and Richardson (1994) also found that any positive motivational effects had at best been 'very modest', and it is 'by no means implausible that the net motivation effect so far has been negative' as Table 14 illustrates.

An alternative source of evidence from those staff who carried out appraisals confirmed the earlier results and indeed it seemed that they were even more sceptical of the system than employees. Even more worrying for the proponents of PRP was the clear evidence of demotivation among staff, with 55 per cent believing it had helped to undermine staff morale and 62 per cent saying it had caused jealousy between them. The main reason for the failure to motivate is the perception by staff that the allocation of performance payments was unfair. Awards were given only to those who had received good ratings, but many respondents felt the appraisal system had been corrupted. Some staff felt that the amount of money involved was not large enough to justify a change in behaviour. Finally, many staff felt that they were unable to improve their performance.

Other research has suggested that PRP – with its emphasis on annual individual performance – has been responsible for a short-termist approach whereby individuals look for quick returns from small-scale projects rather than addressing more fundamental problems (Wilkinson et al, 1992: 15). Of course, it is possible to argue that this simply

Table 14 Staff assessment of their own motivational response to performance-related pay

Has performance-related pay led you to:	Yes	No
	%	%
improve the quality of your work	12	80
increase the quantity of your work	14	78
work harder	9	71
work beyond the job requirements	21	70
give sustained high performance	27	63
improve your priorities at work	22	64
show more initiative	27	61
express yourself with greater clarity	13	67
be more effective in dealing with the public	9	68
improve your sensitivity towards colleagues?	14	63

Source: Marsden and Richardson (1994: 251)

suggests that care needs to be exercised in the choice of performance objectives. If sales targets are seen as the only real objective, then it is likely that long-term customer relationships, as well as management-staff relations, may be threatened. On the other hand, if the latter are flagged up as high priorities in the targets, this might lead to more serious attention being devoted to this area.

An IPM (1992) study on the 'cult of performance' suggested that PRP was perceived more as a way of managing the pay bill than a reward for performance, and many respondents complained that it might motivate 20 per cent of employees but at the expense of the other 80 per cent. Furthermore, a context of rationalisation complicated things further. Other studies, including that by the Institute of Manpower Studies (Thompson, 1992), found that those companies with a performance-management system, of which performance-related pay was often an important part, were no more likely than other companies to have high levels of profit growth. The difficulty of appraisal, the difficulty of formulating objectives, the risk of bias or perceived bias, the inevitable inflationary tendency, high costs of administration, the dubious impact on performance, problems associated with the individual focus, and the difficulty of organising and delivering the necessary degree of managerial commitment are other criticisms levelled at this system (Torrington, 1993b). Furthermore, performance pay stimulates high expectations. People respond to it because there is the prospect of more money, and the prospect has to be of *significantly* more money if it is to be attractive. Therefore, management 'grease-in' the scheme by indicating how *much* one can expect. An enthusiastic, performance-enhancing response (which is the sole purpose of the exercise) will bring with it a widespread expectation of considerably more money, and will not be delivered without the expectation (Torrington, 1993b: 159). Other concerns include the fact that managers are unhappy at marking staff below average, feeling that all their staff are above average. One way to prevent this is to allocate quotas for each category, but this can seem arbitrary. Manual trade unions have been particularly unenthusiastic about PRP, dismissing such systems as unfair and divisive.

There is often a lack of coherent thought behind the introduction of PRP. Storey and Sisson (1993: 140–141) argue that 'in many cases the establishment of formal performance criteria leaves a great deal to be desired – "objectives" and "behaviour" which bear little relationship to work practice are being engineered purely for the purpose of having an individual PRP scheme. In the performance assessment process, which lies at the heart of the individual PRP, there are complaints about subjectivity and inconsistency which are often compounded by lack of attention to the training of managers in carrying out appraisal and to the administrative procedures for monitoring arrangements. The links between performance and the level of pay are not always clear and effective.' It is also apparent that individual PRP sits rather uneasily with a number of other policies which managers profess to be pursuing – especially the emphasis on team work.

> What are the principal benefits to be gained from PRP for employers and employees? Does this general list correspond with experience in your own organisation?

FINANCIAL PARTICIPATION

In recent years there has been a substantial growth in the field of financial participation fuelled by a number of developments in the area. Section 1 of the Employment Act 1982 requires larger quoted companies to provide details of what they have done to maintain (or extend) employee involvement, including 'encouraging the involvement of employees in the company's performance through an employee's share scheme or by some other means', and 'achieving a common awareness on the part of all employees of the financial and economic factors affecting the performance of the company'. Although the Act itself has only had a limited direct impact on organisations, the inclusion of financial involvement is important for the purposes of raising awareness among senior managers. It also reflected the Conservative government's interest in extending financial involvement on a voluntary basis as opposed to other more radical forms of participation. Profit/gain-sharing plans and share ownership are also among the points in the joint IPA/IPM Code of Practice and its associated Action Guide. In addition the Social Chapter makes reference to employee participation in the capital or profits/losses of the European company. Unlike the current British provisions, however, it goes further in requiring a scheme to be negotiated between the management board of the enterprise and the employees or their representatives The emphasis in the 1980s and 1990s on the 'enterprise culture' and 'people's capitalism' is also a background factor. Financial participation has also been facilitated by several pieces of legislation since the 1970s and the number of organisations (and employees) that have taken advantage of share ownership or profit-sharing schemes has increased considerably. However, there has been a tendency to see all the different types of scheme as one of a kind, and this ignores some important differences between the objectives behind the various schemes as well as in their impact.

There are a number of key objectives behind the introduction of financial involvement, although it is likely that several of these are combined in any one rationale. These are:

- *Education-based*: concerned with improving employee understanding of the organisation's position in the market place, its strategy, and the importance of profits for stimulating further investment. Such an approach can also serve as a powerful legitimiser of management actions taken in the interests of all who are employed by the company.

- *Commitment-based*: concerned with increasing employee commitment to, and identification with, the goals of the organisation, and enhancing the loyalty of employees to their employer.

- *Performance-based*: concerned with enhancing both employee and organisational performance. In relation to the former, we are looking at the translation of employee commitment into actual behavioural change, for example increased co-operation with plans, reduced levels of absenteeism, and improved productivity and efficiency. In relation to the latter, this would include increases in profits or share prices, and in the long-term perceived viability of the organisation. The basic argument here is that employees with a stake in the overall success of the unit (plant, division or enterprise) are more likely to work harder and smarter for its ultimate success. Of course, much depends on the degree to which the link is seen as meaningful to – and under the control of – employees.

- *Recruitment-based*: concerned with attempts to attract and also retain employees, especially in a climate where competition between employers for high-quality staff is strong. This explains the high proportion of companies in the financial services sector which have adopted share ownership schemes during the last decade, as well as a similar move by some food retailers. Moreover, this has been a significant factor in the massive growth in selective schemes for senior executives.

- *Defensive motivations*: concerned with other issues which may influence the position of the firm, such as an attempt to deter trade unions from gaining recognition ('killing the employees with kindness'), or in limiting the development of trade union organisation.

- *Paternalist-based*: concerned with the willingness of employers to offer shares or other forms of financial involvement because it is seen as appropriate, given the employer's philosophical stance. Some of the earliest schemes were driven by this kind of motive and it has also been seen as one reason for the emergence of ESOPs both in the UK and the USA. Some may be no more than a desire 'to reward employees for past performance' whereas others may see their scheme as more radical in its aims.

Which of these reasons do you believe are the strongest ones? Do any of these relate to your own organisation? If you do not have direct experience of financial participation, read the article by Wilkinson *et al* (1994) before coming to a conclusion.

In reality, of course, it is likely that there will be a mixture of motives behind the introduction of schemes, and there may be differences in objectives sought within the organisation, especially between different management groups. Indeed, in some cases the rationale will be neither explicit nor well thought through. Some writers have seen financial participation schemes as having some resemblance to an 'act of faith' on the part of management (Baddon, Hunter, Hyman, Leopold and Ramsay, 1989: 280). We now examine three main types of financial participation schemes: share ownership, cash-based profit sharing, and profit-related pay.

Employee share ownership

This is where employee ownership is extended, albeit to a small degree, by using part of the profits generated to acquire shares for employees in the company concerned. There are four sub-categories of scheme in this area; approved profit sharing (known as APS or ADST) introduced in the Finance Act of 1978; Save As You Earn (SAYE), Finance Act 1980; discretionary share option schemes, Finance Act 1984; and employee share ownership plans (ESOPs). The principal point which binds such schemes together is the notion of share ownership, as opposed to cash bonus.

Cash-based profit sharing

This is where a bonus is given to employees based upon the share price, profits or dividend announcement at the end of the financial year. It does not reduce the basic pay of employees if no profits are made in a particular year, and hence is aimed at integrating organisational and employee interests. The main problem with such schemes is that profits can fluctuate as a result of *external* factors and this can seem unfair to employees. While they may be seen by some as little more than a further form of payment, and thus quite distinct from other types of employee involvement, they do at least link some part of employee remuneration to the performance of the company as a whole. Some organisations distribute profits wholly in cash, others offer payment in the form of shares and some offer the opportunity of taking the bonus in both cash and shares. As we shall see below, that also raises certain problems, but the basic principle behind such schemes is that of trying to associate employee effort with company success.

Profit-related Pay

With tax relief available for such schemes, this operates according to the principle that profit-related pay can represent a tax-efficient way in which to finance part of employees' pay, rather than acting as a bonus payment on top of normal salary, as with more conventional profit-sharing schemes. It has been defined as 'a part of employees' pay which varies in relation to the movement in profits of the business or part of the business in which they work' (Duncan, 1988: 186). It differs from profit-sharing in two ways; first, it acts not as a bonus but as part of the payment package; second, it creates a systematic, automatic and regular pay link with profits – in contrast to many profit-sharing schemes where payment is at the discretion of the directors. By June 1994, 1.8 million private sector employees were covered by such a scheme (IDS 564, 1994).

> Prepare a paper for your management team on profit-related pay, making suggestions as to whether this is appropriate for your organisation. Justify your recommendations.

Table 15 Key features of different profit-sharing schemes

Scheme Type	Availability	Tax concessions
Cash	Usually all employees	None
Approved profit-sharing	At least all employees with five years' service	Exempt from PAYE
Mixture of cash and approved profit-sharing	Usually all employees	Profit-sharing exempt from PAYE
Immediate (unapproved) share schemes	Usually all employees	None
Company-wide share options	All employees	None
Save As You Earn (SAYE)	At least all employees with five years' service	Exempt from PAYE
Executive share options	Selected executives	Exempt from PAYE if exercised 3–10 years from grant

Source: IDS Study 539, 1993

A desire to change culture and employee attitudes is a central motive behind financial participation schemes, but the evidence on its effectiveness is mixed. Bell and Hanson's (1984) work for the Involvement and Participation Association (IPA) claims that financial involvement is warmly welcomed by employees and that it is seen as 'good for the company and its employees' (p 27). Other responses, however, cast doubt on the impact of schemes on the commitment and loyalty of employees, and indicate that profit-sharing is seen more in calculative/instrumental terms rather than those associated with greater employee identification and effort. Poole and Jenkins (1990: 50) incline to the optimistic in believing that financial involvement can have a positive effect on employee attitudes, both in terms of increased co-operation and in terms of a greater identification with company goals. However, the calculative (building up a nest-egg) and moral (right for workers to own part of their company) dimensions figure prominently in the case study conducted by Dewe, Dunn and Richardson (1988: 10), and those factors associated with attitudinal change are much less significant. For example, only a small minority felt that the schemes had reduced feelings of 'them and us' or had succeeded in building up team spirit. Yet more evidence to support the view that employees have a primarily calculative orientation to financial involvement can be gleaned from answers to questions about the drawbacks of share savings schemes, namely that employees have to wait too long before making money, and that share price movements are beyond their control. Dewe *et al* (1988: 19) also found that there was a link between commitment and share ownership, but only in the sense that employees who exhibited greater commitment to the organisation were more likely to join the SAYE scheme; there was no suggestion that share ownership actually increased employee commitment.

That schemes tend to have had minimal impact on employee attitudes also comes across clearly from the study by Baddon *et al* (1989), and yet again it is the calculative character of financial involvement which appears most prominent in worker views. The authors argue that management objectives for financial involvement are not being met, partly due to the small size of the benefits (hence leading to their being seen as simply another bonus) but also because of the failure of management to design and implement schemes in a participative manner.

Furthermore, while some studies have found there is a positive relationship between the two factors, there are doubts about the direction of causality of this association. Poole and Jenkins (1990: 95) suggest that improved profits act as a trigger for the introduction of these schemes although they accept that there may be a linkage the other way round, but doubt that it is direct. Their studies show, among other things, that profits are much more likely to be affected by factors other than improved employee performance due to the profit-sharing scheme itself (p 78), and that high profits are essential for maintaining positive employee attitudes to the scheme (p 85). In short, the impact of profit sharing on company performance is likely to be minor, and poor profit announcements may actually have a negative effect on employee perceptions of management and the organisation as a whole.

A number of problems are apparent in profit-sharing and employee share ownership schemes. Firstly, schemes do not usually provide any real control because employees are unable to influence to any great extent the level of profits or the quality of management decision-making within the enterprise. Secondly, investing savings in the firms for which they work can increase employee insecurity. If the employer goes out of business or suffers cutbacks, individuals not only stand to lose their jobs, they might also lose some or all of their savings as well.

Some profit-sharing schemes actually include penalty clauses which reduce or halt pay-outs in the event of industrial action. Black and Ackers' research (1988) at Brown's Woven Carpets described such a situation in this family-owned carpet firm. However, it should also be noted that the inclusion of penalty clauses will not necessarily prevent industrial action given that the level of financial benefit secured from schemes is not very high. Even if a significant proportion of employees hold shares in a company, this does not appear to inhibit employees from striking if this seems legitimate – as at British Telecom in the late 1980s. The trade union response to financial participation initiatives has tended to be lukewarm rather than oppositional, a situation characterised by Baddon *et al* (1989: 248) as 'neutrality at best, a bored hostility at worst, but even the latter not taking on a high profile such as to make the operation of schemes difficult for management'.

One major problem with financial involvement is that it does not link effort to reward in a clear and unambiguous manner, nor is the pay-out made at regular enough intervals to act as a motivator of staff. Because profits or share prices are affected by many factors other than employee performance, it is difficult to conceive of this as a reward for effort. Indeed, due to factors beyond the control of employees, an individual who has worked extra hard during the year may be 'rewarded' with a negligible profit share, or vice versa. Equally, by the time the share announcement is made, so much time has passed since the beginning of the financial year that it is difficult to recall how hard one had been working. All of these problems are especially marked in multi-divisional businesses. This leads to the disembodiment of profit sharing from its alleged motivational base, and to the oft-repeated statement that shares/bonuses are nothing more than an extra payment which causes more or less satisfaction depending upon the amount. Some would argue that employers would be better advised using this money to reward *specific* individuals, say, through a performance-related pay scheme, rather than through a standardised, all-embracing system.

> Why are employees not always keen on profit-sharing? How might you convince staff in your organisation that share ownership is a good idea?

NEW PAYMENT INITIATIVES

Skills-based pay (sometimes referred to as competence-based pay or pay-for-knowledge) schemes have become more prominent in recent years (IDS 500, 1992; IRS PABB 391, 1996). There is no single definition, but these approaches are designed to model pay structures around the idea of skills. Core competences or skills are built into the pay system, and rewarded according to the standard or level achieved. Such an approach encourages skills development and should widen and deepen the skills base of the organisation. Furthermore, it may increase job satisfaction, break down rivalries between groups or units, and increase flexibility as well. Competence-based pay is actually wider than skills-based pay as it incorporates behaviour and attributes, rather than simply skills alone. In many respects it represents a rejection of ideas encountered in job evaluation as, unlike job evaluation, it evaluates the person rather than the job. A job is something an individual employee happens to be doing at a moment in time, rather than a defined thing. There are potential problems with such systems, in that managements need to be thinking some years ahead about what the skill requirements are likely to be. It may create high and unfulfilled expectations among employees if they reach the top of the skills-based pay structure. Some employers in the IRS survey felt that skills which were obsolete were being rewarded.

CONCLUSION

The objective of Chapter 15 has been to review a range of different payment systems, considering their objectives and purpose, their extensiveness, and their advantages and disadvantages in practice. The point has been made that no one type of system is automatically and necessarily superior to the others, and that so much depends upon the context in which the schemes are to function. In this respect, the history and traditions of the workplace and the industry are critical, as too are the attitudes of managements and employees. It is argued that the pay package represents a powerful potential lever in facilitating employee contributions to organisational success, but too often employers adopt pay systems without a full and systematic analysis of the options which are available. Rather than being commonplace, strategic reward management is a rarity, and all that seems to happen is that employers 'shuffle the pack', moving from one scheme to another when deterioration sets in. But we also need to recall that the reward package is somewhat more than the payment system alone, incorporating a range of financial and non-financial benefits; these are considered in Chapter 16.

USEFUL READING

ADVISORY CONCILIATION AND ARBITRATION SERVICE (1991) *Job Evaluation – An introduction.* ACAS, Advisory Booklet No 1.

CANNELL, M. AND WOOD, S. (1992) *Incentive Pay.* London, NEDO/IPM.

FOWLER, A. (1988) 'New directions in performance related pay', *Personnel Management*, November. 30, 4.

INCOMES DATA SERVICES (1994) *Bonus systems.* No 547.

KESSLER, I. (1994) 'Reward Systems' in J. Storey (Ed.), *Human Resource Management: A critical text.* London, Routledge: 254–279.

KINNIE, N. AND LOWE, J. (1992) 'Performance-related pay on the shopfloor', *Personnel Management.* 45, 9.

MAHONEY, T. (1992) 'Multiple pay contingencies: strategic design of compensation', in G. Salaman (Ed.) *Human Resource Strategies.* London, Sage.

MARCHINGTON, M. (1992) *Managing the Team: A guide to successful employee involvement.* Oxford, Blackwell.

STOREY, J. AND SISSON, K. (1993) *Managing Human Resources and Industrial Relations*. Buckingham, Open University Press.

WILKINSON, A., MARCHINGTON, M., ACKERS, P. AND GOODMAN, J. (1994) 'ESOP's fables: a tale of a machine tool company', *International Journal of Human Resource Management*, Vol 5, 1: 121–143.

16 A wider perspective on reward

INTRODUCTION

In the previous chapter we examined a range of different types of payment systems and their relevance to particular organisational contexts. When examining the reward package as a whole, however, it is important to consider other benefits – financial and non-financial – which provide the total reward experience for employees. If we take into account the views on motivation and reward implied by various schools of thought (see Chapter 14), it is clear that pay is only one element of the total reward package. Too often benefits are not seen in a strategic way but taken as 'givens'. Expectancy theory, however, suggests that a more contingent view needs to be taken, and that it may make sense to individualise rewards, a notion which has led to considerable interest in 'cafeteria' benefits.

In the reward-management literature most attention has been focused on pay since this is often seen as a key lever of change, and much less attention has been devoted to benefits such as pensions and sick-pay. Indeed, the other benefits have often been seen as fixed, despite the fact that many employers pay above the statutory minimum. The benefits package has been subject to fads and fashions, with many employers merely reacting by adjusting benefits to address short-term problems such as recruitment and retention, rather than adopting a long-term approach. For example, in the field of pensions, probably the largest item in the benefits package, there has been an absence of strategic thinking (IDS, 72, 1994). It should be apparent from our discussion of motivation that terms and conditions beyond pay can be very significant in the overall reward package. Indeed, benefits are seen as a tangible expression of the psychological bond between employers and those who work for them (IDS 72, October 1994: 12). Benefits have increased dramatically since the post-war period, with what were once considered perks – available only to managerial employees – now having been applied more widely.

The remainder of this chapter is organised as follows: firstly, we look at benefits other than pay, examining pensions and sick-pay so as to illustrate our theme. Secondly, we analyse the steps taken by employers to harmonise conditions, which includes benefits such as pensions and sick-pay, but also the removal of barriers such as separate car parks, canteens or toilets. Thirdly, we discuss non-financial recognition, and the importance of involvement, autonomy and responsibility, before moving on to examine job redesign and total quality management. As Devanna *et al* (1984: 48) note 'organisations tend to think of rewards in a fairly limited way as pay, promotion and benefits ... there are many other rewards that the organisation has to offer that individuals value.'

By the end of this chapter, readers should be able to:

• prepare a case for introducing flexible benefits

• assess the costs and benefits of implementing harmonisation between blue- and white-collar workers

• advise management on the way in which job redesign could be introduced into an organisation.

In addition, readers should be able to understand and explain:

• the nature of employee benefits, such as pensions and sick pay, and their contribution to the total reward package

• the principal characteristics of non-financial rewards and their implications for P&D practice

• the key components of job redesign and total quality management, and the role that these play in providing non-financial recognition.

PENSIONS

Pensions can be seen as a form of deferred pay. They are probably the most widespread of all fringe benefits, with half the working population being members of occupational schemes, despite the fact that most employees show little interest in this area (Friedman, 1990). Occupational pensions developed during the nineteenth century as part of a broader paternalistic-driven personnel policy in gas and public service organisations, in conjunction with various other benefits such as paid leave, sickness and accident benefits. Paternalism was not simply the act of benevolent employers, but it was seen initially as a means of managing retirement (Hannah, 1987), and later for attracting and retaining a good loyal labour force (IDS Focus 72, 1994). After the Second World War pension schemes began to develop as more employees became liable to tax, thus making the tax relief aspects of pensions especially attractive.

There are two types of pension scheme. First, and most extensive, are deferred benefit schemes where the level of pension is calculated as a percentage of the retiring individual's final salary. The second are deferred contribution money-purchase schemes where regular payments are made (by employee and employer) to a pension fund which are then invested – with the employee receiving a pension based on the value of the investment; these represent a minority of schemes. The result of the Social Security Acts 1985 and 1986 led to employees' no longer being required to join a scheme, as well as reduced penalties for those leaving. Those who do leave can take their pension with them – hence, the terminology of 'portable' pensions. The incentive to stay is reduced, although in practice final salary revaluation tends to result in a pension that is less than they would have received if they had remained (Taylor and Earnshaw, 1995). Furthermore, employees can begin personal pension plans for which they receive a National Insurance rebate. The view that pensions were a 'golden handcuff' because of poor transfer values when changing schemes now has less force as a result of changes in legislation which have facilitated greater portability – including better transfer values and the opportunity to opt for a personal pension. Hence, it now seems that employers need to improve their schemes to ensure they have a retention/attraction value. The European Court of Justice judgment requiring employers to equalise pension ages is likely to lead to the introduction of flexible pension ages but this makes it more difficult for employers to use their schemes to determine the age at which employees retire (Taylor and Earnshaw, 1995). Furthermore, the net result will be a rise in the cost of pension provision which may lead some managements to re-evaluate the aims of their funds. WH Smith shifted to a money-purchase scheme in April 1996 as this was seen to provide greater flexibility given that the organisation has high staff turnover (*Personnel Today*, 21 November 1995). The scheme allows staff who leave after working for less than two years to take their money back or leave it in the fund. In effect, this also transfers uncertainty from the employer to the members of the scheme.

The main objectives of occupational pension provisions are: retention; attracting new staff; improving employee relations; and managing the time and manner in which employees retire (Taylor and Earnshaw, 1995). IDS Focus (72, 1994: 8) report that 'top management sees the pension scheme more as part of the furniture than as a considered investment. Small wonder there is concern that employees do not appreciate the value of pension provision if there is such a vague attitude at board level.' Strategic intent was seen to be missing, thus reflecting the distinction between the management of remuneration (which is seen as strategic, and needing to be actively managed) and that of pensions, which is seen separately and related more to welfare. IDS report a paradox in top management concerns about changes in the labour market (for example, demographic change and the end of lifetime employment) and their inability to perceive the possible role that pensions might play in terms of retirement flexibility.

Occupational or company schemes usually involve contributions from both the employer and the employee, although there are non-contributory schemes (that is, only the employer contributes), especially for managerial staff. The Inland Revenue approves schemes (for tax relief) and sets limits on the level of benefits payable – a maximum pension at two-thirds of the employee's final salary. In the UK annual contributions add up to around 15–20 per cent of an employer's annual wage bill, and hence they represent a significant proportion of labour costs.

Changes in legislation in the late 1980s (Social Security Acts 1985, 1986, 1990), judgments of the European Court of Justice, (*Barber* v *Guardian Royal Exchange*), and the new Pensions Act which arose out of the Goode Committee on the reform of pensions, all have important implications. In particular, it seems likely that the government will try to shift some of its current responsibility for old-age pension provision to the private sector. As individuals become more responsible for their old age, they may look more closely at employer provisioning in this area (Taylor and Earnshaw, 1995). There are also implications for P&D professionals who may need to evaluate organisational objectives regarding pension schemes. The Pensions Act also aims to increase the involvement of employees (or pensioners) by giving them a right to nominate or select a number of trustees, and this establishes the need for an internal communications campaign to explain various details of the scheme (Self, 1995).

> How much consideration did you give to the pension scheme when you started work with your current employer, and did it have any influence over your decision to take up employment there? Why do most people treat pensions in a non-strategic way?

SICK PAY

Employees have a right to statutory sick pay (SSP) if they qualify under Department of Social Security rules. Up until April 1994 employers could reclaim 80 per cent of their SSP payments back from the government, and small employers could claim back the full amount of SSP paid after six weeks of sickness absence if their National Insurance contributions were £16,000 or less. However, the Statutory Sick Pay Act of 1994 removed the right of employers to claim back SSP, apart from small employers who can claim 100 per cent of SSP after four weeks of illness. The Act also extended the scope of SSP to include women over the age of 60 in order to harmonise those conditions with men (IDS 556, 1994). SSP payments are made at two rates; a lower rate for those earning less than the standard National Insurance category threshold and a standard rate for others. In order to qualify for SSP, employees have to fulfil a number of requirements – such as periods of incapacity, periods of entitlement, qualifying days and notification of absence.

When introducing the legislation, the government reassured employers that changes in National Insurance would compensate them for the shifting burden of sick pay. Nevertheless, employers appear to have been galvanised by this shift of responsibilities in order to find ways of reducing levels of absence through tighter monitoring – rather than reducing sick-pay benefits. As we saw in Chapter 7, absence management policies have been introduced which include accurate recording procedures, regular absence reports produced for line managers, attendance procedures (including return-to-work interviews), continued monitoring and clearly laid out steps of action to be taken (IDS 556, 1994).

Most employers also have occupational sick-pay schemes which enhance SSP, although there is discretion over eligible criteria and the duration of entitlements as well as refusal to make payments (IDS 556, 1994). It is also important to appreciate that benefits such as sick pay can act as a control mechanism, and that specific entitlements to sick pay reflect the character of the employment relationship. In some organisations, sick-pay entitlement is dependent on length of service, while in others staff are treated on the same basis irrespective of their employment, but none the less there are strict disciplinary procedures (IDS Focus 72, 1994).

For example, at Rover sick pay was harmonised in May 1993 to include both hourly-paid and salaried staff (IDS 556, 1994). All employees are eligible to join the scheme, with maximum sick pay based on a rolling basis from the first day of the current absence and including sickness leave entitlement taken during the previous 12 months. The payments are dependent upon length of service. In cases of long-term sickness, where an employee's sick-pay entitlement has been exhausted, a number of options are available. For employees with more than one year's service, subject to a medical review by the company-nominated medical authority, a further period of paid sick leave of up to six months may be approved (that is, a total of 18 months in all). Subsequently, for those employees with more than five years' service, again subject to a company-nominated medical review, a second extra period of paid sick leave of up to six months may be approved (that is, a total of 24 months' paid sick leave). Harmonisation has been a major force in developments in absence monitoring and control. SSP changes led two-thirds of the organisations which responded to an IRS survey to report they had taken action, or intended to take action, to revise their sick-pay scheme and/or monitoring procedures (IRS 568, 1994; IRS 569, 1994).

There are many other benefits which employees may value – such as company cars, health insurance and holidays, but there is not the space to review each of these here. Perhaps one of the most valued benefits in these uncertain times is job security. While few organisations today guarantee such benefits, some prescribe a lengthy process to be followed before redundancies are invoked, and this may provide some reassurance that terms will be fair and generous – for a wider discussion on benefits, see Armstrong and Murlis (1995: 367–411).

In recent years there has been great interest in the notion of 'cafeteria' benefits. The main reason for such an approach is to maximise flexibility and choice, particularly in the area of fringe benefits which can make up a high proportion of the total remuneration package. Under this system staff are provided with 'core' benefits – including salary – and are offered a menu of other costed benefits (company car, health insurance, childcare, etc) from which they can construct a package of benefits, up to a total value. Such schemes have been popular in the USA, but have not been widely taken up in the UK as a result of administrative complexity and taxation issues, as well as inertia within organisations (Woodley, 1990). During the early part of the 1990s demographic changes have meant there are fewer young people from which to recruit, and this may lead to more diverse workforces which have a different set of remuneration priorities. Some of the ideas on cafeteria benefits sit well with the motivation literature, which stresses that different individuals have different needs and expectations from work. Walkers Snack Foods, the Burton Group and the Mortgage Corporation have all introduced 'cafeteria' schemes, and studies suggest that while only a small minority of organisations currently operate a flexible benefits package, '80 per cent of personnel and finance directors surveyed by benefits consultancy Gissing thought flexible benefits were a good idea' (North, 1995: 29).

How could cafeteria benefits be applied in your organisation?

HARMONISATION

Recent years have seen considerable discussion about the advantages of harmonising benefits to remove status differentials – for example, separate pension or sick-pay provision – as this sends out a message that some employees are second-class citizens, with a different and inferior set of rights. Thus, according to Mullins (1986: 41):

> Further success will be with companies which are highly focused by technology and market expertise, which are able to adapt rapidly to changes in markets and technology. Such companies will have an overwhelming emphasis on cohesion and the fullest identification of their people with the overall business purpose ... There will be no room for differences and divisions which consume energies and are unrelated to the work which has to be done (cited in Price and Price, 1994: 553).

Harmonisation is concerned with the process of reducing differences, normally between manual and non-manual workers. The ultimate aim is to eliminate differences based on the status of employees – hence the term 'single status', or sometimes 'staff status'. The terms can be defined as follows:

- *Single status* is the removal of differences in basic conditions of employment to give all employees equal status. This might grade all staff on the same structure.

- *Staff status* is a process whereby manual and craft employees gradually receive staff terms and conditions, usually after reaching some qualifying standard – such as length of service.

- *Harmonisation* involves the reduction of differences in the pay structure and other employment conditions between groups of employees. Central to harmonisation is a common approach to pay and conditions of all employees. Unlike staff status, harmonisation could involve some staff employees' accepting some conditions of manual employees (Duncan, 1992: 285).

Conditions of employment offering scope for harmonisation may include:

- payment systems and methods of payment
- overtime and hours of work
- shift premiums
- actual times of work
- clocking or other time recording procedures

- sick-pay schemes

- holiday entitlement and holiday pay

- pension arrangements

- period of notice (above the statutory minimum)

- redundancy terms

- lay-off/guaranteed week

- canteen facilities

- fringe benefits such as health insurance and company cars.

Source: ACAS, 1992

The 1980s witnessed an increase in harmonisation, particularly inspired by the practices of Japanese new entrants, and especially on greenfield sites where there was an acceptance among all parties that common terms and conditions were a good idea. For example, none of the three unions involved in the 'beauty contest' for union recognition at Nissan opposed the concept. Wickens (1987: 7) argues that single status is a misnomer – 'it is simply not possible for everyone to have the same status in an organisation – the plant manager has a different status to the supervisor to the line worker simply because of the position held ... what we can do however is to eliminate many of the differences in the way we treat people and end up with the same or similar employment packages. Thus the term "common terms and conditions of employment" is more accurate.' It is becoming increasingly difficult to present a coherent case for continuing distinctions between manual and non-manual workers in terms of separate car parks, toilets and canteens. The roots of such distinctions are deep and historically-based, and in some cases the process of reform has been slow. Perhaps the recession had a double-edged impact here. On the one hand, anything which increased commitment and flexibility was considered important, but it also meant that the money available to facilitate the equalising of conditions tightened.

In the UK, fringe benefits have typically been dependent on the status of the employee, so reflecting class structure, and as such the status divide has proved to be especially resistant to change (Price and Price, 1994: 527). During the industrial revolution in the nineteenth century it became impossible for the single entrepreneur to carry out all the management responsibilities, and so employees were brought in to take over some of these responsibilities. Two key features of this industrial bureaucracy emerged. First, the hierarchy of control was associated with non-manual status, a division of brain from brawn (Arthurs, 1985). Secondly, the number of controlling tiers of bureaucracy was associated with the idea of a 'career' with which loyal and good performance would be rewarded with promotion (Price and Price, 1994). At the same time, the application of scientific management principles was applied to the shopfloor allowing workers little discretion, but highly specific work tasks, pay tied to output, and close discipline, all of which created a low-trust environment (Fox,

1974). By contrast, in the civil service and local government, the greater size of the non-manual workforce, the absence of a manufacturing environment, and the influence of a public sector ethos created less of a divide and, as a result, manual workers have tended to share better pension and sick-pay benefits.

Research in the late 1960s found particular disparities in relation to working hours, attendance, discipline and holidays. Manual workers had to operate according to stricter rules, and the penalties which were applied to them were more frequent and severe. As Price and Price (1994: 528) put it, they (manual workers) 'have to be placed under relatively stringent management control because they cannot be relied upon to behave in a manner that accords with the interests of the company'. Manual workers were disadvantaged in a number of ways: a longer working week; shorter holidays; more likely to suffer deductions in pay; greater irregularity of earnings; pay linked to physical capacity; greater job insecurity; few promotions; stricter rules and discipline; and separate facilities such as canteens, toilets and car parks (Wedderburn and Craig, 1974; Price and Price, 1994).

However, reviewing the evidence some quarter of a century later, Price and Price (1994: 531) report that 'there has been a clear trend towards a narrowing or elimination of differences in treatment.' In particular, leave arrangements (holidays, sick pay and special leave), occupational pensions, and some fringe benefits (product discounts, canteen facilities) appear to have been harmonised. There has also been progress in relation to methods of recording attendance (as clocking has either been abolished or replaced by computerised time-keeping for all employees) and a limited reduction of differences in the working week. However, payment systems and grading structures (with the exception of the introduction of cashless pay) have been more resistant to harmonisation. In an ACAS survey, only one in eight of the respondents who used job evaluation reported an integrated scheme covering manual and non-manual employees (ACAS, 1988b: 7). Non-manual workers benefited from incremental progression through the scales and promotion opportunities, in addition to the annual pay round, while manual workers had to rely solely on the latter.

> What differences in terms and conditions still exist between different groups of employees in your organisation? How would you seek to justify these to a trade union official?

A survey for the BIM (now the Institute of Management) some 20 years ago suggested a number of reasons for employers to harmonise. The list included: to increase employee co-operation; to increase productivity; to improve management–union relations; to reduce labour turnover; and to reduce absenteeism. The reason mentioned most often was 'to increase employee co-operation', and it would be fair to say that this remains a key motivation today. The 1980s witnessed the apparent discovery of human resources as a source of competitive advantage, reflected in the HRM literature which talked of moving from employee compliance to commitment (Walton, 1985). While managers were keen to wax lyrical about the importance of people and the creation of a new corporate culture, demonstrating this in practice has proved to be somewhat more elusive. In the context where common interests are emphasised, it would seem somewhat odd if some groups of workers were treated differently. Important icons in this respect have been the high-profile Japanese implants such as Nissan, Komatsu and Toshiba, whose apparent success in achieving a committed and productive workforce have made them leading-edge companies. The emphasis which managements at these companies have placed on single status – with the removal of separate canteens, car parks and even different types of clothing – have caught the headlines as have the lengths to which these companies have gone to try to reduce perceived status differences (Duncan, 1992: 386).

Moves towards harmonisation have come from two main groups of employers: those who have used it as a tool to change *existing* practices and those who have used it as part of a broader package when establishing on a *greenfield* site. An old example is the ICI Weekly Staff Agreement in the late 1960s, which used the removal of status distinctions to achieve greater flexibility in the utilisation of labour (Roeber, 1975). In relation to setting up a new factory, the Japanese implants have been the most high-profile. At Komatsu, for example, single status was described as one of the biggest lessons to be learnt from Japan. This was not simply a matter of having a single works canteen but it meant that each member of staff had the same appraisal system and criteria. Similarly, the reward structure was also consistent with this message, with all employees (from board to shopfloor) assessed on their performance and accorded increases in salary over and above the annual pay round. Pfeffer (1994: 48) refers to such initiatives as 'symbolic egalitarianism' and suggests they have a role to play in reducing 'them and us' attitudes, and achieving competitive advantage through people. According to Morton (1994: 49), the demonstration of single status was a precondition for flexibility at Komatsu; he argues that if employees do not feel threatened by losing an employable skill, resistance will disappear. The strong emphasis on team work was also a significant factor, with employees recruited for their flexibility and team-orientation. The work siren to start and end the shift was abandoned in favour of individual and supervisor responsibility. Demonstration by example was seen as central and described as 'wearing a hairshirt with sincerity'. This included all staff wearing the company uniform, using the same canteen and car park, working in open-plan offices, and even all taking lunch at the same time (Morton, 1994: 82).

Most employers have adopted a gradualist approach to change, but some have gone for fundamental reform with wide-ranging reviews of terms and conditions. These deals inevitably involve a long consultation process – such as took place at Rover in 1992 when Japanese work practices were introduced together with harmonised conditions and a guarantee of job security (Duncan, 1992: 286). However, these more extensive programmes are more commonly found on greenfield sites, where great care is taken with the whole P&D package so as to help create an appropriate culture (Wilkinson and Ackers, 1995: 352–354).

However, Price and Price (1994) suggest that, while there has been some progress in narrowing the status divide, this has been limited to large companies and high-technology industries. Traditional attitudes, together with the changing structure of industry and some aspects of government policy, have combined to work against business and social forces for change. Historically, senior managers have had little contact with the shopfloor, so depersonalising employment relationships. Given the low-trust dynamic, manual workers – 'hands' – were not to be trusted nor, due to scientific management, were they seen as playing a critical role in the achievement of competitiveness: 'hands' were easily substituted. In contrast, non-manual workers were seen as 'loyal' to the employer and were provided with better conditions and career prospects. However, the growth of white-collar unions, albeit in response to declining prospects for non-manual employees, led to two paradoxical consequences. Firstly, rather than bridging the divide between manual and non-manual workers, white-collar unions tried to preserve their identity. Secondly, employers anxious to keep white-collar staff loyal then tried to 'buy' loyalty to keep them away from unions.

There are a number of factors which seem likely to increase moves to harmonisation. First, new technology cuts across existing demarcation lines (craft, skilled and semi-skilled), and status differentials tend to impede flexibility. Harmonisation is sometimes introduced as a way of 'buying-out' old work practices. The introduction of technology also increases demands and responsibilities on manual workers who are required to be more co-operative rather than compliant, in effect to take on multi-skilling and technician roles. In such circumstances harmonisation can play a key role in trying to make blue-collar workers part of the corporate team.

Secondly, the legislation on sex discrimination and equal pay has narrowed differences between blue- and white-collar workers and has also extended rights – such as maternity pay – to all workers who have sufficient length of service, extending the practice whereby some employers used to provide these benefits solely to white-collar workers. Incomes policies in the 1970s also made it difficult for employers to increase wages, thus moving non-pay issues into the limelight. In addition, the Wages Act 1986 (repealing the Truck Acts) meant that manual workers no longer had the right to be paid in cash, so removing a further obstacle to salary payments. Equal-value issues have also been a force towards an integrated payment structure, based on a common job evaluation scheme (Duncan, 1992: 287). Moreover, as the European Commission continues to press ahead in its moves to harmonise terms and conditions across Europe, the UK appears even more out of step if it maintains different conditions for different groups of workers.

Thirdly, the growth in single-table bargaining and the recent spate of union mergers have also been important forces for change. Indeed, one of the reasons for introducing single-table bargaining (see Chapter 12) has been a commitment by management to harmonise conditions (Marginson and Sisson, 1990) as well as saving management time and reducing conflict between work groups. Similarly, now that many unions (such as UNISON) represent both manual and non-manual workers, it seems anachronistic to maintain status differentials between different groups of workers.

Fourthly, changes in employment structure in recent years have had an impact on lower-level white-collar jobs, which have become increasingly routinised and deskilled with lower prospects for pay and promotion. A gap is now more apparent between clerical employees and professional workers, with little movement between the two. At the same time, many blue-collar jobs have been re-skilled due to technological demands which require technical training. As Price and Price (1994: 542) put it, the 'day of the craftician has dawned in some industries, and more generally craft functions are becoming closely aligned with technical functions'. As a result there is often little to distinguish manual from non-manual jobs.

Despite being part of the conventional wisdom of 'good employee relations' (Arthurs, 1985: 17) there are a number of potential pitfalls to harmonisation. First, there may be cost issues, especially if there are disputes over differentials and if craft unions demand compensation for the erosion of status differentials. It may well be expensive to equalise notice periods, for example, especially in times where constant change puts an emphasis on flexibility. In the short run, costs may well increase even if the longer run offers more benefits. Secondly, workers may be unwilling to see cashless pay as a benefit, so making it necessary to 'buy out' cash payments. However, there could be cost savings in areas of capital costs (two different canteens replaced by a large one, for example), and reducing the administrative costs involved in operating two systems. Thirdly, as with many other management initiatives, supervisors and middle managers are often wary, partly because of confusion over what 'harmonisation' is designed to achieve and also because of insecurity and concern about their 'new' responsibilities (Wilkinson et al, 1993). Some resent the lost status. At Komatsu, for example, supervisors complained that they had spent their working lives trying to achieve staff status, symbolised by being able to wear a suit as opposed to overalls, and now single status had eliminated this recognition of their 'success'.

> What are the obstacles to harmonisation of conditions in your organisation, and what can be done to overcome them?

Price and Price (1994: 553–557) see three factors which might obstruct the development of harmonisation. First, the changing industrial structure in Britain, and in particular the growing number of small firms which do not engage in 'best practice' P&D, might slow down change. Secondly, contracting-out of services, especially in the public sector, might create new status divides between core and peripheral workers. Finally, the government's emphasis since 1979 on deregulating the labour market – for example, through the abolition of wages councils – has tended to reduce, rather than improve, terms and conditions for some parts of the workforce.

NON–FINANCIAL REWARDS AND RECOGNITION

It is important to consider the role which non-financial rewards and recognition play in motivating staff at work, and in this section we examine a number of these. Firstly, we focus on job characteristics. Turner and Lawrence (1965) identify six requisite task attributes. These are variety (in tools, equipment, prescribed workplace), autonomy (discretion to choose work method), required interactions (necessary contact), optional interaction (opportunities for contact), knowledge and skill (learning-time involved), and responsibility (for example, problem-solving). Cooper (1973) lists four intrinsic job characteristics that increase motivation. Firstly, variety, which includes tools, machinery, location, and other people with whom to interact. However, Cooper argues that the value of variety is limited to routine repetitive jobs whereby an increase in variety simply means a reduction in feelings of boredom. Secondly, discretion, which is of two kinds: *means* discretion (the choice of organising the means and terms of work) and *skill* discretion (the choice in selecting appropriate knowledge to solve problems). Thirdly, the contribution of the employee to the total task. It is not the fact of wholeness which is important but the significance of the contribution within the overall structure of the goods or service produced. Finally, goal characteristics are important, such as the difficulty of the goal to be achieved.

Think of jobs you have done in the past. What factors made them satisfying?

How do job characteristics combine to motivate, reward and recognise good employee performance? According to Ford (1969), 'perhaps they have the effect of a shotgun blast; it is the whole charge that brings the beast down' (quoted in Robertson *et al*, 1992: 62). A 'job characteristics model' has been developed by Hackman and Oldman (1976) which incorporates the five core job characteristics they believe are involved in job satisfaction and motivation. These characteristics are:

• skill variety – the range of skills and talents required

• task identity – the extent to which the completion of a whole piece of work is required

• task significance – the impact of the task on others

• autonomy – freedom and discretion in selecting methods and hours of work

- feedback – clear information provided on performance.

According to these writers, if jobs are designed in a way that increase the presence of these core dimensions, three psychological states can occur:

- experienced meaningfulness at work, which is the result of skill variety, task identity and task significance

- experienced responsibility for work outcomes, which is the result of autonomy

- knowledge of results of work activities, which is the result of feedback.

If these do occur then work motivation and job satisfaction will be high and other behavioural outputs – such as attendance – may also be positively affected (Fincham and Rhodes, 1988: 92). Equally, employees with high 'growth-need strength' (GNS) are more likely to experience changes in their critical psychological state when core job dimensions are improved (Robertson *et al*, 1992: 64). It is also important to realise that simply having a highly motivated employee does not necessarily equate with good job performance. Employees also need the necessary skills (training is important) *and* the tools and materials to do a good job. Obviously, a motivated but unskilled employee is unlikely to do a job to the required standard, but neither is a motivated and skilled employee who has had inadequate training or is provided with inappropriate raw materials.

In the 1990s it is perhaps more appropriate to take a less universalistic approach when considering motivation at work. Managements need to try to assess the subjective priorities of their employees, rather than assume and enforce a particular view. It is also the case that attitudes and priorities may change over time. Therefore, as Schein (1965: 61) puts it, managers need to be flexible and accept 'a variety of interpersonal relationships, patterns of authority and psychological contracts'.

There are two common themes relating to non-financial reward and motivation. These are:

Recognition and feedback
Employees' work needs to be valued by employers and hence recognised by them, a line which is taken up by a number of the TQM gurus such as Crosby and Deming. According to Crosby (1980: 218), 'people really don't work for money. They go to work for it, but once the salary has been established, their concern is appreciation. Recognise their contribution publicly and noisily, but don't demean them by applying a price tag to everything.' He argues that it is much more important to recognise achievements through symbolic awards and prizes. However, Kohn (1993: 55) argues that research shows that tangible rewards, as well as praise, can actually *lower* the level of performance, particularly in jobs requiring creativity. According to him, studies show that intrinsic interest in a task (the sense that it is worth doing for its own sake) tends to decline when the individual concerned is given an external reason for doing it.

Extrinsic motivations are not only less effective than intrinsic motivations, they can also corrode intrinsic motivation. People who work in order to get a reward tend to be less interested in the task than those who are not expecting to be rewarded. According to Kohn (1993: 55), when we are led to do something in order to get a prize, we feel that the goal of the prize controls our behaviour and this deprivation of self-determination makes tasks seem less enjoyable. Moreover, the offer of an inducement sends a message that the task cannot be very interesting, otherwise it would not be necessary to bribe us to do it.

Others have argued that providing praise for good work, rather than criticism for poor work, is important. Managers should 'catch staff doing it right'. Token prizes/awards can also play a role as they have symbolic worth even if they are low in financial value (Crosby, 1980: 218). There has been growing interest in this field in recent years and some employers have moved beyond seeing non-financial recognition solely as the watch or clock presented on retirement (Hilton, 1992). Companies such as BT, Rover and British Gas use Marks & Spencers vouchers, while Midland Bank managers use chocolates and gifts in kind (Curry, 1995). These are effective for tax reasons, are seen as being more motivating than cash, and can provide important feedback. Feedback itself needs to be regular, timely and relevant. In other words, employees need to be given feedback more than once a year in a formal appraisal. As far as possible it should relate to a recently completed task and it should also be directly relevant to the employee's work effort/output figures (the establishment as a whole may be too removed from the individual employee).

Involvement, autonomy and responsibility
Research which links participation to higher levels of satisfaction and increased productivity can be found in the social science literature (Pfeffer, 1994: 42). As Blumberg (1968: 123) notes, 'there is hardly a study in the entire literature which fails to demonstrate that satisfaction at work is enhanced, or that other generally acknowledged beneficial consequences accrue, from a genuine increase in workers' decision-making power.' People value the ability to influence their work, but according to Gallie and White (1993: 4), only 32 per cent of employees felt that they could exercise a significant influence over changes in work organisation that could directly affect their jobs. Yet it was this type of influence that was most significantly related to favourability to organisation change and to perceptions of good employee relations. Modern HRM literature appears to endorse this, arguing that employees come to work motivated and interested but are soon alienated by the web of rules and constraints which govern their working lives. If only management could find ways to release and tap employees' creativity – for example, via employee involvement (EI) – their commitment to organisational goals would follow. This belief is also contained within the IPA/IPM Code of Practice (1990: 11) where EI is defined as 'a range of processes designed to engage the support, understanding, optimum contribution of all employees in an organisation and their commitment to it'. It works upon the assumption that common interests are achievable in organisations,

although most managements fail to capture the interest of their staff, partly because communications are ineffective but also because contributions are not welcomed. It is stressed that employees should have the opportunity to satisfy their needs for involvement, autonomy and responsibility through work, perhaps through participation in quality circles or merely by involving employees more in day-to-day matters, so they can agree actions to be taken and be more positive in implementing such measures. Management styles may well need to be addressed as well.

How might these states be achieved? Clearly some of these aspects of management can be integrated into day-to-day management activity, and recognition and feedback can be made part of the corporate culture. However, to illustrate the variety of ways an employer might achieve such goals, we examine two initiatives: Job Redesign and Total Quality Management.

JOB REDESIGN

Job design and redesign is concerned with the allocation of task functions among organisational roles (Cooper, 1974). While early work in this area was largely concerned with matters of efficiency and rationalising work, breaking it down into tiny components in line with Taylor's ideas, modern job redesign has broader aims and looks to balance efficiency and job-satisfaction goals. As there has been increasing recognition that extrinsic rewards (such as pay) are insufficient on their own to motivate employees, more emphasis has been put on intrinsic factors such as job content. Drawing on expectancy theory, the aim is to design jobs which satisfy employee needs so that the work can be performed to a high standard, hence enabling both employee and organisational goals to be satisfied.

Table 16 **Approaches to job design**

To influence skill variety:	provide opportunities for people to do several tasks combine tasks establish client relationships
To influence task identity:	combine tasks form natural work units (eg a typist does all the work of one person instead of some of the work of several people
To influence task significance:	form natural work groups inform people of the importance of their work establish client relationships
To influence autonomy:	give people responsibility for determining their own working system give people responsibility for quality control
To influence feedback:	establish client relationships open feedback channels

Source: Robertson *et al*, 1992: 73

What can be done within your own organisation to redesign work so as to change core job dimensions?

Job rotation is perhaps the most basic type of job redesign. It involves workers' moving from job to job (with similar levels of skill) in an attempt to alleviate boredom. In a supermarket, for example, it might involve shelf-stacking, checkout operating and counting boxes in the warehouse. However, the common criticism is that job rotation is little more than swapping one boring job for another; it can actually be demotivating if it affects a bonus pattern, or breaks up a work group.

Job enlargement involves widening a job so that one or more related tasks are added to the existing one at a similar level of responsibility. This can reduce the repetitiveness of performing jobs of short-cycle operations and may add to motivation for employees if they can see their contribution to the final product or service. However, Herzberg (1968: 18) writes of job enlargement as doing no more than 'enlarge the meaninglessness of the job', and it can actually add to work intensification. It has also been suggested that, while a worker can 'switch off' from one boring job, doing a number of different relatively mundane tasks requires concentration, which is resented if the job is monotonous.

Job enrichment involves a more radical design of the job, perhaps replacing skills designed out by job redesigners in an earlier era. New responsibilities are added, such as production workers taking on some responsibility for maintenance or taking on decision-making roles such as work scheduling. In some cases employees acquire a complete job so that they can see a real purpose to what they are doing.

Autonomous work groups extend job enrichment in that not only is there a wider range of operative/production skills but groups of employees also acquire responsibility for management tasks such as choosing work methods, regulating the pace of work, and allocating and scheduling work. Self-supervision is stressed, and this encourages autonomy. In some cases, groups may even take responsibility for training and recruitment.

Teamworking is perhaps the most recent manifestation of job redesign and involves a group of multi-capable workers who switch between tasks, organise and allocate work, and are responsible for all aspects of production, including quality. Buchanan (1994: 101–103) describes the importance of teamworking within a broader context of organisational change, with high-performance work teams operating without supervision and having wide-ranging responsibilities for production and maintenance. Other changes also take place to support teamworking, including open lay-out, flexitime, the removal of clocking, and a new open management style. This raises a central issue: such initiatives might need to be supported by changes in management style and P&D practices.

What motivates you at work? List the factors which affect your feelings about the job, and rank them. Which tasks are you motivated to do well and which are you not motivated to do well? Explain your conclusions.

TOTAL QUALITY MANAGEMENT (TQM)

Developing and involving people in improvement activities is a key feature of TQM (Wilkinson, 1992, 1994). Unlike quality circles, which were unlikely to succeed because of their peripheral nature, TQM is more likely to succeed because of its holistic approach (Hill, 1991).

Table 17 The differences between quality circles and TQM

Factor	Quality circles	TQM
Choice	voluntary	compulsory
Structure	bolt-on	integrated quality system
Direction	bottom-up	top-down
Scope	within departments/units	company-wide
Aims	employee relations improvements	quality improvements

Source: Wilkinson *et al*, 1992: 5.

TQM is supposed to place a greater emphasis on autonomy and creativity, expecting active co-operation from employees rather than mere compliance with the employment contract. For Hill (1991a: 400–401), participation is 'the central mechanism for improving business quality', one of the key principles of TQM, alongside harder elements such as statistical process control. He argues that everyone, from the senior manager to the ordinary office and shopfloor employee, should participate in the process of identifying and implementing improvements. TQM has important implications for participation and involvement, whether this be in terms of employees' taking greater responsibility for quality and being accountable for its achievement, or in terms of the introduction of teamworking principles into organisations.

If TQM is applied as its proponents suggest, the focus of responsibility for quality is in the hands of those who do the work. This is said to improve motivation by encouraging employees to find satisfaction and continuous improvement in their own work. Furthermore, the supervisory climate is meant to support this, with the fear of failure being discouraged in favour of a *search* for failure. It is felt that individuals who are blamed for mistakes are unlikely to search to put them right. Quality improvement teams, quality circles and steering committees in TQM organisations should involve greater numbers of employees in decision-making than in their non-TQM counterparts. Whilst the experience with quality circles suggests that employees may decide not to participate in such bodies, Hill (1991b: 546–547) attributes this to inappropriate structures, and argues that a failure to create the right framework – rather than employee resistance – is the real obstacle to participation. Furthermore, involvement in such processes is said to reward and recognise employee contributions, improving their motivation, morale, work environment and skills.

The employee involvement aspects of TQM have a number of dimensions. The first is the educative process concerned with creating customer awareness within an organisation. Thus, in manufacturing companies, programmes may be used to show the workforce the end product of the material which they handle, and to meet external customers. In service organisations such programmes represent an attempt to change the corporate culture towards a more market-oriented approach. Second, there may be changes in the conduct of work itself, ranging from restructuring of work organisation – for example, organising work units into cells and the creation of semi-autonomous work groups – to less fundamental reforms which may involve the removal of inspectors, with workers taking responsibility for quality control. The third element consists of committees, quality circles, quality improvement or action teams which may be established on an *ad hoc* basis to solve particular problems, or may be more permanent fixtures. Team members may be drawn from one functional area (as with quality and customer circles) or the teams may have a wider constituency so as to solve cross-functional quality problems – as with quality improvement teams. Teams are designed to improve communication and understanding of cross-functional problems, as well as increase commitment to proposed solutions (Wilkinson *et al*, 1992: 18–20). TQM shifts the focus of responsibility for quality to the people who actually do the work, and as such might represent a transformation from traditional authoritarian top-down decision-making to task-oriented ideals. Its premiss is clearly 'anti-expert' in that all staff can and must contribute. If done properly, this requires a degree of participation which represents a major adjustment to the corporate culture and style of managing for most UK-based organisations. However, criticism has been made of the practice of TQM and how far it actually does offer 'real' participation (Wilkinson and Willmott, 1995).

> Do you think that management initiatives such as job redesign or TQM have made for more satisfying work, rewarding and recognising employee contributions, either at your workplace or more generally?

USING REWARD STRATEGICALLY: AN ILLUSTRATION

Richer Sounds is a specialist hi-fi separates retailer in the UK, which sees customer service as the driving philosophy behind the company. Employees are encouraged to help the customer buy rather than go for the 'hard sell'. Management argues that the company's basic principles are quality products (branded names, etc), value for money and customer service, and point out that while the first two can be controlled by head office, the latter is very much in the hands of the ordinary branch employee or 'colleague' as he or she is known. The company sees reward very broadly in that there is both a payment and a recognition aspect (ie non-financial aspect) to its approach). Pay is above average for the industry with a basic rate supplemented by commission, profit-share and a customer service bonus. A customer service index (CSI) is calculated, with individuals being assessed on several indicators, the main one being customer feedback on service quality. Each customer receipt includes a freepost questionnaire, with the customer invited to assess the level of service provided by the salesperson, who is identified by payroll number on the form.

The individual's bonus is related to the feedback. Thus, if a customer ticks 'excellent', the sales assistant receives an extra £3, if 'poor', a deduction of £3 takes place. These are totalled up at the end of each month and a bonus is paid. The company is at pains to point out that any deductions are far outweighed by the bonuses. Indeed, it is unlikely that anyone with a stream of negative feedback would actually retain their job at Richer Sounds, although management report a relatively high voluntary turnover of new staff, some of whom find that they are uncomfortable with this approach. The peer group is seen as crucial in encouraging good performance, and managers are provided with the results on each individual's performance, which are distributed internally. While many of the incentives focus on the performance of the individual, and staff wear name badges to encourage greater individual responsibility, company performance is also rewarded with a profit-sharing scheme.

The company also believes non-financial recognition is important in motivating staff and has an array of initiatives designed to make working for the company satisfying and enjoyable. Staff performing above and beyond the call of duty receive gold aeroplanes as recognition of their achievement, while wooden spoons are given to staff for acts of amazing stupidity. A suggestion scheme does have a small financial component but the main element is a day trip on the Orient Express for the best two suggestions each quarter. Branches and departments compete in the 'Richer Way League'. This is based on customer service standards and profit, and provides the use of a Rolls-Royce or a Bentley for a week as the prize for the top performing branch. Thus, teamwork is emphasised, and branch staff are encouraged to socialise outside the workplace as a way of consolidating the team identity (for further details see Wilkinson, Redman and Snape, 1996).

> How might the ideas embodied in this approach be applied to your organisation?

CONCLUSION

When managements are reviewing their reward systems, care needs to be taken not only with the choice of suitable payment schemes and benefits packages, but also with the processes by which they are implemented. There are a number of key factors which managements need to take into account when implementing reward systems. This is based on the view that a careful systematic analysis which addresses potential problems is more likely to succeed than an *ad hoc* approach (ACAS, 1992). Firstly, involving employees and their representatives in the process is likely to be helpful: they may add useful knowledge on the issues which affect them and about which management are unaware. It also allows management to sound out employee opinion and hence assess the feasibility of their plans, while employees who have been involved are more likely to accept and understand the system rather than reject it as an arbitrary management imposition. For example, with job evaluation, working parties or panels are usually set up to conduct the actual process of evaluation which ensures there is greater legitimacy to the decisions (subjective as they are) which have been taken. Secondly, it is important to analyse what is wrong with the existing reward system and separate out symptoms from causes, and establish whether or not the scheme is fundamentally flawed or just plagued by implementation problems. Thirdly, it is important to prepare the way by communicating the system, taking care to explain how it is intended to work, and the implications for each group of workers. Finally, it is not enough simply to install the system. It needs to be monitored and reviewed to ensure that it operates in the way that was intended, and that it is judged against established criteria. Given that all reward systems tend to have unintended consequences and decay over time, regular review is critical; there is no such thing as an ideal scheme which can operate for many years without modification (ACAS, 1992; Duncan, 1992).

> To what extent does your organisation follow these steps when implementing new reward systems?

At times when it is difficult for employers to fund pay increases above the rate of inflation and provide a range of generous financial benefits (such as pensions and sick-pay arrangements), attention may need to turn to non-financial recognition and reward. This includes the harmonisation of certain terms and conditions such as clocking on and off, single canteens and car parking arrangements, none of which is likely to be as expensive as financial rewards. It can also include initiatives designed to make work more satisfying and fulfilling, and to seek increases in variety, involvement, autonomy and responsibility through job redesign and total quality management. The gains to be made from these can be extensive and contribute directly to the achievement of organisational success. Recognition can also be through badges, prizes, holidays, and day trips to other organisations which supply raw materials or manufacture or market finished goods from those supplied by the employees concerned. The absolute cost of these sorts of reward is likely to be small, but they have a powerful symbolic significance.

USEFUL READING

ARMSTRONG, M. AND MURLIS, H. (1995) *Reward Management*, Third edition. London, Kogan Page.

CURRY, L. (1995) 'Good for morale, good for business', *People Management*, Vol 7, 7. 42–44.

DUNCAN, C. (1992) 'Pay, payment systems and job evaluation', in B. Towers (Ed.), *A Handbook of Industrial Relations Practice*, Third edition. London, Kogan Page: 258–291.

HILTON, P. (1992) 'Using incentives to reward and motivate employees', *Personnel Management*, September: 49–51.

INCOMES DATA SERVICES (1994) *Employee Benefits*, Number 72.

MORTON, C. (1994) *Becoming World Class*. London, Macmillan.

PRICE, R. AND PRICE, L. (1994) 'Change and continuity in the status divide', in K. Sisson (Ed.), *Personnel Management in Britain*. Oxford, Blackwell: 527–561.

ROBERTSON, I., SMITH, M. AND COOPER, M. (1992) *Motivation: Strategies, theory and practice*, Second edition. London, IPD.

WICKENS, P. (1987) *The Road to Nissan: Flexibility, quality, teamwork*. London, Macmillan.

WILKINSON, A., REDMAN, T. AND SNAPE, E. (1996) 'Richer sounds: Payment for Customer Service' in J. Storey (Ed.) *Blackwell Cases in Human Resource and Change Management*. Oxford, Blackwell: 266–274.

Part 7

INTEGRATING PERSONNEL AND DEVELOPMENT

17 Linking business strategy with personnel and development

INTRODUCTION

The theme running through this final section of the book is integration. This takes two forms, vertical and horizontal, though in practice there might well be extensive links between the two. Vertical integration, the subject of this chapter, refers to the links between the environmental context, business strategy, and P&D policies and practices; this has been referred to as 'external fit' by Baird and Meshoulam (1988) or 'organisational integration' (Guest and Peccei, 1994). In Chapter 18 we consider horizontal integration, the degree to which different aspects of P&D are compatible with each other; Baird and Meshoulam call this 'internal fit', and it can be found in several of Guest and Peccei's other three aspects of integration. In the final chapter in this section, a number of case studies are presented which illustrate some of these links (or lack of them) in various employing organisations drawn from different parts of the public and private sectors. These analyse and assess the way in which employers have sought to promote both vertical and horizontal integration as a component of corporate success. The case studies also demonstrate the difficulties which are likely to be encountered in trying to link together disparate parts of the business or public sector organisation, as well as maintain consistency between separate aspects of P&D.

In recent years there has been a good deal of interest in examining the links between business strategy and P&D, most noticeably since the emergence of human resource management ideas. Although it has become commonplace for leading management gurus to extol the virtues of investing in people and treating employees as the vital component in the achievement of competitive advantage (see, for example, Prahalad, 1995), there has been little systematic analysis of these claims. At one level it is clear that the development of management systems which encourage employees to 'work beyond contract' makes good business sense; other things being equal, committed and motivated employees are likely to increase sales, improve quality and provide high levels of customer service. But no matter how committed and excellent the staff, they cannot make up for low-quality products, poor designs, insufficient investments in technology, unstable exchange rates, collapsed economies, or political upheavals. Equally, even if senior management believes in 'best practice' human resource management, this does not guarantee that first-line supervisors have either the skills or the motivation to put it into effect. Moreover, employing organisations are characterised by political rivalries, departmental splits and functional conflicts which also render problematic the straightforward translation of broad corporate goals into specific workplace practices. To complicate matters yet further, strategies do not emerge in a simple, unilinear top-down direction, but – as we shall see below – are complex, multi-faceted phenomena. In short, not only do we need to analyse the links between business strategy and P&D, we also need to consider the impact of human resource management ideas on emerging business strategies.

By the end of this chapter, readers should be able to:

- apply business planning models to benchmark their own employer's approach to P&D against those of other organisations

- participate in the creation of P&D strategies which contribute to enhanced organisational and individual performance

- advise management on the measures which can be used to evaluate the effectiveness of P&D.

In addition, readers should be able to understand and explain:

- competing meanings of the term 'strategy', and their implications for P&D practice

- how links have been made between business strategy and P&D practice

- the nature of the barriers which prevent the achievement of business strategy in employing organisations.

BUSINESS AND CORPORATE STRATEGIES

Most definitions of strategy in the business and management field stem from the work of Chandler (1962), who argued that the structure of an organisation flowed from its growth strategy. To be worthy of the title 'strategy', actions should be purposeful, encompassing the enterprise as a whole, and long-term in nature. One of the leading British texts on strategy (Johnson and Scholes, 1993: 10) defines strategy as 'the *direction* and *scope* of an organisation over the long term: ideally, which matches its *resources* to its changing *environment*, and in particular to its *markets, customers or clients*, so as to meet *stakeholder* expectations'. Within this perspective, strategy is seen to operate at three levels: corporate strategy relates to the overall scope of the organisation, its structures and financing, and the distribution of resources between different parts of the organisation; business or competitive strategy refers to how the organisation is to compete in a given market, its approaches to product development and to customers; and finally, operational strategies are concerned with how the various sub-units – marketing, finance, manufacturing, and so on – contribute to the higher-level strategies. P&D would be seen as an element at this third level, although Johnson and Scholes, in common with most writers on strategy, do not devote much space to considering the human aspects of organisation.

> How do you account for this apparent discrepancy between the viewpoint that 'people make the difference' and its lack of emphasis – or even mention – by writers on strategy?

This top-down perspective, in which strategies are assumed to be formulated by boards of directors and then cascaded down the organisation, represents the dominant view of strategy in most published literature on the subject. But this 'classical' model is not the only perspective, as Whittington (1993) demonstrates so well. He proposes a fourfold typology of strategy, based upon distinctions between the degree to which outcomes are perceived purely in profit-maximising or pluralistic terms, and the extent to which strategy formulation is seen as deliberate or emergent. The four types are:

- *Classical* (profit-maximising, deliberate): under this conception, strategy is portrayed as a rational process of deliberate calculation and analysis, undertaken by senior managers who survey the external environment searching for ways in which to maximise profits and gain competitive advantage. It is characterised as non-political, the product of honest endeavour by managers who have nothing but the organisation's interests at heart, and who are able to remain above the detailed skirmishes which typify life at lower levels in the hierarchy. This notion of independent professionalism is something which is often used to legitimise management action (Child, 1969; Marchington and Loveridge, 1979). Following a military analogy, the process of strategy formulation is considered to be separate from the process of implementation: as Whittington (1993: 15–17) puts it, 'plans are conceived in the general's tent, overlooking the battlefield but sufficiently detached for safety ... the actual carrying-out of orders is relatively unproblematic, assured by military discipline and obedience.'

- *Evolutionary* (profit-maximising, emergent): from this angle, strategy is seen as a product of market forces, in which the most efficient and productive organisations win through. Drawing upon notions of population ecology, 'the most appropriate strategies within a given market emerge as competitive processes allow the relatively better performers to survive while the weaker performers are squeezed out and go to the wall' (Legge, 1995: 99). Taken to its extreme, it could be argued that there is little point in planning a deliberate strategy since the winners and losers will be 'picked' by forces beyond the influence of organisational actors. Senior managements might, however, see some advantage in keeping their options open and learning how to adapt to changing customer demands.

• *Processual* (pluralistic, emergent): this view stems from an assumption that people are 'too limited in their understanding, wandering in their attention, and careless in their actions to unite around and then carry through a perfectly calculated plan' (Whittington, 1993: 4). There are at least two essential features of this perspective. First, as Mintzberg (1978) argues, strategies tend to evolve through a process of discussion and disagreement which involves managers at different levels in the organisation, and in some cases it is impossible to specify what the strategy is until *after* the event; indeed, actions may only come to be defined as strategies with the benefit of hindsight, by a process of *post hoc* rationalisation when participants in organisations recount stories of recent developments which appear to be rational and carefully planned in retrospect. Quinn's (1980) notion of 'logical incrementalism', the idea that strategy emerges in a fragmented and largely intuitive manner, evolving from a combination of internal decisions and external events, fits well with this perspective. Whittington (1993: 26) uses a political example to illustrate this by arguing that little of what Mrs Thatcher did during the 1980s could have been predicted when she came to power a decade earlier. The second essential feature of the processual view is that it privileges a micro-political perspective, acknowledging the fact that organisations are beset with tensions and contradictions, with rivalries and conflicting goals, and with behaviours which are often geared up to achieving personal or departmental objectives (Pettigrew, 1973; Marchington *et al*, 1993). The challenge to the classical perspective is readily apparent as many of their 'confident assumptions' about long-term goals, cascaded strategies and unproblematic implementation are put in jeopardy (Whittington, 1993: 27).

• *Systemic* (pluralistic, deliberate): the final perspective suggests that strategy is shaped by the social system in which it is imbedded, factors such as class, gender and national culture. Within this viewpoint, strategic choices are constrained not so much by the cognitive limitations of the actors involved but by the cultural and institutional interests of a broader society; the acceptability of state intervention in interventionist countries such as Japan, Germany and France can be contrasted easily with those which are more typical within non-interventionist countries such as Britain and the USA, and has clear implications for strategy (Legge, 1995: 102). The other advantage of viewing strategy from this perspective is that it focuses our attention on the way in which, under the classical approach, management actions may be legitimised with reference to external forces, cloaking 'managerial power in the culturally acceptable clothing of science and objectivity' (Whittington, 1993: 37).

This discussion of strategy has interesting implications for how we view the notion of vertical integration. Under the classical perspective it can be seen as unproblematic, merely a matter of making the right decision and then cascading this through the managerial hierarchy to shop floor or office workers, who then snap into action to meet organisational goals; bureaucracy reigns supreme. The evolutionary view complicates the situation slightly, in that it puts a primacy upon market forces and the perceived need for organisations (which are seen in unitarist terms) to respond quickly and effectively to customer demands. This introduces notions of coercion, power and flexibility into the equation, as opposed to the objectivity which supposedly underpins classical perspectives. The two pluralist perspectives each show up the conflictual nature of organisational life, and demonstrate the barriers to fully-fledged vertical integration in practice, whether this be due to tensions *within* management or to challenges which may be mounted from workers (either through trade unions or as individual employees working without co-operation). It is worth bearing these problems in mind before we examine the principal attempts to link business strategy and human resource management, as many of these have assumed the predominance of classical perspectives on strategy – with obvious limitations. Purcell and Ahlstrand (1994: 49) go some way to incorporating some of the other approaches into what remains essentially a classical perspective (levels of decision-making, upstream and downstream) by stressing the importance of the political dimension to strategy formation, and the fact that it involves a plurality of interest groups.

> Which of these perspectives on strategy is closest to your own experiences at work? Why is this?

LINKING BUSINESS STRATEGY WITH PERSONNEL AND DEVELOPMENT

In Chapter 4 we made a distinction between 'soft' and 'hard' human resource management (Storey, 1989). The former focuses on the *human resource* aspects of people management, on the notion that employees are valuable sources of information and expertise whose desire to contribute to organisational success is prevented by management systems which inhibit creativity and constrain initiative. Employers who believe in this philosophy would probably pursue absolutist or 'best practice' human resource management (Marchington, 1992; Pfeffer, 1994). The alternative conception of human resource management focuses on the *management* of people at work, and the need to ensure that P&D strategies and practices are aligned with, and downstream from, business strategy. These are referred to as contingency approaches or matching models, and they suggest that it is possible to operate with a range of different P&D practices, depending upon the competitive position of the organisation. In one, for example, the 'preferred' style for managing people might be authoritarian and tough, while in another it could be developmental and humanistic. Given pressures to identify the contribution and relevance of P&D to business strategy, it is hardly surprising that many publications focus on the contingent, rather than the absolutist, perspective. Much of this interest has come from studies undertaken initially in the USA, and in particular heavy use has been made of constructs borrowed from marketing and business strategy. Interest in Britain first emerged during the 1970s (Thurley and Wood, 1983).

Four separate contingency approaches are outlined below, and then we draw some more general conclusions about the value and shortcomings of these ideas for determining appropriate patterns of P&D. The four approaches are: the Boston Consulting Group (BCG) matrix; lifecycle models; applications of Porter's work on competitive advantage; and Miles and Snow. A more detailed discussion of contingency models can be found in Legge (1995), Marchington and Parker (1990), Purcell (1989), Purcell and Ahlstrand (1994), Schuler (1989), Storey and Sisson (1993), and Thomason (1984).

> Before reading on, write down what you regard as the most important advantages and disadvantages of contingency models for determining the most appropriate patterns of P&D. Review these lists after reading the next section.

The BCG Matrix
An attempt to make links between the BCG ideal types (star, cash cow, wildcat/question mark, dog) and people management was first made by Thomason (1984), but this has been developed further more recently by Purcell (1989) and in Purcell and Ahlstrand (1994). The BCG model assumes that decisions about P&D are downstream from corporate and business/competitive strategies, and contingent on them as well. Consequently, business strategy is seen as determining the ideal human resource management approach which *should* be adopted by organisations. Accordingly, the P&D policies and practices appropriate for each BCG category can be read off in the following way:

Wildcat/question mark
This type of business has a low share of a fast-growing product market. The overall philosophies guiding the business are flexibility, dynamism and informality, and a relative lack of rules and bureaucracy as attempts are made to gain market share. Its key human resource features are flexible working, both in an individual and a team capacity, a stress on informality and open management styles which aim to encourage employees to work beyond contract, and a minimal P&D presence; in all probability, most P&D activities would be undertaken by line managers, typically without any specific guidance.

Star
This business has a high share of a fast-growing product market. In this situation, one would expect to find much more formalised systems of P&D, as well as a significant functional presence – though it is likely that the primary responsibility for dealing with human resource issues will reside with line managers. These are the businesses in which many of the so-called 'best practice' features of human resource management are likely to be found: careful recruitment and selection decisions to pick the most suitable candidates (in terms of

attitudes as well as technical abilities); internal training and development schemes to foster commitment; individual performance-related payment systems; regular and systematic appraisals; and communications/employee involvement. If trade unions are recognised, the preferred approach might be a single-union agreement or a partnership deal with single-table bargaining. Purcell (1989: 78) suggests that 'technical and capital investment is matched by human resource investments'. It is assumed that the future looks rosy for star businesses provided the market continues to grow and their share remains high.

Cash cow

This is a business with a high share of a slow-growing or even stagnant market. Order, stability, predictability and formalisation are all apparent here, with a feeling of what Gouldner (1954) called an 'indulgency pattern'. There may be tolerance of high staffing levels, inflexibility in operations with little movement expected between tasks and grades, well-established payment systems which reward long service, and a range of welfare services which reflect a degree of paternalism in management approaches to P&D. There are likely to be high levels of unionisation, and long-standing close relationships between P&D specialists and shop stewards, as well as with local union officials. The human resource function is likely to be well-staffed, with a high emphasis on specialisation and being at the forefront of developments in the field. The higher costs of personnel and development-related activities are affordable due to high profit margins, and considered justifiable given their contribution to harmonious labour relations.

Dog

This business is in the worst competitive position of all, with a low share of a slow-growing (or even declining) market. Due to these very difficult business conditions, P&D is likely to face continuing pressures for change and reductions in costs. This may lead to downsizing, lay-offs, short-term working, greater enforcement of management prerogatives, and an emphasis on downward communications. If the organisation has recently shifted from another quadrant, these pressures are likely to lead to conflict and recriminations. The regressive spiral of harsher controls, worker resistance, and further cutbacks only serves to reinforce feelings of doom and gloom on behalf of all the parties.

Lifecycle models

A number of US researchers (for example, Kochan and Barocci, 1985; Lengnick Hall and Lengnick Hall, 1988) have attempted to apply business and product lifecycle models of strategy to the management of human resources in an effort to explain why employers adopt different policies in different situations. More recently, Storey and Sisson (1993: 60–62) have tried to relate this to a British employment context, and they choose to use four categories.

Start-up

During the early stages of business growth, it is felt that flexibility of operation and response is necessary to enable the organisation to grow and develop. The entrepreneurial spirit is central to this phase of business/product development. The P&D implications of this phase point to flexible working patterns, and the ability to recruit and retain staff with the motivation to work hard and develop themselves. The employer's aim is commitment to the business, which can be rewarded to some extent by highly competitive salaries at the outset, but it is also likely that employees will be encouraged to see the potential benefits which may accrue to them in the future. There is likely to be little or nothing in the way of formalised and specialised structures, and in the unlikely event that trade unions are present, their role will probably be minor. As with the wildcat category, it is also unlikely that there will be much in the way of specialist P&D managers, although in larger businesses it is important that the basic philosophy which is set at this stage is appropriate for the business; some start-up businesses may find it more cost-effective to employ consultants to carry out P&D activities.

Growth

This is the stage at which formal policies and procedures begin to emerge, as the organisation finds its market niche and builds upon earlier successes. There is a need to retain expertise, and ensure that earlier levels of commitment are maintained. The human resource implications of this phase are the introduction of more progressive procedures and systems for all aspects of P&D; for example, more sophisticated methods for recruitment and selection, management succession planning, the provision of training programmes, the implementation of appraisal systems, organisation development, and formal compensation structures. In employee relations, the priorities are the maintenance of peace, and the retention of employee motivation and morale (Kochan and Barroci, 1985: 104).

Maturity

As markets begin to mature, and surpluses level out, the business needs to take stock of its activities. By this stage there is likely to be a range of formalised procedures, covering everything from P&D to purchasing. The human resource implications of this phase centre on the control of labour costs. Although training and development programmes may become harder to justify, there may not be any pressure to reduce wages provided the overall wage bill is kept under control. Union representatives, if they are present, are likely to find that previously-good relationships may start to become strained, and management is likely to find itself under increasing pressure to control all types of costs. As with a cash cow which is on the cusp to a dog, this is the time when employees and managers start to question the viability of continued employment into the future. There may be advantages in encouraging staff to leave or become mobile around the business, as efforts are made to improve productivity against a backcloth of worsening competitive prospects.

Decline

The process of decline brings to a head many of the problems which were beginning to become apparent in the previous phase, as the business struggles to survive. In this stage the emphasis shifts to rationalisation and redundancy, with obvious implications for the philosophy of P&D. Most of the policies which have developed through previous years are reconsidered, and indeed may be ditched as the employer seeks desperately to reduce costs. The specialist P&D function could well be disbanded, there may be pay cuts, training opportunities become centred on reskilling and outplacement counselling, and there is an increasing tendency to contract-out services. The human resource culture becomes tense and difficult, and trade unions may find that they are threatened with derecognition or, at best, a marginalised position.

Competitive advantage/Schuler

This model seeks to develop the Porter ideas on competitive strategy for application to human resource management styles. Porter (1985) argues that employers have three basic strategic options in order to gain competitive advantage: cost reduction, quality enhancement and innovation. Schuler and Jackson (1987) draw out the human resource implications of these strategies, and in a later work Schuler (1989) attempts to combine this approach with that of the lifecycle models. Our analysis is restricted to the initial application, which has also been adapted by Storey and Sisson (1993).

Cost reduction

The employer seeks to produce goods and services cheaper than the competition, with no frills and an emphasis on minimising costs at all stages in the process – including people management. The human resource implications of this option are *ad hoc* recruitment and selection, especially for low-grade tasks, low-discretion jobs, minimal levels of training and development, little emphasis on employee involvement, low levels of pay, minimum health and safety standards, and little empathy with staff who are experiencing problems. Non-unionism is likely, although if unions do make an approach they are ignored, or tolerated provided they are not seen as problematic. If a specialist P&D function exists, it is likely to be slim, and have little influence within the enterprise.

Quality enhancement

With this option, the employer seeks to produce goods and services at the highest quality possible, and aims to differentiate itself from the rest of the market on this basis. The P&D implications of this competitive strategy are almost entirely the opposite of those outlined above, and are likely to resonate with 'best practice' human resource management: carefully controlled recruitment and selection; comprehensive induction programmes; empowerment and high-discretion jobs; high levels of employee involvement; extensive and continuous training and development; harmonisation; highly competitive pay and benefits packages; a key role for performance appraisal. There is no mention of unions in the Schuler model, but if they are recognised it is probable that both parties would be keen on maintaining co-operative relations. The human resource function is likely to be well-developed, well-staffed, and highly proactive in helping to shape organisational cultures and change programmes. Close co-operation between human resource and line managers might help to achieve and sustain competitive advantage.

Innovation

Here, groups of highly trained specialists work closely together to design and produce complex and rapidly-changing/adaptable products and services to stay ahead of the competition. The consequences for P&D policies are similar in some respects to the quality enhancement model outlined above, but there is much greater emphasis on informality, problem-solving groups, a commitment to broad and loosely-defined goals, and flexibility. Employee development is likely to be seen as a personal responsibility rather than the employer's obligation, basic pay rates may be low but access to share ownership schemes enables employees to link their fortunes to that of the employer. Again, Schuler does not mention unions, but given the emphasis on individualism, they are unlikely to figure prominently in the organisation.

Miles and Snow

Miles and Snow (1978) identify three effective types of strategic behaviour, associated organisational characteristics and human resource strategies: defender, prospector, analyser. In common with other contingency approaches, they view P&D strategies as downstream from business strategy, dependent upon, and supportive of, the latter. The Miles and Snow categorisation is silent on employee relations issues, in common with a number of other contributions from the USA, but in addition it does not provide clues as to how the P&D function might be organised. Legge (1995: 107–112) provides more detail on this categorisation.

Defender

A defender strategy is characterised by features such as a narrow and stable product market range, a centralised organisation structure, and high-volume low-cost production. The basic human resource strategy flowing from this is 'building', that is, having few ports of entry into the internal labour market, promoting from within, undertaking extensive training programmes, and a reward system which is geared up to internal consistency above all else. Building an extensive and relatively open internal labour market helps to engender employee commitment to organisational goals, and a willingness to undertake tasks which are not constrained by narrow job boundaries.

Prospector

The prospector strategy is built upon change and adaptability, on redesigning product lines, and on growth by moving into new markets, seeking to be at the forefront of developments and opportunities. Given that the employer is not likely to hold sufficient expertise in-house, the basic human resource strategy is one of acquisition and 'buying-in' staff. This means a focus on sophisticated recruitment policies at all levels, with a wide use of psychometric tests to identify and select individuals who can display skills which are highly relevant for the organisation. Reward systems are likely to be results-oriented, short-term in nature and related to specific divisions (product or geographical) of the organisation. Training and development is likely to be targeted at specific problems faced by the employer.

Analyser
The final strategy represents a mix of the other two, and as such the human resource implications are more diverse or mixed depending upon the specific business context. These employers 'allocate' human resources, with a mixture of 'make or buy' decisions, an investment in training which depends upon the situation, and compensation policies which are sensitive both to internal relativities and external comparisons.

> Which of these categorisations makes most sense to you given your own experiences in P&D? Do you see overlaps between these different contingency models? If so, what are these?

There are obvious similarities between some of these contingency models, and parallels may be drawn between P&D practices in some of the different categorisations; for example, between the wildcat and the start-up, or between the star and the quality enhancement strategy. There are also some serious limitations to the models as a whole. First, each of them is deterministic, assuming that it is possible to 'read off' a preferred human resource strategy from a knowledge of business strategy. There are several problems with this assumption. Many organisations do not have clear business strategies, so it is impossible to claim that there are links between them (if they do not exist) and the management of P&D. In addition, the contingency approaches adopt the classical perspective on strategy, in which logical, rational decision-making takes place in an ordered and sequential manner between non-political actors; as we have already seen, such an assumption is unrealistic. Moreover, these models are normative, relying on 'what ought to be' rather than 'what is', resting upon assumptions that there is always one best way to run businesses and manage people in particular situations.

The second problem is that the approaches are all rather static and stylised, not focusing on the processes involved. Evidence suggests that, for example, organisations do not travel in the direction indicated by the lifecycle model, but instead move through a series of recurrent crises as they grow and develop (Legge, 1995: 115). Assumptions also tend to be made about the size, shape and structure of organisations in each of the phases and categories, such that a wildcat is typically seen as akin to a start-up organisation, while a cash cow is often viewed as a long-standing well-known company. The categorisation of 'real' organisations can also be difficult, as Crawshaw *et al* (1994) have shown with their analysis of Sainsbury's; 'good food costs less' implies that the company is stuck in the middle, neither a quality enhancer nor a cost reducer.

The third problem is empirical. There is little evidence to support the notion that links exist between business strategy and P&D, except at a very general level in terms of contrasts between a research-led pharmaceutical company and a service-oriented fast-food chain. The differences in P&D practices between these two types of organisation may be apparent to most observers, but it is more problematic to assess differences between two organisations in separate segments of the same broad product market. It is also difficult to explain the mix of human resource policies within a large, diversified M-form company, since some may appear inappropriate for certain businesses while being in line with those for others; this gets us into questions about how decisions about P&D are made in large organisations, and the choices made about the balance between centralisation and decentralisation (Purcell and Ahlstrand, 1994). This is also relevant to our discussion about horizontal integration in the next chapter, in that even though there may be a broad philosophy which is consistent with business strategy, there may still be contradictions between different elements of P&D practice.

On the other hand, these models are useful for at least two sets of reasons, especially if they are used as a tool for *guidance* rather than a technique for reading off the approach to be adopted. First, each model attempts to predict appropriate human resource strategies from an analysis of business strategies, and at the polar extremes this may fit quite well; for example, it is possible to explain why many British manufacturing companies which had not moved out of mature markets suffered so badly in the 1980s, with such disastrous consequences for the people employed there at the time. Equally, it is easy to correlate the human resource activities of new firms with the wildcat or start-up business strategies. In short, it causes us to question the prescription that all employers should adopt 'best practice' P&D policies irrespective of their market fortunes or business strategies. Second, these kinds of analysis lead P&D practitioners to think more carefully about how they might usefully contribute towards the business, and in particular frame proposals in ways which might be appealing to senior line managers. The case for a new human resource initiative, say in employee development or reward management, might be more persuasive if it is seen to 'fit' with business strategy and conform with the criteria used by senior management – 'conformist innovation' as Legge (1978) termed it.

> Take one of the models we have discussed above, and apply this to a) two different organisations of your choice in different markets, and b) two in the same market. You will obviously need to find sufficient information to enable this to be done, so find published material or talk with other course members about their organisations.

CONVERTING STRATEGY INTO PRACTICE: BLOCKAGES AND BARRIERS

Much of the management literature is based on unitarist principles and classical versions of strategy. It thus presupposes an unproblematic conversion of strategy into practice, and that managers merely need to find the most appropriate methods to put their ideas into effect; the focus tends to be on the tools and techniques rather than on values and behaviour. Once the plans have been laid, so the argument goes, individual managers from different functions and departments willingly follow the senior management line to help achieve higher levels of productivity and efficiency. However, if we reject such superficial assumptions about organisational life, it is then possible to appreciate the possibilities that exist to prevent senior management strategies being operationalised. In this section, we consider the blockages and barriers inherent *within* management circles alone, rather than on relations between management and employees or trade unions which are covered in Chapters 11–13.

The distinction which Brewster *et al* (1983) make between espoused and operational policies represents a useful starting-point for this discussion. Espoused policy is a 'summation of the proposals, objectives and standards that top-level management hold and/or state they hold for establishing the organisation's approach to its employees' (1983: 63). These may or may not be committed to paper, and in many cases are little more than broad philosophical statements about how senior management feel towards staff – such as those within a mission statement, for example about 'employees being a key and valued resource'. Obviously, the phraseology used in these documents is very general, and is capable of interpretation in different ways depending on the circumstances. In contrast, operational policy describes 'the way senior management are seen to *order* industrial relations (and human resource) priorities *vis-à-vis* those of other policies' (1983: 64). This may well be done subconsciously, as well as with intent, since it is reflected in managerial value systems and is clearly moulded by the issues which confront them on a day-to-day basis. If two policies are seen to be in conflict – say, a commitment to healthy and safe ways of working, and a desire to be customer-responsive – then, it is argued, the human resource policies are those which tend to take a lower priority. Brewster *et al* (1983) provide various examples from different industries which illustrate the way in which espoused policies are ignored, amended or ranked in the face of conflicting pressures on organisations.

In order to put strategies into effect, 'champions' are required within organisations; these are managers who have the energy and the ability to lead new initiatives, to ensure that others are persuaded of their value, and are prepared to commit themselves to embedding strategies on the shop floor or in the office. By their nature, however, champions tend to be mobile and career-oriented, often moving to new positions soon after introducing fresh initiatives. As Ahlstrand (1990: 23) notes, in relation to productivity deals at Esso's Fawley refinery, each initiative received a high-profile launch and commanded powerful symbolic significance within the company. The champions made great use of what Barlow (1989) calls 'impression management', making their activities visible to more senior managers, with the result that they were often promoted soon after implementing a new deal. In short, soon after making an impression, champions move on to another post, either inside or outside of the organisation. Those left with responsibility for continuing to progress the new strategies and ideas feel little ownership of them, are less committed to making them work, and in any event want to introduce their own ideas in order to gain promotion themselves. A cycle is set in motion, with the inevitable consequence of fads and fashions, cynicism, and short-termism (Marchington *et al*, 1993).

> Which of the following statements do you support?
>
> a) 'champions are necessary to achieve organisational change'
>
> b) 'champions are ultimately the major cause of failures to achieve change in organisations'
>
> Review the arguments in favour of and against both of these statements.

Conflicts and contradictions can occur within management both on a hierarchical and a functional basis. In this chapter we deal with the former, given that this relates to questions of vertical integration; the latter, interdepartmental conflicts, is dealt with in Chapter 18 as part of the discussion about horizontal integration and links between line managers and their P&D colleagues. Broadly, there are five separate sets of reasons why vertical integration is so difficult to achieve in practice.

First, many middle managers and supervisors do not identify closely with the goals of the employer, but instead view themselves as distinct from senior management. There are several parts to this argument. Scase and Goffee's (1989: 186) conceptualisation of 'reluctant managers' sees persisting class divisions within British employing organisations as the reason why supervisors fail to share senior management views. First line managers might feel that they have escaped from the working class, but are not accepted into the managerial class, to some extent stuck in the middle (Partridge, 1989) and unable or unwilling to align themselves either with workers or managers. They may also have doubts about the validity of senior management's ideas, especially those philosophies which espouse employee involvement and use the language of 'resourceful humans', regarding attempts to empower workers as akin to soft management (Marchington *et al*, 1993: 572). Klein (1984: 90) also notes that supervisors resist employee involvement for a variety of reasons, including a view among some that 'employees are children not adults.' Supervisors also doubt the sincerity of support from senior management, an anxiety which is fuelled as their own job security is lessened and they find little attempt to 'involve' *them* in management decisions.

Feelings of role ambiguity and insecurity have been reinforced by events of the past decade which have seen large numbers of supervisors and middle managers lose their jobs or find that their existing skills are increasingly irrelevant for modern organisational needs. Scase and Goffee (1989: 182) found that middle and junior managers were investing less in their jobs and careers, and getting much more enjoyment and fulfilment out of their leisure and domestic activities. Their ultimate conclusion makes depressing reading for those who believe that vertical integration will be easy to achieve: 'corporations may succeed in cultivating "cultures of excellence" and introducing more flexible organisational forms, but predominant practice in Britain will tend, we suspect, to lead mainly to the *compliance* of reluctant managers' (Scase and Goffee, 1989: 191).

A second constraint on the achievement of vertical integration is that line managers and supervisors are already suffering from work overload, conflicting requirements from senior management, and a lack of explicit rewards for undertaking the human resource aspects of their jobs. Like most other staff, supervisors are being asked to take on extra duties, and are finding it difficult to squeeze yet more into their working hours; as we noted above, in the ranking of operational (as opposed to esoused) priorities, P&D issues come lower down the list than production or customer-focused objectives. It is hardly surprising if line managers concentrate on the achievement of targets which they know will be used to assess their performance at appraisal (for example, meeting production deadlines, having zero defects, or reducing queue lengths) rather than on the regularity of team briefings, opportunities for their staff to engage in self-development, or levels of absenteeism. First line managers pick up signals from their more senior colleagues about the ordering of priorities irrespective of what is contained within the formal mission statement and, understandably, aim to meet these demands rather than more ephemeral, 'soft' human resource goals. In other words, the heavier the work load, the more difficult it is for line managers to satisfy P&D needs; as we shall see in the next chapter, the trend towards greater line management ownership of these topics raises serious concerns about how professional, legal and ethical standards will be maintained.

The lack of training typically provided for line managers and supervisors leads to the third obstacle which prevents the conversion of strategy into practice. Given the prominence which is accorded in mission statements to 'investing in employees', it might be expected that considerable time and effort would be expended on training and development. The reality, however, is rather different, and in practice employee relations training is not a key priority for line managers. Yet more worrying is the feeling that line managers and supervisors may not be sufficiently competent to cope with the responsibilities required to lead change programmes in the workplace (Cunningham and Hyman, 1995). Too often, it would appear, insufficient time is allocated to the training of first line managers because senior managements aim to implement new initiatives with a minimum of delay. This has been particularly apparent from our own studies of employee involvement; training in how to run a quality circle, for example, could consist of little more than a half-hour session on 'how not to communicate' followed by an amusing video illustrating how things went wrong elsewhere. Occasionally, a speaker may be invited from another organisation to explain their approach and answer questions, but there is little attempt to give supervisors the chance to practise their skills (Marchington *et al*, 1993: 573).

A fourth problem is that supervisors do not see any value in being constrained by instructions from senior managers, but wish to retain some flexibility to bend rules at the workplace. This aspect of behaviour – termed 'management commission' by Brown (1973) – allows supervisors to vary the application of rules, to provide themselves with leeway so as to reward, ignore or discipline workers on a selective basis. This can work both to reinforce managerial control over recalcitrant employees, as well as to show leniency or provide a negotiating counter in cases where it is deemed appropriate. This notion of 'deal-making' (Klein, 1984) gives supervisors discretion in handling employees, by allowing staff some flexibility (say, in taking time off) in return for an expectation that they will work harder or stay later in order to complete a rush job. In a sense, this allows supervisors to retain some control over the wage-effort bargain as well as reinforcing their position at the workplace if they are seen as independent from the more oppressive face of management. We noted examples of this in Chapter 11 – the whistling forelady (Armstrong *et al*, 1981: 87) and the three-minute rule (Terry, 1977: 80) – both of which showed the way in which supervisors bent formal rules in return for co-operation on the shopfloor. In these cases, it is apparent that managements can gain from a degree of rule-bending, but this can also work to the detriment of their plans or policies, such as when unacceptable precedents are set in relation to disciplinary issues, or custom and practice is established which detracts from worker performance or customer service.

The final reason why it is so difficult to convert strategy into practice is that managers may be unaware that they are breaking or not following organisational rules, and in the process creating precedents which may run counter to employer goals: Brown terms this 'management by omission'. In these situations, first line managers may not be aware that rules are being broken, as in the case of workers who appear to comply with health and safety instructions, but deliberately flout them when the supervisor is elsewhere. Equally, senior managers may agree to requests from staff which run counter to what has been allowed previously by the departmental manager, so creating awkward precedents. This is particularly problematic in the employee relations area when an agreement in one department may be used as a bargaining counter by workers elsewhere in efforts to improve their pay and conditions. What makes acts of omission so hard to manage is that they are often not noticed until a later date, such as when they are being used to strengthen an employee case against disciplinary action.

> Some might see this discussion as being unduly pessimistic, in its assumption that supervisors are unlikely to support management actions. Can you come to a more optimistic conclusion?

THE PERSONNEL AND DEVELOPMENT CONTRIBUTION TO BUSINESS STRATEGY

So far in this chapter we have analysed the impact of business strategy on P&D policies and practices, concluding that there are many barriers which prevent clear links being made between them. In this section we examine the linkage in the opposite direction, namely the degree to which broad business strategies *reflect* human resource considerations, either in general or through the presence of a specialist P&D function. Once again, the exhortations are made repeatedly, usually supported by anecdotes or case studies from specific organisations; Prahalad (1995), for example, writes about how 'human resources can help to win the future', and how at the moment the most under-leveraged skill in organisations is their staff. Colclough (1983), in her prize-winning essay to the IPM that year, argues that the challenge is 'how to build human resource management into corporate strategy' and asserts that business plans *must* include proper consideration of all the people issues. This can be achieved by drawing the function more into the general management of the business so that 'personnel issues are not seen as peripheral but at the core of the organisation, the heart through which the organisation lives.' All the proponents believe that the P&D function must be fully integrated with the rest of the management team, at whatever level is appropriate. More recently, Sadler (1995: 163) offers a statement specifying the key purpose of a human resource director: 'to ensure that people issues are taken fully into account in all the board's considerations, and specifically that they are given full weight in the determination of the company's objectives; and to provide leadership in all aspects of human resource management.' According to this scenario, the P&D function should be responsible for the propagation of the organisational mission and its ethical stance among other things.

There is little in any of these assertions with which P&D specialists would disagree, and indeed most of them we would applaud. Unfortunately, there are doubts about the extent to which these pleas for a major human resource role in strategic decision-making is achieved in practice. The 1990 Workplace Company-Level Industrial Relations Survey results on large firms – those employing more than 1,000 staff – shows that just 30 per cent had a full-time director of personnel (or related specialism such as industrial relations or training and development). Among foreign-owned companies, the figure was rather higher, at over 50 per cent of all firms, but even so, there are many large organisations which do not have a specialist presence on the board. The proportion of smaller organisations without a full-time specialist on the board is even higher, of course.

There is evidence that having a specialist on the board increases the likelihood that people-management issues will be considered in the formulation of strategic plans (Purcell, 1994), while without a presence these issues are more likely to be sidelined or inadequately discussed. What tends to happen in this case is that P&D professionals are involved in decisions about how to implement policies which have already been agreed (Purcell and Ahlstrand, 1994: 59). This leads them to suggest that P&D practitioners do what they are *allowed* by the board to do. In practice, this means that denying P&D access to strategic decision-making effectively relegates their involvement to fire fighting, sorting out problems once they have arisen; perhaps this accounts for the common perception that P&D professionals are negative and constraining, too often seen as preventing line managers from getting on with their jobs. Drawing upon his long experience with IBM and the NHS, Peach (1989: 38) offers an interesting perspective on this role; he sees, among other things, a strategic P&D function acting as a device to dampen down the oscillations in line management actions. When demand is buoyant, he notes that line managers want to offer above-average pay increases in order to keep production going and avoid disruption, whereas when times are tight they want to get rid of unions. Personnel directors act to prevent wild swings in behaviour and their natural reaction is 'towards the centre'.

It could be argued, of course, that P&D issues do receive consideration even if there is no specialist presence on the board. Indeed, one of the major problems which P&D practitioners face is that all managers regard themselves as experts in people-management, and are therefore reluctant to accept advice from what they see as a support function. While it is true that line managers have plenty of practice at managing people, this is not to say that they are necessarily good at it, nor are they always aware of the implications of their actions. Equally, as we saw earlier in the chapter, human resource issues assume a lower level of priority than many of their other tasks at work, in particular those concerned with meeting short-run production or customer service targets.

Drawing on case study work and accounts by managers themselves, Marchington and Parker (1990: 50–57) have summarised the diverse set of perspectives on whether or not human resource issues are taken into consideration in the determination of business plans. The most common view, already covered in the section on contingency approaches to P&D, sees human resource considerations as downstream from business strategy, a factor of secondary and operational importance. Although this reflects conventional wisdom about the linkage, this is not the sole perspective on the matter. First, some would argue that human resource considerations receive similar attention to other issues, underpinned by an ethos of balanced and competing interests (Fidler, 1981). In much the same way that mission statements specify the employer's obligations and commitment to a range of different interest groups, this perspective places similar emphasis on employee satisfaction as it does on customer service and returns to shareholders. The second view is that human resource considerations are of variable importance, depending upon the issues at hand, becoming more central to management thinking at times of crisis or over decisions about where to locate new plants. This finds support from Peter Wickens' account (1987: 127) of Nissan's decision to locate in the north-east of England. A third view argues that human resource considerations (especially the need for labour control) are implicit in management belief systems, expressed in statements by directors concerning their expectations that their firms would run smoothly and without trouble, that order would be maintained (Winkler, 1974). To ask senior managers whether or not they took explicit account of human resource considerations in decision-making would be to pose the wrong question since such views are so ingrained in their thinking about the world's natural order.

Turning specifically to the contribution which P&D *professionals* (as opposed to P&D issues) can make to business strategies, a number of points emerge. On the basis of his discussions with thirty leading employers drawn from industries such as chemicals and pharmaceuticals, retailing, leisure and hotels, engineering, and utilities, Tyson (1995: 97–102) notes three which are of particular importance: management development, given its key role as a lever to change or reinforce management philosophy, its future orientation, and its visibility; employee relations, given its centrality to issues concerning employee commitment and communications, reward policies, and choices of bargaining levels; and organisation development, due to the part it plays in corporate change programmes, especially those which seek to promote new values and approaches to work relations. Of course, there are many other areas where P&D practitioners can make a contribution that is particularly helpful to line managers in their pursuit of organisational objectives; for example, in human resource planning, recruitment and selection, induction, discipline and dismissal, grievance handling, appraisal, and training for all categories of staff. The trouble with many of these issues, however, is that the impact of the specialist contribution is often hard to quantify in financial terms, and too often the intervention is not what the line manager wanted: for example, when the P&D specialist is asking for an advertisement to be redrafted to reflect the company's equal opportunities policy, or when he or she is urging caution about a disciplinary warning because the evidence is not substantial enough, or when line managers are being reminded about their appraisal interviews. Moreover, given that line managers need to 'own' these issues, great care has to be taken to ensure that their commitment to action is gained; this is a topic to which we return in the next chapter.

> Identify the contribution which you make in your own job to the achievement of line managers' goals. Do not merely list all the activities you undertake, but try to evaluate how this satisfies their needs, the improvements it makes to how they do their jobs, and what decisions they might make without your contribution. Do line managers see you as a positive or a negative force?

The contribution that human resource professionals can make is not restricted solely to issues which are defined primarily as in the people-management field. Marchington *et al* (1993) analysed quality management initiatives in fifteen organisations drawn from the public and private sectors in order to identify the ways in which the P&D function had made a contribution to these programmes. The contribution was apparent at four different phases: in the *shaping* of TQM initiatives through benchmarking, helping to choose consultants, ensuring fit with existing organisational cultures, and in management development; in the *introductory* phase through the facilitation of change processes, communication of key principles and points, training of coaches and team members, and assisting with the development of mission statements; in *reinforcing* quality management through continued communications, redesigning appraisal and pay schemes, teamworking skills, and non-financial recognition and rewards; finally, at the *review* stage, when P&D practitioners could assist with annual TQM reports, prepare and administer employee attitude surveys, and help to gain external accreditation. At all stages, the human resource issues are given due prominence if there is a specialist involvement, something which cannot be guaranteed if this is devolved to line managers.

MEASURING THE CONTRIBUTION OF PERSONNEL AND DEVELOPMENT

We have noted on several occasions the distinction between P&D as a discrete function or set of activities performed by specialists, and P&D as an integral part of every line manager's job. Sometimes, in trying to evaluate the impact of human resource issues on organisational performance, this distinction is ignored, or the ambiguity causes problems in our attempts to assess whether or not P&D adds value. It also helps to explain why human resource specialists are so fond of navel-gazing and questioning the value of their contribution to organisational goals, in a way which does not appear to concern other specialist functions. Guest and Hoque (1994b) suggest three reasons why this might be the case. First, the history and emergence of the profession has always put it in an ambiguous position (welfare or efficiency, intermediary or managerial control function, for example), and with a slimming down of most organisations questions are raised about the need for a separate specialist P&D function, either at headquarters or at the workplace. Second, an ambivalence towards P&D issues is created and reinforced by a UK national culture which puts a primacy on financial control and short-termism to the neglect of longer-term human resource development considerations (P. Armstrong, 1989: 164). Third, the contribution of human resource specialists has always been hard to identify because they work closely with line managers and are dependent on the latter to put systems and policies into effect. Consequently, although 'we may be able to identify the impact of personnel decisions, we cannot always be sure whether the personnel specialists contributed towards them' (Guest and Hoque, 1994b: 41). In other words, while P&D specialists may have set the philosophy and the framework for human resource issues in the organisation, they are ultimately dependent on line managers to put these into effect; on many occasions the negative perceptions about human resource issues may have less to do with the policies themselves than with the way in which line managers have chosen to implement or disregard them.

Of course, this has not prevented analysts from attempting to evaluate the impact of the P&D function, and in many cases this has been seen in negative terms. This is given support by quotes such as Skinner's 'big hat, no cattle' as a way of describing the personnel function (Guest, 1991). In Britain, Fernie, Metcalf and Woodland, (1994: 12) analysed the 1990 WIRS database to come to the conclusion that 'workplaces with a personnel specialist and/or director responsible for personnel matters have very much worse relations than those without such workplace or board specialists.'

> Before reading on, imagine that your general manager has just read
> about this finding and asked for your opinion. How would you respond?

Detailed analysis of this work reveals severe methodological and conceptual problems with the research of Fernie et al. Their dependent variable – employee relations climate – was constructed from responses from the person responsible for personnel matters at the workplace. Responses were made on a seven-point scale, ranging from very good (1), good (3), poor (5) to very poor (7). All but 7 per cent of the sample rated the employee relations climate at their workplace as good or better, with only 2 per cent considering it to be poor or very poor. Notwithstanding this, Fernie et al still decided to differentiate between points 1–3 on the scale, even though conceptually there is little to choose between them, and then developed their argument around differences between the responses of personnel specialists and non-specialists; in 20 per cent of cases, a personnel specialist was present at the workplace, whereas in 25 per cent there was a director responsible for personnel affairs. To argue that because personnel specialists were more likely to rate the climate as good as opposed to very good, this is a sign that relations are *very much worse* is clearly nonsense. Given their propensity for self-criticism, it is also likely that P&D specialists are more likely to veer away from extreme assessments such as 'very good', in favour of 'good'. There are also problems of causality as well; while Fernie et al are convinced that the presence of personnel specialists has caused worse employee relations, it is more likely that P&D specialists have been appointed in order to try to solve these problems (Tyson, 1995: 164).

Guest and Hoque (1994b) also reckon that this research displays a conceptual misunderstanding of how the P&D contribution can be evaluated. As we have seen already, although policies may be developed by specialists, responsibility for operationalising them resides with line managers, and it is unreasonable to assess the P&D contribution by using measures over which specialists have little or no control. They feel it is more appropriate to expect a link between the presence of P&D specialists and the existence of sound human resource policies, as well as a link between the latter and better performance. In short, Guest and Hoque (1994b: 44) believe that the key is effective strategic integration. This means a fit between personnel and business strategies, a set of complementary P&D policies and practices, and a group of line managers who are sufficiently aligned with the P&D philosophy to implement the practices. In terms of the IPD standards, this means vertical integration, horizontal integration, and the gaining of line management commitment to P&D policies and practices.

In another article, based upon an analysis of over 250 separate units within the National Health Service, Guest and Peccei (1994: 224) argue that the best way to assess the effectiveness of HRM and human resource specialists is to ask key stakeholders in the organisation for their assessment. Rather than relying on quantitative measures which may be inappropriate because they are susceptible to influences other than P&D, both within and outside the workplace, this measure reflects the interpretations placed on performance and outcomes by those that matter at the top of the organisation. In some cases, as we shall see in the next chapter, P&D specialists may occupy a high-profile role within the organisation, overtly influencing and guiding the philosophy through an architect or change-agent role. In others, the role may be more discreet, taking place behind the scenes, working closely with the chief executive, influencing him or her, acting as a sounding-board for policy development, or in what is seen as a neutral, cabinet office presence, a hidden persuader. Being a 'power behind the throne' may prove very effective in terms of the contribution to broader business direction, but ultimately it is a precarious role since it is so dependent upon continued support from the chief executive.

There are now several publications which appear to focus on the contribution that P&D can make to bottom-line performance, but each of these tends to focus on *process* issues rather than providing quantitative measures or support for the value of good human resource practices. Tyson and Fell (1986: 90) asked 20 senior personnel specialists to describe the criteria which they felt were used by various stakeholders in the organisation to evaluate their performance. The board, it was felt, reckoned that personnel specialists should:

• be able to sell themselves to management

• have an appreciation of the business

• control personnel costs

• create high-quality manpower resources.

These fit well with Mayo's (1995: 263) scale of human resource credibility, which combines professional expertise with business expertise; the higher that individuals are on both of these axes the more effective their contribution to organisational performance. Similarly, Michael Armstrong (1989: 195–197) argues that, in order to have an impact on the bottom line, the personnel function should take a strategic view of their contribution, aiming to shape the culture and values of the organisation. These 'soft' goals include the following: fostering a performance-oriented environment; stimulating creativity; developing a unified vision of the enterprise; articulating the agenda for change; creating task forces; understanding that people create added value; taking steps to develop flexible working, and so on. While these are all worthy objectives, they are not quantifiable, and thereby run the risk of being seen as vague and imprecise, subject to the criticism that 'performance which cannot be measured, cannot be improved'.

But how can P&D professionals produce measures of effectiveness, given the notoriously difficult problem of assessing their contribution to organisational goals, other than through line managers? Several options are available. First, use can be made of benchmarking exercises through industry clubs, consultants and employers' organisations. One such process, entitled APAC (the audit of personnel activities and costs), is described by Burn and Thompson (1993). This adopts a three-tier approach to assessing the performance of the human resource function. Module one gathers fundamental information about the operation of the department, corporate statistics and cost effectiveness; this can then be compared with organisations of similar size and type in the APAC database. The second module focuses on application, by assessing reactions to the personnel service provided, and the needs of users. The final module recognises the need for professionalism by auditing policies and procedures against legal regulations and codes of practice. The data are broken down into a series of main human resource functions (for example, staffing, employee relations, development, rewards) against which user-satisfaction is assessed (for example, service delivery, communications, professionalism, value). A number of key statistics are produced for benchmarking, which include the following from the complete database, and which are obviously subject to considerable variation between organisations (see Mayo, 1995: 248 for figures):

- ratio of P&D staff to full-time employees   1:95
- costs of P&D function as a percentage of total costs   1.7%
- recruitment costs per new recruit   £950
- training costs per employee per annum   £207
- average days lost per annum through absenteeism   3.8
- labour turnover   15%

> How does your organisation compare with these figures? How can you explain differences between the situation at your organisation and the average?

A second option is to draw up service-level agreements, something which is becoming increasingly common for P&D functions in devolved organisations where local financial accountability is required. These can cover a whole range of aspects of P&D, providing agreements on such matters as payroll management, recruitment advertising, induction, and personnel information systems. According to Mayo (1995: 249), these offer a number of advantages to employers, not least in enabling a more specific statement of service provision which can facilitate auditing, benchmarking, and out-sourcing decisions to be made. There are also dangers with this approach, as the P&D function may find that in trying to satisfy the needs of internal customers it becomes the servant of other functions, sometimes being forced to make agreements which are known to be problematic, especially in the longer term. In short, what is seen as core personnel and development activity is *defined by line managers* rather than being informed by a strong sense of professional judgement. This has major drawbacks because the need to satisfy short-term cost-effectiveness is given prominence without any consideration of the problems which may be created in the longer run.

As part of a service-level agreement, the human resource function can apply TQM processes to a review of its own activities. The precise list of practices obviously depends on the organisation and function involved, but some of the more typical might be:

- undertaking a departmental purpose analysis of the P&D function's contribution to the organisation

- preparing offer and contract letters within a specified time

- advising staff on their terms and conditions of employment

- evaluating training provision on an annual basis

- preparing and disseminating absence and labour turnover data to line managers on a monthly basis

- providing advice on disciplinary matters within a specified and agreed time period.

It is not assumed that the more of these that are undertaken the better. Indeed, going down this route might result in poorer performance because resources are spread too thinly, or the P&D function comes to be seen as the purveyor of the latest fads and fashions which are irrelevant for organisational needs. The key question must be how the function can continually improve its contribution to organisational success. In research carried out for the IPD by Marchington, Wilkinson and Dale (1993b), several organisations made some attempt to draw up and publicise targets or standards for the delivery of HR practices to internal customers, but the most comprehensive was at a company codenamed Software Ltd. This firm gained ISO 9000 System Series Registration in the late 1980s, and quality was embedded into the organisational culture. In 1991, the human resource function produced its own 'simple quality targets of Personnel Products and Services' after discussions with a 'selection of customers'. The overall objective of the function at Software Ltd is to 'provide services for obtaining and maintaining a productive workforce for the group, through the provision of employment policies, services and information for directors, managers and staff; and by liaising, on employment matters, with outside training, recruitment and statutory bodies.' Examples of the products and services provided are shown in Table 18.

A third option, outlined in some detail by Fair (1992), is to generate a series of ratios which can be used to assess the P&D contribution. Adopting accounting conventions, and applying these to human resource activities, brings up a series of measures for practices such as absenteeism, labour turnover, wastage and replacement, selection and assessment, training and reskilling, remuneration and benefits, flexibility, and organisational restructuring. When applied to decisions about out-sourcing, for example, he demonstrates that a shift from employed status to freelance worker can provide significant financial gains for the employer and the individual concerned. Obviously, there are other disadvantages to employing staff on a contract basis – especially in generating commitment to organisational goals – but Fair (1992: 113) argues that the establishment of ratios provides P&D

Table 18 Personnel products and services at Software Ltd

Item	Customer	Level
Offers and contracts	managers	within 24 hours
Administration of induction day and employment presentation	new staff	every month (if sufficient new staff)
Advisory service on all aspects of employment terms and conditions	all staff	within five working days
Advice on dismissal, disciplinary procedures, low performance, etc	managers	within 48 hours of request
Recording of all personal training carried out	quality	all supplied records on personal files
Provision of statistics reports and lists	directors; managers; outside bodies	as agreed with each request

with some form of credibility and legitimacy. As a chief executive of Motorola is reputed to have said, 'if you think training is expensive, try ignorance' (Mayo, 1995: 239).

It is important to realise that there are potential problems with this type of approach unless it is carefully implemented and monitored. By quantifying the P&D contribution, the function basically succumbs to the accountants' vision of how organisations are meant to function. As Peter Armstrong (1989: 160) cautions, 'the strategy of seeking to justify personnel work in accounting terms may cede too much to the dominant accounting culture and may also, in the end, achieve little security for the personnel function'. The use of figures and ratios to measure the P&D contribution might even make it easier for the

> Talk with your colleagues on the course or at the local IPD branch about the use of ratios and service-level agreements. Find out whether the advantages outweigh the disadvantages, and why/why not.

function to be sub-contracted once it becomes known precisely what P&D does and how much it costs (Wilkinson and Marchington, 1994).

CONCLUSION

Many leading commentators argue that an effective linkage between broad business strategies and the practice of P&D is a key factor in the achievement of organisational success. Indeed, management gurus such as Pralahad see the management of an organisation's human resources as the *only* factor which will in the future distinguish the better performers from the rest of the market. In this chapter we reviewed material on this linkage, which we have termed 'vertical integration' in the IPD professional standards. While there are models which can be employed to engineer this linkage (for example, the contingency models outlined in the chapter) and many assertions that vertical integration is crucial to organisational success, the empirical evidence suggests that it is rarely achieved in practice. There are several reasons for this: supervisors and line managers emphasise the attainment of goals other than those relating to human resources; there is only a minority of boards which have a place for a specialist P&D presence, even in larger organisations; it is very difficult, and some would say foolhardy, to measure the P&D contribution to organisational success, especially because human resource *practices* rely upon line managers for their implementation; the British business culture is dominated by accountants and their conventions, as well as being driven by short-term financial considerations, both of which make it difficult to sustain arguments based upon the need to gain long-term and deeply-embedded employee commitment.

But if they are serious about the contribution which the effective management of human resources can make to organisational success, it is up to P&D professionals to demonstrate that they can make a positive impact. The ability to analyse the environmental context, understand the nature of broad organisational strategies, and make recommendations about the most appropriate mix of human resource policies and practices, all help the P&D specialist to gain legitimacy. So too does an understanding of how P&D practices fit together and support each other; this issue – horizontal integration – is the subject of the next chapter.

USEFUL READING

ARMSTRONG, P. (1989) 'Limits and Possibilities for HRM in the Age of Accountancy' in J. Storey (Ed.), *New Perspectives on Human Resource Management*. London, Routledge: 154–166.

BURN, D. AND THOMPSON, L. (1993) 'When personnel calls in the auditors', *Personnel Management*, January: 28–31.

FAIR, H. (1992) *Personnel and Profit: The pay-off from people*. London, IPM.

GUEST, D. AND HOQUE, K. (1994b) 'Yes, personnel does make a difference', *Personnel Management*, November: 40–44.

LEGGE, K. (1995) *Human Resource Management: Rhetorics and realities*. Chapter 4. London, Macmillan.

MARCHINGTON, M. AND PARKER, P. (1990) *Changing Patterns of Employee Relations*. Chapter 3. Hemel Hempstead, Harvester Wheatsheaf.

MAYO, A. (1995) 'Economic indicators of HRM', in S. Tyson (Ed.), *Strategic Prospects for HRM*. London, IPD: 229–265.

PURCELL, J. (1989) 'The impact of corporate strategy on human resource management', in J. Storey (Ed.), *New Perspectives on Human Resource Management*. London, Routledge: 67–91.

SCHULER, R. (1989) 'Strategic human resource management and industrial relations', *Human Relations*, Vol 42, 2: 157–184.

TYSON, S. AND FELL, A. (1986) *Evaluating the Personnel Function.* London, Hutchinson.

WHITTINGTON, R. (1993) *What is Strategy and Does it Matter?* London, Routledge.

18 The responsibility for personnel and development

INTRODUCTION

In Chapter 17 we examined the relationship between P&D and business strategy, otherwise known as vertical integration in the IPD standards. In this chapter we shift to examine *horizontal integration*; that is, the degree to which different aspects of P&D are linked together, and the allocation of responsibilities for the management of people at work. Both of these have assumed prominence in recent years as employers have sought ways in which to achieve 'competitive advantage through people' (Pfeffer, 1994), and both have been central to the continuing debate about human resource management.

For many years criticisms have been made that employers fail to co-ordinate their P&D policies and practices to ensure that employees receive consistent and unambiguous messages from management. For example, actions taken in pursuit of employee relations objectives (in order to reduce headcount) may run counter to those which are pursued in employee development (to promote a learning organisation). Similarly, policies in the area of employee reward (in terms of the predominant payment system, for example) may contradict those concerned with employee resourcing (for recruitment and selection purposes, say). In some cases the problem is exacerbated as a range of approaches are adopted by different specialists, sometimes from different functions. This has occurred in some wide-ranging change programmes which have been led by managers from personnel, corporate communications, and marketing – with consequences which are confusing to the employees on the receiving end of the messages. However, a number of recent studies (Baird and Meshoulam, 1988; Pfeffer, 1994; Huselid, 1995; Wood, 1995) have suggested that clear organisational benefits may flow from a mix of P&D practices which are internally consistent, and designed to coalesce with and support each other. The consequence of this argument is that 'best practice' P&D may be appropriate for *all* types of employing organisation, not just restricted to those which are in particular product market positions – as implied by the contingency models outlined in Chapter 17.

We have seen already in various chapters that P&D has long been engaged in debates about its legitimacy, not least because of its role as a support function and the fact that P&D specialists have often been viewed as a constraint on line managers' freedom to take action. This has come to the fore in recent years as a number of organisations have decentralised decision-making and devolved responsibility for P&D to line managers. At one level this is a beneficial move, as it locates responsibility for P&D at the point where it is most appropriate, that is at the interface between management and managed. It also provides P&D specialists with an opportunity to work more closely with line managers, offering advice and assistance about real-life issues rather than designing and monitoring what may be seen as more abstract policies and procedures. On the other hand, devolution sets some alarm bells ringing: there are worries that the numbers employed in P&D will decline sharply as line managers take more responsibility for issues traditionally dealt with by specialists; there are concerns that line managers possess neither the time nor the expertise to manage P&D in a professional and businesslike manner; moreover, there are doubts that line managers have the inclination to take P&D issues seriously, and that this will have negative implications for ethics and equal opportunities. But the P&D function has also been under threat from consultants as well, with some P&D issues being sub-contracted to external consultants as and when required. In other cases, the P&D function is re-engineered to provide an in-house consultancy service, with or without cash transfers.

Despite the appearance of broad trends such as those outlined above, it is also clear that the organisation of P&D retains a great deal of variety, and that P&D specialists occupy a wide range of roles. Many degree courses make the implicit assumption that human resource issues are strategic, that P&D specialists are able to influence policy and practice, and that change is always taking place. By way of contrast, many personnel assistants spend their time on administrative and clerical work – compiling employee records, issuing reminders about performance appraisals or training programmes, liaising with employment agencies, or generating data from computerised personnel information systems about absence levels. Similarly, the P&D issues which are paramount in one organisation or industry may be irrelevant in another, and those which assume significance in a large multinational may be unheard of in a small independent supplier. Equally, while many P&D specialists will move around between different activities during their careers – say, from training to recruitment and selection, and then to employee relations – others may remain within one broad area for all of their working lives, perhaps moving between different employers and/or between paid- and self-employment. There may be even more diversity of roles in the future as traditional linear careers become less common and individuals move between different forms of employment status and specialism.

What path have you taken into P&D, and how do you see your working life developing? Does it seem likely that you will move between different specialist areas within the P&D function, between functions, and between different forms of paid- and self-employment? Do you envisage a 'career' in P&D?

By the end of this chapter, readers should be able to:

- provide advice on the P&D roles which are most appropriate for a particular organisational context

- formulate and continuously review a statement of P&D policy and its constituent elements

- gain the support and commitment of line managers for selected P&D interventions.

In addition, readers should be able to understand and explain:

- a range of models which describe the roles that P&D specialists may occupy within employing organisations

- the meaning of 'best practice' human resource management and its core elements

- the role of internal and external consultants in the provision of P&D expertise to employers.

MODELS OF PERSONNEL AND DEVELOPMENT

There have been a number of attempts to categorise the work of the P&D function in order to analyse the variety, diversity and complexity of the role. Some writers argue that it is possible to identify *discrete* roles which may be adopted, and which are logically distinct from one another, even if tied together by a single continuum. Others regard the different categories as *cumulative*, with each role building upon the previous one, resulting in categories of increasing complexity. A further perspective suggests that individuals or departments may display *multiple* roles, such that it is possible for more than one category to be in evidence at an organisation at the same time, in relation to different issues and/or filled by different members of the function.

> How would you define the role of the P&D function – if one exists – at your organisation, or the role of the people responsible for P&D issues if there is no specialist department? How well are different aspects of P&D linked together, and do they support or undermine each other?

One of the oldest, and arguably still one of the best, models was that proposed by Karen Legge (1978) about twenty years ago. She argues that in order to gain power and influence, personnel managers needed to adopt one of a series of strategies in their work within organisations. Her first category is *conformist innovation*, in which P&D managers attempt to relate their work and efforts clearly to the dominant values and norms in the organisation, aiming simply to satisfy the requirements of senior managers; this might be seen in the areas of discipline, redundancy, and employee relations where labour costs are kept under strict control. The second category is *deviant innovation*, in which the P&D specialist subscribes to a quite different set of norms, and gains credibility and support for ideas which are not explicitly driven by organisational criteria. These can be reflective of social values (eg concerns about stress, long working hours or empowerment) or legal considerations (eg disability, race or sex equality) whose implementation might appear, at first sight at least, more costly than the adoption of short-term business values. In the 1970s, it was apparent through organisation development initiatives, and more recently with moves towards 'learning organisations'. The final category is a contingent role, that of *problem-solver*, in which the P&D contribution is seen through its ability to identify and resolve problems for the employer, and these obviously vary depending upon the situation. In order to do this effectively, the P&D specialist has to conceptualise the nature of the problem which has to be dealt with before making a diagnosis, and then propose strategies for its resolution. A contingency approach is utilised, albeit drawing upon a body of knowledge such as that developed in the IPD Professional Qualification Scheme.

An alternative classification can be found in Tyson and Fell's (1986) 'building site' analogy. P&D is divided into three models in this categorisation, differentiated along a single continuum defined by a range of internal factors; these are the decision-making approach of the top management team, the planning time adopted for P&D activities, the degree of discretion exercised by P&D specialists, and the extent to which specialists are involved in creating the organisation's culture. The model with least discretion is termed *clerk of the works*, in which all authority is vested in line managers and P&D systems are created in an *ad hoc* way. P&D work is predominantly administrative and clerical, concerned with record keeping and filing, welfare, first interviews for applicants, and maintenance of wages and salary information. The P&D specialist, if one is present, will probably not have come from a human resource background, perhaps being an engineer who now finds it difficult physically to get around the plant, or an accounts clerk. In the middle of the continuum is the *contracts manager*, a role which Tyson and Fell reckon is most likely in industries with a significant trade union presence, where systems and procedures are heavily formalised, and the underlying emphasis is on keeping things under control, trouble-shooting and fire fighting. The employee relations aspect of this model is readily apparent, although the same sorts of principles apply to employee-development activities – in terms of administering, maintaining and evaluating training programmes, for example. Once again, many of the essential people-management functions are undertaken by line managers, although there is a close relationship between them and their P&D colleagues to ensure that practice and policy are integrated. The final model, and the most sophisticated, is the *architect* which, as the name implies, is concerned with grand design at a senior level, with the integration of human resource issues into broader business plans, and with a creative and innovative approach. Under this scenario, P&D practitioners are able to influence change in the organisation and are expected to take the lead in creating the 'right' culture and philosophy for the organisation as a whole. The architect may be regarded as a business manager first and a professional P&D specialist second, and the long time horizons which characterise this role provide opportunities to build a strong senior management culture through team development exercises.

It is tempting to view the Tyson and Fell continuum as one where the P&D role assumes greater maturity as it develops from clerk of the works through contracts manager to architect; this can be applied both to individuals and to the P&D function as a whole, and it can relate to positions in the organisational hierarchy. Similarly, it might also be assumed that the architect role is best, in that it has greatest potential to effect change and influence strategy, whereas the clerk of the works is reactive and low-level administrative in orientation. Tyson and Fell (1986: 24) reject both these assumptions, however, arguing that the choice of model is contingent upon organisational circumstances, and that each of the variants may be found at each level in the hierarchy. They are clear, though, that each model is distinct from the others.

Tyson and Fell's model has been used by Monks (1993) on a sample of Irish organisations, leading her to make a number of refinements to the original categorisation. Overall she suggests that it is possible to identify four categories rather than three; in addition to the clerk of the works (traditional-administrative, in Monks' terms), contracts manager (traditional-industrial relations), and architect (innovative-sophisticated), she claims the existence of a category some way short of the architect, but not a contracts manager; this is termed the innovative-professional, and it applied to over one-third of her sample of 97 organisations. Broadly, the innovative-professional role is characterised by a dismantling of existing bureaucratic systems, while at the same time systemising training to make it more professional and relevant to line managers. These four categories are seen as a continuum running from simple to complex: traditional-administrative ... traditional-industrial relations ... innovative-professional ... innovative-sophisticated. Monks (1993: 36) also suggests that the roles are cumulative rather than discrete; in other words, in organisations where the innovative-sophisticated role is filled, each of the previous three are also utilised, in those which practise innovative-professional there is evidence of the previous two, and so on. In the simplest form, it is merely traditional-administrative. This notion of cumulation versus discrete practice is what really separates the Monks' categorisation from that of Tyson and Fell, rather than the addition of a fourth role.

Shipton and McAuley (1993) also produce a fourfold classification. Differentiating models on the basis of power (low/high) and integration (low/high), they identify a welfare model which is low on both dimensions, describing P&D functions which are traditional and paternalistic, reactive and marginal to broader organisational concerns. The administrative model is much more closely integrated into the organisation, but lacks power because essentially it operates to serve the needs of the senior management team. Shipton and McAuley (1993: 6) feel that these types of P&D function have been particularly vulnerable to dissolution and devolution in recent times. Third, there is the business manager role, which is central to organisational goals and in a position of power, perhaps typified by some of the more optimistic assessments for strategic human resource management; there is resonance here with Legge's conformist innovator. Finally, the *organisation development* role is seen as powerful but lacking in integration, although the description reads rather like Legge's deviant innovator, in that it is seen as challenging the dominant organisational culture.

A further categorisation which has been widely cited recently has been that of Storey (1992a). He proposes a fourfold 'map' based upon two cross-cutting dimensions: the degree to which P&D is strategic or tactical, and the degree to which it is interventionary or not. The former dimension is one which has characterised much work in the management area, illustrating the simple distinction between policy and practice, long- and short-term time horizons, and the level in the hierarchy at which decisions are made. The latter dimension is also well known in the literature, reflecting continuing tensions about the contribution which P&D specialists make to broader organisational decisions, and the extent to which it is possible to measure their contribution in quantitative or financial terms. The four main 'types of personnel practitioner' are as follows. *Advisers* operate at the strategic level and are non-interventionary, providing support for line managers as required, and often working behind the scenes to help shape policies and practices. As we see below, for this reason we prefer to use the Wilkinson and Marchington (1994) terminology of 'hidden persuader' to describe this sort of role. As with the other 'types', most of Storey's examples to illustrate this role are drawn from the employee relations area, and are concerned with allowing plant managers more freedom and authority at the labour-management interface during negotiations. *Handmaiden* is a particularly apt term to describe the role which is tactical and non-interventionary, predominantly led and defined by the needs of their 'customers', the line managers. Like the clerk of the works, the handmaiden is involved mainly in clerical and administrative tasks, such as maintaining absence records, and occasionally on welfare activities and being available for advice. Storey sees this group as submissive, subservient and attendant, responding to short-term requests from customers, and not seeking to change or influence the direction of the organisation; in any event, these individuals lack the power and influence to effect change anyway, and their deference to line managers reinforces their low status. To some extent they are seen as 'neutral agents' mediating the relationship between management and managed. The third type is the *regulator*, a role which is highly interventionary at the tactical level, very much operating as 'old-style' industrial relations fire fighters, working closely with shop stewards, smoothing over problems and managing any discontent which emerges on the shopfloor. As Storey notes (1992a: 176), just because their interventions are at a tactical level it does not mean that they should be misinterpreted as lacking in significance, and in some factories such a role is critical in helping to facilitate stoppage-free production. In addition, although working closely with line managers, Storey suggests that regulators maintain their independence and professionalism through a set of clear P&D goals and an ability to 'deliver the goods'. The final type is the *changemaker*, individuals who are keen to establish relationships with employees on a new footing, seeking ways in which to elicit employee commitment and encouraging staff to 'go the extra mile'. Given all the publicity which has been given to the strategic role of P&D in programmes of change management since the 1980s, it is surprising that Storey found this categorisation so rare in his sample of 'mainstream' companies: these included Rover, Ford, Jaguar, ICI, Whitbread, Plessey, Lucas, the NHS and Bradford Metropolitan Council. He also suggests (1992: 181–182) that changemakers can be proponents of either soft or hard HRM, in the former case tending to highlight the distinctive nature of the P&D contribution, while in the latter demonstrating their worth through a business manager approach.

There are some suggestions in Storey's work that P&D within a single organisation may be represented by more than one role (eg in relation to the handmaiden and contracts manager), but this is not amplified. In Marchington *et al*'s (1993b) research for the IPD on quality management and the human resource dimension, the notion of multiple roles is made much more explicit. In a categorisation which is similar to that of Storey, four types are identified differentiated along two cross-cutting dimensions of level (strategic versus operational) and profile (high versus low). These four types are change agent, hidden persuader, internal contractor, and facilitator, and they are illustrated in Figure 9 below (Wilkinson and Marchington, 1994). While this categorisation was devised initially to analyse the role of P&D practitioners in quality management, it has a wider relevance to other aspects of human resource management as well.

Figure 9 The role of personnel in TQM

The *change agent* is similar to Storey's changemaker, and is characterised by a board-level appointment (or equivalent) which is highly visible to other senior managers. In our study, interviews were conducted with managing directors, line managers, quality managers and union representatives, as well as P&D practitioners, and the view which best summed up the change agent role was the 'engine of change', providing a culture and structure in which TQM could thrive. The *hidden persuader* also operates at a strategic level, but does so in a low-profile manner, working behind the scenes providing 'cabinet office' support for the senior management team, and there are close similarities with Storey's adviser role here. The third category – *internal*

contractor – is rather different from Storey's regulator given that the latter is so closely identified with an old-style industrial relations fixer-type role. The internal contractor's main contribution is at the operational level, and we saw in the previous chapter that this is likely to become more extensive as P&D practitioners are required to demonstrate their contribution to business goals through service-level agreements and clearly laid down performance criteria. Finally, at operational level and low profile there is the *facilitator*, a traditional role whereby P&D provides support of a routine, administrative nature for line managers – in much the same way as Storey's handmaidens, though across the whole P&D arena and not just employee relations.

Perhaps the most important point about this categorisation is that it stresses that the P&D function at one site or one organisation typically plays more than one role. At each of the fifteen organisations studied by Marchington *et al* (1993b: 36), there was evidence of a facilitator role, but at only four was this the *only* role which was filled. Although there were no cases where all four categories were present, there were five organisations where three roles were occupied, and some suggestions that the P&D function had been specifically organised to allow for these multiple roles.

> Consider whether there are circumstances (internal and external to the organisation) under which certain roles are more likely than others, and whether it is possible for P&D practitioners and departments to simply 'choose' the role which suits them best.

It has to be recognised that there are dangers with each of these roles as well. The change agent, while potentially the most influential because of its high profile and strategic contribution, also runs the risk of significant costs if problems occur with any interventions. By taking such a visible role, P&D may create enemies within the organisation, and interventions therefore have to be successful in order to prevent the build-up of overt dissent from elsewhere. The problem for the hidden persuader is almost entirely the opposite of this since P&D may have been chosen by the managing director as a confidante or adviser precisely because of its assumed neutrality. In this situation, continued effectiveness is dependent upon sustained support from its champion and being seen to deliver quality services. The basic problem is that P&D may well be central to the achievement of business objectives, but other managers may be unaware of this contribution; paradoxically, publicising this role too widely can undermine its value. The facilitator suffers from a similar problem, in that the support which P&D provides to line managers (in resourcing, reward, relations or development) is often hard to evaluate and is difficult to isolate from what is typically expected of the function. Line managers do not always recall the source of any assistance from P&D. This is not a potential problem for the internal contractor, due to the very clear and public commitments which are made by the P&D function to its internal customers. However, there are also potential pitfalls with this role as well, ranging from the internal public humiliation due to a failure to meet targets through to the contracting-out of part or all of the function itself. Great care therefore needs to be taken when agreeing targets in the first place.

The contribution of the P&D function might be most difficult to define and evaluate in the case of multi-establishment M-form organisations. Purcell and Ahlstrand (1994: 107–115) identify nine roles which may help corporate personnel departments to assert their authority in an increasingly ambiguous and uncertain future. These are:

- corporate culture and communications

- essential policy formulation and monitoring

- human resource planning in strategic management

- 'cabinet office' services

- senior management development and career planning

- external advocacy, internal advice

- information co-ordination

- internal consultancy and mediation services

- personnel services for small units.

'BEST PRACTICE' PERSONNEL AND DEVELOPMENT

In the previous chapter we spent some time examining a number of contingency models which attempt to relate P&D practice to business strategy. It will be recalled that with these models an assumption was made that specific styles of human resource management were appropriate in certain circumstances and not in others; for example, soft human resource management (sometimes known as 'best practice') might be appropriate for firms which utilise high technology, have a highly-skilled workforce, make products which are sold on the basis of quality rather than low cost, and so on. More recently a contrary argument has gained currency, namely that 'best practice' HRM might facilitate improved performance for *any* organisation, at least in the long term (Pfeffer, 1994). Despite urging caution in applying his ideas too mechanistically, Pfeffer (1994: 27–29) argues that, other things being equal, the utilisation of 'best practice' P&D can lead to competitive advantage. He draws upon case study evidence in support of his assertions, but makes the valid point that not all organisations that practise this form of P&D will *inevitably* have greater success, nor will those employers who consistently ignore these practices *inevitably* be unsuccessful. Huselid (1995: 667) displays none of this caution, basing his conclusions on a study of nearly 1,000 US-owned firms. He asserts that 'the magnitude of the returns for investments in [what he calls] high performance work practices is substantial. A one standard deviation increase in such practices is associated with a 7.05 per cent decrease in labour turnover and, on a per employee basis, $27,044 more in sales and $18,641 and $3,814 more in market value and profits respectively.' The adoption of a range of 'best practice' P&D approaches in a consistent and integrated manner appears to make good business sense according to these statistics. The best-known

British studies (Storey, 1992; Wood, 1995; Wood and Albanese, 1995) have greater similarity with Pfeffer's approach, in that they do not seek to quantify the gains which can be made from 'best practice' P&D, but draw upon case study evidence or less extensive questionnaire survey results to generate their conclusions.

Between them, these authors produce lists of employment practices which should be central to any organisation claiming (and aiming) to be at the forefront of best practice. Storey (1992: 35) identifies 27 points of difference between personnel and industrial relations, and human resource management; the list is broken down into four sections (beliefs and assumptions; strategic aspects; line management; and key levers) which includes under the HRM heading aspects such as an 'aim to go beyond contract', the centrality of HRM to the corporate plan, a key role for line managers, and a low emphasis on standardisation. Under the key levers category are aspects such as integrated selection systems, performance-related pay, harmonisation, individual contracts, teamworking and learning companies. Pfeffer (1994: 30–59) provides a list of 16 (though he argues that the exact number and their precise specification are not important), which includes employment security, selectivity in recruitment, incentive pay, employee ownership, participation and empowerment, teamworking, training and skill development, wage compression and promotion from within. These are held together under an overarching philosophy with a long-term commitment and a willingness to engage in consistent measurement of whether or not high standards are being achieved. Pfeffer (1994: 27) notes 'these are interrelated practices ... that seem to characterise companies that are effective in achieving competitive success through how they manage people.' Wood's (1995: 52) list of 17 'high commitment practices' should be used together since 'it is through the combined effects of such practices that management can most hope to elicit high levels of commitment.' The piecemeal take-up of these HCPs means that many managements miss out on the benefits to be gained from a more integrated approach. Of the 17 practices, these are deemed to be most important: trainability and commitment as major selection criteria, career ladders and progression as an objective for all employees, and teamworking as the predominant system of work for production staff (Wood and Albanese, 1995: 17). To be included under Wood's categories, employers need to demonstrate not only that a policy is in existence, but also that it actually operates in practice: for example, 'training budgets set with at least a two-year financial horizon', 'quality circles which meet regularly', and 'formal assessment for production workers on an annual or bi-annual basis'. Huselid's list contains a total of 13 questions, organised under two headings; these are 'employee skills and organisational structures', and 'employee motivation', and items include information sharing, internal promotion, quality-of-work-life teams, training, selection testing, and appraisal. His questions are somewhat sharper than for the other studies, as these examples indicate:

• What is the proportion of the workforce whose jobs have been subjected to a formal analysis?

- What proportion of the workforce have access to a formal grievance procedure and/or complaint resolution system?

- What is the number of hours training received by a typical employee over the last twelve months?

- What is the proportion of the workforce whose performance appraisals are used to determine their compensation?

- What proportion of non-entry level jobs have been filled from within in recent years?

What is apparent from each study, however, is the importance of horizontal integration, the achievement of a high degree of internal 'fit' if employers are keen to gain major advantages from 'best practice' P&D. This also fits well with the idea that P&D specialists need to have a secure professional and ethical base for their activities, as we saw in Chapter 4. Although the authors do not consider this issue, it might also be the case that employers who are keen on cost reduction strategies and what might be termed 'worst practice' P&D should also aim for internal consistency and horizontal integration between different elements of their human resource practices.

Summarising these studies, it is possible to identify ten clusters of practices which might be seen in an organisation claiming to offer 'best practice' P&D. Many of these can be found in the Japanese firms that have come to Britain since the early 1980s. These are reproduced in Table 19 below, and amplified in the text.

Table 19 Best-practice personnel and development

P&D practice	Storey	Pfeffer	Wood	Huselid
Sophisticated selection	+	+	+	+
Flexibility/teamworking	+	+	+	
Internal promotion		+	+	
Employment security		+	+	
Employee involvement	+	+	+	+
Employee voice				+
Commitment to learning	+	+	+	+
Performance-related reward	+	+	+	+
Harmonisation	+	+	+	
Employee ownership	+	+	+	

How do P&D practices at your organisation compare with this list? How many of them do you have, and are any currently being implemented? Debate with colleagues the feasibility of adopting such a list of 'best practice' P&D.

Sophisticated selection

This is seen as central to 'best practice' P&D in order to recruit high-quality, committed and appropriate staff to the organisation. The use of tests and assessment centres is seen as particularly helpful in this regard. Competencies to be sought at the selection stage include trainability, flexibility, commitment, drive and persistence, and initiative. The key point about 'best practice' selection is that it should be integrated and systematic, making use of the techniques which are appropriate for the position and the organisation, and administered by individuals who have themselves been trained. It also needs to be recalled that recruitment methods need to be capable of attracting a pool of high-quality candidates, and that a comprehensive induction programme represents the final stage of successful selection. See Chapter 6 for more detail.

Flexibility/teamworking

Employees who are willing to undertake a range of tasks, irrespective of job title, in order to meet customer requirements represent the second feature of 'best practice' P&D. This may be seen in the absence of formal job descriptions or broad job grades, but it can be successful only if it operates at a level whereby *all* employees (especially managerial staff) are prepared to be flexible when needed. This is sometimes referred to as 'working beyond contract' or a 'can do' state of mind. It is exemplified by the idea that workers have two jobs: one is to do their designated task, the other is to search for continuous improvements and changes (Morton, 1994). This is further emphasised through teamworking. Some of these teams are likely to be formal and longstanding, meeting on a regular basis, whereas others may be short-lived task forces and function with leaders drawn from among their number rather than because of their position in the formal organisational hierarchy. As with all these practices, their symbolic significance is crucial. See Chapters 2 and 16.

Internal promotion

Once selected and inducted into the organisation, employees need to feel that there are opportunities for advancement, provided they possess the ability. A strong internal labour market, which rewards individuals who continue to demonstrate the competencies shown at selection, appears to result in higher levels of organisational commitment and demonstrates to employees that they are valued by the employer. See the discussions on internal labour markets in Chapters 2 and 5, as well as considerations of the learning organisation and CPD in Chapter 8.

Employment security

This is perhaps the most significant way in which employers can demonstrate to employees that they really are their 'most important resource'. Unlike some of the other 'best practices', this one has to be qualified slightly. Employment security does not mean that employees are necessarily able to stay in the same *job* for life, nor does it prevent the dismissal of staff who fail to perform to the required level. Similarly, a major collapse in the product market which necessitates reductions in the labour force should not be seen as undermining this principle. The principal point about this practice is that it asserts that job reductions will be avoided wherever possible, and that employees should expect to maintain their employment with the organisation. A key factor which facilitates the achievement of employment security is a well-devised and forward-looking system of human resource planning (see Chapter 5) and an understanding of how organisations may be structured to achieve flexibility (Chapter 2). The authors referred to above choose different ways to express this; Pfeffer regards it as part of the 'long-term perspective', while Wood includes 'a policy of no compulsory redundancy', the insulation of core workers by the appointment of temporary staff, and an expectation that *all employees* will have tenure. It is perhaps summed up best by the view that workers should not be treated as a variable cost, but rather viewed as a critical asset in the long-term viability and success of the organisation (Wilkinson *et al*, 1993).

Is it realistic to expect employers to make commitments to employment security, or is it unrealistic to expect employees to be committed to organisations without such assurances?

Employee involvement (EI)

This looms large in all the accounts of 'best practice' P&D, taking a whole range of forms in practice. EI includes: information sharing, especially through cascade or briefing sessions which take place regularly and at pre-arranged times; regular quality circles, QWL meetings, or labour-management teams such as joint consultative committees or task forces; empowerment of non-managerial staff for their own work areas, and a responsibility for their own quality control. The precise mix of EI techniques depends upon the circumstances, but a commitment to its philosophy appears to be the key factor. See Chapter 12 for further discussion.

Employee voice

Only one of the authors (Huselid) specifically mentions this practice, but it seems essential that employees should have the opportunity to express their grievances openly and independently, rather than being able to contribute solely on task-related issues. Employee voice may be achieved through trade union organisation and collective bargaining, through formally established grievance and disputes procedures, or it could be through speak-up schemes which offer employees protection if their complaints are taken badly by managers. Such a stance can be reinforced by 'symbolic egalitarianism' (Pfeffer, 1994: 48 and see 'harmonisation', below), but these are insufficient in themselves. It might also come through partnerships between employers and trade unions. See Chapters 11, 12 and 13 for more details.

Commitment to learning

This is arguably one of the most important elements of 'best practice' P&D, both in seeking to ensure continuing training and development for all employees, but also in terms of improving organisational productivity. The use of the word 'learning' is crucial as it demonstrates employer willingness to encourage and facilitate employee development rather than just providing specific training to cover short-term crises. Different types of measure can be employed to indicate best practice, ranging from fully-fledged 'learning companies' through to EDAPs, and task-based and interpersonal skills training. The time and effort put into training and development is also important, such as the number of days training received by all workers, the proportion of workers who have been trained, the budget set aside for training, or the establishment of agreed training targets over a two-year period. Chapters 3, 8, 9 and 10 deal specifically with this issue.

Performance-related reward

Although there are a number of well-known criticisms of performance-related pay, it is included in all the lists of 'best practice' outlined above. We think it is important to extend this to performance-related *reward*, since this includes other aspects of the total reward package and is not restricted to pay alone. The basic point is that employees should be rewarded, in part at least, for their contribution to organisational performance – whether this is on an individual, team, departmental, or establishment-wide basis. Pay levels may be determined following formal appraisals or they may be linked to some published measure of performance for the team or the unit. PRP is dealt with in Chapter 15, but other elements of the reward package and performance criteria are considered in Chapters 7, 14 and 16.

Employee ownership

This practice is included in three of the lists, but it is a relatively dilute form of employee ownership, typically through schemes whereby staff are allocated shares according to some predetermined formula. The argument for its inclusion in the list is summed up well by Pfeffer (1994: 38): 'employee ownership, effectively implemented, can align the interests of employees with those of shareholders by making employees shareholders too.' He also comments that firms with high shareholder-returns also often have some form of employee ownership. Share ownership is the subject of part of Chapter 15.

Harmonisation

A culture which aims to remove unnecessary status differences also appears regularly as a key component in 'best practice' P&D. This can be seen through egalitarian symbols, such as staff uniforms, shared canteen and car parking facilities, but it is also underpinned by the harmonisation of many terms and conditions of employment – such as holidays, sick-pay schemes, pensions, and hours of work. The principal point behind moves to single status and harmonisation, as we saw in Chapter 16, is that it seeks to break down artificial barriers between different groups of staff, so encouraging and supporting teamworking and flexibility.

The importance of horizontal integration, of the *interdependence* of 'best practice' P&D, cannot be stressed too much. It should be clear from the above analysis that many of these practices are linked together. For example, employees are more likely to welcome EI if their employment and future is seen as relatively secure and their workplace is seen as relatively status-free. Equally, they are more likely to show an interest in EI if their efforts are rewarded with performance-related incentives, share ownership, and access to training opportunities. Similarly, if sufficient care has been taken at the recruitment and selection stage, new recruits ought to be functionally flexible and welcome teamworking, as well as gain promotion in the future. In isolation, or without the support of a strong organisational culture, each of these practices can easily be dismissed as faddish or fashionable; only with a long-term, integrated and comprehensive philosophy do they stand any chance of success.

Drawing from this list of 'best practice' P&D, formulate a statement of personnel and development policy for your own organisation, and explain why it has been formulated in this way.

LINE MANAGERS AND PERSONNEL AND DEVELOPMENT

One of the questions which has frequently been put to PMFP students taking the Management Processes and Functions examination is to 'outline the major criticisms which line managers make about the P&D function, and respond to these criticisms'. Clearly, given the length of the answers, this is a question which has been asked of them on many occasions. Unfortunately, students tend to write significantly more on the criticisms than they usually do on the responses! The criticisms are broadly of four forms. First, P&D professionals are felt to be out of touch with commercial realities, unable to comprehend much about the nature of the business, its customers, or its broad direction. The implication is that P&D practitioners make their decisions based upon a set of principles and ideas, such as welfare or employee rights, which have little relevance for competitive prospects. Second, P&D is seen as a constraint on line managers' freedom to take the kind of action which they feel to be in the best interests of the business. Apparently line managers are particularly frustrated by legal constraints, especially in the area of equal opportunities or individual rights, or about having to negotiate and consult with union representatives. The third criticism is that P&D managers are unresponsive and slow to act, always wanting to check options thoroughly rather than being prepared to pursue a series of actions and not worrying about the consequences until later. The cautious nature of the role was probably emphasised during the 1970s and early 1980s as P&D practitioners struggled to make sense of new legislation and keep their employers out of the courts. Finally, P&D practitioners are criticised for promulgating policies which are seen as fine in theory but hard to put into effect, or inappropriate for their workplace. Employer involvement is usually a prime candidate for assault here, given that it is often viewed as idealistic and naïve, inappropriate for the people who work at their (line managers') place of work; what employees need and respect, according to this line of reasoning, is firm discipline and a heavy dose of fear. In a sense, P&D cannot win the argument because it is criticised both for being too interventionist and too remote. Watson (1986: 204) sums this up well when he states:

If personnel specialists are not passive administrative nobodies who pursue their social work, go-between and firefighting vocations with little care for business decisions and leadership, then they are clever, ambitious power-seekers who want to run organisations as a kind of self-indulgent personnel playground.

Legge (1995: 27–28) terms this problem the 'vicious circle in personnel management'. This emanates from the failure of senior management to involve P&D in mainstream decisions and planning, with the result that 'people' issues are not given sufficient attention at an early stage in the decision-making process. Problems inevitably arise with new initiatives or with routine business issues because P&D has *not* been involved – such as difficulties with poor recruits, inadequately trained staff, stoppages of work, high absence or turnover rates, or generally poor performance. At this stage, P&D is then brought in to help resolve the crisis. This results in fire fighting and short-term solutions to overcome the immediate difficulties, which in themselves merely store up trouble for the future because insufficient time is allowed to introduce the solutions properly. Accordingly, P&D gets the blame for not being able to resolve the problem, and so it continues to be excluded from major decisions, thus completing the vicious circle.

The students who answer the PMFP examination question generally respond by agreeing that there is much to these criticisms, but that with good sense and reason, line managers should be convinced that P&D makes a major contribution to organisational goals and their own (the students') position is therefore indispensable. Given that many of the students do little more than describe their own work instead of answering the question, it is not hard for the examiners to have some sympathy with the line managers with whom these students came into contact! But, it is also possible to speculate that, should line managers be given more autonomy in the P&D area, there might be major problems as well as benefits for organisations.

Things have changed substantially over the last few years, and now line managers take a much greater share of the responsibility for P&D issues. Storey (1992: 194) detected some shifts in the responsibility for P&D issues in the late 1980s and early 1990s, with line managers being at the forefront of various corporate change initiatives, communicating with their staff through team briefings, appraising them for pay purposes, and dealing direct with employees rather than channelling issues through trade union representatives. In Cunningham and Hyman's study (1995: 11), a number of the 45 organisations they examined reported a reallocation of P&D responsibilities towards line managers over the previous three years. More recently, in research for the IPD, Hutchinson and Wood (1995: 9) noted – on the basis of interviews with senior line and personnel managers in 27 organisations – that 22 of them reported greater line management involvement in P&D since 1990. Often the devolution of P&D to the line is accompanied by decentralisation within the organisation, with greater financial autonomy and responsibility locally; sometimes this was the result of privatisation or deregulation. Although decentralisation was a major factor in this trend, other forces were at work as well, notably the need to be more competitive and cost-effective, to be more responsive to customers, and to improve quality. In some cases poor performance from the P&D function in the past was mentioned, but this was never claimed to be a main driver in the change (Hutchinson and Wood, 1995: 5).

Which aspects of P&D are most likely to have been devolved, and are there differences between responsibilities for policy and practice? According to Hutchinson and Wood (1995: 17), P&D lead in the determination of policy across all areas, either having sole responsibility or deciding on policy in conjunction with line management. It is relatively rare for line managers to take the lead on policy issues, either on their own or in consultation with their P&D colleagues. There are no great variations across the subject area, although the P&D influence is slightly more marked with employee resourcing policies (human resource planning or recruitment and selection). It is also interesting to note that some respondents found difficulty in answering the question, arguing that in their organisation P&D and line management worked in partnership, with policy evolving through a series of discussions.

If P&D still appears to lead the development of policy, the picture in relation to practice is somewhat different. Here, line management plays a much greater part according to the respondents, especially in employee resourcing and employee relations, while in employee development and employee reward P&D still has a significant role in most issues. Table 20 (reproduced from *Personnel and the Line*, IPD, 1995: 19) summarises the results of the interviews for 34 separate P&D practices.

Table 20 illustrates that a few P&D practices are now dealt with almost exclusively by the line, albeit following consultation with P&D; these include authorising vacancies, drawing up job descriptions, selection, end-of-probation interviews, and grievance and discipline handling. At the other end of the spectrum, P&D retains responsibility for the selection of recruitment media, gathering references, the administration and running of training courses, and most aspects of employee reward – with the exclusion of individual pay increases, the handling of which shows great diversity across the sample. Perhaps more interesting still is the extent to which responsibility for these practices is shared between line management and P&D; for all but eight practices there is a majority of organisations where consultation is the norm, and of those in which one party or the other dominates, most remain within the P&D domain.

Other surveys show similar results; in an IRS study (IRS *Employment Trends* 566, 1994: 7), devolution to line management was most likely in the areas of recruitment and redundancy interviewing, counselling, and discipline and grievance handling. Conversely, central personnel departments tended to retain responsibility for trade union recognition, pay budgeting and negotiation, job evaluation and benefits administration. Cunningham and Hyman (1995: 11) found that line

Table 20 Personnel/line management involvement
(completed by personnel managers in 25 organisations)

Issues	Line manager	Line in consultation with personnel	Personnel in consultation with line	Personnel department
Recruitment and selection				
Authorising vacancies	10	12	2	1
Job descriptions	5	16	3	1
Selection of media	2	4	12	7
Selection of agency/consultant	0	2	11	11
Screening applications	3	11	6	5
Arranging interviews	2	6	6	10
First interview	3	11	7	3
Subsequent interviews	4	13	5	1
Shortlisting	6	15	4	1
Selection	8	15	1	1
References	1	0	6	17
Individual salary	1	9	9	5
Other terms and conditions	0	5	10	9
Induction	10	4	6	5
End-of-probation interviews	14	6	0	3
Employee relations				
Grievance and discipline	8	15	2	0
Negotiations	1	6	12	4
Disputes	1	10	11	2
Redundancy procedure	0	10	7	7
Welfare/counselling	2	5	8	9
Equal opportunities	1	9	12	3
Training and development				
Analysis of training needs	5	4	13	3
Allocation of training budget	5	4	10	5
Decision on participants	9	10	6	0
Administration of courses	2	2	5	16
Running internal courses	1	3	9	12
Evaluating training effectiveness	4	6	9	6
Pay and benefits				
Job evaluation	0	3	10	9
Deciding on grade	2	2	12	8
Appeals	1	5	7	10
External comparisons	0	0	4	20
Individual pay increases	6	8	6	5
Size of review budget	2	2	7	9
Timing of increases	1	1	8	13

Reproduced from *Personnel and the Line*, S. Hutchinson and S. Wood, IPD, London, 1995 managers were most likely to have responsibilities for human resource management practices such as conducting appraisals, leading quality circles and team briefings, handling discipline and dismissal, and recruitment.

The IPD study also highlighted a number of anxieties which both P&D and line managers had about this increasing devolution of human resource issues to the line, although it should be noted that these were not perceived by the respondents to be major obstacles. There were doubts about the competence of line managers to undertake some of these tasks, especially due to a lack of training and development. Hutchinson and Wood (1995: 23) note that 'lack of resources, a heavy workload, lack of time, and resistance to training from line managers are all reasons why the training is not as good as it could be.' The changes are happening at such a pace that training is not done properly or systematically, and line managers pick things up as they go along. The faddish nature of many management interventions, and the demand for instant success, also relies upon new initiatives being implemented without full and effective preparation (Marchington, Wilkinson, Ackers and Goodman, 1993a). It also helps to explain why line managers often fail to take new ideas seriously, as they expect these to be replaced with the next fashion before too long.

There is also a feeling among line managers that they do not actually *need* any training in P&D issues, a point which comes out strongly from Cunningham and Hyman's interviews. They note (1995: 18) that many supervisors and line managers feel that competence in P&D is gained from a mixture of common sense and experience, and that training is unnecessary. Two quotes from their study sum this up well:

> Most of this [employee relations] is common sense anyway. We have had some training but when an issue comes up it's always in an area where you have had no preparation ... you can deal with it if you consider matters carefully.

> If I went for a personnel manager's job, I would know what to do ... I have had no formal training in these matters, it has just been on-the-job experience using manuals.

This disdain for P&D work is quite worrying, for it contrasts sharply with what they (the line managers) believe is needed to fulfill their own traditional work roles, especially if this is a technical area where knowledge and skills in science or engineering would be considered essential. Most line managers have received little more than rudimentary training in P&D, and for those who were recruited from university more than twenty years ago this would have formed only a minor and insignificant part of their degree programmes. Line managers also feel that they are asked to take on extra P&D responsibilities without any clear and continuing support from their senior managers beyond vague assertions that their efforts are central to organisational success. Without explicit proactive support from senior managers, and recognition and rewards for their work in the P&D area, we can understand why line managers do not take this part of their job too seriously (Marchington *et al*, 1993a: 573).

> What do you see as the major problems in your organisation if more P&D work is devolved to line managers? How might these problems be overcome?

The IPD study (Hutchinson and Wood, 1995: 27–32) identified a number of consequences of greater devolution of P&D work to line managers. Not surprisingly, they foresaw reductions in the number of specialist P&D staff that would be employed by organisations, although this also appeared to suggest a change in role and responsibilities for P&D professionals with a greater emphasis on the development and support of line managers. Persuasion skills might become more important. The reduction in numbers need not necessarily lead to a reduction in status or influence, and indeed those remaining may act more as change agents than facilitators or fire-fighters. This issue is well illustrated by a quote, allegedly from a managing director, which is currently doing the rounds: 'I can't afford to employ two personnel officers on £20,000 each, I can only afford one Human Resource Director on £40,000.' This view is echoed in the requirement for all students on the IPD Professional Qualification Scheme to study core P&D. It is also apparent in the shift from specialist to generalist roles, and the importance which is attached to understanding all aspects of P&D, as well as appreciating how the P&D contribution can be made relevant to the organisation as a whole (Hutchinson and Wood, 1995: 30). It is also clear from the IPD study that both the P&D and the line managers felt that increasing devolution was advantageous for both parties as well as for the organisation overall: devolving 'routine' issues not only allowed line managers to assume control of areas which were important for them, it also released P&D managers to focus on strategic and procedural issues, as well as provide support at times when it was specifically needed.

What skills might be needed by the P&D manager who is working closely with line managers who are accustomed to devolution? Three areas stand out from the IPD study (Hutchinson and Wood, 1995: 33): the formulation of P&D policies and a procedural framework (eg in areas such as recruitment or grievance handling) so as to ensure adherence to corporate policy and legal requirements; the provision of expert advice and guidance on all P&D matters (eg in employment law, equal opportunities, job design, selection techniques, appraisal, training techniques), often through the use of manuals for guidance; and training line managers so that they have the appropriate skills (eg in how to devise a job description, conduct an interview, or engender commitment). This new role is likely to be enhanced by the effective use of information technology; as we have seen at a number of points in this book, IT can be used in many areas of P&D, such as absence monitoring, standard letter production, spreadsheets, personal records, and e-mail.

In order to convince line managers to take advice about human resource issues seriously, two sets of arguments seem relevant, both of which require P&D managers to acquire a better understanding of financial matters, and the ability to provide costings for any recommendations. The first set of arguments concerns the *cost of getting things wrong*: this can be assessed in straight financial terms, such as the cost of a tribunal case for an unfair dismissal, a lapse in safety awareness which results in an accident, the cost of lost orders due to a strike which occurs because an employee-relations issue was badly handled, or the cost of rejected goods due to a lack of effective training. It can also be seen in public relations terms, such that an organisation with a poor record is likely to suffer costs at the recruitment stage through poor-quality applicants or because of staff leaving due to an ineffective payment system, or even through customers who choose not to buy goods or services from the organisation because of its poor image. Costs can also be viewed in 'softer' motivational terms which are reflected in low levels of productivity, unsatisfactory customer service and inadequate quality standards, or through poor levels of attendance and timekeeping, high levels of labour turnover, stress, and general dissatisfaction. Employees of high potential at the recruitment stage can become disillusioned due to deficiencies in any aspect of P&D practice: induction, appraisal, remuneration, training, career development, grievance and discipline handling, and so on. The costs of high labour turnover, for example, need to be viewed not only in terms of the 'lost' employee, but also in terms of readvertising, reinterviewing and reinducting, as well as the time it takes for a new member of staff to reach the top of the learning curve.

The second set of arguments relate to the *benefits of getting it right*. Many of these are the converse of those outlined above: the financial benefits which accrue through higher added value from each well-motivated and productive employee; the public relations benefits which result in the organisation with the image of 'a good employer' being able to attract high-quality applicants; and the 'softer' motivational benefits which flow from low levels of absenteeism, from the positive impact which committed employees make on customers, and from the higher levels of productivity and quality which appear – according to some of the studies referred to earlier – to result from applying 'best practice' P&D.

> Prepare a paper for a general manager which demonstrates the way in which the P&D function is still able to 'add value' in an organisation which has devolved many P&D practices to line managers. Choose any type of organisation for this exercise, and work with colleagues on this if possible so as to increase the range of arguments which you present.

CONSULTANTS AND PERSONNEL AND DEVELOPMENT

Until twenty years ago there were very few consultants offering P&D services to organisations, but since then it is assumed that there has been a rapid growth in their number. However, it is almost impossible to determine the precise number of consultants who operate in the

P&D field; registers are held by the IPD and the Management Consultancy Information Service, and information is available from professional bodies such as the Institute of Management Consultants or the Management Consultancies Association, but there is no obligation upon consultants to register their activities. In the mid-1980s Torrington and Mackay (1986: 34) found that about half of the organisations they surveyed had increased the use of consultants during the previous three years compared with less than 10 per cent which had seen a decrease in their use. For the remainder, usage remained at about the same level. Interestingly, at that time about 60 per cent did not expect the usage of consultants to increase over the remainder of the decade, with the remainder split equally between those who expected an increase and those who thought usage would decline. This finding is important as it puts the use of consultants firmly in its historical perspective, and reminds us that some P&D services have been subcontracted for many years.

The debate about consultants does, however, mask some important differences in their composition, and distinctions need to be made between them. Adams (1991: 44–45) divides consultants into four categories: *specialised in-house agencies*, which are responsible for one or more parts of the P&D remit, but do not operate with an explicit policy of charging for their services; *internal consultancies*, which do charge customers for their work, adopt a profit-centre approach, and perhaps also sell services to organisations other than the 'parent'; *business-within-a-business functions* take this process a step further in that certain aspects of the human resource function are hived off from the P&D department, selling their services both internally and externally; and, finally, *external consultants*, a category which can also be subdivided further, as we shall see below.

Drawing upon the results of an IRS survey, Adams (1991) shows that distinguishing between internal and external consultants is too simplistic. She argues that the P&D function is not subject to a straight core–periphery distinction, in which *all* activities are subcontracted or retained in-house, but that different solutions are adopted by different types of employer for different aspects of P&D. This 'balkanisation' of P&D results in several areas being heavily out-sourced (eg training and development, executive search and selection, the recruitment of temporary staff, and outplacement and redundancy counselling) while other activities are retained principally by in-house units (eg graduate recruitment and other counselling). But, even in the case of training and development it is clear that no one category of consultancy is used exclusively, and almost as many organisations use in-house agencies as use external consultants. These may be used for different parts of the training process but, significantly, all four types are used. The largest growth area in the late 1980s and early 1990s, according to Adams (1991: 47), was the in-house agency; its growth was particularly marked in the areas of training and development, and the recruitment of graduates and temporary staff – two very different categories of employee.

External consultants can also be subdivided into a number of distinct categories as well (Armstrong, 1994: 42). These are:

- large multi-disciplinary firms, such as the leading accountancy practices and management consultants, which provide a whole range of services – including P&D

- specialist human resource organisations, some of which are large and well-established firms providing the full range of P&D support, whereas others are smaller and more specialised, sometimes referred to as 'boutiques'

- small firms or independent consultants, often sole traders, who specialise in one particular field or region, or operate across the whole range of P&D practices; this area has grown considerably in the last ten years due to an increase in the number of retired or redundant executives who offer consultancy services

- academics, some of whom provide consultancy expertise in specific areas in addition to their teaching, research and administrative duties, and who may be a source of up-to-date findings

- organisations such as the Industrial Society and ACAS, which provide consultancy services in addition to their other functions.

There are basically three sets of reasons why employers turn to external consultants rather than using an in-house service (Torrington and Mackay, 1986; Armstrong, 1994; IRS, 1995). First, if consultants are able to provide expertise or time which is not available internally, then there may be a case for using an external organisation. The expertise may be in a particular subject (eg European Works Councils or psychometric testing) or it may relate to process skills. In the latter situation, the external consultant might be able to help managements deal with issues at an organisational level (eg cultural change programmes or internal communications) or at a more basic level (eg helping managers to become aware that their personal style is confrontational or dismissive of others) where it may be difficult for colleagues to help 'unfreeze' problems. In reality, of course, it is often necessary for consultants to demonstrate both process consultancy skills and technical expertise when working with clients. In organisations with an internal human resource function, this group of staff may be overstretched with routine duties so that it is impossible to devote time to specialist projects; a consultant may offer a suitable alternative in this situation.

The second set of reasons relates to the independence of external consultants, the view that they are able to provide an expertise which is (theoretically) free from internal influence. This may be particularly useful in complex and multi-faceted situations which are capable of being interpreted in a variety of ways – in the employee relations field for example. The use of independent consultants to conduct attitude surveys which are overseen by a steering group comprising all sections of the workforce might be one such use, as would recommendations on organisational restructuring. Similarly, it is argued that an outsider's view of issues may help managers and others to resolve problems which had previously seemed insurmountable: a fresh perspective on a problem may be provided, or a summary of views collected by an independent consultant – and then reported back to managers – may lead to shifts in attitudes or behaviour. Merely articulating ideas to a third party who is prepared to 'listen', may cause individuals to put together their thoughts in a more coherent and systematic way. A variant of this approach is where external consultants are employed to help shift senior management opinion within the organisation. This may help to legitimise views which P&D has been trying to articulate without success, but which are now accepted because the external 'expert' consultant is vested with an authority, independence and knowledge which internal managers are not felt to possess.

The final reason is economic and financial, and is especially important if large parts of P&D are out-sourced, or a major project is to be undertaken. If consultants are used on a temporary basis, the costs of employing them are likely to be much less than maintaining an in-house expertise which may not be fully exploited at other times of the year. If senior management is unhappy with the service provided by the consultants, the consultants are unlikely to be contracted again in the future. Undoubtedly there are short-term attractions to employers seeking to reduce quasi-fixed costs in order to retain a competitive edge. Obviously, the costs of consultants varies considerably; Armstrong (1994: 37) reckons that they range from as little as £100 per day through to £1,000. Some of the larger and better-known consultancy firms are at the upper end of this band, whereas academics and independent consultants are likely to be in the middle. Those at the bottom end are likely to be either very inexperienced or unaware of their market value! If managements decide to use consultants on cost grounds, they need to be fully aware of the *complete financial implications* of their employment, realising that the total cost should also include internal management time in putting together the tender in the first place, as well as the costs of implementing recommendations.

> Has your organisation made use of external consultants to undertake some P&D activities? If so, in which aspects of P&D? What was the rationale behind their use, and were the outcomes as expected?

Given the mass of consultants available on the market, and the range of issues on which they can be contracted, it is important to have clear criteria to guide selection choices. The IRS report (1995: 8) suggests that the following are important:

- a high degree of technical competence and evidence of a considerable body of professional expertise; for a large firm, this includes the strength and standing of the team which will undertake the consultancy, not just the reputation of the leader

- a strong track record which can be substantiated, and positive endorsements from previous users

- an empathy with, and understanding of, the business so that recommendations are likely to be appropriate; experience of undertaking work in the same industry or sector may be of value in this respect

- personal attributes such as integrity, honesty and trust, and a clear willingness to subscribe to a code of professional conduct, such as that of the IPD or the Management Consultancies Association

- a down-to-earth attitude such that implementation is seen as a key aspect of the consultancy assignment

- a package which is cost-effective, is directed at the problems which need addressing, and can be delivered on time.

Consultants do not always enjoy a good press. They have been referred to as 'whores in pin-stripe suits' or as the equivalent of twentieth-century witch doctors 'recommending half-baked, theoretical, expensive and unsuccessful remedies to problems they have mis-diagnosed in the first place' (quoted in Baxter, 1996: 67). Armstrong (1994: viii) also recognises that there are some 'cowboys around whose only mission is to sell their simplistic prescriptions to any or all of the problems which beset management'. Against this it is generally acknowledged that good consultants can offer managements expertise which may be lacking within the organisation, and help to facilitate changes which might otherwise not have come to fruition. Clearly it is important to ensure that problems are avoided in the choice of consultants, and the list of points outlined above provides some assistance in how to choose between consultants. It is also necessary to make use of basic project management guidelines in drawing up specifications for consultants before they are offered a contract. Drawing upon Armstrong (1994: 139–141), these can be summarised as follows:

- Take care to ensure that there is a valid and justifiable reason for employing consultants in the first place, that the study is worth doing, and that it cannot be done as well in-house. In relation to training, for example, the Bees (1994: 129–130) suggest that the 'make or buy' decision (whether to go for newly-developed or existing courses) depends upon factors such as the size of the population to be trained, whether the competencies are organisation-specific or general, the speed with which the training needs to be delivered, and the nature of the training.

- Ensure that the objectives and deliverables for the assignment are specified in a way that clearly indicates the desired results. Plan the project so that terms of reference, deadlines, methods of monitoring and review, and reporting arrangements are laid down clearly. Ensure that both parties fully understand their respective roles in the relationship.

- Take care that the project is managed in line with the objectives and deliverables, and that you continue to receive value-for-money services. Wherever possible it is desirable to foster a partnership approach.

- Remember that consultancy projects involve change, so special care is required over the implementation, involvement and communication processes during and after the assignment.

CONCLUSION

The focus in this chapter has been on horizontal integration, the way in which different P&D policies and practices are designed to support each other in order to provide a coherent and comprehensive human resource package. This is not to suggest that there is one best way in which P&D can be delivered, a point which was emphasised when we considered the various models of P&D published in recent times. The situation is characterised by diversity, and it appears that different organisations operate with quite different sets of P&D practices and policies. What matters is adopting the models best suited to specific organisational contexts, although we must remember that many P&D departments lack the power and influence to make such choices anyway.

There is currently a good deal of interest in the concept of 'best practice' P&D – the idea that a specific bundle of human resource policies and practices are inherently superior, and are capable of making a major contribution to organisational success in *all* workplaces. In some situations, say where an employer seeks to gain competitive advantage through cost reduction strategies, this may seem to contradict the arguments put forward in Chapter 17 on external fit and vertical integration. In such a context there will be tensions between different sets of arguments, and human resource specialists may face considerable resistance if they propose the introduction of 'best practice' P&D; to prepare for this, use will need to be made of what Karen Legge calls 'deviant innovation'. In workplaces where employers are pursuing a quality-enhancement or innovation strategy it may be much easier to champion the development of 'best practice' P&D since it is likely to fit well with business objectives. In this case the achievement of both vertical and horizontal integration can be relatively unproblematic.

But P&D professionals do not have exclusive control over human resource *practices* at the workplace, and they are reliant upon line managers to put policies into effect. As we saw in Chapter 17, this can cause problems in evaluating the contribution of P&D to organisational success. For the last few years, however, there has been an even greater emphasis on P&D's being provided by people other than the specialist function, in particular line managers and consultants. Moreover, even in situations where a P&D presence has been maintained, this is now more likely to be the subject of formal external assessment, often through the use of quantitative measures and performance criteria. In short, it is clear that the practice of P&D is in a considerable degree of flux as we enter the last few years of the twentieth century.

USEFUL READING

ADAMS, K. (1991) 'Externalisation versus specialisation: what is happening to personnel?', *Human Resource Management Journal*, Vol 1, 4: 40–54.

ARMSTRONG, M. (1994) *Using the Human Resource Consultant: Achieving Results, Adding Value*. London, IPM.

HUTCHINSON, S. AND WOOD, S. (1995) 'The UK experience', in *Personnel and the Line: Developing the New Relationship*. London, IPD: 3–42.

LEGGE, K. (1978) *Power, Innovation and Problem Solving in Personnel Management*. London, McGraw-Hill.

PFEFFER, J. (1994) *Competitive Advantage through People*. Boston, Harvard Business School Press.

STOREY, J. (1992) *Developments in the Management of Human Resources*. Oxford, Blackwell.

TORRINGTON, D. AND MACKAY, L. (1986) 'Will Consultants Take Over the Personnel Function?' *Personnel Management*, February: 34–37.

TYSON, S. AND FELL, A. (1986) *Evaluating the Personnel Function*. Hutchinson, London.

WILKINSON, A. AND MARCHINGTON, M. (1994) 'Total Quality Management: instant pudding for the personnel function?' *Human Resource Management Journal*, Vol 5, 1: 33–49.

WOOD, S. (1995) 'The Four Pillars of Human Resource Management: are they connected?' *Human Resource Management Journal*, Vol 5, 5: 49–59.

19 Personnel and development in practice

INTRODUCTION

Throughout this book, it has been stressed repeatedly that personnel and development policies and practices can vary significantly between different organisations. Often this is not recognised as practitioners search for models of so-called 'best practice', only to find that they are inappropriate for their own organisational context. Equally, many P&D specialists are unaware of how other organisations operate, particularly if they have spent the majority of their working lives in one industry; it can sometimes come as a shock that policies and practices which are widely practised in their own establishment are not used elsewhere. Moreover, P&D practitioners who hold relatively junior positions within their employing organisation often lack any understanding of *why* their employer pursues certain policies instead of others. It is easy to assume that the approach which is adopted is self-evidently the *only* way in which to manage the organisation.

Some of the key threads running through the IPD Professional Qualification Scheme and the Continuing Professional Development programme encourage members to seek new learning experiences, to question what they do, and to aim for continuous improvement. The purpose of this chapter, therefore, is to provide readers with a series of case studies which describe P&D policies and practices in a number of organisations, and to analyse the links between these and broader business strategies. In some cases, the links are clear and have helped to drive the organisation forward, while in others they are more fuzzy and incoherent. In some cases there is evidence of explicit horizontal integration, while in others there are confusions and conflicts between different aspects of personnel and development. In some cases line managers deal with all aspects of human resource management, whereas in others these are divided between a specialist function and may (or may not) involve the use of consultants to deliver parts of the package.

Each of the cases in this chapter is derived from real-life examples, although some aspects are embroidered in order to enable effective learning to take place. The cases are about 1,000–1,200 words each in length, allowing for an in-depth analysis and, if possible, some groupwork. Readers should be aware of the fact that there are bound to be some gaps in information about the organisations which are described below, but they should be encouraged to add details provided this does not alter the basis of the case. It might also make sense to seek further information about the industry or sector in question, so as to extend the learning that can be gained from these analyses. Moreover, in order to extract full value from the cases, relevant chapters in the book should be read again in order to gather details of specific P&D practices and strategies.

By the end of this chapter, readers should be able to:

• describe the key P&D issues which are important in a range of employing organisations drawn from different sectors and types of employment

• provide advice to employers on suitable P&D practices for their sector or organisation

• advise management on how to tackle a set of human resource problems, providing costings as appropriate.

In addition, readers should be able to understand and explain:

• the meaning of horizontal and vertical integration in a range of employing organisations drawn from different sectors and types of employment

• how responsibility for managing P&D issues is allocated between line managers, personnel and development specialists and consultants

• why styles of managing human resources vary between different employing organisations by accounting for the key variables which influence employers' approaches.

PHOTOCHEM: 'WORKING WITH THE UNIONS FOR COMPETITIVE ADVANTAGE'

Photochem is part of a large US-owned chemical company, Americhem, which employs over 70,000 people worldwide and has interests in a number of different parts of the industry. Photochem is one of the market leaders in the photographic industry, with nearly 90 per cent of its sales outside of the UK, and it competes with Japanese, US and other European firms for market share. Both Photochem and Americhem have been financially stable over a long period, but the last couple of years has seen a dip in profitability and increased monitoring of performance by the American parent company.

Americhem operates at a number of sites in Europe, but the largest manufacturing plant is Photochem's site in Britain, located in the north of England in semi-rural surroundings about 20 miles from a major city. The plant employs about 1,200 staff, less than half the number who worked there ten years ago. All the reductions in staff numbers have been achieved by voluntary means – an early retirement scheme, a freeze on recruitment, the introduction of temporary contracts, and generous severance payments to encourage staff to leave. The site employs a wide range of staff, from highly qualified technical and research personnel through to general labourers and ancillary workers. The spread of qualifications and experience is particularly interesting, in that a quarter of the research staff have doctorates and many have worked for other leading chemical firms, while most of the manual workers left school at 15 and have always lived in the area. In recent years, though, the company has attempted to develop a more effective internal labour market, with all staff now eligible to take advantage of the Employee Development and Assistance Programme (EDAP).

The human resource function enjoys a key role in the company and at site level. The human resources director is on the UK board, heads up Americhem's European division, and has close contact with his American colleagues. The function has an extremely experienced and well-qualified team of seven professionals (as well as the director), all of whom are already IPD members. Human resources is divided up on a business basis, with each individual having total HR responsibility for his or her area, adopting a generalist role for this purpose. These individuals work closely with relevant line managers, dealing with queries and problems as they arise, albeit within an agreed UK company-wide structure. Tensions exist between the needs of individual businesses on site and the desire to maintain consistency and uniformity across the company, but until now this has not led to any problems.

The human resources director is widely respected at Photochem, and he works closely with the managing director in shaping strategy at the plant. The managing director worked in human resources himself earlier in his career, and as such has an affinity for people-management, recognising the importance of integrating human resource policies with broader business goals and objectives. In Porter's terms (see Chapter 17), the company pursues a strategy of quality enhancement, so the personnel and development policies flow from this, in terms of employee development, reward management, employee resourcing, and employee relations. The company is committed to equal opportunities, although it is recognised that the proportion of women in managerial positions is well below target. In many respects Photochem could be regarded as a model employer, but management is not impressed by 'trophy-hunting': it has not sought any of the ISO quality awards, nor has the company decided to go for IIP. Senior management argues that these awards are too often seen in terms of their external public relations value, sidetracking staff from more important and meaningful goals.

Relations with the trade unions are currently very good, having gone through a particularly tense period in the late 1970s. Five separate trade unions are recognised for collective bargaining purposes, each having a distinct sphere of influence. The GMB is the largest union on site, with 500 members, and it represents all production and related workers. The AEEU has about 90 craft workers in membership. Over 95 per cent of eligible staff in these two areas are union members, and a formal closed shop existed until this was outlawed in 1990. APEX-GMB and MSF each have about 200 members, covering clerical grades, technicians, some supervisors and research staff; the density of unionisation in these groups is lower, at about 60 per cent, but is still high for professional staff. The GMB senior steward also acts as the convenor of the joint shop stewards committee, and he spends half his time on union duties; the company has been supportive of the unions on site, providing facilities and time-off as required. The stewards work reasonably well together, although there are some tensions between the blue-collar unions and those representing research staff.

Pay rates at Photochem are above the industry average, but not particularly high in comparison with some other large employers (several of whom are household-name companies) within a twenty mile radius of the company. The human resources director is committed to the present time-based system of pay as he believes it encourages teamworking and a high-quality culture, but he has doubts about the ability of the Europe-wide profit-sharing scheme to motivate and reward staff. He recently attended a seminar on plant-wide incentive systems, and wonders if they may have anything to offer Photochem, especially as there is little contact between the sites. On the other hand, the company is considering a European works council, so contact may increase.

Anxieties about profitability have prompted a world-wide review of activities by a team of US consultants who are working closely with head office. Photochem is due to have its audit soon, and the managing director has asked all the directors, including human resources, to outline some proposals in preparation for this audit. The human resources director has asked all his staff to suggest ideas prior to the meeting, along with a summary of the financial implications of their proposals.

You have been asked to prepare papers on:

- the advantages and disadvantages of single-table bargaining with the unions, as well as a recommendation for action

- a cost-benefit analysis of the EDAP scheme

- the costs and benefits of setting up a European works council

- the advantages and disadvantages of introducing a plant-wide incentive system at the north-of-England site

- a training programme for line managers on how to promote equal opportunities within the company

- an internal review of the work of the human resource function, showing a) how it contributes to successful business performance, b) whether or not human resources should be organised on specialist as opposed to generalist lines, and c) what work, if any, could be contracted out to consultants.

JAPANCO UK: 'THE BROWNING OF A GREENFIELD SITE'

Japanco UK is part of a large Japanese-owned heavy engineering company which employs some 50,000 worldwide. It is one of the market leaders in heavy goods vehicles but is competing fiercely for market share with American competitors. In the mid-1980s it established a greenfield manufacturing site in the north of England as part of a wider strategy to create a global production system. The aim was to provide a base within the European Community so as to avoid import tariffs. As 80 per cent of production is exported, the company is vulnerable to exchange rate fluctuations.

The company employs over 400 workers, most of those on the shop floor being young males. The workforce at the company can be divided into three distinct groups: direct workers (including fabrication, paint and assembly), semi-direct (inspection, maintenance, warehouse), and indirect (both office- and factory-based). While the company has sought to develop an internal labour market, rapid growth in the size of the production unit and high levels of demand have limited the opportunity to develop multi-skilling.

The human resource function enjoys a high status in the company, with the first manager to be appointed in the UK being the personnel director. One of his first tasks was to decide what P&D policies to adopt, drawing selectively on typical features of employment in major Japanese companies. The company emphasises job security, a team-based approach to work, consensus, single status and a company council.

From the outset management insisted it would recognise only one trade union, this being selected following submissions from several unions prior to the start of recruitment. The chosen single union has sole bargaining rights, and rights of representation up to and including supervisory staff. Membership is 30 per cent, although it is higher among production staff. The agreement includes pendulum arbitration, a strike substitute mechanism. The union does face a problem in that its workplace roots are weak, and day-to-day release of representatives for industrial relations activities rely heavily on the discretion of line managers.

The company–union agreement emphasises flexibility in the production processes, with the union recognising and supporting the complete flexibility and mobility of the workforce between jobs and duties within the company and departments. The company operates a batch production system based on teams of 10–12 workers. Tasks are repetitive, but job rotation is practised. There is a strong emphasis on the work team and the team leader, and there is a conscious effort to avoid other relationships which may threaten this. The team leader has a role akin to a working supervisor in terms of direct work, but is also involved in the selection process, appraisal and discipline. Team leaders are trained in inter-personal as well as more technical skills. Workers are expected to be at their workstations ready for work, the official start time for briefing, and although there is no clocking, a register is taken by the team leader. This emphasises the importance of line management responsibility.

Employment terms and conditions are largely harmonised between manual and non-manual employees, including common hours and holidays, free medical cover, and a common pension scheme. The company operates a system of performance review for evaluating employees, which incorporates a wide range of factors – including quality of work, job knowledge, reliability, teamwork, time-keeping, housekeeping performance beyond contract (eg participation in quality circles), and an assessment of employees' career development.

The aim of the company council is not so much to resolve problems but to facilitate the expression of views so that problems do not arise in the first place. There is an assumption that if everyone has the same information and the 'right' attitude, a consensus can be reached. This philosophy is symbolised by round tables and rules discouraging pre-meetings and adjournments. This does place a question mark over the traditional union role, given that representatives are not always required to be union members. The council meets monthly; meetings are chaired by the personnel director with other management representatives including the managing director, the production director and the personnel manager. There are elected representatives from each of the main groups of staff – clerical and secretarial, assembly, maintenance, and team leaders. Its terms of reference suggest that the scope of issues discussed is broad; investment policy and business plans, trading performance, staffing, training and development plans, operating efficiency and quality, work environment and conditions. In practice, however, most of the discussion appears to be focused on production plans and workplace issues.

The induction period, which typically lasts ten weeks, emphasises the 'Japanese way' and the company policy of quality, cost and delivery. Initial training for staff concentrates less on the technical skills to assemble products than on the social skills required for flexibility and teamwork. Workers are expected to take responsibility for quality within their own work area and participation in quality circles is encouraged. The principles of Deming and Crosby with the message of 'do it right first time' are fully operationalised and backed up by the use of the Deming circle (plan, do, check, action). Posters and cartoons around the factory and office are designed to give a user-friendly message that 'quality is attention to detail', 'the customer is the final inspector'.

The expansion of the plant led to considerable promotion opportunities for staff but this has now slowed, and the company is re-examining the existing system in order to provide a clearer career path. Now that start-up problems have been ironed out there is greater effort directed in the human resource development area – a staff development officer took responsibility for training, internal development and performance appraisal. A training centre was established providing opportunities for employees to acquire wider skills (including languages) as well as job-related skills.

The conditions in which the company began production – especially high unemployment levels, small plant size, the careful screening and selection processes – undoubtedly assisted management in creating the initial working climate it wanted. However, three years on, the 'honeymoon' has come to an end. Management now recognises that they will have to work harder to make everyone feel part of Japanco.

Given the extent of changes since Japanco UK started production at this site, now is a very appropriate time to conduct a review of P&D activities. Address the following questions.

- Do you think the benefits which are derived from Japanco UK's induction programme outweigh the costs of its operation?

- Explain how you would implement 'lifetime learning' at the company as part of its career management policy.

- Assume that Japanco decides to establish similar-sized plants in France and Germany. To what extent would the existing company council arrangements act as a template for a European works council, and what advice would you give for the creation of an EWC?

- In Chapter 16, Peter Wickens (ex-Nissan) argued that the term 'single status' is a misnomer. Review this assertion in the light of developments at Japanco UK.

- For which aspects of P&D work do you think it is feasible for supervisors and line managers to take responsibility, and how would you (as a P&D specialist) provide support for them to do this?

- What indicators would you propose for assessing whether or not the 'honeymoon' was coming to an end?

SUPERFOOD: 'QUALITY ENHANCEMENT THROUGH A LOW-SKILLED WORKFORCE'

Superfood is one of the leading food retailers in Britain, employing 75,000 staff at its headquarters and in the 250 stores which are located around the country. The company is organised on a regional basis, with each region containing approximately 15 stores which are served from a number of warehouses spread around the country. Superfood has grown dramatically over the last ten years, both in terms of numbers employed and in the range and type of stores, and it has a continuing problem finding and retaining sufficient high-quality managers to open and run new stores.

The company's mission statement demonstrates its commitment to market leadership through the provision of high-quality customer service, the importance of talented and motivated staff, working in partnerships with suppliers, participation in the local community and, of course, support for the industry and rewards to shareholders. A copy of the mission statement is given to each new employee during the induction programme. In the mission statement the chief executive states that the company's philosophy is to develop and involve staff to ensure that they possess the skills and abilities needed to achieve competitive advantage. Reference is made to training opportunities (both on and off the job), to welfare of staff, to their participation and involvement in teams, and to rewards and benefits at work.

The personnel and development function operates at three separate levels within the company (headquarters, region, and store), and it is headed up by a main board director. This is seen as important in ensuring the contribution of specialist expertise to the board, but also in maintaining links between business strategy and human resource management. Beneath the main board director are a number of other specialist directors, each of whom has responsibility for a particular part of the business. This head office team are the architects behind the development of human resource policies which apply across the business as a whole, as well as playing a leading role in shaping the structure and culture of the company.

Superfood has a recognition agreement with USDAW (The Union of Shop, Distributive and Allied Workers) solely for individual grievance and disciplinary cases and for joint consultation. There is no provision for collective bargaining. Union membership across the company is less than 10 per cent of all staff, and union consciousness is low. A consultative committee structure also operates across the company at regional level, and to some extent fills some of the gaps left open by the lack of union traditions in the stores. These committees take an overview of issues which arise in the stores, and this enables management to detect if common problems are emerging.

Given the continuing growth in the size of Superfood over the last decade, the recruitment and development of managers has been a key activity in the company, and considerable efforts have been made to ensure a steady supply of high-quality applicants who are motivated to achieve high levels of customer service. The company recruits not only from the external graduate market but also by promoting capable internal applicants; it is extremely keen to increase the number of women and staff from ethnic minorities in management positions. A new competency-based recruitment, selection and development programme is about to be launched, and there is provision for mentoring and regular appraisals during the early stages of a new manager's career.

Applicants for shopfloor jobs are evaluated in relation to their ability to provide excellent customer service under seven headings: physical make-up; technical knowledge; general intelligence; customer service; interests outside of work; ability to work under pressure; and domestic circumstances. A number of these are tested via situational questions, designed to assess how well applicants are able to cope with typical customer interactions and difficult service relationships. The importance of selecting the right kind of staff is crucial, both because of their impact upon customers and the high costs of recruitment which are incurred due to high levels of labour turnover (over 30 per cent per annum), especially during the first few months of employment.

Once appointed, induction training takes place under the auspices of a wide-ranging but carefully administered programme. Before taking up any duties, each new recruit is meant to spend several periods of time on basic induction, which is then followed by a further concentrated programme. Over the next twelve weeks more detailed training is undertaken on issues connected with customer care and departmental-specific matters such as correct procedures for meat preparation or baking. The formal induction programme is undertaken within the store by a team of trainers who administer workbooks to the new recruits, including questions about company history, health and safety, and more general rules and regulations.

The need for high levels of customer service is reinforced at all stages of the individual's employment; this is monitored via snap visits by regional managers, by 'mystery shoppers', and by analysing sales by individual checkout operators using electronic means. Disciplinary standards are laid down precisely in the company rule book, and there are specific instructions about standards of cleanliness and dress. Behind the scenes, in the training room, a poster campaign emphasises the more instrumental reasons why employees should deliver high-quality service: 'Satisfied customers who keep coming back again and again strengthen sales and jobs; *customers* make pay days possible!'

Imagine that you have now been at Superfood as a management trainee for twelve months, and you have been asked, as part of your final assessment to present a project on the company's human resource policies and problems. In particular, you have been asked to prepare a paper dealing with the following issues:

- a set of criteria to be used in the company's competency-based recruitment, selection and development programme, with justification for their inclusion

- a case to persuade departmental managers of the benefits of releasing new checkout operators for induction training

- the advantages and disadvantages of departmental managers' undertaking more team-building activities rather than leaving them to the trainers

- a case for or against the derecognition of USDAW

- the relevance of a performance-related payment system for the company, how it would operate in practice, and for which grades of staff

- an evaluation of how the personnel and development function 'adds value' to Superfood, with some attempt to provide costings.

MEDCARE PRIORITY SERVICES: 'MOTIVATING THE WORKFORCE TO IMPROVE SERVICE DELIVERY'

Medcare Priority Services provides the priority services and community care for residents of the local health authority and parts of the neighbouring counties over a wide rural area. The authority is divided between the purchaser and the providers (the units), and the focus of this case is on the priority and community unit which has trust status. It is an extremely diverse organisation providing a wide range of services including acute specialities, care for the elderly, learning disabilities, mental health services, community nursing, and community paramedical services. Around 2,000 staff are employed in the priority and community unit. Over 80 per cent of these are female, and the nursing profession forms 60 per cent of the total numbers employed.

Employee relations issues have traditionally been dealt with at national level through the Whitley Council system, which has allowed little scope for local collective bargaining. However, local consultative committees have been established within the unit, although unit bargaining has not yet been introduced. Several different unions are recognised but the reason is not seen as militant – reflecting its rural location. Attitudes to unions differ quite widely among different groups, which makes it difficult to provide a centralised philosophy. Regrading in the late 1980s caused considerable disgruntlement with the new hierarchy which was seen as having divided good work teams, so leading to ill will. A fundamental problem is the lack of a 'corporate' staff approach, because of the conflicting standpoints of the traditional trade unions and the professional organisations. Unions are concerned that the move to unit consultation has isolated them. In any case there appears to be a division between the representatives in their attempts to follow the national stance of their respective unions, as well as represent rank and file staff at the same time.

A series of governmental and national management initiatives provided the impetus for much of the change which has taken place at Medcare Priority Services. These included the emphasis on customers in the Griffiths Report (1983), the NHS chief executive's drive for all district health authorities to have quality assurance programmes in place by the end of 1989, the NHS and Community Care Act in 1990, and the Patients' Charter. Each of these places a greater emphasis on customer satisfaction and tighter operating procedures; for example, under the Patients' Charter, an emphasis is placed on ready access to services when needed, responsiveness to patients' wishes and expectations, flexibility of provision, and efficiency. The division of authority between provider and purchaser reflects changes introduced under the 1990 Act, thus replacing the system by which regional health authorities arranged health care according to a fixed annual budget. Hospitals have the choice of becoming self-governing trusts outside the control of the district health authorities. For both trusts and directly managed units, the separation of purchasing from the district and other purchasers requires contracts to state in increasingly explicit terms the quality and standard of service which is to be provided. The unit's main purchaser has used the contract process to monitor human resource practices with regular audit visits and the monitoring of a number of factors – including staff sickness levels.

One of the main changes to take place at Medcare Priority Services is in relation to quality. A quality assurance department was established several years ago to raise the profile of quality issues, and this led to the introduction of quality circles in some departments, along with a number of customer surveys. Although some managers were members, the quality circles were not management-led. More recently an employee charter was launched with the aim of providing a supportive working environment for staff and 'caring' for those who care. This was seen as a necessary prerequisite for the further development of customer care. The employee charter laid down guidance for managers on dealing with their staff, which included the following sorts of principles: each member of staff to be treated with respect; the provision of a supportive management environment and performance review; maximum delegation of responsibility; identification of personal training and development needs; maximum security for staff. A 'positive action programme' has been instituted to provide support for these principles; it is described as a package of measures aimed at supporting staff and managers and encouraging excellence.

Much of the activity to date has been geared to the development of an infrastructure via a quality assurance system, customer surveys and the preparation of standards. In addition, there has been an emphasis on cultural change, and management has been particularly keen to relate the day-to-day experiences of staff to quality management concepts. Important benefits have accrued from developing the notion of internal customers, and this has had a significant effect on the quality of relationships between different departments. Compulsory competitive tendering has impacted mainly on the cleaning duties, with staff under contract no longer being seen as part of the ward staff but simply doing their specified jobs.

The human resource function has played a crucial role in these initiatives both under the district regime and more recently as a unit function. In the early days, the district function acted as the champion of quality and introduced the employee charter in order to develop a statement of values and a quality culture for both staff and patients. The district is now effectively the major purchaser and only monitors employment issues through the influence of the contract. Under the current unit structure, a conscious decision was made that human resources should assume responsibility for quality. Rather than having it driven by one group' (eg nursing) and running the risk of other professional groups losing interest, senior management decided that it would be better to have human resources take the lead, as the function was perceived to be 'neutral'.

Considerable emphasis has also been placed on the development of training across the organisation. This has taken many forms: a standard-setting package has been established for clinical and managerial practices; half-day awareness training sessions have been held for all staff; customer-care training is being provided for all staff, not just those who have regular contact with external customers; extra sessions have been included on the management development programmes so as to reinforce the message. Senior management at Medcare Priority Services recognise that the new culture can not be instilled overnight, and its initial aim has been to raise awareness, to be backed up later with ongoing courses and other indications of support for continuous quality improvement. Other human resource initiatives include extensive communications (for example, roadshows for all staff about the trust application), newsletters, and informal employee involvement through briefings at shift changeovers. Although the system of communications is extensive, there are problems with briefings, particularly for part-time and shift workers, as well as those in outlying areas.

The move to trust status also had sizeable implications for the management of human resources, with managers required to prepare information on a range of personnel practices and policies as part of the trust application. For example, data had to be presented on the current skills mix of the workforce, and the organisation's plans for training and development, as did regular and ongoing information on labour turnover and absence statistics, and the results of customer surveys. Managers also look at the mix of staff required for work in the trust and whether to introduce new staff grades supported by NVQs to create a more flexible workforce.

The NHS Management Executive has expressed an interest in developments at Medcare Priority Services, and has asked the human resource director and her team to make a presentation based around the five question areas specified below. If you were part of the human resource team, how would you respond to these question areas?

- In what ways could the human resource function 'add value' to quality initiatives, and what impact has it had in the case of Medcare Priority Services?

- What *specific* P&D practices do you think comprise the personal action programme? Provide examples to illustrate your answer.

- Explain the rationale which underpins the employee development strategy.

- Should management consider introducing single-table bargaining at unit level?

- How can management at the trust improve the effectiveness of employee involvement and communications, especially to workers on atypical contracts and those who spend most of their working time in the community?

MIDLANDS LA: 'DEVELOPING A QUALITY CULTURE IN LOCAL GOVERNMENT'

Modern Metro is a metropolitan council which employs about 8,000 people across eight departments – town clerk's, finance, education, social services, housing, environmental health and trading standards (EHTS), libraries and arts, and technical services – so providing a full range of council services. Numbers employed are likely to fall during the latter part of the 1990s as Modern Metro moves further towards the position of an 'enabling' authority, contracting out more of its traditional core services to private sector companies. At the same time the organisation has already made major changes to its human resource policies and systems, as departments have been obliged to reorganise their activities in an effort to continue delivering services which have been put out to tender. The council is committed to an equal opportunities policy which is aiming to increase substantially the proportion of women in managerial positions by the end of the decade; although exact proportions vary between departments, about 20 per cent of the council's managers are women, compared with a figure of almost two-thirds for the total workforce. In senior managerial positions the council remains dominated by men, although women's support networks have been initiated recently in some departments.

Each of the eight departments is represented on the chief officer's group along with the deputy chief executive and the chief personnel officer. This is the group which is responsible for managing the authority in line with its policy plan and in conjunction with the elected members. Accountability is maintained through the council's committee structure, which covers each area of organisation's interests, and through management boards for certain sports and leisure activities. The council's objectives include the following:

- to improve the quality of service to customers within the resources available

- to introduce a style and structure of local government which ensures that council services are provided in the most effective, efficient and equitable way

- to train, develop, inform and motivate staff to ensure quality and high performance throughout all council services.

Personnel and development is organised both on an authority-wide and a departmental basis. Central personnel is concerned mainly with long-term issues such as organisation and management development, and the provision of legal advice for employment matters. It also co-ordinates personnel and development policies across the organisation. Departmental personnel officers are responsible for specific issues in their own area which, although similar in many respects, also show some variation because of the widely differing sets of staff who are covered; eg professional staff in education versus manual workers in technical services. Given the mass of sites at which council staff are employed, it is impossible to provide a service at every establishment, and a common complaint is that P&D are never available.

Over the last decade the authority has faced major changes in the way it is run, one of the most important being the extension of compulsory competitive tendering (CCT) to white-collar and professional staff, the implementation of internal trading units, and the impact of the Citizens' Charter. Numbers employed have fallen slightly over the last few years, primarily due to CCT for manual workers, although the majority of contracts have been won by in-house tenders. At the same time the Council prides itself on being able to deliver a quality service to customers with one of the lowest ratios of staff–population living in the borough. Many of the contracts that were awarded three years ago are now coming up for renewal, and it is expected that more work will be contracted out.

Trade unionism is well-established at Modern Metro, with recognition for UNISON (following the merger of NALGO, NUPE and COHSE) and the GMB. Density of unionisation is around 60 per cent overall, a proportion which has fallen considerably since the mid-1980s, although the level is much higher among managerial and professional staff. The relationship between management and unions has typically been good, although there have been some minor employee relations problems in recent years. Given governmental constraints on the pay budget (in terms of an 'expectation' about levels of award) and reductions in full-time equivalent numbers employed, discontent and low morale is now proving to be a serious problem in the authority. This is demonstrating itself in a variety of ways, such as problems with attendance and time-keeping, stress-related illnesses, refusals to take on extra work, and a spate of grievances against line managers who are perceived to be adopting a tougher stance than in the past.

For their part, many of the line managers complain that they lack support from their seniors and from the personnel department, and that they are held responsible for performance without having any authority to take action against members of staff who are performing below standard. The disciplinary procedure does not allow for line managers to issue formal warnings, and the process of involving more senior staff (officers of the authority) can be time-consuming and frustrating. At the same time, line managers are responsible for ensuring that the service is delivered in accordance with authority-wide quality standards.

Modern Metro works closely with a local business school, and has agreed that a team of specialists from their management courses should come and conduct a review of activities. You have been chosen as the P&D 'expert' on this team, and you are required to draw up a list of questions which are to be asked of the chief personnel officer and her staff; you must be able to explain why these questions are being asked, and have some broad thoughts on recommendations for action prior to the interview. The key issues are:

• how to improve attendance and time-keeping, including the use of a computerised personnel information system

• how to make the grievance and disciplinary procedures more effective

• how to manage redundancies at the next round of CCT

• whether the introduction of women-only training courses would help to further the achievement of equal opportunities

• how to redesign the existing benefits package, in particular the administration of the sick-pay scheme

• how to devolve more P&D issues to line managers while maintaining a strong corporate culture.

BANKCO: 'OVERCOMING TENSIONS AT BRANCH LEVEL'

Bankco is a medium-sized retail bank which employs about 20,000 staff in the UK. It has over 400 sites nationwide, including 380 branches. In recent years Bankco's profitability has declined as the market has become more fierce, and the deregulation of financial services has eroded distinctions between different types of institutions. In addition, the impact of new technology has been significant.

Bankco traditionally operated a paternalistic human resource policy, in common with other banks. It recruited and trained for a single career structure and a 'cradle to grave' philosophy operated, although in practice it was men who had 'careers' and women who had 'jobs'. Loyalty was a key factor. P&D matters were centralised at the corporate personnel department which dealt with everything from salaries and negotiations to recruitment and discipline.

Within retail banking each organisation provides similar products and hence consumer choice is heavily influenced by convenience and image, the latter partly created by contact with staff. There is thus a clear strategic link between quality of service and staff quality. Yet traditionally, staff have not been recruited or developed for customer contact skills but for technical and administrative ability. With banks wanting to move away from being regarded merely as providers of a money transmission service, to organisations which are engaged in selling of a range of financial products and services, 'tellers' need to become sellers. A new sales culture needs to be developed. The new skills required and the specialists who are needed also have implications for career management structures, and as the branch network is likely to shrink, career opportunities for traditional banking employees are likely to diminish.

Problems in the mid-1980s led to an influx of new managers who were specialists (accountants, marketing and personnel staff) drawn from outside the industry. They took a different view of Bankco and its culture, stressing that profit was not a 'bad' word, and began to move the bank towards more diversified products and services. Given changes in the competitive environment and in business strategies, it was felt important to change management styles and organisational cultures. In particular, it was seen as necessary to place a greater emphasis on business development and the management of performance. Staff needed to be encouraged to show greater initiative and flexibility rather than simply complying with administrative rules. The new P&D policies needed to 'fit' with the new business strategies.

At the centre of the P&D strategy was a remuneration review, which involved replacing the points-based job evaluation system for both managers and the clerical grade. Management desired a more flexible system, especially at the higher level, which would reflect a more market-driven approach: this took the form of a single integrated structure. Performance-related pay was also introduced at managerial level.

These changes were also reflected in the training and management development programmes. There was a trend in the former towards programmes stressing social skills, customer care, and sales and marketing training, all designed to educate staff about the new sales culture. Previously the training emphasis had been on technical training and supervisory skills for clerical and junior management staff.

As individualism strengthened, the relationship with the union also needed to be reshaped. Bankco management revamped its communication policy by implementing team briefing, which was designed to provide a clear management message, achieving the grapevine or the union as the main source of information. Devolving responsibility for P&D issues to the line effectively moved key decision-making away from the union head office function to the shopfloor, where the unions were weak.

It was appreciated that the squeeze on labour costs could lead to problems with the union, and possible detrimental effects on staff morale, so as far as possible the reduction in staff numbers was achieved in an unobtrusive manner via natural wastage and voluntary redundancy. However, the introduction of a new disciplinary code provided the bank with another means to reduce staff numbers by targeting ineffective performers. The bank was successful in reducing its numbers – and hence labour costs – in this first step of a longer-term review of cost structures.

Many of the new initiatives were met with apathy, cynicism and obstruction. Changes in the disciplinary code were regarded as cosmetic: as one manager said, 'Personnel can't bring itself to let go of the reins'. Branch managers showed some cynicism as to the alleged benefits of briefing, some regarding it as yet another 'flavour of the month' from personnel. Furthermore, while senior management emphasised a more positive approach to managing employees, regarding them as a key resource, and attempted to increase co-operation, commitment and identification with Bankco, the policy of reducing staff numbers and assertions of the 'right to manage' gave the impression that a more traditional approach to managing labour was still being practised.

You have been asked to make a presentation to the local IPD branch about how recent changes at Bankco have been managed. Prepare a set of OHPs which will be used during your presentation, including – among other issues – retraining in customer care, the job evaluation system, the role of a computerised personal information system for branch managers, and union–management relations. You also should explain how changes in human resource policies have been influenced by changes in business strategy, and should use one of the contingency models outlined in Chapter 17 as the basis for your argument. In addition, be warned that some hostile questions might be forthcoming given the high profile which the bank has in the area. How might you deal with them, in particular the tensions between the idea that employees are an important asset, and the recent rationalisation, redundancy and dismissal policies?

BLEAK HOUSE: 'PEOPLE ARE OUR MOST EASILY DISPOSABLE COST'

Bleak House is a firm of building contractors which was set up in the middle of the 1980s boom by two partners who left their previous employment at the same time. Both had worked for larger companies but felt frustrated and constrained by what they regarded as 'unnecessary' rules and regulations in these firms, as well as being annoyed that other people were making profits from their efforts. Setting up their own business offered the chance to escape from the drudgery of working for someone else and the possibility of making a lot of money over a relatively short time period. They knew that the market was highly competitive but felt that their previous experience provided an opportunity to be highly successful.

In the first few years business was very good, and the firm grew from about 10 staff up to a peak of 45. The first recruits were drawn from the companies where the two men had worked previously, and were selected for their knowledge of the industry, their willingness to work hard, and their ability to interact with others. One of the new recruits was appointed as the supervisor, and new orders were gained easily due to the quality of the work provided and recommendations from customers. Quite a number of the jobs were for the same customers.

In the early days the firm operated with very few rules and procedures in the P&D area, but given the small numbers employed and the willingness of all employees – including the owners – to get involved in completing jobs on time, this mattered little. Basic wages were low, but the owners gave large bonuses if targets were met, and at the completion of each job there was typically a massive drinking bout. The firm was also notable for the absence of any procedures, discipline being meted out in a harsh and unyielding way, grievances being resolved on a personal *ad hoc* basis. Recruitment was by word-of-mouth, training was non-existent, health and safety rules were short-circuited wherever possible, and the firm survived – and actually did well financially – without any explicit or formal systems.

Two years ago business started to get tighter, the owners spent more time away from the company trying to get new orders, and tempers started to fray. Instead of working together to meet deadlines, people began to blame each other for not completing jobs on time: the owners felt that the workforce was no longer committed to the company, that by not working extra hours they were being disloyal, and that more employees were taking short cuts to ensure that jobs were finished to allow for a long drinking session on a Friday afternoon. The workforce felt that the owners were too interested in their own image, in buying new cars, and in raking off larger profits from the business. A positive working environment turned into a negative and cynical culture.

Several major contracts were lost due to poor-quality work on other jobs, and the reputation of the firm deteriorated. Due to a decline in orders, half the workforce was made redundant – including some of the people who had joined at the outset – and several others were dismissed for misconduct. Three ex-employees filed unfair dismissal claims at the industrial tribunal, but in each case settlements were made outside of court in order to save on costs. Communications, which worked quite well at an informal level during the good days, became non-existent. The absence of procedures has now become an issue as employee relations have worsened, and the owners have become aware that they might be liable for major costs in the event of an unfair dismissal claim's being upheld, or an accident at work occurring which is regarded as management's fault. Moreover, the informal recruitment practices which used to serve the company so well now seem less effective, and several of the more recent recruits have left, or been sacked soon after taking up their posts. Despite all this, however, the firm continues to survive, and the owners are currently hoping for an improvement in the housing market, a reduction in the mortgage rate, or a boost from the Chancellor of the Exchequer to kick-start the economy again. They still have a decent lifestyle, retaining their up-market cars, going abroad on holiday two or three times each year, and engaging in conspicuous consumption, but both feel that things could be so much better if only they could rekindle the culture of the 'good old days' when staff seemed committed and loyal.

You happen to meet one of the owners by chance, and he discovers that you are doing an IPD course. He seems quite interested in what you have to say about 'best practice' P&D, but reckons none of it would work in his firm. Nevertheless, he asks you to spend a couple of days reviewing the firm's P&D policies, providing some advice on what he might do to improve employment relations, provided 'it does not cost too much'. He is particularly concerned about recruitment and selection, on-the-job training, disciplinary procedures, health and safety, and payment systems. He has also heard of the Investors in People award, and thinks that this might help to revive flagging orders and regain his firm's reputation. What will you say in your report, and why?

CONCLUSIONS

These seven cases provide readers with a wide range of examples of P&D in practice. The chemical firm, Photochem, is a market leader and is in an excellent position to develop a range of 'best practice' P&D policies and practices. The trade unions are prepared to work with management to secure competitive advantage, and a number of the P&D practices employed are at the forefront of new developments. A similar situation was apparent at the launch of the Japanese company, and major employee relations gains were made with the introduction of the single-union agreement and flexible working practices. While it was relatively easy to implement some of these 'new' initiatives due to it being a greenfield site, questions are starting to emerge about whether the honeymoon is over. Superfood is in quite a different position from the two manufacturing sites, with a much lower-skilled workforce, high levels of labour turnover and a heavily centralised approach to P&D issues. There have been no employee relations problems in the past. On the other hand, P&D specialists face problems in trying to persuade line managers to take recruitment and selection seriously or release new staff for induction training; because labour turnover is so high, line managers argue there is little point in spending much time on these activities. The fourth and fifth cases are from the public sector, and both of the organisations described here have been through major changes over the last decade due to contracting-out of services and a shift to a more explicit customer-oriented philosophy, as well as decentralisation of P&D to local level. The approaches which have been taken have differed, with the NHS trust aiming to develop a personal action programme to support its customer care and quality initiatives, while the local authority is aiming to tighten up on some of its P&D procedures (eg absence control, discipline, sick pay) yet also trying to develop the potential of its women managers. The financial services company, Bankco, has also undergone major changes in recent years as management have retreated from their long-standing paternalist policies to adopt a more assertive customer-focused strategy. This has led to major reviews of many of the bank's policies, not least in relation to trade union agreements and the relationship between line managers and P&D

specialists. The final case represents a 'bleak house' scenario, one in which changes in business prospects and a more aggressive style of management have combined to limit the opportunity for 'best practice' P&D; indeed, many of the human resource practices are the exact opposite of those which were described in Chapter 18. This is the sort of situation which would test any P&D manager's ethical and professional stance to the full.

As well as dealing with each case separately, readers are also encouraged to compare and contrast their practices, looking for reasons *why* P&D practices might vary between them. It might be worth re-reading some parts of Part 2 in order to identify the contextual factors which influence P&D in such an uneven manner, as well as consider the details which are provided in each of the chapters on substantive issues in the areas of resourcing, development, relations, and reward. In each of the cases, although it is important to identify 'solutions' to the problems which are posed, it is perhaps just as necessary to establish *why* these recommendations are suitable for the particular set of circumstances.

Part 8
REVIEW

20 Examination questions and advice

INTRODUCTION

The purpose of this final chapter is to review readers' knowledge and understanding of the major issues dealt with in the book. This chapter should prove especially useful for those students preparing for the IPD Standards in the area of Core Personnel and Development, in that it provides questions which are similar to those likely to be found on the nationally set examination paper. At the same time, however, it should also prove beneficial to readers who are studying for internally set examinations, since it provides a framework for revision, as well as for those who are interested in posing questions about P&D practices in their own organisation.

The chapter comprises three sections which follow the format of the IPD national examination paper in Core Personnel and Development, and a fourth section which provides general advice on how to tackle the paper. The first section includes three case studies similar to the one which is set in the national examination. If students are trying to simulate examination conditions, each of these questions should take about one hour to complete. In the second section of this chapter, there are 30 questions which aim to test knowledge and understanding through short answers, typically one paragraph in length, which can be completed in 5 to 10 minutes. This style of question forms a new element in the IPD examination assessment portfolio under the Professional Qualification Scheme, not just in Core Personnel and Development but throughout the whole set of modules. The third section contains eight questions drawn from the material which appears in the book and the standards, which require students to produce reports or similar assignments which relate general principles to specific features of organisational practice. Approximately one hour should be allocated for each question.

SECTION A: CASE STUDIES

Advising a recently appointed manager

A new departmental manager was appointed to your organisation six months ago, and has come to ask for advice on how to deal with several issues which have occurred during this time. She has some managerial experience already, but not in your sector of the economy. She has missed out on the training courses offered by the employer due to her starting date, but it is hoped that she will be able to attend them in the next round – yet this is not for a further six months.

There are three problems which need attention. First, one of her longer-serving clerical staff has been absent for approximately 20 per cent of the last six months, including one lengthy absence of six weeks while suffering from stress. This absence was certificated, but it occurred straight after the manager had spoken with this member of staff about mistakes in her work, suggesting that she needed to go through a further training programme. Since that time, there have been a further six absences, all of which have been self-certificated and have lasted between one and five days. On looking back through her files, you find that this is not the first time that a string of absences has occurred, but no formal action was taken in the past. What advice would you give her, and why?

The second issue is that one of the male professional members of her team has been accused by several women managers of harassing and bullying them. The departmental manager also feels that this man has a problem with women, but has no concrete evidence to support her case. The man involved denies the allegations. What do you suggest should happen next?

The third issue relates to the role of the personnel and development function. The departmental manager feels that she is getting insufficient support from P&D, she does not have access to staff files, and if employees have a problem (say, with illness) they telephone central personnel who often fail to get a message through to managers in the department. She would like to have direct and immediate access to a specialist who is located in the department; there are 65 staff employed in the department, but staff are spread over three locations. You decide to bring this issue up at your next monthly personnel and development meeting. What will you suggest, and why?

Consider the financial implications of your recommendations in each case.

Managing change in a privatised organisation

You work for a recently privatised organisation, employing 5,000 people, which is seeking to transform its culture over the course of the 1990s. The organisation employs a large number of managers who have worked their way up the hierarchy since leaving school. Most of the systems and policies were devised at national level, and merely implemented by local managers with little opportunity to adapt them to suit local conditions. Many of the manual and white-collar staff, who are extensively unionised, have been accustomed to high levels of job security in the past. Overall, the environment is one in which change is likely to be difficult to achieve.

Since privatisation the organisation has been led by a new chief executive who worked previously for a large, decentralised manufacturing company, and who is well known for his record of trying to push through changes quickly and without resistance. A new set of managers have been appointed from outside the industry with very clear ideas about change but, in your view, they have little understanding of how the company was managed under the previous regime.

The company has decided to set up a new customer services department (CSD) to handle all customer records, queries and complaints at a central location rather than at a number of geographically dispersed sites, as was the case before privatisation. You have been asked to advise the general manager of CSD on how to deal with the following issues in a way which will convince his senior management colleagues:

• the recruitment and selection of staff for the new CSD, using internal or external sources, or a mix of the two

• the design and implementation of an effective involvement and communications system for CSD, which can be integrated with that for the organisation as a whole

• the evaluation of training and development programmes for managers within CSD

• the implementation of a new remuneration policy at CSD, to be based on performance.

Write brief notes on each issue, summarising your proposed lines of action and their financial implications, as well as indicating *why* it ought to be done.

Delivering P&D to a professional workforce

Softcon is a software engineering consultancy established in the early 1980s on a greenfield site in the south of England. It supplies computer-based systems, products and services to all parts of industry, commerce and central government. It specialises in systems designed for security, air traffic control, and infrastructure software. The external environment has been a difficult one in recent years, and the recession and the contraction of the defence industry has led to increased competition in the industry.

Softcon employs around 200 staff on three sites, and numbers have risen steadily since its foundation – despite the recession. Senior management believe an increase in market share could compensate for contraction in the overall size of the market. Staff are largely made up of professional software engineers, unions are not recognised, and the company operates a number of share option schemes. 70 per cent of staff are shareholders.

Management claims that it has an 'open' culture based on a concept of professional partnership, and work groupings reflect the demands of the business and the particular projects which are being carried out. The rapid growth of the company has made it possible for individual careers to be aligned with company interests. However, in recent months a view has emerged following the results of the staff attitude survey that insufficient attention is being given to staff careers, and that management is becoming obsessed with rules and regulations.

The human resource function at Softcon is small and it is not represented at board level, even though human resource issues have always been important because of the nature of the industry. Line managers have responsibility for managing staff, and this seems to work well for the most part. However, different approaches are taken by different managers and this has led to some inconsistencies which have caused problems. The human resource function has overall responsibility for training and induction. Recently, workshops have been run for middle managers with the aim of getting them to empower staff. The training emphasises the need for staff involvement and agreement in both objective-setting and professional development. In general, however, the human resource function has seen itself as an internal consultant and has a document listing the main products and levels of services it provides.

Review the key points in Chapters 17 and 18 relating to vertical and horizontal integration. Draw up a service-level agreement for Softcon's human resource function on the basis of this, and explain why it has been drafted in this way.

SECTION B: QUESTIONS REQUIRING SHORT ANSWERS

1) Specify the main sources of contractual terms which govern the employment relationship, and provide an example of each source.

2) Describe succinctly what is meant by the term 'the flexible firm'.

3) What are the main services provided by the Advisory Conciliation and Arbitration Service?

4) Provide concise definitions of NVQs/SVQs at Levels 1–5, showing clearly the ways in which they are differentiated.

5) According to Connock and Johns (1995), there are a number of critical success factors for organisations which claim to be practising ethical leadership. List FIVE of them.

6) Distinguish between the terms 'equal opportunities' and 'managing diversity', using an example to illustrate your answer.

7) Provide THREE reasons why human resource planning is important to an organisation.

8) What are the principal differences between a job description and a person specification, and why are both of these important?

9) What are the major advantages and disadvantages of the interview as a selection device?

10) Define 360-degree appraisal, and provide THREE reasons why it might be more useful than traditional appraisal schemes.

11) Identify the key actions which managers need to take in preparing

for, conducting, and following-up a return-to-work interview after a period of absence.

12) Explain briefly Kolb's learning cycle, and specify its key principles.

13) What is meant by the term 'the learning organisation'. Provide an example to illustrate this definition.

14) List FIVE benefits which might flow from a systematic and well-developed system of training.

15) Explain briefly Kirkpatrick's four levels at which training may be evaluated, using examples to illustrate your answer.

16) What are the principal ground rules which need to be observed when designing or selecting an outdoor-based development programme for managers?

17) Specify the major differences between the consultative (problem-solving) and sophisticated paternalist styles of employee relations management.

18) Provide THREE reasons why employers might wish to derecognise trade unions.

19) Using examples, explain the difference between substantive and procedural rules in employee relations.

20) What are the main forms of direct employee involvement used by employers in the late 1990s?

21) List the arguments which P&D specialists might use to persuade line managers that procedures are valuable tools and guidelines rather than millstones.

22) What implications does the distinction between hygiene factors and motivators have for the design of reward management systems?

23) Explain the key differences between a discriminatory and non-discriminatory job evaluation scheme.

24) Why has performance-related pay become more popular in recent times?

25) Identify the major barriers to the achievement of harmonisation in practice.

26) Explain briefly how non-financial rewards and recognition may act as a motivating force at work.

27) Outline the human resource practices which might be found in an organisation which utilises a 'quality enhancement' approach to gain competitive advantage.

28) Provide FOUR reasons why vertical integration is so difficult to achieve in practice.

29) What is meant by the term 'best-practice personnel and development/human resource management'?

30) Why might employers choose to appoint consultants to undertake P&D work rather than using an in-house function?

SECTION C: REPORTS AND OTHER PRACTICAL ASSIGNMENTS

1) As part of your organisation's drive for external accreditation, you have been asked to review your existing P&D policies, assessing the extent to which they are integrated with each other and with broader organisational objectives.

2) Write a paper for your general manager (or his or her equivalent) on the desirability of devolving P&D activities to line managers. Provide examples to support your argument.

3) As part of your organisation's management development programme, you have been asked to deliver a 15-minute talk on 'the value of training and development'. Prepare an outline of your talk, provide examples as appropriate, and explain briefly how you would aim to get your message across to the audience.

4) An employee representative has made an appointment to ask why your organisation's equal opportunities policies have so far failed to deliver complete equality of opportunity for *all* employees. Provide a set of notes outlining what you would say to him or her, and justify your comments.

5) It has come to your notice that line managers are not always following organisational guidelines on recruitment and selection, and you have decided to organise a short session to remind them of those. Provide an outline of what you would include in this session, paying particular attention to how you might persuade them of the merits of following organisational guidelines, and alerting them to the dangers of not doing so.

6) Review your organisation's current policy on union recognition (or non-recognition, as appropriate), and put forward recommendations for future policy. You will need to justify your recommendations, providing information on the costs and benefits of your proposals.

7) How might profit-related pay be introduced into your organisation, and what would be its advantages and disadvantages compared with existing reward schemes?

8) You have been asked to make a presentation to students at a local college on the IPD Professional Management Foundation Programme about the benefits of a computerised personnel information system (CPIS). Describe briefly your own system and demonstrate the way in which this has 'added value' to the organisation. How might it be used more effectively?

EXAMINATION GUIDELINES

The purpose of this final section is to provide students with some guidance about the way in which to tackle examination questions on the Core Personnel and Development paper. A number of general comments are appropriate, given that students tend to make similar mistakes on each part of the paper, but these are supplemented with more specific observations relating to each part.

Four general points are worth making:

• Many candidates fail to answer all parts of a multi-part question, and this is often the case on the compulsory case study. Typically, up to half of those who fail do not provide any costings, even though this is specified in the question. Students need to remember that they are unlikely to gain more than half the available marks if they answer only half the question!

• Many candidates fail to address the question which has been posed, preferring to write what they wish to tell the examiner. While this can be very interesting, it also demonstrates a failure to appreciate the requirements of a 'customer' – if examiners can be seen in that light. Similarly, it is common for students to write an essay rather than a report or draft talk when this is requested. One of the skills that examiners are trying to assess in these papers is the ability of students to write in a clear, concise and convincing manner.

• Many candidates seem to lose sight of the overall objective when answering a question, and provide an unbalanced answer which devotes far too much time to one part of the question, to the detriment of others. Clear planning before starting to write an answer can obviously reduce the likelihood of this particular problem. On some occasions, students seem to feel that making references to well-known academics demonstrates that they understand the principal issues; this is all very well *if* the references are relevant and appropriate, and do not appear to be bolted on to a somewhat peripheral answer.

• Many students fail to locate their answer in the wider commercial and environmental context, showing little appreciation of national trends or longer-run developments in the economy as a whole, or P&D in particular. There is often a temptation to assume that current fads and fashions represent a superior solution to organisational problems, and little recognition that they may be superficial and trite. Moreover, students often fail to recognise the force of existing cultural norms and traditions when putting forward recommendations, somehow assuming that all options are feasible. It is important to show some awareness of the constraints (financial or otherwise) as well as the opportunities when answering questions. One of the things which the Professional Qualification Scheme aims to develop in students is the ability to persuade line managers of the utility of specific P&D recommendations in response to specific organisational problems.

Taking a more positive slant, there are certain guidelines which students might like to bear in mind when preparing for the examination, some of which build upon what has been said in the previous paragraphs. These are:

- Make sure that the material in the whole syllabus is understood, at least to the extent of being able to provide short paragraph-length answers to the questions in section B. In addition, when addressing the case study and report questions in sections A and C, students need to be able to demonstrate a holistic appreciation of P&D.

- Provide examples as appropriate to support a particular answer and argument. These may be drawn from any organisation, not only the one for which the student currently works, and it is useful if contemporary examples are provided as these show that the student is up to date and is reading the professional journals.

- Write concisely and clearly, providing signposts to an answer. There is nothing worse for an examiner (or any reader, for that matter) than having to re-read an answer several times in order to try to identify precisely what the student is trying to say. A clear introduction stating explicitly what will be contained in the answer helps considerably in this respect, as does the use of paragraphs, sections and numbering; the precise technique which is used matters less than the overall impact, and students should therefore use the approach with which they feel most comfortable.

- Ensure that the examination is timed so that an attempt can be made at all sections and all questions. It is worthwhile reiterating that approximately one hour should be allocated to each section on the examination paper. This means that in section B, each question should take between 5 and 10 minutes to answer.

These guidelines should not be seen as some idiosyncratic attempt to impose unrealistic academic standards on IPD students. Rather, these skills are central to all aspects of managerial work: addressing the question which is posed; choosing from alternatives to formulate a realistic answer; justifying and costing a recommendation; writing in a clear and well-structured manner which manages to persuade the reader.

There are a number of more specific comments relating to each of the sections. When addressing the case study, students need to ensure that they understand the case as a whole and are able to identify the key points contained within it. In writing their answers they are expected to draw from the whole syllabus, although there is a need for more detailed analysis of particular sections within it. The recommendations that are proposed need to be costed if this is specified in the question. There is no need to provide highly specific costs – for example, the cost of 20 cups of coffee – but some sort of ballpark figure should be given for the cost of, say, recruitment advertising, the fees for consultants, or a wage claim.

Section B comprises a number of questions which require short paragraph-length answers. These can be drawn from any part of the syllabus, and require students to present fairly basic core information in order to demonstrate their knowledge and understanding of the topics under consideration. The answers in this section need to be concise, but can usefully be supplemented with examples to illustrate the students' understanding of the issue. It is important that all questions in this section are tackled.

In section C, students are required to write a report or provide details on some other practical assignment – such as preparing the outline for a talk, or writing a letter to a newspaper. It is crucial that the format which is specified is observed, so that an *outline* for a talk is presented, or the *notes* for a paper are drawn up, or the *draft* of a letter is written. Students who write essays in response to questions in this section are not going to pass, irrespective of the quality of their answer.

References

ACKERS, P., MARCHINGTON, M., WILKINSON, A. AND GOODMAN, J. (1992) 'The use of cycles: explaining employee involvement in the 1990s', *Industrial Relations Journal*, Vol. 23, 4: 268–283.

ADAMS, K. (1991) 'Externalisation versus specialisation: what is happening to personnel?', *Human Resource Management Journal*, Vol. 1, 4: 40–54.

ADVISORY CONCILIATION AND ARBITRATION SERVICE (1983) *Induction of New Employees*. London, HMSO.

ADVISORY CONCILIATION AND ARBITRATION SERVICE CODE OF PRACTICE (1985) *Disciplinary Practice and Procedures in Employment*. London, HMSO.

ADVISORY CONCILIATION AND ARBITRATION SERVICE (1988a) 'Labour flexibility in Britain', *Occasional Paper No. 41*. London, HMSO.

ADVISORY CONCILIATION AND ARBITRATION SERVICE (1988b) 'Developments in payment systems', the 1988 ACAS Survey, *Occasional Paper No. 45*. London, HMSO.

ADVISORY CONCILIATION AND ARBITRATION SERVICE (1991a) 'Job evaluation – an introduction', *ACAS Advisory Booklet No. 1*. London, HMSO.

ADVISORY CONCILIATION AND ARBITRATION SERVICE (1991b) 'Introduction to payment systems', *ACAS Advisory Booklet No. 2*. London, HMSO.

ADVISORY CONCILIATION AND ARBITRATION SERVICE (1992) *Employment Handbook*. London, HMSO.

AHLSTRAND, B. (1990) *The Quest for Productivity: A case study of Fawley after Flanders*. Cambridge, Cambridge University Press.

AHLSTRAND, B. AND PURCELL, J. (1988) 'Employee relations strategy in the multi-divisional company', *Personnel Review*, Vol. 17, 3: 3–11.

ALDCROFT, D. (1992) *Education, Training and Economic Performance, 1994 to 1990*. Manchester, Manchester University Press.

ANDERSON, G. (1992) 'Performance appraisal' in B. Towers (Ed.), *The Handbook of Human Resource Management*. Oxford, Blackwell: 186–207.

ANDERSON, G., AND EVENDEN, R. (1993) 'Performance management: its role and methods in human resource strategy', in R. Harrison (Ed.), *Human Resource Management: Issues and strategies*. Wokingham, Addison Wesley: 247–273.

ARGYRIS, C. AND SCHON, D. (1978) *Organisational Learning: A theory in action perspective*. New York, Addison-Wesley.

ARMSTRONG, M. (1977) *A Handbook of Personnel Management Practice*. London, Kogan Page.

ARMSTRONG, M. (1989) *Personnel and the Bottom Line*. London, IPM.

ARMSTRONG, M. (1992) *Human Resource Management: Strategy and action*. London, Kogan Page.

ARMSTRONG, M. (1993) *Managing Reward Systems*. Milton Keynes, Open University Press.

ARMSTRONG, M. (1994) *Using the Human Resource Consultant: Achieving results, adding value*. London, IPM.

ARMSTRONG, M. (1995) 'Measuring work: the vital statistics', *People Management*, 21 September: 34–35.

ARMSTRONG, M. AND BARON, A. (1995) *The Job Evaluation Handbook*. London, IPD.

ARMSTRONG, M. AND MURLIS, H. (1991) *Reward Management*, Second edition. London, Kogan Page.

ARMSTRONG, M. AND MURLIS, H. (1995) *Reward Management*, Third edition. London, Kogan Page.

ARMSTRONG, P. (1989) 'Limits and possibilities for HRM in an age of management accountancy', in J. Storey (Ed.). *New Perspectives on Human Resource Management*. London, Routledge: 154–166.

ARMSTRONG, P., GOODMAN, J. AND HYMAN, J. (1981) *Ideology and Shopfloor Industrial Relations*. London, Croom Helm.

ARNOLD, J., ROBERTSON, I. AND COOPER, C. (1991) *Work Psychology: Understanding human behaviour in the workplace*. London, Pitman.

ARTHURS, A., (1985) 'Towards single status', *Journal of General Management*, Vol. 11, No. 1: 17–28.

ASHTON, D. AND FELSTEAD, A. (1994) 'Training and development', in J. Storey (Ed.), *Human Resource Management: A critical text*. London, Routledge: 234–253.

ATKINSON, J. (1984) 'Manpower strategies for the flexible organisation'. *Personnel Management*, August: 28–31.

ATKINSON, J. (1986) 'Flexibility or fragmentation? The United Kingdom labour market in the eighties', *Labour and Society*, Vol. 12, 1: 87–105.

ATKINSON, J. (1989) 'Four stages of adjustment to the demographic downturn'. *Personnel Management*, August: 20–24.

ATKINSON, J. AND MEAGER, N. (1986) 'Is flexibility a flash in the pan?'. *Personnel Management*, September: 26–29.

ATKINSON, R. L., ATKINSON, R. C., SMITH, E. AND BEM, D. (1993) *Introduction to Psychology*, Eleventh Edition. New York, Harcourt Brace Jovanovich.

BADDON, L., HUNTER, L., HYMAN, J., LEOPOLD, J., AND RAMSAY, H. (1989) *People's Capitalism*, London, Routledge.

BAIRD, L. AND MESHOULAM, I. (1988) 'Managing two fits of strategic human resource management'. *Academy of Management Review*, Vol. 13, 1: 116–28.

BAKER, B. AND COOPER, J. (1995) 'Fair play or foul? A survey of occupational test practices in the UK'. *Personnel Review*, Vol. 24, 3: 3–18.

BALADAMUS, W. (1961) *Efficiency and Effort*. London, Tavistock.

BANDURA, A. (1977) *Social Learning Theory*. New Jersey, Prentice Hall.

BARLOW, G. (1989) 'Deficiencies and the perpetuation of power: latent functions in management appraisal'. *Journal of Management Studies*, Vol. 26, 5: 499–517.

BARTHOLOMEW, D. (Ed.) (1976) *Manpower Planning*. Harmondsworth, Penguin.

BARTRAM, D. (1991) 'Addressing the abuse of psychological tests', *Personnel Management*, April: 34–39.

BASSETT, P. (1987) *The New Industrial Relations*. London, Macmillan.

BAXTER, B. (1996) 'Consultancy expertise: a post–modern perspective', in H. Scarbrough (Ed.), *The Management of Expertise*. London, Macmillan: 66–92.

BEARDWELL, I. AND HOLDEN, L. (Eds) (1994) *Human Resource Management: A contemporary perspective*. London, Pitman.

BEATSON, M. (1995) 'Labour market flexibility', London, *Employment Department Research Series, No. 48*.

BEAUMONT, P. (1987) *The Decline of Trade Union Organisation*. London, Croom Helm.

BEAUMONT, P. (1992) *Public Sector Industrial Relations*. London, Routledge.

BEAUMONT, P. AND TOWERS, B. (1992) 'Approaches to trade union organisation', in B. Towers (Ed.), *A Handbook of Industrial Relations Practice*. London, Kogan Page: 123–136.

BEE, R. AND BEE, F. (1994) *Training Needs Analysis and Evaluation*. London, IPD.

BELL, D. (1989) 'Why manpower planning is back in vogue'. *Personnel Management*, July: 40–43.

BELL, D., AND HANSON, C. (1984) *Profit Sharing and Employee Shareholding*. London, IPA.

BEN–SHAKHAR, G. (1989) 'Non–conventional methods in selection', in P. Herriot (Ed.), *Assessment and Selection in Organisations*. Chichester, Wiley: 469–485.

BERRIDGE, J. AND COOPER, C. (1994) 'The employee assistance programme: its role in organisational coping and excellence'. *Personnel Review*, Vol. 23, 7: 4–20.

BEVAN, S. AND THOMSON, M. (1991) 'Performance management at the crossroads'. *Personnel Management*, November: 36–39.

BLACK, J., AND ACKERS, P. (1988) 'The Japanisation of British industry: a case study of quality circles in the carpet industry'. *Employee Relations*, 10, 6: 9–16.

BLUM, S. (1996) 'Technology for the people', *Conspectus*, January: 2–5.

BLUMBERG, P. (1968) *Industrial Democracy: The sociology of participation*. London, Constable.

BLYTON, P. AND TURNBULL, P. (1994) *The Dynamics of Employee Relations*. London, Macmillan.

BOWEY, A. (1975) *A Guide to Manpower Planning*. London, Macmillan.

BOWEY, A., THORPE, R., MITCHELL, F., NICHOLLS, G., GOSNOLD, D., SAVERY, L. AND HELLIER, P. (1982) 'Effects of incentive payment systems: UK 1977–1980', *Department of Employment Research Paper No. 36*. London, HMSO.

BOYATSIS, R. (1982) *The Competent Manager: A model for effective performance.* New York, Wiley.

BOYDELL, T. (1971) *A Guide to the Identification of Training Needs.* BACIE, London.

BRAMHAM, J. (1975) *Practical Manpower Planning.* London, IPM.

BRAMHAM, J. (1994) *Human Resource Planning,* Fourth Edition. London, IPD.

BRAMLEY, P. (1991) *Evaluating Training Effectiveness: Translating theory into practice.* Maidenhead, McGraw-Hill.

BRAMLEY, P. AND NEWBY, A. (1984) 'The evaluation of training part one: clarifying the concept'. *Journal of European Industrial Training,* Vol. 8, 6: 10–16.

BRAVERMAN, H. (1974) *Labour and Monopoly Capital.* New York, Monthly Review Press.

BREWSTER, C. (1989) *Employee Relations.* Basingstoke, Macmillan.

BREWSTER, C., GILL, C. AND RICHBELL, S. (1983) 'Industrial relations policy: a framework for analysis', in K. Thurley and S. Wood (Eds), *Industrial Relations and Management Strategy,* Cambridge, Cambridge University Press: 62–72.

BRISTOL BUSINESS SCHOOL, (1995) *Work and Employment, Issue 3,* Health and Safety in the Workplace, Spring.

BROWN, W. (1973) *Piecework Bargaining.* London, Heinemann.

BROWN, W. (1993) 'The contraction of collective bargaining in Britain', *British Journal of Industrial Relations,* Vol. 31, 2: 189–200.

BROWN, W. AND WALSH, J. (1994) 'Managing pay in Britain', in K. Sisson (Ed.), *Personnel Management* (Second Edition): 437–464.

BUCHANAN, D. (1986) 'Management objectives in techical change', in D. Knights and H. Willmott (Eds), *Managing the Labour Process,* Aldershot, Gower: 67–84.

BUCHANAN, D. (1992) 'High performance: new boundaries of acceptability in worker control', in G. Salaman (Ed.), *Human Resource Strategies.* London, Sage: 138–155.

BUCHANAN, D. (1994) 'Principles and Practices in Work Design', in K. Sisson (Ed.), *Personnel Management in Britain.* Oxford, Blackwell: 85–116.

BURAWOY, M. (1979) *Manufacturing Consent: Changes in the labour process under monopoly capitalism.* Chicago, University of Chicago Press.

BURN, D. AND THOMPSON, L. (1993) 'When personnel calls in the auditors', *Personnel Management.* January 28–31.

BURNETT, D. AND JAMES, K. (1993) 'Body/mind psychology in manager development: a route to enhanced managerial effectiveness', *European Management Journal,* Vol. 11, 4: 466–472.

CANN, P. (1986) 'Improved performance through interactive video', in T. Page (Ed.), *Computers in Personnel: Business and technology–achieving practical solutions.* London, IPM/IMS: 62–66.

CANNELL, M. AND WOOD, S. (1992) *Incentive Pay.* NEDO/IPM.

CARLEY, M. (1995) 'Talking shops or serious forums'. *People Management,* 13 July.

CARLTON, I. AND SLOMAN, M. (1992) 'Performance appraisal in practice', *Human Resource Management Journal,* Vol. 2, 3: 80–94.

CARROLL, A. (1990) 'Principles of business ethics: their role in decision making and an initial consensus', *Management Decision*, Vol. 28, 8: 20–24.

CASEY, B. (1991) 'Survey evidence on trends in non standard employment', in A. Pollert (Ed.), *Farewell to Flexibility*. Oxford, Blackwell: 179–199.

CHAMBERLAIN, N. AND KUHN, J. (1965) *Collective Bargaining*. New York, McGraw-Hill.

CHANDLER, A. (1962) *Strategy and Structure: Chapters in the history of the American industrial enterprise*. Cambridge Mass., MIT Press.

CHILD, J. (1969) *British Management Thought*. London, Allen and Unwin.

CHRYSSIDES, G. AND KALER, J. (1993) *An Introduction to Business Ethics*. London, Chapman and Hall.

CLARK, J. (1993) 'Procedures and consistency versus flexibility and commitment in employee relations: a comment on Storey', *Human Resource Management Journal*, Vol. 4: 79–81.

CLAYDON, T. (1989) 'Union derecognition in Britain in the 1980s', *British Journal of Industrial Relations*, Vol. 27, 2: 214–224.

CLEGG, H. (1970) *The System of Industrial Relations in Great Britain*. Oxford, Blackwell.

COLCLOUGH, J. (1983) 'The business of personnel is the business', *Personnel Management*, November: 21–23.

COLE, G. (1994) 'Learning with computers', *Accountancy*, Vol 113, 1209: 60–64.

COLLIN, A. (1994) 'Learning and Development', in I. Beardwell and L. Holden (Eds), *Human Resource Management: A contemporary perspective*. London, Pitman: 271–334.

COLWILL, N. AND VINNICOMBE, S. (1991) 'Women's Training Needs', in J. Firth-Cozens and M. West (Eds), *Women at Work*. Milton Keynes, Open University Press: 42–50.

CONNOCK, S. (1992) *HR Vision: Managing a quality workforce*. London, IPM.

CONNOCK, S. AND JOHNS, T (1995) *Ethical Leadership*. London, IPD.

CONSTABLE, J. AND MCCORMICK, R. (1987) *The Making of British Managers*. London, BIM.

COOPER, R. (1973) 'Task characteristics and intrinsic motivation', *Human Relations*, Vol. 26, August: 387–408.

COOPER, R. (1974) *Job Motivation and Design*. London, IPD.

COWLING, A. AND WALTERS, M. (1990) 'Manpower planning – where are we today?', *Personnel Review*, Vol. 19, 3: 3–8.

CRAWSHAW, M., DAVIS, E., AND KAY, J. (1994) ' "Being stuck in the middle" or "good food costs less at Sainsbury's" ', *British Journal of Management*, Vol. 5, 1: 19–32.

CRICHTON, A. (1968) *Personnel Management in Context*. London, Batsford.

CROSBY, P. (1980) *Quality is Free*. New York, McGraw-Hill.

CRYSTAL, G. (1991) *In Search of Excess*. New York, Norton.

CUNNINGHAM, I. AND HYMAN, J. (1995) 'Transforming the HRM vision into reality: the role of line managers and supervisors in implementing change', *Employee Relations*, Vol. 17, 8: 5–20.

CURNOW, B. (1986) 'The creative approach to pay', *Personnel Management,* October: 70–75.

CURRY, L. (1995) 'Good for morale, good for business', *People Management,* 7 September 42–44.

DAVIES, J. (1983) 'Evaluating training', in D. Guest and T. Kenny (Eds), *A Textbook of Techniques and Strategies in Personnel Management.* London, IPM: 241–69.

DEAN, C. AND WHITLOCK, Q. (1992) *A Handbook of Computer-based Training.* London, Kogan Page.

DELBRIDGE, R. AND TURNBULL, P. (1992) 'Human resource maximisation: the management of labour under just-in-time manufacturing systems', in P. Blyton and P. Turnbull (Eds), *Reassessing Human Resource Management.* London, Sage: 56–73.

DEPARTMENT OF EMPLOYMENT, (1968) *Company Manpower Planning.* London, HMSO.

DEPARTMENT OF EMPLOYMENT, (1989) *People and Companies.* London, HMSO.

DEVANNA, M., FOMBRUN, C. AND TICHY, N. (1984) 'A framework for strategic human resource management', in C. Fombrun, N. Tichy and M. Devanna, *Strategic Human Resource Management,* New York, Wiley: 37–56.

DEWE, P., DUNN, S. AND RICHARDSON, R. (1988) 'Employee share option schemes; why workers are attracted to them', *British Journal of Industrial Relations,* Vol. 26, I: 1–21.

DICKENS, L. (1988) 'Falling through the net; employment change and worker protection'. *Industrial Relations Journal,* Vol. 19, 2: 139–153.

DICKENS, L. (1994) 'Wasted resources? Equal opportunities in employment', in K. Sisson (Ed.), *Personnel Management in Britain.* Oxford, Blackwell: 253–296.

DICKENS, L. AND HALL, M. (1995) 'The State: Labour Law and Industrial Relations', in P. Edwards (Ed.), *Industrial Relations; Theory and practice in Britain.* Oxford, Blackwell: 255–303.

DICKENS, L., JONES, M., WEEKS, B. AND HART, M. (1985) *Dismissed: A study of unfair dismissal and the industrial tribunal system.* Oxford, Blackwell.

DOERINGER, P. AND PIORE, M. (1971) *Internal Labour Markets and Manpower Analysis.* Lexington, D C Heath.

DONALDSON, J. AND DAVIS, P. (1990) 'Business ethics? Yes, but what can it do for the bottom line?', *Management Decision,* Vol 28, 6: 29–33.

Donovan Royal Commission on Trade Unions and Employers Associations 1965–68 Report Cmnd 3623. (1968) London, HMSO.

DOYLE, B. (1991) 'Disabled workers: legal issues', in M. Davidson and J. Earnshaw (Eds), *Vulnerable Workers: Psychological and Legal issues.* Chichester, Wiley: 93–118.

DUNCAN, C. (1992) 'Pay, payment systems and job evaluation', in B. Towers (Ed.), *A Handbook of Industrial Relations Practice,* Third edition. London, Kogan Page: 258–291.

DUNLOP, J. (1958) *Industrial Relations Systems.* New York, Henry Holt.

DUNN, S. AND GENNARD, J. (1984) *The Closed Shop in British Industry*. London, Macmillan.

EARNSHAW, J. AND COOPER, C. (1996) *Stress and Employer Liability*. London, IPD.

EASTERBY–SMITH, M. AND MACKNESS, J. (1992) 'Completing the cycle of evaluation', *Personnel Management*. May: 42–45.

EDWARDS, P. (1991) 'Industrial conflict: will the giant wake?', *Personnel Management*, September: 26–28.

EDWARDS, P. (1994) 'Discipline and the creation of order', in K. Sisson (Ed.), *Personnel Management in Britain*. Oxford, Blackwell: 562–594.

EDWARDS, P. (Ed.) (1995) *Industrial Relations: Theory and practice in Britain*. Oxford, Blackwell.

EDWARDS, R. (1979) *Contested Terrain*. London, Heinemann.

EGAN, G. (1995) 'A clear path to peak performance', *People Management*, 18 May: 34–37.

ELKINGTON, J. AND BURKE, T. (1989) *The Green Capitalists*. London, Victor Gollancz.

EMPLOYMENT DEPARTMENT (1994) *Resolving Employment Rights Disputes: Options for reform*. London, HMSO.

ENGESTRÖM, Y. (1994) *Training for Change: New approach to instruction and learning in working life*. Geneva, International Labour Office.

EQUAL OPPORTUNITIES COMMISSION (1985) *Job Evaluation Free of Sex Bias*. Manchester, EOC.

EQUAL OPPORTUNITIES COMMISSION (1995) *Equal Pay for Work of Equal Value: A guide to the amended Equal Pay Act'*. Manchester, EOC.

EVANS, A. (1991) *Computers and Personnel Systems: A practical guide*. London, IPM.

EVANS, S. (1987) 'The use of injunctions in industrial disputes: May 1984–April 1987', *British Journal of Industrial Relations*, 25, 3: 419–435.

FAIR, H. (1992) *Personnel and Profit: The pay-off from people*. London, IPM.

FAIRBAIRNS, J. (1991) 'Plugging the gap in training needs analysis', *Personnel Management*, February: 43–45.

FARNHAM, D. (1990) *Personnel in Context*. London, IPM.

FARNHAM, D. (1993) *Employee Relations*. London, IPD.

FARNHAM, D. AND PIMLOTT, J. (1995) *Understanding Industrial Relations*, Fourth Edition. London, Cassell.

FELLS, R. (1986) 'Managing deadlocks in negotiation', *Employee Relations*, 8, 2: 2–7.

FELSTEAD, A. AND GREEN, F. (1994) 'Training through the recession'. *Work, Employment and Society*, 8, 2: 199–214.

FELTHAM, R. (1989) 'Assessment centres', in P. Herriot, (Ed.), *Assessment and Selection in Organisations*. Chichester, Wiley: 401–20.

FELTHAM, R. (1992) 'Safeway plc', in R. Boam and P. Sparrow (Eds) *Designing and Achieving Competency*. London, McGraw-Hill: 104–110.

FERNIE, S., METCALF, D. AND WOODLAND, S. (1994) *Does HRM Boost Employee–Management Relations?*, London, London School of

Economics, Centre for Economic Performance and Industrial Relations Department.

FIDLER, J. (1981) *The British Business Elite*. London, Routledge.

FINCHAM, R. AND RHODES, P. (1988) *The Individual, Work and Organisation*. London, Weidenfeld and Nicolson.

FINEGOLD, D. AND SOSKICE, D. (1988) 'The failure of training in Britain: analysis and prescription', *Oxford Review of Economic Policy*, 4, 5, Autumn: 41–53.

FINN, R. (1994) 'Investors in People: counting the dividends', *Personnel Management*, May 30–33.

FLETCHER, C. (Ed.) (1991) 'Personality tests: the great debate', *Personnel Management*, September: 38–42.

FLETCHER, C. (1992) 'Ethics and the job interview', *Personnel Management*, March: 36–39.

FLETCHER, C. (1993a) 'Appraisal: an idea whose time has gone?'. *Personnel Management*, September: 34–37.

FLETCHER, C. (1993b) 'Testing times for the world of psychometrics, *Personnel Management*, December: 46–50.

FLETCHER, C. AND WILLIAMS, R. (1992) 'The route to performance management', *Personnel Management*, October: 42–47.

FORD, R. (1969) *Motivation through Work Itself*. New York, American Management Association.

FOULKES, F. (1980) *Personnel Policies in Large Non-union Companies*. New Jersey, Prentice Hall.

FOWLER, A. (1988) 'New directions in performance related pay', *Personnel Management*, November: 20, 4: 30–34.

FOWLER, A. (1990a) 'Performance management: the MBO of the 90s?', *Personnel Management*, July: 47–51.

FOWLER, A. (1990b) *A Good Start: Effective employee induction*. London, IPM.

FOX, A. (1966) *Industrial Sociology and Industrial Relations*, Royal Commission Research Paper No. 3. London, HMSO.

FOX, A. (1974) *Beyond Contract*. London, Faber & Faber.

FRASER, J. M. (1966) *Employment Interviewing*. London, McDonald and Evans.

FREIDSON, E. (Ed.) (1973) *The Professions and their Prospects*. London, Sage.

FRIEDMAN, B. (1970) 'The Social Responsibility of Business is to Increase its Profits', *The New York Times Magazine*, 13 September (reprinted in G. Chryssides and J. Kaler (Eds), *An Introduction to Business Ethics*. 1993, London, Chapman Hall: 249–254.)

FRIEDMAN, M. (1990) *Effective Staff Incentives*. London, Kogan Page.

GAGNE, R. (1977) *The Conditions of Learning*. New York, Holt Saunders.

GALL, G. (1993) *Harmony around a Single Table*, Labour Research, June.

GALL, G. AND McKAY, S. (1994) 'Trade union derecognition in Britain, 1988–1994', *British Journal of Industrial Relations*, 32, 3: 433–448.

GALLIE, D. AND WHITE, M. (1993) *Employee Commitment and the Skills Revolution*. London, PSI.

GENNARD, J. AND KELLY, J. (1994) 'Human resource management:

the views of personnel directors', *Human Resource Management Journal*, 5, 1: 15–32.

GHOBANDIAN, A. AND WHITE, M. (1987) *Job Evaluation and Equal Pay*, Department of Employment, Research Paper 17.

GIBB, S. '(1994) The lead body of personnel management: a critique', *Human Resource Management Journal*, 5, 1: 15–32.

GODFREY, G. AND MARCHINGTON, M. (1996), 'Shop stewards into the 1990s', *Industrial Relations Journal*, forthcoming.

GOLD, M. (Ed.) (1993) *The Social Dimension: Employment policy in the European Community*. London, Macmillan.

GOLDTHORPE, J., LOCKWOOD, D., BECHOFER, F. AND PLATT, J. (1968) *The Affluent Worker: Industrial attitudes and behaviour*. Cambridge, Cambridge University Press.

GOODMAN, J., MARCHINGTON, M., BERRIDGE, J., SNAPE, E. AND BAMBER, G. (1996) 'Industrial relations in Britain', in G. Bamber and R. Lansbury (Eds), *International and Comparative Industrial Relations*, Third edition, 1996.

GOSPEL, H. AND PALMER, G. (1993) *British Industrial Relations*, Second edition. London, Routledge.

GOSS, D. (1994) *Principles of Human Resource Management*. London, Routledge.

GOULDNER, A. (1954) *Wildcat Strike*. New York, Harper and Row.

GRAYSON, D. (1987) *Job Evaluation in Transition*, Work Research Unit Occasional paper, No. 36.

GREEN, F. AND ASHTON, D. (1992) 'Skill shortage and skill deficiency: a critique', *Work, Employment and Society*, 6, 2: 287–301.

GREENSLADE, M. (1991) 'Managing diversity: lessons from the United States', *Personnel Management*, December: 28–33.

GREER, C., JACKSON, D. AND FIORITO, J. (1989) 'Adapting human resource planning to a changing business environment', *Human Resource Management*, 28, 1: 105–123.

GRIFFITH, P. (1987) 'Computer–assisted training: the pay–off', in T. Page (Ed.), *Computers in Personnel: From Potential to Performance*. London, IPM/IMS: 47–51.

GRINT, K. (1993) 'What's wrong with performance appraisals? A critique and a suggestion', *Human Resource Management Journal*, 3, 3: 61–77.

GUEST, D. (1991) 'Personnel management: the end of orthodoxy?' *British Journal of Industrial Relations*, 29, 2: 149–175.

GUEST, D. (1995) 'Why do people work?' Presentation to the Institute of Personnel and Development National Conference, Harrogate, October.

GUEST, D. AND HOQUE, K. (1994a) 'The good, the bad and the ugly: employment relations in new non–union workplace', *Human Resource Management Journal*, 5, 1: 1–14.

GUEST, D. AND HOQUE, K. (1994b) 'Yes, personnel does make a difference', *Personnel Management*, November: 40–44.

GUEST, D. AND KENNY, T. (Eds) (1983) *A Textbook of Techniques and Strategies in Personnel Management*. London, IPM.

GUEST, D. AND PECCEI, R. (1994) 'The nature and causes of effective human resource management'. *British Journal of Industrial Relations*, 32, 2: 219–242.

HACKMAN, J. AND OLDHAM, G. (1976) 'Motivation through the design of work: test of a theory' *Organisation Behaviour and Human Performance*, 16: 250–279.

HALL, M (1992) 'Behind the European works councils directives; the European Commission's legislative strategy', *British Journal of Industrial Relations*, 30, 4: 547–566.

HALL, M., CARLEY, M., GOLD, M., MARGINSON, P. AND SISSON, K. (1995) *European Works Councils: Planning for the directive*. Eclipse Group/Industrial Relations Research Unit, London/Coventry.

HANDY, C. (1991) *Inside Organisations: 21 ideas for managers*. London, BBC Books.

HANNAH, L. (1987) *Inventing Retirement: The development of occupational pensions in Britain*. Cambridge, Cambridge University Press.

HARRISON, R. (1992) *Employee Development*. London, IPD.

HART, T. (1993) 'Human resource management – time to exorcise the militant tendency', *Employee Relations*, 15, 3: 29–36.

HAWKINS, K. (1979) *A Handbook of Industrial Relations Practice*. London, Kogan Page.

HEATHCOTE, M. AND KING, J. (1993) 'Measuring and minimising risk', *Personnel Management*. October: 62–64.

HEERY, E. (1993) 'Industrial relations and the customer', *Industrial Relations Journal* 24, 4: 284–295.

HENDRY, C. (1994) *Human Resource Management: A strategic approach to employment*. London, Butterworth.

HERRIOT, P. (Ed.) (1989) *Assessment and Selection in Organisations*. Chichester, Wiley.

HERRIOT, P. (1995a) 'The management of careers', in S. Tyson (Ed.), *Strategic Prospects for Human Resource Management*. London, IPD: 184–205.

HERRIOT, P. (1995b) 'Why do people work?' Presentation to the Institute of Personnel and Development National Conference, Harrogate, October.

HERZBERG, F. (1968) *Work and the Nature of Man*. London, Staples Press.

HERZBERG, F. (1972) 'One More Time: How do you Motivate Employees?', in L. Davis and J. Taylor (Eds), *Design of Jobs*. London, Penguin.

HIGHLEY, C. AND COOPER, C. (1994) 'Evaluating employee assistance programmes', *Personnel Review*, 23, 7: 46–59.

HILGARD, E., ATKINSON, R. L. AND ATKINSON, R. C. (1979) *Introduction to Psychology*, Seventh Edition. New York, Harcourt Brace Jovanovich.

HILL, S. (1991a) 'How do you manage a flexible firm? The total quality model', *Work, Employment and Society*, 5, 3: 397–415.

HILL, S. (1991b) 'Why quality circles failed but total quality management succeeds', *British Journal of Industrial Relations*, December, 29: 541–568.

HILTON, P. (1992) 'Using incentives to reward and motivate employees', *Personnel Management*, September: 49–51.

HOBSBAWM, E. (1968) *Industry and Empire*. Harmondsworth, Penguin.

HOCHSCHILD, A. (1983) *The Managed Heart: the commercialisation of human feeling*. San Francisco, University of California Press.

HOGG, C. (1988) 'Outdoor training', *Personnel Management Factsheet*, No. 9, September.

HOLDEN, L. AND LIVIAN, Y. (1992) 'Does strategic training policy exist? Some evidence from ten European countries', *Personnel Review*, 21, 1: 12–23.

HONEY, P. AND MUMFORD, A. (1981) *The Manual of Learning Styles*. Maidenhead, Peter Honey.

HOPFL, H. (1993) 'Culture and commitment; British Airways', in D. Gowler, K. Legge and C. Clegg (Eds), *Case Studies in Organisational Behaviour and Human Resource Management*. London, Paul Chapman: 117–125.

HOUGHAM, J., THOMAS, J. AND SISSON, K. (1991) 'Ford's EDAP scheme: a roundtable discussion', *Human Resource Management Journal*, 1, 3: 77–91.

HUCZYNSKI, A. AND FITZPATRICK, M. (1989) *Managing Employee Absence for a Competitive Edge*. London, Pitman.

HULME, R. AND BEVAN, R. (1975) 'The blue collar worker goes on salary', *Harvard Business Review*. March–April: 104–112.

HUNTER, L. AND MACINNES, J. (1991) *Employers' Labour Use Strategies: Case studies*. London, Employment Department Research Paper No. 87.

HUNTER, L., MCGREGOR, A., MACINNES, J. AND SPROULL, A. (1993) 'The flexible firm, strategy and segmentation, *British Journal of Industrial Relations*, 31, 3: 383–407.

HUSELID, M. (1993) 'The impact of environmental volatility on human resource planning and strategic human resource management', *Human Resource Planning*, 16, 3: 35–49.

HUSELID, M. (1995) 'The impact of human resource management practices on turnover, productivity and corporate financial performance', *Academy of Management Journal*, 38, 3: 635–672.

HUTCHINSON, S. AND WOOD, S. (1995) 'The UK experience', in *Personnel and the Line: Developing the new relationship*. London, IPD: 3–42.

ILES, P. AND SALAMAN, G. (1995) 'Recruitment, selection and assessment', in J. Storey (Ed.), *Human Resource Management; a Critical Text*. London, Routledge: 203–233.

INCOMES DATA SERVICES (1988) *Teamworking*, No. 419, October.

INCOMES DATA SERVICES/INSTITUTE OF PERSONNEL MANAGEMENT (1989) *Customer Care: The personnel implications*. London, IDS/IPM.

INCOMES DATA SERVICES FOCUS (1992) *Union Recognition, No. 65*, December.

INCOMES DATA SERVICES (1992) *Skill Based Pay*. London, IDS Study No. 500.

INCOMES DATA SERVICES (1993) *Profit Sharing and Share Options*. London, IDS Study 539.

INCOMES DATA SERVICES (1994) *Bonus Systems, No. 547*, February.

INCOMES DATA SERVICES (1994) *No. 556, Absence and Sick Pay Policies*, June.

INCOMES DATA SERVICES STUDY (1994) *Profit Related Pay, No. 564,* October.

INCOMES DATA SERVICES FOCUS (1994) *Employee Benefits, No. 72,* October.

INDUSTRIAL RELATIONS SERVICES (1991) 'Developing managers in the great outdoors', *IRS Employee Development Bulletin 14,* February: 6–9.

INDUSTRIAL RELATIONS SERVICES (1992) 'The role of outdoor-based development: a survey of 120 employers', *IRS Employee Development Bulletin 34,* October: 2–17.

INDUSTRIAL RELATIONS SERVICES (1993) 'Careers guidance vouchers: encouraging employee development at Sainsbury's', *IRS Employee Development Bulletin 37,* January: 6–9.

INDUSTRIAL RELATIONS SERVICES (1993) 'NVQ survey', *IRS Employee Development Bulletin 40,* April: 2–15

INDUSTRIAL RELATIONS SERVICES (1993) 'Customer care training at Elmbridge Council', *IRS Employee Development Bulletin 44,* August: 2–5.

INDUSTRIAL RELATIONS SERVICES (1993) 'The learning organisation', *IRS Employee Development Bulletin 45*: 5–8.

INDUSTRIAL RELATIONS SERVICES (1993) 'Leicester City Council; making complaints pay', *IRS Employee Development Bulletin 46,* October: 8–12.

INDUSTRIAL RELATIONS SERVICES (1994) 'The changing face of recruitment advertising', *IRS Employee Development Bulletin 49*: 2–5.

INDUSTRIAL RELATIONS SERVICES (1994a) 'Ensuring effective recruitment: developments in the use of application forms'. *IRS Employee Development Bulletin 51*: 2–8.

INDUSTRIAL RELATIONS SERVICES (1994b) 'Random selection', *IRS Employee Development Bulletin 51*: 15–16.

INDUSTRIAL RELATIONS SERVICES (1994) 'Assisted development at Peugeot Talbot', *IRS Employee Development Bulletin 53,* May: 2–5.

INDUSTRIAL RELATIONS SERVICES (1994) 'New approaches to employee development'. *IRS Employee Development Bulletin 60,* December: 5–10.

INDUSTRIAL RELATIONS SERVICES (1995) 'EDAP challenges anti–learning culture'. *IRS Employee Development Bulletin 68,* August: 2.

INDUSTRIAL RELATIONS SERVICES (1991) 'Bosch: an industrial relations set–up for a new start'. *IRS Employment Trends 501*: 4–10.

INDUSTRIAL RELATIONS SERVICES (1992) 'Industrial relations developments in the water industry', *IRS Employment Trends 516,* July: 6–15.

INDUSTRIAL RELATIONS SERVICES (1993) 'Decline in multi–employer bargaining charted'. *IRS Employment Trends 544,* September: 7–11.

INDUSTRIAL RELATIONS SERVICES (1994) 'Developments in job evaluation: shifting the emphasis'. *IRS Employment Trends 551,* January: 10–16.

INDUSTRIAL RELATIONS SERVICES (1994) 'The centre cannot hold:

devolving personnel duties'. *IRS Employment Trends 566*, August: 6–12.

INDUSTRIAL RELATIONS SERVICES (1994) 'Sickness absence monitoring and control: a survey of practice'. *IRS Employment Trends 568*, September: 4–16.

INDUSTRIAL RELATIONS SERVICES (1994) 'Sick pay trends, absence control developments and the impact of SSP changes'. *IRS Employment Trends 569*, October: 8–10.

INDUSTRIAL RELATIONS SERVICES (1994) 'First British European Works Councils Established', *IRS Employment Trends 574*, December: 4–7.

INDUSTRIAL RELATIONS SERVICES (1995) 'Single table bargaining: an idea whose time is yet to come', *IRS Employment Trends 577*, February: 10–16.

INDUSTRIAL RELATIONS SERVICES (1995) 'European works councils and the UK', *IRS Employment Trend 581*, April: 13–16.

INDUSTRIAL RELATIONS SERVICES (1995) 'The role of the human resource consultant', *IRS Employment Trend 589*, August: 6–11.

INDUSTRIAL RELATIONS SERVICES (1995a) 'CBI and local government examine sickness absence', *IRS Employment Trends 591*, September: 2.

INDUSTRIAL RELATIONS SERVICES (1995b) 'Counsel for the depressed', *IRS Employment Trends 591*, September: 12–16.

INDUSTRIAL RELATIONS SERVICES (1995c) 'Discipline at work – the practice', *IRS Employment Trends 591*, September: 4–11.

INDUSTRIAL RELATIONS SERVICES (1995) 'Discipline at work 2 – the procedures', *IRS Employment Trends 592*, September: 5–16.

INDUSTRIAL RELATIONS SERVICES (1995) 'Happy families', *IRS Employment Trends 593*: 10–16.

INDUSTRIAL RELATIONS SERVICES (1995) 'Survey of employee relations in local government', *IRS Employment Trends 594*, October: 6–13.

INDUSTRIAL RELATIONS SERVICES (1995) 'Sickness absence', *IRS Industrial Relations Law Bulletin 530*, October: 2–9.

INDUSTRIAL RELATIONS SERVICES (1995) 'The Disability Discrimination Bill: An EOR clause-by-clause guide to its employment provisions, *IRS Equal Opportunities Review, 60*, March/April: 25–34.

INDUSTRIAL RELATIONS SERVICES (1996) 'Skills Based Pay: A survey'. *IRS Pay and Benefits Bulletin 391*, January: 5–10.

INSTITUTE OF MANPOWER STUDIES (1994) *Evaluation of Investors in People – England and Wales, No. 263.*

INSTITUTE OF PERSONNEL MANAGEMENT (1992) *Performance Management in the United Kingdom: An analysis of the issues*, London, IPM.

INVESTORS IN PEOPLE (1995) *Good Practice in Human Resource Management and Investors in People.* Summary of a series of surveys conducted by Cranfield School of Management and the Host Consultancy. London, Investors in People.

INVOLVEMENT AND PARTICIPATION ASSOCIATION (1993) *Towards Industrial Partnership: A new approach to relationships at work.* London, IPA.

INVOLVEMENT AND PARTICIPATION ASSOCIATION (1995) *Towards Industrial Partnership: Putting it into practice – Rhone Poulenc Stavely Chemicals: A case study in movement to single status*. London, IPA.

INVOLVEMENT AND PARTICIPATION ASSOCIATION/INSTITUTE OF PERSONNEL MANAGEMENT (1990) *Employee Involvement in the United Kingdom: the IPA/IPM Code*. IPA/IPM London.

JENKINS, D. (1983) 'Designing and resourcing training', in D. Guest and T. Kenny (Eds), *A Textbook of Techniques and Strategies in Personnel Management*. London, IPM: 215–239.

JENKINS, J. (1983) 'Management Trainees in Retailing,' in B. Ungerson (Ed.), *Recruitment Handbook*. Aldershot, Gower.

JESSOP, G. (1991) *Outcomes: NVQs and the Emerging Model of Education and Training*. Brighton, Falmer Press.

JEWSON, N., MASON, D., DREWETT, A. AND ROSSITER, W. (1995) 'Formal equal opportunities and employment best practice', *Department for Education and Employment, Research Series No. 69*, London, HMSO.

JOHNS, T. (1995) 'Don't be afraid of the moral maze', *People Management*, October: 32–34.

JOHNSON, G. AND SCHOLES, K. (1993) *Exploring Corporate Strategy*, Third Edition. Hemel Hempstead, Prentice Hall.

KAHN–FREUND, O. (1959) 'Labour law', in M. Ginsberg (Ed.), *Law and Opinion in England in the 20th Century*. London, Stevens: 215–263.

KAHN–FREUND, O. (1965) 'Industrial relations and the law: retrospect and prospect', *British Journal of Industrial Relations*, Vol 7: 301–316.

KANDOLA, R. AND FULLERTON, J. (1994) 'Diversity: more than just an empty slogan', *Personnel Management*, November: 46–50.

KANDOLA, R. AND FULLERTON, J. (1994) *Managing the Mosaic: Diversity in action*. London, IPD.

KEENAN, T. (1995) 'Graduate recruitment in Britain: a survey of selection methods used by organisations', *Journal of Organisational Behaviour*, Vol 16: 303–317.

KEEP, E. (1989) 'Corporate training strategies: the vital component?', in J. Storey (Ed.), *New Perspectives on Human Resource Management*. London, Routledge: 109–25.

KEEP, E. (1994) 'Vocational education and training for the young', in K. Sisson (Ed.), *Personnel Management in Britain*. Oxford, Blackwell: 299–333.

KEEP, E. AND RAINBIRD, H. (1995) 'Training', in P. Edwards (Ed.), *Industrial Relations*. Oxford, Blackwell: 515–542.

KELLIHER, C. AND MCKENNA, S. (1988) 'The employment implications of government policy: a case study of public sector catering', *Employee Relations*, Vol 10, 2: 8–13.

KENNY, J. AND REID, M. (1989) *Training Interventions*. London, IPM.

KESSLER, I. (1994) 'Reward systems' in J. Storey (Ed.), *Human Resource Management: A critical text*. London, Routledge: 254–279.

KESSLER, S. (1993) 'Is there still a future for the unions?', *Personnel Management*, July: 24–30.

KESSLER, S. AND BAYLISS, F. (1992) 'The changing face of industrial relations'. *Personnel Management*, May: 34–38.

KESSLER, S. AND BAYLISS, F. (1995) *Contemporary British Industrial Relations*, Second Edition. London, Macmillan.

KINNIE, N. (1985) 'Changing management strategies in industrial relations', *Industrial Relations Journal*, Vol. 16, 4: 17–24.

KINNIE, N. AND ARTHURS, A. (1993) 'Will personnel people ever learn to love the computer?', *Personnel Management*, June: 46–51.

KINNIE, N. AND LOWE, J. (1990) 'Performance related pay on the shopfloor'. *Personnel Management*: 45–49.

KIRKPATRICK, D. (1967) 'Evaluation of Training', in R. Craig and L. Bittell (Eds), *Training and Evaluation Handbook*. New York, McGraw-Hill.

KLEIN, J. (1984) 'Why supervisors resist employee involvement', *Harvard Business Review*, September/October: 87–95.

KNIVETON, B. (1974) 'Industrial negotiating: some training implications', *Industrial Relations Journal*, Vol. 5, 3: 27–37.

KNIVETON, B. AND TOWERS, B. (1978) *Training for Negotiating*. London, Business Books.

KOCHAN, T., McKERSIE, R. AND CAPPELLI, P. (1985) 'Strategic choice and industrial relations theory', *Industrial Relations*, Vol. 23, 1: 16–39.

KOCHAN, T. AND BAROCCI, T. (1985) *Human Resource Management and Industrial Relations*. Boston, Little Brown.

KOHN, A. (1993) 'Why incentive plans cannot work', *Harvard Business Review*, September/October: 54–63.

KOLB, D., OSLAND, J. AND RUBIN, I. (1995) *Organisational Behaviour: An experiential Approach*. Sixth Edition. New Jersey, Prentice Hall.

LANE, C. (1989) *Management and Labour in Europe*. Aldershot, Edward Elgar.

LANGTRY, R. (1994) 'Selection', in I. Beardwell and L. Holden (Eds), *Human Resource Management: A contemporary perspective*. London, Pitman: 230–263.

LAWLER, E. (1984) 'The strategic design of reward systems', in C. Fombrun, N. Tichy and A. Devanna (Eds), *Strategic Human Resource Management*. New York, Wiley: 127–147.

LAWSON, P. (1995) 'Performance management: an overview', in M. Walters (Ed.), *The Performance Management Handbook*. London, IPD: 1–13.

LEGGE, K. (1978) *Power, Innovation and Problem Solving in Personnel Management*. London, McGraw-Hill.

LEGGE, K. (1995) *Human Resource Management: Rhetorics and realities*. London, Macmillan.

LENGNICK HALL, C. AND LENGNICK HALL, M. (1988) 'Strategic human resource management: A review of the literature and a proposed typology', *Academy of Management Review*, Vol. 13, 3: 454–470.

LEOPOLD, J. AND JACKSON, M. (1990) 'Decentralisation of collective bargaining', *Industrial Relations Journal*, Vol. 21, 3: 185–208.

LEWIS, C. (1985) *Employee Selection*. London, Hutchinson.

LEWIS, D. (1990) *The Essentials of Employment Law*, Third Edition. London, IPM.

LEWIS, P. (1992) *Practical Employment Law*. Oxford, Blackwell.

LIMERICK, B. AND HEYWOOD, E. (1993) 'Training for women in management', *Women in Management Review*, 8, 3: 23–30.

LOVERIDGE, R. AND MOK, A. (1979) *Theories of Labour Market Segmentation: A critique*. The Hague, Martinus Nijhoff.

LOWE, J. (1992) 'Teambuilding via outdoor training: experiences from a UK automotive plant', *Human Resource Management Journal*, 2, 1: 42–59.

LUPTON, T. AND GOWLER, D. (1969) *Selecting a Wage Payment System*. Research Paper III. London, Engineering Employers Federation.

MABEY, C. AND SALAMAN, G. (1995) *Strategic Human Resource Management*. Oxford, Blackwell.

McCOLGAN, A. (1994) *Pay Equity – Just Ways for Women*. Institute of Employment Rights, London.

McGREGOR, D. (1960) *The Human Side of Enterprise*. New York, Harper Row.

McHUGH, M. (1993) 'Stress at work. Do managers really count the costs?' *Employee Relations* 15, I: 18–32

McKIDDIE, T. (1994) 'Personnel NVQs: preparing for take–off'. *Personnel Management*, February: 30–33.

McLOUGHLIN, I. AND GOURLAY, S. (1992) 'Enterprise without unions: the management of employee relations in non–union firms', *Journal of Management Studies*, 29, 5: 669–691.

McLOUGHLIN, I. AND GOURLAY, S. (1994) *Enterprise without Unions: Industrial relations in the non-union firm*. Buckingham, Open University Press.

MAHONEY, T. (1992) 'Multiple pay contingencies: strategic design of compensation in G. Salaman (Ed.), *Human Resource Strategies*. London, Sage: 337–346.

MANT, A. (1995) 'Changing work roles', in S. Tyson (Ed.), *Strategic Prospects for HRM*. London, IPD: 30–55.

MARCHINGTON, M. (1982) *Managing Industrial Relations*. London, McGraw–Hill.

MARCHINGTON, M. (1992a) *Managing the team: a guide to successful employee involvement*. Oxford, Blackwell.

MARCHINGTON, M. (1992b) 'Managing labour relations in a competitive environment', in A. Sturdy, D. Knights and H. Willmott (Eds), *Skill and Consent: Contemporary Studies on the labour process*. London, Routledge: 149–184.

MARCHINGTON, M. (1993) 'Close to the customer: employee relations in food retailing', in D. Gowler, K. Legge, and C. Clegg (Eds), *Case Studies in Organisational Behaviour and Human Resource Management*. London, Paul Chapman: 134–143.

MARCHINGTON, M. (1994) 'The dynamics of joint consultation', in K. Sisson (Ed.), *Personnel Management in Britain*. Oxford, Blackwell: 662–693.

MARCHINGTON, M. (1995a) 'Employee relations', in S. Tyson (Ed.), *Strategic Prospects for HRM*. London, IPD: 81–111.

MARCHINGTON, M. (1995b) 'Fairy tales and magic wands: new employment practices in perspective', *Employee Relations*, 17, 1: 51–66.

MARCHINGTON, M. AND LOVERIDGE, R. (1979) 'Non-participation:

the management view', *Journal of Management Studies*, 16, 2: 171–84.

MARCHINGTON, M. AND PARKER, P. (1990) *Changing Patterns of Employee Relations*. Hemel Hempstead, Harvester Wheatsheaf.

MARCHINGTON, M., WILKINSON, A., AND ACKERS, P. (1993) 'Waving or drowning in participation', *Personnel Management*, March 30–33.

MARCHINGTON, M., WILKINSON, A., ACKERS, P. AND GOODMAN, J. (1992) *New Developments in Employee Involvement*, Employment Department Research Paper, Series No. 2.

MARCHINGTON, M., WILKINSON, A., ACKERS, P. AND GOODMAN, J. (1993a) 'Managerial relations and waves of employee involvement', *British Journal of Industrial Relations*, 31, 4: 553–576.

MARCHINGTON, M., WILKINSON, A. AND DALE, B. (1993b) 'The case study report', in A. Baron (Ed.), *Quality: People management matters*. London, IPM: 23–64.

MARGINSON, P., EDWARDS, P., MARTIN, R., PURCELL, J. AND SISSON, K., (1988) *Beyond the Workplace: Managing industrial relations in the multi–plant enterprise*. Oxford, Blackwell.

MARGINSON, P. AND SISSON, K. (1990) 'Single table talk', *Personnel Management*, May: 46–49.

MARSDEN, D. AND RICHARDSON, R. (1994) 'Performing for pay? The effects of "merit pay" on motivation in a public service', *British Journal of Industrial Relations*, 32, 2, June: 243–262.

MARSH, A. I. AND MCCARTHY, W. J. (1968) *Disputes Procedures in Britain Royal Commission*, Research Paper No. 2, Part 2. London, HMSO.

MARTIN, R., FOSH, P., MORRIS, H., SMITH, P. AND UNDY, R. (1991) 'The decollectivisation of industrial relations? Ballots and collective bargaining in the 1990s', *Industrial Relations Journal*, 22, 3: 197–208.

MASLOW, A., (1943) 'A theory of human motivation', *Psychological Review*, 50: 370–396.

MATHYS, N. AND BURACK, E. (1993) 'Strategic downsizing: human resource planning approaches', *Human Resource Planning*, Vol. 16, 1: 71–85.

MAYO, A. (1995) 'Economic indicators of human resource management', in S. Tyson (Ed.), *Strategic Prospects for HRM*. London, IPD: 229–265.

MERRICK, N. (1996) 'Jargon-ridden NVQs back on the defensive', *People Management*, 25 January.

METCALF, D. (1993) *Transformation of British Industrial Relations? Institutions, conduct and outcomes 1980–1990. Centre for Economic Performance*, Paper No. 151. London, London School of Economics.

MILES, R. E., AND SNOW, C. C. (1978) *Organizational Strategy, Strategy and Process*. New York, McGraw-Hill.

MILLER, P. (1996) 'Strategy and the ethical management of human resources', *Human Resource Management Journal*, 6, 1: 5–18.

MILLWARD, N., STEVENS, M., SMART, D. AND HAWES, W. (1992) *Workplace Industrial Relations in Transition*. Aldershot, Dartmouth Publishing.

MINTZBERG, H. (1973) *The Nature of Managerial Work*. New York, Harper and Row.

MINTZBERG, H. (1978) 'Patterns in strategy formation', *Management Science*, 24, 9: 934–948.

MONKS, K. (1993) 'Models of personnel management: a means of understanding the diversity of personnel practices?', *Human Resource Management Journal*, 3, 2: 29–41.

MOORBY, E. (1992) *How to Succeed in Employee Development; Moving from vision to results*. Maidenhead, McGraw-Hill.

MOORE, R. (1994) *Ford EDAP: Breaking through the Barriers in Workplace Learning: Case studies and good practice from around the UK*. Leicester, NIACE: 9–10.

MORGAN, G. (1986) *Images of Organisation*. Newbury Park, Sage.

MORTIMER, K. (1990) 'EDAP at Ford: a research note', *Industrial Relations Journal*, Vol. 21, 4: 309–314.

MORTON, C. (1994) *Becoming World Class*. London, Macmillan.

MULLINS, T. (1986) Harmonisation: the benefits and the lessons', *Personel Management*, March.

MUMFORD, A. (1988) 'Enhancing your learning skills – a note of guidance for managers', in S. Wood (Ed.), *Continuous Development*. London, IPM: 171–187.

MURLIS, H. AND GRIST, J. (1976) *Towards Single Status*. Corby, BIM.

MURLIS, H. AND PRITCHARD, D. (1991) 'The computerised way to evaluate jobs', *Personnel Management*, April: 48–53.

MURPHY, T. (1989) 'Pay for performance: an instrument of strategy', *Long Range Planning*, 22, 4: 40–45.

MYERS, C. AND DAVID, K. (1992) 'Knowing and doing: tacit skills at work', *Personnel Management*, February: 45–47.

NADLER, D. AND LAWLER, E. (1979) 'Motivation: a diagnostic approach', in M. Steers and L. Porter (Eds), *Motivation and Work Behaviour*, Second Edition. New York, McGraw-Hill.

NEWELL, S. AND SHACKLETON, V. (1993) 'The use and abuse of psychometric tests in British industry and commerce'. *Human Resource Management Journal*, 4, 1: 14–23.

NICHOLS, T. (1990) 'Industrial safety in Britain and the 1974 Health and Safety at Work Act: the case of manufacturing', *International Journal of the Sociology of Law*, Vol. 18: 317–342.

NIVEN, M. (1967) *Personnel Management, 1913–1963*. London, IPM.

NOLAN, P. AND WALSH, L. (1995) 'The structure of the economy and labour market', in P. Edwards (Ed.), *Industrial Relations: Theory and practice in Britain*, Oxford, Blackwell: 50–86.

NORTH, S. J. (1995) 'Pick 'n' mix', *Personnel Today*, May, 30–31.

O'BRIEN, G. (1992) 'Changing Meanings of Work', in J. Hartley and G. Stephenson (Eds), *Employment Relations*. Oxford, Blackwell: 44–66.

OLIVER, N. AND WILKINSON, B. (1992) *The Japanisation of British Industry: New developments in the 1990s*. Oxford, Blackwell.

PADDISON, L. (1990) 'The targeted approach to recruitment', *Personnel Management*, November: 54–58.

PARTRIDGE, B. (1989) 'The Problem of Supervision', in K. Sisson (Ed.), *Personnel Management in Britain*. Oxford, Blackwell: 203–221.

PATRICK, J. (1992) *Training Research and Practice*. London, Academic Press.

PAYNE, S. (1995) 'The use of management competencies for selection in the retail sector', UMIST, unpublished MSc dissertation.

PEACH, L. (1989) 'A practitioner's view of personnel excellence', *Personnel Management*, September: 37–41.

PEARN, M. AND KANDOLA, R. (1993) *Job Analysis*. London, IPM.

PEARSON, D. (1994) 'Computer–assisted learning; the Yorkshire Bank experience', *Banking World*, Vol. 12, 4: 48–49.

PEARSON, G. J. (1995) *Integrity in Organizations: An alternative business ethic*. McGraw-Hill International.

PEDLER, M., BURGOYNE, J. AND BOYDELL, T. (1991) *The Learning Company: A strategy for sustainable development*. London, McGraw-Hill.

PENDLETON, A. (1992) 'Employee share ownership schemes in the UK', *Human Resource Management Journal*, 2, 2: 83–88.

PETERS, T. AND WATERMAN, R. (1982) *In Search of Excellence*. New York, Harper and Row.

PETTIGREW, A. (1973) *The Politics of Organisational Decision Making*. London, Tavistock.

PFEFFER, J. (1994) *Competitive Advantage through People*. Boston, Harvard Business School Press.

PICKARD, J. (1991) 'What does the Investors in People award really mean?', *Personnel Management Plus*, March: 18–19.

PICKARD, J. (1995) 'Prepare to make a moral judgement', *People Management*, May: 22–25.

PITT, G. (1995) *Employment Law*, Second Edition. London, Sweet and Maxwell.

PLUMBLEY, P. (1991) *Recruitment and Selection*. London, IPM.

POLLERT, A. (1988) 'The flexible firm; fixation or fact?', *Work, Employment and Society*, 2, 3: 281–306.

POOLE, M. AND JENKINS, G. (1990) *The Impact of Economic Democracy: Profit sharing and employee shareowning schemes*. London, Routledge.

PORTER, M. (1985) *Competitive Advantage: Creating and sustaining superior performance*. New York, Free Press.

PORTER, L. AND LAWLER, E. (1968) *Managerial Attitudes and Performance*. Homeward IL, Irwin-Dorsey.

PRAHALAD, C. K. (1995) 'How HR can help to win the future', *People Management*, 12 January: 34–36.

PRICE, R. AND PRICE L. (1994) 'Change and continuity in the status divide', in K. Sisson (Ed.), *Personnel Management in Britain*. Oxford, Blackwell: 527–561.

PRINGLE, D. (1996) 'NVQs are declared a qualified success'. *Personnel Today*, 16 January.

PURCELL, J. (1979a) 'Applying control systems to industrial relations', *Journal of the Operational Research Society*, Vol. 30: 1037–1046.

PURCELL, J. (1979b) 'A strategy for management control in industrial relations', in J. Purcell and R. Smith (Eds), *The Control of Work*. London, Macmillan: 27–58.

PURCELL, J. (1981) *Good Industrial Relations*. London, Macmillan.

PURCELL, J. (1983) 'The management of industrial relations in the modern corporation', *British Journal of Industrial Relations*, 21, 1: 1–16.

PURCELL, J. (1987) 'Mapping management styles in employee relations', *Journal of Management Studies*, 24, 5: 534–548.

PURCELL, J. (1989) 'The impact of corporate strategy on human resource management', in J. Storey (Ed.), *New Perspectives on Human Resource Management*. London, Routledge: 67–91.

PURCELL, J. (1990) 'The rediscovery of the management prerogative: the management of labour relations in the 1980s', *Oxford Review of Economic Policy*, 7, 1: 33–42.

PURCELL, J. (1994) 'Personnel earns a place on the board', *Personnel Management*, February: 26–29.

PURCELL, J. AND AHLSTRAND, B. (1989) 'The impact of corporate strategy and the management of employee relations in the multi–divisional company', *British Journal of Industrial Relations*, 27, 3: 397–417.

PURCELL, J. AND AHLSTRAND, B. (1994) *Human Resource Management in the Multi-Divisional Company*. Oxford, Oxford University Press.

PURCELL, J. AND SISSON, K. (1983) 'Strategies and practice in the management of industrial relations', in G. Bain (Ed.), *Industrial Relations in Britain*. Oxford, Blackwell: 95–120.

QUINN, J. (1980) *Strategies for Change: Logical Incrementalism*. Homewood IL, Irwin.

RAINBIRD, H. AND MAGUIRE, M. (1993) 'When corporate need supersedes employee development', *Personnel Management*, February: 34–37.

RAINNIE, A. (1989) *Industrial Relations in Small Firms: Small isn't beautiful*. London, Routledge.

RAMSAY, H. (1991) 'The community, the multinational, the workers and their charter: a modern tale of industrial democracy', *Work Employment and Society*, 5, 3: 541–566.

RANDELL, G. (1994) 'Employee Appraisal', in K. Sisson (Ed.), *Personnel Management in Britain*. Oxford, Blackwell: 221–252.

REDMAN, T. AND SNAPE, E. (1992) 'Upward and onward: can staff appraise their managers?', *Personnel Review*, Vol. 21, 7: 32–46.

REID, M. AND BARRINGTON, H. (1994) *Training Interventions: Managing employee development*, Fourth Edition. London, IPD.

REID, M., BARRINGTON, H. AND KENNY, J. (1992) *Training Interventions: Managing employment development*, Third Edition, London, IPM.

REILLY, B., PACI, P. AND HALL, P. (1995) 'Unions, safety committees and workplace injuries', *British Journal of Industrial Relations*, 33, 2: 275–288.

REITSPERGER, W. (1986) 'British employees: responding to Japanese management philosophies'. *Journal of Management Studies*, 23, 5: 563–586.

RIBEAUX, P. AND POPPLETON, S. (1978) *Psychology and Work: An Introduction*. London, Macmillan.

RIMINGTON, J. (1995) *Valedictory Summary of Industrial Health and Safety since the 1974 Act*. Paper presented to the Electricity Association. Aviemore, Scotland, April.

RIX, A., PARKINSON, R. AND GAUNT, R. (1993) *Investors in People: A qualitative study of employers*, Employment Department Research Series No. 21.

ROBERTS, C. (1984) 'Who will bite the closed shop ballot?', *Personnel Management*. October.

ROBERTS, C. (Ed.) (1985) *Harmonisation – Whys and wherefores*. London, IPM.

ROBERTS, I. AND WILKINSON, A. (1991) 'Participation and purpose: boilermakers to bankers', *Critical Perspectives on Accounting*, 2, 4: 385–413.

ROBERTS, K., AND CORCORAN-NANTES, Y. (1995) 'TQM, the new training and industrial relations' in A. Wilkinson and H. Willmott (Eds), *Making Quality Critical: New perspectives on organisation change*. London, Routledge: 194–218.

ROBERTSON, I. AND MAKIN, P. (1986) 'Management selection in Britain: a survey and critique', *Journal of Occupational Psychology*, 59, 1: 45–57.

ROBERTSON, I., SMITH, M. AND COOPER, D. (1992) *Motivation*. London, IPM.

ROEBER, J. (1975) *Social Change at Work: the ICI weekly staff agreement*, London, Duckworth.

RODGER, A. (1952) *The Seven Point Plan*. London, National Institute for Industrial Psychology.

ROGERS, C. (1969) *Freedom to Learn*. Ohio, Charles and Merrill Publishing Company.

ROGERS, J. (1989) *Adults Learning*. Buckingham, Open University Press.

ROSE, M. (1978) *Industrial Behaviour*. Harmondsworth, Penguin.

ROTHWELL, S. (1995) 'Human resource planning', in J. Storey (Ed.), *Human Resource Management: A critical text*, London. Routledge: 167–202.

RUBENSTEIN, M. (1992) *Making the Visible and Invisible – Rewarding womens work*. Equal Opportunities Review: 23–32.

RUBERY, J., TARLING, R. AND WILKINSON, F. (1987) 'Flexibility, marketing and the organisation of production', *Labour and Society*, 12, 1: 131–51.

SADLER, T. (1995) *Human Resource Management: Developing a strategic approach*. London, Kogan Page.

SAGGERS, R. (1994) 'Training climbs the corporate agenda', *Personnel Management*, July: 42–5.

SALAMON, M. (1992) *Industrial Relations: Theory and practice*, Second Edition. Hemel Hempstead, Prentice Hall.

SARGENT, A. (1989) *The Missing Workforce: Managing absenteeism*. London, IPM.

SCASE, R. AND GOFFEE, R. (1989) *Reluctant Managers: Their work and lifestyles*. London, Unwin, Hyman.

SCHEIN, E. (1988) *Organisational Psychology*. New Jersey, Prentice Hall.

SCHULER, R. (1989) 'Strategic human resource management and industrial relations', *Human Relations*, 42, 2: 157–184.

SCHULER, R. AND HUBER, S. (1993) *Personnel and Human Resource Management*, Fifth Edition. New York, West Publishing.

SCHULER, R. AND JACKSON, S. (1987) 'Linking competitive strategies with human resource management'. *Academy of Management Executive*, 1, 3: 207–219.

SCOTT, M., ROBERTS, I., HOLROYD, G. AND SAWBRIDGE, D. (1989) *Management and Industrial Relations in Small Firms*. Department of Employment Research Paper, No. 70. London, HMSO.

SELF, R. (1995) 'Changing roles for company pensions', *People Management*, October: 24–26.

SELWYN, H. (1975) *The Law of Employment*. London, Butterworth.

SENGE, P. (1990) *The Fifth Discipline: The art and practice of the learning organisation*. London, Century.

SHACKLETON, V. AND NEWELL, S. (1991) 'Management selection: a comparative survey of methods used in top British and French companies', *Journal of Occupational Psychology*. Vol. 64: 23–36.

SHEARD, A. (1992) 'Learning to improve performance', *Personnel Management*, November: 40–45.

SHIPTON, J. AND MCAULEY, J. (1993) 'Issues of power and marginality in personnel', *Human Resource Management Journal*, Vol 4, 1: 1–13.

SINCLAIR, A. AND EWING, J. (1993) 'What women managers want: customising human resource management practices', *Human Resource Management Journal*, 3, 2: 14–28.

SISSON, K. (1993) 'In search of human resource management', *British Journal of Industrial Relations*, 31, 2: 201–210.

SISSON, K. (Ed.) (1994) *Personnel Management: A comprehensive guide to theory and practice in Britain*. Oxford, Blackwell.

SISSON, K. AND TIMPERLEY, S. (1994) 'From manpower planning to strategic human resource management?', in K. Sisson (Ed.), *Personnel Management: A comprehensive guide to theory and practice in Britain*. Oxford, Blackwell: 153–184.

SKEATS, J. (1991) *Successful Induction: How to get the most from your new employees*. London, Kogan Page.

SMITH, A. (1971) 'Developments in manpower planning', *Personnel Review*, 1, 1: 44–54.

SMITH, P. AND MORTON, G. (1993) 'Union exclusion and the decollectivisation of industrial relations in contemporary Britain', *British Journal of Industrial Relations*, 31, 1: 97–114.

SMITH, M. AND ROBERTSON, I. (1993) *The Theory and Practice of Systematic Personnel Selection*. Basingstoke, Macmillan.

SMITH, P., FOSH, P., MARTIN, R., MORRIS, H. AND UNDY, R. (1993) 'Ballots and union government in the 1980s'. *British Journal of Industrial Relations*, 31, 3: 365–382.

SNAPE, E., REDMAN, T. AND BAMBER, G. (1994) *Managing Managers: Strategies and techniques for human resource management*. Oxford, Blackwell.

SNAPE, E., REDMAN, T., AND WILKINSON, A. (1993) 'Making the transformation? Human resource management in building societies'. *Human Resource Management Journal*, 3, 3: 43–60.

SPARROW, P. (1992) 'Human resource planning at Engindorf plc.', in J. Winstanley and J. Woodall (Eds), *Case Studies in Personnel*. London, IPM: 252–259.

SPARROW, P. AND HILTROP, J. (1994) *European Human Resource Management in Transition.* London, Prentice Hall.

STAMMERS, R. AND PATRICK, J. (1975) *The Psychology of Training.* London, Methuen.

STEEDMAN, H. AND WAGNER, K. (1987) 'A second look at productivity, machining and skills in Britain and economy', *National Institute Economic Review,* No. 122, November: 84–96.

STEERS, R. AND RHODES, S. (1978) 'Major influences on employee attendance: a process model'. *Journal of Applied Psychology,* 63, 4: 391–407.

STOREY, J. (1985) 'Management control as a bridging concept', *Journal of Management Studies,* 22, 3: 269–291.

STOREY, J. (1986) 'The phoney war? New office technology: organisation and control', in D. Knights and H. Willmott (Eds) *Managing the Labour Process:* 44–66.

STOREY, J. (Ed.) (1989) *New Perspectives on Human Resource Management.* London, Routledge and Kegan Paul.

STOREY, J. (1992a) *Developments in the Management of Human Resources.* Oxford, Blackwell.

STOREY, J. (1992b) 'HRM in action: the truth is out at last', *Personnel Management,* April: 28–31.

STOREY, J. (Ed.) (1995) *Human Resource Management: A critical text.* London, Routledge.

STOREY, J. AND SISSON, K. (1993) *Managing Human Resources and Industrial Relations.* Buckingham, Open University Press.

STURDY, A., KNIGHTS, D. AND WILLMOTT, H. (Eds) (1992) *Skill and Consent: Contemporary studies on the labour process.* London, Routledge.

SUMMERFIELD, J. AND VAN OUDTSHOORN, L. (1995) *Counselling in the Workplace.* London, IPD.

TAYLOR, S. (1992) 'Managing a learning environment', *Personnel Management,* October: 54–55.

TAYLOR, S. AND EARNSHAW, J. (1995) 'The provision of occupational pensions in the 1990s: an exploration of employer objectives', *Employee Relations,* 17, 2: 38–53.

TEAGUE, P. AND GRAHL, J. (1992) *Industrial Relations and European Integration.* London, Lawrence and Wishart.

TERRY, P. (1977) 'The inevitable growth of informality', *British Journal of Industrial Relations,* 15, 1: 76–90.

THOMASON, G. (1984) *A Textbook of Industrial Relations Management.* London, IPM.

THOMPSON, M. (1992) *Pay and Performance: the employer experience'* Brighton, Institute of Manpower Studies, Report No. 218.

THOMSON, A. W. J. AND MURRAY, V. V. (1976) *Grievance Procedures.* Farnborough, Saxon House.

THURLEY, K. AND WOOD, S. (Eds) (1983) *Industrial Relations and Management Strategy.* Cambridge, Cambridge University Press.

TOPLIS, J., DULEWICZ, V. AND FLETCHER, C. (1991) *Psychological Testing: A manager's guide.* London, IPM.

TORRINGTON, D. (1988) 'How does human resource management change the personnel function?'. *Personnel Review,* 17, 6: 3–9.

TORRINGTON, D. (1993a) 'How dangerous is human resource

management: a reply to Tim Hart', *Employee Relations*, 15, 5: 40–53.

TORRINGTON, D. (1993b) 'Sweets for the sweet: performance–related pay in Britain'. *International Journal of Employment Studies*, 1, 2: 149–164.

TORRINGTON, D. AND HALL, L. (1991) *Personnel Management: A new approach*. Hemel Hempstead, Prentice Hall.

TORRINGTON, D. AND HALL, L. (1995) *Personnel Management: Human resource management in action*. London, Prentice Hall.

TORRINGTON, D. AND MACKAY, L. (1986) 'Will consultants take over the personnel function?' *Personnel Management*, February: 34–37.

TOWERS, B. (Ed.) (1992) *A Handbook of Industrial Relations Practice*. London, Kogan Page.

TOWNLEY, B. (1989) 'Selection and appraisal: reconstituting social relations', in J. Storey (Ed.), *New Perspectives on Human Resource Management*. London, Routledge: 92–108.

TRADES UNION CONGRESS (1994) *Human Resource Management: A trade union response*. London, TUC.

TRAINING AND DEVELOPMENT LEAD BODY (1995) *N/SVQ Level 4: Human Resource Development*. London, HMSO.

TURNER A. H. (1962) *Trade Union Growth, Structures and Policy*. London, Allen and Unwin.

TURNER, A. AND LAWRENCE, P. (1965) *Industrial Jobs and the Worker*. Boston, Mass, Harvard University Graduate School of Business Administration.

TUSON, M. (1994) *Outdoor Training to Improve Employee Effectiveness*. London, IPD.

TYSON, S. (1995) *Human Resource Strategy: Towards a general theory of human resource management*. London, Pitman.

TYSON, S. AND FELL, A. (1986) *Evaluating the Personnel Function*. London, Hutchinson.

UNDY, R. AND KESSLER, I. (1995) *The changing nature of the employment relationship*, Presentation to the Institute of Personnel and Development National Conference, Harrogate, October.

VINNICOMBE, S. AND COLWILL, N. (1995) 'Training, mentoring and networking', in S. Vinnicombe and N. Colwill (Eds), *Women in Management*. London, Prentice-Hall: 74–91.

VINNICOMBE, S. AND STURGES, J. (1995) 'Strategies for change – company cases', in S. Vinnicombe and N. Colwill (Eds), *Women in Management*. London, Prentice–Hall: 110–121.

VROOM, V. (1964) *Work and Motivation*. Chichester, John Wiley.

WADDINGTON, J. AND WHITSTON, C. (1995) 'Trade unions: growth, structure and policy', in P. Edwards (Ed.), *Industrial Relations: Theory and practice in Britain*. Oxford, Blackwell: 151–202.

WALKER, J. (1992) *Human Resource Strategy*. New York, McGraw-Hill.

WALTERS, B. (1983) 'Identifying training needs', in D. Guest and T. Kenny (Eds), *A Textbook of Techniques and Strategies in Personnel Management*. London, IPM: 175–213.

WALTERS, M. (Ed.) (1995) *The Performance Management Handbook*. London, IPD.

WALTON, R. (1985) *From Control to Commitment in the Workplace.* Harvard Business Review, 63, March–April: 76–84.

WALTON, R. AND McKERSIE, R. (1965) *A Behavioural Theory of Labour Negotiations.* New York, McGraw-Hill.

WARD, P. (1995) 'A 360–degree turn for the better', *People Management.* 9 February: 20–25.

WARR, P. (1982) 'A national study of non-financial employment commitment, *Journal of Occupational Psychology.* 55, 4: 297–312.

WATSON, T. (1977) *The Personnel Managers: A study in the sociology of work and employment.* London, Routledge and Kegan Paul.

WATSON, T. (1986) *Management, Organisation and Employment Strategy.* London, Routledge and Kegan Paul.

WATSON, T. (1994a) *In Search of Management: Culture, chaos and control in managerial work.* London, Routledge.

WATSON, T. (1994b) 'Recruitment and selection', in K. Sisson (Ed.), *Personnel Management: A comprehensive guide to theory and practice in Britain.* Oxford, Blackwell: 185–220.

WEDDERBURN, D. AND CRAIG, C. (1974) 'Relative deprivation in work', in D. Wedderburn (Ed.) *Poverty, Inequality and Class Structure.* Cambridge, Cambridge University Press.

WHITE, P. J. (1992) 'Pay, payment systems and job evaluation', in B. Towers (Ed.), *A Handbook of Industrial Relations Practice.* London, Kogan Page.

WHITTAKER, J. (1992) 'Making a policy of keeping up to date', *Personnel Management*, March: 28–31.

WHITTAKER, J. (1994) 'Personnel NVQs: a big step forward', *Personnel Management*, August: 28–29.

WHITTINGTON, R. (1993) *What is Strategy and Does it Matter?* London, Routledge.

WICKENS, P. (1987) *The Road to Nissan: Flexibility, quality, teamwork.* London, Macmillan.

WICKENS, P. (1995) *The Ascendent Organisation.* London, Macmillan.

WILKINSON, A. (1992) 'The other side of quality: soft issues and the human resource dimension.' *Total Quality Management*, 3, 3: 323–329.

WILKINSON, A. (1994) 'Managing human resources for quality', in B. G. Dale (Ed.), *Managing Quality*, Second Edition. Hemel Hempstead, Prentice Hall: 273–291.

WILKINSON, A. (1995) 'Towards human resource management? A case study from banking'. *Research and Practice in Human Resource Management*, 3, 1: 97–116.

WILKINSON, A. AND ACKERS, P. (1995) 'When two cultures meet: new industrial relations in Japanco', *International Journal of Human Resource Management*, 6, 4: 849–871.

WILKINSON, A. AND MARCHINGTON, M. (1994) 'Total quality management: instant pudding for the personnel function?'. *Human Resource Management Journal*, 5, 1: 33–49.

WILKINSON, A., MARCHINGTON, M. AND ACKERS, P. (1993) 'Strategies for human resource management: issues in larger and international firms', in R. Harrison (Ed.), *Human Resource Management.* Addison-Wesley: 85–109.

WILKINSON, A., MARCHINGTON, M., ACKERS, P. AND GOODMAN, J.

(1992) 'Total quality management and employee involvement', *Human Resource Management Journal*, 2, 4: 1–20.

WILKINSON, A., MARCHINGTON, M., ACKERS, P. AND GOODMAN, J. (1994) 'ESOPS fables: a tale of a machine tool company', *International Journal of Human Resource Management*, 5, 1: 121–143.

WILKINSON, A., MARCHINGTON, M., GOODMAN, J. AND ACKERS, P. (1993) 'Refashioning industrial relations: the experience of a chemical company over the last decade', *Personnel Review*, Vol 22, 3: 22–38.

WILKINSON, A., REDMAN, T. AND SNAPE, E. (1996) 'Richer sounds: Payment for customer service?', in J. Storey (Ed.), *Blackwell Cases in Human Resource and Change Management*. Oxford, Blackwell: 266–274.

WILKINSON, A. AND WILLMOTT, H. (Eds) (1995) *Making Quality Critical: New perspectives on organisational change*. London, Routledge.

WILSON, S. (1992) *The Evaluation of Performance Management at Manchester Airport*. UMIST, unpublished MSc dissertation.

WINCHESTER, D. AND BACH, S. (1995) 'The state; the public sector', in P. Edwards (Ed.), *Industrial Relations: Theory and practice in Britain*. Oxford, Blackwell: 304–334.

WINKLER, J. (1974) 'The ghost at the bargaining table: directors and industrial relations', *British Journal of Industrial Relations*, 12, 2: 191–212.

WOOD, R. AND BARON, H. (1992) 'Psychological testing free from prejudice', *Personnel Management*, December: 34–37.

WOOD, SUE (Ed.) (1988) *Continuous Development*. London, IPM.

WOOD, S. (1995) 'The four pillars of human resource management: are they connected?' *Human Resource Management Journal*, 5, 5: 49–59.

WOOD, S. AND ALBANESE, M. (1995) 'Can we speak of a high commitment management on the shop floor?' *Journal of Management Studies*, 32, 2: 1–33.

WOOD, S., WAGNER, A., ARMSTRONG, E., GOODMAN, J. AND DAVIS, J. (1995) 'The "industrial relations system" concept as a basis for theory in industrial relations', *British Journal of Industrial Relations*, 13: 291–308.

WOODLEY, C. (1990) 'The cafeteria route to compensation', *Personnel Management*, May: 42–45.

WOODRUFFE, C. (1992) 'What is meant by a competency?, in R. Boam and P. Sparrow (Eds), *Designing and Achieving Competency*. Maidenhead, McGraw-Hill: 16–30.

WOODRUFFE, C. (1993) *Assessment Centres: Identifying and developing competence*. London, IPM.

YOUNG, J. (1991) 'Computer–assisted learning and banking: A major development', *Journal of European Industrial Training*, 15, 4: 17–20.

Index

The People and Organisations Series

PROFESSIONAL QUALIFICATIONS

This series has been commissioned specially for students setting out on a professional career in personnel and development. The Institute of Personnel and Development's new professional qualification scheme is offered from July 1996. It comprises three parts:

- core management
- core personnel and development
- any four from a range of more than 20 generalist and specialist electives.

The series starts by addressing core personnel and development and four generalist electives: employee reward, employee resourcing, employee relations, and employee development. Together, these cover the personnel and development knowledge requirements for graduateship of the IPD (or their N/SVQ Level 4 equivalents).

INFORMATIVE AND COMPETENCY-BASED

Each of these core texts follows the syllabus closely and should constitute students' main source of ideas, information, and guidance. The emphasis is as much on skills development as on theory, so students will gain a firm foundation for applying and using their knowledge in a variety of situations. The books include mini-cases and examples drawn from a wide spectrum of organisations and employment contexts.

AUTHORITATIVE

Each book is written by the chief examiner in the relevant area, follows the syllabus closely and provides essential reading not just for students taking the IPD Professional Qualification Scheme but for all those undertaking courses with a human resource management component.

SERIES EDITORS

Mick Marchington is professor of human resource management at the Manchester School of Management, UMIST, where he has worked since the mid-1980s. He is currently chief examiner for Core Personnel and Development and has played a major part in the redesign of the Professional Qualification Scheme. He has written widely elsewhere on employee relations and human resource management, specialising in the areas of employee involvement, workplace industrial relations, human resource management in retailing and, more recently, on the links between HRM and total quality management. He wrote the chapter on employee relations in *Strategic prospects for HRM* (1995, IPD) and also contributed to the IPD's research report on *Quality*.

Mike Oram is a human resource professional whose career has also spanned general management, information systems, legal affairs, and academia. He has for many years been at the forefront as group personnel manager and company secretary with the Prestcold Group and as director of personnel and corporate affairs with Toshiba (UK) Ltd. He is co-author of *Re-engineering's missing ingredient: the human factor* (1995, IPD) and is also a fellow of the IPD. As the IPD's vice-president for Membership and Education he has been closely involved in discussions leading up to the new qualification scheme.

EMPLOYEE REWARD

Michael Armstrong

Reward is one of the central creative accountabilities for all personnel professionals. When used effectively as a strategic tool, it can play a key role in communicating values, promoting flexibility, and maximising individual contributions to organisational objectives. This book sets out the central competences that all practitioners need in their portfolio.

Decisions about pay are inevitably influenced by local labour markets, the wider national and international context, the state of the economy, and beliefs about whether money, fringe benefits, and less tangible forms of remuneration can genuinely motivate employees. Michael Armstrong demonstrates to students how employers:

- evaluate, price, and analyse jobs and roles while ensuring competitiveness and equal pay for work of equal value
- design graded structures, pay spines, and newer broadbanded systems
- integrate reward with performance management
- forge links with individual, team, and corporate results; skills-based pay, competence-based pay, and incentive schemes
- determine the right levels of benefits, allowances, and pensions
- reward directors, executives, expatriates, and sales staff.

Michael Armstrong is one of Britain's best-known authors and an acknowledged authority on reward. He has been closely involved in drafting the Employee Reward module of the new IPD professional standards and is now the chief examiner for this module.

... seems set to become the Wisden of UK employee reward matters ... this is the most definitive and up-to-date book [on reward issues] available. Buy.

Duncan Brown, Principal, Towers Perrin

1996 432 pages Paperback ISBN 0 85292 623 5   £19.95

EMPLOYEE DEVELOPMENT

Rosemary Harrison

Building on the success of her best-selling book, *Employee Development* (1992, IPD), in the IPD's Management Studies Series, Rosemary Harrison has created a completely new text to take full account of the changes in the new syllabus requirements and the wider training scene.

The book is divided into four parts and covers the following areas:

- employee development and the business
- the context for employee development
  - national and international context
  - organisational and professional context
- developing the corporate curriculum
- promoting organisational learning and advancement.

Rosemary Harrison is a graduate of Kings College, London University. Since 1989 she has been lecturer in human resource management at Durham University Business School where she is also director of its human resource development unit. She has worked as a consultant in many British private- and public-sector organisations and has written several books on human resource management and development. She has recently been appointed chief examiner in employee development for the IPD's new Professional Standards.

1997 488 pages Paperback ISBN 0 85292 657 X   £19.95

EMPLOYEE RELATIONS

John Gennard and Graham Judge

To help prospective personnel managers develop the necessary skills, the authors have taken a wholly pragmatic managerial perspective. The book is written to the syllabus requirements and combines theory with practice to enable all students to apply their knowledge and understanding in unfamiliar or difficult situations.

Each chapter contains exercises, mini case-studies, and examples of real-life situations from all sectors of industry, commerce, and public authorities.

The book is divided into two parts and covers:

- employee relations organisations
- employee processes
- outcomes of employee relations
- employee relations management and the corporate environment
- negotiation skills – general overview
- handling grievances
- handling disciplinary matters
- bargaining
- devising, implementing and monitoring schedules
- evaluating new employee relations management.

John Gennard is professor of human resource management at Strathclyde Business School. He is also the IPD's chief examiner for employee relations.

1997 288 pages Paperback ISBN 0 85292 654 5   £19.95